Competitors

Outwitting, Outmaneuvering,
and Outperforming

Competitors

Liam Fahey

John Wiley & Sons, Inc.

New York • Chichester • Weinheim • Brisbane • Singapore • Toronto

This book is printed on acid-free paper. ∞

Published by John Wiley & Sons, Inc.

Published simultaneously in Canada.

This publication is designed to provide accurate and authoritative information in regard to the subject matter covered. It is sold with the understanding that the publisher is not engaged in rendering professional services. If professional advice or other expert assistance is required, the services of a competent professional person should be sought.

Library of Congress Cataloging-in-Publication Data:

Fahey, Liam, 1951–
    Competitors : outwitting, outmaneuvering, and outperforming / by
Liam Fahey.
      p.   cm.
    Includes bibliographical references and index.
    ISBN 0-471-29562-0 (cloth : alk. paper)
    1. Business intelligence. 2. Competition. 3. Organizational
learning. I. Title.
  HD38.7.F34   1999
  658.4′ 7—dc21
                                            98-23546

Printed in the United States of America.

10 9 8 7 6 5 4 3 2 1

Dedicated to
my wife, Patricia;
my daughter, Michelle;
and my son, Kevin.
I can now tell them
that the book is finished.

PREFACE

STRATEGY IN ANY BUSINESS (OR NONBUSINESS) CONTEXT IS MEANINGLESS WITHOUT reference to customers and competitors. The dominant aim of strategy in the product marketplace is to deliver superior value to customers compared with current (and potential) rivals. A persistent and unavoidable challenge in the perennial battle to enhance and sustain superior marketplace customer value is to stay one or more steps ahead of the competition. Simply emulating what competitors do cannot lead to superior financial performance.

Winning strategies do not fall like manna from heaven. Rather, they stem from the ability to outwit, outmaneuver, and outperform current and potential rivals. An entrepreneurial strategy—that can generate distinctive change in the marketplace—is more likely when an organization outwits its rivals. It can do so by anticipating changes in marketplace conditions, identifying opportunities, and determining how to affect marketplace change faster and better than its rivals.

But outsmarting rivals by itself does not lead to marketplace success. It is also necessary to outmaneuver them by developing the right products, partnering with leading customers, executing more effective differentiation, and managing alliances and networks more strategically.

The ultimate test of outwitting and outmaneuvering rivals is the extent to which they are outperformed in terms of marketplace results, capability or competency development, and financial performance. Who is first to market with innovative products? Who penetrates the market more quickly? Who develops the capabilities necessary for the next generation of competition? Who generates higher margins and greater profitability?

A comprehensive and thorough understanding of competitors is thus an essential ingredient to developing and executing winning strategies. Organizations, therefore, need integrated analysis frameworks to identify and assess the current and potential strategies of current and future competitors. The intent of this book is to provide such analysis frameworks.

Focus of Book

The notion of competitor learning constitutes the integrating theme underlying these analysis frameworks: creating knowledge that informs decision makers and influences decision making through learning about and from the actions, words, and organizational attributes of current and potential competitors. Learning about competitors must never be allowed to become an end in itself. The purpose of competitor analysis is thus not to learn about competitors; it is to use that learning to make the right decisions and to make them faster and better than rivals.

This book emphasizes analysis and assessment—the transformation of data (generated by attention to competitors) into outputs that are relevant to decision making. It therefore highlights the roles of competitor analysts—whether professional staff or senior managers—in adding value for decision makers at all levels in the organization.

Premises Underlying Competitor Learning

Several premises underlie the content and focus of the competitor learning approach advocated in this book:

- Analysis of competitors must be just as attentive to *potential* rivals as to current rivals.
- Decision makers need to learn about and from competitors' actions *before* they execute them.
- Learning associated with competitors' *future directions and actions* is often radically different from that derived from competitors' current and past states and actions.
- Analysis of competitors should lead to extensive learning about the *broader competitive arena*—customers, channels, suppliers, technology, and competitive dynamics.
- Only by knowing current and potential competitors can any organization truly *know itself.*
- Learning occurs through *assessment,* rather than description, of the current and future states of competitors.
- Analysis of competitors should lead to identifying possible future decisions as well as reframing some existing decisions.

These premises conflict in many respects with competitor analysis or *competitor intelligence* work as practiced in many organizations today. In particular:

- The orientation is often to refine and perfect competitor data (rather than drawing preliminary inferences to determine, among other things, whether the data is worth collecting).

- Competitor analysis outputs are frequently strong on description (the "what-so") but weak on assessment of implications (the "so-what").

- There is a prevalent presumption that the value of data resides in its extensiveness and precision (rather than its contribution to decision making).

- The learning derived from attention to smaller rivals, emerging and potential rivals, and functional substitute and even invented rivals is largely neglected.

- Alternative projections of competitors' future strategies receive scant attention.

- Little emphasis is placed on the analysis of competitors as a source for learning about customers, distribution channels, suppliers, technology, and marketplace change.

- Alternative logics or lines of reasoning pertaining to competitors' current or potential actions are not created and assessed.

Purpose of the Book

This book is intended to serve as a road map to any group of individuals in any type of organization who want to use competitor learning for two related purposes:

- To learn about competitors but also to learn about the broader competitive environment and their own organization.

- To leverage that learning in making and executing decisions.

In particular, the three parts of the book aim to:

1. Provide a thorough conceptual and practical understanding of the role of competitor learning in making and executing strategy.

2. Develop and illustrate specific analytical tools and techniques that can be used to describe and assess the present and potential states of current and future competitors.

3. Suggest ways to avoid many of the organizational errors associated with competitor analysis.

Audience of the Book

This book is explicitly intended for managers and others involved in the analysis of current and potential competitors. It will be particularly useful to:

- Staff specialists who need to scan, monitor, and project the strategies and actions of competitors.
- Managers of such functions as marketing, sales, manufacturing, R&D, and engineering who track competitor activity in their specific domains.
- Executives who need to know what competitor questions to ask and how they might be answered.
- Management consultants who conduct analysis of individual or multiple competitors for their clients.
- Security analysts and other professionals who monitor specific organizations and their competitors.
- Academics and students who want to be able to analyze organizations and their competitors.

Structure of the Book

The book is divided into three parts.

Part One, "A Framework for Competitor Learning," provides the conceptual underpinnings of the approach to competitor learning advocated in this book. Chapter 1 outlines the framework for thinking about strategy and introduces the notions of outwitting, outmaneuvering, and outperforming current and potential rivals. Chapter 2 develops the model of competitor learning, and Chapter 3 outlines key concepts that are central to the frameworks of analysis presented in Part Two. Chapter 4 provides a detailed understanding of signals, perhaps the critical concept in the interpretation and assessment of competitors' actions or intentions.

Part Two, "The Analysis of Individual (and Multiple) Competitors," then details how to analyze individual (as well as groups of) competitors. It addresses how to identify a competitor's marketplace strategy, activity/value chain, alliances and relationships, networks, assumptions, assets, capabilities and competencies, organizational infrastructure, and culture. It concludes by showing how scenarios can be used to project any competitor's plausible alternative future strategies. A central theme in Part Three is assessment—the identification of implications. Each chapter addresses implications pertaining to the competitor(s), the future states of the competitive marketplace, and your own organization.

Part Three, "An Organizational Perspective on Competitor Learning," highlights some of the organizational issues involved in analyzing current and potential competitors. Its purpose is to demonstrate how to avoid critical errors that are commonly made as organizations endeavor to develop and leverage competitor knowledge.

Research, Consulting, and Teaching Bases of the Book

This book reflects almost 15 years of researching, consulting, and teaching in the domain of analyzing competitors. Its genesis dates back to a modest research project conducted in the mid-1980s when I was a faculty member at the Kellogg Graduate School of Management at Northwestern University. Its purpose was to investigate the tools and techniques employed by companies to depict and analyze their industry and broader macroenvironment. An overriding conclusion of this study was that large U.S. corporations did not utilize a formal and comprehensive analysis framework to identify, assess, and project the strategies and actions of current or potential rivals.

I initially tested a preliminary form of the analysis frameworks for individual competitors with two sections of the Executive MBA program and two sections of final quarter MBA students at Kellogg. The analysis frameworks were further extended and refined at Boston University during the late 1980s and early 1990s.

During the past 10 years, I have presented and tested these competitor analysis frameworks in many public seminars in the United States, Canada, Europe, and Southeast Asia under the auspices of such organizations as the Planning Forum (now the Strategic Leadership Forum), the President's Association, the Institute for the Study of Business Markets (located at Pennsylvania State University), and Management Centre Europe. The reactions and responses of managers in many of these seminars greatly aided their continual refinement and application.

Applying the analysis concepts and frameworks in live organizational settings represents the ultimate learning laboratory—analyzing real competitor issues and challenges confronting management teams. I have had the good fortune to be involved in analysis projects in a diverse array of firms in North America and Europe over the past decade or so.

My fondest hope is that the long journey reflected in the pages of this book will aid and abet organizations' efforts to identify and analyze their current and potential competitors as a means of enhancing the effectiveness of their marketplace strategies.

LIAM FAHEY

Needham, Massachusetts

ACKNOWLEDGMENTS

I OWE A SUBSTANTIAL INTELLECTUAL DEBT TO MANY SCHOLARS WHO HAVE LAID THE groundwork for much of the thinking and analysis addressed in these pages. Although they are too many to list, a few deserve special mention because their work has greatly contributed to the conceptual development underpinning specific chapters: Peter Senge (Chapter 2), V. K. Narayanan (Chapter 3), Gary Hamel and C. K. Prahalad (Chapter 6), Michael E. Porter (Chapter 7), Benjamin Gomez-Casseres (Chapter 9), Ian Mitroff (Chapter 10), Kurt Christensen (Chapters 11 and 12), Gerry Johnson (Chapter 15), and Peter Schwartz (Chapter 16).

This book simply would not have been possible without the support and cooperation of far too many people to name individually. A sincere word of thanks must be extended to the many organizations over the past 10 years that have allowed me to test and develop my ideas about how to do competitor analysis in workshops, presentations to managers, and consulting projects. The persistent probing and questioning of these organizations challenged me to continually refine and extend the tools and techniques presented in this book.

The following individuals gave me detailed and constructive comments on one or more chapters: Lynn Behnke, Dave Burgess, Ben Gomez-Casseres, John Camillus, Kurt Christensen, George Day, Dave de Long, Phil Dover, Marjorie Lyles, Steward Early, Jeffrey Ellis, Sam Felton, Dick Hammer, Jan Herring, Bernie Jarowski, Gerry Johnson, John Martin, Bill Meinhardt, Tom Neubert, Tom Nagle, V. K. Narayanan, Jap Paap, Charles Perrotet, Farshad Raffi, Robert Randall, Aleda Roth, Allan Shocker, Dan Simpson, Tassu Shirvani, Rajendra Srivastava, and Mohan Subrami. Few authors have been so fortunate to have chapters treated as works-in-progress by such a conscientious and critical set of academics, practitioners, and consultants. Their insights are evident in every chapter. I thank each and every one of them.

A special word of thanks to my many MBA students at Northwestern and Boston Universities who tested and adapted these analysis frameworks as part of their class projects. They have educated me in ways that they can never appreciate.

Domique Lakos and June Kavorkian gave unstintingly of their time to type and retype innumerable renditions and variations of many charts and figures. Their patience and good humor were always a joy to behold.

Finally, this book is dedicated to the three persons who gave this journey meaning and without whom it would not have a purpose: my wife, Patricia; my daughter, Michelle; and my son, Kevin. No longer do they have to ask: When will you be finished with that book?

L.F.

CONTENTS

PART ONE

A Framework for Competitor Learning

PART TWO

The Analysis of Individual (and Multiple) Competitors

PART THREE

An Organizational Perspective on Competitor Learning

PART
ONE

A Framework for Competitor Learning

Outwitting, Outmaneuvering, and Outperforming Competitors

JUST A FEW DECADES AGO, COMPETITION IN MOST INDUSTRIES COULD BE APTLY likened to a traditional horse race in which companies jockey fiercely for market share. Consistent with this metaphor, the company with the fastest, strongest horse—in other words, the most resources—usually won. Nowadays, however, the croquet game in *Alice's Adventures in Wonderland* could also be a metaphor for competition in many industries. That is, the realities change—so expect the unexpected. Nonetheless, if we still choose to apply the race track metaphor to the current marketplace, a number of disclaimers and warnings to participants are required:

- All rules are subject to change without notice.
- The prize money may change at short notice.
- The route and the finish line will likely change after the race starts.
- Bets may be made at any time during the race.
- New entrants may join the race at any time.

- Racers are on-line at all times and may alter their plans based on the most current information.
- Racers may form alliances.
- All creative strategies that are not specifically against the law are allowed.
- Governmental laws may change (sometimes retroactively).

The characteristics of an ideal competitor have also changed. Tiny but agile, information-based entrepreneurial firms now run neck and neck with organizational behemoths endowed with deep pockets and greater resources. Nowadays, the advantage goes to the firm that can most quickly rethink its strategy for winning while adapting to frequent changes in the competition.

But many basics of the marketplace "horse race" concept still apply. Racers—the companies that make products or services—create strategies that will gain them advantage with those who control the prize money—customers. Winning is measured in terms of getting and keeping customers from current and even future rivals—competitors. As the race progresses, racers adapt and amend their strategies as they observe, and anticipate, the actions and reactions of both competitors and customers. The stakeholders—those with an "interest" in the race, such as current and future customers, investors, and company managers—make bets on the race. The racers need to convince investors they will continue to be a winner in the race. To devise successful strategies, racers need to have an intimate understanding of competitors and customers.

The Strategy Game

Updating the familiar companies-in-a-horse-race metaphor in light of current business conditions makes it clear why all businesses must prepare for sudden and dramatic changes in rivalry among competitors to win customers and why there is a need for rivals to outwit, outmaneuver, and outperform each other. However, the concept of market rivalry as a complex game provides a better-running metaphor for the intricacies of competition described in this book. The game analogy offers a powerful way to capture the variety, complexity, and turbulence of modern rivalry as played out in old and new industries alike.[1] Some observers see the give-and-take, move and countermove, of market rivalry in terms of war or battle. A game better depicts rivals competing in multiple locations simultaneously and also moving in multiple (product or geographic) directions simultaneously. In addition, it better suggests the continual state of the ebb and flow of competition as some rivals succeed for a period, only to be quickly surpassed by others. Finally, it reflects the reality that leading-edge organizations like to think of themselves as shaping how rivalry unfolds—in the language of some strategists: the rules of the competitive game.

The strategy game involves five key elements:

1. The competitors or rivals.
2. The arenas in which they confront each other.
3. The stakes they win or lose.
4. The chips that are needed to participate in the game.
5. The methods by which score is kept.

To play the strategy game successfully, you have to understand the function of each element.

The Competitors: The Game's Participants

The interplay of the five key elements shapes the game's context and rules. Competition evolves as firms become more practiced and experienced. As they lay the foundation for tomorrow's success while competing to win today, they become more intelligent, networked, entrepreneurial, and ambitious.

Intelligent Competitors either become more intelligent or fall prey to rivals or to astute acquirers. Companies that survive continually enhance both their intellect and intelligence. Without corporate leadership that supports sustained (re)invigoration of both intellect and intelligence, the capabilities needed to win atrophy.

Intellect is broadly defined[2] as an organization's capacity to think (to perceive and understand) and to learn (to recognize and correct errors in its knowledge and processes of learning).[3] The collective intellect of many organizations has been improved through their commitment to train and develop managers at all levels; to surface and challenge prevailing mental models of their business, its environment, and the best market strategies; and to build the capacity for organizational renewal and, in some instances, reinvention.

Intellect is fueled by a flow of intelligence—data and information—that informs decision makers and influences decision making.[4] Winning organizations recognize that intelligence becomes obsolete very quickly in an information-driven society, and when it does, intellectual supremacy can't last. Consequently, companies need to continually update and extend what they know through interactions with customers, distribution channels, suppliers, competitors and sociopolitical entities, and employees with diverse talents and backgrounds. With effective management, these interactions become opportunities to test and develop the organization's intelligence about the future as well as the present. Cutting-edge companies employ scenario learning, simulations, and other future-oriented analysis tools to structure data and information about their environment from many sources. Such tools enhance an organization's ability to study competitive rivalry in an array of possible futures.

Networking Firms in many types of industries including automobiles, computers, software, pharmaceuticals, financial services, health care, and electronics can now be described as networked enterprises.[5] Organizations as diverse as Sun Microsystems, Unilever, Prudential Insurance, Daimler-Benz, and Motorola configure themselves through alliances and relationships in ways that were unthought of a few years ago. They form interconnected information and contractual webs that extend their contacts far beyond traditional boundaries. One pharmaceutical firm now has an interconnected web of research sites around the world, most of which it does not own or control. Such networks often radically transform organizations' assets, capabilities and competencies. These networked organizations are able to pursue opportunities unavailable to, or too expensive for, individual businesses. As a result, they foster new forms of rivalry and change the competitive landscape in ways that were unthinkable a decade ago.

Entrepreneurship The willingness of even large mature firms to change both the context of the strategy game and its marketplace rules, reflects the spread of entrepreneurship.[6] Once only small, young organizations saw the advantage in initiating new marketplace directions, changing their market's historic frame of reference, and departing radically from the traditional modes of marketplace behaviors. Now many organizations, large and small, act on the premise that the essence of strategy is to be different from rivals, to provide distinct (and preferably unique) value to customers, and to do so in ways that make it difficult for competitors to play catch-up.

Corporate leaders often have their best opportunity to create an entrepreneurial culture when their organizations are in dire straits. Mature companies all too often do not adopt radical change until they have no other choice. Downturns in performance caused Ford, Digital Equipment, Xerox, IBM, British Petroleum, Siemens, and Phillips, to embark on strategy renewal initiatives. Even exemplars of Japanese manufacturing success during the 1970s and 1980s such as Matsushita, Honda, and Toyota had to risk radical innovation and, in some cases, to reinvent their strategies, after they fell on difficult times.

Ambition The best way to understand the key industry players who are aggressively changing the game's context and rules is to first assess their ambitions and aspirations.[7] We should assume, whether or not their strategic intent or vision is explicitly communicated, that they aspire to lead the marketplace, to set the pace in technological change, and to create new ways of attracting and retaining customers. They are attempting to "grasp beyond their reach" and to "strive for stretch goals."[8] The actions of firms such as America Online, General Electric, Nestlé, Computer Associates, and Bertelsmann A. G. reveal that their sights are set not just on winning but on attaining domination of their product segment. They drive to be the marketplace and technological leader rather than just first among equals in the pack.

The Arenas: Where the Game Is Played

As a consequence of the changes wrought by intelligent, networked, entrepreneurial, and ambitious players, the strategy game now plays simultaneously in multiple arenas. Competitors confront each other in, and must win in, the end-customer, distribution channel, factor, institutional and geographic arenas (see Figure 1.1). Strategy must attract, win, and retain end-customers and distribution channel members, as well as suppliers or vendors, and must have the support of other institutional entities such as governmental agencies, industry or trade associations, technology sources, and community groups.[9]

Customers For many decades, strategy was viewed predominantly as a battle to capture end-customers by providing either better *or* cheaper offerings. Now the customer battleground gets rethought and remapped continuously as businesses compete to offer products and services that are better *and* cheaper. Cutting-edge firms are even customizing their offerings.

This high-speed rivalry to serve customers even occurs across what previously were considered unrelated industries. Once secure product-customer segments have fallen prey to assault from newer products: multiple segments within financial services now compete against each other; telephone, television, cable TV, and electronic segments are increasingly intermingled; and substitutes spawned by technology allow new competitors. To cite another example, it may be only a matter of time before teleconferencing displaces a major portion of the most profitable air travel business.

Channels Distribution channels such as wholesalers, distributors, retailers, and value-added resellers, represent an increasingly intense battlefield in almost all markets or competitive domains.[10] Getting into (and remaining

FIGURE 1.1
The Locales of Rivalry

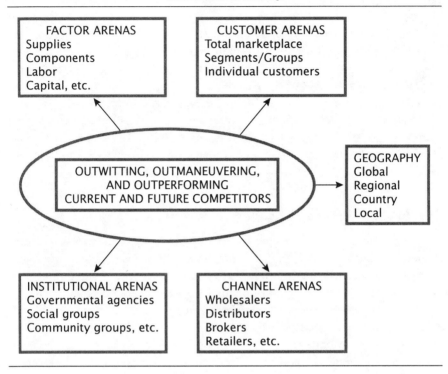

in) the right channels, is now a fundamental strategic challenge for almost all enterprises. Many firms such as the VF Corporation (clothing), Procter & Gamble (consumer goods), and Compaq (computers) reward their managers handsomely for winning battles in their channel wars. Marketplace innovation now includes finding opportunities to compete in new channels through the Internet and newer telecommunications developments. Unless such challenges are met and the channel battles are won, an organization won't come in first in the race to get its products and services to end users.

Factors The factor marketplace—the competition for raw materials, components, labor, capital, and information, to name just a few factors—is now another intense battle zone. When firms have to match the product variety and prices of rivals everywhere on the globe, they must pay greater attention to the sources of factors, the quality of factor inputs, and cost management. This in turn elevates the importance of intellect and intelligence as factors that can overcome low labor costs or cheap raw material. Intelligent, networked players recognize that the quality and availability of factors severely constrain their product opportunities and choices. Increasing attention is being devoted in many organizations to winning in their critical factor markets.

Institutions In many instances, winning in the product, channel, and factor marketplaces can no longer be accomplished without a comprehensive plan for succeeding in the institutional or political arena.[11] Networked, intelligent, and entrepreneurial players don't leave to chance their relationships with other market participants—suppliers, distributors, end-customers, technology sources, industry and trade associations. They must also interface effectively with sociopolitical entities such as community groups, public policy and social interest groups, standards-setting bodies, and governmental agencies. Many corporations have found themselves ultimately outmaneuvered in the product and factor marketplaces by the adept actions of their rivals in the institutional arena.[12]

Geography As the world economy moves into the twenty-first century, competition is no longer confined by national or even continental boundaries. The ambitions of successful business enterprises now stretch well beyond their local or historic geographic area. Winning entails anticipating developments in multiple geographic markets and determining how best to preempt or attack rivals across regions, often necessitating trade-offs between operations in geographic areas. Even small businesses can compete globally with firms of all sizes through the Internet. With almost instantaneous global communications, what transpires in one geographic area can quickly affect rivalry in other areas.

The Stakes: What You Get When You Win or Lose

The rewards of winning in the strategy game get larger and more precarious. At the same time, losing becomes more crippling and more difficult to overcome. In some product markets, only the consistent winners can stay in the game, so players must determine and assess their bets based on benefits from future successes and the costs of losing.[13]

Winning Strategy bets get bigger all the time. Dominance of a market segment or an entire competitive domain is frequently a company's driving focus; and leadership of the next generation of product or technology is often its immediate driving goal. Firms as diverse as General Electric, Honda, Disney, Procter & Gamble, Nestlé, and Sony, as well as many smaller less well-known entities, now aim for global marketplace leadership, a high-stakes gamble.[14]

Success becomes more elusive as many firms stretch themselves to the limits of their grasp by making acquisitions or buying market share that they can only afford if the economy keeps growing rapidly. As evidenced in the computer, software, automobile, fashion, and other industries, winners may not enjoy their success for long either. Moreover, the amount of capital required to be a major player continues to increase. Some food firms spend in excess of $20 million merely introducing their product to the marketplace. Ford invested $6 billion in its new "global" automobile. All phases of business activity, from research and development through engineering, manufacturing, marketing, and distribution absorb substantial investment. "Bet-the-ranch" decisions are becoming more common for all sizes of firms.

Losing   The managerial, technological, and product challenges of getting back into the competitive race once a company has fallen behind are enormous for most firms. So the costs of losing a decisive battle have become larger, more painful, and less amenable to remedy. Some firms can recover from financial losses but not from loss of brand loyalty and deterioration of customer goodwill, respect and admiration of supply and distribution channels, and of cooperation from technology sources. A firm that suffers any of these setbacks is saddled with burdens that hinder its chances of successfully getting back into the game after a misstep. Successful turnarounds in which firms regain substantial lost market position such as Harley-Davidson in motorcycles, Ford in automobiles, and Sears Roebuck in the retail sector, are rare. General Motor's multibillion-dollar, multidecade investment in its Saturn division illustrates the enormity of the challenge confronting even the richest firms when they try to regain their former glory in an industry segment.

The Chips: What Is Needed to Play the Game

Companies tally what it takes to play in the strategy game in chips—the resources required to be a successful player. A transformation is occurring in the concept of resources. Financial balance sheet items such as capital, plant and equipment, and inventory, though necessary, are no longer the dominant building blocks of corporate competitiveness in the long run.[15] Another recent change of thought is that ultra high product quality, the focus of much attention in the 1980s when U.S. and European firms were incessantly compared with Japanese competitors, now is the industry standard. Only by meeting the highest product standard can a company be certified as a supplier in many industries, so quality no longer can be the major source of sustainable differentiation.

Knowledge The steel industry provides a striking illustration of how knowledge has become both the new strategic engine and the business currency. For decades, scale was the decisive competitive advantage in this so-called commodity business. Then in the 1970s and 1980s, steel customers wanted specialty products, and small companies prospered by switching the basis of competition to knowledge—about markets, customers, processes, products, service, and raw materials. In recent years, the invention of lightweight steel for automobiles has turned steel production into a high-tech enterprise. Pioneering steel companies such as Nucor and Chaparral Steel recognized their workers and forepersons as knowledge workers and as partners in innovation and process reengineering at a time when their antediluvian competitors were still fighting the labor wars of the 1960s.

Knowledge results when the intellect (the capacity to think) does purposeful work using data and information. It generates new products, powers new processes, and spawns new materials. It affects all levels and functions in organizations; every individual is now a knowledge worker.[16] Firms that formerly understood their purpose narrowly: as makers of products and services—now see their enterprise broadly: as generators and users of knowledge. To maintain their competitiveness, players need continual replenishment of knowledge about customers' tastes, changes in competitors' behaviors, technology developments, and future marketplace dynamics.

Relationships Linkages with organizations outside the corporation are essential to competitiveness for an obvious reason: few organizations have the wherewithal (capital, knowledge, capabilities) to go it alone with any hope of continuously winning in the strategy game.[17] Linkages come in many forms: the range of alliances, informal relationships, and networks is diverse and constantly evolving. Corporations have been acting with ever greater ingenuity by crafting linkages with rivals, channels, customers, suppliers, and technology sources.

Perceptions Perceptual chips[18] such as brand loyalty, corporate image, and competitive reputation[19] underpin strategic initiatives. An organization's image and reputation in the eyes of the different groups that compose its stakeholders—(current and potential) customers, competitors, and suppliers—may determine the success or failure of its efforts to introduce new products, to change how it competes in the marketplace, or to seek governmental support of its interests.

These perceptual assets can be difficult to measure and can disappear quickly. They take inordinate sustained effort over many years to cultivate, yet they can dissipate overnight if a firm blunders. Their value can decline and even disappear not because of anything the firm itself does but as a result of the actions of competitors. Some organizations are not even aware that they possess these chips until they are surprised by marketplace events that reveal a dramatic change in stakeholder perceptions. In contrast, firms that depend on image-based marketing—clothes designers, soft drink makers, entertainment packagers—make customer perceptions the focus of extensive and continued investment and commitment.

Capabilities and Competencies Knowledge, relationships, and perceptions contribute to and benefit from skills, capabilities, and competencies. What organizations do well—their distinctive capabilities and competencies—can be leveraged for marketplace advantage. Identifying the capabilities and competencies needed to generate successful new products is central to winning. The recent emphasis[20] upon what organizations do, as opposed to the asset configuration they possess, is well placed.

Keeping Score: Tracking and Anticipating Winners and Losers

Keeping score requires explicit attention to the following questions:

- Who is winning and losing in each arena?
- Who is controlling the stakes?
- Who is reconceiving the rules and redeploying assets in creative ways?
- Who is redefining how score is kept?

Score can be measured and monitored in many ways. There are relevant parameters (or indicators) for each question and for individual arenas, stakes, and chips. Tracking who is winning and losing in each arena requires separate indicators for support of customers (e.g., market share, product usage); support of channels (e.g., acceptance of products, shelf space); support of suppliers (e.g., suppliers' willingness to partner, prices charged); and support of institutional entities (e.g., court decisions, commitments of community groups).

Keeping score must address not just the past and present, but also the future. Thus, parameters must be developed to help anticipate who will win and lose in the various arenas. For example, parameters pertaining to new products (as an indicator of who will win in the channel and customer arenas) might include development of specific measures for tracking knowledge (e.g., hiring new types of people), relationships (e.g., changes in alliance relationships) and capabilities and competencies (e.g., development of technological prowess).

Changing the Way the Game Is Played

Organizations seek to win by affecting the strategy game in two separate though highly related ways. First, they endeavor to reshape the game's *context:* the players, arenas, stakes, chips, and scorekeeping. Second, they aim to change its *marketplace rules:* how end-customers, channels, factors, and institutions are attracted, won, and retained.

Reshaping the Game's Context

Ambitious, intelligent, networked, and entrepreneurial firms are not satisfied with adhering to the game's prevailing conditions. They recognize that flux breeds opportunity. They understand that unless strategy is entrepreneurial and relentlessly seeks new opportunities in and around the competitive arenas, they can not get ahead of the competition, much less stay there. They know that if they do not create marketplace change, others will do so. Thus, they seek to alter to their own advantage each element in the game: the structure of the game's combatants, the configuration of the arenas, the nature of the stakes, the composition of the chips, and parameters and criteria by which score is kept.

Firms use a number of levers to alter these elements.

Restructuring Players   Few firms hesitate to restructure the game's combatants to their own advantage. Firms alter the number of players or change their own position relative to other players.[21] Alliances, mergers, and acquisitions are *direct* means of *reducing* the number of existing rivals. Food giant Heinz, for example, through a series of acquisitions greatly reduced the number of players in the pet food business. The development of networks[22] linking suppliers, producers, channels, and end-customers is another increasingly common ploy to alter the configuration of players. Investments in embryonic entities and emerging rivals are used by many firms such as Microsoft and Du Pont to preempt the emergence of potential players.

The successful introduction of new products, product line extensions, and substitute products *indirectly* may topple the old game's player structure by causing the decline and exit of the previously dominant players.

Reconfiguring Arenas   Firms dramatically reconfigure the terms of competition by maneuvering in each of the arenas: customers, channels, factors, institutions, and geography. *Product* advances often force competitors to play catch-up. By continually introducing new products and extensions of existing products, firms such as Intel, Microsoft, Disney, Rubbermaid, Nucor, 3M, and Hewlett-Packard, never let competition in the *end-customer* arena stagnate. Japanese automobile manufacturers, much to the surprise of the then dominant U.S. and European rivals, changed the competitive context of luxury car segment with the introduction of the Lexus, Infiniti, and Acura brand names. Similarly, Black & Decker launched its attack on the professional tool market with an extended product line under the DeWalt brand name. In both the auto and tool manufacturer cases, rivals soon discovered they were in a new game.

Firms endeavor to build linkages with distribution *channels* that induce favorable treatment and in some cases inhibit the entry of rivals. The integration of logistics and information systems resulting in the rapid movement of products, better service, less inventory, and lower cost has established such tightly bound linkages between many organizations and their distribution channels that rivals have enormous difficulty entering or even sustaining their position in these channels. The collaboration between Procter & Gamble and Wal-Mart involving tight integration of product ordering, inventory control, and logistics is a classic case in point.

By the same token, many organizations have preempted rivals' moves by developing exclusive relationships with the providers of components and raw materials, the sources of *factor advantage.* Many firms choose to jointly develop components, raw materials, technologies, and supplies with factor providers.[23] In some instances, firms integrate backward by acquiring existing sources or developing their own supplies internally, thus either increasing or decreasing the number of factor providers as well as the volume of supply.

In the *institutional* arena, companies use the courts, legislatures, governmental agencies, and industry standard-setting groups to shape competitive conditions to their own advantage. Many firms, including Intel, AT&T, Apple, and Motorola, have resorted to the courts to restrain or punish new entrants (through protection of patents and other intellectual property rights). Others have sought to erect entry barriers (quotas, duties, and the protection of prevailing subsidies). Leaders in the television receiver, electronics, automobile, and steel industries, have appealed to governmental agencies to prohibit competitive practices that they claimed provided "unfair" advantages to rivals.

Reshaping Stakes One intended consequence of many firms' efforts to win in the various arenas as previously discussed is to escalate the stakes— the benefits of winning and the costs of losing. To stay the course with rivals, many firms now find that major strategic moves such as an important new product introduction or the redesign of manufacturing operations are often bet-the-ranch decisions. Success is essential to fund the next round of product development and engage in the next stage of marketplace rivalry; failure jeopardizes involvement in that product sector and sometimes puts at risk the entire organization. Chrysler's introduction of the minivan, Digital Equipment Corporation's introduction of its Alpha chip, and Lotus Corporation's market launch of Lotus 123 are classic examples of the enormity of the new product introduction stakes.

Reconceiving Chips   The pace of rivalry is such that no firm can now afford to take its resources for granted. Even firms in what many perceive to be low-tech businesses, such as textiles, shoes, furniture, paint, and books, are feverishly pursuing new knowledge that might radically reshape established products or traditional ways of manufacturing and distributing them. In high-tech businesses such as electronics, firms that include IBM, Apple, Motorola, Intel, and Microsoft have fashioned multiple alliances with entities all across the activity/value chain[24] to develop and apply new types of knowledge and capabilities that they did not possess, and could not develop or acquire quickly enough on their own.

Redefining the Score   Changes by companies in players, arenas, stakes, and chips also affect how they define and measure the score. The accepted norms for performance parameters may change or firms may establish new parameters. Many firms have redefined or rescaled customer satisfaction from narrow product functionality to include all aspects of interactions with customers. The Japanese automobile manufacturers redefined "quality" for many consumers. Other companies have increased the rate of product enhancements, upgrades, and speed to market. An increasing number of businesses make the development of knowledge and its application across product lines or business sectors a critical parameter. Some firms have initiated major efforts to develop new capabilities and competencies (and monitor their progress in doing so against specific competitors) as one element in their scorecard to determine who will win in the future marketplace.

Changing the Game's Marketplace Rules

Within a strategy game's context or conditions, competitors strive to attract, obtain, and retain the support, commitment, and involvement of end-customers, channel members, factor suppliers, and institutions. Over time, however, established practices and norms emerge—what we shall refer to as marketplace rules—pertaining to how best to package and distribute products, create image and reputation, deliver service, build relationships, and set price. Yet, the players must continuously seek new ways to differentiate themselves; otherwise they are unable to deliver distinctive value to channels and end-customers. Virgin Airways by modifying its airplanes, providing limousine services for its business class customers, and crafting a new image of higher value but at lower prices for its coach customers, dramatically altered how the game was played between trans-Atlantic rivals in the airline business. In short, the marketplace rules are in a continuous state of flux.

Modes of Competition   Several modes of competition can be employed within the end-customer and channel arenas to get and keep customers. Although rivals compete in many distinct ways, firms can make eight key choices to distinguish and differentiate themselves in the eyes of customers and channels: product line width, product features, functionality, service, distribution or availability, image and reputation, selling and relationships, and price.[25] Sustainable differentiation is more likely to occur when all the modes of competition are working in concert.

Focus   Companies make the choices previously noted to accomplish three distinct, though related, tasks: attracting, winning, and retaining customers and channels. Attracting customers is a prelude to winning or acquiring them. What attracts customers is often not what wins them: brand name and product reputation influence customers to try a product such as an automobile or personal computer; functionality and better-than-expected price may be what compels them to make the purchase. Why customers buy initially often has little to do with why they repurchase; customers have to be continuously rewon.[26]

Levels   Marketplace rules can be changed at three distinct but related levels: the *aggregate* marketplace or, more narrowly, a competitive domain; a product-customer *segment* such as a niche within a competitive domain; and *local,* an individual customer or channel member.

At the *aggregate* level, rivals compete for a share of customers' attention and resources. All products ultimately compete for customers' limited income or cash flow. More narrowly, rivals compete for a slice of a particular industry or competitive domain: a group of related products. Ford, General Motors, Chrysler, Volvo, Toyota, Honda, and other automobile manufacturers strive for a share of current and future automobile sales. To attract customers into their showrooms, they try to build name recognition, reputation for product functionality, and brand loyalty.

Competitors confront one another more directly within and across product-customer *segments* or niches such as the luxury, mid-size, or compact product segments of the automobile market. The rivalry is more intense and direct. The intent is to win market share and position for the next rounds of rivalry.

All rivalry ultimately is acted out at the *local* or micro level. Each individual customer selects among rivals' offerings. At this level, the game is typically zero-sum: purchasing one rival's offering means lost opportunity for other competitors. A customer who purchases a BMW automobile is lost to other manufacturers for that purchase.

Trends Whatever the level of rivalry, at least four trends are evident in how organizations strive to change the marketplace rules. First, most firms' pursuit of differentiation is characterized by the switch from providing "products" to delivering "solutions." No longer do most organizations conceive what they offer or deliver to customers as solely or predominantly the functionality and features associated with their product. Rather, they view their offering as a solution: it represents a response to multiple needs and wants related to specific products. Customers not only want an automobile that is superbly functional but also want service that is convenient, spare parts that are reasonably priced, and high resale value.[27]

Second, increasingly, customers want custom-tailored solutions—customization. So an organization's offering range no longer should be limited to discrete types or forms. Companies must create an offering or solution that meets each customer's specific needs and wants. Ideally, each customer interaction becomes a mutual learning opportunity.

Third, the days when a company could be confident that its competitors' product line would remain stable have passed and the norm is now relentless change: continuous product and solution enhancement has become more the norm.[28] Any complacency about change, any satisfaction with solution success, any delay in redeploying the fruits of past success, opens the door wider to competitors. The intent is to continually set "the bar" of success at a higher level for existing and potential competitors.

Fourth, the switch from an emphasis on price/performance to price/value has been a long-term trend and lies at the core of all efforts to differentiate products or solutions. Value is denominated in both tangible dimensions such as product functionality, features, and service, and intangible dimensions such as image, reputation, and relationships. Providers of technology-based solutions such as manufacturing control systems can no longer emphasize only the performance and reliability of what they offer. They must also provide superior service and develop intimate working relationships with individual customers so that the value perceived and realized by customers goes well beyond the functionality of the tangible product.

Winning: Outwitting, Outmaneuvering, and Outperforming

To succeed in changing the strategy game's context and marketplace rules, companies must pay close attention to current and future competitors. To win, you have to understand your competition. Competitors can blindside you by initiating change before the need for it becomes apparent. That's why winners pay premiums for managers who outwit rivals. The firm's own strategy initiatives may be preempted by the moves of competitors. One or more competitors may simply do better what the organization is doing. To win against opponents, companies need strategies for three related tasks: outwitting, outmaneuvering, and outperforming competitors. Each task is distinct. Each is necessary but not sufficient for sustained competitive success.

Outwitting Competitors

Outwitting rivals means to outthink or to outsmart them. It involves detecting, anticipating, understanding, and instigating change in the competitive arenas more quickly and more incisively than rivals.

To consistently outwit opponents, companies must be the first to *detect* how the strategy game is changing. Signs of change include:

- How are the players becoming more intelligent, networked, entrepreneurial, and ambitious?
- What changes are occurring in the arenas?
- What organizational, competitive, and macroenvironmental[29] forces are propelling them and which organizations are driving them?
- How are the stakes changing, who is causing them to change, and how are they doing so?
- What chips are being created or augmented, who is doing so, and how are they being leveraged?
- How are the parameters and criteria in keeping score changing?

Managers thus must be willing to challenge conventional wisdom and see beyond mere data—to derive signals from the data about emergent change.[30]

The organization that *anticipates* faster and better than competitors how the game will change, or how it could change, is likely to have a head start in transforming such change into opportunity. Outwitting requires that organizations anticipate change before it happens. Thinking about the future is unavoidable: today's actions and commitments are played out in the marketplace at some future date. Backward thinking is increasingly required: it is the capacity to envisage a future and then trace backward to determine what actions would be necessary to make that future happen.[31] To anticipate well, an organization must be obsessed with inquiry. Data about rivals, arenas, stakes, chips, scorekeeping, and marketplace rules, are tinder for burning discussions about issues, questions, possibilities. For example, a customer's problem indicates a possible product innovation; the responses to a rival's actions suggest the need for a new way of doing business; a new technological capability opens up a new market opportunity.[32]

Detecting and anticipating change in and around the marketplace challenges the organization's *understanding* of the present and the future. Managers must be willing to re-examine and reinterpret their own knowledge: what they know about the competitive environment and their own organization. They must cultivate the art of "seeing things differently."

Detecting, anticipating, and understanding change is never sufficient. To outwit competitors, an organization must think through how it can foster and take advantage of change. That is, how it can alter the game's context and rules for its own gain.

Organizations must do their thinking efficiently and effectively. Outwitting rivals requires setting priorities for thinking about competitive issues. Those organizations that focus on internal operating issues and neglect external market concerns have their priorities reversed. To win in the marketplace, organizations should instead emphasize learning about how changes in the game's context, and rules can then be translated into marketplace opportunities. The development and deployment of organizational capabilities and competencies to expand market opportunity merit equal attention.[33]

Outwitting rivals also necessitates the capacity to renew one's own thinking, frame of reference, or perspective. In the face of pervasive environmental change, organizations convinced that their own view of the world is permanent cannot adapt. A stubborn commitment to obsolete beliefs, assumptions, perceptions, and projections caused many longtime industry leaders to stumble at different periods in their history. At crucial moments, IBM, Digital Equipment, General Motors, Sears Roebuck, and Kmart, as well as many less visible smaller firms, failed to adapt to the manifest change in their product-markets or competitive domains.[34]

Outmaneuvering Competitors

Successful organizations learn to quickly think, act, learn, and then act again, but smarter the second time. This maneuvering is what firms do to compete: the actions they take, the moves they make. Maneuvering means changing elements in the strategy game's context and rules.

Competitors can be outmaneuvered when an organization *preempts* rivals by restructuring the players, reconfiguring the arenas, reshaping the stakes, reconceiving chips, or redefining scorekeeping. For example, a competitor might acquire a potential new entrant before its product offerings impact the customer and channel arenas. Being first to the marketplace with new products is a classic means of preempting rivals.

An organization also outmaneuvers rivals by being more *skillful* at particular tasks. Corning outmaneuvers most rivals through its ability to manage alliances. Rivalry is now intense among firms in many competitive domains to develop more enduring relationships, to extend knowledge, to enhance perceptions, and build superior capabilities and competencies.[35]

Preempting and outdoing rivals involves *cooperative* arrangements with other entities rather than going it alone. Competitors might be outmaneuvered by aligning with a critical channel, an emerging new supplier, a large end-customer, or a highly visible community interest group. Lotus has aligned with numerous other entities in its efforts to make its Notes software the industry leader.

Despite the historic emphasis on the channel and customer arenas, organizations now also view maneuvers in the *factor* and *institutional* arenas as increasingly critical to long-run success. With a view to preempting or outdoing rivals, organizations strive to attain guaranteed supply of scarce raw materials, to lock in critical components, to get capital on the most preferential terms, to obtain rights to scarce know-how, and to secure key human resources. Organizations also maneuver in the institutional arena to prevent restructuring of the rivalry (such as seeking regulatory prohibition of mergers, alliances, or acquisitions), from launching new products (such as challenging their copyright or patents in the courts), and from entering specific geographic markets (by appealing to local governments and other interest groups). Organizations maneuver to obtain governmental, labor, and local community support for building plants by entering into public negotiations with institutional leaders in multiple geographic areas.

Some firms outmaneuver rivals by reshaping the *stakes* in one or more arenas. Many large firms now use networks to develop products more quickly (and thus be first to the market); in this way, they integrate and extend knowledge possessed by different entities in the network while lowering their own product development costs. The result is that the stakes are reshaped for rivals. If they don't act quickly, their current products will lose their advantage; the costs for not acting quickly also increase, in some cases dramatically so.

Moves in the arenas always involve the deployment of *chips*. Outmaneuvering rivals entails the development of superior *relationships* with multiple entities in each arena. In the automobile industry, Ford and Saturn are now reputed to have developed exemplar partnerships with many of their *factor* suppliers. Some firms now install full-time sales and service representatives in large commercial and corporate *end-customers* to inhibit penetration by rivals. Some firms have outmaneuvered rivals by continually advancing the state of *knowledge* relevant to specific products, technologies, or competitive domains: Intel in microprocessor chips, Merck in some pharmaceutical products, and IBM in many integrated system and software solutions.

Outmaneuvering rivals is the essence of changing the marketplace rules. Moves may preempt or outdo rivals along each mode of competition with a view to attracting, winning, and retaining customers: product line width can be narrowed or extended; features can be added or subtracted; functionality can be improved; service can be created or revamped; distribution can be structured; image and reputation can be sharpened; selling and relationships can be targeted; and price can be segmented.[36]

Outperforming Competitors

Thinking and maneuvering generate outcomes such as new products introduced, market share gained, and financial returns achieved. However, indicators such as these only reveal who is winning and losing to date: they capture current performance as a result of past actions. In many instances, they are poor measures of future performance. Thus, identification and assessment of results must go beyond who *has* won or lost: it must assess which competitors are positioning themselves to win in the marketplace of tomorrow—and how they are planning to do so—before the results or outcomes are evident for all to see *in* the competitive arenas.

Any consideration of outperforming competitors begs two fundamental questions: What are the relevant performance *parameters* (or measures)? What are the *criteria* against which performance is assessed? Answering these questions in turn raises further issues: How is the short-run and the long-run best integrated? What are the relevant parameters to anticipate future success? How are technological, marketplace, and financial parameters reconciled? Against which competitors should performance be assessed?

Such questions about tomorrow's marketplace address whether the organization (or competitors) is *creating a new strategy game.* The net effect is to invent a business: new products, new customer needs, a new way of doing business.[37] Critical parameters might include:

- Who is creating new customer needs that do not exist today?
- Who is establishing new product configurations that do not exist today?
- Who is establishing new channels to reach old and new customers?
- Who is reinventing the stakes such that others are confined to playing catch-up roles?

- Who is creating new capabilities and competencies as the source of new products and customer needs?
- Who is creating new knowledge that will drive competencies and products?

Creating a new game emphasizes winning in the future by creating a new competitive space. At any point in time, few organizations will be creating a new strategy game. Thus, performance always must be assessed with regard to *reconstructing an existing strategy game*. The focus is changing the game's context around *existing* product configurations, or more likely, extensions of existing products or solutions. To cite two recent examples: a number of firms have announced alliances to reconstruct the TV news and sports segments pioneered by CNN and ESPN respectively.

Key parameters might include:

- Who is introducing, or plans to introduce, the next generation of the product?
- Who is establishing new relationships with channels?
- Who is redefining relationships with factor suppliers?
- Who is using the institutional arena advantageously?
- Who is reinventing the stakes such that others are confined to playing catch-up roles?
- Who is reconceiving chips such as knowledge, perceptions, and capabilities?

At the most micro level, as rivals are creating or reconstructing the strategy game, performance can be assessed with regard to *shifting the current marketplace rules*. Critical parameters include:

- Who is winning or losing share in existing products?
- Who is establishing new levels of customer satisfaction?
- Who is recomposing the standards of customer satisfaction?
- Who is leading product and customer functionality?
- Who is dominating the price-value relationship?
- Who is the leader in each mode of competition?

Outperforming competitors must be assessed along the three levels: creating a new strategy game; reconstructing an existing game; and shifting the current marketplace rules. Each level emphasizes the importance of comparison with rivals. Attention to each level serves a purpose. Neglect of any level greatly misconstrues an organization's performance.

Interconnections between the Three Elements

Thinking and maneuvering are so interlinked as to be almost inseparable: thinking precedes, is concurrent with, and follows action.[38] By learning from the results and consequences of its own actions, as well as those of others, the organization tests and refines its thinking.

The parameters and criteria used to assess performance serve to focus both thinking and action. If creating a new strategy game rather than shifting current marketplace rules is what preoccupies management, then what managers think about (the substance of outwitting) and the actions they take (the substance of outmaneuvering) will differ accordingly.

The strategy game makes sense only in the strategist's mind.[39] It is the strategist who interprets actions or maneuvers. It is the strategist who sees patterns where others might see only discrete or incongruent actions.

Strategy: Rivalry and Competitors

The preceding discussion suggests a number of overarching conclusions about rivalry and competitors. Rivalry occurs at three levels: thinking (outwitting), acting or behaviors (outmaneuvering), and results or performing (outperforming). Rivalry takes place in multiple arenas: rivals compete to attract, win, and retain customers, channels, suppliers, and institutions. Rivalry is thus about much more than competing for customers. Rivals maneuver to win factor supplies; to develop chips; to create superior perceptions; to build support from institutional entities.

Rivals themselves are changing. No longer can they adhere to the strategies that made them historically successful. Many now recognize that execution of change is critical. Many are reinventing their chips: knowledge, relationships, capabilities, and competencies. Many are changing how they define and keep score to take better account of new realities.

Competitors are an essential window on the current and future competitive environment. They shape the strategy game's context and its marketplace rules. Their current and future strategies must be considered by any organization seeking to outwit, outmaneuver, and outperform them. Consideration of competitors raises a barrage of questions that are addressed in this book.

Against Whom Does the Organization Compete?

Identifying relevant competitive domains does not by itself indicate current and potential competitors. Each must be considered as an input to the outwitting, outmaneuvering and outperforming process. Each may radically shift the content and meaning of strategy. Each carries distinct action implications. To cite merely one common consequence of not considering current and potential competitors, attempts to develop and sustain differentiation are likely to be aimed at the wrong rivals. The organization then learns it has outmaneuvered and outperformed its target rivals but lost to other competitors that it did not "see" as part of its competition.

What Do We Need to Know about Competitors

Outwitting, outmaneuvering, and outperforming place specific demands on what an organization should know about its current and potential rivals. For example, outwitting compels analysis of the thinking or mind-set underlying rivals' current or projected strategies. Outmaneuvering suggests the need to identify what competitors are likely to do under different marketplace or organizational conditions. Outperforming compels attention to what goals competitors are pursuing. The concepts and analysis frameworks presented in each chapter in this book are intended to grapple with this central question: what does an organization need to know about its competitors (and the forces, such as customers, that affect them)?

What Are the Implications for the Organization?

Organizations do not generate knowledge about competitors (and as a consequence about each of the competitive arenas) for its own sake. Rather the purpose is to generate knowledge that informs decision makers and influences decision making. Thus the emphasis throughout this book is on the use of such knowledge in strategy development and execution.

How Does the Organization Engage in Competitor Learning?

Competitor knowledge must be fostered and developed. It involves specific analytical processes: gathering data about competitors; applying tools and techniques to categorize, codify, structure, and analyze the data; drawing inferences and insights from the analysis; and making use of the analysis in decision making. These analysis tasks are the focus of every chapter in this book. They are all embedded in the concept of competitor learning—to which we now turn in Chapter 2.

Competitor Learning

OUTWITTING, OUTMANEUVERING, AND OUTPERFORMING COMPETITORS IS ABOUT THE creation of change: changing the strategy game's context and its marketplace rules. Since change in and around the arenas discussed in Chapter 1— end-customers, channels, factors, institutions, and geography—is the norm, strategy is thus always conditional on some understanding of the future.[1] In the face of pervasive and dynamic change, the old ways of doing things— the firm's long-held recipes about how to win in the marketplace and how to manage internally—are not likely to generate continued success. When strategy no longer contains an entrepreneurial content, the organization has sown the seeds of its own demise. The result inevitably is organizational decline and ultimately death. Innovation and entrepreneurship are the only sources of long-run salvation in a constantly changing marketplace.[2]

Strategy, as the creation and exploitation of change, is unavoidably dependent and predicated on learning. Change can not be created or leveraged in the absence of learning about both the external environment and the organization itself. Learning about change in and around customers, suppliers, distribution channels, technology, and the social, political, and economic milieu furnishes an understanding of the current competitive context as well as key inputs in developing "alternative futures."[3] It is in *future* competitive contexts that the capacity to outwit, outmaneuver, and outperform competitors is most severely tested. The central thesis in this book is that attention to current and future competitors[4] provides a critical focus for learning about both the external environment and the focal firm.[5]

The nexus between strategy and competitor learning must be considerably more closely interwoven than is the case in most organizations today, for at least two reasons. First, change in the customer, channel, factor, and institutional arenas is increasingly pervasive, discontinuous, and unpredictable. As a consequence, "mental models" of the competitive environment and the future are often incongruent with the actual external world.[6] Each organization must continually relearn what change is occurring and what forces are driving it.

Second, in part due to change in the external arenas, each organization must continually renew, reinvigorate, and reinvent itself. The bases of historic success become the seeds of future failure.[7] In the absence of systematic attention to learning, knowledge becomes obsolete, skills stagnate, and capabilities and competencies deteriorate. Managing and leading organizational change is the handmaiden of successfully crafting and exploiting change in the marketplace.

This chapter examines the role of competitor analysis in fostering the nexus between strategy and learning. We begin by defining what learning is and detailing a model of competitor learning including the linkage between learning and knowledge. We then note how competitors serve as a source of learning and identify four types of competitor learning. Two distinct modes of competitor learning, guided and open-ended learning, are next outlined. Finally, some key errors, and their implications, in the processes of learning or knowing are noted and discussed.

A Model of Competitor Learning

In organizational settings, learning is not engaged in for its own sake. It is focused, instrumental and purposeful: it is not just (about) the acquisition or creation of knowledge. The outputs of learning must be integrated into decision making; they must inform decision makers, influence decision making, and guide action.[8] Competitor learning therefore cannot stop with the generation of knowledge *about* competitors: the knowledge must be put to use. An organization truly learns if the output of its learning—whether referred to as knowledge or something else—is recognized as (potentially) useful in decision making. Learning therefore *should* cause the organization to reflect on its own actions and those of others.[9] As a consequence, learning should extend the range of the organization's choices and its possible behaviors and actions.[10]

A model of competitor learning that integrates both knowledge generation and knowledge use is presented in Figure 2.1. The model is segmented into two related learning domains: building knowledge about competitors

FIGURE 2.1
Competitor Learning

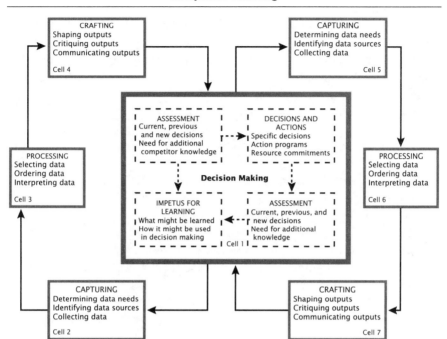

(as well as about customers, channels, suppliers, and other facets of the competitive environment) and using that knowledge in decision making. Learning as used throughout this book involves both knowledge generation and knowledge use.

Both knowledge generation and knowledge use involve four separate though intimately interrelated learning activities: capturing (inputs), processing (inputs), crafting (outputs), and decision making (using the outputs). Each cell in Figure 2.1 constitutes one of these activities. As evident in the following discussion, it is not easy to draw clearly demarcated conceptual or pragmatic boundaries around each activity: what takes place within one cell affects the other cells. Each of these four activities is crucial to understanding learning in organizations. Each activity is briefly discussed.

For purposes of illustration, we shall use the example of a firm, Omega, learning about a new product introduction by a competitor, Alpha. Omega historically had been the product leader; Alpha had been a persistent follower but had never been able to make a breakthrough product introduction that would catapult it into a position of market leadership.

Competitor Knowledge Generation

Impetus for Learning Learning takes place as individuals and groups engage in decision making and the routines of organizational life (Cell 1). Although developing and using knowledge is an implicit part of decision making and day-to-day routines, individuals and groups in organizational settings pay relatively little attention, for the most part, to explicitly reviewing, critiquing and augmenting their stock of knowledge. Thus, learning typically requires some type of impetus. Learning in the form of seeking new competitor knowledge or challenging existing knowledge is initiated or provoked in many ways and for many different purposes (as described later in this chapter).

An impetus for learning is typically neither a single event nor an isolated impulse. Rather, it involves a sequence of tasks[11] or considerations, each of which contributes to decision makers making the commitment to embark on learning, that is, to go through the learning activities depicted in Figure 2.1.

Decision makers are initially *sensitized to learning:* something causes them to consider learning about competitors. It may or may not be associated with competitors' actions or words.

They consider *what might be learned.* Any effort to engage in competitor learning presumes that something specific about one or more competitors will be learned. Sometimes, decision makers have only a vague intuition as to what might be learned.

They consider how what might be learned *could be used in decision making.* Again, decision makers may or may not have a clear sense of how specific decisions might be affected. It is not uncommon to find executives expressing a hunch that if they knew more about a competitor's technology development and application, they might change some of their present or planned technology programs and commitments.

In our new product illustration, some senior managers in Omega were sensitized to the need for competitor learning when a member of the salesforce informed them that he had been told by a customer that a salesperson from a competitor (Alpha) passed some comments about a major new product line that the firm would introduce within the next 12 to 15 months. Some senior executives in Omega were immediately concerned because if the new product line succeeded, it would likely mean a significant decline in the sales of Omega's principal product group, unless some type of preemptive or retaliatory action was taken.

Capturing Irrespective of the impetus for competitor learning, it requires inputs: data about competitors (Cell 2). Data may be in any form, may be about any facet of competitors, and may be received from different types of sources both inside and outside the organization.[12] Data is thus the raw material of learning. The acquisition of inputs typically involves a number of tasks.

The first task in capturing is *determining data requirements*. Often it is not clear to decision makers what data is required.[13] To guide data collection, it is useful for decision makers to consider what data might be ideal before they seek and interact with primary data sources.

Capturing necessitates *identifying data sources*. Again, frequently it is not self-evident what data can be obtained from sources internal or external to the organization.

Capturing also requires *collecting data*. Many different data collection processes and techniques are available.

Omega quickly determined that it needed to identify how far Alpha had progressed in product development, how long it would be before the product might be launched, and what the key characteristics of the product might be. It collected competitor data from many types of primary and secondary sources[14] using multiple modes of data gathering. It scanned several electronic databases to quickly pull together recent data about Alpha in various secondary publications. It questioned its own customers and those of other competitors (including Alpha's) for any data about Alpha's product development activities. It also interviewed technology and industry experts.

Processing Data do not speak for themselves. They require the intervention of one or more individuals: they must be processed[15] (Cell 3). A number of tasks typify processing.

Processing begins with *selecting data*. Individuals identify the data they consider relevant and important (as well as the data they may ignore). They do so either consciously or subconsciously.

Processing also requires the *ordering of data*. Individuals employ formal and informal tools and techniques to array and organize the selected data.

Data are selected and ordered to facilitate the individuals who *interpret* them. Interpretation implies that individuals imbue data with meaning. Meaning accrues when individuals bring some "logic" (a mode of thinking or reasoning), to bear on data. The interaction of logic and data thus gives rise to "interpretation." Any logic or reasoning to make sense of data entails judgments—the essence of interpretation. Different logics[16] are embedded in analytical tools and techniques to derive insights that are not evident from looking at the raw data alone.

Detecting relevant indicators and extracting from them signals[17] of past, current, and future states of competitors reside at the core of selecting, ordering, and interpreting data. Omega identified a number of indicators of Alpha's intention to launch the new product line:

- Statements made by Alpha's salespersons to customers.
- Statements made by Alpha's managers at an industry trade show.
- Changes in its manufacturing processes.
- Commitments made to the distribution channels.

Crafting Processing leads to outputs (Cell 4). However, outputs don't just happen; they must be crafted. As shown throughout this book, outputs take many forms including descriptions of competitors' strategies, alliances, assumptions, capabilities and competencies, and organization. They also include projections of competitors' future strategies. Outputs entail not just descriptions and projections of competitors' current and future states, but also interpretations (or judgments) concerning implications for competitors and the focal firm.

Outputs are crafted to inform decision makers and influence decision making. To do so, they typically must add to the organization's prior knowledge. They constitute new items of knowledge, changes to prior knowledge, or reenforcement of existing knowledge. The quality of the outputs, in terms of their increments of knowledge, and their impact on decision making, reflects the "value-added" of those doing the analysis.

Crafting also typically involves some specific tasks. Outputs need to be *shaped* or configured. Multiple options always exist in shaping or "formatting" outputs: they may be rich or slight in details; they may emphasize data and logic on the one hand, or implications on the other; they may exhibit only one or multiple logics; they may or may not include opposite interpretations and inferences, and their implications.

As outputs evolve, they need to be *critiqued.* This is in part, a continuation of processing: challenging and evaluating the interplay of data and logic that underpin specific interpretations, inferences, and implications. Multiple analytical and organizational options also exist in critiquing outputs.

Finally, outputs need to be *communicated* to decision makers and others within the organization.[18] They are not shaped and critiqued for their own sake. Multiple options also exist in how outputs are communicated.[19]

Omega's principal output was its conclusion that the competitor was indeed committed to introducing the new product line. Among other items, it projected:

- When the product would be introduced.
- What the configuration of the line would be.
- The principal features of the products.
- How the product line would be distributed.
- What the rate of market penetration might be.
- How the competitor might respond to the moves of other competitors.

Knowledge in Use

Assessment The central tenet in the learning model depicted in Figure 2.1 is that the generation of competitor knowledge is necessary but not sufficient. Decision makers must continually assess knowledge outputs for their decision relevance (Cell 1). Assessment[20] thus furnishes in part the link between competitor knowledge and action. In the absence of assessment, competitor knowledge is likely to remain in the nice-to-know category.

Assessing outputs for their decision relevance includes a number of tasks. Decision makers evaluate the implications of competitor knowledge for *current and previous decisions.* Outputs may suggest speeding up or slowing down the making of specific decisions or the execution of past decisions.

Decision makers *search for new decisions.* Outputs sometimes generate decisions that are new to the organization or to which managers had previously paid little heed.

Decision makers typically consider the *need for additional competitor knowledge.* Decision makers thus may decide to engage in further capturing, processing, and crafting.

Omega assessed the implications for itself of Alpha's impending product introduction. It considered the potential effects on the sales of its own product line, the reaction of distribution channels to supporting its product line, whether it should speed up its own product development plans and whether it could do anything to inhibit its existing customers from switching to the Alpha's potential new product. These assessments informed its decisions and subsequent actions.

Decisions and Actions Competitor learning therefore results in the generation of new decisions and actions and/or changes to prior decisions and action programs. The distinction between new and prior decisions and actions is central to learning. Assessment often surfaces decisions that were not previously considered. It also often reconfigures decisions already under consideration and leads to modifying the execution of prior decisions and commitments.

Omega made a number of decisions or commitments to action in anticipation of Alpha's new product launch:

- It committed to investigating the importance of an emerging technology to its customers—a new decision (the technology was identified by analyzing the competitor's potential product).
- It committed resources to speeding up its own R&D efforts.
- It launched a marketing and promotion program designed to build the firm's brand name and customer loyalty.

Capturing Decisions and actions of competitors and our own organization generate further data (Cell 5). Again, decision makers need to determine data requirements, identify data sources, and collect the requisite data.

Progress in executing the actions noted and consequent results were carefully tracked by Omega. It monitored[21] how well its own R&D activity was progressing, how various distributors and end-customers were responding to its new programs. It also simultaneously monitored Alpha's actions and their consequences before, during, and after the product launch. It tracked the response of the distribution channels and end-customers to the formal announcement of the new product line. It tracked the product rollout. It monitored how different types of customers responded to the new product.

Processing The data generated through the monitoring previously noted must be selected, ordered, and interpreted (Cell 6).

Among other things, Omega was able to draw inferences about Alpha's commitment to winning with its new product, about the behaviors of customers in different market segments in response to its own actions and Alpha's product introduction.

Crafting Processing the results and consequences of the focal firm's own actions and those of competitors leads to outputs (Cell 7). As is the case with Cell 4, outputs need to be shaped, critiqued, and communicated. Outputs include new knowledge—something the organization did not previously know (e.g., that a particular competitor has an extremely tight working relationship with a particular distribution channel), confirmation of existing knowledge (e.g., that customers would eagerly switch to a competitor) or rejection of prior knowledge (e.g., that a competitor was not strongly committed to staying in a particular product line).

Omega developed a small set of pivotal outputs pertaining to Alpha's actions in the marketplace:

- Alpha's new product was attracting new customers.
- Alpha's new product was succeeding in attracting away some of Omega's own customers.
- Alpha was likely to intensify its efforts to gain market share more quickly.

Assessment The outputs are again factored into ongoing decision making (Cell 1). Again, they may affect prior decisions and action plans or lead to new ones. Also, they may lead to the commitment to develop further competitor knowledge.

It became evident to Omega's managers that customers were willing to switch to the new product in far greater numbers than was initially expected. This in turn led to two decisions: to move more quickly than originally planned to get the firm's own new product into all distribution channels and to reduce prices on existing products as one means of holding onto existing customers.

The Competitor Learning Process: Some Principles

The competitor learning model illustrated in Figure 2.1 and discussed earlier reflects a number of widely shared learning principles. Each principle has specific implications for the approach to the analysis of current and future competitors advocated in this book.

Learning is a *continuous process:* it occurs over time. As illustrated in the Omega-Alpha case, learning evolves as the organization gathers data, processes it into outputs, assesses the outputs, takes action, monitors and reflects on the consequences of its actions and factors these outputs into decision making. It is a journey, not a destination, because change in the organization's external and internal environment, as noted earlier, is unrelenting, pervasive, and unpredictable. As soon as learning begins to stagnate, the organization's knowledge begins to slide into mythology (as explained later in this chapter).

Learning is a *cognitive process. Individual* decision makers make sense of the world around them: they select and order data; they imbue data with meaning; they draw inferences from incomplete data and partial analysis; they continually challenge their prior stock of knowledge. Thus, the wide variety of analysis tools and techniques presented throughout the remaining chapters are intended as aids to interpretation.

Learning also is a *collective process.* Although the difficulties in transforming individual learning into organizational learning are legend,[22] it cannot occur unless multiple individuals are intimately involved in all the learning activities noted in Figure 2.1. Learning truly occurs when individuals share their knowledge, challenge each other, and reflect on each other's judgments and assessments.[23] The frameworks of analysis presented in each chapter are intended to serve as the medium for collective learning.

Learning cannot be disassociated from decision making and action. As represented in Figure 2.1, *learning and doing are inseparable:* knowledge generation and knowledge use are inextricably interrelated. Learning generates knowledge that is embodied in action; action, in turn, generates further knowledge and learning.[24] Thus, as manifest in Figure 2.1, and as evident in the subsequent chapters, heavy emphasis is placed on the decision and action implications of competitor knowledge generation for the focal organization.

In part as a means of overcoming human frailties and organizational impediments (many of which are discussed later in this chapter), learning necessitates an *unrelenting commitment to question raising.* Inquiry is driven by a concern with questions rather than answers. Answers reflect a closed mind; questions reflect an openness to new data, views, logics, and challenges. Pervasive, discontinuous, and unpredictable change—much of it the result of the emergence of new competitors and actions of existing competitors—renders question raising a learning imperative. Each chapter offers many sets of questions as guides to the relevant analysis.

Learning is not just about accumulating (often apparently unrelated) data, no matter how new they are to the organization. Real insight comes from capturing *underlying structures:*[25] patterns that are revealed through ordering, selecting, and interpreting data. Thus, the analysis tools and techniques proposed in this book address how to detect patterns in current, emerging, and projected competitors and in the marketplace strategy, alliances and networks, assumptions, competencies, technology, and organization of individual competitors and groups of competitors.

Competitor learning is not an end in itself. Its intent is to better understand the *interface between the organization and its environment* as one input to outwitting, outmaneuvering, and outperforming current and future competitors. Thus, emphasis is placed throughout this book on competitor learning as the source of both preemptive and responsive actions.

Finally, learning in any context is severely handicapped unless there is a shared understanding of a number of key *concepts.*[26] Thus, key concepts pertaining to each chapter are defined and explicated before the relevant analysis frameworks are presented.

Refining the Notion of Knowledge

It is evident in the preceding discussion that learning and knowledge are closely linked. Knowledge is both an input to and output of learning. It is not created out of a blank slate; individuals and organizations always enter into learning with some given stock of tacit[27] and explicit knowledge about customers, suppliers, technology, products, and their own organization. However, learning changes the stock of knowledge: the presumption in all models of learning is that individuals, groups, and organizations possess the capacity to alter and augment what they know—their prevailing stock of knowledge.

The Elements of Knowledge

But what is knowledge? Although there are no generally accepted definitions of what constitutes knowledge, we can broadly conceive knowledge as the *stock* of what an individual or group of individuals know, or consider that they know. Individuals must have some basis for knowing: they must be able to offer some data and logic for what they claim to know. Stated differently, individuals must be able to justify what they hold as "knowledge."[28]

But a stock of what? The conception of knowledge advocated here is driven by a concern with what decision makers ought to know as they participate in decision making. Five separate though interrelated knowledge elements are suggested: the *facts* decision makers work with, the *perceptions* they hold, the *beliefs* they adhere to, the *assumptions* they accept, and the *projections* that inform their view of the future (see Figure 2.2). Because of change within and outside an organization, decision makers must continuously substantiate and justify the stock or content of each of these knowledge elements. Because of their importance in competitor learning, each of the knowledge elements as they pertain to competitors is briefly discussed.

Facts These are unambiguously true statements or assertions. They thus predominantly *describe* competitors' past or present states. Despite the desire and efforts in many organizations to develop a fact base about competitors, surprisingly little competitor data meets the test of facts in the sense that they are true or verified.[29] Moreover, facts about competitors are always

FIGURE 2.2
The Elements of Competitor Knowledge

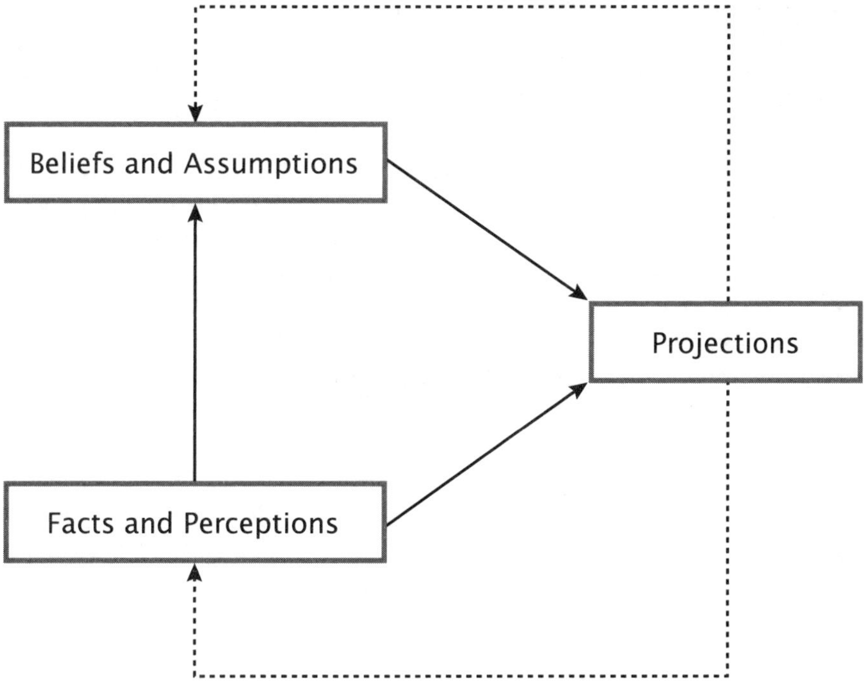

time dependent: because competitors are continually undergoing change, what is true today about a competitor may not be so tomorrow. Also, the more refined and specific the analysis, the greater the difficulty in generating facts. Descriptions of a competitor's financial situation may meet the test of facts at a general level (e.g., the competitor's financial condition is quickly deteriorating) but many of the details may be difficult to verify in any acceptable way. An understanding of competitor facts by themselves is of limited use as an input to decision making: the facts need to be processed and their implications derived. Knowledge (about any topic or subject) in organizational settings must be viewed as considerably more than a store of facts.

Perceptions Organizational members may hold impressions or opinions that do not meet the strict test of facts. Some of these perceptions are translatable into facts; others are not. However, whether or not perceptions are verifiable, individuals are still justified in holding them: there is data and logic to support them. As with facts, they are also predominantly descriptive. However, they refer to competitors' future as well as their past and current states.[30] Perceptions typically are of the form, "we think" or "it is our opinion that. . . . " Perceptions can refer to descriptions of microlevel[31] components of a competitor such as "we think its manufacturing process technology has been allowed to deteriorate" or "we think its managers tend to be very aggressive and compulsively competitive" or to descriptions of macrolevel components such as "we believe the competitor's marketplace strategy is becoming customer oriented."

Perceptions constitute a large part of the stock of any organization's competitor knowledge.

Beliefs Cause-effect relationships in the form of A leads to B are beliefs. They often connect or relate one or more facts and/or perceptions with other facts and/or perceptions. Thus, they are distinct from merely descriptive statements. Beliefs pertain to competitors' past, current, or future states.[32] Examples might be that the competitor's decline in market share has led to lower profitability or that a competitor's enhanced cash flow will result in greater investment in R&D leading to the revitalization of its product line within the next few years.

It is especially important to test beliefs for their justification. Because they represent a causal view of the world around us, they exert a strong influence on the way we think and how we act. If the logic or reasoning that supports a belief is not made explicit, it is difficult to evaluate the bases for holding or adhering to it.

Assumptions The organization takes for granted or considers that it must take for granted certain assumptions about competitors.[33] They are the "givens" about competitors that decision makers accept for the purposes of decision making. They may include some facts, perceptions, and beliefs. Assumptions may refer to competitors' past, current, or future states. Managers might assume that a particular competitor will not introduce a new product for some specific period or that a set of competitors will not be able to develop a specific type of competence. As with perceptions and beliefs, assumptions may be explicit or tacit. Explicit assumptions are those the organization consciously decides to adopt. Tacit assumptions are givens (about competitors) that decision makers are not conscious of or are not aware they have made,[34] for example, that a particular organization is not a competitor. As with perceptions and beliefs, it is often necessary to muster considerable data and logic to justify particular assumptions.

Projections These refer to justified or substantiated judgments[35] about the future. A critical element in competitor knowledge is projections of competitors' future states: assessments that go beyond facts and perceptions but that are sometimes heavily influenced by beliefs and assumptions. Projections are a critical output of competitor analysis.[36] Projections of competitors' future strategies as well as changes in their alliances, assumptions, assets, capabilities and competencies, and technology are addressed in later chapters. Projections that are accepted as "givens" become assumptions for decision-making purposes.

Learning and Knowledge

Knowledge as Input and Output

A distinguishing feature of knowledge, as defined, is that facts, perceptions, beliefs, assumptions, and projections always embody and reflect the judgments of one or more individuals.[37] As noted, such judgments are made explicitly or implicitly. Thus, at any point in time, an individual's or group's stock of competitor knowledge—facts, perceptions, beliefs, assumptions, and projections, pertaining to competitors—is the result of *prior* judgments (especially in Cells 1, 3, and 6 in Figure 2.1).

The stock of knowledge prevailing at any point in time serves as an input to the learning process (Cells 1 and 2 in Figure 2.1). As illustrated in the Omega-Alpha case discussed earlier, as a result of judgments and inferences[38] drawn by decision makers, new knowledge evolves: the prior facts, perceptions, beliefs, assumptions, and projections change.

Knowledge and Mythology

Since knowledge is the product of individuals' judgments, what often passes for knowledge is not consistent or congruent with the reality outside or inside the organization. Individuals' judgments are in part a consequence of the simplifications necessarily embedded in their mental models of the world around them. Knowledge is thus likely to become inconsistent with the environment for two principal reasons. First, individuals are innately reluctant to change their knowledge structure, even in the face of considerable evidence of the need to do so.[39] Second, as discussed in Chapter 1, the persistence and pervasiveness of change in and around the competitive arenas render it necessary to continually update the stock of knowledge.

A mismatch between an organization's prevailing knowledge and environmental change is rendered even more likely when we consider that a central challenge in learning is to develop knowledge (facts, perceptions, beliefs, assumptions, projections) pertaining to the future. In competitor learning, decision makers strive to develop projections about competitors' likely future strategies including their reactions to the focal organization's own potential moves. These projections need to be monitored; those that do not capture what competitors actually do need to be corrected.

To the extent that congruency between an organization's stock of knowledge and its external environment does not exist, erroneous or mistaken knowledge prevails; what organization theorists refer to as mythology.[40] To the extent that mythology exists, an organization is handicapped in its efforts to outwit, outmaneuver, and outperform competitors. A fundamental purpose of (competitor) learning is therefore to expose and correct such knowledge errors.

Learning as the Detection and Correction of Knowledge Errors

If learning is about the creation of useful knowledge, then it can be viewed as the detection and correction of errors in the organization's knowledge (its facts, perceptions, beliefs, assumptions, and projections) and processes of knowing.[41] Detecting and correcting these errors reduces mythology. As illustrated in Figure 2.1, knowledge errors (as distinct from errors pertaining to processes of knowing)[42] are detected in two ways: through the acquisition and development of new knowledge (Cells 1, 2, 3, and 4) or through reflection on action[43] (Cells 1, 5, 6, and 7). We shall consider the latter first because of the emphasis here on knowledge use.

An organization takes an action (e.g., changing price or the content of an advertisement) or a set of actions (e.g., the distribution, pricing, promotion, and service activities involved in a new product introduction) based on some given base of knowledge (Cell 1). The consequent results either match or mismatch the organization's base of facts, perceptions, beliefs, assumptions, or projections. A mismatch that is detected constitutes a *revealed* error.

Such errors are common. To cite merely one example: A competitor responds more quickly and more aggressively to an organization's moves (such as the launch of a new marketing program) than had been anticipated. Instead of reacting passively, the competitor initiates a set of countermoves intended to blunt the organization's expected first mover advantage. The error in assessing the competitor's likely reactions might reveal underestimation of the competitor's assets and capabilities (facts and perceptions), its underlying commitment to retaining its market position (assumptions) and its plans to extend its market share (projections). As these errors are identified, they can be corrected. This learning (the new increments to the organization's stock of knowledge) then serves as part of the input to the next set of decisions.

However, a match between the results or outcomes of decisions and actions, and knowledge, sometimes entails *concealed* errors, that is, errors in the stock of knowledge that have not been revealed. Concealed errors are critical because if a number of such errors exist, much of what is presumed to be knowledge is actually mythology. The organization might (mistakenly) decide that a competitor did not respond to its new product introduction because it was not willing to bear the necessary cost of doing so (a perception or assumption). However, if the real reason was the difficulty the competitor encountered in concluding an alliance with a new supplier so that it could launch the next generation of technology, the error might be revealed later by the competitor's public announcement of its planned new product introduction.

Learning also is caused when new knowledge, independent of the organization's own actions, is acquired and used in decision making. A report by a management consulting firm indicating the emergence of a new technology likely to result in a new line of products may challenge existing facts and perceptions (e.g., no new products are under development by existing competitors or likely new entrants), beliefs (e.g., growth in total sales of the current product line will lead to increased profits for all competitors) and assumptions (e.g., competitive rivalry in the marketplace is not likely to be upset for next year or so). The challenge to prevailing knowledge is particularly strong if the technology is being developed by an organizat that is not now seen as a current or prospective competitor. Such *revealed* errors can then be corrected.

Single-Loop and Double-Loop Learning

Learning, as the detection and correction of errors, has widely varying decision and knowledge implications for outwitting, outmaneuvering, and outperforming competitors. Single-loop and double-loop learning afford a simple way of depicting these differences (see Figure 2.3).[44]

Single-loop learning occurs when the organization detects and corrects errors in its knowledge and processes of learning without changing the thrust of its strategies, action plans, and objectives. It is intended to facilitate more effective and efficient execution of the existing strategy. Although single-loop learning allows for successive refinements and replacements of actions, it does not challenge either the core content or direction of the organization's strategies, or the stock of knowledge underlying them. Knowledge developed about competitors (Cells 2, 3, and 4, or 5, 6, and 7) is not used to question whether the strategy is the right one. Since single-loop learning and its associated actions occur within a closed or self-correcting decision-making and knowledge system, the potential to outwit, outmaneuver, and outperform competitors is severely constrained.

Single-loop learning is evident in the Omega-Alpha case discussed earlier. Omega used the knowledge developed about Alpha to adjust and adapt its strategy but not to seriously question whether it was the right strategy. For example, Omega speeded up the introduction of its own new product and modified how it marketed and promoted its products. Yet it did not question whether the product already in an advanced state of development was the right product or what other strategies might have been more appropriate in

FIGURE 2.3
Single-Loop and Double-Loop Learning

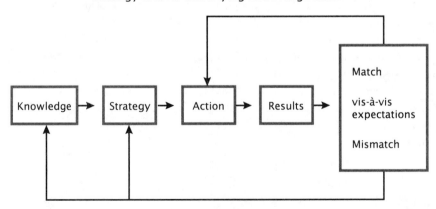

Single-Loop Learning
Change occurs within the confines of the existing
strategy and its underlying knowledge base.

Double-Loop Learning
Strategy and its underlying knowledge base
are challenged and may be changed.

competing against Alpha's new product. Learning is used to reinforce prior knowledge and to further support or reinforce commitment to existing strategies and actions.

In double-loop learning, on the other hand, the organization's knowledge and its strategies, in addition to its action plans and behaviors, are open to question. Double-loop learning processes reflect an open system: inquiry occurs as to why changes in strategy or knowledge are required or appropriate. Learning causes direct challenges to the organization's knowledge—its facts, perceptions, assumptions, beliefs, and projections—some of which may be long held and widely shared within the organization. It also causes review and critique of the processes of learning or knowing.

In the Omega-Alpha case, double-loop learning in the case of Omega would be reflected in analysis of whether this was the right product to introduce, whether the product should have been introduced at this time, whether it was introduced in the right way, and whether the organization should remain committed to the sequence of planned follow-up products. It also would be reflected in assessments of its underlying beliefs and assumptions about customers; whether some other competitor such as a potential new entrant might be a more serious rival than Alpha; projected rates of product sales; and, likely competitors' responses to its own actions.

Unlearning

The capacity to engage in critical self-reflection (such as explicating and critiquing the organization's stock of knowledge) that resides at the heart of double-loop learning (and, to a lesser degree, in the case of single-loop learning) presumes a capacity to unlearn. Without unlearning, learning is greatly inhibited.

Unlearning makes way for new knowledge and thus enhances the likelihood of new behaviors. As decision makers move through the cells in Figure 2.1, they are confronted with the need to unlearn significant parts of their knowledge including their implicit perceptions and projections of the future. Analysis of a competitor's marketplace strategy sometimes suggests significant shifts in customers' buying behaviors and preferences, indicating the need to question and perhaps replace long-held facts and perceptions about customers. In the face of competitor change, an organization's facts, perceptions, beliefs, assumptions, and projections sometimes quickly become outdated and obsolete.

Also, analysis of competitors often causes organizations to unlearn how they *do* things. Increased exposure to how one or more competitors provide high quality but differentiated service to different customer groups has caused many organizations to "unlearn" their historic modes of providing customer service.

Competitors as a Source of Learning

As noted, the impetus for competitor learning occurs in many different ways. Yet irrespective of how it is caused, four distinct types of competitor learning merit attention. Organizations attentive to fostering each type of competitor learning are more likely to outwit, outmaneuver, and outperform competitors.[45]

The Impetus for Competitor Learning

The impetus for competitor learning (Cell 1) emanates from at least three distinct sources. Each source leads to single-loop learning such as minor adjustments to existing strategies and action plans or to double-loop learning such as the decision to create a new strategy game or to dramatically reconstruct an existing game, or to significant changes in the stock of knowledge. Organizations aware of the different stimuli for competitor learning are better prepared to detect and create opportunities to marshal their learning resources and capabilities.

Organizations often decide to *initiate* competitor learning (Cell 1) in the absence of specific competitor change. It occurs as part of a larger effort to understand the environment or to avoid surprises by engaging in a dedicated effort to anticipate competitor change.[46] Frequently, organizations gather extensive data on current or anticipated competitors as one element in an industry analysis or broader scan of environmental change.

Competitor change causes an organization to reassess its competitor knowledge (Cells 2 and 3). Learning is *triggered* by change in competitors' behaviors, words, or organization attributes.[47] The change is detected by the organization itself or it is brought to its attention by third parties such as consultants, customers, or suppliers. The Omega/Alpha case discussed earlier was triggered by Alpha's potential product introduction, which was detected by a customer's comment to one of Omega's salespersons. Surprise moves by a competitor are especially likely to cause reassessment of competitor knowledge. The announcement by a competitor that it is ceasing development of a particular product line could cause extensive reassessment of the prevailing facts, assumptions, and projections pertaining to the competitor. More generally, a competitor's initiative such as the commitment of extensive resources to an R&D project, or the announcement of a new alliance, or the enhancement of a manufacturing process, if viewed as a significant competitive threat, may cause the organization to try to learn why the initiative was embarked on, its likelihood of success, and how it might be preempted or counteracted.

Organizations also learn through monitoring and assessing the consequences of their own actions (Cells 1, 5, 6, and 7). Such learning is thus *activated* due to the organization's own initiatives and behaviors. An organization introduces a product or lowers price in one distribution channel or makes an announcement at a trade show, and then carefully monitors the responses and actions of other entities such as competitors, channels, and end-customers. Such initiatives provide a rich opportunity for detecting and correcting errors in areas such as the organization's beliefs and assumptions about customers' brand loyalty, price sensitivity, and proclivity to defect to competitors' offerings. This opportunity for learning is often missed in many organizations.

Each impetus is central to ongoing competitor learning. Initiated learning is often an inherent element in organizations' periodic or ad hoc efforts to depict, anticipate, and understand environmental change. It reflects the commitment of organizations to creating and leveraging change rather than merely responding to events. Triggered learning, on the other hand, embodies a commitment to understanding competitor change as it unfolds. It suggests that an organization should always be in a learning mode since learning can be triggered at any time. Activated learning recognizes that an organization's own decisions and actions offer a learning opportunity: the organization learns from the responses of competitors, customers, and other entities.

Types of Competitor Learning

Whatever its impetus, four distinct though related types of competitor learning are worthy of note. Each type is distinctive along the four core learning activities: what data is acquired, how it is processed, what outputs are created, and how they are integrated into decision making and linked to action. Some relationships among the four competitor learning types are noted in Figure 2.4.

Descriptive Learning Learning *about* individual competitors or learning that *describes* competitors is the most basic level of competitor learning. It involves capturing and processing data and information about a competitor in order to describe and delineate its innumerable facets and features. As addressed in Chapters 5–16, such data and information is processed and crafted into outputs such as *descriptions* of any competitor's marketplace strategies, activity/value chain, alliances and networks, assumptions, assets, capabilities and competencies, technology, and organization, and projections of future competitive moves. These descriptions are then assessed for their contribution to decision making. For example, a description of a major competitor's assumptions about the emerging marketplace might cause an organization to (better) identify its own assumptions and to speed up or slow down asset commitments to product development or new marketing programs.

FIGURE 2.4
Types of Competitor Learning

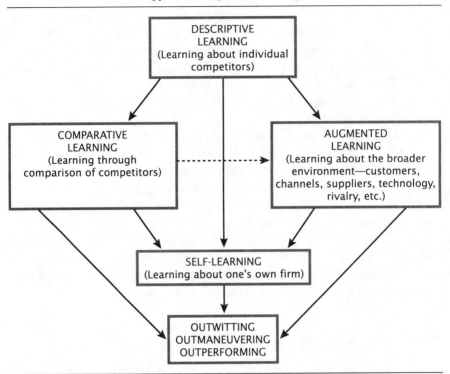

Comparative Learning   Comparative learning occurs when two or more competitors are compared and contrasted. It especially entails analysis of outputs (Cells 4 and 7). It is frequently necessary to compare and contrast the projections of two or more competitors' future strategies (Cell 4) as a means of anticipating which competitors are likely to do what and when. It is also often necessary to compare and contrast how competitors are responding to the focal firm's own initiatives and why they are responding as they are (Cells 6 and 7).

Descriptive learning furnishes the inputs to comparative learning. Many of the concepts and analysis tools detailed in Chapters 5–15 such as marketplace strategy, activity/value chain, assumptions, resources, and competencies, facilitate comparisons across two or more competitors.

Comparative learning generates insights and inferences that cannot be derived by examining individual competitors in isolation. For example, comparison of look-alike and emerging functional substitute competitors[48] often identifies the deficiencies in long-established products. Contrasting rivals' assumptions sometimes lead to fundamental questioning of one competitor's strategy that heretofore seemed on the right track.

Augmented Learning Extensive learning beyond descriptive and comparative learning is *caused* by attention to competitors. In many respects, descriptive and comparative learning are only a means rather than an end: they afford a means to augmented learning (and of course learning about one's own organization) that in turn informs decision making.

Augmented learning refers to knowledge generated about the environment surrounding the organization and its competitors that is useful in decision making. It arises when individuals ask: How does learning caused by attention to competitors indicate current, emergent, and potential change in and around end-customers, distribution channels, vendors and suppliers, technology, patterns of alliances and networks, and governmental policies? The identification of new look-alike competitors, or emergent or potential substitute competitors, sometimes indicates a decisive shift in the domain of the relevant competitive arena or industry. A competitor changing its assumptions about what it takes to win in a particular market may cause an organization to radically recast its own fundamental assumptions about future products, customers' needs, or channel requirements.

Augmented learning assumes significance in part because it is enormously difficult for organizations to comprehensively scan, monitor, and project environmental change. Analysis of competitors generates signals of current, emerging, and potential change in the customer, channel, factor, institutional, and geographic arenas, noted in Chapter 1.[49] The analysis of competitors thus directs the organization's attention to what should be scanned, monitored, and projected in the environment surrounding competitors.

Self-Learning Descriptive, comparative, and augmented learning provide the means to attain self-learning. Although learning about one's own organization is always embedded to some degree in descriptive, comparative, and augmented learning, it must be an explicit focus of competitor learning. Self-learning stems from explicitly comparing and contrasting one's own organization to one or more competitors. It thus involves the application of the principles of comparative learning to one's own organization.

Self-learning is relevant to every cell in Figure 2.1. Comparing and contrasting itself to current and future competitors allows an organization to challenge and critique its strategies in the marketplace, its most pervasive operating norms, and its most deeply held knowledge (Cell 1). Self-learning is fundamental to the identification of an organization's competencies and capabilities, constraints and vulnerabilities, sources of asset advantage, and points of potential marketplace leverage. Numerous examples of the application of self-learning are provided in this book.

Self-learning is important because an organization's learning is severely restricted if it reflects only on itself—it needs an external referent point. It can be argued that it is only by knowing other organizations that it is possible to fully know one's own organization. Reference to current, emerging, and potential competitors is always needed to avoid the biases inherent in self-referential assessments. Competitors provide one such critical referent point.

Two Modes of Competitor Learning

The four types of competitor learning just discussed—descriptive, comparative, augmented, and self-learning—either individually, or in some combination, result from two fundamentally distinct though complementary ways of managing the learning activities depicted in Figure 2.1. These two modes of learning, guided and open-ended, involve a distinct impetus, give rise to (often radically) different inputs, involve different approaches to processing the inputs, and often generate different outputs leading to distinct decision implications. Both modes can result in either single-loop or double-loop learning. Each mode has specific benefits and limitations. Each is widely used in organizations. Each contributes in different ways to the efficiency and effectiveness of competitor analysis. The implications of the two learning modes for integrating competitor analysis and decision making are addressed in Chapter 17. The two modes are briefly outlined here because of their relevance to and importance for the frameworks of analysis presented in the remaining chapters.

Guided Learning

Guided learning can be initiated, triggered, or activated.[50] Whatever the impetus, it is propelled or guided by a focus on prevailing and anticipated decisions and concerns within the focal organization. Two central decision-focused questions guide learning (Cell 1):

1. What are the focal organization's current and anticipated decisions (or decision domains)?
2. Given these decisions, what does the organization need to know about its competitors?

These two questions in turn give rise to four *central learning* questions:

1. What do we know about the competitor?
2. What can we learn about the competitor?

3. What is the difference between what we know and what we can learn—the knowledge difference or knowledge increment?

4. Who will be able to use the knowledge increment in making decisions and which decisions will it enhance?

These two sets of questions undergird the *guided* identification and analysis of individual competitors. They contribute to determining competitor *intelligence needs,*[51] that is, what the organization needs to know about competitors as an input to decision making. The dominant premise in guided learning is that decision makers are able to identify a priori what intelligence they require and how that intelligence will contribute to decision making.

A comparison of intelligence needs to the existing stock of knowledge indicates an *intelligence gap.* In identifying intelligence gaps, an organization must critically evaluate its stock of competitor knowledge and be willing to admit its deficiencies and limitations. If it does not do so, it is all too easy to overestimate the quantity and quality of its competitor knowledge.

Each component of the analysis framework to identify current and potential competitors, as well as each component of the analysis of individual competitors, such as marketplace strategy or assumptions, is guided by a specific understanding of the component,[52] key questions that need to be asked, and a sequence in which the questions can and should be asked. In this way, determining data requirements, identifying data sources and gathering data (Cell 2) are guided by an understanding of look-alike competitors or the elements of marketplace strategy or assumptions. Data selection, data ordering, and interpretation, the central tasks in processing (Cell 2), are guided by specific a priori questions about matters such as marketplace strategy or assumptions. The outputs (Cell 4) are guided, indeed constrained, by the questions asked and the consequent processing. For example, a description of a competitor's current marketplace strategy will be delineated along the a priori elements or configuration of marketplace strategy.

Open-Ended Learning

A dangerous fallacy in any knowledge structure or learning process is that decision makers know what they need to know. The intelligence that decision makers say they want to make a decision is often not what they need.[53] What an organization needs to learn about its competitors is therefore unavoidably a central and nontrivial issue in any systematic approach to competitor learning. A concern with efficient and effective learning[54] makes this issue all the more important.

In open-ended learning, descriptive learning is used as the catalyst for comparative, augmented, and self-learning. The driving force is the opposite to that in guided learning: the desire is *first* to develop knowledge about competitors and then to derive implications for the organization's current and future decisions. Open-ended competitor learning is driven by three *learning and decision* questions:

1. Who are the organization's current and future competitors?

2. What are the major alternative plausible futures or scenarios around the strategic and operating direction of individual (and multiple) competitors over different time periods?

3. What are the implications of these alternative futures for the competitive context of the organization and the organization itself?

In open-ended learning, intelligence needs—what the organization needs to know for current and future decision making—are not articulated a priori. There is no presumption that the organization knows what decisions it will be making or what intelligence is required.

The search for data about current and future competitors is thus unconstrained. In open-ended capturing (Cell 2), no presumptions are made about the types of data that should be collected, the best data sources, or data usefulness. Data gathering is thus as open-ended as possible.

Processing also is driven by open-ended inquiry (Cell 3). To the extent possible, individuals suspend their organizational concerns, roles, and involvement. They strive to step outside their own mind-sets and worldviews. Processing provokes open-ended learning when individuals ask questions that are not constrained by their own knowledge. The presumption is that many potentially insightful signals are thus detected that otherwise would be missed. Open-ended learning challenges organizational members to transform data into judgments rather than fitting data to a priori mental models. The intent, as reflected in the first two questions previously listed, is to develop an understanding of the present and future and *then* to derive organizational implications (Cells 4 and 1).

Processing results in *knowledge increments* (Cell 3): the difference between the organization's prior knowledge and the outcomes of its learning. For example, through an analysis of technology signals, the organization could develop a scenario indicating the competitor's likely future product introductions. Such descriptive learning then becomes part of the intelligence base from which decision implications are derived.

Only *after* data have been processed and crafted into descriptions of competitors' futures does the focus shift to identifying implications for the organization—comparative and self-learning (Cell 1). Given an identification of current and future competitors and projections of their strategies and operations, implications for the organization are then derived.

Linking the Two Learning Modes

The two learning modes are essentially opposite sides of the same coin. Although their points of departure and modes of processing are clearly different, both open-ended and guided learning ultimately lead to assessment of implications of competitor change for the focal organization.

Each learning mode influences the other. Guided learning often generates points of departure for open-ended learning. For example, if guided analysis of a competitor indicates emerging technologies, they then become the focus of open-ended scanning and monitoring[55] processes. Open-ended learning often generates issues and questions that then become the focus of guided learning.

Learning Processes: Detecting and Correcting Errors

As discussed earlier, an organization's stock of knowledge is always an output or consequence of prior learning and an input to current learning. The content of an organization's stock of knowledge at any point in time is greatly affected by errors that go undetected and uncorrected in its processes of learning (or knowing), that is, how the organization goes about generating and using knowledge in decision making. These organizational errors are distinct from the errors in the organization's knowledge (stock) that were previously discussed.

Some key errors in organizations' processes of learning pertaining to each of the four learning activities in the competitor learning model that affect guided and open-ended learning are noted in Tables 2.1 and 2.2, respectively. Although distinct organizational errors are associated with guided and open-ended learning, a few of the more common errors that affect both modes of learning, and their implications for efficient and effective learning, are briefly noted in this section to highlight the importance that must be attached to both analytical and organizational considerations in any model of competitor (or other) learning.

Capturing The analytical and organizational data errors noted in Tables 2.1 and 2.2 (and the data errors discussed in Chapter 3) often significantly inhibit both guided and open-ended learning. Here are two common examples. First, individuals often neglect the data that already exists *within* their own organization: thus, they seek external data before they identify,

TABLE 2.1 Errors in the Processes of Guided Learning

Activity	Errors	Implications
CAPTURING		
Determining data needs	Narrow conception of competitors	Inefficient data gathering
Identifying data sources	Lack of familiarity with internal and external data sources	Limits variety in data considered in processing
Collecting data	Overemphasis on quantitative data	
	Little triangulation of data	
PROCESSING		
Selecting data	Use only a select set of (familiar) tools and techniques	Limits range of questions that will be posed
Ordering data	Dominance of one logic in analyzing data	Absence of clash of logics limits scope of reflection
Interpreting data	Satisficing—adopting first reasonable inference	Constrains variety in inferences that can be drawn
	Processing seen as one-time event	
	Same set of individuals continually involved	
CRAFTING		
Shaping outputs	Adherence to a constricted set of formats	Routines around formats and satisficing obviates outputs that challenge prior knowledge
Critiquing outputs	Emphasis on providing what satisfies decision makers	
Communicating outputs	Orientation toward answers, not questions	Communication routines overwhelm substance of what is to be communicated
DECISION MAKING		
Current and prior decisions	Presumption that decision makers know what decisions need to be made	Decision making closed to unexpected outcomes
New decisions	Presumption that decision makers know what they need to make decisions	Decision makers shy away from open-ended inquiry
Additional knowledge	Ignore or downplay decisions not in keeping with a prior understanding of decisions	As a consequence, double-loop learning becomes difficult to initiate

TABLE 2.2 Errors in the Processes of Open-Ended Learning

Activity	Errors	Implications
CAPTURING		
Determining data requirement Identifying data sources Collecting data	Become obsessive about gathering all potentially useful data Specify data needs too narrowly Become overly selective in choice of data sources Relentlessly pursue all data sources	Data gathering becomes interminable and thus processing is gravely slowed Data gathering takes place too quickly and thus processing is compromised
PROCESSING		
Selecting data Ordering data Interpreting data	Reject data if its value is not readily apparent Development of multiple logics leads decision incapacity Unwillingness to bring in individuals who do not share the group's or the organization's assumptions	Sense-making gets bogged down in conflict between two or more logics Sense-making occurs too quickly due to lack of competing logics
CRAFTING		
Shaping outputs Critiquing outputs Communicating outputs	Arrive at outputs too quickly Spend little time developing outputs that will challenge prevailing knowledge Make little effort to communicate outputs beyond those who ask for them	Outputs do not challenge prevailing knowledge or current processes of decision making Outputs do not reach individuals/groups who could benefit by having their stock of knowledge and decision processes challenged
DECISION MAKING		
Current and prior decisions New decisions Additional knowledge	Inability to break out of prevailing conception of competition and competitors Accept too quickly initial implications Do not challenge prior knowledge base underlying prior decisions	Fundamental open-ended questions are not raised If they are raised, premature closure in thinking occurs If premature closure does not occur, wrong decision makers are involved—can't make change happen

challenge, and extract insight from what they already know or consider that they know. In guided analysis, external search frequently degenerates into a hunting-and-fishing expedition to demonstrate due diligence in data gathering rather than a search to identify and challenge the prevailing stock of knowledge or to fill in data gaps.

Second, learning is inhibited by an absence of familiarity with existing data sources both inside and outside the organization. The quality and speed of learning is thus severely hampered; this is especially so in open-ended learning.

Processing Multiple errors are common in selecting, ordering, and interpreting data. Processing must not be allowed to become dependent on one individual or the same set of individuals. Multiple logics[56] (or mental models or frames of reference) are required to generate alternative meanings, inferences, and outcomes in both guided and opened-ended learning. Only by doing so is it possible to continually challenge the prevailing stock of knowledge.

Similarly, tools and techniques to analyze data must be varied. Dependence on one or a small set of analytical tools and techniques constrains the range of potential insights. Adherence to a narrow range of tools and techniques, or using them to ask only a narrow range of questions, unwittingly constricts an organization to single-loop learning.

Processing is sometimes viewed as a sequence of one-time events or as a series of project-specific tasks. Learning is therefore less likely to be cumulative since there is often little connection between the isolated events or tasks. This is especially the case if they are performed by different sets of individuals.

Crafting Outputs are often shaped by the need to conform to preordained formats instead of fitting outcomes of analysis to the needs of decision makers or the peculiarities and complexities of what is being investigated.

An embarrassing error that too often dominates the efforts of organizations to engage in either guided or open-ended learning is the frequency with which outputs are shaped and communicated to provide the "answers" that decision makers are looking for or have stated they want. Outputs are generated to support and confirm suppositions, inferences, or conclusions that were drawn or derived *before* processing occurred. The perceived need to conform to a preestablished format and satisfy decision makers discourages alternative views and perspectives, and suppresses uncertainty from outputs.

Decision Making How decisions are made also gives rise to multiple errors in the processes of learning or knowing. Decision makers presume they know which are the most important decisions or which decisions need to be made. Yet guided, and more frequently, open-ended learning generates decisions that were not on managers' agendas.

Relatedly, decision makers presume that they know what knowledge they need for decision making. Frequently, this is not the case. Consequently, learning is short-circuited or guided in the wrong direction.

In many instances, learning largely ceases once decisions have been made or action committed to. The rituals of single-loop learning drive out reflections on the relevance of the underlying knowledge, the correctness of prior decisions, or a willingness to ask previously unthought of or suppressed questions. In short, decision makers may not recognize the need to initiate competitor learning.

 ## Summary

Considerable attention must be devoted to avoiding the errors in both an organization's stock of knowledge and its processes of learning if competitor learning is to maximally inform decision makers about competitors and, more broadly, the strategy game, as discussed in Chapter 1. Central to avoiding these errors is understanding a number of key concepts, which is the subject of Chapter 3.

3

Core Concepts

MUCH CONFUSION EXISTS IN BOTH THE LITERATURE AND PRACTICE OF COMPETITOR analysis because many key concepts are inadequately defined, poorly developed, and badly communicated. This is especially unfortunate because concepts are central to learning. They are the fundamental building blocks in any analytical framework or methodology. Moreover, concepts only have value when individuals share a common understanding of their meaning and usefulness. Regrettably, concepts such as data, information, intelligence, and learning often have multiple meanings even within the same organization. In one large corporation, the concept of competitor analysis itself led to considerable confusion until it was discovered that individuals attached different meanings to the term: some viewed it as the analysis of a set of competitors; others viewed it as the analysis of individual competitors; others confined it to the analysis of competitors' products. The lack of attention to concepts, and to developing shared meanings around key concepts, contributes to both ineffective and inefficient competitor learning.

This chapter identifies and elaborates a number of key concepts central to competitor learning. It begins by reviewing the role and importance of concepts. It describes three distinct levels of competitor analysis, and then distinguishes between analysts and decision makers, and efficient and effective competitor learning. Three concepts central to competitor learning are next discussed in detail: data, information, and intelligence. The chapter concludes by delineating four fundamental analysis processes: scanning, monitoring, projecting, and assessment.

The Role and Importance of Concepts in (Competitor) Learning

Concepts underlie and influence each competitor learning activity: capturing, processing, crafting, and assessment (the cells in Figure 2.1). Concepts developed in the following chapters such as marketplace strategy, activity/value chain, assumptions, and capabilities and competencies serve a number of roles. They influence what decisions receive attention, what data is considered, what analysis is conducted, what outputs accrue, and how the outputs are integrated into decision making.[1] In short, they shape the perspective, frame of reference, and philosophy that underpin how organizations approach competitor learning (see Figure 3.1).[2]

How concepts influence *what* we think about often is not fully appreciated. Concepts focus and frame what decisions managers pay attention to (Cell 1 in Figure 2.1). For example, (the concepts of) outwitting, outmaneuvering, and outperforming competitors, as discussed in Chapter 1, help guide the substance and focus of managers' thinking. Outwitting causes managers to identify and reflect on their own assumptions—which are often implicit or tacit. Changing the concept of performance from an exclusive emphasis on market share and financial considerations to include also the development of resources and competencies causes a shift in the relevant performance criteria.

Concepts shape *how* managers think. They partially structure the logic[3] or thought process that is brought to bear on data (Cell 3 in Figure 2.1). Alliances

FIGURE 3.1
The Role of Concepts in Competitor Learning

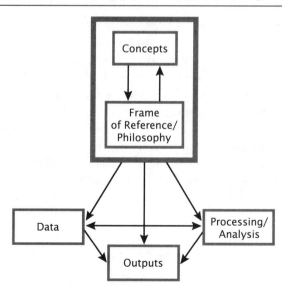

and network analysis predisposes individuals to look for linkages among and between several organizations, the intent and motivation underlying the establishment of these linkages, as well as the reasons for changes in alliances and networks over time.

Concepts *shape the data* that are sought or attended to (Cell 2 in Figure 2.1). As illustrated in Chapters 5–15, the types of data required is a function of the analysis scheme embedded in one or a series of concepts such as marketplace strategy, assumptions, and competencies. For example, the concept of marketplace strategy requires the collection of specific types of data about products, customers, modes of competition, and goals.[4]

Finally, as depicted in Figure 3.1, concepts directly and indirectly *influence and shape outputs*[5] (Cell 4 in Figure 2.1) through their impact on what managers think about, how they do so, and the data to which they pay attention. If decision makers and others involved in competitor analysis are not familiar with concepts such as a customer-focused activity value chain, special relationships, or competencies, outputs will not reflect analysis generated by these concepts.

Competitor Analysis: Three Levels

Competitor analysis takes place at three levels: a system of competitors, an individual competitor as a whole, and specific components of a competitor. Each level constitutes a distinct focus for competitor learning.

A System of Competitors

At the *system* level, analysis addresses multiple competitors. The intent is to map the competitive terrain, that is, to identify the competitors competing within some specified industry, business segment, or competitive context.[6] System is used in a generic sense: the specific focus may be what is generally referred to as an industry, such as the pharmaceutical, computer, or hotel industry or, an industry segment such as the biotechnology, ethical drug, or cardiovascular segments of the pharmaceutical industry. Mapping the competitive terrain requires identifying current and potential look-alike and substitute competitors. A principal shortcoming of system level analysis in many organizations is that potential competitors receive minimal attention, thus sowing the seeds of future competitive surprises.

Individual Competitors:
Macro- and Microlevel Analysis

Once current and potential competitors are identified, competitor analysis then switches to developing a comprehensive understanding of individual competitors (or groups of competitors). Despite an avalanche of books in the past decade on the topic of "competitor intelligence,"[7] a glaring void in almost all of them is the absence of any comprehensive, coherent, and integrated framework of analysis to guide competitor learning. What they offer for the most part are sets of topic areas[8] that should be addressed, checklists of questions that should be asked, and types of data that should be collected.

The competitor analysis framework proposed in this book segments into two related levels (see Figure 3.2). The focus of macrolevel analysis is competitors' marketplace strategies.[9] It is macro in the sense that the purpose of any organization is to win in the marketplace: to create or reconstruct a strategy game; to attract, win, and retain customers. Marketplace strategy (and its results) is the ultimate test as to whether an organization is outwitting, outmaneuvering, and outperforming its rivals.

Microlevel analysis furnishes description and understanding of the other framework components or elements of them: activity/value chain, alliances and relationships, networks, assumptions, assets, capabilities and competencies, technology, and organization infrastructure and culture. Chapters 7-15 address each of these framework components. These components are micro in the sense that how well they are managed strongly influences whether marketplace strategy wins. Fundamental insight into the nuts and bolts or functioning of a competitor is acquired at the micro level.

Microlevel concerns are the focus of most analysis tools and techniques. For example, financial tools and techniques permit intensive analysis of the financial assets and condition of competitors. Cultural analysis tools and techniques facilitate dissecting the competitor's culture—its values, norms,

FIGURE 3.2
The Competitor: An Analysis Framework

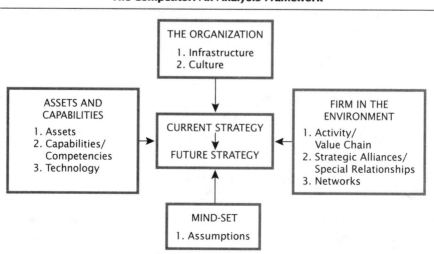

beliefs, and modes of behavior.[10] However, one must integrate microlevel and macrolevel analysis to paint a picture of the competitor as a total entity.

Building Bridges between the Three Levels

The three levels of analysis are interrelated in many ways. The analysis outputs in each level serve as an input to the other levels. System-level analysis identifies individual competitors, or classes of competitors, that warrant competitor level analysis. On the other hand, microlevel outputs sometimes suggest directions for system-level analysis. For example, if a microanalysis of a specific competitor's technology indicates the emergence of a number of related technologies, it warrants a system-level analysis of competitors around a set of emerging technologies.

Analysts and Decision Makers

Many organizations fail to distinguish between competitor analysis as an *analytical activity* and as an *organizational function or unit.* Any individual, irrespective of his or her organizational position, department or function, can execute one or more of the key activities associated with competitor learning discussed in Chapter 2: gathering relevant data, processing data and information, creating outputs and using them in decision making. For example, senior line managers often collect critical competitor data from sources often not available to others in the organization. Every individual should be viewed as a current or potential competitor analyst. Otherwise, the benefits of competitor analysis are unnecessarily circumscribed.

Decision makers are thus a subset of analysts. They use the outputs of competitor analysis in the making of decisions. The distinction between analysts and decision makers is made in part because individuals learn,[11] not organizations. They generate knowledge and use that knowledge in decision making; in turn, they learn by observing and reflecting on the consequences and implications of their decisions and actions.[12]

The role of the competitor analyst has become a full-time position for one or more individuals in an increasing number of organizations. In some organizations, these competitor analysis professionals (CAPs) now constitute a dedicated staff department or function.[13]

Efficient and Effective Competitor Learning

Two concepts central to competitor learning are efficient and effective learning. Efficient competitor learning refers to the learning input-output ratio: the greatest learning output (change in knowledge) for some given level of learning resources. Resources include the number of analysts, their skills and experience, discretionary cash, time availability, and data and information. Efficiency poses many (competitor) analysis challenges: how to identify key decisions (Cell 1); how to gather the right competitor data quickly and with the least cost (Cell 2); how to develop sustained relationships with many different types of data sources (Cell 2); how to quickly process data and information (Cell 3) and to craft them into outputs (Cell 4) that are useful to decision makers (Cell 1).

Effective competitor learning addresses the output-decision relationship. To be effective, competitor learning must inform and influence decision makers. Ideally, effective competitor learning causes decision makers to make better decisions and to make them faster (Cell 1). Effective competitor learning may bring new decisions to the attention of decision makers, provoke them to think differently about specific decisions, and cause them to speed up or slow down the making of specific decisions.

Efficiency and effectiveness both need attention. However, great care must be taken in making judgments as to what is efficient and effective. In open-ended learning, a narrow-minded pursuit of efficiency may limit potential effectiveness. Open-ended modes of inquiry such as exploratory and unfocused discussions with different types of primary data sources run directly counter to many prescriptions for efficient data collection. In guided learning, providing data and information that responds to decision makers' identification of their intelligence needs contributes to ineffective competitor learning if decision makers have misidentified the competitor knowledge they need.[14]

Efficient and effective competitor learning requires that analysts clearly understand the distinctions between data, information, and intelligence, and the implications of these distinctions. These terms are used loosely in many organizations resulting in considerable "noise" in every competitor learning activity. Hence, the need to define and review each of these fundamental terms.

Competitor Data

Data constitutes the basic raw material in competitor learning (see Figure 2.1). In its broadest sense, data consists of *raw* bits and pieces *about* competitors. Data is raw because it is almost always inchoate, disjointed, and unintegrated. Examples of raw data include reports about competitors' actions by members of the sales force; articles in the industry's publications; material downloaded from a competitor's Internet site; comments by the competitor's managers to security analysts; and announcements by the competitor about its proposed new products. Data remains raw until it is subjected to the judgment and assessment of an analyst.

Data Categories

The data *about* any competitor falls into three broad categories: the behaviors of the competitor, statements by or about the competitor, and organization change.

Behaviors Individual actions or a pattern of actions (or inactions) are referred to as behaviors. The array of actions competitors engage in is immense. This book makes evident how distinct types of behaviors are categorized and arrayed depending on the concept or analysis tool or technique that is employed. For example, marketplace strategy addresses competitors' actions with regard to products and customers, and how they attract, win, and retain customers. On the other hand, behaviors relating to competitors' networks address actions pertaining to alliance partners and other external entities with which they possess relationships.

Statements The words used by competitors themselves or by others about them are statements. The words may be in written or oral form. As with behaviors, the scope of topics about which competitors make statements is enormous: financial results, new product introductions, closure of plants, mergers and acquisitions, personnel changes and expectations about the future, to name but a few.

The contexts or situations in which competitors make statements or use words are also extensive. They include settings in which organization members make *prepared* statements such as meetings with security analysts, their annual general meetings, industry and trade shows, and appearances before governmental agencies. Many different types of *announcements* such as appointments of new personnel, organization structure changes, formation of alliances, and strategy shifts such as the addition or deletion of product lines or movement into new geographic areas, represent another form of statements. Statements are also an inherent component of many different types of *regular business communications* such as annual reports, submissions to different governmental agencies, product promotion material, service literature, and reports to industry and trade associations. In making these three types of statements, many different subunits of a competitor's organization such as investor relations, public relations, the CEO's office, sales, service, local plants, board of directors, and heads of the various functional areas, issue a bewildering array of documents to a multitude of external audiences. They do so in part because they are required by law or because it is a necessary business function.

Prepared remarks, announcements, and regular business communications are *formal* statements: they are typically in written form; they are issued with the approval of the competitor; and they go through regular channels such as scheduled meetings with external parties (e.g., security analysts, the media), press releases, advertisements, and communications to suppliers, distributors, and customers.

Informal statements, on the other hand, are always oral comments delivered by the competitor's personnel to external parties. They may or may not be authorized by the competitor. Since they are oral, they are not transmitted through regular channels, though they are often eventually carried in such channels. Informal statements include remarks by salepersons to customers or by purchasing personnel to suppliers, observations by R&D personnel in response to audience questions at the conclusion of a formal presentation at an industry or technology conference, or comments by a CEO at an industry or trade association meeting.

Organization Change Competitor data extends beyond behaviors and words. Change in each of the framework components noted in Figure 3.2 extends the raw material or data about a competitor from which analysts make judgments and derive insights. As discussed in detail in Chapter 4, unless analysts are alert to change in a competitor's assets, capabilities and competencies, extensive competitor data is missed.

Organization change is not isolated from behaviors and words. Behaviors shape changes in assets or assumptions or organization culture. Changes in a competitor's financial balance sheet are in part the consequence of investments such as research and development, equipment, personnel, and multiple other types of actions. And, competitors often make statements about key (organization) changes in assets, alliances, networks, and organization infrastructure.

Data Characteristics

Lack of understanding of the implications of different forms of data for drawing inferences and interpretations contributes to many of the errors noted in the concluding section of Chapter 2. Although data assumes many forms, a number that are particularly common and important are briefly discussed. Some analysis issues pertaining to each data form are also noted.

Quantification Important competitor data that is quantitative includes sales figures, financial condition and performance, projected scale of investment, plant capacities, and number of employees. Even aspects of a competitor frequently presumed to be nonquantitative such as assumptions and culture possess quantitative aspects. Assumptions often refer to quantifiable elements such as expectations about the growth rate of specific product-customer segments or the extent to which the competitor will be able to enhance its production capacity.

Despite its importance and usefulness, however, analysts need to recognize that not all data is quantifiable. More importantly, analysts must recognize that quantitative data does not necessarily generate superior insights to nonquantitative data and, as evidenced in many later chapters, that nonquantitative data often generates insights that simply cannot be obtained from numbers. Quantitative data only yields insight when used in context.[15]

Time   Whether pertaining to behaviors, statements, or attributes, all data is time bound: data can only refer to the past, present, or future. Time always constitutes one aspect of the context of data. The analyst must know what the relevant time period is; otherwise, data is difficult if not impossible to interpret. The statement that the competitor's annual sales growth is 15 percent assumes distinctly different implications if it refers to the past 2 years or to the projected growth rate for the next 10 years.

Precision   Varying degrees of preciseness or accuracy are also associated with competitor data. While in general more accuracy is desirable, analysts need to recognize that it does not come without costs and the degree of accuracy required is a function of its contribution to decision making.[16] For example, firms sometimes spend considerable resources trying to get more precise figures on competitors' market shares. But what is the value of the increased precision? What difference will it make if the competitor's market share is determined to be 30 percent or 28 percent? In some businesses, it may make a tremendous difference; in others, the difference may be only marginal.

Descriptions and Opinions   Another useful way to categorize data is to distinguish between description and opinions. Descriptive data includes delineations of competitors' behaviors (what the competitor has done or is doing), statements (what the competitor has said or is saying) or organization change (e.g., changes in some of the competitor's assets). Descriptive data, when it is verified, is the basis of facts, the first element of knowledge noted in Chapter 2.

Opinions refer to judgments, inferences, or interpretations drawn by someone about competitors' behaviors, statements, and organization change. They are judgments in the form of "I think . . ." or "I believe. . . . " Opinions about competitors may be expressed by individuals internal or external to them. Opinions that have not yet been verified, or which may be difficult to verify, often give rise to perceptions, the second element of knowledge discussed in Chapter 2.

Sources of Data

Data is obtained from an extraordinary number of sources. Data sources can be categorized as either primary (people) or secondary (written documents), and internal or external to the competitor. Thus, it is possible to classify data sources into four types: internal-primary, internal-secondary, external-primary, and external-secondary. (See the appendix for a brief sample of these data sources.)

Some Common Data Errors

Common misconceptions about data stifle firms' efforts to do more effective and efficient competitor analysis.[17] Each of the following errors flows in part from a rather primitive conception of what data is, and in particular, a lack of understanding of the distinctions raised in this chapter between data, information, and intelligence.

A Lot of Data Is Required for Competitor Analysis to Be Useful This is simply not so. Analysts will never have complete data; partial data is always the norm. The art in competitor analysis is how to make use of limited data. A small amount of data can be extremely useful. One firm, as part of its data gathering, discovered that a small regional competitor was planning to build a new plant that would allegedly quintuple its capacity (Cell 2 in Figure 2.1). Although the firm did not know with complete certainty when the plant would come onstream, whether it would quintuple or merely double its capacity, or to which products the plant would be dedicated, this single bit of data compelled the firm to analyze (Cell 3), and later, to significantly alter its assumptions about future business conditions in that region (Cell 4). And, as a consequence of its changed assumptions, it had to consider new strategy possibilities (Cell 1).

However, great care must always be taken when acting on limited or isolated data. The dangers inherent in the temptation to act on a single piece of data are demonstrated by the case of another small company that heard from a distributor that its principal competitor planned a new plant that would be operational within a year.[18] Only when the company searched for corroborating data did it discover that the competitor was indeed beginning to build a new plant, but that it would not come onstream for at least two years, and that if the competitor's profits did not improve, the plant might be shelved altogether. Because of the additional data, the company decided to wait and see what would happen rather than immediately altering its strategy as initially intended.[19]

Data Should Be as Accurate as Possible   In general, the more precise and accurate the data (both quantitative and nonquantitative), the better the analysis. But in many instances, it is a poor use of analysts' time and resources to seek more precision. For example, with regard to a competitor's sales promotion program, what is the value in determining that it is $2.6 million or $2.7 million? If the extra $100,000 makes a significant difference to the focal firm's decision making, then the added precision may be worth the effort. But if the added precision makes little or no difference to the outcome of the analysis, then the time and energy can be more productively expended on the analysis of some other issue or question.

The Most Wanted Data Is the Most Needed Data   There is a very common presumption that the data "we want" is, in fact, data that is needed. The only data "needed" is that which is potentially useful for making a decision. Thus, needed data must always be distinguished from nice-to-know data. If this distinction is not kept in mind, a lot of data collection is driven by purposes other than the desire to generate outputs that are useful in decision making.

In competitor analysis, analysts often seem to possess insatiable appetites for data. This appetite is particularly voracious when the distinction between needed and nice-to-know data is forgotten. Consider an example. A manager became very enthused about obtaining more extensive data on a competitor's manufacturing costs. The initial estimates by his own competitor analysis team was that manufacturing costs represented about 5 to 8 percent of the competitor's total costs. The manager asked the team to provide a more specific estimate. When the manager was asked how the added data might be used in the making of specific decisions, he could not give an answer, but he did remark "It would still be nice to know."

Needed Data Cannot Be Obtained   Another common fallacy is that the data that is truly needed for effective competitor analysis cannot be obtained. In practice, there is little data about competitors that is not accessible. Some data is easily obtained; other data requires ingenuity and perseverance, but there is little about competitors' behaviors, statements, and attributes that cannot be tracked and ascertained if the firm decides it needs that data and commits the necessary resources to obtaining it.

Competitor Data Mostly Exists Externally   Having worked on the analysis of many competitors, I would estimate that 80 percent of the competitor data required for studies of established competitors[20] already exists *within* the focal organization. The data, however, is not in any convenient form: most of it exists in the heads of the company's employees, and the rest is buried in reports, studies, analyses, and other documents that all too often are ignored or forgotten when analysts begin to study competitors. Much of this data was obtained from sources external to the firm, but it now exists inside the organization.

To Get the Data We Need, We Must Engage in Unethical and Illegal Behavior
Given the diversity of data sources, the extensiveness of available data, and the many legal and ethical ways to gather competitor data, there is no need to employ questionable or illegal practices.[21] Some firms that have resorted to questionable methods have been shocked to discover the data they sought either already existed within their own organization or could easily have been obtained through legal and ethical means. One firm that regularly phoned competitors under the pretense that it was a customer[22] in order to obtain their latest products, found that its salespeople often legally received these same products from their clients.

The ground rules for data gathering can be reduced to one prescript: If there is any doubt about the ethical basis or legality of individual behaviors or actions, do not engage in them. It is the only way to avoid not just actual difficulties but the appearance of impropriety.[23]

Generating Competitor Information

Data is necessary but not sufficient for learning. It must be processed (Cell 3): it must be selected, ordered, and interpreted. Data do not speak for themselves; they require the intervention of the analyst. The product of analysts bringing their judgment to bear on data is information. Information is thus the result of the intersection of data and logic. As such, it becomes an output in the competitor learning model (see Figure 2.1). Once information is assimilated[24] by one or more individuals, it becomes knowledge.[25]

Transforming Data into Information: The Role of Logic

Data and logic constitute the ingredients of processing. Neither alone is sufficient. Logic embodies the capacity to order and organize data so that inferences can be derived and judgments made. Logic often involves a series of judgments that constitute a "story" or a "line of argument." Judgments typically entail making causal connections among data points.

The importance of explicating logic is that it allows others to see how and why an inference or conclusion is derived from data. In the manufacturing case cited earlier, once the logic underlying the conclusion that the competitor's new plant will not come onstream for at least two years is explicated, then analysts and others can evaluate the quality of its reasoning such as causal links in the argument, and search for conflicts in the data. For example, analysts might assess whether the time necessary to obtain all the required building permits is over- or underestimated.

Forms of Information

Information also comes in many forms. It too may be either quantitative or nonquantitative; historic, current, or prospective; precise or imprecise; and descriptive or speculative.

Key Characteristics of Information

Information is *evaluated* data. It is the product of some degree of processing (Cell 3). It has thus been given context by the analyst.

Since information is a product of analysts' judgments, it is always to some degree *biased*. The bias is predominantly a function of analysts' logic: our modes of thinking and analysis are influenced by our background, training, experience, and cognitive orientations. Information is also biased by the data analysts choose to consider or disregard.

Information is much *smaller in volume* than data. An extensive amount of financial and other types of data may go into generating a competitor's cashflow projections. A competitor's assumptions are extracted from many different types of data. A wide variety of data is needed to project and assess a competitor's product development activities.

Some Information Errors

As with data, a number of fallacies are associated with information.

Misplaced Concreteness   The fallacy of misplaced concreteness[26] is perhaps most common. When analysts quantify their judgments about many different facets of competitors such as projections of cash flows, sales, and production levels, greater faith is often invested in these calculations than is warranted. What is often ignored are the assumptions underlying the numbers.

Misconstrued Structure   Analysts also sometimes misconstrue patterns or the underlying structure in a set of data. For example, they might misidentify the connections across a competitor's activity/value chain or derive a set of assumptions that misrepresent those actually held by the competitor.

Exaggerated Relevance Analysts frequently fall into the trap of presuming that the information they generate is decision relevant. As the list of unused reports and ignored analyses in many organizations attests, just because information is developed does not mean that decision makers will find it useful—thus, the importance of the distinction between information and intelligence.

Competitor Intelligence: Knowledge in Use

Competitor learning is driven by the desire to generate intelligence—knowledge that informs decision makers and influences decision making. Only data and information that are actually *used* in decision making should be considered intelligence. The pursuit of intelligence constitutes the essence of competitor learning and distinguishes it from what passes for competitor analysis in many organizations.[27] Nicely bound and profoundly titled reports that provide considerable data and information but remain unopened or are quickly forgotten are not "intelligence." The ultimate test of an organization's competitor analysis is the extent to which its outputs become intelligence (the shift from Cell 4 and Cell 7 to Cell 1 in Figure 2.1).[28]

Both data and information lead to intelligence. A single item of data such as a saleperson's report that a competitor has discussed key characteristics of a new product with some customers or a rumor that a competitor is considering extending its production capacity for particular products may be quickly incorporated into decision making.[29] The analyst identifies possible responses to the potential new product introduction or the extended product output. Consideration of the implications for the competitor's strategy if the rumor of additional production capacity proves true compels the analyst to identify and assess different responses. The data is now being used by the analyst to create intelligence—outputs that are useful in decision making.[30]

It is not necessary to use data and information immediately in decision making. Data and information may sit on the decision maker's shelf, or reside in the decision maker's mind, for some time before being incorporated into analysis.

Types of Intelligence

Intelligence can be categorized in a number of ways. Since intelligence is knowledge-in-use, its *content* can be categorized in terms of the *knowledge elements* discussed in Chapter 2: facts, perceptions, beliefs, assumptions, and projections. Each knowledge element, as illustrated in the remaining chapters in this book, forms a distinct general type of intelligence that affects decision making in a variety of ways.

Since intelligence is the data and information that informs decision making—the knowledge-in-use—it makes sense to categorize intelligence using decision relevant criteria. Thus, intelligence includes these key types:[31]

- *Marketplace Strategy Intelligence.* Data and information that informs the making and execution of marketplace strategy.
- *Decision-Specific Intelligence.* Data and information that informs and influences the making and execution of specific decisions such as new product, manufacturing investment, or pricing decisions.
- *Issue Intelligence.* Data and information that informs decision makers and analysts about one or more issues, that is, topic domains that are being explored before specific decisions are identified and formulated.[32] Competitor issues might include: What new competitors may emerge in the foreseeable future? What technologies will lead to the development of substitute products? Why are competitors changing how they compete in the marketplace?

Some Intelligence Errors

Although many fallacies evident in the way organizations understand and approach intelligence are identified and discussed in Chapter 17, two merit particular attention here.

Decision Makers Need Not Be Involved Intelligence is more likely to evolve when decision makers are involved in knowledge generation. If processing (Cell 2) and crafting (Cell 3) are separated from the use to which outputs are put (Cell 1), then analysis is likely to generate only data and information (and not intelligence).

Intelligence Is Self-Evident Intelligence requires analysts, and especially decision makers, to think: to ask how the data and information might be used in decision making. Consider the following example. In one firm, top management was getting fragmentary reports (data) from its sales force about changes in a competitor's pricing behavior. On analysis of these reports, the management concluded that the competitor was systematically lowering its prices (information). This information, however, did not qualify as intelligence until management asked: Did lower prices mean the competitor was seeking to gain market share or was it merely trying to scare off a potential entrant into the market?

Scanning: Gathering Competitor Data

Guided and open-ended knowledge development and use necessitate a number of distinct though related analysis processes: scanning, monitoring, projecting, and assessment.[33] Each process elaborates and refines the tasks within the learning activities or cells noted in Figure 2.1.

Open-Ended versus Guided Scanning

Descriptive learning is impossible in the absence of scanning. *Open-ended* scanning entails surveillance of all competitor-related primary and secondary data sources (Cell 2). Unrestricted scanning personifies the open-ended approach: the intent is to scan or search all available data sources (both internal and external to the focal organization) for data pertaining to all current and potential competitors. There are no a priori restrictions on the tasks in capturing: determining data needs, identifying data sources, or collecting data. Neither are there restrictions on who can or should do the scanning.

Guided scanning is more common. It is restricted to selected primary and secondary data sources; it typically searches for data pertaining to a specific facet of a competitor. Analysts often decide to scan all electronic databases for data about a specific competitor or set of competitors or about some component of the analysis framework depicted in Figure 3.2 such as assets or technology. As emphasized throughout this book, scanning often focuses on *internal* primary and secondary sources.[34]

Two Modes of Scanning

Open-ended and guided scanning can be segmented into two modes. In its *prospective* mode, scanning tries to identify *early* indicators of *potential* competitor changes and issues—what is commonly referred to as an early warning system. Scanning is thus aimed at alerting the organization to potentially significant competitor changes *before* they have fully formed or crystallized.[35] Successful scanning, therefore, should draw attention to changes in competitors' strategies well before they take place. For example, a scan might unearth that a competitor has announced it is committing significant funds to research and development with the intent of creating a product breakthrough. The potential new product could provide the signal of a major shift in the competitor's marketplace strategy.

Scanning in the prospective mode therefore is especially useful when competitor change takes time to unfold. This gives the focal organization time to work out implications for its actions. Since the competitor's new product might take two or more years to develop, the firm possesses plenty of time to transform data into intelligence: to assess the implications for its own strategy.

In focusing on *current and retrospective* competitor change, scanning generates a number of distinct types of outputs including "surprises" and competitor issues requiring action on the part of the focal organization. A scan may pick up that a competitor is about to introduce a new product or modify its current product line. When this data is translated into information such as projections of the competitor's sales, it may warrant immediate decisions such as the commitment to change the firm's own product line or to realign product prices. In this case, scanning feeds directly into and influences current and imminent strategic and operating decisions.

Some Key Characteristics of Scanning

Scanning is the most ill-structured and ambiguous process in competitor learning. Especially at the system and macro levels, the relevant data is essentially unlimited. A scan for indicators of potential look-alike and substitute competitors confronts inherently scattered, vague, and imprecise data. Moreover, the primary and secondary sources of such data are many and varied.

Open-ended scanning is especially ambiguous. This is so in part because analysts do not know (precisely) what data they are looking for. In scanning for indicators of potential competitors, the analyst is not able a priori to anticipate every type of indicator or which data sources will generate them. In scanning a security analyst's report of a particular competitor, the analyst may be searching for interesting clues or indicators about the competitor's current and future strategies but may not be able to articulate a priori what those indicators might be.

Scanning is difficult to structure and circumscribe in part because useful indicators about competitors often show up in unexpected places.[36] Thus, the purview of search must be broad, but search guidelines are difficult to formulate.[37]

When Scanning Is Most Useful

Scanning is especially useful when the analyst knows relatively little about the competitive domain or individual competitors. At the system level, scanning is particularly productive when the analyst's focus shifts to a group of competitors to which the organization has paid little if any attention. This circumstance may occur for a number of reasons: foreign competitors may enter the firm's geographic markets; substitute competitors may emerge; small regional competitors may begin to expand their horizons. Also, the firm's own strategic moves may transform entities into competitors that were previously considered noncompetitors. The future direction of the firm's own strategies may also suggest groups of competitors that should be scanned.[38]

At the competitor level, *guided* or *open-ended* scanning typically provides extensive data about a specific competitor in a relatively short time. In most instances, a search of secondary sources such as security analysts' reports, financial sources, trade and industry press, and electronic databases as well as phone calls to selected primary sources[39] can quickly generate extensive broad-brush data on individual competitors.

Monitoring: Tracking Competitor Change

Comparative, augmented, and self-learning require data and information that scanning alone is unable to provide. They necessitate monitoring or tracking competitor change over time. Monitoring is a core element in capturing and processing (Cells 2 and 3 in Figure 2.1). Its purpose is to assemble sufficient data to discern and delineate[40] the extent to which specific competitor change is taking place. Because it involves selecting, ordering, and interpreting data, monitoring generates information.

Monitoring What?

Monitoring may be relatively guided or open-ended. *Guided* monitoring tracks specific types of competitor change for predetermined reasons. It has a number of distinct foci: trends, patterns, and sequences of events or streams of actions. Quantitative trends refer to change along single numerical items or indicators[41] such as market share, sales of individual product lines or product types, specific cost items (such as cost of particular raw materials or total advertising expenditures). Nonquantitative trends might be change along indicators such as key values espoused by the firm (e.g., a commitment to providing higher quality service to customers) or relationships with external entities (e.g., building a closer working relationship with a particular supplier).

Patterns consist of a cumulation of interrelated trends. A variety of cost trends might add up to indicate that a competitor is successfully reducing its manufacturing costs or its total delivered cost to customers. A set of marketing trends might indicate that a competitor is committing itself to compete aggressively in particular product-customer segments.[42]

Sequences of events or streams of actions also serve as important foci of monitoring. Monitoring events and actions around building a new plant, or launching a new product, or restructuring a sales force may indicate how rapidly these changes are being implemented, whether bottlenecks are occurring, and whether key target dates are being met.[43]

In *open-ended monitoring,* the dominant premise is that analysts do not know what should be monitored or what can be learned by monitoring specific competitor change. Thus, analysts select, order, and track as many indicators as possible, even if there is no apparent or immediate rationale for monitoring specific indicators. The intent is to first develop a description of trends, patterns, and sequences of events; only then do analysts look for interactions and interrelationships among them.

The Outcomes of Monitoring

In both focused and open-ended monitoring, three types of outcomes are common. First are the descriptions of trends, patterns, and sequences. Some of these may then become the focus of projecting. Second, monitoring may suggest other facets of competitor change that should be monitored. Third, monitoring sometimes indicates areas for further scanning.

Some Key Characteristics of Monitoring

In both *guided* and *open-ended* monitoring, the data search is more focused and more systematic than in scanning. It is more focused because analysts are guided by specific questions, or in some cases, the types of hunches that may be generated during scanning. Systematic implies that analysts have a general sense of the change parameters they are investigating. For example, in tracking a competitor's sales, or costs, or asset fluctuations (such as access to raw materials, cash flow, or sales force personnel) or service delivery, analysts typically possess a clear understanding of the variables or indicators they are tracking and the types of changes that are likely.

As monitoring specific changes progresses, the data frequently moves from imprecise and unbounded to reasonably specific and circumscribed. In tracking the evolution of a competitor's research and development alliance, early indicators include statements about the need for the alliance, announcements about the content and direction of the alliance, the roles of each alliance partner and the actions they must take. Continued tracking imbues each of these changes with details and clarity.

A number of data interpretations and judgments are unavoidable in monitoring, especially in *open-ended monitoring.* As a number of trends or a sequence of events or actions are tracked or a potential pattern emerges, judgments must be made as to what data are relevant, what the valid and reliable data sources are, how the data fit together, how conflicts in the data can be reconciled, and when data are sufficient to declare that a pattern is evident.[44] Each of these judgments attests to the important role of logic in the process of monitoring.

When Is Monitoring Most Appropriate?

Monitoring is essential when specific aspects of a competitor are deemed especially important to understanding the competitor's strategy, and as a consequence, to determining the focal firm's own strategy. For example, if the competitor's assumptions are different from those of other rivals, tracking indicators of these assumptions (in the form of specific behaviors, statements, and attribute change) assumes added importance.

In addition, since the intent of monitoring is to depict and understand competitor change, monitoring is more appropriate to the extent that change is taking place. The more uncertain the (potential) direction of competitor change, the more important is monitoring.

Projecting: Understanding Future Competitor Change

Scanning and monitoring generate the data inputs required for the two core tasks in descriptive learning: identifying competitors and delineating their *current* strategies and key micro components. However, that is not sufficient given competitor learning's emphasis on knowledge about both the present and the future.[45] Decision making requires a future orientation (Cells 1, 4, and 7 in Figure 2.1). At the system level, it requires a projection of likely future competitors. At the macro level, it needs a projection of what strategies competitors are likely to pursue. The intent of projecting is to provide these projections. It is thus central to competitor learning.

What Is Projected?

The range of possible projections is evident when we consider the three levels of analysis noted earlier. At the system level, projections focus on the emergence, entry, and exit of competitors, changes in strategic groups, and changes in the composition of competitors that are likely to find themselves in direct confrontation or rivalry. At the competitor or macro level, the focus is on projecting changes in the competitor's marketplace strategy: the direction the competitor's strategy is likely to take. At the micro level, the thrust of projections is around specific components of the competitor;

for example, what changes are likely to evolve within the competitor's activity/value chain, what alliances the competitor is likely to enter, or how the competitor's capabilities and competencies are likely to change.

Two Types of Projections

Projecting entails two conceptually separable though integrally related types of projections. The first concerns *simple* projections based on trends (change along single indicators) and patterns (change along multiple indicators) pertaining to the competitor that are evident and which can be expected, with some margin of error, to continue unabated for some period of time in the future. Simple projections are in large measure extrapolations of competitor activity, that is, projections based on the assumption that the future is driven by the past and the present—in forecasting terminology, they flow from a closed perspective on the future. Simple projections might entail projecting continuation of the competitor's current strategy or of specific trends or patterns such as greater use of its sales force in creating value for customers or further movement toward a specific type of culture.

Complex projections, on the other hand, relate to *alternative futures* that may come about not only on the basis of current change (that is, what competitors are currently doing) but also on the basis of judgments by the competitor regarding events that may take place or that may be made to happen by the competitor itself or outside entities. These represent possible futures. Possible futures are best captured in the form of scenarios. A scenario might be developed around the plausibility of a competitor adapting radical departures from its current strategy such as the introduction of a distinctively new product line[46] or engaging in a series of related acquisitions or divestments.

Guided and Open-Ended Projecting

In *guided* projecting, the emphasis is on system and competitor changes of importance to the organization. Simple projections and alternative futures are crafted because there is a presumption that what is being projected has implications for the focal organization. Only those facets of system and competitor change that are expected to have significant implications for the organization typically receive extensive attention.[47] In this sense, projecting is more focused than scanning or monitoring. It inherently requires that the organization identify fairly precisely what aspects of the system of competitors and of individual competitors it wishes to project.

In *open-ended* projecting, simple projections and alternative futures are crafted *before* implications for the organization are considered. Assessment occurs only after projecting. Judgments about the value of specific projections are delayed until they are developed. As with scanning and monitoring, open-ended projections sometimes lead to unanticipated insights into evolving and potential system and competitor change.

Some Characteristics of Projecting

Since the focus, scope, and goals of projecting are more specific than in scanning and monitoring, developing projections is usually a much more logical and rigorous activity. Many projecting techniques are available, ranging from simple extrapolation techniques to methodologies involving multiple participants making projections in a number of iterations such as scenario development, which involves individuals laying out different paths of likely future developments.

Irrespective of the technique employed, as illustrated in many later chapters, developing projections involves numerous data interpretations and judgments. Collectively, these interpretations and judgments constitute the causal connections or "logic" that is central to any projection connecting the present to the future. How strong is the supporting and refuting evidence that the trend or pattern will continue, intensify, or broaden in scope? What underlying forces within or outside the organization are driving these changes, and how strong are they?[48]

Some Key Characteristics of Projections

Projections are not predictions in the sense that they foretell or prophesize what is going to happen. Rather, they indicate what might happen in the future, given careful consideration of all the available data and information.

Projections may be broad or narrow in scope. There is no simple algorithm as to what the scope or focus of projections should be. For example, useful projections might be developed around a competitor's future pricing behavior or the competitor's entire strategy.

Assessment: Identifying Implications of Competitor Change

Competitor learning requires that analysis goes beyond describing and projecting competitor change (the functions of scanning, monitoring, and projecting). It is necessary to asses the consequences and implications of competitor change. Intelligence, the bridge between knowledge generation and knowledge-in-use, is the ultimate outcome of assessment. As described in Chapters 5–16, assessment addresses the system, competitor, and micro levels. Since assessment is extensively treated in each of the remaining chapters, a number of its key elements are briefly introduced here.

The Extent and Direction of Competitor Change

An initial focus in assessment is to develop a thorough understanding of the relevant competitor change. It is essential to understand how a competitor is changing its marketplace strategy: whether it is adding new products, or deleting existing product lines, or adding new items to some of its existing lines, or altering how it is differentiating its products from rivals, or doing all of these. The extent and direction of change guides the questions that analysts should ask.

Signals of Marketplace Change

Competitor change is also assessed for signals of current and projected change in and around the product and factor marketplaces—the end-customer, channel, factor, and institutional arenas. For example, change in one or more competitors' marketplace strategies often portends change in customers' needs, buying behaviors, and the dynamics of rivalry.[49] Such augmented learning, although frequently overlooked in the way many organizations do competitor analysis, is a critical output of assessment.

Competitor Consequences

Also frequently overlooked in competitor analysis in many organizations is the value of assessing consequences[50] for competitors themselves. Signals of marketplace change often have consequences for a competitor's current and projected marketplace strategies. Also, any projected strategy that a competitor might pursue has consequences for its assets (e.g., how will it obtain the necessary assets?), and its capabilities and competencies (e.g., how will it develop capabilities required by the strategy but which it does not now possess?).[51]

Implications for the Focal Firm

The integrating purpose of competitor learning is assessment of implications for the focal firm (self-learning). Implications must be addressed at both the macro and micro levels.[52] Macro implications pertain to its current and future marketplace strategies. Strategy implications are the essential rationale for engaging in competitor learning: the intended outcome is the ability to outmaneuver and outperform existing and potential competitors.

At the micro level, implications can be identified for each of the analysis components noted in Figure 3.2. For example, by comparing and contrasting two or more competitors' assumptions, the focal organization may derive specific insights into its own assumptions, and thus augment its potential to outwit these (and other) rivals.

Summary

This chapter has outlined a number of concepts central to understanding and executing competitor analysis. Concepts such as data, information and intelligence, and efficient and effective learning, shape how individuals think about competitor analysis. Concepts such as scanning, monitoring, projecting, and assessment reside at the heart of how any organization practices competitor analysis. An organization needs to have a shared understanding of these concepts if its competitor analysis efforts are not to become both inefficient and ineffective.

CHAPTER

4

Signals

SIGNALS ARE PERHAPS THE MOST CENTRAL CONCEPT IN COMPETITOR LEARNING. PERceiving, interpreting, and assessing signals is essential to every activity in the competitor learning model (see Figure 2.1) but especially to processing: selecting, ordering, and interpreting data and information. Signals are a core element in every facet of the identification and analysis of current and potential competitors. They contribute greatly to both efficient and effective competitor learning. Without an understanding of what signals are and how they are interpreted and assessed, the analysis of competitors becomes unwieldy, confusing, and unproductive.

Since our focus is the analysis of competitors, this chapter examines signals primarily from the perspective of the *receiver*. The intent is to develop an analysis framework for the identification, interpretation, and assessment of signals. The chapter begins by delineating what a signal is and describing three distinct but related functions of signals. It continues with a description of the analyst's role in signal analysis. The concepts of indicators and signals are next distinguished as a prelude to the identification of multiple types of indicators, followed by sections devoted to what signals indicate and the linkages between signals and change. Some critical characteristics of signals are then noted. The process of analyzing signals is detailed using the example of a competitor's purchase of an equity stake in a supplier. Finally, some common errors in the analysis of signals are noted.

Understanding the Nature of Signals

A signal is an inference drawn by an individual in some specific context from data and information[1] about a competitor pertaining to some past, current, or future state of, or actions by, the competitor. Signals thus require three items: (a) *data and information* that give rise to *indicators* from which *signals* are inferred; (b) an *individual* who draws the *inference(s)*; and (c) a *context* in which the inferences are drawn. Signals result from the interpretation of indicators within some context—hence, they are inferences. They give rise to the assessment of *consequences* for the competitor(s) and *implications*[2] for the focal firm (see Figure 4.1).

When viewed as inferences, signals cannot exist without analysts.[3] A signal, defined as an inference, cannot be sent; it can only be constructed by an individual. It is one or more individuals who detect indicators and draw inferences from them. Thus, a competitor's preannouncement of the launch of a new product is an indicator, not a signal. It becomes a signal when an analyst draws an inference from it that the competitor is willing to bet a lot of resources to become the dominant player in a particular product sector. Similarly, the appointment of a new president, who has no experience within the industry, is an indicator from which multiple tentative inferences might be immediately drawn. One inference might be that the competitor is likely to move in some new strategic direction and/or it will speed up its commitment to execute some previously announced marketplace strategy moves.

A signal as an inference is fundamentally distinct from its usage in both nonbusiness literatures and common parlance. A presumption in electrical engineering, for example, is that a signal sent from Point A is precisely the signal picked up at Point B. In the inanimate world of engineering, there is no room for misspecification or misinterpretation of what is sent. This is obviously not the case in organizational settings. Even when indicators such as the actions and words of a competitor are fully and accurately picked up by an organization, individuals unfamiliar with the competitor's context often do not draw any inferences from them. Even with an understanding of the relevant context, individuals frequently draw different inferences or they

FIGURE 4.1
Signals: The Analysis Process

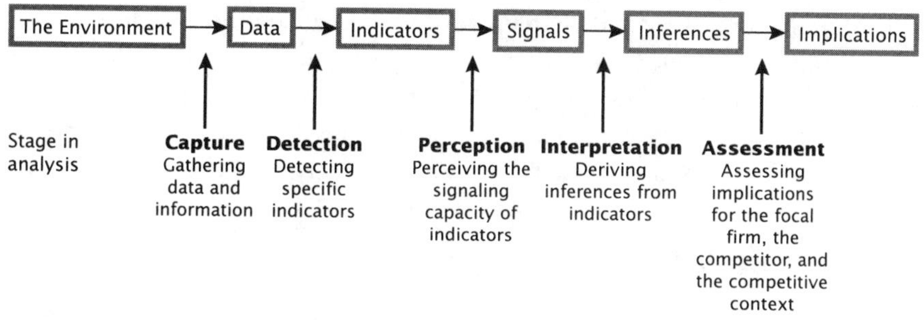

| Stage in analysis | **Capture** Gathering data and information | **Detection** Detecting specific indicators | **Perception** Perceiving the signaling capacity of indicators | **Interpretation** Deriving inferences from indicators | **Assessment** Assessing implications for the focal firm, the competitor, and the competitive context |

draw inferences that later prove false, which is the case when what is inferred does not occur.

A signal defined as an inference is also distinct from the way signals are typically treated in the strategy, economics, and related, literatures. For example, Porter defines a (market) signal as "any action by a competitor that provides a direct or indirect indication of its intentions, motives, goals or internal situation."[4] Heil and Roberstson, on the other hand, assert that "competitive market signals are announcements or previews of potential actions intended to convey information or to gain information from competitors."[5] Both definitions illustrate how authors interested in rivalry among competitors have not distinguished between indicators and signals, and have tended to downplay or ignore the importance of the inferencing process and to emphasize only one type or a small set of indicators.

Signals are distinguished from indicators for a number of reasons. First, not all indicators give rise to signals (inferences). Signals arise only when analysts recognize the signaling capacity of data or indicators. For example, one company had meticulously cataloged a number of actions and statements by a competitor including an increase in its manufacturing capacity, a buildup of inventory of some product types, and comments about the importance of gaining market share. However, no one drew an inference that the competitor was about to dramatically reduce prices in some of its product lines. Thus, all signals stem from indicators but not all indicators necessarily give rise to a signal (or confirm or refute a previously derived signal).[6] Second, a single indicator sometimes gives rise to more than one inference. Conversely, multiple indicators often are the source of a single signal; for example, a sequence of actions by a competitor such as its moves in the marketplace or a series of resource commitments is frequently the basis of an inference or signal. Third, others have tended to greatly understate the availability and range of indicators although they are far more extensive than market actions and preannouncements.[7] Finally, the definition and conception of signals advocated in this chapter places a heavy onus on understanding the role of the individual who detects indicators and draws the signals.

Signals as inferences go to the heart of the value added by analysts. They add value through their ability to go beyond data collection and description; by drawing inferences, they perceive more than is in any single data point or set of indicators. As the remaining chapters in this book illustrate, without the capacity to develop reasoned inferences about competitors' likely strategic moves and behaviors, outwitting rivals is largely impossible.

The Functions of Signal Analysis

The overriding function of perceiving and analyzing signals is to create competitor intelligence: knowledge that informs decision makers and infuses decision making. Signals facilitate and enhance competitor learning in at least three related ways: by focusing analysis; by constituting the evidence that allows inferences to be drawn; and, by compelling reflection on the part of analysts.

Focus Analysis Learning occurs when analysts' attention is stimulated and focused.[8] Signals stimulate and focus competitor analysis in a number of ways. The *search* for indicators, whether guided or open-ended, is the principal focus of competitor data collection. In scanning, the intent is to capture indicators that reflect past, present, or future competitor change. In monitoring, the focus may be a stream of indicators pertaining to marketplace strategy or to a specific microlevel component such as activity/value chain, assumptions, assets, or capabilities.

Second, signals focus attention on *change* in and around competitors.[9] Thus, in *guided* learning, the analyst might scan and monitor indicators of a competitor's intent to change its strategy or to modify its activity/value chain. Signals thus sharpen the analyst's purview: the analyst is primed to pick up indicators that might signal likely changes in the competitor's marketplace strategy or in the activities that constitute the competitor's value chain. In *open-ended* learning, the analyst is attentive to all indicators, irrespective of their immediate capacity to generate signals.

Constitute Evidence One or more signals (inferences) typically undergird analysts' projections of competitors' future marketplace strategies or other behaviors, and assessments of their competitor consequences and focal firm implications. More specifically, it is the data or indicators and the logic or reasoning associated with individual signals that buttress such projections and assessments.[10] For example, if an analyst concludes (draws an inference) that a specific competitor has adopted a goal of attaining 10 more market share points within a three-year time period, one might reasonably ask what evidence, such as specific indicators and logic, support that judgment. The supporting indicators might include recent plant extensions and the completion of a long-term contract for key raw material supplies that will facilitate production of the necessary volume of product, as well as statements by the CEO and head of marketing indicating their desire to be "the dominant market leader within five years."

Compel Reflection An implicit but often overlooked function of signal analysis is to cause analysts to continually reflect on both the stock of their own knowledge—their facts, perceptions, beliefs, assumptions, and projections—as well as their modes of thinking or processes of learning.[11] It is all too easy to develop an apparently compelling logic buttressed by some available data; however, conviction cannot be substituted for reflection and insight. The signal analysis process, detailed later in this chapter, compels analysts to reflect on the judgments, and in particular, the evidence and reasoning underlying them, that are inherent in each of the acts in signal analysis noted in Figure 4.1. Thus, signals provide an opportunity for analysts to continually question their own knowledge and also the prevailing assessments (shared knowledge) within their organization of what competitors are doing or are likely to do and why.

Perceiving and Using Signals: The Role of the Analyst

Signals as inferences result from the deliberation and analysis of individuals. The analyst's role in creating and using signals is segmented into five related steps (see Figure 4.1). Each step pertains specifically to one or more of the learning activities depicted in Figure 2.1: capturing data and information about the competitor (Cells 1 and 2); detecting indicators (Cells 2 and 3); perceiving indicators as signals (Cell 3); interpreting signals (Cells 3 and 4) and, assessing the signal's implications (Cells 1 and 4). Each step is briefly delineated and discussed, using a competitor's price reduction as an illustration.

Guided and open-ended scanning and monitoring, as discussed in Chapter 3, furnish the data and information that are a prerequisite to the detection of indicators—*an act of capture*. In our pricing example, the competitor's price announcement is the initial data captured. The analyst then gathers data to determine the specifics of the pricing move (the extent of the price reduction, its timing, what products it applies to, etc.) and its context (whether other competitors have reduced price, product sales trends, etc.).

Extracting indicators out of data and information requires an *act of detection*. It often involves clarifying and specifying the details or "content" of the indicator.[12] Sometimes an indicator consists of individual data points such as a change in market share or the appointment of a new executive. In the pricing case, the analyst outlines the competitor's prior pricing moves, the context in which those moves were made, and the results that ensued.

Recognizing an indicator's capacity to serve as a signal requires an *act of perception* on the part of the analyst. Without this perceptive act, the signaling capacity of indicators is missed and hence both the efficiency and effectiveness of competitor analysis is greatly jeopardized. It is the intervention of the analyst that allows signals to emanate from, or more precisely, be derived from indicators. In the pricing case, the analyst must recognize that the price move may give rise to a signal of the competitor's future behaviors and intentions. Initially, the analyst may have little insight into what the price move signals: it requires that data pertaining to the price move be organized and a logic developed that allows the data to be ordered and interpreted.[13]

Determining what the price move signals requires an *act of interpretation.* In the pricing case, the analyst must judge whether the price reduction signals that the competitor is embarking on an effort to quickly gain market penetration, or that it is firing the first salvo in launching a protracted battle to gain market share, or that it reduced price reluctantly only because it anticipated a similar move by another competitor and does not want to lower prices any further.

Context is critical to interpretation. Without an understanding of the competitor's current and past marketplace strategy (including its pricing behaviors), its performance results and the nature and history of the rivalry among competitors in the marketplace, it is simply impossible for any analyst to interpret what the pricing move signals (and thus what its implications may be).

Finally, the analyst must judge the competitor consequences and focal firm implications of what is signaled: *an act of assessment.*[14] The implications of signals are also often assessed for other competitors and the industry in general.[15] In the pricing case, if the price reduction is interpreted as a signal of the competitor's intent to initiate and engage in a protracted price battle to gain market share, the analyst needs to assess whether the competitor has the resources to sustain a price war, what share gain the competitor might need to obtain before it would consider the price move a success and whether the competitor would need to expand its production capacity to sustain its price initiative. Answers to these questions help determine the possible implications for the focal organization. For example, if the competitor is committed to gaining substantial market share, the focal firm may have little choice but to take drastic action.

Because of the role and importance of signals in competitor learning, several comments pertaining to the analysis of signals merit emphasis. First, each of the acts noted earlier (capture, detection, perception, interpretation, assessment) is unavoidable in the process of signal analysis. Second, each contributes to both the efficiency and effectiveness of competitor learning. Third, analysts need to hone their skills with respect to each act. If analysts are not accustomed to viewing data and information as a source of indicators (and thus as a source of signals), many potential signals will be missed. Fourth, as discussed later in this chapter, analysts need to understand the role of both logic and data in the derivation of inferences. Fifth, to avoid the pitfalls and traps associated with interpretation and assessment,[16] signals need to be subjected to the analysis process detailed in the penultimate section of this chapter. Sixth, the outputs of interpretation, and the decisions and actions due to assessment, need to be continually reviewed; changes in the context of signals sometimes lead to changes in what they indicate and their implications. Finally, analysts engage in signal analysis over time; it is rarely a one-time event. Hence, the analyst typically cycles back and forth[17] through the acts or steps noted in Figure 4.1.

Indicators: The Source of Signals

Data and information about competitors constitute the indicators from which signals are derived. As noted in Chapter 3, data ultimately consists of competitors' behaviors or actions (including the absence of behaviors), statements, and organization change.

Behaviors Most actions or behaviors (a pattern among actions) of any competitor possess some degree of signaling capacity:[18] one is able to draw inferences from them about other behaviors or actions of the competitor or about change in one or more of its microlevel components such as assumptions, competencies, or organization infrastructure or culture. There are four distinct types of indicators stemming from actions or behaviors:

1. **Marketplace indicators** pertain to a competitor's actions in the marketplace—the end-customer and channel arenas noted in Chapter 1. Since they are addressed in detail in Chapters 5 and 6, it is sufficient to note here that they pertain to *products* or solutions (e.g., the introduction of new products, modifying existing products), *customers* (e.g., changing distribution channels, dropping specific end-customers), and *how the competitor competes* (e.g., changes in advertising, promotions, prices). Since they occur in the open, marketplace indicators are visible to third parties.

2. **Organizational indicators** refer to actions *within* the boundaries of the competitor's organization. Organizational actions include decisions, commitments of resources, and changes in internal policies, procedures, and practices. Chapters 7–15 identify multiple types of organizational action indicators pertaining to each microlevel component. Some organizational actions are publicly visible such as the appointment of a new CEO, major organization structure changes, or changes in its capital structure; whereas others are much less publicly visible such as changes in manufacturing processes, incentive systems, or raw material procurement practices.

3. **Relational indicators** refer to actions a competitor takes pertaining to all entities other than product marketplace entities (competitors, channels, and end-customers) such as suppliers, research bodies, governmental agencies, public interest or community groups—the factor and institutional arenas noted in Chapter 1. The visibility of these actions also varies.

4. **Inaction** also is often an indicator. However, inaction is not unbounded; all inactions are not indicators. There must be some grounds for expecting action; the absence of specific action in a given set of circumstances

may be detected as a potential indicator.[19] For example, if a competitor does *not* lower prices in response to another organization dropping its prices, it may be trying to "send a signal" that it does not wish to engage in price competition and/or that it is able to hold its customer base without lowering its prices.

Statements Words, in the form of statements, also constitute indicators. As with behaviors, four distinct types of indicators merit noting. Each has distinct characteristics that affect its role as a source of signals:

1. **Preannouncements** are competitors' statements pertaining to *future* actions or intentions. Competitors frequently announce that they are going to do something such as withdraw from a market, extend a product line, hire new personnel, or search for new alliance partners. Widely different motivations spur competitors to make preannouncements.

2. **Postannouncements** are competitors' statements pertaining to actions they *have already taken* or are in the process of taking. Such announcements pertain to many matters: the appointment of a new CEO, personnel promotions, research breakthroughs, product introductions or modifications, or entry or exit from specific product-customer segments.

3. **Commentary** in the form of *scripted* statements by competitors also constitutes a rich source of indicators. Commentary is often associated with pre- and postannouncements. Other times it is not. Competitors provide commentary on many matters including observations on the current state and likely future direction of their industry or specific product-customer segments, assessments of their present and expected performance results, and explanations of specific decisions (e.g., the entry into or exit from product-customer segments).

4. **Informal** or unscripted words are also a source of signals. Sometimes they are associated with pre- and postannouncements. For example, members of a competitor's sales force may pass comments to customers about the firm's intention to revamp its product line or change prices. Executives sometimes say more than they intended in responding to questions in a press interview or at a trade or industry show. Even unscripted comments made by executives and others *within* their own organization sometimes find their way into public forums. For example, internal newsletters are often widely disseminated.[20]

Although discussions of signals often emphasize competitors' behaviors or actions to the neglect of words, the role and importance of the latter should not be overlooked. First, as noted, words often *predate* behaviors. Announcements of new plant construction, for example, often precede the consequent addition to industry capacity by months or even years. Thus, words allow others to anticipate and prepare for changes in competitors' behaviors. Second, words almost always aid in understanding the competitor's past, current, or projected behaviors. Commentary is often intended to explain a competitor's planned actions. Third, in some instances, words allow analysts to infer significant changes about the context of a competitor's current and intended behaviors, even though the content or sequence of behaviors themselves does not change. The CEO who reiterates that his organization does not intend to withdraw from a product-customer segment can change the perceptions of the actions of his organization.

Organization Change: Elements and Attributes What an organization does and says are not the only types of indicators (or sources of signals). As illustrated in Chapters 5-15, changes in the constituent elements of each component—marketplace strategy, activity/value chain, alliances and relationships, networks, assumptions, assets, capabilities and competencies, technology, organization infrastructure and culture—also serve as distinctive and valuable indicators. For example, changes in key asset types[21] (capital, cash, marketing skills, technical knowledge, customer image and reputation, supplier relationships, inventory) frequently constitute useful indicators. Changes in the competitor's balance sheet and income statements can be informative indicators. An increase in the competitor's credit lines with its financial institutions may generate a signal of its intent to undertake a major strategic initiative such as an acquisition.[22]

To cite one more example of component indicators, changes in the competitor's culture—the values, beliefs, norms, and behaviors[23] of its members, also constitute indicators. Changes from engineering or manufacturing values to customer and marketplace values often constitute indicators of major and pervasive organization change, with major implications for each element of marketplace strategy.

As described in Chapters 5-15, each component is characterized by a number of distinct attributes: ways in which changes in the component as a whole, or specific elements of it, are delineated and assessed. For example, the key attributes of assets are their availability, specificity, sustainability, replicability, and substitutability.[24] Changes in these attributes are often insightful and unique indicators. If an asset such as cash or access to a particular component becomes less available to a competitor, it may indicate the need for multiple changes to how the competitor operates.

Attribute changes are considered as a separate source of indicators for a number of reasons. They provide a more aggregative level of indicators than simply changes in one or more elements of a component. They broaden the range of indicators beyond actions and words. They extend the scope of indicators to include the results of behaviors and actions. Thus, analysts must take a broader purview in scanning and monitoring competitors.

Finally, changes in component elements and attributes cannot be separated from behaviors, words, or inaction. Organization change, action, and words are always interrelated. Management actions such as hiring new personnel or initiating a series of alliances frequently cause change in infrastructure and culture elements and attributes. Commitments of assets lead to change in capabilities and competencies. Changes in component elements and attributes may in turn lead to actions and words. If an asset such as specific technological knowledge becomes more replicable or substitutable, the competitor often has little choice but to take action such as embarking on new product development initiatives or changing its marketplace strategy.

Information

Information, as noted in Chapter 3, is created by analysts. It is noted here because it is a much overlooked source of indicators. It is analysts who generate behaviors (patterns in actions), all change in component attributes and much change in component elements. To cite a common example, projected cash flows and consequences derived from them for a competitor may indicate choices that are likely to confront the competitor and, therefore, its potential marketplace strategies or specific behaviors. A less obvious example is that changes in a competitor's assumptions (typically an output of extensive data ordering, selecting, and interpreting) sometimes serve as an indicator of significant changes in strategy.[25] Thus, as a competitor becomes more and more convinced that truly distinct customer segments are emerging, it is likely to differentiate its offerings to meet the specific needs of these distinct customer groups.

Indicators: Signals about What?

As noted, indicators become signals when analysts draw inferences from them or use them to make judgments about a competitor. But, what might indicators signal about competitors? Or, stated differently, what are signals able to indicate? It is insightful to discuss these questions with regard to the three levels of competitor analysis noted in Chapter 3.

At the system level, indicators signal change within and around the industry or competitive arena. In particular, indicators are scanned and monitored to indicate change such as the potential entry of additional look-alike competitors, the emergence of substitute competitors, the exit of competitors, potential moves by competitors from one product-customer segment to another and changes in the nature and intensity of rivalry among competitors.

At the competitor or macro level, as delineated in Chapters 5 and 6, indicators are searched for and analyzed to indicate change in the competitor's marketplace strategy. Signals indicate change in scope (potential changes in the products the competitor provides and the customers it chooses to serve), in posture (how the competitor competes in the marketplace), and in goals (what the competitor is trying to achieve).

At the micro level, as delineated in Chapters 7–15, signals indicate change in each of the micro components of analysis noted in the previous chapter (see Figure 3.2): activity/value chain, alliances, special relationships and networks, assumptions, resources, capabilities and competencies, technology and organization.

Signals and Change

The relationship between signals and change is complex and often not well understood. Change pertains to each stage and each act noted in Figure 4.1. Competitor change, as reflected in competitors' behaviors, words, inaction, and organization elements and attributes, is the source of indicators. The indicators, in turn, give rise to signals. Assessment identifies change implications for the competitor, the system of competitors, and the focal firm.[26] Although signals sometimes indicate continuation of, or commitment to, the status quo, they typically indicate change with respect to some facet of the system of competitors or of an individual competitor. Change captured along indicators often leads to other signals of change about the competitor.

Signals and the Timing of Change

Signals indicate past, current, or future competitor change. The timing of indicated change often has major action implications for the focal firm.

Prospective Signals   Prospective signals indicate *future* competitor change: the analyst derives inferences about competitor change that has not yet taken place. Preannouncements, by definition, generate prospective signals. Marketplace indicators often serve the anticipatory function: the competitor's actions in the marketplace allow the analyst to infer or judge that specific other changes are likely. For example, withdrawal from one product-customer segment may be a precursor to increased aggressiveness in and commitment to another segment. Organization changes such as an inventory increase and decline in cash reserves may be harbingers of price reductions.

Retrospective Signals   Although prospective signals are the exclusive focus in most treatments of signals,[27] they also can indicate past change. Retrospective signals assume significance to the extent the change is important and the analyst is unaware of it. For example, announcements often indicate that the competitor has already changed its manufacturing process or has initiated a new approach to servicing its customers. Retrospective signals therefore indicate significant competitor change necessitating major responses. Scanning frequently unearths indicators that lead to retrospective signals.

Current Signals Some signals also indicate ongoing change. Marketplace signals typically indicate changes the competitor *is* executing. Indicators such as changes in product features signal how the competitor is trying to attract, win, and retain customers. Words often refer to change that is in process. Organization changes such as inventory decline and cash flow increases are often the source of signals of changes in the competitor's sales volumes.

Anticipated Signals Sometimes an organization first identifies potential options or courses of action confronting a competitor such as different marketplace strategy alternatives or different locations in which a large manufacturing plant might be built.[28] There may be little, if any, immediate evidence to support these possibilities. It then asks what indicators would signal the choice or execution of one option as opposed to others. Thus, the search is for signals of a specific event, result, or choice. These signals are anticipated in that the analyst is systematically seeking indicators,[29] often without knowing what type of indicator may transpire, or what its source may be.

Confirming and Refuting Change

Some indicators or, more precisely, the signals derived from them, serve the critical role of initially alerting the analyst to change—past, current, or future. It is then almost always necessary to seek other indicators (signals) to confirm or refute the change.

Alerting Signals An alerting signal is the one which *first* draws the analyst's attention to a specific competitor change. As noted in Chapter 3, a primary intent of scanning is the generation of alerting signals. Alerting signals address past, present, or future change. The importance of capture and detection noted earlier is now evident: analysts often possess indicators without recognizing what they might signal. The first signal of change such as the development of a new product line, or entry into new product-customer segments, or a radical shift in how the competitor wishes to compete in the marketplace, may indicate potential major changes in the competitor's marketplace strategy. Alerting signals quickly focus the analyst's attention and cause critical reflection on prior presumptions about the competitor.

Confirming Signals Because competitor change is ongoing, the analyst is likely to detect a sequence of indicators over time that relate to a specific type of competitor change. Thus, many signals confirm or support prior signals, or more precisely, previously drawn judgments or inferences. Table 4.1 shows a sequence of indicators relating to a competitor's decision to completely revamp its customer service function. The hiring of a new customer service manager generated the alerting signal: the replacement of the prior manager allowed the first inference to be derived that the competitor was intent on "beefing up" its service function.

Actions frequently confirm statements. The assignment of additional salespersons to a specific territory might confirm a statement by a member of the competitor's management team that it intended to aggressively pursue market share. Actions also often reinforce other actions, as in a sequence of actions intended to gain market share. It is not unusual to find statements confirming or supporting earlier statements. Organization attribute change, as noted in Chapters 5–15, also often plays an important role in confirming initial inferences.

Refuting Signals Inferences drawn from later indicators sometimes refute or disconfirm prior signals—the inferences drawn from prior indicators. A competitor's action(s) may indicate something quite opposite to that inferred from prior actions and/or statements. The announcement of an acquisition (giving rise to a signal of intent to enter a particular product-customer

TABLE 4.1 A Competitor Enhancing Its Customer Service

Indicators	Inferences
Hired new "customer service manager"	Alerts analyst that competitor is going to upgrade and renovate the quality of its service to customers
Reorganized customer support and service unit (CSSU)	Initial confirmation of alerting signal
CSSU now reports to VP of marketing (rather than sales)	Signals increased importance of service by the competitor
Initiating new training programs for sales force	Service is to be enhanced for all key customer segments
Emphasizes customer service in advertising	Service is of value in attracting and retaining customers
Comment of president: Customers expect quality in service as well as in the product	Service is becoming part of the competitor's mind-set—it will be institutionalized
Customer to our salesperson: ABC is now doing things for us they never did before	Confirms that service is being institutionalized and leveraged

segment) would refute prior statements of the competitor's management team that it did not intend to participate in this marketplace sector. Given the credibility and commitment associated with an acquisition as a signal of intent, the action outweighs the words.

The Signal Analysis Process

The signal analysis process portrayed in Figure 4.1 involves complex acts of data capture, indicator detection and signal perception, interpretation, and assessment. The intent of this section is to develop a more incisive understanding of each act, and how they relate to each other, before turning to the analysis of individual or multiple signals (see Figure 4.2).

Indicator Content: Clear versus Ambiguous

A signal is difficult to interpret and assess if the relevant indicator(s) are poorly delineated. Ambiguity about indicators occurs in many ways: words, actions, and organization attributes are sometimes unclear, confusing, or contradictory. Descriptions of informal, or unscripted, statements may be at odds. Different members of the sales force may present inconsistent reports of what a competitor's sales manager actually said to key customers. The particulars of behaviors such as emerging new product features, customer

FIGURE 4.2
The Signals Analysis Process: Some Key Elements

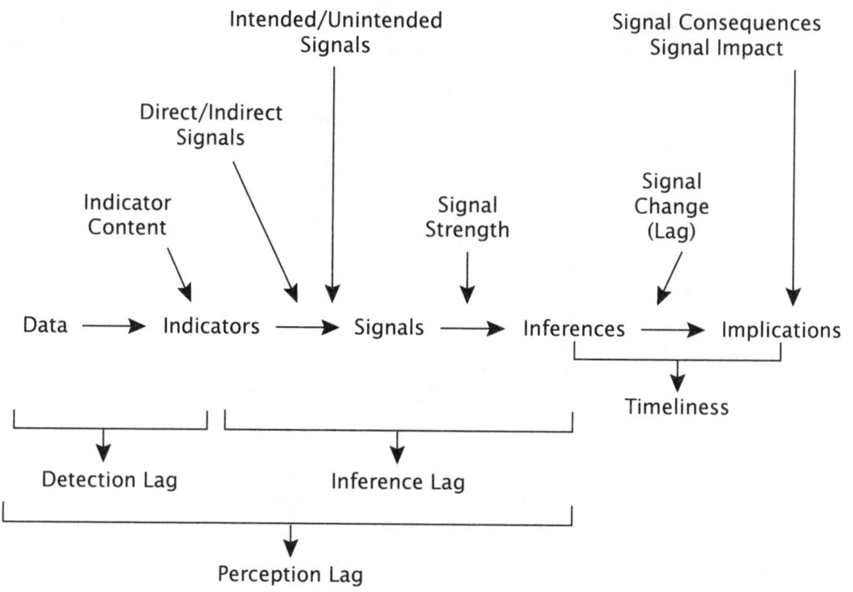

service changes, and even price changes sometimes take time to correctly specify. Some organization attribute changes are especially ambiguous. Changes in the leadership, purposes, and stability of a competitor's network are often difficult to pin down.

Even indicators associated with *intended* signals (to be discussed shortly) are sometimes ambiguous. For example, reports of preannouncements may vary considerably in different trade publications. Statements intended to "send a signal" may be attributed to different individuals within the competitor.

Not surprisingly, indicators generating *alerting* signals are sometimes quite unclear and ambiguous. This is so in part because analysts are not expecting a particular indicator or they do not fully recognize an indicator's signaling capacity; thus, the content of the indicator remains ambiguous in their mind. For example, a manager who was told by a business acquaintance about a number of statements that an executive from one of his competitors had made at a trade conference could not recall with much precision a few weeks later what the executive was alleged to have said.

Sometimes competitors deliberately cause indicator ambiguity by taking actions that are, in part, intended to confuse rivals or to conceal from them a long-term strategy or action plan. Actions such as raising and lowering prices in different product lines, or in different geographic segments, are sometimes intended to conceal from rivals the pricing changes the competitor plans to make at a later time. Also, statements are frequently intentionally vague. On occasion, statements are deliberately untrue—what is referred to as misinformation.[30]

When indicators are reasonably unambiguous, analysts are able to concentrate on signal interpretation and assessment. When indicators are ambiguous, analysts tend to become preoccupied clarifying the indicators rather than extracting and refining inferences. Competitor learning becomes inefficient if analysts do not test whether the ambiguous indicator leads to inferences with significant implications. If the manager noted in the previous paragraph does not derive and test the implications of different inferences from the competitor's alleged statements, he is likely to waste considerable time determining precisely what the executive said.

Indicator (and Signal) Context: Specific versus Fuzzy

Even in the presence of clear indicators, signals are more difficult to interpret to the extent that their context is ill-specified or fuzzy. A preannouncement of an alliance for joint product development is difficult to interpret and assess without prior knowledge about the alliance partners including their R&D and other capabilities, their recent and anticipated marketplace performance, as well as the product development activity of other competitors. It is even more important for an intended signal. Without knowledge of the context, it is difficult to make judgments about its motivation—why it is being sent or what response it is intended to evoke.[31]

Indicators to Signals: Direct versus Indirect

Signals (and indicators) are direct or indirect. Signals are direct when the inference refers to indicator(s) from which it is being drawn. Stated differently, indicators pertaining to A allow inferences to be drawn about A. All the inferences about a competitor's efforts to enhance customer service shown in Table 4.1 are direct: each inference and its associated indicator refers to some facet of or action involved in providing customer service.

Indirect signals require the analyst to draw inferences about one thing from something else: indicators about A allow inferences to be drawn about B. For example, indicators about a competitor's strategy in Europe such as changes in how it competes might (indirectly) allow signals to be drawn about potential changes in its strategy in the U.S. marketplace. Changes in manufacturing process often allow signals to be derived about potential changes in how the competitor is likely to differentiate its products in the marketplace in terms of product line breadth, functionality, features, and services.[32]

Indirect signals especially require the analyst to think carefully through the logic or reasoning that links the indicator(s) and the inference(s). It is therefore a good example of how signals compel analysts to engage in reflection—one of the functions of signals noted at the beginning of this chapter.

Signal Intent: Intended versus Unintended

Although the perspective in this chapter is that of the receiver or generator of signals, it is still important to remember that competitors sometimes wish to "send a signal"[33] to others. An intended signal is a specific inference that one or more competitors (or others) are expected to derive from particular actions, words, and/or associated organization change—the indicators.[34] Signals are intended when the competitor determines what it wants to convey (the inference it wishes to be derived), to whom it wants to send the signal (the receivers), what the signal's purpose or intent is (often in the form of action expected of the recipient), and how it can convey the signal (the indicators that are expected to cause a signal to be received). These are interrelated choices. An organization may endeavor to send a signal to a foreign competitor (the intended recipient), by its actions such as replicating each of the foreign competitor's incentives to the trade and distribution channels and announcements such as a commitment of R&D funds to develop the next generation of product as a means of preempting the foreign competitor (the indicators that convey or communicate the signal) that it will not allow the competitor to gain easy access to the U.S. marketplace (the intended signal or inference), so that the competitor might reconsider its decision to enter the U.S. marketplace (the signal's purpose).

Competitors try to signal each other (and other third parties such as customers, suppliers, distributors, and governmental agencies) about any or all the items noted earlier under the heading, Indicators: Signals about What. Signals about its own current or future strategy are intentionally conveyed by an organization to its competitors for many reasons: to help avoid debilitating rivalry in the marketplace; to preempt competitors from engaging in specific behaviors; or, to entice competitors into behaviors or words that are deemed to be in the best interest of all in the industry.[35]

Of course, what is intended by the sender need not be what is captured, detected, and interpreted by the receiver. Analysts, therefore, as receivers, must subject intended signals to the analysis process detailed in the final section of this chapter.

Although most of the literature focuses on intended signals, signals are predominantly unintended or inadvertent. Indeed, they arise in multiple ways. The competitor's behaviors and words allow different signals to be derived than were intended: others draw inferences from the behaviors or words beyond what the competitor intended. Unintended signals arise when the competitor is not aware that its behaviors, words, inaction, and organization change are serving as the source of signals for others. Also, indicators that are the product of analysis, that is, information, are an especially rich source of unintended signals. Change in a competitor's network attributes such as its purpose and leadership process may give rise to strong signals of change in its marketplace strategy or in its commitment to a particular type of research and development. To cite a more common example, a decline in cash flow allows signals to be derived about the competitor's ability to carry through on an announced capital expenditure program. Indeed, the competitor need not be aware of either of these types of organization change, yet they serve as a signal (of potential competitor change) to others.

Signal Perception Lag: Short versus Long

As illustrated in the service example (see Table 4.1), a sequence or pattern of indicators is typically associated with significant competitor change such as change in how competitors compete, and in their underlying assumptions, competencies, and technologies. Organizations often detect indicators only in the later stages in the sequence. In detecting indicators and perceiving signals, analysts need to be aware of two distinct types of lag, each of which directly affects both the efficiency and effectiveness of competitor learning.

Detection Lag Detection lag is the length of time between when an indicator becomes available and its detection by the analyst. Detection lag is zero when the analyst becomes aware of the indicator as it occurs. Such might be the case with many types of statements and some types of actions. Some degree of lag, however, is typically associated with indicator detection.

Inference Lag Inference lag is the length of time between when an indicator is detected and the analyst draws a signal from it. For many reasons, analysts often do not immediately recognize the signaling capacity of data and information in their possession. The alerting signals would have been perceived earlier had analysts been attentive to the signaling capacity of the data and information they already possessed or data and information readily accessible to them.

Signal perception lag is the cumulation of detection lag and inference lag. The shorter the signal perception lag, the longer an organization has to amend or change its strategies and behaviors. A major purpose of scanning, monitoring, and projecting is to aid analysts in shortening perception lags.

Signal Inferences: Strong versus Weak

Signals arise when inferences are drawn from direct and/or indirect indicators. Whether a signal is intended or unintended, inferences drawn by an analyst vary greatly in strength, defined as the extent to which they are credible.

The strength or credibility of inferences depends on both the data and the logic. Data includes the nature, extent, and reliability of the indicators. Indicators reflecting capital outlays or other asset commitments add greatly to inference strength. A number of supporting and reinforcing indicators, as illustrated in the customer service example (see Table 4.1), adds to inference strength. A statement that an analyst has personally heard is typically more reliable than third-party reports.[36]

Interpretation, the core of a signal, requires a logic or "story" in the form of one or more causal connections or lines of argument that link the inference(s) to one or more indicators. A logic is stronger to the extent there is no competing or alternative plausible explanation or rationale linking one or more indicators to an alternative inference. There are often competing logics in the case of indirect signals. Analysts therefore must always be careful to challenge the logic giving rise to any indirect signal.[37]

Weak inferences are those for which there is only a little supporting data, or data that is conflictual, and/or a noncompelling logic or competing logics. A small price reduction to a single customer alone would generate only a weak signal that the competitor was launching a massive price war against its major competitors. While it might serve as an alerting signal of potential price change, inferring that it was the competitor's first blow in a major price war would require a mammoth leap of judgment.

A strong inference does not mean that what is inferred or indicated will come to pass. Rather, it asserts that an inference has been drawn for which there is substantial evidence and compelling logic. A strong inference may prove incorrect in that what was indicated (as interpreted by the analyst) did not transpire or something else occurred. The possibility that strong inferences may be incorrect attests to the importance of the reflection function of signals discussed earlier: the judgments at the heart of any inference must be continually open to critique and modification.

Signal Change: Continuous versus Discontinuous

Competitor signals are inferences about competitor change. However, the indicated change may be minimal or extensive. Signal change is the degree to which the change indicated by the signal is different from the status quo; that is, what the competitor is doing now, or what was previously believed or expected. The status quo as the essential referent in assessing degree of signal change requires that analysts know what the competitor is now doing or is projected to do.

The continuum of change ranges from zero to extreme discontinuity. A competitor's words and behaviors often signal little, if any, change for the immediate future in its marketplace strategy. On the other hand, many prospective signals indicate dramatic change. Preannouncements sometimes signal complete reversals in a competitor's behaviors such as an announcement of an impending alliance by a competitor that had always vowed it would go it alone. Postannouncements may also indicate significant discontinuities.

The greater the degree of signal change, the greater the uncertainty of its outcomes. Thus, the greater the necessity to review the indicators and logic giving rise to the signal and to assess the signal's consequences for the competitor and implications for the focal firm.

Signal Change Lag: Short versus Long

The change indicated by a signal most frequently is not contemporaneous with the indicator. The length of time between when an inference is derived and when what it indicates will take place (or has taken place) is defined as signal change lag. Preannouncements necessarily entail some degree of change lag.

Change lag ranges from zero to many years. It is zero when the indicator and the change it indicates are contemporaneous. Such is the case, when a competitor surprises its rivals by introducing its new executive vice president at an industry show or trade association meeting. Other signals have a very short lag time. Some preannouncements are associated with or lead to immediate change. Personnel changes often take effect within days; joint marketing programs can be initiated within weeks. Retrospective signals also may have short or long lags associated with them.

On the other hand, long signal lag is common. Organizational actions such as the hiring of new personnel with specific types of knowledge and skills may not result in new product introductions for a number of years.

Signal Timeliness: Early versus Late

The pragmatic import of signals is that they not only facilitate understanding and anticipation of competitors' strategy changes, but also give the firm more time to develop preemptive or other types of response. Signal timeliness refers to the amount of time an organization has to respond to or take action after an intended or unintended signal has been derived. It is a function of perception lag and change lag. The shorter the perception lag (the earlier a signal is derived) and the longer the change lag, the greater the amount of time the firm has to respond to a competitor's signal. A firm that infers from comments of a senior executive at an industry conference that a competitor will build a new manufacturing plant leading to significant new product functionality and features has considerably more time to put in place its own strategy than if that inference was only derived one year later when the competitor announced the types of products that would be manufactured in the plant.

Signal Consequence: Significant versus Minor

The change indicated by signals may lead to significant or minor consequences or results for the *competitor*. Some signals indicating adherence to the status quo have minor consequences with regard to change in strategy or asset commitments. Other signals such as an inference that the competitor is likely to aggressively pursue market share indicate the need for the competitor to significantly alter its prior investment plans or to reconfigure its complete approach to winning a particular market segment.[38]

Signal Impact: High versus Low

Degree of impact refers to the extent to which a signal leads to favorable or unfavorable implications or results for the focal firm. Signals indicating the launch of a new breakthrough product line, or a massive cost reduction program, or the hiring of a highly experienced marketing team by a competitor frequently portend substantial potential negative impact on the focal firm's marketplace and financial performance. Signals also may indicate positive implications. For example, a competitor's potential new product may suggest a new market opportunity for the focal firm.

High-impact signals require much greater scrutiny on the part of the analyst. Thus, degree of impact guides analysts' allocation of their time and resources. These high impact signals often suggest further scanning and monitoring to seek (other) confirming or refuting indicators. They also compel the analyst to reflect whether the signal challenges or even refutes long-held assumptions about the competitor, the marketplace, or itself, or about anticipated results from its current strategy.

A signal's degree of impact is not constrained by its other characteristics. Signals with a small or large degree of change may have high or low impact. In many product areas, a small price change or a minor improvement in manufacturing capability has significant impact on costs, margins, and profits. Signals with short or long change lag may have high or low impact. Many times, a signal that allows a strong inference has low impact. The firm has reliable and extensive data (e.g., a statement by the marketing manager, comments by customers, and observations in a trade publication) that a competitor is already in the process of reorganizing its sales force, but its implications (in the judgment of the focal firm) are minimal in terms of gaining market share or building stronger relationships with customers.

Weak signals sometimes have long-term high impact. Often, although rumors constitute classic weak signals, they are the initial (alerting) indicator that a significant competitor change is about to take place (such as an acquisition or the hiring of a distinguished new CEO) with potentially high-impact implications for the focal firm.

Analyzing Signals

Analysis of signals requires careful indicator detection, signal interpretation, and assessment. A *guided* analysis framework relevant to both individual and multiple signals is shown in Figure 4.3. A competitor's announcement of its (ongoing) negotiations to purchase 40 percent of a supplier is used to illustrate the analysis, a summary of which is provided in Figure 4.4.

What Is the Content of the Indicator(s)?

One or more indicators give rise to a signal. The alerting indicator was a rumor circulating in the industry that the competitor was looking at its supply options. The formal announcement by the competitor in the form of a brief press release that it "is currently in the midst of negotiations to purchase a 40

FIGURE 4.3
Analyzing a Signal

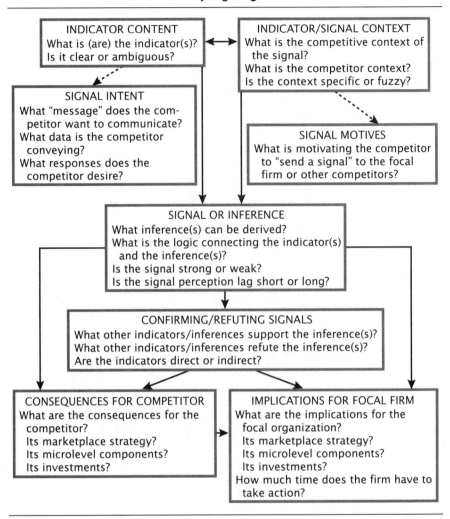

percent stake in a supplier" constituted a strong confirming signal. The commentary in the press release laid out the rationale for the potential purchase at this point in time. Thus, there was now both credible data and a convincing logic that the competitor was serious about taking action at the supplier end of its business.

The initial indicator was a single data point—a rumor. It was then followed by the announcement. It in turn was quickly followed by a series of

FIGURE 4.4
Analyzing a Signal: Purchase of an Equity Position in a Supplier

What Is the Indicator?
Announcement of the purchase of a 40% stake in supplier.

What Is the Signal's Context?
Competitor did not have a prior ownership position in any supplier.
Competitor had 20-year relationship with supplier.
Competitor has not enhanced its market share position or financial
   performance for 5 years.

What Does Signal Indicate?
Intends to develop a "partnering relationship" with supplier.
Importance attached by competitor to components provided by supplier.

What Is the Signal's Intent?
Wants to inform its competitors that it not only wishes to stay in this
   business but wants to begin taking the initiative in the business.
Wants to compel competitors into assuming similar investments.
Wants competitors to review whether or not they should stay in the
   business.

What Motives Underlie the Signal?
Fear that the supplier will form a relationship with a competitor and
   thus lock it out.
Unless this move (and others) are made, it will not be able to develop
   a sustainable position.

Are There Confirming or Refuting Signals?
Statements to the effect that opportunitites exist in the industry.

Assessing the Signal's Implication?
 For the Competitor:
   It is likely to become more of an initiator—can expect superior products.
   It will need to change many of its procedures and processes to
      make the new partnership work.
 For the Focal Firm:
   Its historic strategy will no longer be sufficient for marketplace success.
   It will have to reshape its product development.
   It must speed up its directions.

management comments that appeared in the trade and national press—a
pattern of statements. However, considerable ambiguity existed as to
when the purchase would actually occur (the initial announcement said it
would be completed within two months but that then became a point of
issue in later managerial comments) and under what conditions it would be
completed.

What Is the Context of the Signal?

Clarity in indicator content never obviates the need for an understanding of the relevant context. In the absence of such understanding, misleading or false inferences are more likely to be derived. The competitor's performance was at best holding steady. It did not have an ownership position in any supplier. It had a 20-year relationship with the supplier in which it had announced its intention to acquire a 40 percent stake.

What Is the Signal's Intent?

Intent refers to what the competitor wishes to convey to its rivals (and perhaps others such as customers and vendors) and what response(s) it wishes to provoke. The immediate message conveyed in the purchase preannouncement was clear: the potential purchase of a 40 percent stake in the supplier within two months, subject to certain (unstated) conditions being agreed on by the two parties.

However, the analysts in the focal firm believed that the intent went beyond the desire to convey a signal to competitors about an imminent purchase of a stake in a supplier. The underlying intent in the judgment of the analysts was that the competitor wished not only to stay in the business but to assume a greater technology leadership role than previously. Thus, the reaction the signal was intended to elicit from competitors was the conclusion that, to continue in the business, they would have to either invest in their suppliers or invest in the development of their own components and supplies.

What Does the Signal Indicate?

Inferences (signals) intentionally transmitted to competitors via specific indicators sometimes allow analysts to draw further inferences beyond the intended inference(s) and preferred response(s). Once the signal's content, context, and intent are delineated, the analyst is able to make (further) judgments as to what the intended signal indicates. These inferences, as asserted throughout this chapter, lie at the heart of signal analysis.

In this case, the analysts inferred that the potential purchase of the stake in the supplier allowed some indications to be drawn about the competitor, its relationship with the supplier, and the broader competitive arena. It indicated that the competitor attached a high degree of importance to the type of components provided by the vendor and that it could not or would not undertake to develop and manufacture these components itself. It indicated that the competitor believed it could develop a partnering relationship with the vendor. It also indicated that success in the product segment would be increasingly driven by component technology.

Are There Confirming or Refuting Indicators (Signals)?

The signal's intent and what it indicates constitute inferences: they are interpretations drawn by analysts. Even though they are logically derived and consistent with each other, analysts must ask what other indicators confirm or refute these inferences. Confirming signals add to the alerting signal's strength.

In this case, the analysts quickly reviewed behaviors, words, and organization change of the competitor prior to the announcement for indicators that might have signaled a prospective relationship with a vendor. No direct signals were found although an analysis of the competitor's product development history and its performance record indicated the need for new product development or, at a minimum, enhancement of existing products and thus the need for potential joint product development with a supplier of a key component.

However, a number of indicators confirmed the inferences drawn about the competitor, its relationship with the supplier, and the broader industry. Some statements by members of the competitor's management team about the future technology direction of these components lent support to the inference about the importance of the components. Its success in partnering with distributors and some end-customers might serve as a weak, indirect signal of its ability to develop and foster a cooperative relationship with the component supplier.

What Motives Underlie the Signal?

In the case of intended signals, the motives of the sender must be examined. The intent of a signal can only be understood in relation to its motives or causes. Although they are related, a clear distinction must be drawn between the motivation underlying the decision to send a signal and the motivation underlying the behaviors or actions that are the focus or subject of the signal. The analyst must investigate what is motivating the competitor to "send the signal" and why specific responses are desired. Identifying the underlying motives often paints a very different picture of an individual signal or pattern of signals—its impact or implications may be considerably enhanced or reduced.

In this case, the competitor was motivated to send the signal via its public announcement to counteract rumors in the industry that the competitor was about to make a major investment that might severely negatively affect some of its current relationships within the industry.

Two motivations might underlie the potential investment. First, the competitor might have been fearful that the supplier would form a relationship with one or more other customers, that is, the competitor's rivals, and thus jeopardize, if not lock it out of, access to a critical component. A somewhat different motivation might be that the new partnership, benefiting from the competitor's financial wherewithal, could lead to considerable product development with regard to this key component and thus serve as the basis for significant marketplace advantage.

What Are the Signal's Implications?

Knowing what a signal indicates as well as its intent and motives are critical inputs to determining what it portends for both the competitor and the focal firm as well as the broader competitive environment.

Major *consequences* were likely to ensue for the competitor. If it was able to leverage its new relationship, it could become much more of a product leader. Its capacity to upgrade its product quality (i.e., functionality) would be greatly enhanced. At a minimum, its future products would likely be considerably superior to its past products. However, the operational challenge would be to fashion a real partnership with the supplier, something which it had never previously accomplished.

For the focal firm, there was little doubt among the analyst team that this was a *high-impact* signal. It indicated a significant threat to the firm's current market share position and that its current mode of operations would not be a sufficient platform for future marketplace success. Hence, it had little choice but to develop and evaluate different strategy alternatives.

Errors in Signal Analysis

Signal analysis is the essence of competitor learning. Thus, it is especially appropriate to identify and discuss critical errors in the acts of detection, perception, interpretation, and assessment from the perspective of learning.

A common error that inhibits learning is the failure to distinguish between indicators and signals. As a consequence, some indicators are not detected; the signaling capacity of data is often not appreciated; and people tend to draw only one inference from one or more indicators. In short, each of the functions of signal analysis noted earlier—focusing analysis, constituting evidence and compelling reflection—is severely handicapped.

This error is further confounded when analysts fail to search for alerting signals and to then seek confirming and refuting signals. Learning by hypothesis development and testing is thus considerably less likely. If analysts are not attentive to deriving inferences that do not fit with their current knowledge, such as their projections of how a competitor will adapt its marketplace strategy to changing competitive conditions, then much learning about competitors, the competitive environment, and their own organization will not occur or will be delayed.

Misinterpretation, that is, the derivation of false inferences,[39] also inhibits learning, if it is not detected and corrected. Such is more likely to occur when the logic generating a signal is not explicated. Without explicit logic connecting indicator(s), context, and inference(s), it is impossible for other analysts to know why one inference rather than another was drawn. Also, the logic or reasoning connecting the indicator(s) to the signal(s) cannot be tested, challenged, or refined.

Treating signal analysis largely as a one-time event obviates the learning that necessarily accrues when it is viewed as a continuous process. An inference about which strategy alternative a competitor might choose in response to a rapid decline in its performance or unexpected strategic initiatives on the part of one or more rivals, suggests the need for further indicator detection, and confirmation or refutation of the initial or alerting signals, and so on.

Finally, if inferences are not viewed as projections of what could happen, the opportunity for focused learning is missed. The merit of anticipated indicators is that they direct analysts' attention to what a competitor might do. When analysts identify a priori the indicators that allow signals to be drawn about how a competitor is responding to a new product introduction or to a new sales and promotion campaign, they are more likely to capture these indicators and derive signals from them faster than might otherwise be the case.

Summary

The efficiency and effectiveness of competitor analysis is greatly enhanced when analysts understand the distinctions between indicators and signals, and the processes of signal analysis outlined in this chapter. Efficiency is augmented when analysts recognize the variety of possible indicators, the signaling capacity of different types of indicators, and the differences among the five distinct analysis acts noted in Figure 4.1. Effectiveness is improved when analysts understand the distinct functions of signals and are able to move beyond indicator detection to project competitor consequences and focal firm implications. As the remaining chapters make evident, signal perception, interpretation, and assessment are central to every domain of competitor analysis.

The Analysis of Individual (and Multiple) Competitors

CHAPTER

5

Marketplace Strategy: Scope and Posture

CAPTURING AND ASSESSING COMPETITORS' STRATEGIES IN THE END-CUSTOMER AND channel arenas—the marketplace in which customers choose among rivals—is central to the concept of winning outlined in Chapter 1. An organization outwits its rivals by more quickly detecting changes in customers' needs, anticipating rivals' product change, ascertaining faster how to create value for customers, and achieving greater learning from the actions of different rivals. An organization outmaneuvers its rivals by being the first to introduce a particular product, creating a sole source relationship with a distribution channel, and delivering superior value to customers—in short, changing the marketplace rules to its own advantage.[1] Outperforming rivals is reflected in such parameters as number of new products introduced, market share gained, levels of customer satisfaction or excitement created, and positioning for the future in terms of image, reputation, and relationships established.

An understanding of competitors' current marketplace strategy is also central to the competitor analysis framework advocated in this book (see Figure 3.2). It is a prerequisite to projecting competitors' future strategies. Without an understanding of a competitor's current and potential marketplace strategy, as discussed in Chapters 7 through 15, it is difficult to interpret and assess its alliances and networks, assumptions, assets, capabilities and competencies, technology, and organization infrastructure and culture.

This chapter begins by elaborating the three core elements in marketplace strategy: scope, posture, and goals. Because of its importance to outwitting, outmaneuvering, and outperforming rivals, posture—how a competitor attracts, wins, and retains customers—is addressed in some detail. A methodology for detecting scope and posture is then presented.[2] The final section of the chapter enumerates a number of common errors in the identification of scope and posture.

Since this is the first competitor analysis framework component addressed (see Figure 3.2), the intent in this chapter is to provide a general explication of the learning model described in Chapter 2 (and summarized in Figure 2.1). It illustrates execution of the tasks within each learning activity, and the relationship between data, indicators, and inferences.

The Elements of Marketplace Strategy

Marketplace strategy embodies *where, how,* and *why* an organization seeks to attract, win, and retain customers. Every organization continuously confronts three related marketplace questions: What product-customer segments is the organization in or does it want to be in? How does it compete or want to compete in these marketplace segments? What is the purpose of being in these segments?[3] The answers to these three questions—what product-customer segments the organization is in, how it competes in them, and what its goals are—constitute the three elements of any organization's marketplace strategy: scope, posture, and goals (see Figure 5.1).

Scope: Product-Customer Segments

Product-customer scope defines the marketplace space the competitor occupies: what products the competitor puts in the marketplace and what customers purchase them. Scope consists of position and direction. *Position* refers to the product-customer segments the competitor occupies at any point in time. Direction embodies a competitor's product-customer moves over time. Moves occur either with regard to products or customers or both. Adding or deleting product lines and adding or deleting product types within a product line represent product moves.[4] Adding or deleting geographic areas, distribution channels, or customer types represent customer moves.[5]

Products and customers are categorized and depicted in many different ways. Depicting the competitor's product-customer position and direction is a more specific application of mapping the broader competitive or industry

FIGURE 5.1
Marketplace Strategy: Three Elements

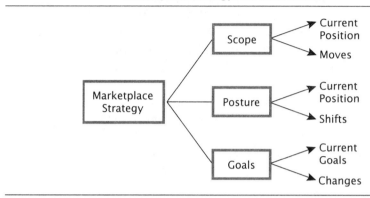

terrain. Products can be segmented into product classes, lines, types, and items.

Customers are also segmented in many distinct ways. The relevant bases to segment end-customers are dependent on the product. For many consumer products and services, customer demographics such as age, sex, income level, ethnic background, and geographic location are employed. For industrial and commercial products, segmentation bases such as type of industry, application or use, and geographic location are often appropriate.

Increasingly, organizations use different categories of needs or benefits as a dominant means of segmenting customers. Customers' needs relate more directly than demographic variables to what organizations should do to attract, win, and retain customers.

Distribution channels provide a distinct but related picture of a competitor's position and direction.[6] Rivals often choose distinctly different channels by which to reach end-customers or product users.

Competitive Posture

Posture embodies *how* a competitor competes in the marketplace to attract, win, and retain customers: how it differentiates itself from current and future competitors as perceived and understood by customers. Posture is always viewed *from the customer's perspective:* it is what the customer perceives, sees, and understands. Posture also is segregated into position and direction.[7] Position refers to how a competitor competes at any particular point in time. Direction refers to changes in posture over time.

But how do organizations compete to attract, win, and retain customers? The range of *generic* modes of competition that are applicable to most organizations is not unlimited. Eight such modes are noted in Table 5.1. In general terms, organizations compete along the same generic modes irrespective of the competitive domain or product. Firms in industries as diverse as insurance, airlines, semiconductors, home furnishings, paint, videotapes, wine, and books compete along such generic modes as product line width, features, functionality, service, availability, image and reputation, selling and relationships, and price.

Each generic mode embodies multiple dimensions (see Table 5.1), and specific indicators are associated with each individual dimension.[8] Because of the importance of the generic modes of competition to shifting the marketplace rules and to the management of every micro component,[9] each is briefly discussed.

Product Line Width Product line width refers to the competitor's range of products. Its dimensions are specific product types and items. The width of a product line is often of great importance to distributors and retailers due to scale economies and the reduced need to work with other suppliers. One-stop shopping is also of great value to some end-customers or users of many industrial and commercial products. Some firms focus on a narrow product line (compared with competitors) and promote their specialization and expertise to specific classes of customers.

Product Features Products vary greatly in terms of features such as design, style, shape, and color. Automobile rivals continuously try to distinguish their products with myriad features such as the design of the dashboard, digitally controlled door locks, and tinted windows, to name just a few. Features in service products such as financial services include terms and conditions (e.g., length of loan and interest rates), waiting period before a loan is granted, and volume of paperwork to be completed by the applicant.

Functionality All products by definition serve some use or functionality for customers. In broad terms, functionality is viewed as how a product satisfies some bundle of customer needs and wants.[10] The dimensions of functionality are highly product specific. The relevant performance dimensions vary greatly for such products as automobiles, computers, furniture, toys, and videos. However, functionality is also relevant to services or intangible products. Performance in the case of life insurance might include such dimensions as the type of coverage provided, when the coverage becomes available, and in what form it will be provided.

Service Customers don't just buy a tangible product (such as an automobile or a chair) or an intangible product (such as life insurance or market

TABLE 5.1 Posture: Modes, Dimensions, Indicators

Modes of Competition	Possible Dimensions	Sample Indicators
Product line width	Breadth of product lines Breadth of types within lines	Product lines and items
Features	Physical aspects of individual products Packaging Terms and conditions	Shape Style Color Design
Functionality	Performance Reliability Durability Ease of use Taste Shelf life	Speed Breakdowns Customer perceptions
Service	Maintenance Installation Help line Training Technical assistance Repair Response time	Contracts Service announcements and programs Customer reports Speed of competitor's responses
Availability	Distribution channels Amount Delivery	Individual channels
Image and reputation	Image of the company Image of products Reputation for rapid response time Reputation for best value	Content of advertising Actions and words of customers Third-party reports
Selling and relationships	Customer coverage Detailing of products Relationships with distributors Relationships with end users	Actions of sales force Frequency of calls Judgments of channels Customer's comments
Price	List prices Discount prices Price-performance Price-value	Actual prices Channel/Customer assessments

research). An ever-growing set of services are provided to channels and end-customers. As with functionality, its dimensions are highly product specific. Among common service dimensions are repair, maintenance, warranties, customer hot lines, education about product features and functionality, and training about product use.

Availability Products, even in the same competitive domain, frequently vary greatly in their availability: the range of distribution channels through which they are available to end-customers. Wide or select distribution is sometimes a significant source of differentiation. Some firms select distribution channels to augment the image and reputation of their products and services. Availability's dimensions are the channels through which the product is available.

Image and Reputation All organizations and products by virtue of their existence create some image and reputation in the mind-set of customers. The dimensions of image and reputation are also many. Customers develop perceptions over time about all the dimensions of functionality and service noted in Table 5.1 as well about the firm itself.

Selling and Relationships How an organization sells its products and develops relationships with channels and end-customers is often a powerful source of differentiation. Many firms have established such tight relationships with their distribution channels and/or end-customers that rivals have extreme difficulty getting a hearing. Selling and relationships also encompass multiple dimensions including breadth of customers reached, frequency of calls, extent of selling or detailing, relationship with distribution channels, and friendliness of the competitor's personnel.

Price Customers compare and contrast not only the prices charged by competitors but the benefits associated with each rival's prices. Increasingly, customers in all product areas are more concerned with the price/value relationship than with the price/performance relationship.[11] Price dimensions include list prices, discount prices, price-performance, and price-value.

Direction incorporates change in the generic modes of competition. Few organizations leave their posture unchanged for extensive periods; to do so augments their vulnerability to attack by competitors who differentiate and make themselves more appealing to customers. For many years, Sears failed to change its posture; only when it had lost massive market share to competitors and its sales had actually declined in many outlets did it change its posture by adding branded products (product line width), reorganizing the layout of stores (features), emphasizing ease of purchase (functionality), paying greater attention to customers (service), upgrading perceptions of its product range and service (image and reputation), and reducing prices.

Some Observations on Posture Essential to understanding a competitor's posture (and rivalry among competitors) is that it always must be delineated along several of the generic modes of competition. Customers can (and do) simultaneously assess multiple rivals along a number of competition modes.

Firms are rarely successful when their posture depends on only one competition mode. Despite claims by many organizations that they "compete based on price," they must still provide certain (minimum) levels of value to customers along other modes of competition such as specific product features, particular types of functionality, some degree of availability, and an image or reputation that is not repugnant. Some firms have discovered that when customers are dissatisfied with product performance or service, the lower price quickly proves ineffective in retaining them. Each mode of competition possesses the potential to contribute to the overall value perceived and experienced by customers.

When viewed from the perspective of customers, the modes of competition are highly interrelated. For example, as service becomes more important in many businesses, it is increasingly difficult to separate from functionality. The speed and efficiency of service in fast-food restaurants such as McDonald's is difficult to disentangle from their functionality.

When viewed from the perspective of customers, the modes of competition are either reinforcing or conflictual. Service often is not consistent with the desired image of functionality; selling and relationships are perceived as "arrogant," yet the competitor's advertising and promotional literature emphasizes its reputation for "friendliness"; low price may be seen as inconsistent with distribution through selective channels.

Organizations rarely compete in the same way across all products or even within related product-customer segments. They emphasize different generic modes *or* different dimensions within the same mode. Automobile firms emphasize distinct features across their product lines, provide different levels of service, and endeavor to build different levels of relationship with customers.

As illustrated in Table 5.1, each generic mode of competition breaks down into a number of distinct dimensions. However, the relevant dimensions— and associated indicators—of each mode of competition are always product dependent. For example, image and reputation in the case of a hotel chain includes such dimensions as customers' perceptions of speed of check-in, friendliness and courteousness of hotel staff, cleanliness of rooms, quality of food, and the value-price relationship.

Each dimension of any mode of competition in turn has multiple indicators associated with it. For example, technical assistance, a dimension of service that is often important with many industrial products, involves identification of product needs, assessment of product or application uses, and provision of technical knowledge regarding the product and its uses. Performance, a key dimension of functionality in the case of automobiles, typically assumes an array of indicators including gasoline consumption (miles per gallon), road handling, speed with which the car is able to go from zero to 60 miles per hour, and from 60 miles per hour to zero.

Posture shapes an organization's customer-based advantage. How the competitor competes along the generic modes furnishes customers with the basis to differentiate the firm and its product offerings from competitors. Posture, however, often does not translate into customer-based advantage. Customers sometimes do not view how the competitor chooses to compete as important or as a source of value. Many firms have discovered that low price (compared with that of rivals) is often not seen by customers as a reason to purchase their products. Many firms have added dimensions to their service only to discover that customers did not value the new service options.

Goals

Scope and posture represent the behavioral elements of marketplace strategy. The actions inherent in scope and posture such as adding products, altering service, and changing price are the means to some ends. However, the behaviors and actions inherent in scope and posture do not by themselves reveal *why* these choices are made. The presumption is that the organization has some purpose, or goal, in selecting or modifying its scope and posture.[12] An understanding of a competitor's goals provides answers to the why questions: Why does the competitor possess a specific product-customer scope and why is it adopting a particular posture? An analysis of goals is the focus of Chapter 6.

Types of Marketplace Strategy

Identification and analysis of competitors' marketplace strategy is greatly facilitated by the availability of a typology or classification of marketplace strategies. A typology provides a shorthand by which analysts label and communicate different types of strategies. Although a number of typologies exist, they tend to be too "coarse-grained" or all-inclusive. Typologies such as differentiation, cost, and focus,[13] offer categorizations or distinctions between strategy types that are too broad or crude for the purpose of specifying, comparing, and contrasting with sufficient preciseness the position and direction of competitors' scope, posture, and goals. The typology of marketplace strategies offered in this chapter flows from the identification and analysis of (the direction of) a competitor's scope and posture and their comparison with that of competitors.

Product-Customer Scope A competitor's coverage of product-customer segments and change in it over time reveal the position and direction of its marketplace scope. Product and customer scope generate four distinct types of marketplace coverage (see Figure 5.2). Each type of scope is often found within a specific "industry" or competitive domain. Each type of scope is only meaningful in reference to one or more competitors. Scope moves such as the addition or deletion of products or customers indicate a competitor's direction across these scope domains.

A *niche* domain involves a narrow product line and narrow customer coverage. These rivals are specialists in terms of both products and customers. Examples include the law practice that only deals with estate planning; the soft drink firm that sells only its own brand of bottled water in one small geographic area; the automobile firm that offers only a very expensive car to an exclusive clientele (e.g., Rolls-Royce).

A *spread* domain entails a narrow product line that is aimed at a broad spectrum of customer segments. For example, a firm might specialize in the design and development of dictionaries (a narrow product line), but they might be sold through many types of distribution channels to the mass market.

A *proliferated* domain involves a wide product line that serves a narrow customer base. A specific region, a select set of industrial customers, and particular distribution channels represent some of the common foci in narrow customer bases. Many firms offer a wide product line but do so in a restricted geographic region.

FIGURE 5.2
Scope Focus

	Customers	
	Narrow	**Wide**
Products Narrow	Niche	Spread
Products Wide	Proliferated	Blanket

A *blanket* domain is attained when the competitor is in (almost) every product-customer segment. Marriott in motels and/or hotels, IBM in computers, General Motors in automobiles, represent examples of firms with blanket domains.

Posture The modes of competition can be combined or integrated to constitute multiple distinct postures. The following are common types:

- *High End.* A "high-end" posture combines an "up-market" image, unique features, and high price. It is especially common in consumer markets. The product is intended to make a statement about its owner or user. Rolls-Royce and Porsche in automobiles, and Rolex in watches are well-recognized examples.

- *No Frills.* At the other end of the image, features, and price spectrum is a "no-frills" posture. The emphasis is on basic functionality: the product gets the job done. A classic example is the airline that does not provide advance ticketing, preassigned seats, or food service.

- *One-Stop Shopping.* Many different organizations now craft a posture that is intended to meet all the needs of their industrial, commercial, or individual customers with regard to a specific range of products. One-stop shopping is the essence of the marketplace strategy adopted by retailers such as Home Depot and Wal-Mart.

- *Performance Superiority.* Some organizations build their posture around performance superiority in terms of combined functionality, features, and service. They endeavor to stay ahead of competitors by continually upgrading the functional solution they offer customers. Compaq in computers and Intel in semiconductors are frequently referenced examples.

- *Distinguished Support.* Many organizations offer customers a level and extent of support in the form of "services" that is unmatched by their rivals. They aid and assist customers in every possible way prior to and during purchase; they advise customers how to use their solutions; they quickly provide an answer to any query or question a customer might ask.

- *Customer Involvement.* Other organizations develop a tightly knit working relationship with their customers. Sometimes it centers around sharing personnel. Often, it is reflected in partnering for multiple purposes: to more fully understand the customer's specific needs; to develop and test solution prototypes; to track product use and application; to extend solution applications and use in the customer's operations or facilities. Many manufacturing firms now dedicate themselves to creating and enhancing intense customer involvement with their corporate and commercial customers.

Customization constitutes a unique integration of the modes of competition. It exists when the competitor can adapt its product or solution to the needs of individual customers.[14] Stated differently, customers are able to customize or tailor their own product or solution. It necessitates tailoring a unique solution along the modes of competition for each customer or small groups of customers. Customization is perhaps most obvious in personal and professional services. The hairstylist who can create any kind of hairdo that customers might request exemplifies customization. It is also becoming increasingly common in manufactured products and different types of services. Customers will soon be able to select many different features in the automobile, software, or textbook they intend to purchase.

Competitor Focus In seeking to outwit, outmaneuver, and outperform competitors, organizations frequently choose to compete directly—go head-to-head—against rivals: enter the product-customer segments they occupy (pursue a similar scope), and adopt a somewhat similar posture (standardization) or distinct posture (differentiation or customization). Or they try to avoid direct confrontation. It is therefore possible to categorize strategies with regard to their competitor focus. There are four distinct competitor-focused strategies:[15]

1. *Frontal* confrontation is the most direct form of competition. It takes place when an organization enters a competitor's product-customer segment(s) with a largely similar product and competes to win that competitor's current and potential customers. Many automobile manufacturers have launched a direct frontal attack on Chrysler's minivan by introducing their own varieties of this product line.

2. A *flanking* focus occurs when an organization enters an adjacent product-customer segment and endeavors to avoid frontal confrontation. The organization introduces products "above" or "below" those of one or more specific competitors. For example, many Japanese firms in such product domains as television receivers, radios, motorcycles, copiers, and medical equipment, used smaller versions of existing products to enter the U.S. marketplace. The intended customers may or may not be those of specific competitors.

3. *Encirclement* is another frequently employed mode of confrontation. It consists of surrounding a competitor's product-customer domain: the firm provides a broader product array and goes after a wider array of customers.

The competitor then finds itself in both intense horizontal competition, that is, competing against rivals within a product line, and perpendicular competition, that is, competing against other product lines. It typically accrues over many years of rivalry. Japanese television set manufacturers have now encircled their U.S. and European rivals. Sony has encircled many consumer electronic competitors in several product areas.

4. *Bypass* is a frequently employed response when rivals threaten or deplete a firm's marketplace position. Competitors seek to bypass each other by moving to the next generation of product.[16] It is becoming more common as organizations seek to escape intense competition[17] and to establish a new basis of customer-based and competitor-based advantage. Technology often lies at the core of bypass moves. Kodak's stated goal to produce all electronic cameras is a clear commitment to bypass its current camera rivals.

A Typology of Marketplace Strategies   Combining the scope, posture, and competitor focus permits a shorthand description of a competitor's marketplace strategy. Although many combinations of scope, posture, and competitor focus are possible, some are more common than others. Many Japanese firms such as Toshiba, Toyota, and Honda, in the early years of their entry into the U.S. marketplace, adopted a niche scope, with an emphasis on functionality and price differentiation, using a flanking attack on the entrenched U.S. competition. At the other end of the spectrum, some firms are now endeavoring to attain a blanket scope, through customization, with the intent of encircling or even bypassing rivals. Some organizations such as many software providers persist with a niche scope and frontally attack rivals by differentiating along every possible mode of competition.

Indicators of Scope and Posture Change

Scope change is *directly* indicated by change in products (such as the introduction of new products or the deletion of product items) and change in the customers pursued (such as adding or dropping distribution channels or end-customers). Changes in each of the microlevel components may *indirectly* signal past, emerging, or potential change in marketplace strategy.[18]

Scope and Posture Change as Signals

Changes in marketplace strategy also serve as signals. New product introductions and additions to product lines often are the source of signals of marketplace strategy changes that go beyond the product introduction itself. They indicate significant departures from the competitor's historic strategy, for example, a move away from a niche focus, thus alerting analysts to a new *strategic* direction. Similarly, changes in the competitor's modes of competition indicate more encompassing posture shifts. For example, a new sales force initiative to develop closer relationships with distribution channels or end-customers may serve as the alerting signal that the competitor intends to put in place a posture predicated on collaborative relationships rather than historic arm's-length relationships.

Change in marketplace strategy frequently alerts analysts to change in microlevel components. Major change in scope and posture is an especially strong signal of change in the competitor's underlying assumptions[19] and product or organization technologies.[20]

Capturing the Executed Marketplace Strategy

Every organization by definition has an *executed* or implemented marketplace strategy: it possesses some product-customer scope; it manifests some type of posture; its scope and posture reflect particular goals. Irrespective of whether an organization believes it has a strategy, its behaviors and (inferred) goals constitute an implemented or implicit marketplace strategy. The products the organization puts in the marketplace and how they are distributed, delivered, promoted, serviced, and priced add up to an executed strategy.

Not only do organizations have an executed marketplace strategy but it is largely *visible* to others. Even though extensive "digging" may be necessary, it is well-nigh impossible for any organization to conceal the scope and posture of its marketplace strategy: the behaviors that constitute these elements are executed in the daylight of the marketplace. It is difficult for a competitor to conceal its offerings in the marketplace, the prices it charges for its products, the manner in which they are distributed, the content of its advertising, or how its sales force is deployed.[21] Thus, they are visible or evident to others or, at a minimum, can be tracked and traced by anybody intent on doing so.

A major rationale for isolating and developing the notion of marketplace strategy in the context of competitor analysis is that all competitors possess at least an implicit marketplace strategy and it can be detected in every case. Moreover, competitors often have little economic or other type of rationale for wanting to conceal these behaviors; quite the contrary, it is often in their own self-interest to publicize these behaviors and actions to end-customers, channels, suppliers, stockholders, and even competitors. For example, to build customer awareness, competitors often go to great lengths to publicize the introduction of new products or major product modifications as well as the addition of new distribution channels, reduction in prices, or the augmentation of service, warranties, or technical support.

Key Marketplace Strategy Attributes

Three attributes of marketplace strategy—coherence, entrepreneurialism, and degree of stretch—are particularly informative in identifying and assessing change in a competitor's marketplace strategy.

Coherence A competitor's marketplace strategy is coherent to the extent that its scope, posture, and goals are consistent and integrated. Without a reasonable degree of coherence within and across scope, posture, and goals, a competitor's marketplace strategy will be heading in multiple directions simultaneously. The result is confusion for the competitor's stakeholders including its customers (as well as a lack of direction within the competitor's own organization).

Entrepreneurialism A competitor's marketplace strategy is entrepreneurial to the extent it creates change in the marketplace.[22] Each element of marketplace strategy—scope, posture, and goals—affords entrepreneurial opportunity: products can be truly innovative; posture can build genuine differentiation; and goals help point the organization in distinctively new directions. Without entrepreneurial content, as noted in Chapter 1, it is not possible for marketplace strategy to be successful in the long term.[23]

Degree of Stretch Competitors' marketplace strategies vary greatly in their degree of stretch: the extent to which they are pursuing goals that are apparently beyond their resources; the extent to which their goals are more ambitious than rivals'.[24] Degree of stretch compels consideration of whether a competitor is likely to be able to attain its goals, and if it does, what the marketplace consequences will be.

Identifying the Competitor's Marketplace Scope

Identifying competitors' marketplace strategy requires a methodology to capture and depict scope, posture, and goals. Central to the methodology is that analysts have a thorough understanding of the concepts of scope, posture, and goals, dimensions and indicators pertaining to each, what data or "footprints in the sand" to search for, and where and how to do so.

Because of its visibility, scope generally is not difficult to capture. However, often it is not self-evident. Some surprises usually arise in delineating a competitor's range of products and breadth of customers. Thus, although they are interrelated sides of the same coin, it is useful to separate identification of products and customers. The steps and questions that drive a *guided* analysis are shown in Figure 5.3.

FIGURE 5.3
Identifying a Competitor's Scope

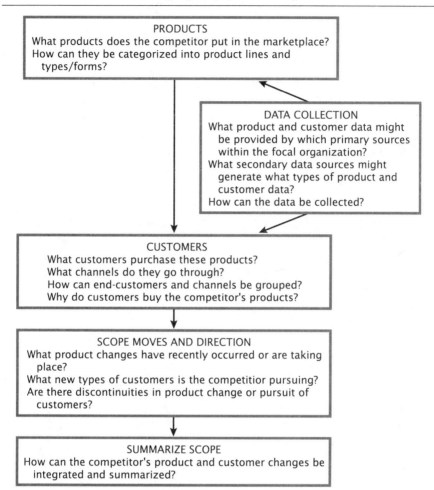

A yogurt competitor is used to illustrate the analysis. Its brand name is one of the recognized market share leaders in most geographic regions. It has been slowly taking share from some of its leading rivals. The focal firm has a strong regional brand image but is not present in many other regions. It is considering how it might enter some of the regions in which it does not have a presence.

Identify Current Products

Delineating a competitor's product[25] range is the essential first step in describing its marketplace strategy. Doing so presents a number of challenges in selecting, ordering, and interpreting product-related data. Some of these challenges pertain to how to categorize the competitor's products. One way of doing so is to use the classic product tree: from product classes down through product lines and types, and if necessary, to the level of product items. The product portfolio can be developed across the corporate, sector, business unit, and product group levels.

How product lines, types, and items are categorized is peculiar to each product class. The characteristics of products such as features (e.g., size, style, design), functionality, and price serve as common bases of categorization. Thus, the offerings of beer, shoe, insurance, and software competitors are categorized quite differently. Also, any competitor's offerings might be categorized in different ways for different analysis purposes.

With a modest degree of familiarity about a competitor and its competitive context, *guided* inquiry typically generates quite quickly a "first-cut" of its product portfolio *before* any data are collected from other internal or external sources.[26] First-cut refers to the output generated by one or more analysts based solely on their knowledge of the competitor. The yogurt competitor's products were grouped into product lines based on product content (regular, light, and new) and further subdivided by package or container size (see Figure 5.4).

FIGURE 5.4
Yogurt Competitor's Current Strategy—Customer Demographics

Identify Current Customers

As noted earlier, identifying customers revolves around answering two related questions: Who buys the competitor's products? and why do they do so? The "who" question addresses customer "demographics" and the "why" question is concerned with customers' needs and preferences.[27] There are no straight and fast rules as to which question should be answered first or which question is easier to answer. However, rarely is it sufficient to answer either question alone: each lends insights into the other; each adds unique insight into customers.

Once products are identified, distribution channels and end-customers are related to each product level in terms of both demographics and needs and preferences. The difficulty in doing so is contingent on the nature of the products and the competitive domain. For many industrial and commercial products, identifying first-cut customer demographics at the product line and product type levels is often straightforward. Members of the focal organization know in broad terms which types of customers buy which specific products. This is especially so if the competitor's product-customer segments are reasonably similar to the focal firm's.

Given a modest degree of familiarity with the business and competitive context, it is usually possible to approximate customer demographics such as geographic location, family type, and income level at the product line and product type levels in the case of consumer products. Even a first-cut analysis typically proves enormously insightful. Figure 5.4 shows an initial breakdown of customers by age and household group for the yogurt competitor, based on an analysis of the competitor's advertising and promotion literature as well as the focal firm's own market research.

Customer demographics provide essential parameters about product-customer segments such as size, types of customers, and location. Embedded in the demographic parameters are customer needs and preferences.[28] Because the ultimate purpose of marketplace strategy is to attract, win, and retain customers, customer needs and preferences represent a critical segmentation base. Organizations of all types are finding that customer needs and preferences are a viable and insightful means of segmenting customers. Needs and preferences reveal why customers buy the product and thus are directly related to the success of competitors' postures or their ability to differentiate themselves from others.

Segmenting customers by needs and preferences is often more difficult than by demographics. It requires a thorough understanding of what benefits customers derive from the product, what purchasing criteria they employ, and how they use the product. A number of need categories and usage situations were initially developed in the yogurt analysis (see Figure 5.5).

FIGURE 5.5
Yogurt Competitor's Current Strategy—Customer Needs

		Usage Purposes			Usage Situations		
		Health	**Diet**	**Fast Food**	**Lunch**	**Snack**	**Breakfast**	**Dessert**

Product Lines and Package Size

	Health	Diet	Fast Food	Lunch	Snack	Breakfast	Dessert
Light	●	●		●	●	●	●
Regular			●	●	●	●	●
New	●	●					●

Each category represents a different set of reasons for purchasing and consuming yogurt.

As noted, channel analysis is often essential to understanding the customer side of scope. This is especially so in the case of industrial products. In view of the limited array of distribution channel options in any product area, assuming some knowledge of the industry context, it is usually much easier to identify a competitor's distribution channels than its end-customer demographics, and needs and preferences. A variety of distribution and retail channels were employed by the yogurt competitor to move its products to end-customers (see Figures 5.6 and 5.7).

Gather Data about Products and Customers

Data collection is best viewed as a series of iterative steps involved in determining data needs, identifying data sources, and collecting data.[29] Each step is guided by what is learned in prior steps. First-cut outputs guide data requirements determination and collection in several ways. They help identify (a) key gaps in analysts' knowledge[30] about competitors' products and customers, (b) specific questions that need to be asked of different types of primary data sources, and (c) different types of data to seek in secondary data search. The identified gaps in knowledge (e.g., uncertainty about the range of types or items in a particular product line) serve two purposes: they

FIGURE 5.6
Yogurt Competitor's Current Strategy—Distribution Channels

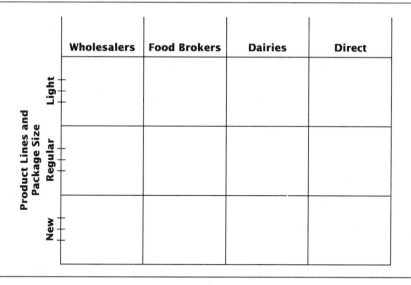

FIGURE 5.7
Yogurt Competitor's Current Strategy—Retail Channels

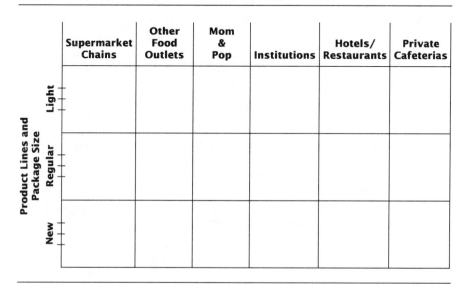

motivate analysts to eliminate the knowledge deficiencies and they suggest specific foci for data collection.

Efficient competitor learning is greatly aided by the identification of relevant primary and secondary data sources *prior* to data collection. Doing so avoids the blind and redundant data search procedures that often characterize the early stages of competitor data gathering in many organizations: outside sources are searched for data that already exists within the focal organization. Thus, analysts must ask themselves what primary data sources possess what types of product and customer data, and what secondary sources will be most useful.[31]

Efficiency is often greatly aided by conducting initial inquiry with internal organizational members. Sales, marketing, and service personnel typically possess considerable data on competitors' products thus leading to an initial refinement of the first-cut output. Once internal sources are exhausted, analysts are then in a better position to refine the questions they want to pose to external sources such as end-customers, retailers, distributors, industry experts, and others.

Similarly, a search of internal archives and databases is advisable before turning to external secondary searches. Many organizations systematically collect competitors' product brochures, product announcements, and related product data gathered by members of the sales force and others. Larger organizations now develop their own electronic databases on competitors' products. Various departments and units also often collect competitor data pertaining to their own specific functional purposes. Sometimes it is not obvious that these units might have competitor data. For example, in some firms, engineering personnel who spend time with customers often analyze their purchasing criteria and habits.

Many types of organizations now conduct systematic research on customers' needs and preferences using either external consultants or internal teams. This research involving comprehensive surveys of and interviews with customers (and sometimes observations of customers) identifies distinct customer groups based on specific needs and preferences.

Identify Moves and Direction

Scope is dynamic: competitors continually change products and seek new customers. Insightful patterns are usually revealed by mapping competitors' current and historic product-customer moves.[32] The relevant *direct* indicators, as noted previously, include all product changes and the addition and deletion of channels and end-customers. Depicting competitors' moves and their direction is important because they often serve as the source of strong signals of future marketplace strategy:[33] changes in products and the customers pursued reveal the trajectory of the competitor's evolving marketplace strategy.

Scope moves are indicated graphically or listed in chronological form. Thus, analysts devise multiple ways to shape, critique, and communicate the outputs of data capturing and processing.[34] Recent moves and their overall direction for the yogurt competitor clearly indicated a thrust toward continued scope extension (see Figure 5.8). New additions to its fleet of delivery trucks and new agreements with a number of dairies indicated the competitor's commitment to enhancing its distribution capability. The addition of product line items indicated a direction toward continued product proliferation.

Changes in scope are sometimes discontinuous: the trajectory does not manifest an evolutionary path. The introduction of distinctly new product lines, fundamental change in existing products, and the pursuit of new classes of customers represent discontinuous change. Capturing such change, whether it has already occurred or is occurring, is important because it often constitutes strong alerting or confirming signals of departure from the competitor's historic marketplace strategy.

FIGURE 5.8
Yogurt Competitor's Current Strategy—Scope: Moves and Direction

Indicators / Scope		Distribution Channels	Retail Outlets	Consumers
	Customers	Adding more trucks (direct) Seeking extended coverage through dairies	Adding shelf space in many outlets Aggressively adding new institutional outlets and restaurants	Trying to create new customer needs through product development
Products — Light		Extending light line		
Regular		Extending regular line		
New		Added two new types Announced that two new types were being developed		

Summarizing and Articulating Scope

Ultimately scope must be integrated, categorized, and summarized so that it can be succinctly described and easily communicated.[35] All the product and customer data must be synthesized into a pithy depiction (via charts and figures) and statement of the competitor's current and past scope and its direction. The yogurt competitor's marketplace strategy was summarized as tending toward a blanket focus via the moves indicated in Figure 5.8. The competitor's scope and marketplace goals were clearly to provide the most complete product offering of any yogurt provider and to reach all categories of distribution, retail, and end-user customers.[36]

Specific judgments are unavoidable in the interpretations necessary to generate these types of outputs. To determine whether a competitor is tending toward a niche, spread, proliferated, or blanket scope, its product width and customer breadth must be compared with that of one or more competitors, including the focal organization. The goals associated with scope moves, as discussed in Chapter 6, also necessitate judgments requiring explication of both data and logic.

Open-Ended Inquiry

The identification of scope, as discussed, exemplifies a *guided* analysis: a sequence of steps that guide data capturing and processing. However, if a competitor's scope has not been previously delineated or if analysts have little knowledge of the competitor, *open-ended* inquiry in the form of an unconstrained scan of primary and secondary data sources dominates the early stages of data search and scope delineation.

The challenge is to develop a listing of product lines and types, and associated customers. Many secondary sources such as industry and trade publications, popular and business press (both local and national), governmental records, consultant and industry studies, typically contain product data. Material placed in the public milieu by competitors such as product catalogs, price lists, and advertising and sales campaigns often provide specific and detailed product data. Primary sources such as distributors, retailers, customers, technology experts, and industry and trade associations often furnish rich detail on competitors' product offerings.

Primary data sources such as interviews with industry experts, technology experts, distributors, end-customers, trade and industry association personnel, are more useful than secondary sources in identifying and understanding both customer groups and specific customers. For many industrial and commercial products with limited customers, primary data sources can help to identify individual customers within specific regions, industries, or other buying groups (and their decision-making criteria).

Identifying the Competitor's Marketplace Posture

Identifying the competitor's posture is closely related to scope determination. Once key product-customer segments are determined, a *guided* analysis (see Figure 5.9) identifies and assesses how the competitor competes along each of the eight generic modes of competition discussed earlier across the major product-customer segments.

FIGURE 5.9
Identifying a Competitor's Posture

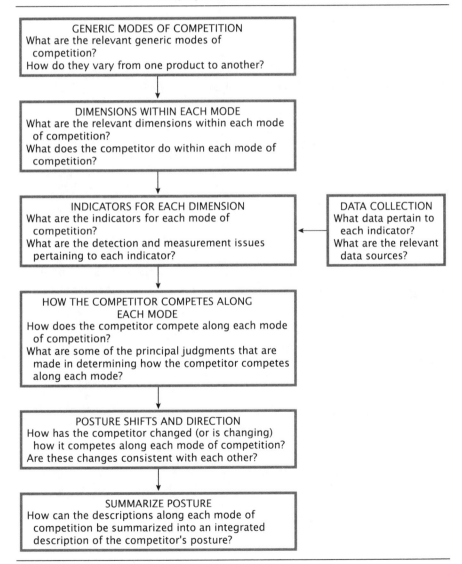

GENERIC MODES OF COMPETITION
What are the relevant generic modes of competition?
How do they vary from one product to another?

DIMENSIONS WITHIN EACH MODE
What are the relevant dimensions within each mode of competition?
What does the competitor do within each mode of competition?

INDICATORS FOR EACH DIMENSION
What are the indicators for each mode of competition?
What are the detection and measurement issues pertaining to each indicator?

DATA COLLECTION
What data pertain to each indicator?
What are the relevant data sources?

HOW THE COMPETITOR COMPETES ALONG EACH MODE
How does the competitor compete along each mode of competition?
What are some of the principal judgments that are made in determining how the competitor competes along each mode?

POSTURE SHIFTS AND DIRECTION
How has the competitor changed (or is changing) how it competes along each mode of competition?
Are these changes consistent with each other?

SUMMARIZE POSTURE
How can the descriptions along each mode of competition be summarized into an integrated description of the competitor's posture?

Configure Generic Modes of Competition

The relevance and applicability of the generic modes of competition noted in Table 5.1 are assessed for each competitive domain. Because of the differences across industries and markets, it is sometimes necessary to reconfigure the generic modes. Some industrial firms have separated service into presale and postsale service. The generic modes in the case of the yogurt competitor are identified on the left side of Table 5.2. The modes of competition heavily influence the data that is required as well as how it is collected and processed.

TABLE 5.2   The Yogurt Competitor's Posture

Modes	Dimensions	Indicators	Sample Data
Product line width	Width of lines	Number of lines	Four
	Depth of lines	Number of types	Twenty plus
Features	Content	Level of fat	Varies by line
	Packaging	Size of package	6–32 oz.
Functionality	Shelf life	Months	Lasts 12–18
	Taste	Customer perceptions	Minimal diff. vs. competitor's
Service	Delivery	Order response	Fast, < 3 days
		Out of stock	Almost never
	Channel support	Product returns	Accepted
		Shelf management	On agreement
Availability	Distribution channels	Types of channels	All major channels
Image and reputation	Desired product image	Content of advertising	Nutritious rich taste Low-calorie
	Position vs. competitors	Price focus of advertising	Premium upscale
Selling and relationships	Customer coverage	Number of salespersons	Highest number among competitors
		Call frequency	Above industry average
	Relationship with channels	Cooperative promotions	Large number and extensive
		Statements by the channels	Positive, supportive
Price	Price comparison	List prices	Close to highest
		Discounted price	Few discounts
	Price-value	Customers' perceptions	Surveys reveal very positive value profile

Identify Dimensions within Each Generic Mode

Once the generic modes are tentatively identified, the challenge then is to determine how the competitor competes within each mode of competition. This requires the identification of the key *dimensions* within each mode of competition. This is perhaps the critical task in a *guided* analysis of posture: as we shall see, dimensions determine the relevant indicators, which in turn determine the relevant types and sources of data.

Analysts must ask what the competitor does within each mode of competition and how it is done. For example: What does functionality mean in the case of each specific product? What types of service does the competitor provide and how does it deliver this service to different customers? How is the competitor trying to create specific types of image and reputation?

The key dimensions of each mode of competition in the case of the yogurt competitor are shown in Table 5.2. These dimensions were largely identified a priori by the team conducting the analysis. First-cut specification of dimensions serves to document analysts' understanding of how the competitor competes and thus serves as a benchmark for learning.[37] As the analysis progresses, analysts track not only how much they are learning about how the competitor competes but also their own understanding of each mode of competition and how they interrelate.

Dimensions may be relevant to the distribution channels or end-customers or both. For example, in the case of functionality, shelf life is relevant to both channels and end-customers. Taste is principally relevant to customers, yet it has implications for channel sales.

Identify the Indicators for Each Dimension

Each dimension of each mode of competition has specific indicators associated with it. Unless indicators are identified, it is impossible to scan and monitor change in the dimensions. Indicators thus focus the collection and analysis of competitor data.

Appropriate indicators vary markedly across the generic modes (see Table 5.2). The indicators of the dimensions of selling and relationships are radically different from those for service and functionality. Indicators also vary dramatically within some modes. Sometimes the relevant indicators are not immediately obvious or objectively measurable. These differences have critical implications for identifying data sources and data characteristics. For example, the indicators of taste—a dimension of functionality—are customers' perceptions or assessments of taste. Unlike the indicators of the other dimensions of functionality, customers' perceptions are not visible or measurable along some physical scale.

Gather Data along Each Dimension

In a *guided* analysis, dimensions and indicators (see Figure 5.9) serve to focus data search. What a competitor does along the relevant indicators for each generic mode must be systematically scanned and monitored. For example, in capturing how a competitor competes in the case of image, it might be necessary to assemble data on indicators pertaining to dimensions such as brand name, reputation for speed of delivery and adequacy of service, elements that are emphasized in advertisements, characteristics of packaging, and behaviors of the sales force.

Efficiency in data collection requires determination of existing and potential internal and external (primary and secondary) data sources. Many data sources are appropriate for multiple purposes. End-customers typically provide data on each mode of competition and on many competitors. By way of institutionalizing data sources and data search processes,[38] and enhancing both the efficiency and effectiveness of data gathering, the analyst must identify and categorize data sources for each of the generic modes of competition. Thus, analysts must know which are the relevant data sources for each competition mode and how best to collect and obtain the data. A sampling of internal and external data sources that have been found useful in determining competitors' posture are noted in Table 5.3.[39]

Table 5.2 provides some of the raw data for the yogurt competitor. The data is raw in that it represents the *descriptive* behaviors and actions of the competitor along each generic mode. For example, the listing under service shows the order response time, the amount of out-of-stock items, whether product returns are accepted, and if shelf management is incurred.

Collection and specification of the *raw data* along the indicators of the relevant dimensions for each mode of competition is emphasized for three reasons. First, it is often not apparent how the competitor competes along any single dimension. By providing analysts with a focus for collecting, selecting, ordering, and interpreting data, the identification of dimensions and indicators helps them to document and describe what the competitor is actually *doing*. For example, a computer manufacturer was surprised to discover that one of its competitors used off-site locations as its dominant means of providing key elements of service in one geographic area. Second, without this database, confusion is likely to reign as to how the competitor actually competes. It is not uncommon to observe intense debates about what service competitors actually provide to customers. Given the propensity of many firms to offer discounts, rebates, and other special offers, it is sometimes unclear what prices customers actually pay.

Third, as shall be apparent in the next step, once data is assembled along the relevant indicators, analysts then focus on the data as evidence to buttress sound judgments.[40]

TABLE 5.3 Posture: Sample Internal and External Data Sources

Generic Modes of Competition	Sample Internal Sources	Sample External Sources
Product line width	Marketing sales and other personnel Industry studies conducted by the firm's own personnel	Competitors' product catalogs Industry/trade associations Industry specialist consulting/data firms Trade/industry press

Features	Sales, marketing, engineering personnel
	Product observation
	Various product analyses conducted by range of internal personnel
	  Product tear-downs
	  Product trials/comparisons
	  Sales force analysis
		Industry/trade publication product reviews
		Competitors' promotion material
		Consultants' product review
		Specialist product assessment groups
		Customer-oriented publications

Functionality	Reverse engineering Manufacturing sales and other personnel assessments Product comparison studies	Customers' reports Retailer comments Distributors Specialist trade/industry observers Competitors' sales literature
Service	Service personnel comparisons Special studies conducted across multiple types of customers	Assessments of end-customers and channel members Competitors' sales and marketing materials Third-party assessments
Availability	Distribution and logistics personnel Sales force reports	Customers' survey Reports of channels Competitors' statements Studies by industry specialists and other third parties
Image and reputation	Marketing, sales, and advertising personnel Special tracking studies of competitor's individual promotions and advertisements	Competitors' advertising and promotion content Perception of end-customers and channels Research and surveys by others
Selling and relationships	Sales force reports Assessment by executives and others after visiting customers and channels	Interviews with selected end-customers and channel members
Price	Marketing, sales and service personnel Sales force reports Interviews with customers and channels	Competitors' price lists Retail and channel price lists and actual prices Interviews with end-customers

Determine How the Competitor Competes along Each Generic Mode

The raw data about dimensions is recast or aggregated into judgments about how the competitor competes along each mode. These judgments are central to processing: it is another form of ordering and interpreting data to generate required outputs (Cells 3 and 4 in Figure 2.1) that are useful to decision makers.

Figure 5.10 indicates how the yogurt competitor was judged to be competing along each mode. Each item in Figure 5.10 summarizes the data pertaining to a specific mode of competition.

The data shown in Table 5.2 serves as the evidence for the judgments inherent in the interpretations shown in Figure 5.10. Decision makers and

FIGURE 5.10
The Yogurt Competitor's Integrated Posture

Modes of Competition	Summary Description	Integrated Posture
PRODUCT LINE WIDTH	Product lines cover all available products	DISTINCTIVE IMAGE:
FEATURES	Innovative features Distinctive and unique packaging	
FUNCTIONALITY	Lasts as long as rivals' Customers say it tastes better than rivals	
SERVICE	Fast and responsive service to channels	Creates a high-end image and reputation as the best tasting yogurt, with superior service to, and strong relationships with channels, and, for which it charges the highest prices.
AVAILABILITY	Distribution to all possible channels	
IMAGE AND REPUTATION	Upscale, premium image Strong brand loyalty	
SELLING AND RELATIONSHIPS	Strong channel relationships	
PRICE	High prices across all product lines	

strategists therefore return to the data in Table 5.2 to assess whether the evidence strongly or weakly supports the judgments and the logic reflected in Figure 5.10.

Identify Posture Shifts

As with scope, posture also changes over time. A clear, succinct statement of the competitor's prevailing posture, as shown in Figure 5.10, provides the baseline for the identification and analysis of posture shifts over time. The detection of posture change, including its direction, intensity, and goals, is an important input to projecting a competitor's future marketplace strategy.

Historic profiles of a competitor's posture indicate its shift over time. Change along the indicators relevant to each dimension are scanned, monitored, and profiled. For example, changes in advertising themes indicate modifications in image and reputation that the competitor wishes to establish. A series of price reductions might indicate that the competitor wishes to position itself at the lower end of the price spectrum for a specific range of its products. *Indirect* indicators are sometimes especially important in anticipating posture shifts. The hiring of a new advertising agency may indicate a major shift in the image objectives of a competitor's posture. The restructuring of a sales force may indicate potential shifts in how the sales force will "sell" to different types of customers.

The yogurt competitor's current posture moves, and indicators of potential moves, pertaining to each competition mode are shown in Table 5.4. The analysts interpreted these moves collectively as indicating that the competitor was striving to build value for its customers, that is, channels and users, along each mode of competition. It was thus making it more difficult for any rival to use any single mode of competition as a basis of differentiation. Moreover, the indicators of potential moves also suggest that the competitor was not willing to rest on its laurels. In most instances, it planned to reinforce and extend the direction or thrust along each mode of competition.

Summarize and Articulate the Competitor's Posture

The aggregation of the interpretations along each competition mode provides an integrated description of the competitor's current posture. By adopting the widest product line in the business, with innovative features and packaging, fast national distribution, and creating a unique, upscale, premium image, the yogurt competitor was able to charge a substantial price premium (Figure 5.10). Its multiple forms of differentiation contributed to a high-end posture.[41]

TABLE 5.4 The Yogurt Competitor's Posture Shifts

Modes of Competition	Shift Along Each Mode of Competition	Indicators of Future Direction
Product line width	Adding lines and items	Product development
Features	Adding new package sizes	Management statements
Functionality	No apparent physical change in the product but increasing promotion of superiority in taste (through advertising)	Manufacturing commitments
Service	Helping retailers with their order processing and shelf management	Sales force and channel comments
Availability	Adding new channels Seeking added sales in existing channels	Management and channel statements
Image and reputation	New advertising program to strengthen image	Advertising agency statements
Selling and relationships	Sales force spending more time with retailers	Sales force channel and management statements
Price	Increasing prices	Management statements regarding strategy

The importance of succinctly articulating a competitor's posture and its direction resides in two factors. First, it provides a sharp focus for comparative, extended, and self-learning.[42] Second, it is easier for analysts and decision makers to see and understand the competitor's posture as summarized and integrated in Figure 5.10 than as depicted in its raw form in Table 5.2.

Open-Ended Inquiry

Open-ended inquiry makes no presumptions as to the content of posture, the indicators to search for, or the relevant data sources. Analysts attempt not to allow themselves to be influenced by any a priori conception of posture—how competitors compete against each other to attract, win, and retain customers. Rather, the spirit and thrust of open-ended inquiry is to gather posture-related data without any prior conception of the dimensions of posture that might emerge, to detect indicators as the search proceeds, and to order and interpret data by searching for patterns.

Some Errors in Identifying Scope and Posture

Since errors in marketplace strategy assessment are addressed at the conclusion of Chapter 6, this chapter concludes with the identification of some common errors in capturing and delineating competitors' marketplace scope and posture. These errors are cast in terms of the competitor learning model (see Figure 2.1) and the related learning principles presented in Chapter 2. They are emphasized here because of their applicability to each component in the competitor analysis framework. Later chapters address each error in greater detail.

Although the intent of both *guided* and *open-ended* approaches is to generate a *description* of scope and posture, a critical error is for analysts to embark on data gathering without any shared understanding of the elements of marketplace strategy or their key dimensions. Data capture thus becomes grossly inefficient: analysts have little guidance as to what types of data to gather. It also becomes gravely ineffective: analysts have difficulty transforming data into some description of the competitor's scope and posture (that is then useful in decision making).

The absence of a shared understanding of scope and posture contributes to a fundamental error: the failure to develop an a priori specification of modes of competition, their key dimensions, and potential indicators. Analysts are then unable to execute a *guided* approach. Also, they are less able to quickly generate a tentative first-cut of scope and posture. Determination of data needs, relevant data sources, and potential data collection methods are less likely to be systematically considered.

A common error in both guided and open-ended approaches is to cease processing *before* sufficient (raw) data has been collected and ordered. That is, analysts quickly make *final* judgments about how the competitor competes (such as those evidenced in Figure 5.10 and Table 5.4). Analysts are inclined to draw conclusive inferences about a competitor's posture from one or a small number of indicators, and often from the first indicators that are detected. Alerting inferences are not noted and then confirmed or refuted through the detection of further indicators.[43]

Another pervasive error is not to identify and *explicate* the judgments or reasoning that gives rise to interpretations or inferences as data are captured and processed over time. Both the data and logic must be made available: the learning of others within the organization rests on the data and logic being available for review and critique.

Although they are described sequentially, the processes depicted in Figures 5.3 and 5.9 are highly recursive: analysts move back and forth between steps. A serious error, therefore, is not to continually critique and reflect on the outputs of capturing and processing. As data is collected, processing often suggests a refinement of the first-cut specification of the modes of competition or the dimensions within a single mode. Learning is thus driven by the persistent attention to *questions* (e.g., should we modify and refine specific modes of competition or our present delineation of customers) and the continual (re)formulation of questions.

As with all the other framework components, analysts integrate an extensive swath of disparate and sometimes conflicting data in distilling and summarizing descriptive pictures of the individual dimensions of a competitor's current and emerging scope and posture (see Figures 5.4 and 5.5; Table 5.2). It is analysts who imbue data with meaning. Selecting, ordering, and interpreting data—processing—lies at the heart of the value-added created by analysts. A grave error, therefore, is the unwillingness on the part of decision makers and other analysts to develop interpretations or inferences. Without doing so, it is impossible to get beyond mere data.

Although they are presented separately in this chapter, analysts inevitably find themselves simultaneously identifying dimensions of scope and posture. Another regrettable error, therefore, is to lose sight of the big picture: how scope and posture (and goals) are related. Analysts must therefore continuously distinguish between the forest and the trees.[44] Although marketplace strategy can be described in varying levels of detail, ultimately, it is the *underlying structure* of the competitor's marketplace strategy (how scope, posture, and goals interrelate to constitute strategy) that is of interest rather than such factors as the individual product types within a particular product line or the individual dimensions within a specific mode of competition.

A final error worth noting is the tendency to emphasize description of scope and posture rather than the types of change occurring in them. Change in scope and posture (see Figure 5.8 and Table 5.4) serves as an indicator of further change in marketplace strategy or change in one or more microlevel components such as the activity/value chain, assumptions, or capabilities and competencies. Without attention to change in scope and posture, these signals are likely to be missed.

 ## Summary

Scope and posture are captured and described by tracking and integrating the competitor's behaviors in the marketplace. Distinct types of scope and posture are often identified across competitors. Patterns in scope and posture change serve as key indicators of marketplace goals, the topic of Chapter 6.

CHAPTER

6

Marketplace Strategy: Goals

THE CONCEPTS OF OUTWITTING, OUTMANEUVERING, AND OUTPERFORMING COMPETI-tors presume that the organization has some sense of what it wants to achieve or accomplish. Individual actions (such as introducing a new product or lowering price) and behavior patterns (such as a series of scope moves or posture shifts) are engaged in to achieve some purpose or ends—goals. Goals thus constitute a critical element in strategy: they address the *whys* behind a competitor's behaviors. As noted in Chapter 1, goals are particularly linked to both the importance and the relevance of outperforming competitors.

This chapter begins by addressing the relationship between behaviors (scope and posture) and goals, and highlights the role of goals in understanding strategy. It then presents a hierarchy of goals and distinct types of goals that are found in most organizations. Guided and open-ended approaches to identifying competitors' goals, as well as key errors that are common in doing so, are then delineated. The chapter next outlines a framework for the assessment of competitors' marketplace strategies. Finally, a number of errors commonly associated with assessment are noted.

Because goals must always be inferred, a primary focus in this chapter is the derivation and use of inferences. The role of logic or reasoning in furnishing links between indicators and inferences receives particular attention. A second learning emphasis is the introduction of the key elements of assessment.

Understanding Goals

Goals are broadly defined as what the competitor is striving to attain or the results it seeks. As such, goals (the ends) and behaviors (the means) are two interrelated and inseparable components of marketplace strategy.[1] Neither one alone is sufficient to provide an understanding of a competitor's strategy. Behaviors without goals are blind; without some sense of what the competitor is trying to achieve, behaviors in the context of scope and posture are meaningless. Goals without supporting behaviors are empty: goals give meaning to actions. Without an articulation of how they are to be achieved, goals are merely statements of desire or hope.

Goals vary greatly in the extent they are espoused, explicated, and documented within organizations. Since behaviors are rarely aimless, even if a competitor's goals are not explicit, implicit goals still drive its behaviors both at the level of strategy and individual actions. It is thus the competitor's implicit goals that in many cases are captured by analysts. To the extent the competitor is not aware of its own implicit goals, the analyst is likely to generate a better understanding of the competitor's goal structure than members of the competitor's own organization.

Roles of Goals in (Understanding) Strategy

Goals serve two primary but related roles as a component of strategy. At the macro level, goals are the purposes underlying, motivating, and inspiring the competitor's behaviors: they provide a rationale for the existence of the organization,[2] aspirations for its stakeholders, and motivation for its members. Clearly articulated, widely disseminated, and well-understood goals often serve as a rallying cry or unifying and integrating force *within* organizations.[3]

At the micro- or suborganization level, goals provide context, meaning, and explanation for individual behaviors.[4] This is especially important in relation to competitors' behaviors. The launch of a product line extension by a competitor is understood and interpreted quite differently depending on whether its purpose is to capture a specific customer segment, preempt another competitor's anticipated product introduction, position the competitor to launch the next generation of the product, or accomplish some combination of these goals. Some organizations' commitment to providing superior service to select individual customers appears to be irrational, or at least economically unjustifiable, until it is understood in the context of a goal to leverage winning and retaining some key accounts as the means to attract and win the next set of customers.

At both levels, goals address the "why" questions: Why is the competitor engaging in these behaviors? Why is it pursuing its current scope and posture? Why is it ignoring other strategy options? Why might the competitor pursue a different strategy at some point in the future? Thus, the analyst must dig beneath the competitor's behaviors (and words) to develop an understanding of what goals are driving them.

Understanding a competitor's goals is central not just to capturing its current marketplace strategy but to anticipating and projecting its marketplace moves including its reactions to the moves of others. Goals facilitate *anticipation* of competitors' scope moves, posture shifts, and other changes in behaviors in a number of ways. First, goals indicate a competitor's likely product-customer choices. For example, if the competitor defines its product-customer domain or business as "the publishing of books" it is likely to seek product opportunities within this domain and to avoid product choices outside it such as publishing comics or distributing videos or movies. Second, goals as statements of aspirations always offer a criterion by which to evaluate current goal attainment.[5] A gap between aspiration and attainment—often referred to as a performance gap[6]—indicates the extent to which a competitor may be inclined or impelled to make strategic moves. If the competitor is exceeding its financial and marketplace goals, it may lack the urgency associated with poor performance to make significant changes in its strategy or operations.

Goals help in other ways to facilitate anticipation and determination of competitors' responses to the moves of others. Goals often indicate not just resource commitments but emotional commitments. Competitor-focused goals such as the aim to take market share away from a specific competitor or to beat a particular competitor to market with a new product introduction[7] sometimes reflect intense personal and organizational passion and conviction.

A Hierarchy of Goals

Every organization manifests some hierarchy or structure of goals. Although the terminology involved in goals is a semantic jungle, a goal hierarchy broadly applicable to multi- or single-business organizations is shown in Table 6.1. The hierarchy of goals exhibits a number of features. Goals are directly related to the organization's structure; broad, long-term goals are evident at the higher end of the hierarchy and specific, short-term goals are found at the lower end; goals at each level influence goals at all levels below it. Each level adds insight into a competitor's goals. In moving down the hierarchy from intent and vision to operating goals, the goals become more

TABLE 6.1   Goals: Four Interrelated Levels

Definition	Time	Focus/Purpose	Sample Content	Sample Indicators
INTENT/VISION:				
What the firm wants to achieve or how it sees itself in the long run	Long-run: can be a 5-to 20-year time frame, and sometimes longer	To provide a broad, collective challenge that stretches and energizes the organization	To put a computer in every home To integrate voice, data, and video and make it available to every home owner	Senior management statements Linkages among strategy thrusts, investment programs, and commitments
STRATEGIC THRUSTS/ INVESTMENT PROGRAMS:				
The major strategy/ marketplace and resource commitments	Medium-run: often 3 to 5 years, and sometimes more	To operation-alize attain-ment of the intent/vision	New products Research and development programs Development of a network of alliances and relationships	Senior management statements Announcements Product change Investment and resource commitments
OBJECTIVES:				
Results to be achieved in the medium run	Short to medium: time line to attain strategic thrust/ investment goals	To establish focused and measurable targets in key result areas	Launch a new product each year Penetrate each major channel Achieve gross margins of 20%	Specific management statements Statements by others Action programs
OPERATING GOALS:				
Specific, short-term tasks or accomplish-ments	Short-run: typically months to one year, some-times a little more	To provide clear guidance to short-run activities and tasks	Complete product line extension Attain specific market share in each customer segment Improve particular operating and cost efficiencies	Management statements Statements by others Action programs

specific with regard to content and time. Specific indicators are germane to each level.

Intent or Vision Many organizations are driven by one or a few overarching, long-run goals that imbue the organization with a collective challenge, shared vision and sense of mission or purpose. Such goals have been designated by others as strategic intent,[8] vision,[9] and superordinate goals.[10] For example, one organization's intent and vision is to make multimedia a reality: to integrate voice, data, and video and make it available to every homeowner. Intent and vision provide the glue connecting what otherwise might appear to be disconnected or isolated investments, activities, and behaviors.

Strategic Thrusts/Investment Programs To be realized, intent and vision must be transformed into significant marketplace (i.e., product and customer), and technology, organization, and related investment commitments. Even if a competitor is not guided by an overarching intent and vision, specific goals are still associated with its major marketplace thrusts and investment programs.[11] Such thrusts and programs often take three to five (and in some cases considerably more) years to come to fruition. Examples of thrusts and investments include commitments in research and development (R&D), product line extensions, alliances, new manufacturing facilities, and new marketing capabilities. The following representative goals might be associated with each of these thrusts and investments: reorient R&D to products that are new to the marketplace; extend product lines to attract new segments of customers; use alliances to build a significant marketplace position in leading Asian or European countries; build new manufacturing facilities for new product development and introduction; develop new marketing capabilities to outmaneuver specific competitors across major customer segments.

Objectives Objectives operationalize strategic thrusts and investment programs: they set desired results to be achieved in the medium- to long-range future.[12] A set timetable for their attainment is typically established. For example, a business unit's strategic thrust to penetrate the Asian market might be guided by these objectives: launch each product line in each Asian country within three years; attain 20 percent of the Asian market within four years; achieve average gross margins of 20 percent; and be represented in every major distribution channel in each country.

Operating Goals These are discernible, short-term tasks or accomplishments that the organization intends to achieve in pursuit of its objectives.

An objective of launching each product line in each Asian country during the next three years might have associated with it specific goals pertaining to product development, marketing programs, sales force activities, access to distribution channels, coverage of particular geographic areas, and advertising commitments. Operating goals contain the parameters[13] along which their attainment is monitored and measured.

Goals and Organization Levels

As noted, goals are associated with different levels of a competitor's organization. Although they are conceptually and operationally linked, the substance and focus of intent/vision, strategic thrusts/investment programs, objectives, and operating goals are distinctly different depending on the organization levels found in typical multibusiness corporations (see Figure 6.1). At the corporate level, intent and vision set the strategic direction for the entire corporation. At the sector level (i.e., a group of related businesses), intent and vision establish what the group of businesses within the sector want to become or achieve. Each division or business unit may also possess its own intent and vision. As one moves from the corporate to the business-unit level, intent and vision become more focused and specific.

Strategic thrusts and investment programs at the corporate, sector, and business-unit levels, aimed at realizing the intent and vision often involve

FIGURE 6.1
A Framework for Goals Analysis

Goal Level \ Org. Level	Corporate	Sector	Business Unit	Product Line
Strategic Intent/ Vision				
Strategic Thrusts/ Programs				
Objectives				
Goals				

acquisitions, mergers, divestments, alliances, and partnerships as well as investments in many domains of research and development. These tend to be more specific and focused as one moves from the corporate to business-unit levels.

Categories of Goals

A competitor may pursue many different types of goals at each organizational level and within each goal level. Marketplace goals address what a competitor wants to achieve in the marketplace, that is, with customers and channels. They are central to understanding marketplace strategy. Competitor-focused goals are sometimes intimately related to what the competitor is trying to achieve in the marketplace. Although they are distinct from marketplace goals, financial and technological goals are essential to developing an integrated picture of what is driving a competitor either at the level of the total organization or at subsidiary organization levels.

Marketplace Goals These goals refer to what the competitor is trying to do or wants to achieve in the marketplace. In line with the notion of marketplace strategy developed in Chapter 5, marketplace goals can be delineated with regard to scope and posture. At the corporate and business-unit levels, marketplace goals are often a major component of strategic intent and vision, as is evident in Table 6.1. At an aggregate level, marketplace goals can be related to scope focus: the extent to which the competitor aims to achieve a niche, spread, proliferated, or blanket marketplace coverage.[14]

Although marketplace goals ultimately make sense only in the context of both products and customers, it is frequently useful to disaggregate *scope* goals to the level of product and customer goals. Product goals, as illustrated in the multimedia example noted earlier, typically lie at the heart of *intent/vision*. Broad product goals at the level of *strategic thrusts/investment programs* might include whether the competitor is trying to be a product leader or follower, wants to extend, retain, or contract its product line or desires to change or retain its product design and features.

Customer goals, up and down the four goal levels, indicate the extent to which the competitor is emphasizing different customer segments, the degree to which the competitor would like to penetrate specific customer segments, and how the competitor would like to position its products and, in many instances, its entire organization, in the minds of customers.

The integration of product and customer goals is reflected in such *objectives* as relative superiority of products (e.g., to provide a greater degree of customization than competitors) and direction of product-customer focus (e.g., expansion into new regional or foreign markets). Typical *operating goals* might include attaining X percent market share within two years in a specific distribution channel or geographic region.

Any competitor's *posture* also has specific marketplace goals associated with it. Competitors engage in specific modes of competition to attract, win, and retain customers. To understand how this broad goal is attained, however, it is essential to identify and assess *investment programs* associated with the posture dimensions as well as the *objectives* and *operating goals* of the modes of competition employed by the competitor. Goals at these two levels that might be associated with specific modes of competition are noted in Table 6.2.

Competitor-Oriented Goals   As illustrated in many of the examples in this chapter, competitor-oriented goals are often a central focus at each goal level—intent/vision, strategic thrust/investment programs, objectives, and operating goals. For example, statements of intent or vision almost always refer explicitly or implicitly to current and potential competitors. In some instances, competitor-oriented goals serve as the dominant driving or overarching goal; they provide the explanation of the organization's overall strategy.

Each of the competitor-focused strategies noted in Chapter 5—frontal, flanking, encirclement, and bypass—directly manifest distinct strategic thrusts/investment programs and associated objectives and goals. For example, a flanking competitor-focused strategy aims to avoid direct frontal competition with one or more competitors. But it also aims to take overall market share from these competitors through its ability to attract customers away from them. A principal objective may be to avoid provoking or inciting the flanked competitor(s) into retaliation. Competitor-oriented goals therefore are not only closely related to but shed further light on competitors' marketplace goals.

Technological Goals   Technological goals are difficult to disentangle from marketplace and competitor-oriented goals. The scope and impact of technological change renders technological goals ever more important in understanding firms' strategies.[15] Marketplace success is increasingly a function of what organizations are able to do in both product and process technologies. As discussed in Chapter 13, technology should be viewed broadly to include firms' basic and applied research and development as well as technology application in all organizational areas.

Technological goals are relevant to each goal level. They can be denominated along several dimensions including new product development, entry into and exit from specific technologies, process technology development, and enhanced operational efficiencies.

TABLE 6.2 Posture: Some Objectives and Operating Goals

Modes of Competition	Objectives	Operating Goals
Product line width	To add a new product line To prune existing product types within a particular line	To introduce new types or items within the next quarter To bundle products for a special promotion
Features	To add new features To reinforce existing features	To add or eliminate specific features
Functionality	To redefine endurance and reliability To be the recognized performance leader within 3 years	To add specific increments to performance parameters (e.g., improve safety)
Service	To add new service dimensions To integrate service dimensions into distinct service options for specific customer groups	To provide specific new service options for distinct customer sets To provide specific types of assistance to individual channels
Availability	To add new channels To increase product flow through existing channels	To add a certain number of outlets To increase product flow by 5%
Image and reputation	To enhance name/brand recognition beyond all competitors To build the best reputation for customizing solutions	To improve brand awareness by 10% in a particular customer group
Selling and relationships	To be the preferred vendor to all key channels within 3 years To have a close working relationship with all key customer accounts	To have each salesperson call on each channel at least twice by quarter To have a product development agreement with specific key end-customers or users
Price	To develop the best price/value relationship	To achieve the highest rating on industry-wide customer value/ satisfaction scores

Financial Goals An organization's efforts in the marketplace are intended to generate financial returns. Financial goals reveal the level of economic performance the competitor hopes to attain. Many firms publicly identify their aspirations in terms of such financial goals as shareholder value, return on investment or equity, cash flow, margins, profit, and leverage. The attainment of such goals depends on how effectively and efficiently the organization achieves its marketplace, competitor, and technological goals.

Dominant Goals

The task of identifying and analyzing competitors' goals is made somewhat easier because one or two goals often dominate or drive each goal level. Such dominant goals serve as an integrating focus for all other goals. Strategic intent and vision, at the apex of a competitor's goal hierarchy, when they are clearly articulated and widely communicated, constitute dominant or driving goals.

Sometimes driving goals are visibly espoused at levels below intent and vision. Many U.S. firms have vociferously communicated their commitment to shareholder value enhancement as the criterion by which all strategic thrusts and investment programs are to be assessed. In some instances, technological goals strongly prevail at the level of objectives. Sometimes, marketplace goals dominate at the level of operating goals.

Changes in Competitors' Goals

Goals are rarely static. That competitors change goals at any of the four levels noted in Table 6.1 should not be a surprise. If they did not, competitors would be neither adapting to nor responding to the environment; they certainly would not be taking strategic initiatives. In many instances, changes in their economic performance compel organizations to change goals. In other instances, unexpected opportunities cause goal change.

All types of goals, irrespective of the goal or organization level, change over time. Even intent and vision undergo change, ranging from a modest refocusing to a radical recasting as evident in the efforts of many multidivisional firms to forgo many years of diversification to concentrate on a set of related businesses or technologies.

Changes in corporate, sector, and business-units goals are often significant. Many publicly traded U.S. firms have changed their dominant financial goal from ROE or ROI to enhancement of shareholder value. In order to concentrate on core businesses, a large number of firms have recently divested many of the entities they acquired during the diversification era of the late 1970s and early 1980s. These actions reflect dramatic shifts in marketplace (and, relatedly, financial and technological) goals.

Even in the short-run, competitors sometimes make sudden and dramatic changes in their goals. This may occur with regard to any type of goal and at any organizational level. Firms frequently announce shifts in strategy that involve extensive goal change, such as the introduction of new products, withdrawal from particular product-customer segments, establishment of strategic alliances, and major alterations in how they want to compete. Frequently, these announcements catch many competitors by surprise.

Goal Change as Signals

The function of goals in anticipating competitors' marketplace moves discussed earlier implies the importance of goals as signals. Goal changes often constitute strong, high-impact signals of competitors' emerging and future behaviors. Goal change may precede, follow, or be concurrent with major changes in behaviors.

Change in intent/vision and strategic thrusts/investment programs often signal major shifts in marketplace strategy, commitments to specific products and customer segments, technological activities, and organization configuration. For example, when many U.S. firms began to pursue shareholder value enhancement as their dominant goal, it signaled a strong likelihood that organizational units that did not contribute to value creation would be divested or dramatically reshaped.

Changes in objectives may also signal large-scale organizational change. The emergence of customer-oriented objectives and the relative decline of technological objectives are often crucial signals of competitors' desire to compete based on quality, as defined by the experience of customers, as opposed to quality defined in terms of technological standards and internal operating norms and procedures. This switch in objectives often reflects a desire to conduct all phases of business in a new, customer-driven manner.

Indicators of Goals and Goal Change

The range of potential indicators of goals and goal change is extremely broad. All the indicators noted in Chapter 4 serve to indicate goals and goal change. Marketplace, organizational, and relational behaviors and inactions are often critical goal indicators. They may serve as either direct or indirect indicators though the incidence of indirect indicators is more common since goals are rarely explicitly associated with behaviors.

Statements frequently serve as alerting indicators; firms make many different types of announcements about their plans and intentions. However, great care must be taken not to take such goal announcements merely at their face value: confirming (and refuting) behaviors and organization attribute change should be sought. Goals that are not translated into behaviors are merely words.

Organization attribute change sometimes is a powerful source of *anticipated* indicators of goal change. For example, a decline in product functionality may indicate the need for the competitor to refocus its goals on building and promoting product quality. The analyst then scans and monitors for indicators of increased attention to product quality such as changes in personnel, in manufacturing processes, in procurement of raw materials and suppliers, and in statements ascribing greater importance to product quality.

Identifying Goals

Guided and open-ended approaches to goal identification are both driven by the search for indicators that allow inferences (signals) to be drawn about the competitor's goals. The purpose is to build a picture of the competitor's current goal structure and to identify signals of goal change. The emphasis

FIGURE 6.2
Identifying a Competitor's Goals: The Process of Deriving Inferences

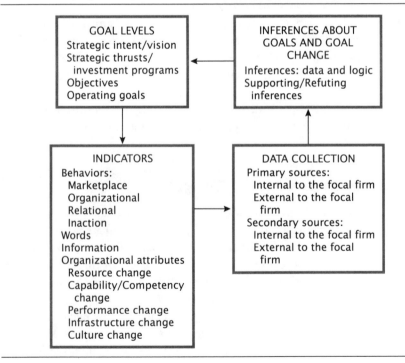

in each approach is on patterns among indicators: inferences that reinforce and confirm initial signals.

Guided goal identification presumes some a priori configuration of goals, such as depicted in Table 6.1, an understanding of the relevant types of potential indicators, familiarity with internal and external data sources, and a recognition of the need to derive inferences about the competitor's current goals and apparent goal change. These four sequential steps (see Figure 6.2), a priori goal levels, indicators, data collection, and inferences, represent the core phases in guided goal analysis. A more refined set of specific steps and associated key questions are noted in Figure 6.3. (As shown in later chapters, key indicators of marketplace as well as technological, financial, and

FIGURE 6.3
Identifying a Competitor's Goals: Steps and Questions

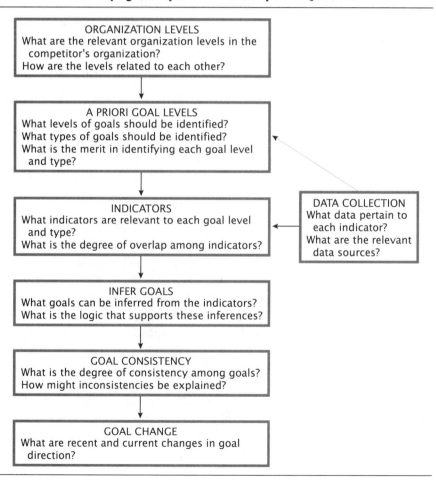

competitor-focused goals are identified as part of the analysis of competitors' activity/value chains, alliances and networks, assumptions, assets, capabilities and competencies, technology, and organization.)

Marketplace Goals

The identification of *marketplace* goals must be closely integrated with the delineation of competitors' scope and posture, as discussed in Chapter 5. The steps in the analysis outlined here are highly iterative. The yogurt competitor discussed in Chapter 5 will be used for illustration purposes.

Identify Organization Levels A useful point of departure is to identify the relevant organization levels in the competitor because, as noted earlier, distinct marketplace strategies (in terms of scope, posture, and goals) are associated with each level.[16] A multibusiness corporation typically possesses a complex set of organizational elements and relationships. An understanding of the organization structure alerts the analyst to the need to discern goals at each organizational level, the likelihood of varying emphasis on the different types of goals across the levels, and the need to be aware of potential goal interrelationships.

Identify a Priori Goal Types It is often useful for analysts to consider *a priori* what types of marketplace (and other) goals they should pay attention to at each organization level. For example, analysts might consider whether *objectives* pertaining to image and reputation (such as brand recognition or reputation for service) need to be analyzed.

Identifying a priori goals helps ensure that specific types of goals are not over- or underemphasized. Both familiarity with and lack of knowledge of a competitor lead analysts to overemphasize, downplay, or even ignore specific types of goals. Analysts in many U.S. firms tend to overemphasize financial and market share goals, thus downplaying broader marketplace goals and sometimes neglecting technological goals. Lack of prior knowledge about a competitor may lead analysts to impose the goal structure of their own organization on the competitor. The relevant goals may vary by organization level, strategy type, product or industry type, age of competitor, performance results, and other factors.

Search for Indicators The search for goal indicators at each goal level—intent/vision, strategic thrusts/investment programs, objectives and operating goals—is informed by the determination of scope and posture. Current scope and posture reflect, at least implicitly, some marketplace goals. Scope moves and posture shifts, as discussed in Chapter 5, are especially useful as a basis for inferring marketplace goals: they manifest what the competitor is trying to achieve.

Table 6.3 shows many of the relevant indicators and the goal structure that was derived from them in the case of the yogurt competitor. Specific indicators are associated with each goal that is derived at each goal level. Also, individual indicators are often relevant at different goal levels.

TABLE 6.3 Yogurt Competitor's Marketplace Goals

Goal Level	Goal Content	Indicators
Intent/Vision	To be recognized as the market leader in innovative, high-image yogurt products	Management statements Strategic thrusts Investment programs
Strategic thrusts/ Investment programs	1) Develop products	Investments, alliances Marketing programs
	2) Penetrate new and existing consumer groups	Product introductions Channel changes Management statements
	3) Enhance image	Advertising/Promotion Management commitments
	4) Solidify and extend trade distribution	Management statements Trade statements Sales-force activity
Objectives	1) Add to each line every year	Announcements of specific products
	2) Gain two market share points for each of next 2 to 4 years	Extension of plant shifts Two vendor contracts adding new volume
	3) Reinforce image with existing and new consumers	Advertising content Management statements
	4) Reach "maximum" penetration of each retail outlet type	Management statements Sales-force activity Trade statements
Operating goals	1) Introduce specific products	Announcements
	2) Gain specific market share in each type of outlet in each region	Management statements Sales-force comments to customers
	3) Add additional trade promotion and advertising programs within a year	Sales/Promotion materials Sales-force comments
	4) Add additional outlets in each geographic region within one year	Competitor's meetings with customers Sales-force literature

Infer Goals The content of each goal level—intent/vision, strategic thrusts/investment programs, objectives and operating goals—is *inferred* by analysts. Thus, analysts' judgments must be buttressed by both data and logic. For example, the logic and data associated with the objective, gain two market share points for each of the next two to four years (see Table 6.3), is the following: The extension of the plant shifts results in additional volume of X; The two vendor contracts generate a further additional volume of Y; If annual market growth of Z is assumed, and competitors do not increase sales, X and Y added to the competitor's current sales would give it a market share gain of two points over the next few years.

Both direct and indirect indicators give rise to signals of goal content and direction. In the case of the market share objective discussed in the previous paragraph, the two vendor contracts and the extension of plant shifts constitute important *indirect* indicators of the goal to increase market share. The analyst must draw the connection between one set of variables (extension of plant shifts and vendor contracts) and another variable (market share)—a connection that sometimes is not obvious.

Review for Coherence As goals are identified at each level, it is necessary to check for consistency within each level and across levels. Although there is no presumption that a competitor's goals are coherent either within or across levels, the consistency check compels analysts to ask questions that otherwise might go unheeded. For example, with regard to the *objective* of gaining two market share points for each of the next two to four years, the analyst should ask whether other goals support or impede that objective. Each of the other objectives—adding to each product line each year, reinforcing image with existing and new customers, and reaching "maximum" penetration of each type of retail outlet—if achieved would aid in attaining the market share goals.

Identify Goal Change Goal direction is just as important to know as goal content at any point in time. Changes in direction of goals and/or reinforcement of goal direction constitute critical indicators of emerging and future marketplace strategy. In the case of the yogurt competitor, a number of key goal changes were detected (see Table 6.4). Cumulatively, they reveal a competitor that is committing itself to extending and reenforcing its position as marketplace leader.

Other Goals

The identification of competitor-focused, technological and financial goals follow a similar set of steps to that outlined above. Table 6.5 shows the structure of these goals for the yogurt competitor.

TABLE 6.4 Yogurt Competitor's Changes in Marketplace Goals

Intent/Vision	Greater commitment to the overall intent/vision
Strategic thrusts/Investment programs	Additional emphasis on new products
	Greater attention to new customers
	New emphasis upon further penetration of existing customers
	New commitment to enhancing and furthering image
	Continued aim to penetrate the trade
Objectives	A significant new increment in market share
Operating goals	Using new products to build image and reputation with both the trade and consumers

Open-Ended Search

An open-ended approach to the identification of goals is useful for several reasons. It counterbalances the tendency to impose the focal firm's goal hierarchy and priorities on other organizations. Analysts frequently fall into the trap of focusing on goals that their own organization emphasizes. It also serves as a check on the compilation of behaviors such as marketplace scope and posture.

In an open-ended search, the analyst ignores any prior analysis of the competitor, is not constricted by an a priori structure of goals, and does not impose any constraints on data search or data sources. The search is for direct and indirect indicators of goals and changes in goals.

The focus in data capture is unconstrained. Analysts scan both primary and secondary sources. It is now possible to quickly scan all available secondary data sources through the use of electronic databases and review available reports such as the output of security analysts, industry and trade associations, consultants, industry watchers, and governmental studies. Many of the competitor's own written outputs or publications can also be scanned such as annual reports, filings with governmental and regulatory authorities, advertising, and promotion materials.

As with scope and posture, a central element in any extensive open-ended search is a scan of primary sources both inside and outside the focal organization. The range of primary sources noted in the prior chapter is also relevant to goals. Individuals often provide data in the form of their opinions about competitors' goals that serve as alerting signals: the analyst then seeks confirming or refuting evidence.

TABLE 6.5 Yogurt Competitor's Marketplace and Other Goals

Marketplace	Competitor-Focused	Technology	Financial
INTENT/VISION:			
To be recognized as the market leader in innovative, high-image yogurt products	To compel all competitors to be followers	To use technology to generate new products and to reduce costs	To be most profitable firm in the business
STRATEGIC THRUSTS/ INVESTMENT PROGRAMS:			
1) Develop products 2) Penetrate new and existing consumer groups 3) Enhance image 4) Solidify and extend trade distribution	To preempt specific competitor's moves To be seen by the trade to be the strategic leader in the marketplace To make key investments faster than competitors	To develop products To develop innovative packaging To reduce manufacturing costs	To seek a balance in returns from investment programs
OBJECTIVES:			
1) Add to each line every year 2) Gain two market share points for each of next 2 to 4 years 3) Reinforce image with existing and new consumers 4) Reach "maximum" penetration of each retail outlet type	To introduce products before competitors To enhance image and reputation relative to competitors To demonstrate functional superiority	To facilitate additions to each product line To upgrade packaging on each product line To reduce manufacturing costs by 10%–15% over 2 years	To achieve specific profit targets by: product line customer group channel type To generate specific levels of cashflow
OPERATING GOALS:			
1) Introduce specific products 2) Gain specific market share in each type of outlet in each region 3) Add additional trade promotion and advertising programs within 1 year 4) Add additional outlets in each geographic region within 1 year	To attract specific channels away from particular competitors To attain greater sales in some specific channels than particular competitors	To facilitate introduction of new products To complete packaging changes on one line To change some manufacturing operations	To exceed budgeted revenues for all products in all geographic areas

Errors in Identifying Goals

Because inferences are central to identifying competitors' goals, this section draws attention to errors pertaining to the derivation of inferences. Each error is addressed in more detail in later chapters.

An error on the part of many analysts is the tendency to resist the interpretations or judgments that lie at the heart of inferences about competitors' goals. Such judgments, as emphasized throughout this book, are unavoidable. Analysts must therefore address how they can improve their inference derivation capabilities.[17]

A critical error is to overemphasize goal content at the expense of change in goal direction. Since goal change is often an indicator of change in marketplace scope and posture, and many types of change in microlevel components, critical inferences about the direction of marketplace strategy change are therefore likely to be missed.

Since a competitor's goals, especially at the level of strategic thrusts/investment programs, objectives, and operating goals, can change at any time, and sometimes precipitously, analysts should always specify anticipated indicators of change in key goals. This prescription is more honored in the breach than the observance. Hence, analysts are often slow to detect change in a competitor's goals.

Inferences pertaining to goals are typically derived from a pattern across indicators. As illustrated in the yogurt case, patterns derived from indicators associated with a competitor's scope moves and posture shifts, allow analysts to draw inferences about such goal changes as market share, introduction of new products, or penetration of existing market segments.

Inferences about goals are frequently indirect. Market share goals might be derived from manufacturing output and technology changes. A fundamental error therefore is not to recognize the goals-signaling capacity of specific indicators, that is, to possess the indicators, but not to see or derive alerting or confirming/refuting inferences.

A common error is not to carefully articulate the logic that connects one or more indicators to an inference about goals. This is an especially critical error to the extent the inferences are indirect. If the case supporting an inference is not available to others, it becomes extremely difficult to challenge and perhaps refute the logic.

Analysts sometimes do not sufficiently challenge inferences about goals by developing countervailing logics, that is, assembling the strongest possible data and reasoning to refute a specific inference. It is only through such challenges that it is possible to fully test the strength of an inference.[18]

An error that is easily overlooked is the failure to check for consistency within and across the goal levels. Since goal content and direction are the product of inferences, conflicts in what is inferred easily arise. Among other benefits, it provides analysts with another reason to carefully develop the logic connecting one or more indicators with an inference and to make the logic available to others.

Assessing Scope, Posture, and Goals

Any competitor's marketplace strategy must be assessed with reference to one or more rivals including the focal firm. Such assessment is critical to determining whether and how a competitor is outwitting, outmaneuvering, and outperforming its look-alike and substitute rivals. It is thus essential to comparative and extended learning as well as self-learning. As underscored in Chapters 7 through 15, it also guides the microlevel analysis of competitors. The steps in the analysis and key associated questions are noted in Figure 6.4. The yogurt competitor is used for purposes of illustration.

Strategy Coherence, Entrepreneurialism, and Degree of Stretch

Before subjecting a competitor's marketplace strategy to performance assessment, it is useful to evaluate it for coherence, entrepreneurialism, and degree of stretch. A critical review of these marketplace strategy attributes often raises fundamental concerns and issues with regard to strategy direction, design, and execution.

It is particularly critical to evaluate *coherence* between behaviors (scope and posture) and goals. Incongruence is sometimes especially apparent in the case of espoused goals: organizations frequently articulate specific goals, yet engage in behaviors suggesting different goals. The methodology suggested in this and Chapter 5 captures, detects, and interprets the competitor's actual behaviors and (inferred) goals. Often, inferred goals are closer to the competitor's actual goals (the goals that are actually inspiring, motivating, and sustaining behaviors) than its espoused goals.

Incongruence *within* inferred marketplace goals and *across* goal types is common. Market-share goals may not be supported by new product rollout goals. Market-share goals may be inconsistent with cash flow enhancement goals. Inconsistencies alert analysts to choices (decisions) that confront or will confront the competitor. The yogurt competitor's goals exhibited a high degree of consistency. Marketplace, technological, and financial goals were mutually reinforcing. For example, the financial goals of increasing margins and overall returns were aided by attainment of the marketplace goal of increasing market share while achieving the technology goal of reducing unit manufacturing and other costs.

FIGURE 6.4
Assessing the Marketplace Strategy: Guiding Questions

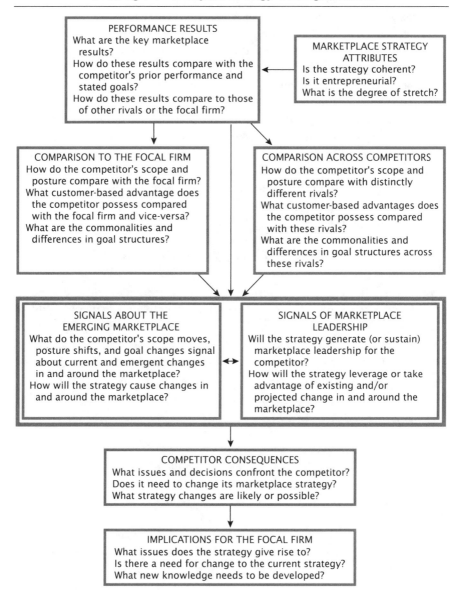

PERFORMANCE RESULTS
What are the key marketplace
  results?
How do these results compare with the
  competitor's prior performance and
  stated goals?
How do these results compare to those
  of other rivals or the focal firm?

MARKETPLACE STRATEGY
ATTRIBUTES
Is the strategy coherent?
Is it entrepreneurial?
What is the degree of stretch?

COMPARISON TO THE FOCAL FIRM
How do the competitor's scope and
  posture compare with the focal firm?
What customer-based advantage does
  the competitor possess compared
  with the focal firm and vice-versa?
What are the commonalities and
  differences in goal structures?

COMPARISON ACROSS COMPETITORS
How do the competitor's scope and
  posture compare with distinctly
  different rivals?
What customer-based advantages does
  the competitor possess compared
  with these rivals?
What are the commonalities and
  differences in goal structures across
  these rivals?

SIGNALS ABOUT THE
EMERGING MARKETPLACE
What do the competitor's scope moves,
  posture shifts, and goal changes signal
  about current and emergent changes
  in and around the marketplace?
How will the strategy cause changes in
  and around the marketplace?

SIGNALS OF MARKETPLACE
LEADERSHIP
Will the strategy generate (or sustain)
  marketplace leadership for the
  competitor?
How will the strategy leverage or take
  advantage of existing and/or
  projected change in and around the
  marketplace?

COMPETITOR CONSEQUENCES
What issues and decisions confront the competitor?
Does it need to change its marketplace strategy?
What strategy changes are likely or possible?

IMPLICATIONS FOR THE FOCAL FIRM
What issues does the strategy give rise to?
Is there a need for change to the current strategy?
What new knowledge needs to be developed?

Inconsistencies across the dimensions of posture are also common. This is especially likely if posture is undergoing significant change. For example, organizations trying to move from a predominantly product functionality and features mode of differentiation to include perceptual and relationship differentiation often encounter difficulties in maintaining consistency across the posture dimensions. The tendency to sell based on product performance (functionality) and features is often difficult for sales force members and others within the organization to abandon or downplay. Again, the analyst is alerted to the need to monitor specific indicators within particular posture dimensions. The yogurt firm's posture was tightly integrated: all modes of competition were geared to developing and sustaining a high-end image at prices considerably above the majority of rivals.

Degree of entrepreneurialism, unlike coherence, requires comparison to competitors. The yogurt competitor's marketplace strategy was not radically entrepreneurial: it was introducing new products, seeking new customers, and extending and upgrading its posture. Yet, it was not in any sense reinventing the yogurt business; it was largely extending and refining prevailing business practices.

However, the yogurt competitor was exhibiting a modest degree of stretch in its strategy. Its marketplace (and financial) goals were highly aggressive (compared with rivals): it was dedicated to turning the market-share battle into a zero-sum game. Yet its strategy was not a stretch for its assets: it had ensured the necessary product supply (in part through agreement with vendors) and it possessed the necessary financial wherewithal.

Delineate Strategy Results

Strategies generate results: they ultimately succeed or fail to attract, win, and retain customers. Delineating and assessing strategy results in each of the arenas noted in Chapter 1 resides at the core of "keeping score."[19] Distinct parameters can be developed for each scorekeeping or assessment arena.[20]

Delineating and evaluating the realized (and potential) results of competitors' marketplace strategies necessitate some parameters (indicators) and evaluation criteria. Marketplace parameters, such as those noted in Table 6.6, are essential to monitoring and measuring marketplace strategy success or failure. Key parameters include product development and introduction, penetration of distinct product-customer segments, penetration of and acceptance by the major channels, and customer satisfaction.

Key strategy results for the yogurt competitor along a number of parameters are noted in Table 6.7. It is evident that its strategy is generating improved performance: all key parameters including revenue growth, market share, and profitability show enhanced performance.

TABLE 6.6   Assessing Marketplace Strategy: Delineating Actual Results

Parameters		Criteria
Sales:	Units	The competitor's own past performance
	Revenues	The competitor's own goals and
	Market share	expectations
Users:	Penetration by segment	Other competitor's performance, goals,
	Customer satisfaction	and expectations
	Image/Reputation	
	Relationships	The focal firm's performance, goals, and
	Margins/Profits	expectations
Channels:	Share per channel	
	Support from channel	
	Image/Reputation	
	Relationships	
Products:	Margins/Profits	
	New products	
	Product enhancements	

TABLE 6.7   Assessing the Yogurt Competitor's Marketplace Strategy Results

	Parameters	Criteria
SALES	1) Total revenues increased by 3%	Sales did not grow as fast as the competitor had predicted
	2) Revenues increased for all product lines in all regions	But, sales increase was larger than that of any national rival
	3) Profit margins enhanced marginally	Resulting in being the only firm to make a significant gain in market share
	4) Total market share increased by 1.5%	
CONSUMERS	1) Image/Reputation as measured by a third party's surveys improved	Penetration of some customer segments not as great as forecast by the competitor
	2) More use in each customer (demographic) segment	Reputation as high-end yogurt being extended against all rivals
CHANNELS	1) Opening new channels	Outperforming most rivals in opening new channels
	2) Greater penetration of each channel	Penetration in some channels not as great as forecast by the competitor
	3) Image/Reputation improving among channels	
	4) Stronger relationships with channels apparent	Strong channel relationships and image only getting stronger
PRODUCTS	1) Has achieved broadest product range	Extending its lead in product range against all rivals
	2) Creating new products and customer needs	

However, it is never enough merely to delineate performance: it is always relative. It must, therefore, be assessed in relation to several criteria: the competitor's own past performance and current goals and expectations; other competitors' performance and goals; and the focal firm's own performance and goals. Each of these criteria generates distinct insights into a competitor's success or failure and its consequences.

Comparison with the Focal Firm

Very limited understanding of any competitor is possible in the absence of comparison to rivals.[21] It is in comparisons across current and potential competitors and to the focal firm that the descriptions of scope and posture emphasized in Chapter 5 become so useful.

Self-learning, as discussed in Chapter 2, is central to competitor learning. Perhaps nowhere is self-learning more closely linked to action and decision making than in the comparison of a competitor's marketplace strategy with the focal firm's. Such comparisons generate immediate insight into *how* and *why* the focal firm (or the competitor) is winning or losing in the marketplace.

Scope position and moves can be directly compared using product-customer charts (Figures 5.4 through 5.7). Among other things, such comparisons quickly reveal whether the two organizations are competing in the same competitive domains or are heading in the same product-customer direction.

Posture (including posture shifts) can be compared and contrasted along the relevant generic modes of competition such as functionality, service, or image and reputation. The output of this analysis is the identification of the customer-based advantages possessed by each organization along each mode of competition. The resultant analysis in the yogurt example is shown in Table 6.8. The entries in the column, Competitor's Advantage, indicate the advantage that the team conducting the analysis judged the competitor to hold over their own organization.

Insight into customer-based advantage stems from analysis at the level of individual modes of competition. Consider functionality in the case of the two yogurt competitors (see Table 6.8). Although no taste differences were discernible by customers in a number of "taste tests," the competitor was still judged by customers to have superior taste. Although the shelf life of both competitors' products was essentially similar, the trade believed that the competitor's products had a longer shelf life. Thus, a challenge confronted the focal firm: how to remedy the perceptual disadvantage it confronted with both users and the trade.

A comparison of goals reveals commonalities and differences in goal structures, with implications for current and potential marketplace rivalry.

TABLE 6.8 Assessing the Yogurt Competitor's Marketplace Strategy: Customer-Based Advantage Compared with the Focal Firm

Mode/ Dimension	Competitor	Focal Firm	Competitor's Advantage	Data/Data Source
Product line width	Broadest in the market	Narrow by comparison	Trade leverage	Trade behaviors and interviews
Content packaging	Varied Varied/New sizes	Higher Less variation	User appeal Logistic and trade volume	Surveys Analysis of trade
Taste	No actual difference	No actual difference	Alleged superiority	Trade tests Surveys
Shelf life	12–18 months	12–18 months	Perceived difference	Statements by trade
Delivery	Fast, < 3 days Responsive	About same	Slightly faster	Trade and industry press and interviews
Distribution channels	Broad and expanding	Narrower	Greater availability Cost efficiencies	Trade interviews Press analysis
Image	Premium, upscale	Local, "Good value"	Stronger brand identification	Surveys Trade
Sales force	Blanket coverage	Selectively used	More able to target and build sales	Trade competitor's statements
Trade relationship	Strong	Strong in own region	National leverage	Trade interviews
Price	Highest	Medium	Greater perceived value	Sales data Surveys

In the yogurt example, both firms were striving to gain market share. However, the larger, national firm (the competitor) was exhibiting an ambitious intent and vision that would necessarily create a zero-sum game: assuming a continuance of the low annual total market growth rate, it could only attain its market share goals by taking share away from other competitors. If it were to continue its recent success in gaining market share, the focal firm could not but come under increasing competitive pressure to retain its current market share.

Comparison across Competitors

Comparison across multiple competitors (comparative learning) is an extension of comparison to the focal firm. Greater value is derived from this analysis to the extent that competitors with distinctly different marketplace strategies are compared and contrasted.

The scope and moves of multiple competitors can also be depicted on one or more product-customer segment grids. These grids indicate in which product-customer segments competitors are horizontal and/or vertical rivals. They also indicate which competitors are tending toward niche, spread, proliferated and blanket scope positions.

Posture especially invites comparison to competitors. As noted in Chapter 5, a competitor's posture may vary greatly from one product-customer segment to another. Thus, it is often necessary to depict and compare competitors' postures across product-customer segments. In the yogurt example, a comparison of postures across different customer segments such as institutions, hotels, restaurants, and private cafeterias, revealed that some rivals used distinctly different pricing tactics across segments and that some rivals were endeavoring to build distinctly different relationships across these segments. As a consequence, the focal firm would have to tailor its posture to individual segments (or, more specifically, groups of customers within these broad customer segments).

Comparisons of goals across competitors reveal (among other things) whether rivalry is likely to become more intense and in which product-customer segments it will become so. In illuminating the "whys" behind competitors' current (and anticipated) scope moves and posture shifts, comparison of their goals often signals emerging clashes at one or more levels of the goal hierarchy discussed earlier. For example, two firms in the yogurt business were committing themselves at the level of strategic intent and vision to be "the most recognized brand name, market leader and most profitable yogurt firm." At the level of objectives and operating goals, it was even more evident (through their actions) that rivals were aiming to substantially increase their market share in the same product-customer segments.

Signals about the Emerging Marketplace

Competitors' marketplace strategies typically give rise to signals of emerging change in and around the marketplace—augmented learning. A competitor's scope, posture, and goals may signal emergent and potential change in product evolution, customer needs, customers' responses to different product offerings, distribution channels, the likely direction of competitive dynamics and rivalry, and what it will take to win in the emerging marketplace.

The necessary indicators often reside in how customers and channels are responding to the competitor's changes in scope and posture. One consumer food firm inferred the emergence of ethnic foods as a rapid growth market from consumer response to a competitor's new product introduction. In the yogurt example, based on the success of different competitors with different customer groups, the focal firm inferred that the yogurt market was tending toward separate customer segments with distinct needs and that this was the case for both channels and consumers. As a consequence, the focal firm would have to consider how it could employ different forms of differentiation across product-customer segments, something it had never previously done.

Signals of Future Marketplace Leadership

Assessment of marketplace leadership requires consideration of the competitive context within which rivals seek to outwit, outmaneuver, and outperform each other. The purpose is to assess whether a competitor's marketplace strategy is likely to generate and sustain leadership in one or more product-customer segments. Sometimes, assessment of a competitor's marketplace strategy indicates potential future leadership despite relatively poor performance results to date.

Three specific tests are required: conditions, vulnerabilities, and assumptions. The vulnerabilities and assumptions tests to some extent refine the conditions test.

The *conditions* test compels the analyst to ask whether the competitor's current marketplace strategy (and the projected strategy as indicated by scope moves, posture shifts, and goal direction) "fits" or can take advantage of the prevailing and anticipated marketplace conditions. Thus, the conditions test enforces consideration of how a competitor might be seeing the current and potential competitive environment differently than its rivals— and thus outwitting them.

Two questions typically need to be critically considered: (a) How will the strategy leverage or cause marketplace change such as change in customers' tastes, technology developments, change in related products? (b) How will the strategy generate and sustain customer-based advantage? Assessments developed in comparisons with the focal firm and across competitors as well as in signals about the emerging marketplace constitute important inputs to this analysis.

In the yogurt case, the competitor's strategy was geared to leveraging the propensity of a large segment of consumers to sufficiently value high-image products that they were willing to pay a price premium. It was also committed to enhancing its relationship with the trade, and in many instances, completely revamping its relationship with some channels.

The *assumptions* test compels the analyst to identify the assumptions about the marketplace underlying the competitor's strategy. It is then necessary to assess their validity by asking what current or anticipated environmental conditions support or refute these marketplace assumptions. In the case of the yogurt firm, two assumptions were identified as critical: (a) consumers would continue to pay a price premium for its brand, and (b) new customer segments could continue to be developed. Should either of these assumptions not prove true, the competitor's marketplace strategy would be in dire jeopardy.

The *vulnerabilities* test forces the analyst to identify those environmental conditions to which the strategy may be vulnerable. The assumptions test suggested some vulnerabilities. What are the consequences if consumers become more price conscious? What might competitors do to create a more favorable price-value relationship for themselves in customers' minds?

Consequences for the Competitor

Assessment in each of the preceding areas suggests consequences for the competitor. If assessment of marketplace performance or results reveals a performance gap, then the competitor may have to consider dramatic changes in its overall marketplace strategy. Even if the competitor's performance to date exceeds its goals and expectations, it is appropriate to consider what the competitor will have to do to sustain its strategy. A strategy that generates marketplace success can quickly lead to internal constraints and vulnerabilities such as product supply, access to raw materials and components, distribution capability, and service prowess.

Two overriding consequences for the yogurt competitor were evident. First, its stretch goals compared with those of competitors (and the presumption that it would continue to stretch its goals even further) implied that it would probably have to become increasingly entrepreneurial: it would have to develop new products, extend existing lines, attract new customer groups, and develop more means of successful differentiation. The competitor could not sit on its laurels, especially since many of its competitors including the focal firm, had not yet responded to its initiatives.

Second, its immediate market share goals suggested it would have to quickly lure new customers to its high-end image, high-priced product lines. It would thus have to significantly augment and continually monitor its marketing, distribution, and sales activities. Since its posture was intended to create and sustain comparatively high prices, it did not wish to resort to price reductions as a means of attracting and retaining customers.

Implications for the Focal Firm

The purpose of competitor learning is not just to develop knowledge about competitors and the current and emerging competitive environment, but to inform and aid the focal organization's own decision making. Thus, assessment in each of the preceding areas should generate intelligence—knowledge that is relevant to marketplace strategy and other decisions.

Knowledge As competitors' marketplace strategies are identified and assessed, changes required in the focal firm's stock of knowledge—its facts, perceptions, assumptions, beliefs, and projections—can be determined and assessed. Such change may include how competitors are competing or are likely to compete, customers' responses to competitors' postures, emerging conditions in the marketplace, and what it will take to win against specific rivals. Explication and consideration of such knowledge change often results in decision makers developing a more comprehensive and accurate understanding of their own organization's marketplace strategy: where the firm competes (scope), how it competes (posture), and what it strives to achieve (goals).

For the focal yogurt firm, some facts and perceptions about its own marketplace strategy did not stand the test of scrutiny: for example, that distribution channels saw its service as significantly superior to specific rivals and that its lower prices (compared with the national rivals') was the number one reason customers said they purchased its brand. Analysis of competitors also called into question a number of the firm's long-held assumptions. The competitor's manifest goal of taking market share from others was a distinct challenge to the firm's assumption that its larger rivals would not increase their sales aggressiveness in its local region in the near future. The firm's cherished belief that if it kept its prices significantly lower than its national rival's, it would gradually take market share away from them was also abandoned. Its explicit projections about future marketplace dynamics were now radically different than its prior depiction of how rivalry would unfold.

Marketplace Strategy Assessment of competitors' marketplace strategies often directly impacts immediate and long-term decisions about the focal firm's scope, posture, and goals. It sometimes gives rise to decisions that are new to the focal organization, that is, they arise explicitly as a consequence of the analysis of one or more competitors. More frequently, it changes the perspective on existing decisions. It may also lead to "issues," that is, substantive areas that require further analysis.

As a result of its assessment of its major competitors, the yogurt firm evaluated and challenged each of a set of strategy options it had previously identified. In particular, it appraised one option that had previously been favored by senior management: that it should aggressively enter contiguous geographic regions and launch a frontal assault on the entrenched competitors in these regions. Its newly acquired knowledge about the competitor discussed earlier, as well as other competitors and the emerging marketplace, led it to shy away from this option—in short, double-loop learning. In particular, the apparent absence of distinctive customer advantage compared with the competitor (see Table 6.8), led the executive team to estimate that the competitor (and probably some other competitors) could quite easily defend their position and make it a very unprofitable adventure.

With regard to winning in its current geographic regions, the yogurt firm began to consider whether and how it could augment its appeal to customers along each mode of competition and, as a consequence, raise prices to a level much closer to the dominant major competitors. It developed a set of plans to add value along each mode of competition. For example, it decided to emphasize its regional origins in its advertising and sales promotions. It also decided to build a stronger relationship with key retail accounts by having one or more managers visit each account to discuss how they could provide more service and sales support.

Microlevel Analysis Assessment of competitors' marketplace strategy, as noted, typically generates issues and questions for the focal firm's own microlevel analysis: its activity/value chain, alliances and networks, assumptions, assets, capabilities and competencies, technology, and organization.[22] Marketplace strategy implications such as those previously discussed give rise to specific microlevel component considerations. Some specific implications are briefly noted.

The need to add value for customers in its current geographic area raised inevitable issues for the yogurt firm's activity/value chain. For example, the provision of superior service to the trade generated specific issues for a number of activities: What extra burdens would be placed on the firm's sales force? Would the service function need to be reorganized? How could the firm's outbound logistics be better integrated with the inbound logistics of distributors and retailers? To add value for customers, how could the focal firm's activity/value chain be best managed?

If one or more of the large national competitors were to compete more aggressively in the firm's local market area, a serious question emerged as to whether the firm had sufficient marketing capability to win. Indeed, an issue that required considerable attention was what marketing capability the firm possessed: To what extent was it able to develop new opportunities or to build and extend image and reputation?

Errors in the Assessment of Marketplace Strategy

Since this is the first explication of assessment, the intent in this section is to note a series of errors that are applicable to the assessment of each framework component. Each error is discussed in greater detail in later chapters.

Learning as the generation and use of knowledge suggests that assessment of marketplace strategy must be a continual process: it cannot be postponed until all capturing, processing, and crafting have been fully completed. Thus, a cardinal error is not to execute preliminary assessments: to fail to identify implications of what is being learned during processing. Analysts therefore must continually cycle through the key learning questions noted in Chapter 2.[23]

Another fundamental error is to ignore or downplay (marketplace strategy) attribute change. The failure to identify and assess (in)coherence within and across scope, posture, and goals implies that analysts may not fully understand a competitor's marketplace strategy.[24] Unless changes in the modes of competition are related to each other and to changes in goals, analysts cannot fully understand the content and direction of the competitor's marketplace strategy. A failure to assess the entrepreneurial content of a competitor's marketplace strategy lessens analysts' ability to know how it differs from rivals.

Assessing a competitor's strategy results, as noted earlier in this chapter, always requires both parameters and criteria. An error that constrains learning is to adopt a narrow set of parameters and/or narrow criteria. Varying parameters and criteria lead to different insights.

Ignoring signals of emerging and potential marketplace change—augmented learning—severely shortchanges assessment. Such signals are often central to outwitting and outmaneuvering rivals. For example, by understanding the assumptions and vulnerabilities associated with the competitor's marketplace strategy, the focal yogurt firm is now able to identify key indicators to monitor that will alert it to emerging change in the marketplace.

Judgments about a competitor's marketplace strategy always depend on the referent point: hence the need for comparisons across multiple types of look-alike, as well as functional substitute, rivals. If only the dominant look-alike rivals are used as a point of reference in assessing a competitor's marketplace strategy (or the focal firm's), then significant learning, as discussed in the last section of this chapter, will also be missed.

In many organizations, competitor consequences receive little attention. Assessment does not address whether and how the competitor could sustain its current strategy, or which vulnerabilities and constraints it might confront if the strategy proved more successful than expected.

A critical assessment error evident in many organizations is the failure to systematically assess the focal firm's own marketplace strategy: for example, what customer-based advantage it possesses, what constitutes the basis of the advantage, and how distinctive it is compared with rivals. The failure to assess such advantage along each mode of competition (see Table 6.8) is one reason judgments by many organizations about their own customer-based advantage are often so wrong.

The central knowledge error is not to use assessment of competitors' marketplace strategies to reveal, challenge, and enhance the focal organization's stock of knowledge about such factors as end-customers, channels, marketplace dynamics, and what it takes to win in the marketplace. Without explicit attention to the need to identify and challenge prevailing stocks of knowledge, double-loop learning is jeopardized and single-loop learning is limited.

Finally, as analysts avoid each of the preceding errors, they glean greater insight into how (and why) the competitor is outwitting, outmaneuvering, and outperforming the focal firm and/or other rivals (and thus how the focal firm might better outwit, outmaneuver, and outperform its rivals).

A Final Note: Which Competitors' Marketplace Strategy Should Be Analyzed?

As noted, a common error is to analyze only, or predominantly, the marketplace strategies of the market leaders. However, given the ebb and flow of success in most end-customer and channel arenas, other types of competitors must receive attention. By analyzing one or more rivals in the following categories of competitors,[25] significant new increments of knowledge can be added, no matter how extensively the leading market share rivals are analyzed.

Unexplained Success (or Failure)   If decision makers and other analysts are at a loss to explain why a rival, or class of rivals, has begun to win (or lose), it is usually a candidate for analysis. This criterion also helps to screen which of the larger market share players may need to receive more dedicated attention. If they are small(er) market share players, often they are succeeding because they are doing something different from the large(r) rivals.

Small Share Rivals   Sometimes very small share rivals, often niche players as described in Chapter 5, provide distinctively different postures and goals compared with larger rivals. To the extent this is so, one or more of these rivals merit attention. Sometimes they provide insights into how to win that can be leveraged by larger players.

Recent Entrants   Recent entrants probably cannot win simply by emulating existing players. To the extent they appear to be pursuing a distinctive customer-based advantage, they become desirable candidates for marketplace strategy analysis.

Emerging Entrants An often neglected category is one or more emerging entrants: organizations that are about to enter the market. Searching for indicators of their likely marketplace strategy and analyzing how it might be similar to or different from that of the focal firm and other current rivals often generates extensive insights into potential marketplace dynamics, and thus why some rivals might win rather than others.

Substitute Product Rivals Current and emerging substitute rivals often receive systematic attention only after they have begun to win. Once they have been identified, it is almost always necessary to identify and assess their marketplace strategy as a means to determine and evaluate how the solutions they offer are attracting customers or will do so. In most instances, they provide a distinctly different referent point than any of the look-alike rivals noted earlier.

Invented Rivals An invented rival is one that does not now exist. Analysts create a competitor and then determine what type of marketplace strategy it might pursue. For example, analysts might imagine a competitor that would result from the entry of an organization in a related industry and then attribute to it a marketplace strategy that would reflect how it competes in its current industry.[26] Invented rivals can be used to challenge and assess both the focal organization's current strategy and possible strategy alternatives.

 ## Summary

Identification and assessment of the marketplace strategy of one or more competitors is essential to developing knowledge not just about competitors but about the broader competitive arenas and the focal firm. It serves as a critical means to challenge the firm's current strategy. Without such an external referent point, the understanding of executives and others about their own organization's marketplace strategy—what it is, the sources of its success, what customer-based advantage it generates, and whether it can be the basis of future success—may be filled with mythology.[27] Moreover, assessment of competitors' marketplace strategy is a prerequisite to analysis of their microlevel components—to which Chapters 7 through 15 are dedicated.

The Activity/ Value Chain

WINNING REQUIRES THAT AN ORGANIZATION NOT ONLY MUST OUTWIT, OUTMANEUVER, and outperform its current and future competitors in the marketplace but also in how it manages itself. How an organization structures, operates, and integrates all its major activities such as research, manufacturing, marketing, and sales, critically affects each marketplace strategy element—scope, posture, and goals.

Using the concept of the value chain, the purpose of this chapter is to delineate a framework of analysis that identifies and assesses any competitor's major work activities. It is a preliminary step in analyzing the inner workings of a competitor and how these work activities are connected to external entities such as suppliers, distribution channels, and end-customers. Understanding how a competitor manages its core work activities is central to identifying and assessing every other microlevel component: alliances and relationships, networks, assumptions, assets, capabilities and competencies, technology, and organization infrastructure and culture.

This chapter begins by delineating two distinct views of an activity or value chain (A/VC) that offer distinctly different but related ways to categorize and integrate a competitor's major activities. The body of the chapter addresses how to identify and assess a competitor's A/VC. It concludes by noting some common errors in A/VC analysis.

This chapter further details many of the tasks within the four core learning activities. Its integrating theme is the recursive nature of competitor analysis. It illustrates the role and importance of moving back and forth among the steps typically involved in identifying and assessing any A/VC. It highlights the interaction between capturing and processing, with particular emphasis on detecting indicators, identifying data sources, and collecting data. It also illustrates the importance of refining outputs: how provisional findings are continually shaped and critiqued.

Understanding Activity/Value Chains

While many tools and techniques have been developed to decompose and understand organizations, few offer the scope of analysis, richness of detail, and extensiveness of insight obtainable from A/VC analysis. It addresses not only core activities such as research, manufacturing, and sales, but how they are linked to the factor, channel, and end-customer arenas. The discipline involved in applying A/VC analysis to competitors results in a thorough depiction of what activities they engage in and how they manage them.

What an Activity/Value Chain Is

Some organizations have found it difficult to apply A/VC analysis to competitors. This is in part due to an incomplete or misguided understanding of what an activity/value chain is, and how activities and the subelements or tasks within them, should be defined and related. It is necessary to begin, therefore, by delineating what we mean by an activity/value chain.

To provide products or solutions to customers, any organization must engage in activities such as designing the product, producing it, and delivering it. Activities refer to the core or central chunks of the work performed by the organization.[1] The classic value chain depicts a sequence of activities that must be performed by an organization to transform inputs (such as raw materials, components, and supplies) into a product delivered to customers. Thus, typical activities include inbound logistics (acquiring and transporting raw materials, components, and supplies), manufacturing or operations (transforming the inputs into a product or solution), outbound logistics or physical distribution (getting the product out to customers), marketing (learning about customers' needs and making them aware of the product and its virtues), sales, and service.[2]

Two types of value chain are useful in analyzing competitors. The conventional or classic value chain connects upstream suppliers to the downstream channels and end-customers (see Figure 7.1). It is the A/VC framework of analysis[3] most commonly applied in organizations. It incorporates each activity—and the linkages among them—involved in transforming inputs into the organization's products. It is an inside-out perspective: the emphasis is on the organization itself and its connections to suppliers and customers. It is most applicable to organizations that produce a tangible

FIGURE 7.1
The Conventional Value Chain: A Sequence of Activities

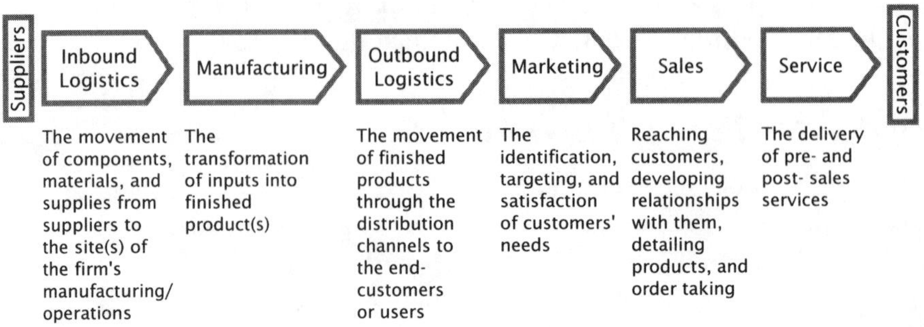

Suppliers	Inbound Logistics	Manufacturing	Outbound Logistics	Marketing	Sales	Service	Customers
	The movement of components, materials, and supplies from suppliers to the site(s) of the firm's manufacturing/ operations	The transformation of inputs into finished product(s)	The movement of finished products through the distribution channels to the end-customers or users	The identification, targeting, and satisfaction of customers' needs	Reaching customers, developing relationships with them, detailing products, and order taking	The delivery of pre- and post- sales services	

product although it is also applicable to organizations providing a service or nontangible solution.

However, an A/VC can be approached from a different perspective—that of customers. A customer-focused activity chain emphasizes the activities an organization engages in to learn about customers' needs, and to work with customers in the design, development, testing, delivery, installation, and maintenance of solutions (see Figure 7.2). It is especially applicable to organizations that provide services (or intangible products) to their customers and that must work closely with them in solution design and delivery such as software, systems integration, insurance, banking, publishing, and advertising providers.

These two A/VCs are complementary. In many instances, it is appropriate to use both. They provide distinct but related learning. The conventional value chain facilitates an overview of what a competitor does, from accessing suppliers through manufacturing the product to servicing customers. The customer-focused activity chain, on the other hand, begins with identification of customer needs and requirements, and development of the product or solution concept. It then identifies and details all activities involving direct and indirect interaction with customers. The customer-focused activity chain is becoming more important as organizations partner more with customers in solution design and delivery, and move to more intricate forms of customization.

The Relevant Unit of Analysis

A business unit or division rather than the broader corporation is clearly a more appropriate organizational unit for A/VC analysis. Given that General Electric is in a dozen or more fundamentally distinct businesses such as financial services, aircraft engines, plastics, lighting, and medical systems, it makes no sense to refer to General Electric's (corporate) value chain.

FIGURE 7.2
Customer-Focused Activity Chain: A Sequence of Activities

Identify customer needs/ requirements	Develop product/ solutions concept	Develop/ produce prototype/ working model	Product/ solutions testing
How the competitor goes about under- standing customers' current and evolving needs	How the competitor fleshes out initial configu- rations of the potential products/solutions	How the competitor creates one or more working proto- types or models	What the competitor does to test the product/solution before it is developed/ assembled/ installed/sold

Produce/ assemble batch/mass	Sales	Delivery/ installations	Service
How the competitor produces/ assembles products/ solutions on and off customers' sites/locations	What the competitor does to "sell" its products/ solutions to existing and potential customers	How the competitor installs/delivers the product/ solution to customers and/or sites-locations	How the competitor provides different forms of service to customers

However, the mistaken impression has been created within some organiza-tions that a business unit or product group possesses only one A/VC. Any single business may possess a number of A/VCs: the activities and especially the tasks within activities may vary greatly from one product (group) to an-other. Different products may require different raw materials, use different forms of logistics, employ different modes of manufacturing, use different physical distribution systems, and require different types of sales and ser-vice functions. Because of the discretion available to organizations in de-signing and executing customer-focused activity chains, even for two related solutions, a competitor may manifest two quite different activity chains.

Importance of the Activity/Value Chain

Any organization's raison d'être, embodied in its marketplace strategy, is to provide superior value to its customers (compared with current and prospective rivals). As demonstrated later in this chapter, any A/VC reveals how a competitor goes about generating and sustaining customer value.

Thus, it allows analysts to directly connect the "insides" of a competitor to the content of its marketplace strategy.

However, the A/VC encompasses more than what goes on inside the competitor. As noted, it also reveals critical linkages to external entities such as end-customers, distribution channels, suppliers, logistics providers, technology sources, and those entities with which the competitor has an alliance or other form of relationship.

Distinguishing between Activities and Tasks

Much of the difficulty encountered by many organizations in applying the value chain concept to both their own organization and competitors stems from a lack of appreciation of the distinction between *activities* and the subelements or *tasks* that constitute activities. It is for this reason that considerable attention is devoted later in this chapter to the issues involved in identifying and specifying activities and their constituent tasks.

Part of the difficulty in distinguishing between activities and tasks is that a priori depictions of A/VCs, such as those shown in Figures 7.1 and 7.2, must be adapted to the business that each competitor is in. For example, for many competitors in the computer, pharmaceutical, and chemical industries, a strong argument can be made that research should be added to the conventional value chain (see Figure 7.1).

Irrespective of how activities are defined, each must be broken down into constituent tasks, as shown in Figures 7.3 and 7.4. Judgments are always involved in demarcating tasks and in relating tasks to each other within an

FIGURE 7.3
The Conventional Value Chain: Generic Activities and Sample Tasks

Inbound Logistics	Operations	Outbound Logistics	Marketing	Sales	Service
Purchasing	Engineering	Order processing	Product development	Order processing	Presales support
Shipping	Machining	Packing	Brand development	Selling	Postsales support
Inspection	Assembling	Shipping		Point-of-sale promotion	
Warehousing	fabrication	Inspection	Promotion		On-site service
Material handling	Quality control	Warehousing	Advertising		Off-site service
	Maintenance		Pricing		
JIT delivery					
	Facilities operations				

FIGURE 7.4
Customer-Focused Activity Chain: Sample Activities and Tasks

Identify customer needs/ requirements	Develop product/ solutions concept	Develop/ produce prototype/ working model	Product/ solutions testing
Meet with customers	Develop alternative concepts	Develop one or more prototypes	Present to customer
Study customer's operations	Test concepts with customers	Test prototype designs	Deploy in customer's facility
Specify broad product/solution requirements	Test concepts with experts	Establish performance	Monitor initial operations
	Define potential		

Produce/ assemble batch/mass	Sales	Delivery/ installations	Service
Produce final product	Call on customers	Process order	Hot line
Develop operations for multiple production/ delivery	Detail product	Ship product	Phone customer
	Demonstrate product	Customer setup	Customer site visits
Resolve operations issues	Document customer responses/ requirements	Installation	
		Trial run	

activity. Part of the difficulty in rendering these judgments is that organizations possess considerable discretion as to how they configure the tasks within any activity. For example, direct competitors often segment marketing into quite distinct tasks. It is also sometimes relatively easy to change the configuration of tasks within an activity.

Attributes of an Activity/Value Chain

Although many attributes could be considered in the case of any A/VC, for the purpose of understanding a competitor, four are particularly insightful: extraconnectedness, intraconnectedness, uniqueness, and value adding.

Extraconnectedness An A/VC may be poorly or well connected to or integrated into external entities such as suppliers, channels, or end-customers. Such integration occurs in many ways: through the use of information technology, logistics management, procurement practices, and the exchange of personnel.[4] Sometimes, customer-focused activity chains are so intimately integrated into the activities of customers that it becomes difficult to distinguish the competitor from its customers.[5]

Intraconnectedness Two types of internal connectedness must be considered: across tasks within an activity and across activities. Activities are interconnected to the extent that two or more activities are integrated in such a way that greater value is created and/or greater cost efficiencies are affected. Activities become disconnected in many ways: activities are given or assume conflicting goals; the organizational units responsible for implementing activities or specific tasks are poorly coordinated; personnel across units do not see eye to eye. To the extent that disconnects occur within or across activities, customer value is likely to be deprecated and costs are likely to increase.

Uniqueness If all competitors created the same types of external and internal connections across their A/VCs, they would likely provide the same types and levels of customer value.[6] By developing different links to suppliers and customers, and by configuring intraconnectedness, an organization is more likely to create and sustain distinctive value for customers. Dell Computer eliminated third-part distributors and began selling directly to corporations and consumers. Compared with traditional steel mills, the minimills reconfigured every significant activity and the connections among them. In doing so, they provided customer value that the traditional manufacturers simply could not match.

Value Adding An A/VC affects value in three ways. How the A/VC is managed results in adding or deprecating value to channels and end-customers, to "customers" inside the organization, and to increasing or lowering the organization's cost structure. Generating value for channels and end-customers is the direct link to marketplace strategy and the ultimate purpose for engaging in the activities represented in any A/VC. Each activity influences the value-creating capabilities of others. If the deliveries provided by inbound logistics are not coordinated with manufacturing schedules and requirements, manufacturing is severely handicapped in its ability to produce products or solutions desired and valued by channels and customers. How well (or badly) design, coordination, and integration within and across activities is affected directly lowers (or increases) costs.

Indicators of Change in Activity/Value Chains

Both direct and indirect indicators are critical to identifying and monitoring competitors' A/VCs. As the examples in this chapter illustrate, direct indicators are associated with each task within each activity. However, indirect indicators sometimes assume importance. For example, in developing "first-cut A/VCs," indirect indicators often generate alerting signals of the existence of particular activities and the tasks within them. These alerting indicators assume added significance when analysts have little a priori sense as to what activities will emerge.

Change in Activity/Value Chains as Signals

Change in the configuration and integration of activities often leads to strong signals of change in marketplace strategy. Changes in activities such as research, manufacturing, and distribution frequently lead to change in offerings to customers, in the range of customers pursued, in specific modes of competition, and in goals pertaining to market share, desired image, and channel coverage. Of particular importance is the role of A/VC change as an *indirect* signal of marketplace strategy change. Changes in the tasks involved in manufacturing are often a strong indicator of a competitor's commitment to upgrading a product's features and functionality. A reconfiguration of logistics often leads to more rapid delivery and lower prices.

A/VC change also provides strong, and often early, signals of change in many microlevel components. This is especially so in the case of capabilities and competencies, and technology.[7]

Identifying the Competitor's Activity/Value Chains

The identification and assessment of competitors' A/VCs is a step-by-step process. A/VCs typically evolve from rough first-cuts[8] to detailed depictions of multiple activities showing the complex interrelationships among the tasks within and across the activities. Irrespective of the level of detail sought, a number of steps characterize the *guided* identification of A/VCs (see Figure 7.5). For purposes of illustration, a computer competitor is used in the case of the conventional value chain, and an integrated systems provider in the case of the customer-focused activity chain.

Impetus for and Purpose of the Analysis

The impetus[9] for A/VC analysis stems from a diverse array of circumstances. Decision makers may not know why a particular competitor is winning. Sometimes decision makers do not know how a competitor is able to do certain things, such as provide products or solutions at a specific cost. Sometimes, it is a competitor's use of technology that triggers an interest in

FIGURE 7.5
Identifying a Competitor's Activity/Value Chain

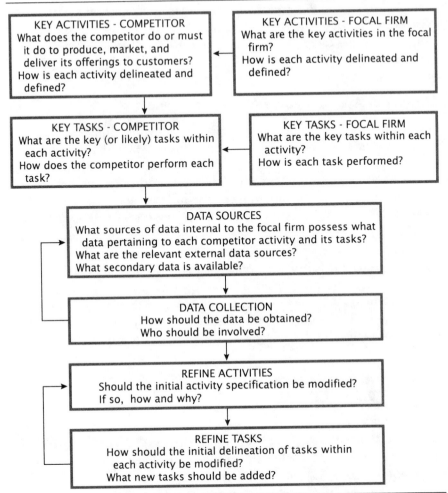

learning how a competitor is organizing and managing itself.[10] Decision makers sometimes want to determine how a new entrant is likely to compete in the marketplace or how a competitor might respond to its actions.[11] Other times, decision makers want to benchmark their organization against the "best-in-class"[12] in their competitive domain.[13]

In the two cases discussed in this chapter, the impetus for the analysis was clear and significant. In the computer case, some senior managers wanted an explanation as to why the competitor was outperforming the focal organization in developing and sustaining differentiation along nearly every mode of competition. In the systems integration case, decision makers wanted an answer to a specific question: Why was the competitor able to design and deliver a completely integrated solution much more quickly than the focal firm?

Whatever the impetus and purpose, it is imperative that before analysts embark on an A/VC analysis, they articulate what might be learned and how the learning might be used in decision making.[14] Doing so motivates the need to do the analysis, guides the types of issues and questions that are explored, and focuses analysts' attention on the implications of the analysis. By learning how the competitor designed and managed its key activities to always outperform rivals in adding value for customers, the computer firm might be able to reconfigure its own activities to close the gap in the short run, and learn how to leapfrog the competitor in the long run. By learning how its competitor was able to design, deliver, and install an integrated system so quickly, the integrated systems firm hoped to reconfigure "what it needed to do and how it needed to do so" to shorten the time gap between itself and the competitor while adding more value to customers (in greater functionality, better service, and superior working relationships).

The level of complexity and detail required in delineating an A/VC is a function of the purpose of the analysis. Since few issues are so fundamental to understanding a competitor as delineating its key activities, even a rough first-cut depiction is often sufficient to identify and develop a preliminary understanding of key linkages across activities and key linkages to suppliers, and channels and end-customers. On the other hand, a thorough understanding of a competitor's cost structure or how a competitor brings products to the market so quickly necessitates a considerably more refined and detailed A/VC analysis.

Identifying Provisional Activities

Identifying activities (and the tasks within them) is driven by a central guiding question: What does the competitor do, or must it do, to create, produce, market, deliver, and enhance its offerings to customers? Reflecting the ambiguity of the concept of activity discussed earlier, as well as the variation in activities across organizations, analysts typically find it necessary to (re)define activities and tasks a number of times as they select, order, and interpret data.

Analysts with only a modest familiarity of a competitor are normally able to identify broad-brush activities that a competitor engages in, or must engage in, to provide offerings for customers. Analysts take the activities identified in Figures 7.1 and 7.2 as one point of departure. In the computer case, analysts were quickly able to determine that the competitor engaged in each of the activities in the conventional value chain—inbound logistics, manufacturing, outbound logistics, marketing, sales, and service and support.

However, terms such as inbound logistics and marketing contain little meaning until they are specifically described and delineated in the context of a particular competitor. Thus, given their knowledge of the competitor (and of the business more broadly), analysts must ask: How should each of these activities be circumscribed and defined? In the case of the computer competitor, how does inbound logistics connect suppliers to the competitor's manufacturing locations? Is marketing really separate from sales and service? Should service be designated as a separate activity? These types of questions cause analysts to carefully consider how each activity should be demarcated and delineated. Analysts in the computer case chose the term "supplier logistics" instead of inbound logistics because they wanted to emphasize the importance of connections to suppliers.

In the integrated systems provider case, analysts were quickly able to identify a *tentative* series of activities that the competitor engaged in or must engage in. The team traced what the competitor would have to do from initial contact with a customer, through design and development of the integrated system, to installation and postinstallation actions. The team could do so largely for two reasons. Their familiarity with the integrated systems business allowed them to quickly identify activities (and tasks) that would almost certainly have to be completed by any firm in the business. They were able to modify these activities because of their knowledge of the competitor built up over a number of years of competing intensively against it for the accounts of many different types of customers.

In many instances, as indicated in Figure 7.5, analysis of the focal firm is helpful in *suggesting* key activities that a competitor might engage in. It is especially useful to do so if analysts are not familiar with the A/VC concept or if they have not previously conducted an A/VC analysis. At a minimum, it sharpens their understanding of individual activities, and in particular, the tasks within activities. Identifying the focal firm's own A/VC encourages analysts to ask whether the competitor engages in the same activities, and if so, what the relevant indicators might be. As a consequence, analysts are better able to determine what types of data should be collected and what might be specific data sources.

Particular emphasis needs to be placed on asking what the competitor must do, or probably needs to do, to facilitate its marketplace strategy. Sometimes analysis of change in key dimensions of marketplace scope, posture, and goals indicates to analysts a need to include or redefine specific activities.[15] In the computer case, the competitor's introduction of a stream of new products and its continued enhancement of functionality led the analysts to adopt a broad conception of manufacturing: it should not be viewed as merely the assembly and integration of components.

Identifying Provisional Tasks within Activities

Identification of the tasks within each provisional activity requires a much greater degree of familiarity with the competitor. For long-established competitors, it is sometimes surprisingly easy to identify a first-cut depiction of tasks. Individuals within the focal organization often possess considerable insight into what competitors do. For example, members of the purchasing function frequently are able to detail how a competitor procures components, from which suppliers they are obtained, what the relevant prices are, and how they are transported to specific manufacturing sites. Knowledge of one's own organization typically generates a useful listing of tasks that the competitor might engage in. At a minimum, it compels analysts to ask whether the competitor performs the activity in the same way. Also, the execution of some tasks are directly observable such as marketing, sales, and service programs and through visits to manufacturing and distribution sites.

The tasks eventually identified in the computer and systems integration cases are shown in Tables 7.1 and 7.2, respectively.

However, two distinct paths were involved in identifying these tasks.

In the computer case, the analysis team identified a preliminary list of tasks within each activity. Each member of the team worked with individuals associated with each activity *within the focal firm* to determine what the preliminary listing of tasks should be. For example, one team member worked with individuals in the purchasing department to identify the key tasks in supplier logistics, and which tasks the competitor employed, and how it did so.

In the systems integration case, the analysis team identified a preliminary listing of tasks based on their knowledge of the business and the competitor.

TABLE 7.1 Computer Manufacturer's Value Chain: Activities and Key Tasks

Supplier Logistics	Manufacturing	Distribution	Marketing	Sales	Service and Support
Procurement of components	Internal plant operations	Order processing	Developing the product concept	Order development	On-site service
Shipping systems	Component fabrication and assembly	Packing	Extending and enhancing the brand	Developing channel relationships	Post-sales support
Just-in-time delivery	System integration	Shipping Installation	Pricing	Customer research	Consulting services
Quality control and enhancement	System testing		Advertising		Service engineers
			Promotion		
			Customer education		

TABLE 7.2　Customer-Focused Activity Chain: Activities, Functions, and Indicators

	ACTIVITIES		
Initial Client Contact	*Identify Customer Needs/Requirements*	*Develop Solution Concept*	*Test and Accept Proposed Solution*
TASKS:			
Initial cold calls on prospective customers	Study customer's operations	Develop alternative solution configuration	Develop one or more solutions (prototypes)
Presentation of potential solution content and benefits	Document customer's needs	Test alternatives with groups in customer's organization	Assess solution design
Document customer responses/issues/ questions	Document broad potential solution concept	Test alternatives with experts	Modify/accept solution
		Delineate potential solution	Establish performance standards
INDICATORS:			
Number of calls	Steps in analyzing customer's operations	Number of solutions developed	Number of proposed solutions
Types of organizations	Individuals involved	Types of solutions discussed	Steps in assessing solution design
Executives spoken with	Types of needs identified	Teams involved	Who is involved in the assessment
Whether presentation was made	Existence of a customer's needs document	Individuals involved	Criteria used for solution acceptance
Elements in its content	Description provided by customer personnel	External experts	Types of performance standards
Number of issues, etc.		Comments by customer personnel	
Types of issues		Elements of the solutions	
Types of post-meeting follow-up to issues		Meetings held between senior customer personnel and competitor personnel	

They then interviewed key individuals within the focal firm as a means of developing a refined preliminary listing of tasks. It was this listing that served as the focus of the first interviews with customers—the primary source of data.

Even in the early stages of identifying provisional activities and tasks, analysts should anticipate and detect *alerting signals* of internal and external connectedness. In the integrated systems case, interviews with colleagues alerted analysts to the success the competitor had attained in coordinating all activities: it appeared to be able to deliver an integrated system faster

	ACTIVITIES		
Prepare for Installation	*Installation*	*Installation Monitoring*	*Post-Installation Service*
TASKS:			
Procurement of components	Rollout of installation plan	Monitoring system evolution	Extending system design
Off-site organization preparation	Sequence of installation steps	Managing organizational issues	Adding specific technical capabilities
On-site training and development	Learning during installation	Correcting system problems (within the design)	Managing organizational problems
Development of installation schedule and procedures		Refining system design	
INDICATORS:			
Types of components procured	When formal installation was begun	Who does the monitoring	Changes made to system design
Supplier(s) of each type	Key actions taken to initiate rollout	Issues that arise	Meetings to discuss possible changes
Mode of delivery	Organization initiatives to facilitate rollout	Actions taken	Technical changes
Locations of off-sites		Corrections made to the system	Organizational issues
Customer's member participation	Key steps in installation plan	Refinements to the overall design	Organizational changes
Decisions taken	Sequencing of steps		
Types of training	Involvement of key customer members in each step		
Groups to be trained			
Goals of training			
Individual items in the schedule	Individuals assigned to monitor installation		
Sequencing of items			
Who approved the schedule			

than any of its rivals, including the focal firm. Analysts then identify what data they should collect to determine how the competitor builds connections across activities, and to customers and suppliers.

Indicators and Data Sources

Identification of indicators and data sources exemplifies how closely processing (ordering, selecting, and interpreting data) is intertwined with capturing (determining data needs, identifying data sources, and collecting data). As activities and tasks are identified, analysts detect relevant indicators. As indicators are, in turn, generated from many different sources, and as data is gathered along indicators, activities and tasks are redefined.

Indicators for each preliminary activity in the integrated systems example are noted in Table 7.2. These indicators emanated from a number of related data sources. First, as analysts identified each provisional activity, they *asked themselves* what tasks are associated with it. For example, initiating client contact might involve a number of tasks: initial cold calls, dissemination of promotional material, initial client presentation, documenting customer context, and assessing likelihood of the customer committing to working with the firm.

They then asked what indicators could be used to verify whether and how the competitor executed each task, and also to monitor change in the task over time. For example, indicators associated with initial cold calls might include individuals making the calls, types of organizations called on, number of calls, executives spoken with, and customers' accounts of the calls.

Second, analysts *asked their colleagues* to describe how the focal firm executed each activity and its constituent tasks. These descriptions allowed the analysts to refine some indicators and to add others that had not occurred to them.

Third, analysts also asked their colleagues to describe what they knew about the competitor. These descriptions also alerted them to relevant indicators.

These steps suggest the merit of extensively using *internal* data sources before interacting with external primary sources.[16] As demonstrated earlier, in the case of the integrated systems provider, internal sources help tentatively identify activities and key tasks, provide a preliminary understanding of them, and suggest what indicators are relevant. Internal personnel also identify possible external primary and secondary data sources.

Many internal primary data sources contribute to identifying activities and tasks. Key internal sources and examples of the data they provided in the computer example are shown in Table 7.3. Procurement personnel provided extensive data on suppliers and the logistics function. Manufacturing personnel were able to provide significant data on facets of the competitor's manufacturing processes, the types of technologies involved in its production, and how it integrated both inbound and outbound logistics into its manufacturing tasks.

It is also necessary to identify external sources pertaining to each activity. Often, external sources specific to an individual activity quickly generate critical data. In the computer case, a consultant specializing in logistics was extremely helpful in depicting how the competitor was changing key logistics tasks.

TABLE 7.3 Internal Data Sources and Types of Data Provided

Data Source	Date Types
Procurement personnel	Names of competitors' suppliers
	Their locations, products, and prices
	Nature of relationships with specific customers
Logistics personnel	Types of logistics used by individual competitors
	Names of competitors' logistics providers
	Services provided
	Costs associated with types of services
	Cost and customer value advantages/disadvantages associated with use of specific types of logistics providers/services
Manufacturing personnel	Location of competitors' manufacturing operations
	Steps/stages in manufacturing processes
	Types of technologies used
	Cost estimates
	Constraints/vulnerabilities associated with types of manufacturing operations
Research and development personnel	Overview of competitors' R&D thrusts
	Types of research programs
	Individual projects
	Stages/steps in the way individual competitors do R&D
	Alliances and relationships involved in specific research programs/projects
Marketing personnel	Details of competitors' marketing programs
	Specific tasks that individual competitors do
	Involvement of other third parties in each task such as channels and customers
	Customer responses to individual marketing programs/initiatives
Sales/Service personnel	Descriptions of competitors' sales organizations
	Specific programs/actions taken by sales force
	Types of service provided to different types of customers
Line management	Descriptions of competitors' actions in the marketplace
	Relationships with suppliers, channels, and end-customers

In the customer-focused activity chain, customers are the critical external data source. A small set of customers, often no more than four or five, is sufficient to specify in considerable detail a competitor's activity chain.[17]

It is sometimes necessary and useful to engage third parties such as consultants or specialist data-gathering organizations as *collectors* of data. If an organization wants to get the analysis executed as quickly as possible, using third parties can expedite data collection. Third parties are especially useful when an organization wants to conceal from its rivals that it is conducting A/VC analysis. Also third parties enhance data quality: external data sources such as customers sometimes feel more inclined to speak openly with a consultant or other third party.

It should be evident from the preceding that the recursive interplay between indicators and data sources augments the efficiency of guided A/VC analysis. Indicators and associated data sources relevant to each activity and key tasks should be identified before any systematic or extensive data gathering occurs. In this way, data search is guided and analysts' time is not expended in blind data searches. Second, internal data sources serve as a guide to appropriate external sources including customers. Third, as data is gathered, indicators are detected, and these in turn, suggest further data needs.

Refine Activities and Tasks

As data is processed, analysts (re)define individual activities and (re)construct the tasks within each activity. As an aid to (re)defining and circumscribing individual activities (and tasks), analysts ask the following types of questions:

- How important is the activity to understanding what the competitor does?
- How does the activity contribute to developing value for customers?
- Are the tasks within the activity connected to each other?
- Are the tasks operationally separate from the tasks in other activities?
- Are there different ways in which the tasks can be designed, managed, and executed?
- To what extent does each activity require assets—personnel, capital, physical assets, and managerial time?

Consideration of these types of questions challenges each delineation and demarcation of activities and tasks. The intent is to spur analysts to generate a full and complete understanding of the competitor. In the systems integrator case, analysts struggled to delineate the activity and associated tasks involved in developing and testing the solution concept. Eventually they decided that it consisted of two activities: developing the solution concept, and testing and accepting the proposed solution. Each activity was critical to the value delivered to customers; each entailed a set of separate but related tasks; each could be managed in different ways; and each required specific assets and managerial expertise.

As an A/VC is refined, it is useful to test it among internal colleagues. They may raise issues and questions that challenge activity definition, the allocation of tasks across activities, and the inferences that are drawn. These in turn lead to further data collection and A/VC refinement.

Indeed, it is typically useful to develop two or more depictions of activities and tasks. These separate A/VCs lead to issues, questions, and insights that are missed if only one A/VC is developed. For example, in the integrated systems example, it would have been possible in the early stages of data collection to develop two or more tentative customer-focused activity chains. One chain might have emphasized the learning that occurred within the competitor: what knowledge the competitor was trying to develop; how it was doing so; and, how it was being put to use within each activity. The other chain might have emphasized the completion of tasks; what is largely illustrated in Table 7.2.

In defining and discussing what constitutes activities, analysts truly learn not just about the competitor but also about their own organization and the broader business.[18] Distinct shifts occur in analysts' knowledge, even if they are not always fully aware of these shifts. For example, in distinguishing between the two activities—develop solution concept, and test and accept proposed solution—analysts could not help but develop an enhanced understanding of what was required to generate a solution that customers would value. Who did what to win in bidding situations was no longer a "black box" to any individual involved in analyzing what was entailed in these activities, how they were connected to each other, and how they provided value to customers.

Open-Ended Inquiry

An open-ended orientation spurs analysts to question and redefine the definition and content of individual activities, the tasks within them, and connections across activities and tasks. This becomes especially important when competitors with distinct A/VCs are analyzed. It serves as an antidote to imposing one's own A/VC on competitors.

Errors in Identifying Activity/Value Chains

When analysts fail to appreciate the role and importance of the recursive nature of competitor learning, each of the following errors is more likely to occur. These errors are emphasized here in part because they are relevant to the analysis of each microlevel component.

One debilitating error is the pursuit of the perfectly detailed A/VC *before* analysts ask what they are learning and how the new knowledge might be used in decision making. Refinement of A/VCs can be taken too far. Even first-cut A/VCs, as demonstrated, lead to tentative inferences and implications that generate new insights for decision makers. Such preliminary assessments aid in determining how much further A/VC analysis should be taken.

At the other end of the spectrum, however, is another common error: analysts cease development of the A/VC as soon as they generate an initial first-cut. Without asking what could be learned by further A/VC delineation, analysts forgo the opportunity to extend their learning. These analysts do not pose the central learning questions noted in Chapter 2.[19]

Another error that curtails both the efficiency and effectiveness of A/VC analysis is not to develop an initial first-cut A/VC based on analysts' own knowledge of the competitor and/or that of other internal colleagues. Analysts rush to gather data from external primary and secondary sources but without knowing what data they should seek, which sources might provide what types of data, how that data could be used to delineate the A/VC, or how the data could be used to confirm or refute analysts' own a priori judgments. Thus, among other things, analysts lose an opportunity to test and refine their own knowledge—a facet of recursive learning that is emphasized in many later chapters.

In developing and refining first-cut A/VCs, analysts must be attentive to avoiding another common tendency: imposing the A/VC of their own organization on competitors. This error is more likely when analysts collect minimal data from external sources. It also limits the potential self-learning that accrues.[20]

A frequent error is to follow too slavishly particular depictions of the value chain. These may be the work of well-known strategy authors, the preferred value chain configuration of particular consulting firms, or the value chain model advocated by one or more managers within the organization. Whatever the source of the information, analysts need always to delineate activities and tasks that represent the situation of a particular competitor rather than to configure the data to fit a preordained A/VC model. Otherwise the potential value added of analysis is severely circumscribed.

A related error is a tendency to impose one model of an A/VC, irrespective of its source, on all competitors. Analysts seek indicators that confirm a prior model of an A/VC rather than creating A/VCs that are specific to each competitor. Among other consequences, the opportunity for extensive comparative learning is lost.

Assessing the Competitor's Activity/Value Chain

Assessing competitors' A/VCs compels analysts to take an integrated and comprehensive view of how competitors manage themselves. Delineating the attributes of, and current change in an A/VC, sets the stage for comparing and contrasting A/VCs across competitors and with the focal organization. In discussing each step (see Figure 7.6) in assessment, particular emphasis is placed on identifying implications for the focal firm.

Attributes of the Activity/Value Chain

Assessment of an A/VC's attributes generates initial insights into why and how value is generated and for whom. Generation of these insights exemplifies the role of judgments in processing,[21] the importance and role of indicators, and the need to discern and assess patterns that go beyond individual data points.

In the integrated systems provider example, the competitor was intimately *connected to its customers.* Each activity was integrated into the workings of the customer through the interrelationships and interactions of personnel from both organizations. The partnering relationship was embodied in codevelopment of the design and execution of each activity such as how the customer's need was established and elaborated and how the solution concept was developed.

The competitor was also tightly *connected to its suppliers.* In some instances, suppliers were present in deliberations with customers. The competitor developed parts of the solution concept in conjunction with individual suppliers. Customers reported that suppliers provided the competitor with different options to present to them.

The activity chain also was highly *connected internally.* For each customer, the competitor assigned a team to oversee the execution of each activity and coordination across activities. Thus, information about the customer flowed freely across the activities. In part because of the intimacy of its connection to the customer, the competitor was also able to move quickly and freely back and forth across the activities. For example, the competitor in agreement with the customer, could move backward from prototype development to (further) identification and consideration of the customer's needs. Moreover, internal connectedness of the activities allowed more and more parallel development and execution of activities.

Internal and external connectedness, as outlined, were themselves interconnected. The oversight team that served as the linchpin of internal integration and coordination also drove and guided involvement with customers.

Compared with four major look-alike rivals (including the focal firm), the competitor's activity chain appeared to be *unique* in at least two ways.[22] Linkages to customers and suppliers were interwoven in almost every activity through the use of the oversight team. Second, the competitor seemed to have a greater ability to move back and forth through the activities than any other rival.

FIGURE 7.6
Assessing a Competitor's Activity/Value Chain (A/VC)

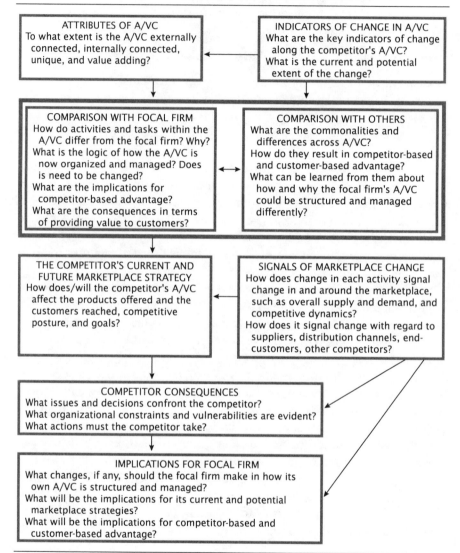

The activity chain *added value* to customers in multiple ways. First, the intimacy attained through the external connections previously discussed led to strong perceptions[23] by customers of involvement, commitment, and contribution on the part of the competitor. Second, the tight-working relationship with customers led to system designs that were typically appropriate to their business operations. Third, the competitor appeared to be continually reducing the time required to design, deliver, and install a fully functioning system, thus increasing the price-value relationship for customers.

Indicators of Change in the Activity/Value Chain

Capturing (and projecting) key changes along the A/VC is not only a critical input to the remaining steps in assessment, it also draws analysts' attention to what the competitor may consider most important to winning. Change is sought both within and across activities. The major changes detected have significant implications for the focal firm, in part, because they frequently reflect how the competitor has outwitted and outmaneuvered rivals. They also indicate areas in which the competitor believes it must outperform rivals.

In the integrated systems case, three key changes were detected. First, the competitor was endeavoring to further integrate all activities to the extent it could execute activities in parallel rather than in sequence. The intent was to continually shorten the development and delivery time cycle, and hence, to develop superior value for customers. Two indicators were key to this inference: the managing team appeared to be spending more time with customers, and customers were reporting that the competitor was emphasizing doing things in parallel rather than serially. If the competitor succeeded in doing so, it would further raise the bar for the focal firm: it would have to enhance its own development and delivery time even more than originally anticipated.

Second, based on customers' comments, the competitor was spending more time developing and testing the solution concept with customers. The intent was to limit later problems in solution design, installation, and service—each of which added to the development and delivery cycle time. If the competitor could "get it right the first time," then the focal firm would be confronting an ever-improving competitor.

Third, the competitor was increasingly using its service activity to learn about customers' needs and how to fulfill them. It was not content with merely providing an effective integrated system: it wanted to learn about customers' reactions to the installed system, their assessment of the competitor as a vendor, and ways that its overall solution could be enhanced for future customers.

Linkages to Other Microlevel Components

The centrality of A/VC analysis to competitor learning is evident in its linkages to other microlevel components. Alliances and relationships are related to each activity and to the entire A/VC in the form of networks.[24] Activities provide a useful means to categorize and assess assets.[25] How well competitors perform activities contributes directly to identifying and assessing their capabilities.[26] Changes in A/VCs often alert analysts to change in assumptions. Assumptions in turn often constrain competitors' choice of A/VC and how A/VC change is executed.[27]

Comparison with the Focal Firm

Comparing and contrasting the A/VC of one or more competitors with its own A/VC compels the focal firm to critically assess how it manages its own business: how it designs and manages each activity, and the connections across them, as well as connections to customers and suppliers. Learning occurs when the focal firm assesses whether and how it is *outperforming* these rivals with respect to specific activities and across the entire A/VC. This involves asking what the focal firm does differently than its rivals and vice versa. The intent is to identify relative competitor advantage: what the competitor does better than the focal firm and vice versa. In this way, competitors' A/VCs provide a critical means for any organization to challenge its own knowledge about itself.

In the integrated systems case, comparison with the dominant competitor revealed two distinct activity chains; in short, two distinct ways of managing the business (see Figure 7.7). These differences can be summarized in terms of the choice and design of activities and the performance attained. Again, these differences generated specific implications for the focal firm.

The focal firm designed and executed each activity as a set of stand-alone tasks. Unlike the competitor as described, each activity was managed by a specific group of individuals who then "handed-off" the results of their work to the next group. Each group was largely composed of individuals from a particular organization unit or department. Groups manifested a strong tendency to review and redo the work of earlier groups. Since activities were completed serially, it was not a surprise therefore to discover that the focal firm took considerably longer than the competitor to complete an integrated system.

Since there was not a set of individuals with overall responsibility for interface with the customer, management of the entire customer-focused activity chain tended by default to "fall between the cracks." It was little wonder then that customers reported great difficulty in finding someone within the focal firm who was clearly in charge—the opposite of what was reported by customers of the competitor.

With the computer competitor, the focal firm was able to identify a number of areas *within* each activity in which the competitor was outperforming it (see Table 7.4). Each of these bases of competitor advantage stemmed

FIGURE 7.7
Competitor's and Focal Firm's Customer-Focused Activity Chains

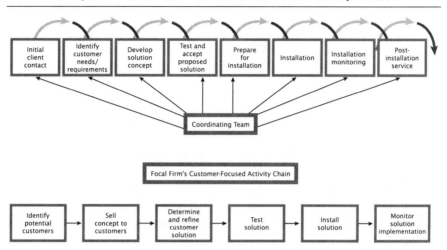

TABLE 7.4 Computer Manufacturer's Value Chain: Competitor-Based Advantages

Supplier Logistics	Manufacturing	Distribution	Marketing	Sales	Service and Support
Higher component quality—less reliability problems Low inventory and related costs—potentially lower costs to customers More integrated logistics with suppliers—lower cost and more timely deliveries	Superior fabrication and assembly and testing —better features and more reliability Improved plant design and operations—greater ability to customize products	More efficient distribution—lower costs to customers More specialized distribution—faster delivery of spare parts	Understanding customer needs—products tailored to what customers need Developing customer awareness—customers do not make unwise commitments to rivals	Customer issues detected and respon-ded to—rapid turn-around of product problems, etc. Working with other channels —lower sales costs and less customer confusion	On-site service and rapid repair—less downtime Educate customers —extend uses and applica-tions Variety of service and support—customers have confidence in the vendor

from execution of the tasks within each activity. Thus, analysts had to think through how the tasks within each activity combined to generate each competitor-based advantage. For example, the competitor's supplier logistics involved procuring components from a select set of suppliers known for their product quality and working closely with them to coordinate procurement and shipping. Thus, it both enhanced component quality and reduced inventory costs.

These assessments result from judgments about selecting, ordering, and interpreting considerable competitor data and specific indicators. The judgment that the competitor performed superior fabrication, assembly, and testing in its manufacturing resulted from a number of direct indicators including observation of the competitor's plant by a number of consultants, comments about the plant by former employees and by a few of the competitor's managers to an industry/trade publication, as well as descriptions of the manufacturing technology by vendors. Indirect indicators included product teardowns, and product functionality and features. These judgments entail both data and logic, the ingredients of inferences, as discussed in Chapter 4.

Self-learning, however, is further advanced when analysts assess how each competitor-based advantage within each activity might contribute to generating and sustaining value for customers. It is these judgments that compel analysts to critique and challenge how well the focal firm performs along its own AV/C and whether and how they contribute to generating value for customers.

For example, the computer competitor had developed an intimate partnering relationship with component and supply vendors resulting in higher component quality, lower inventory and related costs, and more integrated logistics with suppliers (see Table 7.4). These in turn led to a number of distinct value contributions for customers: less product reliability problems, more timely deliveries, and low(er) costs. The focal firm now had a foil or benchmark against which to assess its own performance in the domain of supplier logistics.

Comparison with Multiple Competitors

Learning ensues when different types of competitors are chosen as the frame of reference.[28] For example, since new entrants often must do something distinctive along the A/VC to generate customer advantage, their current or potential A/VCs generate insights that cannot be obtained by comparison with multiple current look-alike rivals.

It is especially useful to categorize *look-alike* competitors based on differences in their marketplace strategy, as discussed in Chapter 5. The A/VC associated with a niche competitor may be radically distinct from that of a blanket competitor. Competitors with a posture built around product functionality and features may emphasize different activities than those with a posture intended to create superior image, relationships, and high price.

One category of competitor frequently overlooked in A/VC analysis is *invented* competitors: a competitor that analysts create for the explicit purpose of configuring and projecting a plausible A/VC. Thus, the focal computer firm might invent a competitor with the following key elements: A Japanese computer manufacturer builds an alliance with a small American competitor to manufacture computers in a Southeast Asian country; it enters into codevelopment agreements with a number of small but growing U.S. software providers; and it then enters into distribution agreements with several specific channels. The focal firm then conjectures as to what the resultant activity chain might look like. Even first-cuts of such activity chains lead to significant learning. For example, one firm discovered the importance of building strong relationships with its key suppliers when senior managers convinced themselves how easy it might be for a new entrant (the invented competitor) to attract away many of its long-established suppliers.

Comparisons with multiple competitors reinforce the importance of the "peeling the onion" metaphor.[29] It is not necessary to execute a full-fledged or completely detailed A/VC analysis to derive significant insights. A first-cut analysis sometimes reveals key distinctions across individual competitors or groups of competitors. In the integrated systems case, a first-cut analysis based on preliminary interviews with customers or other external data sources could identify fundamental differences across competitors with regard to key activities and linkages across them. It could reveal differences in installation and service practices thus giving the focal firm a benchmark against which to assess its own installation and service processes. Such an initial assessment might then lead to further data collection and processing.[30]

The Competitor's Current and Future Marketplace Strategy

Competitors' A/VCs are always directly and indirectly related to their current and potential marketplace strategies. In a detailed analysis, each activity is related to the three elements in a competitor's marketplace strategy—scope, posture, and goals. In particular, each activity is assessed for its contribution to customer-based advantage: the value it generates directly or indirectly for customers (see Table 7.5). Such assessments compel analysts to ask whether competitor-based advantages, such as those noted in Table 7.4, translate into value for customers.

Competitors' A/VCs impact product range, variation within product lines, and the type and extent of customers reached. The systems integration competitor's A/VC allowed it to continually enhance the customization of

TABLE 7.5   Computer Manufacturer's Value Chain: Customer-Based Advantages

Supplier Logistics	Manufacturing	Distribution	Marketing	Sales	Service and Support
Partnership relationship with some vendors	State-of-the-art design, assembly and testing	Integrated distribution system	Commitment to product development	Customer research and feedback	Customer-focused service and support
⬇	⬇	⬇	⬇	⬇	⬇
More security of supply Enhanced quality Same or lower cost	Superior functionality Greater capacity to customize	Faster delivery Lower cost	Products more user friendly and offer greater value	Products and support organization more tightly linked to customers	Greater capacity to extend uses and applications for customers

its solutions. The computer competitor's A/VC also facilitated its movement toward greater customization.

Individual activities directly and indirectly affect posture—individual or multiple modes of competition. Sometimes the logic involved in weaving these connections needs to be made explicit and then challenged.[31] Consider for example, supplier logistics in the case of the computer competitor. Its management of supplier logistics contributed directly to specific modes of competition. Its partnerships with some vendors resulted in greater security of supply of key components, thus ensuring that the competitor could continue to broaden its product line and upgrade functionality and features. By reducing component and other logistics costs, the competitor if it chooses could reduce prices or use the extra margin to augment service, image, reputation, and selling and relationships.

Marketplace goals including market share, desired image and reputation, and value delivered to customers, are often indicated by assessing the goals the competitor seeks to achieve within and across activities (see Table 7.6). Sometimes, the logic is direct. The computer competitor's goal of enhancing manufacturing so that it could better customize product configurations allowed strong inferences to be drawn about its goal of customizing solutions for customers. More often, the linkages are indirect. The goals of purchasing high-quality supplies and components and to lessening dependence on one supplier indicated the computer competitor's commitment to enhancing product functionality—the performance and reliability of its products.

TABLE 7.6 Computer Manufacturer's Value Chain: Goals within and across Activities

Supplier Logistics	Manufacturing	Distribution	Marketing	Sales	Service and Support
Reduce cost of raw materials	Improve plant efficiencies and cost	Meet or beat all customer order com-mitments	Anticipate and shape customers' needs	Take and refine orders	Provide full service and support
Lessen dependence on one supplier	Customize product con-figurations	Develop the most efficient shipping system	Develop superior image	Detail specific customer needs	Customize service to meet individual customer needs
Purchase high-quality supplies and com-ponents	Attain highest possible levels of functionality	Provide rapid spare parts delivery	To be perceived as having highest price/value	Document customer issues and problems	To reduce, if not eliminate, downtime
Continually increase quality of purchases			To educate users so that they will get maximum value from products	To support and reinforce channel activities	

On the other hand, it is useful to test marketplace goals identified as part of determining and assessing a competitor's (marketplace) strategy against goals attributed to individual activities and to the entire A/VC. If analysts had previously determined that the computer competitor aimed to achieve a 10 percent gain in market share, in part by lowering its prices, they could now assess whether the competitor was managing its individual activities, as well as the connectedness across activities, so that it could both manufacture the necessary product supply and lower its costs.

Signals of Marketplace Changes

Change in competitors' A/VCs is frequently a source of signals of potential change in the factor, channel, and end-customer arenas.[32] Such signals require analysts to make explicit connections between what competitors are doing, or may do, along their A/VCs, and how these actions might affect competitive conditions in each arena.

Change in the "upstream," or front-end, of the conventional value change—supplier relationships, inbound logistics, and operations or manufacturing—provide weak or strong signals of change in *factor* markets. In the computer case, the competitor's goals to reduce the costs of its raw materials, to lessen its dependence on one supplier, and to purchase higher quality supplies and components, indicate that rivalry is likely not only to become more intense for these factors but that the market for some factors might (further) divide into segments around high(er) and low(er) cost/quality.

Change in "downstream," or back-end, activities such as marketing, sales, and service often signals future change in the channel and end-customer arenas. The computer competitor's commitment and efforts to further customize its offerings to the needs and situation of individual customers could portend a significant change in the nature of rivalry. In the near future, rivalry might center around the ability to customize solutions as opposed to simple product functionality or price.

Competitor Consequences

Competitor consequences are identified around three related items: issues and decisions confronting the competitor (some of which stem from its current or potential marketplace strategy), constraints and vulnerabilities associated with the A/VC, and how to (better) leverage the A/VC over time. Each of these items contributes to identifying action plans and investments that must be made to build the organization that can win in the marketplace, including linkages to suppliers, channels, and end-customers. These consequences go to the heart of any competitor's ability to outwit, outmaneuver, and outperform rivals.

Comparison with the focal firm and other competitors, in conjunction with consideration of linkages to current and future marketplace strategy, lead to the identification of *issues and decisions* that either confront the competitor now or will do so in the future. It takes time to tease out and consider such issues and decisions. Analysts find themselves moving back and forth among the steps identified in Figure 7.6. Consideration of the attributes of any competitor's A/VC always leads to an enumeration of possible issues or decisions. These factors are then further explored as analysts compare and contrast the competitor's A/VC with those of the focal firm and other rivals. Issues and decisions generated by such comparisons also cause analysts to reconsider prior assessments of the A/VC's attributes and indicators of potential change.

In the judgment of the analysis team, three *issues* confronted the systems integration competitor: how to continue to shorten its total solution development and delivery time; how to further integrate activities; and how to develop stronger relationships with its principal suppliers. The extent to which it successfully managed each of these (related) issues would strongly influence its ability to continually add value over time for its customers—to outmaneuver and outperform its rivals.

Several *decisions* also confronted the systems integration competitor. Specific decisions were associated with each issue. It would have to decide which suppliers it would retain as "strategic partners" and with which new suppliers it would like to develop such a relationship. It also faced a decision regarding how best to integrate suppliers into its "selling process."

Another way to sharpen the understanding of issues and decisions facing a competitor is to assess the *constraints and vulnerabilities* associated with its A/VC. Constraints are those factors that limit what the competitor is able to do. All individual activities and entire A/VCs, by definition, entail constraints. The computer competitor had clear constraints associated with each activity (see Table 7.7). Issues and decisions with crucial implications for the competitor's marketplace strategy emanated from the constraints evident in its manufacturing operations. Plant capacity would limit product supply; an aging labor force might inhibit adoption of new technology and thus product functionality and features; and its current manufacturing process technology, which was rapidly becoming inferior to a number of rivals, would limit product supply and quality. The competitor, whether it knew it or not, would have to make a number of decisions to deal with these constraints.

TABLE 7.7 Computer Manufacturer's Value Chain: Constraints and Vulnerabilities

Supplier Logistics	Manufacturing	Distribution	Marketing	Sales	Service and Support
CONSTRAINTS:					
Number of suppliers Capacity of suppliers Experience of procurement personnel	Plant capacity Aging labor force Limitations of existing technology	Commitments to logistics firms and channels constrain major moves	Marketing mind-set Number of personnel Ability to reach new customers	Number of sales personnel Time spent with existing and new customers	Number of personnel Knowledge and training of personnel
VULNERABILITIES:					
Historic relationship with one specific supplier Capacity of suppliers to be technology leaders	New process technologies	Capital invested in distribution might be of little value if rivals develop new and superior methods to deliver products	Inability to change own historic marketing routines New entrants who may do things very differently	Customers seeking knowledge and support that can be supplied by existing sales personnel	Major changes in technologies New types of customers seeking new services and types of support

Vulnerabilities are those internal or external factors that could impede the competitor from achieving its goals. They are associated with individual activities or the entire A/VC. They also highlight issues and decisions. The computer competitor (see Table 7.7) faced particular vulnerabilities. Its manufacturing process, although superior to the focal firm's, was extremely vulnerable to new manufacturing process technologies. The competitor thus faced a decision as to when it should invest in the new technologies and whether a new production plant would be desirable. A significantly different vulnerability was whether the competitor could break out of its historic ways of doing marketing: its marketing mind-set might inhibit its ability to explore emerging opportunities.

Patterns also emerge across issues and decisions to reveal A/VC-wide consequences. Many issues and decisions in the case of the computer competitor pertained to technology, thus suggesting the importance of technologies across all activities for both competitor-based and customer-based advantage.

How the competitor might resolve issues and decisions generates potential action and investment programs. These programs must be considered in conjunction with the competitor's potential marketplace strategies. For example, if the computer competitor were to more intensively pursue a customization strategy, analysts might ask what technology investments were required to facilitate the strategy. It might then develop an action program around investments in technologies to build tighter linkages with suppliers, to move to the next generation of manufacturing capability, and to enhance customization through connecting marketing, sales, and service activities.[33] Analysts might then develop a tentative timetable for these actions and explore their results. For example, how would the new manufacturing technologies enhance product functionality and features? How long would it take rivals to catch up to this advantage?

It is often appropriate to develop and assess a different type of action and investment program: How could the competitor better leverage its current A/VC, and enhancements to it, in the immediate future for marketplace strategy purposes? In the case of the systems integration competitor, analysts might develop an action plan that would allow it to further shorten its core development and delivery cycle time, thus allowing it to reach and serve a greater number of customers with its current asset base. A major benefit of developing such programs about competitors is that analysts can explore how these actions might be developed and exploited for the focal firm.

Implications for the Focal Firm

Implications for the focal firm must be considered in the context of linkages between its own A/VC and its current and potential marketplace strategy.

Failure to relate A/VC and marketplace strategy may lead to recommended changes in the design and management of the A/VC that may inhibit winning in the marketplace.

Implications for A/VC design are assessed at two levels: the entire A/VC and individual activities. Entire A/VC design revolves around three sets of questions:

1. What A/VC is required given planned and potential marketplace strategy changes?
2. How can the existing A/VC be better leveraged?
3. What might be the ideal A/VC design?

Consideration of these questions quickly leads to assessment of the attributes of the focal firm's current A/VC. In the worst case, though not an uncommon one, when compared with current, emerging, and invented competitors, the focal firm's A/VC transpires as poorly connected externally and internally, offering little uniqueness, and delivering inferior customer value. Its limitations and deficiencies become manifestly evident. Such was the case for the systems integration focal firm discussed in this chapter.

Even when the focal firm's A/VC compares favorably in terms of competitor-based and customer-based advantage with multiple types of competitors, it is still useful to depict what an ideal A/VC might be. Emerging, projected, and invented competitors often influence ideal A/VC design more than current look-alike competitors. For the systems integration firm, an ideal A/VC configuration could well be an extension and elaboration of its dominant competitor: a set of high value-adding activities that are tightly connected to customers and suppliers, and are tightly integrated internally. Based on action programs developed as part of assessing competitor consequences, the focal firm, in a short time, was able to lay out an ideal A/VC configuration that was radically distinct from its current A/VC configuration.

If the ideal A/VC configuration generates significant customer value, it typically gives rise to specific issues and decisions for the focal firm. The choices it makes to resolve these issues and decisions generates a set of specific action implications—an action plan to move the current configuration toward the ideal.

Two issues dominated the systems integration firm's analysis. First, how to radically redesign its customer-focused activity chain so that each activity was intimately connected to customers and so that a high degree of intra-connectedness was achieved: How could it put the ideal A/VC into practice? Second, how could it ensure that superior customer value was generated (compared with the current dominant competitor)? Discussion and analysis of these issues required the participation of all organization functions, units, and hierarchy levels.[34]

The action program that ensued was nothing short of a fundamental business redesign. It included:

- The appointment of a senior management team to oversee the design and delivery of every customer solution.

- A fundamental redesign of all activities, based in part on input from customers.

- The specification of the tasks involved in each activity and how tasks were related across activities.

- The establishment of ideal timelines for the completion of each activity and key tasks.

- The development of a review process for building into each activity learning that inevitably occurs as part of the design and delivery of each solution.

Errors in Assessing Competitors' Activity/Value Chains

Many of the errors noted here are intended to highlight and illustrate some reasons why organizations often do not learn as much as they should from A/VC analysis. Some of these errors are evident even in organizations that do a good job of delineating and describing competitors' A/VCs. They are also more likely to occur when analysts do not appreciate and understand the recursive nature of assessment (and identification).

A common error is that assessment tends to become excessively focused on the competitor's A/VC: detecting internal change in the A/VC, documenting the extent and direction of the change, and assessing its consequences within and across activities (intraconnections). While such understanding is a necessary part of assessment, learning that emphasizes knowledge-in-use redirects analysts' attention to extraconnections—the links between a competitor's A/VC and customers and suppliers, and other signals of change in the current and emerging marketplace.

Even in absence of the preceding error, analysis of the A/VC and marketplace strategy is often poorly interconnected. In particular, change in A/VC is not directly linked to change in marketplace strategy. The emphasis throughout this chapter on an A/VC's externally focused attributes—extraconnectedness, uniqueness, and value adding—is intended to build concern with marketplace strategy implications into each phase of assessment.

Many times, the interconnections between A/VC and marketplace strategy change are not readily apparent. In the computer manufacturer example, the effects of change in supplier logistics and relations on functionality, features, service, and price had to be teased out and analyzed. Because of the prevalence and importance of these indirect inferences, the logic or reasoning that connects A/VC and marketplace change must be carefully articulated and explicated—something that often is done only sparingly, if at all.

Connections to suppliers, or more broadly, the factor arena, sometimes receive only passing attention. Yet, as both case examples in this chapter illustrate, linkages to suppliers affect many individual activities, integration among them, and as a consequence, the value delivered to customers.

An error that must be noted concerns "breadth versus depth" in the range of competitors' A/VCs analyzed: the A/VCs of one or only a few (largely similar) look-alike competitors are assessed to the neglect of other categories of current and potential rivals. As noted, invented competitors are often a powerful source of learning. So also are smaller or niche players, recent and emerging entrants, and substitute product rivals.

A pervasive error is not to consider and develop what an ideal A/VC might look like. Because ideal A/VCs change the referent point from rivals' current A/VCs, potential implications for the focal organization are likely to be missed. Analysts need to be willing to imagine and speculate beyond what is happening today.

Finally, an error noted in many other chapters also pertains to assessment of A/VCs: self-learning takes a backseat to assessment of competitor consequences. By constantly comparing and contrasting its own A/VC with those of rivals, critical issues, decisions, and questions are raised earlier than might otherwise be. The purpose of analyzing any competitor's A/VC is not to understand how and why the competitor manages its core activities but to leverage that learning to outwit, outmaneuver, and outperform all rivals.

 ## Summary

Activity/value chains provide a useful point of departure to disentangle and analyze any competitor's way of doing business—how it manages its core work activities. The knowledge generated is directly linked to key issues and questions about the competitor's current and potential marketplace strategy. As a framework of analysis, it also serves as a useful input for identifying and assessing each microlevel component. The ultimate benefit of the analysis is self-learning: how the focal organization can enhance its own marketplace strategy, and better manage its own activity/value chain(s) and other microlevel components.

CHAPTER

8

Alliances and Relationships

MANY ORGANIZATIONS NO LONGER DEPEND ON THE CHIPS THEY OWN OR FULLY control to win either today or tomorrow. They recognize that alliances and relationships with other entities are fundamental to outwitting, outmaneuvering, and outperforming competitors. They outwit their rivals by identifying more quickly whom they should align with, the benefits of such alignment, and how these alignments might best be interrelated and integrated. They outmaneuver competitors in the way they attract alliance partners, sustain and enhance these relationships, and leverage them for mutual gain. They outperform competitors in the way they use alliances to acquire and enhance assets, build and augment capabilities and competencies and, ultimately, to achieve superior marketplace and financial returns.

Alliances and relationships thus transform the concept of a competitor. If an organization is competing against Ford, Apple, or Citibank, in the automobile, computer, and banking domains, respectively, it is not just competing against these entities in their narrow legal form but against the total combination of all their alliances and relationships. Thus, to ignore or downplay competitors' alliances and relationships almost certainly results in misconstruing their current and potential strategies, assets, and capabilities and competencies.

The chapter begins by addressing what we mean by alliances and relationships, their prevalence and importance, and their key attributes. The bulk of the chapter is devoted to identifying and assessing individual alliances and relationships. Patterns among a competitor's alliances and relationships are then briefly considered. The final section of the chapter addresses the identification of a competitor's potential alliances.

Analysts must be prepared to move back and forth through the steps in any guided analysis of individual alliances or special relationships. Thus, this chapter also highlights the recursiveness of competitor learning. It emphasizes the role and importance of projecting the evolution of individual alliances and special relationships. It illustrates how anticipated indicators contribute to projecting which alliances a competitor is likely to enter and to projecting potential evolutions of an individual alliance or special relationship.

Understanding Alliances and Special Relationships

An *alliance* is a formal economic relationship between a competitor and some other entity. Alliances are typically with another entity in the competitor's competitive domain such as a factor supplier, distribution channel, end-customer, technology source, or a rival. Alliances constitute formal relationships in that the competitor enters into some sort of explicit contractual relationship with one (or more) of these entities. Alliances constitute economic relationships in that they involve an agreement to commit resources over some period of time.

A *special relationship* is an informal relationship with a competitive domain entity such as those previously noted or with a sociopolitical entity such as a community or public interest group, governmental agency, political party, or labor union. These relationships are special in that they involve long-term interaction and understanding between the parties. They are informal in that they are not (typically) predicated on some form of contractual agreement. Special relationships assume importance in part because they often underpin, and in some cases, grow out of formal relationships (alliances).

The Prevalence and Importance of Alliances

The business press reports many new alliances every day. Almost all business enterprises have one or more alliances. Most large corporations have multiple alliances. The annual reports of most corporations list alliances announced or advanced in the prior year.

Alliances are increasingly a critical feature of individual business sectors. Industries as diverse as automobiles, computers, newspapers, airplanes, and office furniture, are marked by alliances between rivals and between rivals and various suppliers, vendors, distribution channels, and end-customers. Moreover, alliances serve to break down the barriers between individual industries or competitive domains.

For many firms, alliances are fundamental to new product development, acquisition of raw materials and components, access to new technologies, entry into distribution channels and, in many instances, obtaining and retaining key corporate or commercial end-customers.

Types of Alliances

The identification and analysis of alliances is rendered somewhat difficult due to the multiple types of alliances and breadth of potential partners (see Figure 8.1). While the alliances noted in Figure 8.1 are far from exhaustive, they suggest the options that are available to any organization as it considers what types of alliances to create and with which other organizations it might align.

The Evolution of Alliances

Essential to scanning, monitoring, projecting, and assessing alliances is an understanding of how they evolve over time. Most types of alliances are the result of a complex and time-consuming undertaking. It frequently takes months, and in some cases, one or more years, for two or more parties to agree to enter into an alliance. Frequently, an alliance is announced well in

FIGURE 8.1
Types of Alliances with Different Entities

	Joint Ventures	Contracts	Licensing Agreements	Ownership Modes
Raw Material Sources				
Component Sources				
Logistics Providers				
Competitors				
Technology Sources				
Distribution Channels				
End-Customers				

advance of its consummation in the form of a written agreement or signed contract. It sometimes takes months, if not longer, to work out the details of the alliance: who is to do what, when, how the parties are to work together, and so on. For many joint ventures, product development, and licensing agreements, it requires years to bring a product to market.

The scope, purpose, and direction of an alliance also change over time. As the partners get to know each other, they learn about each other's goals, assets, capabilities, and culture. Marketplace conditions also change, invoking the partners to modify or alter the alliance's goals, timeline, or asset commitments. Sometimes, the actions of one or more governmental agencies causes the partners to shift from previously announced alliance plans and commitments.

Alliances sometimes fail. It is estimated that more than 50 percent of manufacturing joint ventures do not last more than seven years. Licensing agreements sometimes do not generate winning products in the marketplace. More generally, alliance partners occasionally agree to disengage from each other. Special relationships often fall apart when a new management team takes the helm at one of the parties and it is not able to sustain the bonds established by the prior managers.

Key Attributes of Alliances and Relationships

While alliances and relationships have many key attributes, four in particular merit attention from the perspective of competitor analysis. Change along each attribute—direction, mutuality of interest, commitment, or contribution—affects how an alliance is likely to evolve.

Direction Direction refers to change in the goals of an alliance. As indicated throughout this chapter, the goals associated with an alliance change for many reasons.

Mutuality of Interest Organizations align because they are able to do something together that either one alone cannot do. However, the interests of each partner can, and do change.

Commitment The partners can add to or deplete their emotional and resource commitments to the alliance. Such commitments are critical to attainment of the alliance's goals. Even if an alliance continues to be of mutual interest, one or both partners may not be in a position to add to or meet their resource commitments. Also, other demands on the organization's time and attention detract from managers' emotional commitment to a particular alliance.

Contribution   Alliances differ considerably in their direct or indirect contribution to a competitor's marketplace strategy. Current or anticipated contribution may change due to the actions of either partner.

Alliances and Special Relationships—Indicators

Analysts need to seek indicators during three distinct phases of an alliance: anticipated indicators that suggest a competitor's need to develop an alliance; indicators that allow the monitoring and tracking of alliance evolution; and, indicators to facilitate the projection of alternative paths an alliance may take in the future. Anticipated indicators for both alliances and relationships are often indirect; for example, changes in marketplace strategy results sometimes indicate a need for a particular kind of alliance. Also, when an alliance fails or a relationship disintegrates, analysts need to pay attention to indicators that facilitate analysis of why it occurred.

Alliances and Relationships as Signals

Alliances are central to competitor learning because they often give rise to strong, high-impact signals of change in a competitor's emerging and future marketplace strategy. In some cases, a single alliance dramatically alters scope, posture, and goals. Alliances are often the source of signals of new products and product line extensions, of the business segments where a competitor intends to commit its resources, of how it plans to compete against specific competitors, and of the goals it wants to pursue.

Alliances are also a frequent source of indirect signals of significant change in every component of the competitor analysis framework. As illustrated later in this chapter, analysts need to carefully explicate and test the logic connecting alliances and special relationships to change in individual microcomponents such as capabilities and competencies, assumptions, and organizational culture.

Identifying Alliances

Alliances are typically highly visible. They are thus difficult, if not impossible, to conceal. In almost all cases, firms announce either their intention to enter into an alliance or that they have already done so.[1] Indeed, many firms are anxious to publicize an alliance because of the statement it makes about their commitment to a particular business or market segment, or product innovativeness or intent to extend the frontiers of technology. A guided approach to identifying alliances is shown in Figure 8.2.

FIGURE 8.2
Identifying Alliances

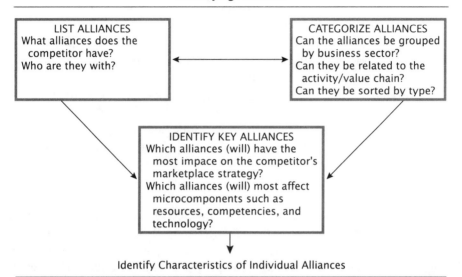

LIST ALLIANCES
What alliances does the
   competitor have?
Who are they with?

CATEGORIZE ALLIANCES
Can the alliances be grouped
   by business sector?
Can they be related to the
   activity/value chain?
Can they be sorted by type?

IDENTIFY KEY ALLIANCES
Which alliances (will) have the
   most impace on the competitor's
   marketplace strategy?
Which alliances (will) most affect
   microcomponents such as
   resources, competencies, and
   technology?

Identify Characteristics of Individual Alliances

ALLIANCE PARTNERS
Who is each partner?
What do we know about
   their marketplace
   strategy?
What do we know about
   their microcomponents?

TYPE OF ALLIANCE
What is the specific
   type of alliance?
Are there any
   peculiarities?

CONTEXT OF ALLIANCE
What are the relevant
   competitive conditions?
What are the motivations
   of the partners?

PURPOSE OF ALLIANCE
What are the stated goals of the alliance?
How do the goals fit with each partner's own context?

TERMS OF ALLIANCE
What is the resource contribution of each partner?
What are the roles and responsibilities of each partner?
What is the duration of the alliance?
What are some key milestones?

EVOLUTION TO DATE
What has been the alliance's history to date?
What have been the significant developments in its evolution?

List Alliances

Because of their visibility, a scan of secondary electronic databases generates a listing of most of a competitor's alliances. It can be abetted by a scan of the competitor's own secondary materials such as annual reports, 10K (and other mandatory financial) statements, other governmental submissions, and public relations materials.[2]

These scans pick up alliances at different stages of their evolution. Some may be only at the announcement stage; negotiations may still be ongoing about the alliance's terms and conditions. Some may be announcements of agreements that have only recently been signed. At the other end of the spectrum, a scan picks up alliances that have been in existence for many years.

It should not be overlooked that these scans also alert analysts to competitors' need for alliances and to potential alliances. Sometimes, organizations actually indicate in one or more public forums, or in written statements, that they are seeking a specific type of alliance partner or that they need one or more alliance partners to accomplish some purpose such as entering a new geographic market or creating new products.[3]

Categorize Alliances

Because most large corporations such as Du Pont, General Electric, Ford, and Westinghouse and most smaller organizations are involved in so many different alliances, even a preliminary categorization permits insights that cannot be attained by simply eyeballing a listing of alliances or by considering individual alliances in isolation. It especially helps in the identification of key or critical alliances.

Alliances can be quickly grouped in related ways. First, they can be segmented by the relevant business sector or product domain of the competitor. It is not unusual to find a wide disparity in the propensity of sectors or business units of firms to enter into alliances.[4] It is usually revealing to relate alliances to a specific activity/value chain, as demonstrated later in this chapter. Also, if a competitor has a large number of alliances, categorizing them into joint ventures, contracts, licensing arrangements, ownership modes, and so on indicates the competitor's propensity to develop specific types of alliances.

Identify Key Alliances

Because even relatively small competitors often possess several alliances, a preliminary assessment[5] to determine which are most important to a competitor's current and future marketplace strategy enhances both the efficiency and effectiveness of the analysis of alliances. Key questions include asking which alliances (could) contribute to:

- A particular strategic intent or vision?
- Products new to the marketplace?
- New products for the competitor?
- Change in the competitor's existing products?
- Significant increments in value-added for customers through changes in the competitor's posture?
- New ways of competing to attract, win, and retain customers?

Tentative answers to these questions are continually reassessed[6] as analysts proceed through the remaining steps in identifying and assessing alliances.

Characteristics of Individual Alliances

The data generated to list a competitor's alliances typically permit the determination of many key characteristics of both individual alliances and patterns across alliances. This section addresses only the characteristics or details of an individual alliance.[7] For purposes of illustration, we will use a component manufacturer's product development alliance with an engineering firm (see Figure 8.3), which is referred to as "CompAll."

Alliance Partner(s) It is always necessary to identify the alliance partner. In the case of CompAll, the alliance partner is an engineering firm with a design and development specialty in a particular range of industrial components.

However, knowing the name of the alliance partner and other general data such as its sales revenue, location, and names of its senior managers, should not be confused with understanding its business strategy or key microcomponents such as its activity/value chain, assets, or organization. If the analysts are unfamiliar with the partner, extensive analysis may be required to get to know it.[8]

Type of Alliance The type of alliance is almost always described in the announcements associated with the alliance. However, because such variation exists within types of alliances such as joint ventures and licensing agreements, analysts must be careful not to be lulled into falsely believing they know the details of an alliance simply because they are able to slot it into some preordained category.

FIGURE 8.3
A Component Manufacturer's Product Development Alliance: Key Characteristics

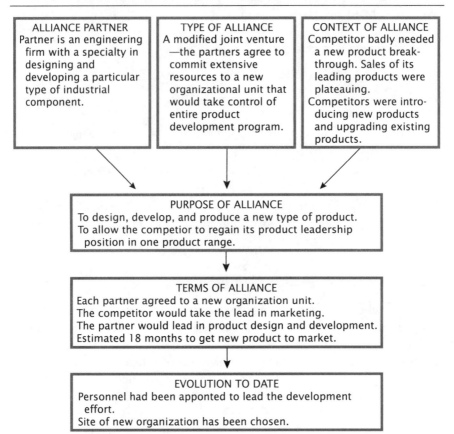

The component manufacturer's alliance was essentially a joint venture. The partners agreed to create a new organizational unit, CompAll, that would develop and execute the product development program.

Context of Alliance Alliances are initiated, developed, and executed in very different competitive and competitor contexts, which must be understood before signals are derived. Increasing or declining market growth, the recent emergence of new entrants, or anticipated changes in key technologies, illustrate the importance of understanding any alliance's current and anticipated marketplace context *before* inferences are drawn about its key attributes—direction, mutuality of interest, commitment, or contribution.

The component manufacturer had failed to meet its announced goals with a number of recent product introductions. Moreover, sales of many of its long-established products were faltering. Its rivals were taking market share from it through upgrading existing products and introducing new products. Thus, the alliance's potential contribution to the firm's future marketplace strategy could be enormous.

Purpose of the Alliance Even alliances of the same type manifest quite distinct purposes. Although alliance announcements typically identify some broad purposes, it is often necessary to dig beneath the stated goals to understand why particular goals were chosen (or announced), and why they might change over the life of the alliance.

The CompAll alliance had one overriding goal: to design, develop, and produce a new type of product. Success with the new product would in turn allow the competitor to regain its leadership position in at least one segment of this broad product category.

Terms of Alliance Alliances also vary greatly in their terms. Key terms to be addressed include the principal asset contributions of each party (what each party brings to the alliance; e.g., expertise or financial commitment), the roles and responsibilities of each party (who is charged with doing what), the duration of the alliance (is the alliance entered into for a specific period?), and key milestones (e.g., when contracts will be signed, when a product is likely to be introduced).

The CompAll alliance committed both partners to creating a new organizational unit that would be funded equally by them. In announcing the alliance, they estimated that it would take at least 19 months before the new product could be introduced to the market. The component manufacturer would take the lead in marketing and promotion. The partner would lead the product design and development activities.

Evolution to Date A recording of the history of the alliance to date provides a description of its evolution.[9] Depending on the type of alliance, a modest historical description provides a basis for assessing its potential success or failure. A retrospective scan of public and company-specific materials, as discussed, is necessary to furnish the historical data specific to a particular alliance.

The CompAll alliance had only recently been announced. The partners were still working out how they would work together in the new organizational unit.

Open-Ended Inquiry

The identification of a competitor's alliances in its early stages is essentially open-ended inquiry: analysts search all available primary and secondary data sources, without little a priori sense as to what types of alliances the competitor possesses. Open-ended discussion with secondary data sources such as suppliers, end-customers, technology experts, and management consultants often generates surprising details and insights. The spirit of open-ended inquiry is also necessary for preliminary categorizing of alliances and identifying of key alliances. To the extent that analysts retain an open mind, they are more likely to develop alternative approaches to grouping alliances and questioning how and why any particular alliance is likely to contribute to marketplace strategy and/or specific microcomponents.

Identifying Special Relationships

Special relationships are not nearly as visible or evident as alliances or networks. They are generally only recognized or detected once analysts have developed extensive knowledge about a competitor. The steps and key questions central to a *guided* approach to identifying special relationships are noted in Figure 8.4. A small competitor of a large electronics firm that has successfully introduced a series of product extensions is used for illustration purposes.

Detecting Special Relationships: Potential Indicators

Because competitor analysts typically devote little attention to special relationships and secondary data sources provide few direct indicators of them, before guided data gathering occurs, it is necessary to identify other organizations with which the competitor has some degree of formal or informal interaction, and why these relationships might be special. Analysts thus generate *alerting* indicators of potential special relationships. First, *existing alliances* often suggest the presence of special relationships. An alliance sometimes leads to two or more organizations working closely together in ways that were never intended by its original terms and conditions. A bond develops between the partners that runs much deeper than could ever be ascertained by reading the legal or other documents associated with the alliance. Relationships evolve between the personnel in the partner organizations such that their commitment to each other extends well beyond the explicit alliance agreements.

It is sometimes possible to surface special relationships by identifying those organizations with which the competitor has had an *enduring business relationship*. Factor suppliers, distribution channels, end-customers, logistics providers, and technology sources, among others, merit consideration. The activity/value chain analysis, and alliance and network analysis can surface many of these organizations.

FIGURE 8.4
Identifying a Competitor's Special Relationships

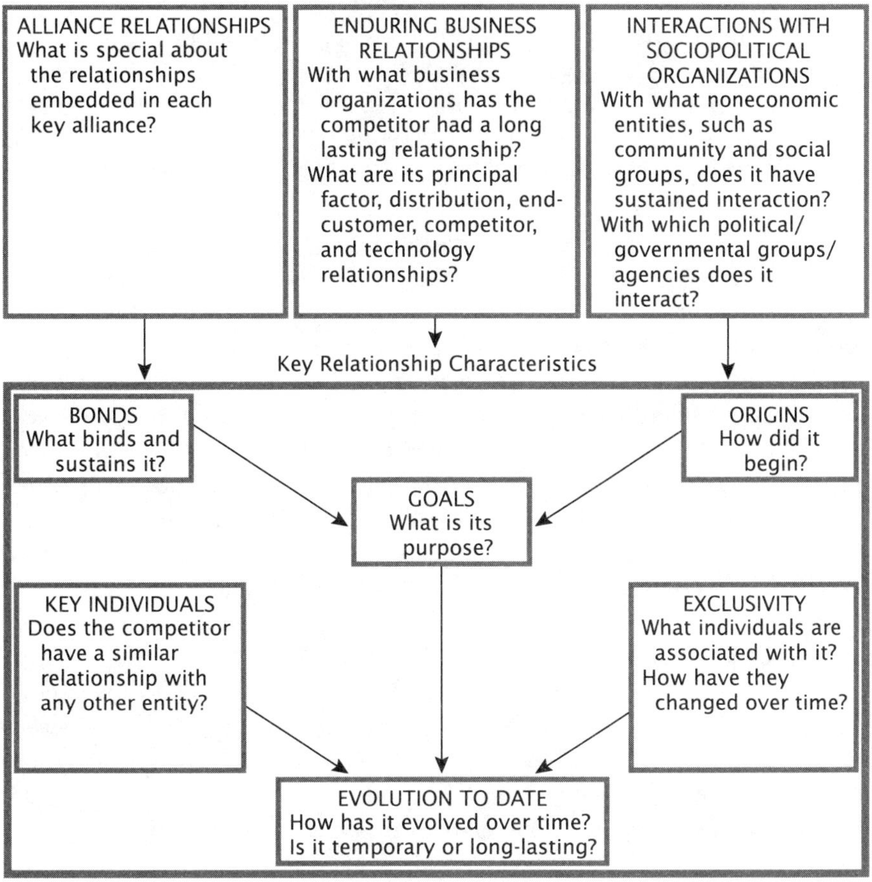

ALLIANCE RELATIONSHIPS	ENDURING BUSINESS RELATIONSHIPS	INTERACTIONS WITH SOCIOPOLITICAL ORGANIZATIONS
What is special about the relationships embedded in each key alliance?	With what business organizations has the competitor had a long lasting relationship? What are its principal factor, distribution, end-customer, competitor, and technology relationships?	With what noneconomic entities, such as community and social groups, does it have sustained interaction? With which political/ governmental groups/ agencies does it interact?

Key Relationship Characteristics

BONDS What binds and sustains it?		ORIGINS How did it begin?
	GOALS What is its purpose?	
KEY INDIVIDUALS Does the competitor have a similar relationship with any other entity?		EXCLUSIVITY What individuals are associated with it? How have they changed over time?
	EVOLUTION TO DATE How has it evolved over time? Is it temporary or long-lasting?	

Special relationships are also generated by identifying those organizations in the *social, political, and cultural milieu* with which the competitor has had a long-term relationship or seems to be developing a close working relationship. Electronic data searches provide few, if any, indicators of their existence. They are captured and confirmed only through interactions with individuals active either in the competitive domain or in and around the sociopolitical organizations themselves.

The Role of Primary Data Sources

Secondary data sources provide few direct indicators of special relationships. It is through interaction with individuals both internal and external to the focal firm that the "special" side of a competitor's relationships are typically unearthed. It is only through such individuals that they are confirmed.

Individuals in all entities *associated with the competitor* such as customers, channels, vendors, governmental agencies, sociopolitical groups, experts, and industry observers, among others, are potential sources of rich data. These individuals sometimes are able to describe the history of a relationship, its origins, its current state including difficulties and uncertainties, and its likely evolution.[10] Often only one or two individuals are required to develop a strong sense of the special side of a relationship. In the case of the small electronics competitor, engineers in an original equipment manufacturer (OEM) detailed how they had worked with the electronics firm in testing emerging product designs, and end-customers talked freely about the history and intimacy of their relationship with the firm.

The focal firm's own customers, vendors, and channels, as well as experts, governmental agencies, consultants, and others with whom it has some association, also serve as critical data sources. Vendors or suppliers are often painfully aware of the special side of the relationship their own competitors (other suppliers or vendors) have with their customers. Channels often have extensive understanding of the relationship their own rivals (other channels) have developed with their suppliers or vendors and customers. It was one of its own vendors that informed the large electronics firm of the relationship its small competitor had developed with a local university.

Individuals internal to the focal firm often are able to identify some of a competitor's special relationships: what the relationship is and what makes it special. This is especially so if the firm has competed against the competitor for a number of years. Purchasing managers are often able to describe the bonds connecting individual competitors and specific suppliers.

Key Relationship Characteristics

Once a relationship is identified, or even suspected, the focus of inquiry shifts to determining what, if anything, makes it special. Several items need to be addressed.

Bonds Every special relationship manifests some glue or bond that binds and sustains the relationship. Sometimes it is as straightforward as the friendship between specific individuals in the respective organizations. It may be a relationship based on ethnic, religious, or regional commonalities. Sometimes it is a shared interest in a specific technology or social issue.

Different bonds were evident in each of the electronics competitor's special relationships. In the case of its relationship with a local university, graduates continued to work with their former professors. The competitor had developed a close working relationship over a long number of years with manufacturing and purchasing personnel in one end-customer. Senior executives had developed a close affinity with key personnel in the standards-setting body by working with them on industry issues.

Origins The special side of relationships often emanates from their origins—how the relationship began.[11] Two family-owned organizations founded by individuals who knew each other or hailed from the same local area may maintain close ties for many years.

The electronics competitor's special relationship with the local university evolved as its graduates began to seek advice and counsel from their former professors. Its special relationship with a software development vendor evolved out of a joint agreement to work on a particular software problem. They began to exchange personnel as a means of learning more about each other's issues and opportunities. The standards-setting body had initially approached the competitor to be one of its lead spokepersons on a particular issue.

Goals Every special relationship has some overriding purpose(s). One pharmaceutical firm's special relationship with the FDA (Food and Drug Administration) was intended to get its products through FDA review processes as quickly as it was legally possible to do so.[12] A special relationship's purposes also focus and reinforce the underlying bonds.

The electronic competitor's special relationship with the local university was intended to give it early access to emerging product research. Its relationship with the software development vendor was intended to speed up its product design and development. Its relationship with the original equipment manufacturer generated understanding of the product needs of a specific class of customers.

Key Individuals Relationships are special not so much between organizations as between specific individuals within them. Relationships between older members of founding families and between sales force and purchasing personnel are classic examples. It is important to identify the key relevant individuals because the special side of relationships often disintegrates once these individuals are no longer present.

Graduates and professors were the key individuals in the electronics competitor's relationship with the local university. More specifically, one professor had been the leading source of key research. With the standards-setting body, the relationship was between the founding owners of the firm and one or two key technology experts who were central to the board's standard-setting practices.

Exclusivity The marketplace importance of special relationships often rests on their exclusivity: the other party only holds a special relationship with a particular competitor. The exclusive relationship potentially conveys many benefits and advantages to the competitor.

Because of the proximity of the university to the electronics competitor's headquarters and major plant, the relationship was especially strong, even though it was not exclusive. Although the analysis team was not certain, it appeared that the software development vendor did not exchange personnel with any of its other customers.

Open-Ended Inquiry

Identifying special relationships is essentially open-ended: analysts do not know where such relationships lurk, what data sources may lead to them, or what indicators are relevant. Thus, they are often surprised when specific relationships are unearthed. The points of departure noted in Figure 8.4—alliance relationships, enduring business relationships, and interactions with sociopolitical organizations—are therefore only intended as ways to initiate the search. However, once analysts are cognizant of the notion of special relationships, they search for alerting indicators in secondary sources and in most interactions with individuals inside and outside their organization.

Assessing Alliances

Assessing an individual alliance is guided by the analysis framework shown in Figure 8.5. We will continue with the industrial component competitor's product development alliance, CompAll, for illustration purposes.

Alliance Record to Date

If the alliance has been in existence for some time, it is necessary to assess its record to date. The parameters and criteria are to some extent specific to the type of alliance. Some parameters[13] relevant to many different alliance types include actions taken in pursuit of the alliance's goals; decisions made by the alliance partners, adherence to originally stated timelines; degree of cooperation between the alliance partners; contribution to the competitor's marketplace strategy.

Criteria provide a reference point against which the parameters are assessed. Some general criteria include the alliance's originally stated goals; comparison with similar alliances of other competitors; comparison with similar alliances of the focal organization.

Since the CompAll alliance was announced only a month or so previously, few parameters were available for assessment. However, both internal and

FIGURE 8.5
Assessing an Alliance

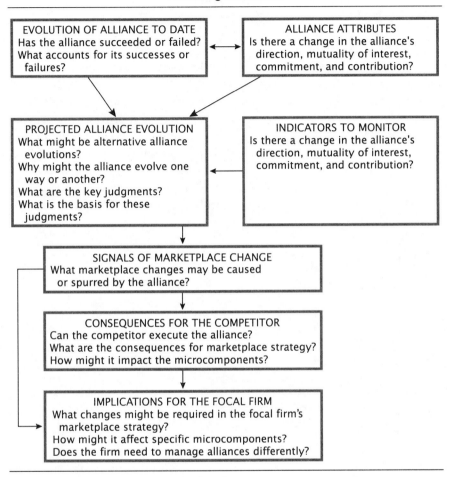

EVOLUTION OF ALLIANCE TO DATE
Has the alliance succeeded or failed?
What accounts for its successes or
  failures?

ALLIANCE ATTRIBUTES
Is there a change in the alliance's
direction, mutuality of interest,
commitment, and contribution?

PROJECTED ALLIANCE EVOLUTION
What might be alternative alliance
  evolutions?
Why might the alliance evolve one
  way or another?
What are the key judgments?
What is the basis for these
  judgments?

INDICATORS TO MONITOR
Is there a change in the alliance's
direction, mutuality of interest,
commitment, and contribution?

SIGNALS OF MARKETPLACE CHANGE
What marketplace changes may be caused
  or spurred by the alliance?

CONSEQUENCES FOR THE COMPETITOR
Can the competitor execute the alliance?
What are the consequences for marketplace strategy?
How might it impact the microcomponents?

IMPLICATIONS FOR THE FOCAL FIRM
What changes might be required in the focal firm's
  marketplace strategy?
How might it affect specific microcomponents?
Does the firm need to manage alliances differently?

external primary sources noted that both partners had made a number of statements confirming their commitment to making the alliance work.

Project Alliance Evolution

Alliance assessment is more concerned with how an alliance will evolve than with its past or current state. How an alliance evolves determines its strategic implications for both the competitor and the focal firm. Thus, it is imperative to project likely alternative alliance evolutions.

Alliance projection entails answering the types of questions noted in Figure 8.5. It requires the analyst to project different evolutions of the alliance depending on different asset contributions and organizational commitments of the partners, key events and milestones, what might go wrong and how it might be corrected, and how success might be further leveraged.

One projection of the CompAll product development alliance is shown in Table 8.1. As is evident from this table, analysts must make judgments about the key decisions and actions that the alliance partners might take over some time period. In essence, analysts must ask themselves what the partners must do to make the alliance a success.

Some inputs to the critical judgments necessary to develop projection about what the alliance partners must do and when are often provided by the partners themselves. Announcements and commentary on them by the alliance partners often explicitly detail key events or milestones and the associated timeline. Analysts can ask members of their own organization and outside experts what steps would be typical of a particular type of alliance and whether the participating parties tend to execute alliances in a particular way.

TABLE 8.1 Projected Evolution of a Product Development Alliance: From the Vantage Point of July 1996

Time	Stages in Alliance Evolution	Indicators
May 1996	Alliance was announced	Announcements
June–July 1996	New stand-alone organization was structured	Stages in research evolution
	Key personnel were appointed	
August–November 1996	Key development programs will be initiated	Stages in organization development
	Some research relationships will be developed with other organizations	
	Organization structure will be further elaborated	
	More personnel appointments will be made	Personnel changes
December 1996– June 1997	Development work will be carried out in multiple sites	Resource commitments
	Major resource commitments will be made	
	Business relationships will be tested and developed with other units within the competitor's parent	
July–December 1997	Prototypes will be tested in laboratory and on customers' premises	Marketing/Sales announcement and commitments
	Marketing and sales programs for new product will be put in place	
January–March 1998	Product will be introduced in the marketplace	

Indicators to Monitor over Time

Since individual alliances evolve over time, monitoring is required. However, guided monitoring necessitates anticipated indicators—identification of the indicators that should be tracked as the alliance evolves. Relevant indicators include key decisions and their execution, major events and their consequences, key milestones, organization evolution, and key stages in research progress.

Key anticipated indicators associated with the CompAll alliance are also noted in Table 8.1. Indeed, sets of related indicators are relevant to each time period in the evolution of the alliance. Thus, organization indicators such as specific personnel appointments, alignments with external entities, and establishment of roles and responsibilities are key indicators in the early stages of the alliance's evolution.

Signals of Marketplace Change

The projected evolution of alliances is a source of signals of marketplace change in multiple ways. If the CompAll alliance leads to a new product, current rivals (including the focal firm) are likely to experience radically different forms of rivalry as customers switch to the new product. Some modes of competition are also likely to shift in importance: product functionality and features may become more important in attracting, winning, and retaining customers than price.

Consequences for the Competitor

Before consequences for marketplace strategy and microcomponents are determined, it is necessary to assess *what* the competitor must do to execute the alliance and whether it *can do* so.

Alliance Execution Projections of alliance evolution suggest actions required to make the alliance a success. The CompAll product development alliance, as shown in Table 8.1, necessitated hiring key personnel, initiating a product development program with specific research and development initiatives, execution of these initiatives in different locations, commitment of financial resources at different times, and if a product was indeed created, the development of marketing, distribution, and sales programs.

Analysts can now ask the following analysis questions:

- Do the partners have the requisite financial assets to execute the alliance?

- Do the partners have the human resource experience and skills to transfer to the new organization?
- What are the attributes of the partners' cultures that might facilitate or inhibit their working together?
- From where will the alliance acquire the knowledge required at different stages of development of the product?
- Do the partners have the emotional commitment to stick with the alliance in the face of development setbacks?

Many specific questions can be posed pertaining to each major action item or stage in the projected alliance evolution. As actions and results are monitored over time, analysts generate much of the data necessary to assess progress in executing the alliance.

Marketplace Strategy Once different ways in which the alliance might evolve are detailed, it is then possible to address marketplace strategy consequences. Each major alliance is assessed for its direct and indirect impact on marketplace scope, posture, and goals. Anticipation of these consequences accords the focal firm a long(er) lead time in determining its own marketplace strategy implications.

In the CompAll new product development example, its success in developing and launching the new product would indicate a new strategic direction. The product would be new to the marketplace; it would be intended to retain many of its existing customers but also to attract many new customers; its goal would be to leapfrog all existing competitors in generating market attention and excitement. If the product proved successful, the competitor might well have a launching pad for the generation of a whole new business segment.

Indirect marketplace strategy consequences occur in multiple ways as a result of many types of alliances. An alliance often leads to a lower cost structure which in turn allows the competitor to charge lower prices or to extend its service, product features, and functionality. An alliance with a vendor resulting in higher quality components enhances product functionality and features.

Microcomponents What it takes to execute an alliance is further tested and refined by assessing the alliance's consequences for each microcomponent. Also, each microcomponent is assessed with regard to how it might constrain or impede execution and evolution of the alliance. How well these consequences are managed determines whether desired marketplace strategy consequences, such as those previously discussed, are realized.

An alliance often relieves or eliminates a constraint or vulnerability along a competitor's activity/value chain (A/VC) or exposes its limitations and vulnerabilities. In the CompAll case, the competitor essentially had to create an A/VC specific to the new product: a new way of doing research, manufacturing, marketing, sales, and service. As it configured each of these activities and the connections among them, CompAll might be able to establish an innovative way of doing cooperative research and development and a significantly enhanced way of manufacturing the new product (compared with its current manufacturing processes).

Relatedly, an alliance sometimes reinforces and leverages a competitor's capabilities and competencies or exposes their limitations and weaknesses. In some instances, an alliance creates or augments a particular capability or competence to the point that it moves the competitor ahead of all rivals in its ability to do something or other.

The asset consequences of an alliance are to some extent embedded in the discussion of A/VC and capability or competency consequences. Organizations sometimes simply do not have the assets to execute an alliance. Specific financial, human, technological, knowledge, or political assets peculiar to the needs of a particular alliance are not available to the competitor.

What it takes to execute an alliance is sometimes incongruent with the competitor's *mind-set*. In some instances, an alliance is a strong indicator of a change in the competitor's assumptions about what it takes to be successful in the business or the future direction of a particular competitive domain, thus alerting the focal firm to potential marketplace strategy change. Such was the case with the CompAll new product development alliance.

The necessary actions may or may not fit with the competitor's *culture* and way of doing business. To the extent they do not, difficulties are likely to transpire in bringing the alliance to fruition. A particular challenge for the CompAll alliance was whether the electronics competitor might impose its own research and development oriented culture on the new organizational unit. To the extent it did, CompAll would most likely find it difficult to move with the speed and alacrity that the projected product development timeline demanded.

Implications for the Focal Firm

Even a single alliance sometimes has significant implications for the focal firm's marketplace strategy, microcomponents, and how it manages its own alliances.

Marketplace Strategy Marketplace strategy consequences for the competitor often generate implications for the focal firm's marketplace strategy.

The focal industrial component firm quickly determined that its current marketplace strategy was grossly insufficient to win against CompAll should the new product reach the marketplace with its announced characteristics. Thus, it was immediately confronted with the challenge of determining how best it could change its strategy: how it could develop or acquire a similar or superior product. The alliance had confronted the focal firm with a strategic issue it had not anticipated.

Microcomponents Implications for the firm's microcomponents derive in part from marketplace strategy implications. For example, the need to radically shift from its current marketplace strategy typically calls into question some core assumptions. Implications also stem in part from the microcomponent consequences for the competitor. For example, if an alliance extends and upgrades a competitor's marketing capabilities, the focal firm is left with little choice but to reassess its own marketing capabilities or how the competitor might be outwitted and outmaneuvered by developing or enhancing other capabilities.

In the CompAll example, the need for the focal firm to develop or acquire a new product compelled assessment of assumptions pertaining to change in the marketplace, the adequacy of the firm's own assets, the sufficiency of its capabilities and competencies, and the appropriateness of its culture.

Managing Alliances Finally, assessment of competitors' alliances inevitably compels the focal firm to consider how it determines what alliances it requires, identifies potential alliance partners, develops alliance relationships, fosters and develops individual alliances, and creates and sustains linkages among its alliances.[14] For example, as attributes of competitors' alliances—direction, mutuality of interest, commitment, and contribution—are addressed, questions quickly arise about the attributes of the focal firm's own alliances. The direction of the CompAll alliance immediately caused the focal firm to assess to what extent any of its own alliances could contribute to a product to rival CompAll's potential product.

Errors in Identifying and Assessing Alliances

Errors are frequently evident in the analysis of alliances. Some of these errors directly relate to the need to continually monitor and project the evolution of individual alliances.

Decision makers fail to recognize or downplay the potential competitor consequences and focal firm implications of a current or an announced alliance. Hence, alliances receive little systematic attention in competitor analysis in many organizations.

Analysts sometimes prematurely cease detailing the characteristics of a key alliance. As a consequence, they fail to fully understand the alliance. Knowing that the alliance is a joint venture with a small competitor indicates little of its terms and conditions.

A related error in describing an alliance is failing to make inquiries of primary sources: the data generated from secondary sources, such as database searches, are not tested and challenged with pertinent primary sources. Thus, the data employed are often somewhat outdated and judgments about the alliance's direction, commitment, and contribution are missed.

Sometimes by not categorizing alliances and by not pursuing the types of questions noted earlier, analysts move too quickly to determining which alliances are key. Extensive publicity accorded an alliance does not imply that it is or will be a key alliance.

Perhaps the gravest error is not projecting likely evolutions of the alliance. Hence, analysts do not test their implicit assumptions about the viability of the alliance. Neither do they identify anticipated indicators; therefore, they are only able to analyze the alliance as it unfolds.

Assessing Individual Relationships

Individual or multiple special relationships are assessed in much the same way as alliances. We will continue to use the small electronics firm's special relationships for illustration purposes (see Figure 8.6).

Evolution of Relationships to Date

As with alliances, special relationships typically evolve in quite different ways. The relationship of the small electronics firm, with a particular university had extended and intensified over a number of years as the university's graduates were promoted into senior positions and the university's research work became even more central to the firm's product development thrust. Its relationship with an original equipment manufacturer was of relatively recent vintage, yet its potential as a source of customer learning and product adaptation was enormous. Its relationship with both the software development vendor and the original equipment manufacturer had evolved and intensified over a number of years.

Projected Evolution

Special relationships often decay. Key individuals retire, resign, or move to other organizations. Competitive change renders a particular relationship less necessary or useful. Rivals intervene with inducements that attract away

FIGURE 8.6
Assessing a Competitor's Special Relationships

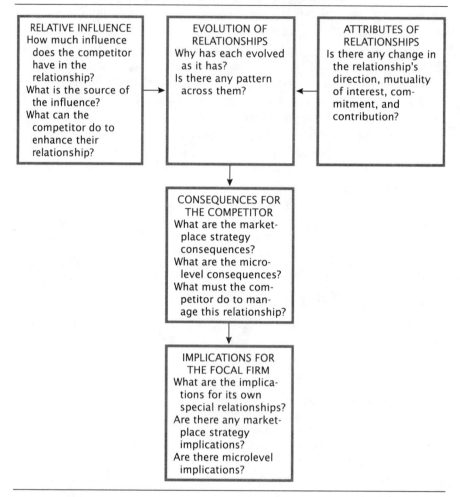

either party. Thus, it is important to assess any relationship's likely future evolution: analysts cannot presume that it will extend and intensify.

A simple projection of a special relationship is sometimes extremely insightful as to its potential consequences and implications. One baseline projection is to presume that the relationship will remain intact for some period of time and then identify the competitor consequences and the focal firm implications. Other projections can be developed around what might happen that would serve to reinforce or disentangle the special relationship. Yet other projections are built around worst-case outcomes for the competitor (e.g., how quickly might a relationship come apart) and best-case outcomes (e.g., the relationship becomes stronger and leads to a major product breakthrough or a new form of customer advantage).

If all the small electronics firm's special relationships dissipated within a year or two, the consequences for its product development, as will be discussed, would be disastrous. A different projection could address new special relationships the competitor might develop with other vendors, original equipment manufacturers, and end-customers. These relationships might then allow it to extend its product line or refocus its posture.

Relative Influence

Relationship projections hinge to some extent on the relative influence of the competitor and the other party. Assessments of the relative degree of influence are inherently difficult, in part because a competitor typically possesses varying degrees of influence across its special relationships, its influence may wax and wane over time, and the degree of influence also varies across different facets of any particular relationship.

Relative influence is partly a result of the extent to which the parties are dependent on each other. Considerations of the elements of what constitutes the special relationship discussed earlier—bonds, origins, purposes, key individuals, and exclusivity—provide indicators of relative dependence and influence. In the case of the small electronics firm's special relationship with the university, the competitor's influence was most likely increasing as it developed and enhanced its own knowledge base and as students with similar or superior qualifications became more readily available from other institutions. By the same token, its influence with the standards-setting body was probably declining as more and more organizations became involved in its various activities.

A further difficulty is that analysts sometimes allow their own presuppositions to color their (preliminary) assessments. This bias was greatly in evidence when analysts in a pharmaceutical firm initially dismissed the likelihood that a competitor could have any influence over the manner and speed that the FDA or any other federal agency would review its submissions and presentations. Only when it was discovered that the competitor adhered to all the FDA stipulations and requests, and demonstrated its willingness to do so, did it become evident that it had worked hard over a number of years to build a solid, open, and honest working relationship with the agency.

Consequences for the Competitor

Special relationships are important because they sometimes have significant marketplace strategy and microlevel consequences. They are the source of new products; they cement linkages to channels and end-customers; they allow distinctive forms of posture; they facilitate operational efficiencies that otherwise would be impossible.

For the small electronics firm, the combined effect of its special relationships on product development was enormous. Its university relationship gave it continued access to new product ideas and extension possibilities for its current products. Its involvement with one software development vendor greatly aided the design and development of some key product features. Its involvement with both the OEM and the major end-customer was intended to generate new product ideas and better ways of extending the applicability of existing products.

Implications for Focal Firm

The competitor's special relationships had high-impact marketplace strategy implications for the large electronics firm. The competitor's ability to introduce a stream of product upgrades had given it significant customer-based advantage reflected in substantial market share gains. The focal firm now had to more fully commit to developing and introducing a range of products that would at a minimum reconstruct the strategy game and shift the marketplace rules[15] in its favor. The small competitor became in effect one of a number of wake-up calls for the larger, more complacent, focal firm.

More directly, the success of the smaller competitor caused the focal firm to critically review the state of its own special relationships: which ones it had (and did not have), with whom, how well they were managed, and to what extent they were leveraged. The outcome of this assessment was two sets of action implications. First, there was a need to develop the special side of existing relationships. Tighter bonds had to be created and sustained with suppliers, channels, and end-customers. Second, it needed to better leverage many relationships. For example, its relationship with a number of end-customers could be better utilized in all phases of product development and testing.

Errors in Analyzing Special Relationships

The errors noted in relation to the analysis of alliances also pertain to special relationships. Some errors more specific to special relationships are noted here.

The most substantial error is to ignore special relationships entirely. This occurs when the concept of such relationships is not part of analysts' mental model of competitor learning.

More generally, perhaps, analysts often do not make detection and assessment of special relationships a persistent focus of their competitor scanning and monitoring. If special relationships are not at the forefront of analysts' mental models of what needs to be understood about competitors, attention to them will occur only if it is provoked in some way or other.

Frequently, analysts do not dig beneath the surface of an alliance to discern what is special about the competitor's involvement with the alliance partner(s). The alliance is not pursued beyond its formal terms and conditions.

Every special relationship has a context: its history, the reasons for its existence, and the forces within and external to the parties that sustain it. A fundamental error is the failure to develop a sufficient sense of the context of a relationship as a prelude to inferring what is special about it.

It is also often presumed that what is special about a relationship will continue, or will extend and intensify. Anticipated indicators of change are thus not developed. Change in the relationship is then detected only after its consequences are visible for all to see.

A common error is not to investigate the personal side of a special relationship—Who are the participants, what are the bonds that bind them, and what are the reasons for them? The elements that make the relationship special are thus poorly understood, critical indicators of change in it are not anticipated, and fundamental changes in the relationship are more likely not to be detected.

Identifying and Assessing Patterns among Alliances and Relationships

Over time, most organizations manifest distinct patterns in their alliance behaviors. Analysts search for indicators that suggest specific patterns (for a guided approach, see Figure 8.7) or they search for patterns across many different types of indicators (an open-ended approach). These behavior patterns reveal how alliances are used to facilitate and attain specific marketplace strategies and/or particular organization purposes such as building specific competencies. These patterns also provide essential background or context for the analysis of individual alliances. The more common patterns are highlighted here.

Sometimes there is a common marketplace strategy purpose to a sequence or set of alliances. For example, many firms have used alliances with different types of distribution channels to gain access to new geographic markets. A dominant goal is to gain global market coverage as quickly as possible. Some firms use alliances with large end-customers or users to more quickly develop and test products.

Individual competitors often exhibit a tendency to enter into a specific type of alliance. For example, one telecommunications firm noted that a particular competitor used codevelopment alliances to design and develop the next generation of key components.

FIGURE 8.7
Identifying and Assessing Patterns across a Competitor's Alliances

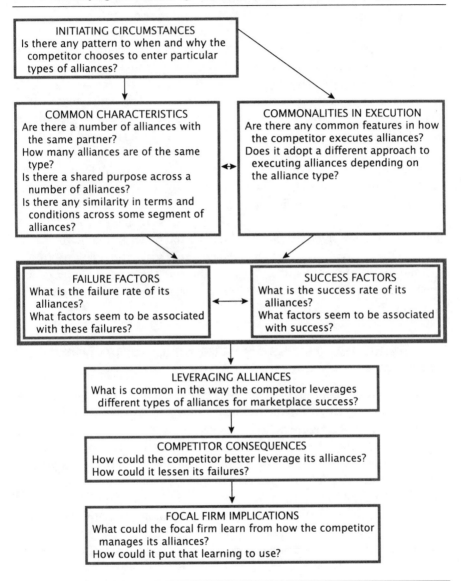

INITIATING CIRCUMSTANCES
Is there any pattern to when and why the competitor chooses to enter particular types of alliances?

COMMON CHARACTERISTICS
Are there a number of alliances with the same partner?
How many alliances are of the same type?
Is there a shared purpose across a number of alliances?
Is there any similarity in terms and conditions across some segment of alliances?

COMMONALITIES IN EXECUTION
Are there any common features in how the competitor executes alliances?
Does it adopt a different approach to executing alliances depending on the alliance type?

FAILURE FACTORS
What is the failure rate of its alliances?
What factors seem to be associated with these failures?

SUCCESS FACTORS
What is the success rate of its alliances?
What factors seem to be associated with success?

LEVERAGING ALLIANCES
What is common in the way the competitor leverages different types of alliances for marketplace success?

COMPETITOR CONSEQUENCES
How could the competitor better leverage its alliances?
How could it lessen its failures?

FOCAL FIRM IMPLICATIONS
What could the focal firm learn from how the competitor manages its alliances?
How could it put that learning to use?

It is not uncommon to find a degree of commonality in the terms and conditions of alliances. Thus, agreements with various distribution channels tend to have a somewhat similar incentive structure.

Not surprisingly, a high degree of consistency is evident in how individual competitors execute alliances. Indicators pertaining to the evolution of an alliance, as discussed earlier, allow patterns to be detected in how long it takes to consummate an agreement, the stages involved in making the alliance happen (such as the steps taken to affect a manufacturing joint venture), how progress is monitored and evaluated, and the types of corrective actions taken.

The reasons alliances (and sometimes even special relationships) break down and dissipate sometimes constitute another insightful pattern. One large firm discovered that its most significant corporate competitor had extreme difficulty sustaining alliances with most other entities in its industry because of its distinctive culture. Its alliance partners were unable to adjust to its entrepreneurial style of decision making and its abhorrence of formal procedures and detailed budgets.

Conversely, the factors associated with the successful execution of alliances also indicate why some competitors are able to create and leverage alliances and others cannot. Some firms such as Corning work hard at building a culture that understands why alliances are necessary, how to develop and sustain them, and how to transfer learning from one alliance to another.

Anticipating a Competitor's Potential Alliances

Outwitting and outmaneuvering competitors requires that analysts go beyond identification and assessment of existing and announced alliances. They must also address competitors' potential alliances: those they may need to undergird marketplace strategy change, to leverage capabilities or competencies, or to alleviate constraints and vulnerabilities. Both guided and open-ended inquiry are appropriate. One framework for *guided* analysis is shown in Figure 8.8.

(Anticipated) Indicators of Need for Alliances

Indicators of the need for an alliance emanate from many of the steps already addressed in this chapter and from other framework components such as marketplace strategy, activity/value chain, capabilities and competencies, and technology. Assessment of competitor consequences of one or more alliances also often indicate the need for a specific type of alliance. For example, if a particular alliance does not meet the competitor's need for a specific supply of a particular component or it does not provide sufficient distribution channel reach into a new geographic region, one or more alliances may be required to make up for the shortfall. Similarly, assessment of constraints and vulnerabilities along a competitor's activity/value chain[16] sometimes clearly indicate a need for particular alliances. Alliances are often the only way that competitors can quickly alleviate supply constraints

FIGURE 8.8
Identifying a Competitor's Potential Alliances

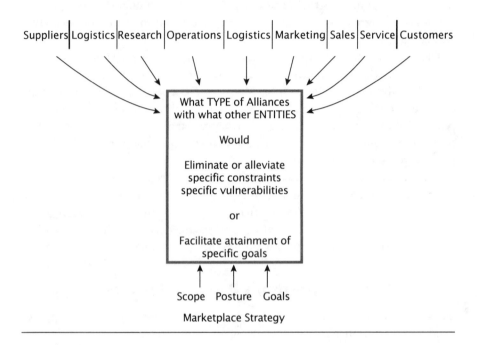

Suppliers | Logistics | Research | Operations | Logistics | Marketing | Sales | Service | Customers

What TYPE of Alliances
with what other ENTITIES

Would

Eliminate or alleviate
specific constraints
specific vulnerabilities

or

Facilitate attainment of
specific goals

Scope   Posture   Goals

Marketplace Strategy

for critical components, deficiencies in integrated logistics, and research competencies in particular product areas. Changes in a competitor's marketplace strategy such as the development and introduction of new products or the pursuit of new classes of customers may require alliance partners to conduct different types of research or to avail of existing distribution channels.

As an aid in identifying potential alliances, analysts determine an array of *anticipated* indicators that would suggest individual competitors' needs for alliances. Anticipated indicators serve to guide analysts' search for potential alliances: they are systematically applied to individual competitors. As noted, anticipated indicators of the need for alliances include inability of existing or proposed alliances to meet specific product or supply requirements, specific constraints and vulnerabilities, marketplace strategy goals that exceed the competitor's production ability or ability to reach specific geographic segments.

Indicators of Interest in Potential Alliances

Detecting a need for alliances sensitizes analysts to be alert for indicators that reveal a competitor is interested in affecting alliances. Analysts then scan and monitor both primary and secondary data sources for prean-nouncement indicators that suggest the competitor is considering an al-liance, or is likely to enter into an alliance, *before* a formal announcement of its intention to do so occurs. Even though most organizations' contacts and conversations with prospective alliance partners are confidential and shrouded in secrecy, individual firms often make statements to the effect that if the right alliance partner came along, they would be interested in holding discussions, or that they are always holding talks with prospective alliance partners.

Availability of Alliance Partners

Potential alliances presume the existence of available partners. Once the need for a particular alliance is identified, analysts identify potential al-liance partners. The more specific the goals and requirements for an al-liance partner, the more focused is the scan to identify the range of available entities. For example, a need was identified for a telecommunications com-petitor to develop an alliance with a supplier with strong current and potential capability in two particular technology areas. These two tech-nologies then guided the scanning of available industry directories, and interviews with technology, supply, and industry experts, to identify poten-tial alliance partners.

Competitor Consequences

By projecting possible consequences of one or more potential alliances, an-alysts are able to assess what the results might be, whether and how a com-petitor might be able to execute the alliance(s), and whether and how it might be able to leverage the alliance(s).[17] Results are assessed for the com-petitor's marketplace strategy and specific microlevel components. For ex-ample, if the telecommunications competitor noted earlier developed one or more alliances with suppliers having the right technology capabilities, then the firm could radically upgrade its product line, and potentially secure a significant customer-based advantage over all rivals. Results for activity/value chain configuration, and in particular the alleviation or elim-ination of constraints and vulnerabilities, are often significant.

Focal Firm Implications

Anticipating a competitor's potential alliances often identifies a number of potential implications for the focal firm. Potential change in one or more competitors' marketplace strategy often has significant implications for the firm's own strategy. If potential competitor alliances alleviate major activity/value chain constraints and vulnerabilities, the focal firm may have to reappraise its own activity/value chain commitments: they may not generate the competitor-based advantage initially projected. Finally, consideration of competitors' potential alliances may identify alliances the firm itself may need. Articulation of how a competitor might execute a potential alliance, its marketplace strategy and other results, and its implications for the focal firm, often compel decision makers to critically review their own perceptions, beliefs, assumptions, and projections about their own marketplace strategy, future competitive dynamics, and whether and how they might win.

 ## Summary

Alliances and relationships focus the analyst's attention beyond the legal boundaries of a competitor. They necessarily cause analysts to ask questions and to raise issues that are unlikely to surface if analysts address only a competitor's marketplace strategy and activity/value chain. Moreover, they reinforce the importance of going beyond description of the current state of an alliance or relationship (or indeed a pattern across alliances and relationships) to projecting their likely future paths.

Networks

NOTHING MORE CLEARLY DEMONSTRATES THE NEED FOR BROAD-BASED FRAMEWORKS of competitor analysis than the emergence and prevalence of networks—the complex linkages an organization possesses with many other entities including suppliers, distribution channels, end-customers, technology sources, public policy interest groups, and even competitors. No longer is it sufficient to analyze competitors as stand-alone organizations.[1] In computers, software, pharmaceuticals, airplane manufacturing, automobiles, plastics, and many types of electronic goods, competition is now as much between networked enterprises as it is between individual stand-alone firms.[2]

For many firms, networks are central to winning. These interconnected webs of alliances and relationships greatly extend a firm's access to many different assets, allow it to develop new and distinctive capabilities and competencies, and facilitate its staying power in the face of rivals' strategic moves. Leaders in many industries have outwitted their rivals by anticipating the need for a network, identifying the entities that should be part of the network, and designing possible network configurations. They outmaneuver rivals by attracting "best-in-class" entities such as the most innovative supplier of a particular component, creating relationships among the entities that inspire and sustain commitment to the network, and doing so quickly. They outperform rivals in the way they use networks to create new products, to quickly bring products to market, and to gain market penetration.

This chapter begins by defining networks. Next, distinct network types are delineated, and the prevalence of networks and their strategic importance are briefly outlined. The body of the chapter describes how to identify and assess a network. The concluding section identifies common errors in network analysis.

This chapter focuses on the role of analysts in integrating the core learning activities (decision making, capturing, processing, and crafting) through use of the core learning questions that were briefly introduced in Chapter 2. The specific intent is to demonstrate how capturing, processing, and crafting are directly linked to assessment. The discussion extends and reinforces the recursive nature of competitor learning highlighted in Chapter 8. To demonstrate integration and feedback among the learning activities, the steps involved in identifying and assessing networks are commingled (as opposed to being discussed separately as occurs in several other chapters).

Understanding Networks

What a Network Is

A network is an interconnected set of alliances and relationships. Typically, the web of interconnected entities has one organization as its node, as shown in Figure 9.1, in the case of a computer firm. The nodal organization is always the network initiator and leader. Each entity fulfills a specific function or role within the network.

Network members can be any entity along the industry chain: raw material providers, component suppliers, logistics organizations, competitors, distribution channels, and end-customers. Networks also often include many other entities typically involved in an industry including banks and other suppliers of capital, consulting organizations, and technology sources. Sometimes networks include universities, government agencies, and social and political interest groups.

Types and Purposes of Networks

Networks can be categorized in terms of their structure or composition and goals. Although there is some overlap among them, five types of networks merit special attention:[3]

1. *Vertical network.* Alliances and relationships across the activity/value chain constitute a vertical network. Each element in the network contributes to the performance of one or more activities. Almost every firm has some form of a vertical network. The network's aim is to help the firm win today and to position it to win tomorrow.

2. *Technology network.* Many firms now develop alliances and relationships with multiple technology sources. The general goal of such networks is to ensure that the firm gains or retains technological superiority.[4]

3. *Development network.* The intent of some networks is to develop new products, processes, or materials. The alliances and relationships are

FIGURE 9.1
A Computer Competitor's Network: The "Raw" Form

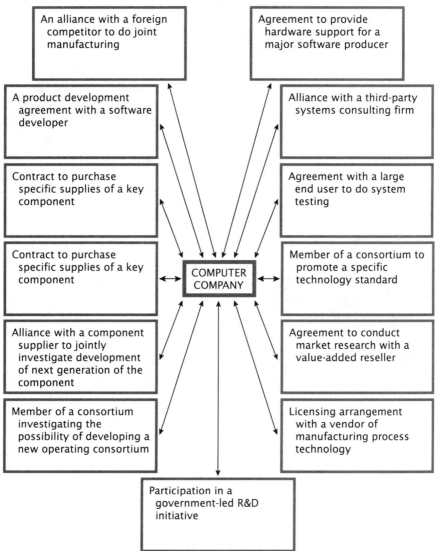

coordinated and managed with a view to creating a solution or technology that is new to the marketplace. Few firms have the resources to develop a continual stream of new products, processes, and materials without the benefit of multiple development networks.

4. *Ownership network.* Ownership networks are the essence of the Japanese keiretsu. Firms such as Mitsui, Toyota, Honda, Mitsubishi, Matsushita,

and many others, possess an ownership position in many different suppliers, some channels, and one or two financial institutions. The intent of a keiretsu is to create a mutuality of interest among many different entities so that they will work cooperatively to achieve common goals. Some U.S. firms such as GE, Microsoft, and Du Pont also develop ownership positions in a large number of other enterprises.

5. *Political network.* A political network is a group of entities that come together to achieve some purpose in the political, regulatory, and judicial milieu such as lower tariffs on imported raw materials or the protection of favorable tax policies. Such networks are almost always temporary in nature: once their purpose is attained they tend to dissipate. However, the relationships forged in any single political network facilitate the development and execution of other political networks. Some firms are especially capable in mobilizing, energizing, and leading such networks.

The Prevalence of Networks

Networks are evident in every industry. Each large firm in the automobile industry is the node in a complex network that involves one or more competitors, multiple types of suppliers, technology sources, and dealers. Every large pharmaceutical firm is now part of a complex network with links to competitors, biotechnology entities, distribution channels, and end-customers such as hospitals, research institutions, and government agencies.

Networks are not just created by large firms. Many smaller firms develop some form of a vertical network in pursuit of their strategic goals. A complex of alliances and relationships pertaining to each activity allows smaller firms access to key knowledge, technology, and markets.

The development of a network is increasingly the means by which new organizations seek to grow and prosper. Consider the case of DreamWorks (see Figure 9.2). Three individuals form a partnership and then entice many different entities to enter into some form of alliance or relationship with them so that they can make and distribute movies and multimedia entertainment products. This development network has attained considerable prominence in the rapidly changing entertainment industry in less than two years.

A Single Firm's Networks

Analysis of networks is made more complex because an individual firm is frequently simultaneously involved in multiple networks. In some, it is the nodal enterprise; in others, it is merely one of the interconnected entities.

Any large firm with multiple distinct product or business sectors (e.g., Allied Signal, Westinghouse, Motorola, Emerson Electric, Du Pont, Siemens,

FIGURE 9.2
A New Organization's Network: DreamWorks

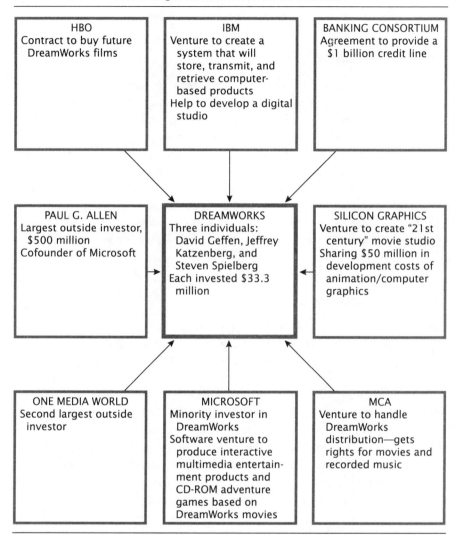

Olivetti) is likely to have multiple vertical networks across its business sectors or business units. Indeed, a product or business sector may have distinct networks around its individual product lines or groups. Even predominantly single industry firms such as Merck, Procter & Gamble, and Microsoft possess distinct vertical networks around specific product groups or lines.

Firms like these are typically involved in many technology and/or development networks (e.g., Microsoft is continually augmenting its network around its operating system and corporate network systems solutions).

Any firm, almost irrespective of its size, may also be a member of multiple political networks. It may find itself on the same or opposite sides with any particular network member from one issue to another.

Network Evolution

A network does not spring into being all at once. It takes a firm many years to develop a vertical or technology network. Alliances and relationships are added to the network over time. The leading auto manufactures have spent at least two decades augmenting and extending their networks.

Many of these firms probably did not realize they were creating networks. They simply added alliances and relationships to gain access to specific assets, technologies, or markets. However, as it becomes aware that it is creating a networked enterprise, the nodal organization chooses alliances and relationships that fill out the network by seeking entities that may give it access to particular technological capabilities or unique components, or to specific national markets or channels of distribution.

Network Attributes

Irrespective of the type of network, four distinct though related attributes merit attention: structure, leadership, purpose, and stability. Change occurs along each attribute, and sometimes precipitously.

Structure Rivals' networks most often embody distinct structures: different compositions of alliances and relationships. For example, two or more vertical networks frequently manifest different configurations of suppliers, channels, rivals, and end-customers. One network may have only one supplier; another may have multiple suppliers. Some vertical networks, such as those occurring in the automobile industry, may evidence a small number of primary suppliers,[5] which in turn, are linked to many secondary suppliers.

Leadership Networks require significant investments of managerial attention and time. Leadership refers to those who lead the network and how they do so. In vertical networks, leadership rests in a single organization (the nodal enterprise). In technology and development networks, leadership is sometimes shared among two or more members: different members may lead in the execution of specific network tasks.

Purpose One of the difficulties in developing and sustaining a network is creating a sense of shared purpose among its members. Some networks manage to establish an integrating purpose that binds and integrates the commitment and contribution of all or most members. Others find it difficult to do so.

Stability Networks also vary greatly in their stability: the extent to which network structure and composition remain constant over time and the extent to which members support and reinforce each other. Network instability is likely to arise as the interests of members diverge. Unstable networks find it difficult to achieve their integrating purpose or to coherently react to the moves of rivals.

The Marketplace Strategy Importance of Networks

As the examples in this chapter illustrate, networks frequently facilitate and generate extensive change in each marketplace strategy element: scope, posture, and goals. Vertical, technology, and development networks often underlie new product introductions, extensions of existing products, and the integration of existing products. Through their global reach, networks allow firms to serve new customer segments. The pursuit of new strategic intents or marketplace visions increasingly requires developing and leveraging one or more networks.

Marketplace strategies must be viewed as rivalry between networks rather than stand-alone corporate entities. It is not just Hewlett-Packard competing against IBM, General Motors competing against Honda, or Unilever competing against Procter & Gamble. Rivalry is between the networks these firms and their rivals have created within specific product areas such as computer workstations, midsize automobiles, and detergents.

Indicators of Network Change

Direct indicators pertain to each network attribute. Exit and entry of members, and developments in alignments among individual members, indicate change in network structure and stability. Sometimes a subset of network members develop closer working relationships over time, which may positively or negatively affect structure and stability. Statements and actions are often significant direct indicators of change in network leadership and purpose. For example, the nodal organization may issue comments about what it wants to achieve with the network. Actions of network members may indicate change in the leadership roles: for example, when members launch new product development activities, contribute new capital to the network, or extend their own alliances and relationships with non-network members, it may herald an extended leadership role for them within the network.

Indirect indicators are sometimes the source of alerting signals of network change. A downturn in the nodal organization's financial or marketplace performance may cause it to consider change in one or more of its networks. Changes in its senior management ranks, such as the recruitment of individuals from firms known for their astute network management, may also auger impending network change.

Network Change as Signals

Networks give rise to both strong and weak signals of change in marketplace strategy, and many microlevel components including assumptions, assets, capabilities and competencies, and technology. As discussed later in this chapter, change in each network attribute is a source of signals, some of which may indicate discontinuous and short lag change. A single change in a network's structure such as the addition of a new alliance partner is sometimes the alerting signal of significant marketplace strategy change such as the potential development of a new product. Perceiving and interpreting these signals requires an understanding of the network that goes beyond the analysis of any one of its links.

Identifying and Assessing a Competitor's Network(s)

The guided steps in identifying and assessing competitors' networks (see Figures 9.3 and 9.4) frame the analysis that is necessary to understand a network's attributes as well as its consequences and implications. A major rival of a leading computer manufacturer is used for illustration purposes. The competitor, also a well-established computer provider, had launched a series of product advances but had not yet succeeded in becoming the undisputed market leader in a relatively new product sector. However, it had outperformed the focal firm in launching new products and committing the research and development that would be required to create and introduce the next two or three generations of the product.

A Comment: The Role and Importance of Analysts

Identifying and assessing networks demonstrates the importance of the role of analysts in each competitor learning activity: assessment, capturing, processing, and crafting (see Figure 2.1). Analysts are not idle bystanders in any of these learning activities: they continually make judgments[6] as they capture and process network data and craft it into useful decision-relevant outputs. Analysts revisit their judgments as they circle back and forth through these activities: knowledge about competitors' networks is created, articulated, and reflected on.

FIGURE 9.3
Identifying a Competitor's Network

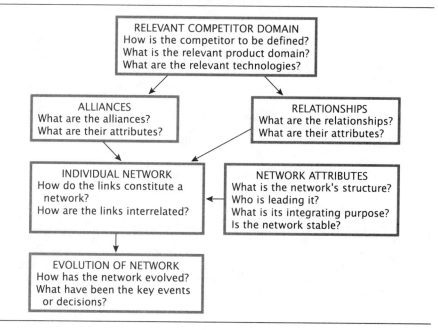

As with other microlevel components such as activity/value chain, assumptions, and capabilities and competencies, the role of analysts assumes added importance because they often have little sense of the eventual network configuration. Sometimes, analysts are surprised by the network structure that emerges: they have little idea of the breadth and complexity of the linkages between the competitor and other entities. They thus need to adopt the spirit of open-ended inquiry: as each alliance or relationship is identified, analysts need to ask in what ways the network might be reconfigured.[7]

Impetus for Network Analysis

An interest in competitors' networks arises in many ways. Sometimes it is *triggered* by observations of their efforts to develop alliances and relationships with multiple other entities. Analysts begin to query what the competitor is trying to do. Sometimes it is triggered by recognizing how a competitor is able to develop new products, gain access to markets, or tap into the technological knowledge and capabilities of other organizations.[8]

The computer firm was *sensitized* to the existence and importance of competitors' networks in several related ways. First, key decision makers became concerned that the focal organization had been outwitted and

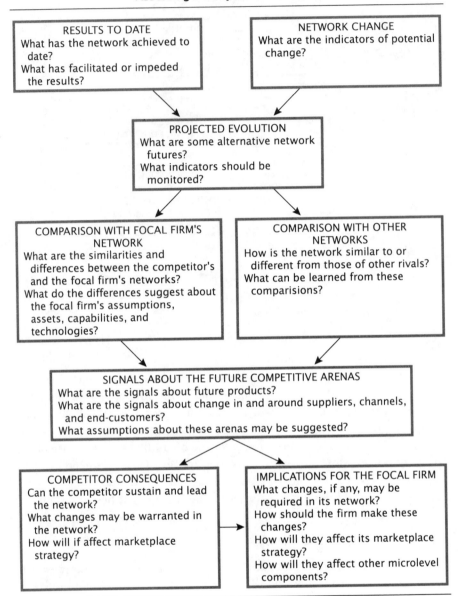

FIGURE 9.4
Assessing a Competitor's Network

outmaneuvered by specific competitors that had developed a series of alliances with key component and supply vendors, channels, end-customers, and technology sources as well as with other rivals. These competitors appeared to be doing things that they could not do on their own. Second, the firm had been surprised by the speed with which some competitors introduced new products, reinvigorated product lines, and imbued these products with technology that they had not developed in-house.

Guiding Learning Questions

Guided learning is driven by focused questions. The analyst team assigned to study competitors' networks began by applying the core learning questions:

- What do we know about competitors' networks?
- What might we learn about their networks?
- What is the knowledge increment?
- What difference would the new knowledge make to decision making and who could use it?

The team quickly concluded that they knew relatively little about each major competitor's current networks, history, or potential evolution. Network analysis had never been a focus of attention. However, they felt they knew a considerable amount about many competitors' individual alliances and relationships.

Yet it was not obvious to everyone in the focal firm that a research effort should be expended to study how and why competitors were networked. What *might be learned* by identifying and assessing any competitor's network required discussion. As they asked network-related questions, a central focus of learning emerged:

- Why were networks apparently more evident with some competitors?
- What accounted for network success and failure?
- When did networks contribute most to marketplace strategy?
- How might this learning be applied in the focal firm?

The *gap* between what they knew and needed to know was extensive and significant. So were the potential *implications*. If the focal firm could develop and enhance its own networks, it might be able to develop new products or extend existing product lines. A number of difficulties in managing component suppliers might also be resolved.

Crafting a Preliminary Network

A network structure evolves (in diagrammatic form) as analysts add alliances and relationships. Each network presents a number of unavoidable judgments:[9] What is the relevant network domain? Which alliances and relationships should be included? How should the alliance be configured? What is the role of each network link?

Network Domain   Because of the many different types of networks, and the likelihood that a competitor is involved in a multiplicity of networks, an initial task is to specify the network domain: the relevant competitor, products, and technologies. In some technology, development, ownership, and political networks, it is not obvious who the competitor is. For example, in the case of three companies, Apple, Motorola, and IBM, coming together to develop a new PC technology, specification of "the competitor" is not self-evident. It is certainly not any one of the three firms alone. It is essentially the network created by these independent firms.

Because a competitor often is a participant in many networks, it is always essential to identify the relevant product focus. In some instances, it is a product sector or group of related products. Such would be the case if one were detailing Motorola's network in its semiconductor business or IBM's network in its workstation business. Often, the relevant focus is a specific product line. Sometimes it is an individual product: a pharmaceutical firm may delineate the product development network of a competitor that is bringing together diverse research and development organizations from many parts of the globe.

In the computer firm case, the network domain was all the technologies pertaining to one product area of a single firm. These included component product technologies, manufacturing technologies, product content technologies, and the technologies to facilitate reaching and interacting with channels and end-customers.

Identify Alliances and Relationships   The central data collection task is to identify the competitor's alliances and relationships in the relevant network domain. The data collection methods outlined in Chapter 8 generate a listing of individual alliances and relationships (see Table 9.1). Descriptive data including whom the alliance or relationship is with, its purpose, and history to date, may also be included in the listing.

Raw Network   A network is never evident from a mere listing of alliances and relationships. Analysts must create it. It begins to take form when a pathway connecting the alliances and relationships to the competitor is identified and delineated in diagrammatic form. It is a step-by-step process: each alliance and relationship is individually entered into the network. The resulting first-cut network for the competitor is often a node (the competitor) and a set of arrows that show a system of alliances and relationships (see Figures 9.1 and 9.2).

Even at this early stage, extensive learning occurs. Analysts begin to understand the complexity of the network structure—the alliances and relationships that constitute the network's configuration. Some hints of a

TABLE 9.1 Listing of Computer Competitor's Alliances and Relationships

1) A product development agreement with a software developer

2) Contract to purchase specific supplies of a key component

3) Member of a consortium investigating the possibility of developing a new operating consortium

4) Agreement to conduct market research with a value-added reseller

5) Agreement with a large end-user to do system testing

6) An alliance with a foreign competitor to do joint manufacturing

7) Contract to purchase supplies of a key component

8) Participating in a government-led R&D initiative

9) Alliance with a component supplier to jointly investigate development of next generation of the component

10) Licensing arrangement with a vendor of manufacturing process technology

11) Alliance with third-party systems consulting firm

12) Member of consortium to promote a specific technology standard

13) Agreement to provide hardware support for a major software provider

---

network's purpose may also be inferred. For example, analysts considering the DreamWorks network (see Figure 9.2) begin to get a sense of the network's intent to create certain types of movies and to develop new and distinct movie production capabilities.

Reconfigured Network   Often true understanding of a network's structure and purpose only begins to emerge when the raw network is reconfigured to clarify connections to the competitor and connections among entities within the network. Analysts are thus presented with another opportunity to order, select, and interpret data such that one or more outputs are crafted that are simply not evident from the raw data—the listing of alliances and relationships (see Table 9.1) and the raw network (see Figures 9.1 and 9.2).

It is often useful to reconfigure a raw network by indicating the link between each alliance or relationship and the competitor's activity/value chain. For the computer competitor (see Figure 9.5), specific alliances were associated with each major activity. Analysts can now begin to assess how these alliances enable the competitor to manage and execute each activity. To do so requires an understanding of the role and contribution of each network link.

Role of Each Network Link   Each alliance or relationship contributes to understanding what the network is intended to achieve, what it may be able to achieve, and how it may do so. For example, a large end user's role in system

FIGURE 9.5
A Computer Competitor's Network: Alliances and Relationships along the Activity/Value Chain

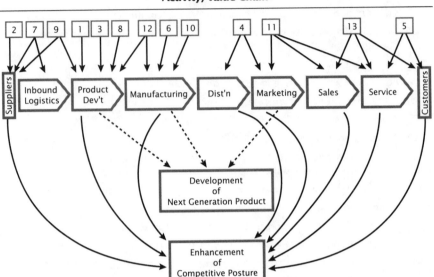

testing serves as a critical link in the computer competitor's product development, testing, and learning *before* the product or solution is announced and launched (see Figure 9.5). Many of the bugs in the solution are detected and corrected in a real user's work environment. The competitor thus quickly gains significant benefit from the customer's extensive knowledge of the product, its application, and its limitations and merits.

The two component alliances in the case of the computer competitor (see Figure 9.5) offer it the possibility of developing leading components, and thus superior product functionality.

Sometimes, the contribution of an individual link only becomes evident when it is viewed in the context of the entire network. For example, the computer competitor's membership in a government-led R&D initiative could lead to technology breakthroughs that would in turn give rise to extensive product innovations. The competitor's network of links in this product domain to suppliers, channels, and other technology sources might allow it to leverage these technology developments more rapidly than many of its rivals.

Attributes of the Network

As the network is being described and reconfigured, analysts identify and assess its attributes. Doing so serves at least two purposes. First, it compels analysts to consider whether a genuine network is present or merely a small set of unrelated alliances. Second, if a network is evident, it focuses analysts' attention on the network as a whole rather than its individual parts. This is especially important if analysts were previously preoccupied with one or two alliances. As analysts consider each attribute, they begin to identify possible consequences: what issues and decisions the state of each attribute generates for the competitor.

As illustrated in the following discussion, identifying and assessing a network's attributes involves detecting and interpreting a pattern across both direct and indirect indicators. Thus, assessments of each attribute require analysts to consider the entire network and not just isolated segments of it.

Structure The computer competitor's vertical network was composed of itself as the lead firm, with two major alliance partners, and many minor partners. The major alliance partners were providers of key components. Each component was critical to the final product or solution; each partner was widely recognized as the leader in its respective technologies; the computer competitor had a tight working or special relationship with senior executives in each component partner.

Two competitor consequences quickly emerged. First, was the network structure and composition sufficient to sustain and extend the competitor's current product leadership in the short to medium run? Second, what links, if any, should be added to the network? Although answers to these questions could not yet be tendered with any degree of confidence, raising them at this early stage of the analysis sensitized the analysts to critical potential competitor consequences.

Leadership The structure indicated significant elements of the network's leadership process. The competitor, reflecting its position as the node in the network, was unambiguously the initiator and driver of the network. It had put the alliances and relationships in place over a number of years. Almost all of the alliance partners were considerably more dependent on the competitor than vice versa.

Yet two leadership challenges were evident. First, the competitor would need to lead in a different way as technologies, products, and markets changed. It would no longer be in a position to dominate some key alliances with vendors and value-added resellers. Leadership would require developing true partnering relationships, something that the analysts believed the competitor had not yet practiced.

Second, leadership based on partnering relationships would be a challenge to the firm's historic culture. It would require a significant shift in some of its apparent values and beliefs; it had always taken great pride in its ability to develop products based on its own technology accomplishments.

Purpose Viewed solely from the competitor's perspective, the integrating purpose of the network in the opinion of the analysts was to position the competitor to win in the long run—to generate and deliver solutions that would keep it ahead of all its rivals. Although this inference was not derived from any direct indicators, a pattern was evident across a number of indirect indicators: alliances with component suppliers, software developers, and a systems consulting firm were intended to move the competitor toward the next generation of solutions; statements by the competitor's senior managers referred to the need to be involved with the leaders of each major technology; and the competitor's senior managers provided supporting rationales for entering into particular alliances and relationships.

An evident challenge was how the competitor could sustain and reinforce a sense of purpose throughout the network, or more specifically, among the primary links in the network. This challenge was closely related to the need to develop true partnering relationships—and the supporting culture.

Stability The primary links in the network had been sustained for a number of years. The competitor had a long-term relationship with each of the two major suppliers, the third-party consulting firm, and many of the other alliance partners.

Despite the apparent current stability, the computer competitor's leadership prowess would be severely tested as the position of existing network members changed and as it attracted new entities to the network. For example, if one of the network's component suppliers were enticed to join another network or if it judged that it was not obtaining its just rewards from involvement in the network, the computer competitor would have to adjust the inducements available to it. The stability of the network was dependent on the actions of the competitor.

Network History

It should be evident from this discussion that understanding a network's history provides essential background for assessing network attributes. It also yields important indicators of its likely future development and direction. Among the questions that should be addressed are:

- Over what time period has the network evolved?
- What has been the sequence in which key alliances or relationships were put in place?
- What have been some of the significant events?

The computer competitor had forged its network over the course of four or five years. Its propensity to enter into alliances had greatly increased in the prior two years. Previously, the firm had for many years largely disdained formal alliances unless it felt they were absolutely necessary.

Preliminary Assessment

It is all too easy for analysts to become preoccupied with network specification. The contribution of a preliminary assessment to refining the network and to shaping decision relevant outputs[10] is thus missed. Both *guided* and *open-ended* approaches are useful at different stages of a preliminary assessment.

What Is Being Learned As the network structure emerges and its key attributes are assessed, analysts must carefully identify what is being learned and how that learning can be put to use. As a first-cut network emerged (see Figure 9.1), the analysis team was able to point to key information that was being generated about the competitor:

- The scope, integration, and purpose of the network.
- How each link in the network was contributing to the overall network purpose.
- Potential costs, limitations, and vulnerabilities of the network.

At this stage, each element of what is learned is tentative. Yet they guide the next stages in the analysis. They do so in part by generating learning when the competitor's network is compared with the focal firm's. Some of the preliminary judgments included:

- The focal firm's network is by comparison poorly designed and managed.
- The competitor may have outwitted the focal firm by more quickly recognizing the benefits of a network and what the composition and purpose of the network should be.
- The competitor may have outmaneuvered the focal firm by aligning with key component vendors, channels, and value-added resellers, thus making it more difficult, and in some cases impossible, for the focal firm to develop an alliance with these entities.

Analysts find it unavoidable, even in the earliest stages of network specification, not to ask questions about the competitive context in which the network is embedded. Such *augmented* learning emanates from the following types of questions:

- Which network members are the dominant product or solution leaders in their domain?
- Which members are technology leaders or followers?
- Which members are involved in other networks? What role do they play in these networks?
- What is happening in the relevant competitive domain or "industry" that could affect the role and contribution of each member to the network?

Detailed consideration of these and related questions leads analysts to examine competitive issues that go beyond analysis of any individual network. For example, the analysts decided to examine rivalry among the suppliers of key components to ascertain which suppliers were likely to be product and technology leaders two or three years hence. Answers to this question influence firms in determining which suppliers to seek as members of their network.

What Might Be Learned   As analysts reflect on what they have learned, they must also determine what could and should be learned through further network analysis. Doing so guides the next steps in identifying and assessing the network, and motivates and energizes analysts to complete the analysis.

Perceiving what might be learned usually does not drop like manna from heaven. Rather it evolves out of discussion and dialogue among analysts as they consider and reflect on what the next steps in the analysis might be, what knowledge might be gained from each step, and how that knowledge might be useful to specific decision makers.

As analysis of the network progressed, the analysts identified several key items of learning that might emanate from a fully detailed network and its assessment. Some pertained to the competitor's network itself:

- How the competitor was able to sustain and lead the network.
- How the network might be usefully extended.
- How its purpose might change over time.
- Different ways in which the network might be leveraged by the competitor.

As noted, analysis of any competitor's network always leads to augmented learning. Analysts derive insight into different stages in the activity/value chain such as the forces shaping actions of suppliers, channels, or end-customers. Thus, the analysts identified some key desired elements of augmented learning:

- Why were some suppliers eager to commit themselves to a network and others would not do so?
- How would networks change rivals' marketplace strategy?

Ultimately, self-learning is required as one input to decision making. The analysts thus identified some desired items of learning for their own organization, each of which would contribute to designing and leading its own networks:

- What might be alternative structures for its own network?
- How might these networks enhance the firm's current marketplace strategy?
- How might they lead to strategy breakthroughs?

Difference between Desired and Existing Knowledge Analysts also need to identify and review the desired *knowledge increment:* the difference or gap between what they know (or believe they know) and what they want to know. How much needs to be learned—the knowledge increment—affects how analysts go about learning.

If the knowledge increment is large, analysts likely need to launch a full-scale learning program: extensive scanning and monitoring of the competitor; one or more teams to process the data; and, careful linkage between learning outputs and decision making.

In this case, the analysts concluded that there was indeed a substantial knowledge gap. In particular, they did not know:

- Whether and how the competitor had outwitted and outmaneuvered its rivals through its network.
- How the competitor might develop and extend its network.
- How the network might be leveraged for future business success.

One side-benefit of assessing the knowledge gap is that analysts need to articulate and reflect on what they think they know about the network. In reviewing what they believe they know, that is, facts, perceptions, beliefs, assumptions, and projections about the network, analysts must provide the data and logic that support and buttress the alleged knowledge.

Implications of Resolving the Knowledge Gap Resolving the knowledge gap must generate value for decision making; otherwise, it is merely an analytical exercise. Thus, analysts must determine, even if it is only in a preliminary way, how the knowledge increment could *enhance the quality of decision making.* Analysts must consider at least three related questions:

1. How will what is learned generate new issues or decisions, or inform current decisions?
2. Who can use the new knowledge in decision making?
3. How will closing the knowledge gap assist the focal firm to outwit, outmaneuver, and outperform current and future competitors?

Refining the Network

The preliminary assessment stimulates analysts to continue reconfiguring the network. As analysts address the questions noted under the heading, What Might Be Learned, they move beyond merely identifying and describing the links in the network to delineating and assessing how the network as a whole operates to achieve its apparent or stated purposes. As these questions receive attention, analysts begin to develop a deeper understanding of the network and its attributes.

Refining Attributes

One output of the deeper understanding of a network that is gradually developed is refinement of network attributes—structure, leadership, integrating purpose, and stability.

Structure is continually reconfigured. The data and logic underpinning judgments about leadership, purpose, and stability are reviewed and extended.

Projecting Network Evolution

As with any individual alliance, a network's implications depend on how it will evolve. Since networks are notoriously difficult to manage, and many networks suffer from internal conflict and strife, projecting network evolution is hazardous. Thus, drawing on the philosophy of scenarios,[11] it is advisable to develop three or four projections of plausible network evolutions. Alternative projections also sharpen the insights that stem from the core learning questions.

The range and extent of projections developed depend on the type of network. For example, projections about the future of a technology or development network might address different time paths around which the specific technology or product, process, or material might be developed. Each projection involves specific judgments about how the network members might collaborate with each other, and how quickly they could accomplish particular tasks such as integrating two technologies or making a technological breakthrough.

Projections about the future of a business created around a network (such as DreamWorks) might examine distinctly different business futures: the business takes off and becomes a success; the business grows but sluggishly; the business runs into major stumbling blocks and fails. Again, each projection makes explicit judgments about how the network is structured, how well the network members work together, and whether they can successfully take to market whatever products or solutions they create.

For the computer competitor, one projection might be built around an extension of the current network: the competitor continues to extend the network by aligning with other component vendors, software specialists, and other technology sources, to develop the next one or two generations of product within the next two years. Other projections might be the extension of the network but without the competitor being able to make any product breakthroughs for three or four years, or maybe not at all.

Each of these projections requires analysts to identify how the network might evolve and what the timeline of key events might be. In the case of the computer competitor continuing to extend its current network, analysts need to project what new alliances it might create, when it might do so, and in what sequence. The projection does not need to be completely accurate for it to lead to insightful implications.[12] A projection might not identify the actual component, channel, or other type of partners with which the competitor would eventually align. Yet by identifying the likelihood of such alliances, it is possible to derive relevant competitor consequences and focal firm implications.

Assessment of such projections connects directly to the core learning questions. Projections often serve to identify a knowledge gap. They indicate what analysts need to know. Since projections draw attention to plausible future network alternatives, analysts are able to assess what the competitor would have to do to make each future unfold or to avoid a specific future unfolding.[13] Analysts also consider what the implications of each projection could be for the focal firm. In this way, each projection leads to outputs that are decision relevant.

Beyond a Competitor's Network: Augmented Learning

As indicated, assessment of networks generates immense augmented learning about emerging and potential products or solutions, technology developments, stages in the activity/value chain and connections among them, and marketplace rivalry. The steps described for preliminary assessment are applicable to augmented learning.

Competitors' networks are often a source of strong signals of future products and solutions. Projections of each network lead to depictions of products or solutions likely to be in the marketplace at some future point. Projections of multiple computer competitors' solutions provide the basis for scenarios about solution or product rivalry. Analysts are thus able to compare and contrast a number of specific future competitive environments to the prevailing marketplace. They can then assess whether and how specific competitors could outwit and outmaneuver other rivals and the focal firm.[14]

Networks also generate weak and strong signals of technology developments. Often network change is the source of weak technology signals: the data are sparse and logic is not convincing but the apparent or potential network change suggests that significant technology change could occur. A comment by a senior executive of the computer competitor, in an industry conference presentation, stressed the need for computer and software organizations to work together to establish a dominant technology standard. This was the alerting indicator about the potential efforts of that firm to create a network with the explicit aim of establishing that technology standard.

The establishment of networks and change within them are often the source of strong technology signals. Many networks in the electronics, computer, software, health care, and financial services industries are explicitly intended to develop new technologies, to combine existing technologies, or to establish specific technology standards. NationsBank, for example, has taken a leadership position in inaugurating an on-line banking network to compete with established home-banking powers such as Intuit.

Much can be learned about current and future change in individual stages along the activity/value chain and in connections among them. An assessment of computer and electronic firms' networks always generates insights into current and potential developments in factor markets: the suppliers and vendors of components. Changes in networks' configuration and stability sometimes significantly affect supply availability on the open market, rivalry among suppliers, and the development of products by individual suppliers. For example, the commitment of suppliers to enter exclusive relationships with a single customer sometimes seriously affects the availability and quality of supply to other customers.

Comparison with the Focal Organization

A direct comparison of one or more networks to the focal organization provides a unique lens for self-learning. A comparison of network attributes (structure, leadership, purpose, and stability) helps orient the learning questions toward the focal organization:

- What is being learned about the focal organization? For example, in what ways is its network (or the absence of a network) the source of specific asset, capability, or vulnerability issues?
- What should be learned about the focal organization? For example, what types of network might it develop and why should it do so?
- What is the knowledge gap? For example, how long might it take to develop a specific type of network?
- What are the marketplace strategy implications for the focal firm?

Identification of differences and similarities between the networks of a competitor and the focal firm generates and frames many issues and questions about the focal firm's network. The firm can assess whether its network is poorly or well structured and led, has clear or ambiguous goals, and is relatively stable or unstable. The focal computer firm quickly discovered that its network was poorly developed and configured compared with the competitor's: it had not developed alliances and relationships to augment and extend each of its core business activities and was now beginning to suffer the results. The absence of an established network had constrained the focal firm from generating the assets and capabilities required for new product development and to execute its strategy in the channel and end-customer arenas. It had depended on its own assets and capabilities for far too long. It was thus extremely vulnerable to the new product advances of its rivals.

These types of assessments in turn spawn issues and questions about the focal firm's own *potential* network configuration and evolution. Indeed, it may be the case that the focal firm begins to project potential networks it had never before envisaged. The focal computer firm could now project at least three specific network configurations. One might be an extension of the competitor's current network. Its integrating purpose would be to do better what the competitor is already doing. A second projection might be a distinctly new type of network structure. It would include key foreign suppliers and perhaps an alliance with one or more current competitors. Its integrating purpose might be to develop a new range of products—in short, to establish a new strategy game. A third projection might entail one or more extensions of its own current network. These might be created in part as a foil against which the other projections might be judged, and partly, to assess whether merely extending the current network would alleviate some of the constraints, limitations, and vulnerabilities previously noted.

The focal computer firm's *knowledge gap* turned out to be extensive and important. It needed to learn what network configurations might be possible and what their implications might be. Projections such as those just discussed would indicate what types of network the firm could develop, how long it would take to do so, and what it could hope to gain in terms of customer- and competitor-based advantage—issues to which we return when addressing focal firm implications.

Comparison with Other Competitors

Extensive augmented and self-learning is generated by assessing the networks of a competitor (and the focal firm) against those of other rivals. Again, the central learning questions are applicable:

- What is being learned about networks?
- What augmented learning could be generated?
- What is the knowledge gap? For example, what do we know about how different types of rivals use networks to win and what should we know?
- What are the implications for marketplace strategy and individual microcomponents?

Differences across *look-alike* competitors' network structure, leadership, purpose, and stability, reveal distinct approaches to winning, and signals of what it will take to win. A visual inspection of a set of vertical or technology networks identifies a competitor with *unique* network elements such as linkages to a particular type of component supplier, or linkages that involve outsourcing specific activities such as logistics or information management, or a linkage to a technology consortium. These unique network elements lead to specific questions about how the competitor is outwitting, outmaneuvering, and outperforming rivals. For example, outsourcing logistics or involvement with a technology consortium may indicate an understanding of the industry and its likely future direction that was not detected by other rivals.

Changes in network attributes provide early though sometimes weak signals of competitors' views of what it will take to win in specific product domains. The addition of new linkage—a component supplier, a codevelopment alliance, a licensing agreement, involvement in a basic research activity with a university or some other type of specialist research organization—indicate what the competitor considers essential to developing particular products or to how it must compete to win.[15]

Changes in network attributes sometimes generate strong signals of competitors' strategic intent or marketplace vision. A sequence of changes in network structure as well as in leadership and purpose are often an early and strong signal of competitors' product development goals, especially for technology networks.

Great latitude also exists for analysts to create *invented* networks, (networks that do not now exist but could be devised by one or more rivals). Invented networks allow decision makers to see what a competitor might actually look like several years hence. Moreover, they also provide a distinctly different point of reference to current rivals' networks, and in most instances to competitors' projected networks.

Assessing Competitor Consequences

If a competitor does not exercise leadership, its network is likely to deteriorate and disintegrate. Network structure and composition often need to be changed: potential new network members emerge; existing members lose their ability to contribute or are overshadowed by nonmember counterparts; relationships among existing network members may need to be altered. To some extent, network goals are always in a state of flux. The roles and responsibilities of the network leader may need to be adapted to the changing contributions of network members and to events in the broader competitive environment such as competitors' research and development breakthroughs, product introductions, or changes in legal and regulatory conditions.

Thus, analysts must address the learning questions to competitor consequences:

- What do we know now about consequences for the competitor?
- What can we learn about them? What do we need to know?
- What is the knowledge gap?
- How would knowledge about competitor consequences affect the focal firm's implications?

Competitor consequences are influenced by whether the network is achieving its *integrating purpose*. If it is not, then the competitor has little choice but to reconfigure the network, reinvigorate its own leadership of it, or change its goals. The computer competitor's network was well on its way to achieving its integrating purpose: the network was likely to contribute significantly to the competitor's next generations of solutions.

However, attainment of the overarching purpose always depends on the competitor's execution capability. Generation of the new solutions would have to be led by the computer competitor. In view of turbulent technology change in and around the computer industry, the competitor could not rely on its current network members to keep ahead in the strategy game: either in changing the strategy context or the marketplace rules. Thus, some specific *leadership* consequences confronted the competitor:

- It would need to bring new knowledge and technology capability into the network—new network members.
- It would need to integrate the new knowledge and technology into the network's product development activities.
- It would need to continually reinforce and support relationships with many network members.

In view of the difficulties inherent in leading any network, as well as the competitor's limited success in leveraging networks, its success in leading this network could not be taken for granted.

A concern with what might be learned should prompt analysts to ask what the consequences might be if the network were to realize its goals—if it successfully developed the next one or two generations of products. The importance of this line of questioning often becomes evident when analysts are surprised by the lack of returns or benefit to the competitor. A number of questions merit attention:

- What might be the marketplace results? What advantage would the competitor possess over specific rivals?
- What might be the financial results?
- How might these results help it to outwit and outmaneuver rivals in the next generations of the product and its associated technologies?

Answering these questions, however tentatively, requires consideration of multiple rivals' networks.[16] In the judgment of the analysts, even if the computer competitor realized all its product goals, it was not likely to be dramatically ahead of some of its rivals. Although rivals were taking different approaches to product development, it was certain that most of them would bring to market many new solutions. This observation served to reinforce analysts' judgments about the importance of the competitor's execution capability: the results would hinge on how well it led and managed the network.

The strategy issues and leadership concerns about execution capability gave rise to *organization* issues. Questions were raised pertaining to the competitor's organization:

- Did it have a set of managers with the capability to develop, nurture, and leverage a network?

- Did it have a culture that supported the development of working relationships with different network members?

- How would various elements of its infrastructure[17]—its current structure, systems, decision-making processes—help or hinder execution of the necessary network tasks?

How well the competitor managed these organization issues would greatly influence whether and how it would be able to leverage the network.

Even if it appears that the network's purposes are being attained, as with the computer competitor, it is usually insightful to identify what the competitor must do to ensure their achievement or to make the network even more successful. Among other things, analysts can then monitor these tasks.[18] The following items must always be considered:[19]

- What additional linkages would aid in achieving the network's purposes?

- How might the competitor enhance network execution?

- How might the competitor better leverage the network?

Assessing Focal Firm Implications

Implications can be assessed for marketplace strategy, microlevel components, and networks. Each assessment sheds light on the other two. Determining strategy implications allows analysts to integrate many of the focal firm's issues and concerns noted in the earlier assessment steps.

Marketplace Strategy Projection and assessment of competitors' networks often lead to significant marketplace strategy implications that directly challenge the focal firm's current and planned strategies, their underlying assumptions, and anticipated results. Because networks are often strong indicators of competitors' future strategy direction, these implications go beyond those emanating from an assessment of competitors' *current* marketplace strategies or activity/value chains.

The gravity of the implications depends on whether one or more competitors in the judgment of the focal firm's analysts have outwitted and outmaneuvered it by using networks to affect the strategy game's *context* to their own advantage. If they have, or are on their way to doing so, then the focal firm must confront two central questions:

- What customer- or competitor-based advantages have specific competitors created?

- What does the firm need to do to catch up to, or preferably, to get ahead of them?

The computer firm was faced with serious strategy implications. First, by building the network required to create new generations of products, the competitor was raising the stakes considerably: a major new business opportunity was being created for all potential combatants; the financial costs and technology learning needed to participate in this product-customer segment were extensive; and the inability to do so would essentially mean that the focal firm would find it extremely difficult to get back into this product domain.

Second, the new solutions would change the marketplace rules. They would give the competitor the broadest solution range; they would create new forms of functionality, with distinct new features; they would extend the competitor's image and reputation as the solution leader; they would allow the competitor to achieve price premiums, at least in the short run, when rivals would not have comparable solutions. Thus, as competitors, including the focal firm, became solution followers, they would find it even more difficult to change the marketplace rules to their advantage.

If the competitor reached its product targets, the focal firm simply would have inferior product and technological solutions. Worse, it would have wasted one or two years: it would be further behind in terms of product quality, appeal to customers, and brand recognition in the general marketplace. The danger of losing key customer accounts was judged to be a real possibility. Its own product development plans would need to be radically altered.

Microlevel Components These strategy implications also gave rise to some significant microlevel component implications. First, due to the need to change its solution development plans, the focal firm had little choice but to review its *assumptions* about the future state of the industry, the strategies and actions of competitors, what it took to succeed in the business, and its own assets and capabilities. For example, its current assumptions about the solutions that would be in the marketplace two or three years later grossly understated their technological content. One benefit of considering these strategy implications was that many of the firm's assumptions, although widely shared within the firm, had remained largely implicit—and thus untested and unchallenged.

Second, grave questions emerged about the sufficiency of the focal firm's *assets and capabilities* to outmaneuver and outperform its rivals. In the view of the analysts, the firm would have to augment its technology knowledge, and supplier and customer relationships, to win against this competitor and other rivals. Also, its current manufacturing capability was not flexible enough to support movement to significantly new products.

Networks Strategy and microcomponent implications lead to an assessment of the focal firm's *own network*. They provide a backdrop against which the firm assesses the adequacy of its existing network, how its structure might be amended, and what its goals should be. These network implications inevitably raise issues pertaining to other microlevel components.

Of most immediate concern is how the focal firm could better leverage its network, or more precisely, the elements of a potential network that are already in place. If existing alliances and relationships are not being fully leveraged, significant opportunities may exist for the firm to enhance performance in the short run and to lay the groundwork for longer term success.

The analysts concluded that the firm would have to develop a network of alliances and relationships that went considerably beyond its existing network if it harbored any ambitions to be a market leader in this segment of the computer industry.

Errors in Identifying and Assessing Networks

Many organizations fail to extend analysis of alliances to include networks or simply identify partial or "quick and dirty" network configurations. Thus, since network analysis will be new for most firms, the intent of this section is to note errors that are likely to arise when applying the learning questions emphasized throughout the chapter.

An initial error is not to determine a knowledge gap: the difference between what analysts know (or consider they know) and what they believe they need to know about a competitor's network(s). By not identifying and evaluating the knowledge gap, analysts are less likely to ask penetrating questions about how knowledge of competitors' networks extends their understanding of individual competitors. Also, not doing so is likely to lead to prematurely ceasing network development and assessment because analysts will fail to appreciate how what is learned can affect decision making.

Yet attention to the knowledge gap is not sufficient for efficient or effective learning. The central learning questions compel early assessment of what it being learned about a competitor's network(s). Failure to develop preliminary assessments contributes to inefficient analysis: key questions about the competitor's network are more likely to be missed, and unfocused data gathering is probable.

Failure to conduct preliminary assessments also contributes to ineffective analysis: analysts are less likely to continually refine what needs to be learned, to identify or refine key elements in the knowledge gap, and to determine how and why the competitor is using networks to win.

Implicit in the two preceding errors is the absence of a clear focus on how the competitor is using one or more networks to win. The following questions ensure that analysts maintain the link between networks and winning at the forefront of assessment:[20]

- How has the competitor outwitted its rivals in the way it has detected and anticipated the need for one or more networks and how to leverage them for marketplace success?

- How is the competitor outmaneuvering its rivals in the way it is structuring its network(s) and developing cooperative relationships with key entities in its factor, channel, end-customer, and institutional arenas?

- How is the competitor outperforming its rivals in the way it is leveraging its network(s) to create a new strategy game or to reconstruct an existing game and/or to change the marketplace rules to its own advantage?

An emphasis on preliminary and continual assessment is intended to avoid the error of not relating what is learned about competitors' networks to implications for the focal firm. As illustrated with the focal computer firm, implications must be assessed for current and potential marketplace strategy, microlevel components, and for developing and leveraging the firm's own networks.

A critical aspect of the recursive nature of competitor learning is that assessment—the identification of implications for the focal firm—leads in turn to issues and questions that must be investigated about competitors' networks. Hence, analysts must always be willing to go back and forth between assessment of focal firm implications and competitor consequences.

As analysts apply the learning questions, errors may occur. A simple yet consequential error is not (re)configuring a network in multiple ways. Each configuration of a network is likely to lead to new insights and questions. In this way, processing or analysis must be viewed as a recursive activity: one configuration of a network leads to a more profound understanding of another.

As part of processing, each network link must be thought of as a source of potential signals. In this way, the error of overemphasizing description and detail to the detriment of interpretation is less likely.[21]

The need for recursive learning is also exemplified in the tendency of network attributes to change over time, and sometimes, precipitously. A failure to recognize the learning that accrues from monitoring, projecting, and assessing network attribute change is a fundamental error.[22]

A likely error is for analysts not to appreciate the necessity for an open-ended approach to network analysis. Even as they strive for efficiency in analysis, analysts will find it beneficial to suspend their preconceptions as to the likely final network structure, to be willing to seek new data sources, to follow up unexpected indicators, and to ask varied questions of primary data sources. The open-ended orientation is especially necessary in its early stages of identifying and reconfiguring network structure as analysts struggle to process myriad discordant and disparate data.

Summary

The identification and assessment of competitors' networks requires decision makers and other analysts to adopt a broader and more encompassing understanding of what is meant by a competitor—it is not simply a stand-alone single organization. Analysis of a competitor's networks generates insights into the competitor and the broader competitive context that cannot be obtained from any other framework component. Networks thus provide unique insights into how a competitor is, or is likely to, outwit, outmaneuver, and outperform its rivals.

CHAPTER

Assumptions

EXPLICATING AND ASSESSING THE CONTENT OF COMPETITORS' STRATEGIES—THE WHAT, how, and purpose of competitors' behaviors in the marketplace—is insufficient to outwit them. Managers need to understand the "whys" behind competitors' current and potential strategies: Why are they pursuing their current strategies? Why might a competitor pursue one strategic alternative rather than another? Why do some competitors not seriously entertain specific alternatives? Why has a competitor adhered to a particular strategy long after it would appear desirable to do so?

These *why* questions bring into sharp focus the importance of understanding competitors' mind-sets. While mind-set has been defined in many different ways, assumptions are always at its center. Thus, capturing a competitor's assumptions provides a powerful means to posit answers to these questions.

This chapter begins by defining assumptions, delineating their importance and pervasiveness, and highlighting some reasons why assumptions always must be inferred. It then details the methodology to determine and assess competitors' assumptions as well as common errors associated with assumption analysis in many organizations.

Because assumptions always must be inferred, this chapter emphasizes the derivation and interpretation of inferences or signals. It demonstrates the critical role of evidence based on data and logic in signal analysis. Because of the nature of assumptions, outwitting competitors receives particular attention in this chapter.

Understanding Assumptions

Definition and Importance of Assumptions

Assumptions are broadly defined as what the competitor takes for granted or as a "given" or must take for granted.[1] For example, a competitor about to launch one of its products in a new geographic region might assume: (1) It will be able to adhere to its published launch plan, (2) no competitor will follow it into the marketplace for at least a year, (3) it will obtain extensive support from specific distribution channels, and (4) sufficient customers will be persuaded to purchase the product to achieve a market penetration level of 10 percent by the end of the first year.

Assumptions always drive or guide strategy. Any (competitor's) strategy is always premised on some assumptions about the future: what new technologies will emerge; whether customers will switch from one competitor to another; whether new competitors will enter the marketplace. Absence of change in key assumptions explains why many competitors often do not change the core elements in their strategy for long periods. As demonstrated later in this chapter, a major change in a competitor's assumptions is likely to lead to a significant change in its strategy. Assumptions allow us to get underneath or behind a competitor's actions and words—to understand the whys that drive a competitor's current and potential strategy.

Competitors' Awareness of Their Own Assumptions

Assumptions contribute greatly to outwitting competitors in part because the detection and assessment of a competitor's assumptions does *not* depend on a presumption or requirement that the competitor is aware of its own assumptions. Quite the contrary. The argument here can be made in two distinct ways. Central to the assumption analysis framework presented in this chapter is that assumptions are derived from the competitor's behaviors (its decisions, actions, and inactions) and words. Analysts draw inferences or make judgments about what the assumptions are, or must be, given some set of behaviors such as the competitor's marketplace strategy, or management of its activity/value chain, or a pattern in its alliances and relationships. Analysts thus derive competitors' assumptions from the outside looking in. The analysis framework presented in this chapter is therefore independent of the assumptions competitors actually make or think they make.[2]

Second, organizations rarely fully explicate their own assumptions. Even when they attempt to do so, they may not detect their "true" or actual assumptions. Thus, *tacit* assumptions are often more important in guiding action than explicit assumptions.[3]

One consequence of decision makers in competitor organizations not explicating or knowing their own assumptions is that (given a methodology to detect and assess assumptions) the focal organization ends up knowing a competitor's assumptions better than the competitor itself. As a result, it is in a powerful position to outwit the competitor.

Assumptions about What?

A competitor makes explicit or tacit assumptions about its external environment and its own organization. Assumptions are often made about facets of the relevant competitive terrain or industry such as: the scope or definition of the competitive domain; its rate of potential growth; the likelihood of new entrants; changes in competitive dynamics; and the actions of individual domain members such as customers, distribution channels, suppliers, and other competitors. Assumptions about emerging and projected technology change are increasingly critical in many competitive domains. Most organizations make assumptions about the macroenvironment—the social, political, regulatory, and technological milieus outside or surrounding the competitive domain.

Decision makers make assumptions about their own organization. Key assumptions often pertain to the organization's ability to attract assets such as knowledge, skills, raw materials, and capital; its capacity to develop and leverage specific capabilities and competencies; its commitment to execute its strategies and plans; and its ability to develop alliances, relationships, and networks.

Key Attributes of Assumptions

The following five attributes of assumptions enable analysts to identify a competitor's key assumptions and to assess their importance in understanding its likely strategic moves:

1. *Validity.* Assumptions may or may not be true in the sense that they correctly reflect the current or future context and conditions within or outside the competitor. Often assumptions are wrong or invalid in that they misconstrue what the competitor is actually able to do or they misinterpret or misstate what will happen in the competitor's competitive domain.[4]

2. *Breadth.* Assumptions may refer to a few or many domains including customers, technology, industry growth, competitors, or governmental action. The narrower the range of domains, the greater the competitor's vulnerability to change in other domains.

3. *Consistency.* Competitors' assumptions also vary greatly in the degree to which they are consistent or congruent. For example, assumptions that presume the entrance of multiple new competitors and a slowing of overall

competitive domain growth may be at variance with an assumption about market share gain.

4. *Dispersion.* The power of core or fundamental assumptions is extended if they are widely dispersed among (key) personnel across the competitor's organization. This is often the case. The large U.S. automobile firms assumed for many years that their U.S. customers were more interested in style than in functionality and performance.

5. *Endurance.* Dominant assumptions are also often enduring. Sometimes they endure for years. The styling assumption of the U.S. automobile firms lasted for many years.

Core or Fundamental Assumptions

All assumptions are not equally important. Core or fundamental assumptions underlie or are critical to a competitor's strategy or most of its key decisions. Usually, the list of core assumptions is short; rarely does it exceed more than six or seven. The central challenge in assumption analysis is to extract a competitor's core assumptions from what initially is likely to be a long laundry list of raw or individual assumptions. Change in core assumptions usually leads to substantial change in strategy. In some instances, change in core assumptions leads to a reversal of past decisions or asset commitments.

Assumptions Must Be Inferred

Assumptions always must be *inferred;* they are the outcome of analysts' judgments. Analysts connect what is often highly disparate data or indicators and asserted inferences (assumptions). Since assumptions are always inferred, it is essential to identify the evidence that supports them. It is also necessary to challenge assumptions by continually asking what evidence is available that refutes them.

Analysts have no choice but to infer assumptions. This is so for at least three reasons. First, competitors often do not know what their assumptions are: their mind-set is dominated by tacit assumptions. Second, competitors rarely make their assumptions public; thus, analysts must construct them. Third, even if competitors did make their assumptions public, it is imperative that analysts independently derive and test such articulated assumptions because competitors may incorrectly derive them, or even if they are correctly derived, they may not fully disclose them to external audiences.

Because inferencing has such a critical role, the detection, perception, interpretation, and assessment[5] of assumptions is first and foremost a *thinking* exercise. Understanding and using a competitor's assumptions never reduces to a mechanical routine. It requires developing and testing logics that connect indicators and inferences. Different individuals often develop distinct logics, thus, leading to different inferences or assumptions.[6]

The importance of thinking, or the logic capability of analysts, is evident in every stage of the inferencing process. The data are likely to be discordant and ambiguous; the initial inferences are often weak; the evidence is sometimes contradictory; the competitor consequences and focal firm implications are often not immediately obvious. The analyst therefore must create and process the data. Central to processing is the need to explicate the logic that connects data or indicators and the inferred assumptions: the basis for the judgments that are unavoidable in crafting and testing assumptions. The logic generating one or more assumptions is challenged through invoking the strongest possible supporting and refuting data.

Indicators of Assumptions

Assumptions are *inferred* from both direct and indirect indicators. The relevant indicators are principally competitors' behaviors and words. They refer to past, present, and future time periods. Often *individual* behaviors or words (statements) such as changes in pricing, the purchase of new machinery or operations technology, or announcements to augment a specific category of assets or to carry out a program to enhance existing capabilities and competencies, constitute the *alerting* indicators of assumptions, or change in assumptions.

Assumption Change as a Signal

Changes in competitors' assumptions often constitute long-lag, high-impact signals of discontinuous change in marketplace strategy and microlevel components. It is especially important to note that assumptions sometimes generate longer-lag signals than changes in performance results or changes in strategies (see Figure 10.1). Performance results generate indicators of whether current or past strategies are successful. However, they are notoriously poor as a source of early signals of the need for strategy change or its

FIGURE 10.1
Assumptions as Signals of Strategy Change

ASSUMPTIONS	STRATEGY	RESULTS
e.g.,	Scope	Market share
Industry change	Posture	Profits
New technology	Goals	Technology
Potential alliance		leadership
Etc.		

likely occurrence.[7] Changes in marketplace strategy generate indicators of emergent change (change already underway). On the other hand, changes in assumptions often generate even earlier signals of future change in marketplace strategy (and its potential performance results).

Identifying Competitors' Assumptions

Identifying (and assessing) a competitor's assumptions is one of the toughest but most enlightening tasks in competitor analysis. It places a heavy burden on analysts' judgments. The thought process is different from many managers' prevailing modes of thinking. These problems are exacerbated in most firms by the absence of an analytical framework to guide data collection, interpretation, and assessment. The intent of this section is to provide such a framework. A *guided* analysis is outlined in Figure 10.2. The analysis of a competitor of a provider of surgical instruments is used for illustration purposes. The competitor seemed to be especially buoyant about the industry's immediate prospects. It was also endeavoring to be the technology leader in several product categories.

Assimilate Prior Analysis

Assumption identification is guided in that assumptions are derived from marketplace strategy and microlevel components. Framework components not yet analyzed should be assessed for their potential contribution to identifying assumptions. Because core assumptions are reflected in major decisions and actions, analysts typically identify the competitor's key current and recent marketplace strategy decisions and actions as well as those pertaining to each microlevel component. It is always useful for analysts to identify decisions and actions they expect the competitor to confront or undertake in the near future.

Identify Recent Indicators (and Signals)

This is always a critical step. If key framework components such as marketplace strategy or activity/value chain analysis have not been conducted recently, capturing up-to-date indicators is of the utmost importance because they often suggest inferences about the future that differ from those in the prior analysis. In some instances, current signals contradict or refute earlier signals. Some recent signals pertaining to the surgical instrument competitor are noted in Table 10.1.

Even a single signal sometimes has significant strategic and operating implications leading to a potential shift in assumptions about the competitor. The election of three new outside directors (see Table 10.1) might constitute

FIGURE 10.2
Identifying a Competitor's Assumptions

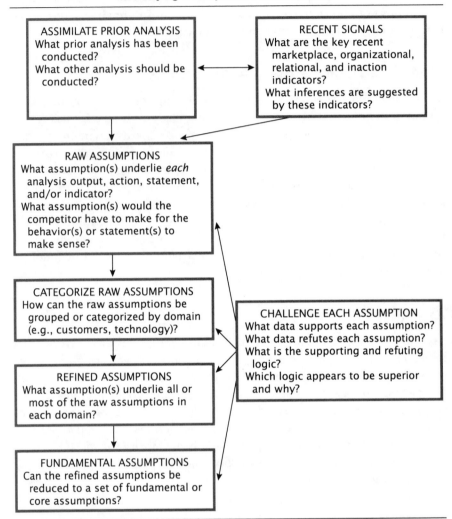

an alerting signal of the competitor's emphasis on positioning itself for much greater long-run competitiveness as well as on taking actions to improve short-run performance.

List Raw Assumptions

Raw assumptions form the core of assumption identification. The assumptions are raw in that they relate to *individual* or *sets* of behaviors (e.g.,

TABLE 10.1 Surgical Instruments Competitor: Recent Signals

Indicators	Inferences
Announced that one plant's production has increased by more than 30% in the past 3 months	Associated cost reductions will lead to price reductions
	Some customers may be likely to enter into long-term contracts if product quality is not compromised in added output
A new order entry and delivery process instituted on a trial basis with large key customers	New process will increase competitor's attractiveness to these customers (especially if waiting time for delivery is reduced)
Elected three new outside directors to the board	Competitor will show greater emphasis on both long-term commitments and short-run performance improvement
CEO intimated that the firm would probably raise prices again before the end of the year	Competitor is suffering even worse margin pressures than previously believed

dimensions of posture) or words and have not yet been categorized, related to each other, or prioritized. The intent is to generate a laundry list of all apparent or raw assumptions that underlie the competitors' specific behaviors and words.

Two questions dominate the derivation of *raw* assumptions:

1. What assumptions underlie the specific behavior or words?

2. What assumptions would the competitor have to make for the behaviors or words to make sense?

Both questions always need to be asked because frequently the task is to ascertain what assumptions the competitor would have to be making to justify or rationalize specific actions.[8]

Table 10.2 shows some of the raw assumptions derived from the surgical instrument competitor's marketplace strategy. The two questions noted previously are asked with regard to the content or substance of each major element of marketplace strategy: scope, posture, and goals. For posture, one might ask what assumptions underlie, or must underlie, the surgical instrument competitor's approach to product line width, features, functionality, service, availability, image and reputation, selling and relationships, and price? One raw assumption pertaining to most of these modes of competition is noted in Table 10.3.

TABLE 10.2 A Surgical Instrument Competitor's Marketplace Strategy Raw Assumptions

Raw Assumptions	Evidence
New product and product extensions are critical to competitive success	Continual stream of new products and product modifications
	Statements by key managers
Product functionality must be continually enhanced	Continuous improvements
	Emphasis on product features in marketing and sales
Customers require involvement in product design and development	Frequent usage trials with surgeons
	Statements about what surgeons and other hospital personnel consider important in a vendor
Customized service offers powerful potential advantage	Tailoring service "deals" to meet needs of individual hospitals and individual surgeons
Customers are not price sensitive if product quality and service are superior to that of rivals	"Deals" for customers
	Upgrading product features
	Statements to press
	Statements by customers

It is also imperative to identify the raw assumptions underlying specific *change* in each element of marketplace strategy (changes in scope, posture, and goals) or changes in other framework components such as activity/value chain, assets, or organization. Changes, especially recent ones, are more likely to reflect or signal current or emerging shifts in underlying assumptions. Detection of such changes helps to ensure that key signals have not been missed.[9]

The process outlined here is both pedantic and repetitive but it is unavoidable. Raw assumptions make up the database from which the competitor's core assumptions are derived. Unless analysts systematically consider the assumptions underlying behaviors such as changes in marketplace strategy, in individual activities along the activity/value chain, in alliances and networks, in assets, in capabilities and competencies, and in organization infrastructure and culture, key assumptions are likely to be missed.

Categorize Raw Assumptions

It is impossible to identify core assumptions simply by reviewing or assessing a hodgepodge of unrelated raw assumptions; they are too disaggregated. The list of raw assumptions must therefore somehow be grouped and categorized.

TABLE 10.3 Sample Raw Assumptions Underlying Each Posture Component

Modes of Competition	Sample Assumptions
Product line width	New products and product line extensions are essential to stay ahead of increasingly aggressive rivals
Features	Some customers are highly sensitive to particular features
Functionality	Functionality is best enhanced by working closely with selected customers
Service	Service must be tailored to the needs and wants of individual customers
Availability	Customers will continue to be willing to buy directly from the focal firm
Image and reputation	Reputation for technology leadership and development leads many customers to quickly test and adopt the firm's new product offerings
Selling and relationships	Close working relationships with key customer accounts are important to their involvement in product design and development—and hence, product adoption
Price	Early adopters of new products are not price sensitive

One useful way to do so is to use a priori categories or domains such as the industry or competitive domain (customers, suppliers, distribution channels, other competitors), the macroenvironment (social, economic, political, and regulatory change), technology, the competitor itself, and the competitor's strategy. In some instances, if the focal firm is a dominant player or product leader, it should be included as a category.

The surgical instrument competitor's assumptions were categorized into groups including historic customers, new customers, competitors, technology, the future direction of the industry, and the competitor itself. The raw assumptions pertaining to technology are shown in Table 10.4. These assumptions were initially derived by examining the competitor's marketplace strategy, alliances, and investments (among other facets of the competitor).

The importance of noting the evidence for each assumption is again apparent when raw assumptions are categorized. Each technology raw assumption is challenged and critiqued by asking whether the "evidence" supports, or is sufficient to establish, the existence of the assumption. Consider the assumption, "Current customers value the firm's commitment to technology development" (see Table 10.4). Some statements by the competitor's sales force (at trade shows and to customers) provide a reasonable basis for asserting the existence of the assumption. However, it is not sufficient evidence to assert that the assumption is either widely shared within the competitor or that it is an important assumption.

TABLE 10.4   A Surgical Instrument Competitor's Technology Raw Assumptions

Raw Assumptions	Evidence
The firm's own proprietary technology will continue to generate new products	Assertions by the CEO Investments in technology Pursuit of patents Defense of patents
Current customers value the firm's commitment to technology development	Statements by the firm's sales force
New customers will see added value in the firm because of its historic technology prowess	Statements in promotional literature Assertions by the firm's CEO
New manufacturing technology will lead to substantial cost reductions and product development	Statements by manufacturing personnel
New information technologies will eliminate existing problems in order taking and fulfillment	Announcement of investments in these technologies

Identify Refined Assumptions

Because of the unavoidable overlap in raw assumptions and the fact that only a few core or fundamental assumptions underlie an organization's current or future strategy, it is necessary to consolidate the raw assumptions. At first glance, this appears to be a difficult, if not, impossible task. However, the analysis processes suggested here offer a number of checkpoints and balances to increase the probability that the competitor's actual[10] core assumptions are extracted.

Typically, it is possible to reduce each domain of raw assumptions to one or two refined assumptions. Again, there is no magic formula. Analysts must ask two questions:

1. What assumption(s) would seem to underlie all or most of the raw assumptions in a particular domain (such as customers or technology)?
2. What evidence supports the refined assumption(s)?

The surgical instrument competitor's raw technology assumptions were reduced to two refined assumptions (see Table 10.5). The two refined technology assumptions address distinct foci: one focuses on the external marketplace; one focuses on the competitor's internal organization—its cost structure.

The reduction of raw assumptions to refined assumptions involves judgments and logic. Thus, it is essential to identify the evidence that supports

TABLE 10.5 A Surgical Instrument Competitor's Technology "Refined" Assumptions

Refined Assumptions	Evidence
Technology can give the firm significant customer-based advantages in almost all dimensions of posture	Investment in specific technologies
	Customer statements and actions
	Statements by the firm's personnel
Technology can lead to significant cost reductions in both products and customer service	Investments in specific technologies
	Statements by the firm's personnel

each reduced or refined assumption. Analysts or decision makers can now review, critique, and raise questions about the evidence briefly indicated for the two refined assumptions in Table 10.5. Consider the evidence or logic for the refined technology assumption, "Technology can give the firm significant customer-based advantages in almost all dimensions of posture." The firm had made significant investments in technologies to augment features, functionality, service, and image; many customers had expressed how much they valued the competitor's technology capabilities; many customers had switched to the competitor's products; and many of the competitor's personnel stated bluntly (in many different ways) that technology was the source of the value the firm had historically provided to customers.

Part of the explication and test of the prevailing logic is to identify the opposite of each refined assumption and then seek evidence that supports each opposite assumption. This test of logic is imperative for both refined and core assumptions. The evidence is drawn from any of the data and information developed as part of any prior analysis or as part of assumption derivation. To test the refined technology assumption, the analysts sought data to suggest that technology would not give the competitor a significant customer-based advantage along posture's modes of competition. They did find some statements by the competitor's personnel that technology's benefits as perceived by customers could be short-lived and that technology must be continually upgraded. However, it was their judgment that the refined assumption was strongly upheld.

Identify Core or Fundamental Assumptions

The refined assumptions are then further reduced to fundamental or core assumptions. This step involves analysis of the refined assumptions across domains represented by the refined assumptions. The intent is to identify the small set of core assumptions that are truly fundamental to understanding the competitor's mind-set. Since they are the product of analysts' judgments; evidence is needed to support them. The surgical instruments competitor's

TABLE 10.6 A Surgical Instrument Competitor's Fundamental Assumptions

Fundamental Assumptions	Evidence
Rate of growth in total industry sales will average 10%–15% for the next 5 years	Product investments Capacity investments Statements of CEO and marketing manager
No competitor is now in a position to launch a series of major product innovations	Statements made by senior managers (e.g., "nobody is positioned to challenge our product leadership in the near term")
Continued enhancements in differentiation (posture) will sustain the firm's marketplace leadership	Decisions and actions along each mode of competition Statements (e.g., "our commitment to adding value for customers keeps us ahead of all rivals")
Technology investments leading to new products are key to long-term marketplace leadership	List of technology investments Statements (e.g., "our technology thrust will generate continual new products and extensive product modification")
No substitute products are on the horizon	Technology investments Statements (e.g., "our product line is secure from invasion")
Surgeons will continue to insist on the most technologically sophisticated products	Technology investments Repeating the statements by surgeons

fundamental assumptions and some supporting evidence are shown in Table 10.6.

Each core assumption emanates from further evaluation of the refined assumptions and the evidence supporting them. Often, linkages across the refined assumptions give rise to core assumptions. Consideration of the refined technology assumptions and new product assumptions led to articulation of the core assumption, "Technology investments leading to new products are key to long-term marketplace leadership."

Challenge Each Fundamental Assumption

Even fundamental assumptions that seem self-evident at first glance need to be challenged and critiqued. The experience of many organizations is that obvious assumptions sometimes do not stand the test of scrutiny.

Two questions constitute the challenge to each fundamental assumption:

1. What data (and associated logic) supports or refutes the assumption?
2. Which data (and associated logic) appears to be stronger?

These questions compel analysts not only to detail the logic and data that both supports and refutes each fundamental assumption but to compare and contrast them. As in previous stages in the analysis, the supporting and refuting data may come from any prior analysis or from the derivation of the raw, refined, and fundamental assumptions. Much of the data is likely to refer to the competitor itself: not just its behaviors and words but its alliances and networks, assets, competencies, and organization infrastructure and culture.

The logic supporting or refuting each fundamental assumption also must be spelled out. Often the debate in challenging assumptions is around alternative "logics" rather than the validity of the evidence, per se. For the second fundamental assumption noted in Table 10.6, "No competitor is now in a position to launch a series of major product introductions," two distinct logics were operative. The first logic was that current look-alike competitors did not possess the technological resources or capabilities to generate one or more new product innovations within the next two or three years. The second logic held that although the competitor's technology assets and capabilities were deteriorating, one of two or three competitors could still, through carefully chosen alliances and partnerships, launch a major product innovation within two or three years.

Fortunately, for most fundamental assumptions, the data and logic are often overwhelmingly in one direction or the other. Typically, fundamental assumptions, because of the emphasis on evidence at the raw and refined stages, are supported.

When the evidence is mixed, or perhaps leaning in the direction of refutation, a number of analysis options are available. Analysts sometimes choose to reconcile the disputed evidence by changing the assumption so that the evidence and logic are decisive in one direction or another. Indeed, small changes are sometimes decisive. In the preceding example, changing "a major product innovation" to "a series of product innovations" eliminated much of the debate.

As the example just cited illustrates, when fundamental assumptions are refuted or seriously challenged, significant learning often accrues. Analysts and decision makers must recognize that this can and should be the case.

Open-Ended Inquiry

Open-ended inquiry is unavoidable if analysts know little about the competitor. Moreover, it also serves as a useful control for guided analysis: analysts compare and contrast the assumptions generated through open-ended inquiry with those generated through guided analysis. Since many of the analysis tasks are similar to those in guided analysis, differences are highlighted here.

Assimilate Indicators Open-ended inquiry begins with the assimilation of indicators such as the competitor's behaviors, words, attribute change, and information (that is, outputs of analysis conducted by analysts such as cash flow analysis or sales projections). Unlike a guided analysis, these indicators are not organized around individual framework components such as marketplace strategy, activity/value chain, or competencies.

Derive Assumptions The process of deriving raw assumptions is largely similar to guided analysis. Raw assumptions are derived from each indicator. They are then categorized around domains to generate refined assumptions. Unlike guided analysis, the domains stem purely from the data; they are not guided by any a priori set or listing of possible or preferred domains. Refined and fundamental assumptions are then derived.

Open-ended inquiry is highly iterative. An emphasis on seeking confirming and refuting data at the level of raw, refined, and fundamental assumptions means that analysts search for further indicators (evidence) as the process unfolds.

Errors in Identifying Assumptions

The most critical error is the all-too-frequent tendency not to identify competitors' assumptions at all.[11] Not only are the potential insights about competitors' assumptions not obtained, but their contribution to understanding other microlevel components is also missed.

The overarching error perhaps is the desire to reduce assumption identification to a mechanical exercise. Since the identification (and assessment) of assumptions is essentially a *thinking* activity, analysts inevitably must deal with conflicting evidence. Judgments reside at the heart of the process.

All too often, analysts do not (or are reluctant to) challenge assumptions by means of developing the strongest possible counterargument or logic. Assumptions are sometimes presumed to be self-evident. The logic connecting data or indicators and inferences (the assumptions) derived from them are not spelled out so that they can be reviewed and critiqued by others. This error, in part, reflects the desire to reduce assumption identification to a mechanical exercise.

Sometimes the subtleties involved in refining and restating assumptions are not appreciated. A rewording of an assumption may make a substantial difference both to whether a competitor actually holds the assumption and to its validity. With the surgical instrument competitor's fundamental assumptions, there is a world of difference between these two assumptions: no competitor is in a position to launch a single product innovation; no competitor is in a position to launch a series of product innovations.

A final error worth noting is that the contribution of recent indicators is often overlooked. As noted, recent indicators such as reactions to rivals' decisions or statements by senior executives often allow the derivation of signals that are distinctively different from those derived from prior marketplace strategy or microlevel analysis. These signals thus constitute critical evidence for emerging or potential *change* in a competitor's assumptions.

Assessing Competitors' Assumptions

Competitors' assumptions are assessed in a number of ways (see Figure 10.3). Assessing key attributes often generates critical competitor issues and challenges. The validity of refined and fundamental assumptions is always tested by reference to the broader environment. Assumptions are also prioritized to determine which ones are truly key to understanding the competitor's mind-set. Comparison to other competitors and the focal organization gives rise to considerable comparative and self-learning. Competitors' assumptions are also a powerful source of augmented learning: they generate signals about the evolving and future marketplace. We continue to use the surgical instruments firm for purposes of illustration. Again, the emphasis is on outwitting competitors.

Key Attributes of Assumptions

Before a competitor's fundamental assumptions are compared and contrasted to the focal firm's, or signals are derived from them, it is essential to understand their key attributes—validity, breadth, consistency, dispersion, and endurance.

Validity Assessment of refined and core assumptions immediately raises issues about their validity. Since validity refers to the "truth" of an assumption, not whether the competitor holds it, two questions must be posed:

1. Is the assumption congruent with the current reality within or external to the competitor?
2. Is the assumption consistent with expected change within or external to the competitor?

Because a competitor makes or adheres[12] to an assumption does not mean that it is true or valid. Stated differently, identification and evaluation of the

FIGURE 10.3
Assessing a Competitor's Assumptions

ATTRIBUTES OF ASSUMPTIONS
Are the fundamental assumptions few in number, pertaining to many domains, enduring and robust?

IMPORTANCE OF ASSUMPTIONS
Which assumptions make the most difference to the competitor's current or future strategy?
What are the implications if each assumption was reversed or radically changed?

VALIDITY OF ASSUMPTIONS
Are the assumptions congruent with the current or future reality within or external to the competitor?

ABSENCE OF ASSUMPTIONS
What assumptions does the competitor not appear to be making (that might have been anticipated)?
How would these nonassumptions affect its current assumptions?

STRATEGY AND ASSUMPTIONS
What marketplace strategy do the fundamental assumptions suggest?
What are the differences (if any) between the suggested strategy and the actual strategy?
What strategy alternatives might be constrained by the assumptions?
Which assumptions would have to change before specific strategy alternatives might be chosen?

SIGNALS OF CHANGE IN ASSUMPTIONS
What assumptions appear to be changing?
What are the indicators of these changes?

COMPARISON WITH FOCAL FIRM
How are the competitor's assumptions similar to or different from the focal firm's?
What are the implications of the different assumptions?

COMPARISON WITH OTHER COMPETITORS
How are the competitor's assumptions similar to or different from those of other competitors?

SIGNALS ABOUT MARKETPLACE CHANGE
What inferences can be drawn from the competitor's assumptions about evolving and potential marketplace change such as product change, customer focus, competitive dynamics?

DECISION IMPLICATIONS
What are the implications for the focal firm's current and potential decisions?
What new decisions are suggested?

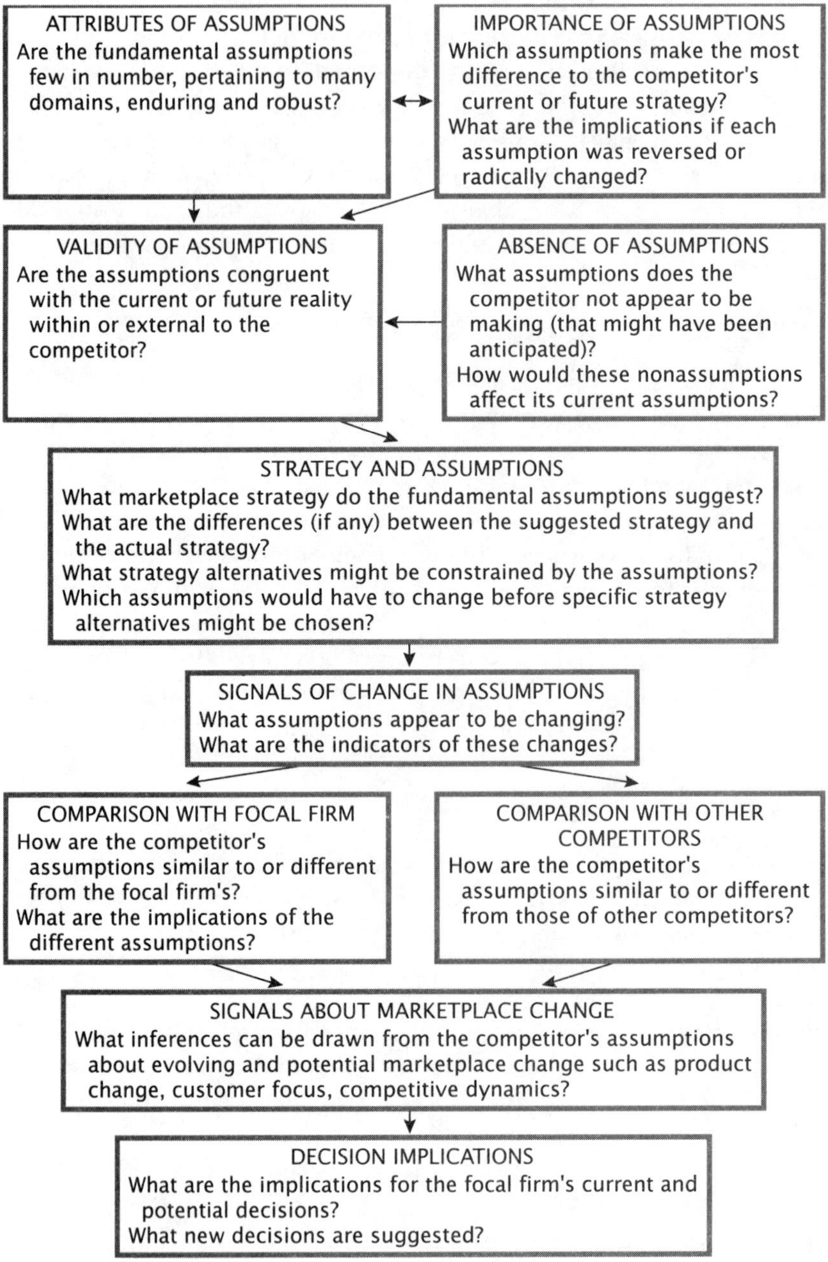

evidence for an assumption, as emphasized throughout this chapter, is intended to verify that a competitor *holds* that assumption. In most instances, that is quite distinct from an assertion that the assumption represents the world internal or external to the competitor.

Assumptions pertaining to both the competitor itself and the external environment should be tested for their validity.

Consider again the surgical instrument competitor's fundamental assumptions (see Table 10.6). The evidence appeared to be overwhelming that the competitor did indeed hold each assumption. However, irrespective of whether the competitor was explicitly cognizant of each assumption, real issues of validity pertained to at least two assumptions: "No substitute products are on the horizon," and "No competitor is now in a position to launch a series of major product innovations." There was some evidence that both of these assumptions were to some extent "wrong" or untrue: substitute products were in the process of development, and one small competitor was in the process of positioning itself to dramatically upgrade its only product line.

Breadth The surgical instruments competitor's core assumptions referred to a relatively wide set of domains: growth of industry sales, competitors' new products, posture, technology, substitute products, and surgeons' product preferences. However, the analysts noted that the core assumptions were considerably more oriented toward the external environment than the competitor itself—a point to be discussed later.

Consistency (In)consistency can be assessed with regard to any two or more assumptions. Two key questions are:

1. How do the assumptions support or contradict each other?
2. Do the assumptions lead to similar or different outcomes?

No dramatic inconsistencies were apparent in the surgical instruments competitor's core assumptions.

Dispersion Widely dispersed assumptions are reflected in more integrated (and thus more predictable) behaviors and marketplace strategies. Based on the number of individuals from whom analysts had found statements, they made the judgment that the core assumptions were most probably widely shared across the surgical instruments competitor.

Endurance It was also the analysts' judgment that most of the surgical instruments competitor's core assumptions had proved enduring: the firm's actions and statements over a number of years were largely consistent with the assumptions. However, enduring assumptions always raise questions about their future validity. If the environment is changing, the possibility is strong that the assumptions may become (or are already in the process of becoming) incongruent with the evolving environment. This seemed to be the case with the surgical instruments competitor.

Prioritize Assumptions: Which Are Most Important?

All refined and core assumptions do not provide equal insight into a competitor's current or potential strategies and other behaviors. Some assumptions are more important than others. Prioritization of assumptions refers to the process of identifying those assumptions that make the most difference to a competitor's current or future behaviors.

One way to identify the most important assumptions is to pose the following three questions:

1. What difference does it make to the competitor's current strategy or potential strategy if each assumption proves false or correct?
2. Which assumptions seem to make the most difference to specific strategy alternatives?
3. What are the strategy and decision implications if the opposite of the assumption proves correct?

If an assumption makes little difference to current or future change in the competitor's marketplace strategy, most likely it is not an important assumption. In one financial services firm, a raging debate occurred as to whether economic growth over the next one or two years would be 2.5 percent, 2.7 percent, or 2.9 percent. After intense discussion, it was agreed that estimates within this range would have little differential impact on the organization's performance—hence, economic growth within this range was not an important assumption.

Analysts should also test an assumption's importance against specific strategy alternatives and specific decisions. For example, if "We must depend on income from operations as the primary source of investment capital" is one of a competitor's fundamental assumptions, one might ask to what extent it would allow or inhibit specific alternatives such as embarking on a major market share acquisition program or internally developing new products.

A critical test of an assumption's importance is to analyze the strategy and decision implications if the opposite of the assumption proved correct.[13] In the case of the surgical instruments competitor, if the opposite of its assumption, "No substitute products are on the horizon for the next two to three years" is actually the case, then perhaps a serious challenge to its marketplace strategy is emerging. The data and logic buttressing this inference would then need to be severely critiqued.

Absence of Assumptions

It is often revealing to identify assumptions the competitor does not appear to be making but which might have been anticipated. When the competitor's behaviors and words do not seem to reveal expected assumptions (or more specifically, assumptions about specific domains), the analyst's attention is directed toward reviewing the analysis in case either behaviors and words have been overlooked, or some inferences have not been drawn.[14]

Analysts were surprised to see that none of the surgical instruments competitor's fundamental assumptions addressed the firm's own assets or capabilities. It seemed to be making a general assumption that it had, or could obtain, the necessary assets and capabilities to execute its preferred strategies. This assumption might be particularly critical in fulfilling its technology needs.

The Competitor's Marketplace Strategy and Assumptions

The relationship between the competitor's current marketplace strategy and potential strategy directions constitutes the essential rationale for detecting and assessing assumptions. Given the identification of a set of fundamental assumptions (as well as the refined and raw assumptions from which they are derived), several issues merit analysis.

What Marketplace Strategy (Direction) Do the Fundamental Assumptions Suggest? It is often insightful to develop a strategy outline that would be consistent with or flow from a competitor's core or fundamental assumptions. Assumptions always suggest direction of change in marketplace scope, posture, and goals. Although it is difficult to do, analysts must try to forget or ignore their knowledge of the competitor's actual marketplace strategy. Among other benefits, it may indicate inconsistencies among the assumptions.

The surgical instruments competitor's fundamental and refined assumptions generated a number of signals of marketplace strategy directions. For example, it is likely to introduce new products (stemming from Assumptions 4 and 6 in Table 10.6), to emphasize posture change and enhancement to win and retain customers (Assumption 3), and to seek further increments in market share (Assumptions 2, 3, and 4).

What Are the Differences (if Any) between the Suggested Marketplace Strategy and the Actual Strategy? The marketplace strategy direction suggested by a competitor's refined and core assumptions may be at odds with its current marketplace strategy. This may be so for two reasons. First, the assumptions may be derived from signals of potential or future change that are not yet reflected in the competitor's current or actual strategy. Second, analysts may be picking up changes in the competitor's assumptions that the competitor may not be aware of.[15]

The only significant difference determined in the case of the surgical instruments competitor pertained to the rate and extent of new product development. The assumptions suggested that product development (both products new to the competitor and the revamping of existing products) would be a much more evident feature of the competitor's marketplace strategy than heretofore. If this proved to be true, the competitor would be a much more formidable rival than previously.

What Strategy Alternatives Might Be Constrained by the Assumptions? The *constricting* power of mind-set is easily demonstrated by identifying strategy alternatives that would be inhibited, if not prohibited, by the competitor's assumptions.

To do so, it is necessary to develop possible strategy alternatives, some of which may be radically different from the competitor's current marketplace strategy, and then ask how each alternative might be facilitated or inhibited by the competitor's assumptions.[16] For the surgical instruments competitor, a marketplace strategy driven by a goal of diversifying into unrelated surgical instrument products might receive little enthusiastic support within the firm given its high expectations of growth in its existing product sectors, its assumption that enhancement of existing products will generate considerable further sales, and its assumption that its existing business was not threatened by the emergence of substitute products.

Which Assumptions Would Have to Change before Specific Strategy Alternatives Might Be Chosen? Consideration of strategy alternatives that might be constrained by prevailing assumptions leads in part to identifying which assumptions would have to change before specific alternatives might be chosen. As discussed in the preceding paragraph, the assumption of no threat of substitute products would have to change before the surgical instruments competitor would seriously consider some significant changes in its marketplace strategy such as "milking" some of its products rather than investing heavily in them for future market penetration.

Relatedly, it is also possible to ask in the event of change in each assumption (such as the opposite of the assumption proving true), which strategy alternatives might then be considered. For example, if the surgical instruments competitor were to conclude that continued enhancement in differentiation was *not* sufficient to sustain its leadership position in most of its existing products (the opposite of its existing assumption), it might then (consider) dramatic change to its prevailing marketing strategies.

The purpose of identifying these assumptions is that they then become a focal point in anticipating and monitoring assumption change in one or more competitors.

Signals of Change in Assumptions

The preceding analysis confirms the importance of isolating and assessing key signals of assumption change. Although refined and fundamental assumptions are often enduring and dispersed within a competitor, they change over time. In some instances, as noted, they change quickly and may result in the opposite of the prior assumption becoming accepted. Often, the changes are more subtle such as an increase or decrease in the rate of expected industry growth. The sooner such signals are derived, the longer the lead time in anticipating their competitor consequences and focal firm implications.

Two key questions need to be addressed:

1. What are the alerting and confirming/refuting indicators of change in individual assumptions?
2. How are the changes in assumptions related to each other?

An announcement that the surgical instruments competitor planned to extend its plant capacity served as the alerting indicator of an increase in the expected rate of growth in total industry sales (one of its fundamental assumptions). Further statements to that effect as well as statements from suppliers initially confirmed the seriousness of the intent. Purchase of equipment then served as a conclusive indicator that the firm was committed to the plant extension.

Frequently, changes in assumptions are related. Change across a number of assumptions may be consistent with an expectation of growing or declining industry sales, or a more or less competitive marketplace.

Comparison with the Focal Firm

Comparison between the assumptions of one or more competitors and the focal firm represents one of the most enlightening forms of self-learning. This is so for at least three reasons. Often, an organization does not know what its own *actual* assumptions are. Comparison with competitors provides the motivation and the means to discover what they are. Often, decision makers are surprised to discover which assumptions they actually hold. Finally, recognition of these assumptions leads to challenging questions about the current marketplace strategy, potential strategy alternatives, and other decisions. The experience of an industrial products company is used here to illustrate this kind of self-learning.[17]

Identify Own Assumptions   Many firms in the process of identifying competitors' assumptions discover, much to their surprise and horror, that their own assumptions have not previously been clearly and completely explicated. The challenge therefore is to do so. The relevant analysis process is the same as that described in this chapter for competitors.

Managers in the focal industrial products firm found that they had paid only lip service to assumptions. In the words of the firm's president, "We did a masterly job of concealing from ourselves what our assumptions were or should be." They charged a group of analysts with the task of identifying the assumptions underlying the firm's strategy.[18] They began by outlining the strategy documented in the firm's strategic plan.

Review the Assumption Context   The learning occurs in the comparison of the two assumption sets. However, analysts must understand the context in which each competitor operates; otherwise, they are likely to attempt invalid comparisons. Two questions are operative:

1. *Are the assumptions being derived for competitors in broadly similar product-customer segments?* If competitors are (largely) in two distinct product-customer segments, great care must be taken in comparing assumptions about products, customers, competitors, distribution channels, and future direction of the industry, to name but a few. For example, it is valid to compare assumptions pertaining to customers held by rivals that offer functional substitute products.

2. *Are the assumptions about the same phenomena?* Many errors in assumption analysis occur due to failure to carefully review to which phenomena assumptions refer. Although they often get lumped under customers, quite distinct assumptions sometimes pertain to distribution channels and end-customers. Assumptions about "the rate of market growth" may refer to different growth parameters (e.g., growth in unit sales versus growth in dollar sales) and different understandings of the market (e.g., different geographic markets or different channels).[19]

In the industrial product example, both competitors had competed against each other for many years with essentially the same types of products, going through mostly similar channels, in the same geographic region.

Compare the Assumption Sets Learning is generated through the identification of similarities and differences between the assumption sets. It is important to identify both. Similarities indicate shared conventional wisdom or "recipes." The greater the similarity, the less likely that the competitors are doing anything that surprises each other. Differences in assumptions focus attention on why rivals have had or have distinct strategies or behaviors.

Assumptions can be compared with respect to marketplace strategy or with respect to specific domains such as customers, technology, future direction of the industry, or the broader macroenvironment.[20]

Despite the similarity in competitive context, comparison of fundamental assumptions between the industrial product firms revealed pivotal differences (see Table 10.7). Indeed, they appeared to be almost polar opposites. To take one example: the competitor seemed to be assuming that distinct customer segments existed while the focal firm was making the assumption that little difference existed in purchasing criteria across customers.

Test the Validity of Conflicting Assumptions In testing the validity of assumptions,[21] two questions need to be raised:

1. *Do the differences in assumptions make a difference and to what?* There is a tendency to get bogged down in testing the validity of assumptions (e.g., are they congruent with apparent or expected environmental conditions) *before* concerns are raised about whether the differences have any implications for current or potential decisions. A number of managers in one financial services firm spent agonizing hours hotly debating whether their own firm's estimate of economic growth or that of one of their major rival's was a more reliable forecast. Only later did they discover that the difference led to only minor implications for key strategy issues.

TABLE 10.7 Comparison of Fundamental Assumptions: Industrial Products Firm and Its Competitor

Focal Firm	Competitor
Customers purchase products for the same reasons	Distinct market segments exist
One marketing strategy is sufficient for all customers	Differentiated marketing is required
Technology is not important in this industry	Technology development is key to competitive success
Many product-market segments are highly mature	Many key product-market segments are in the early stages of development

2. *Which assumptions are more congruent with current and prospective realties?* It is usually necessary to break this analysis into two segments: test for congruence with prevailing environmental conditions and with potential conditions. This is especially so if the assumptions pertain to key environmental uncertainties: conditions and events that are outside the control of any one competitor such as anticipated industry growth or the threat of substitute products.

In this case, the evidence was overwhelmingly in favor of the competitor's assumptions. Increasing product differentiation, greater variety in customer purchasing criteria and firms' postures, all suggested that distinct market segments were emerging.

Comparison with Other Competitors

Competitor learning is greatly augmented by comparing and contrasting assumptions across competitors. Distinct assumptions about products, customers, what it takes to succeed in the business, and the role of technology, among others, are often identified. In particular, early, though sometimes, weak signals of competitors' emerging or potential strategy change are gleaned.

Learning is enhanced when competitors with distinct assumptions are contrasted. Thus, the choice of competitors for comparative assumption analysis is crucial. One useful rule of thumb is to choose competitors with manifest differences in their marketplace strategies or in how they have positioned themselves across the activity/value chain. Some organizations have found it extraordinarily insightful to compare and contrast assumptions with functional substitute competitors and even some extended competitors. Such competitors lead to revealing assumptions about product and customer functionalities.

In the surgical instruments case, comparison with other major look-alike rivals revealed that none of them were as buoyant about the immediate future of the industry: they all appeared to be expecting a lower overall market growth rate. Thus, analysts' attention was focused on the evidence supporting the competitor's assumption of a 10 percent to 15 percent growth rate for the succeeding four or five years. If the assumption held up, the competitor might well have significantly outwitted its rivals.

Signals of Marketplace Change

Change in competitors' assumptions sometimes generates early signals of change in and around products or solutions, customers, channels, and competitive dynamics. These signals also often have a long change lag. Their interpretation and assessment is essential to outwitting rivals.

In the surgical instruments case, the competitor's fundamental assumptions (see Table 10.8) indicate that product change will almost certainly intensify: the competitor is committed to the technology investments that will generate new products, and surgeons will continue to seek technologically more sophisticated offerings. The competitor's technology commitments may in turn cause other rivals to extend and enhance their own product development investments. Competitors that appreciate and understand possible product trajectories and their associated competitive dynamics are likely to be in a better position to outmaneuver their rivals.

However, it is often differences in assumptions across competitors that offer particular outwitting capacity. The focal firm's own fundamental assumption that "competitors are beginning to specialize by product type and customer focus (i.e., type of surgery)" suggests emerging differentiation across product-customer segments. If this assumption is correct, it suggests the need for a fundamentally different approach to marketplace strategy: from largely undifferentiated marketing to several types of differentiation. Competitors mired in historic modes of competitive dynamics would have little chance of winning in the new environment.

Competitor Consequences

Competitor consequences with regard to its own assumptions, marketplace strategy, and microlevel components, may range from minor to

TABLE 10.8 Fundamental Assumptions: Surgical Instrument and Focal Firm

Competitor	Focal Firm
1) Rate of growth in total industry sales will average 10%–15% for the next 5 years	1) Industry growth is slowing; will not exceed average of 6%–8% over next 5 years
2) No competitor is now in a position to launch a series of major product innovations	2) Competitors are beginning to specialize by product type and customer focus (i.e., type of surgery)
3) Continued enhancements in differentiation (posture) will sustain the firm's marketplace leadership	3) Emergence of new substitute products are on the verge of changing the competitive context
4) Technology investments leading to new products are key to long-term marketplace leadership	4) Enhancements to existing products will not be sufficient for long-term marketplace success
5) No substitute products are on the horizon	5) Alliances will be necessary to quickly benefit from emerging technologies
6) Surgeons will continue to insist on the most technologically sophisticated products	6) Surgeons and hospitals will continue to demand the state-of-the-art technology

major. Assessment of assumption attributes—validity, breadth, consistency, dispersion, and endurance—often provides a preliminary indicator of the extent of the consequences. For example, competitors committed to *invalid* fundamental assumptions are predetermined to lose in the marketplace. Nothing short of a radical shift in assumptions is required to avoid performance decline. However, the challenges in shifting to new assumptions or mind-set are among the most difficult that confront any organization.

Even competitors with valid fundamental assumptions must be committed to continual assumption assessment. Unless they do so, they essentially forfeit their ability to outwit competitors. Thus, the challenge for many organizations, especially those outmaneuvering and outperforming their rivals, is to systematically and strenuously critique their own (historic) assumptions.[22] This is perhaps the central challenge facing the surgical instruments competitor. In view of the marketplace leadership position of its principal product line, the competitor is likely to find it difficult to give up fundamental assumptions that are losing validity such as those about industry growth, competitors' introduction of new products, and the absence of substitute products.

To the extent that assumptions are changing (or have already changed), they suggest emerging or potential change in marketplace strategy and microlevel components. Sometimes, however, assumption change indicates change in marketplace strategy and microlevel components that the organization is not able to execute. Thus, although marketplace strategy changes are not realized for some time (in some cases for a number of years), questions must be raised as to whether and how the competitor could execute the suggested strategies. For example, does the competitor possess the assets or capabilities and competencies to develop, manufacture, sell, and service the new products that might be suggested by a change in assumptions? For the surgical instruments competitor, the potential change in its total industry assumption growth rate (from mid-single digits to 10 percent and 15 percent for the next 5 years) raised grave questions as to whether the competitor could surmount its current operating capacity constraints to exploit the projected market growth.

Focal Firm Implications

Implications must be assessed with regard to the focal firm's own assumptions, and to its marketplace strategy and microlevel component decisions or actions.

Assumptions Comparison with one or more competitors compels the focal firm to identify, assess, and refine its own assumptions. Because of the importance of assumptions in outwitting competitors, each merits brief consideration.

The analysis of competitors' assumptions often results in more extensive and thorough delineation of the focal firm's own assumptions because the firm has not previously focused on this task. By obtaining a systematic understanding of its own assumptions, the focal firm can identify hidden influences in its decision making. A critical implication, therefore, is that by identifying its own *actual* assumptions, the focal firm can discern how it is being (or might be) outwitted by rivals. The focal surgical instruments firm discovered that it had to carefully consider the product and organization implications for itself if the competitor's assumption of 10 percent to 15 percent industry growth rate proved correct.

Once assumptions are identified, it is then possible to assess them: Are they valid? Are they consistent? Are they dispersed? How long have they endured? What decisions and actions do they suggest? What gaps are evident in the assumptions? To determine which assumptions the focal firm wants to accept for decision making, the assumptions are subjected to the same analysis delineated for individual competitors.

Since assumption assessment never ceases, refinement of assumptions merits continual attention. The central challenge is to continually test assumptions against current and anticipated change. The surgical instruments firm decided that it had to determine the relevant indicators along which it could monitor its own assumptions. Commitment to outwitting rivals demanded that it detect the need to change its fundamental assumptions before competitors did so.

Marketplace Strategy Explication and refinement of assumptions require assessment of the need to modify existing strategies. A dominant output of comparing and contrasting assumptions is sometimes recognition among a management team of the need to change strategy before the marketplace indicators of this need (including the actions of competitors) are readily apparent. Recognizing the need to change strategy removes what is often the most pervasive and inhibiting barrier to actual strategy change.

Consideration of assumptions immediately generated a crucial question for the surgical instruments firm: How could it use what had been learned to generate a winning marketplace strategy in the emerging and future competitive arena? Assuming the validity of its fundamental assumptions and the signals about the future marketplace, the firm had little choice but to significantly change its current marketplace strategy: to add new products (some of which would be new to the marketplace); to differentiate across product-customer segments (something the firm had not previously done); and to heighten its expectations or goals about what it could achieve in the marketplace (to set specific new product introduction targets; to stretch itself to become the dominant marketplace leader, at least in some product-customer segments). The firm would have little choice but to craft a new strategic direction in the marketplace.

Microlevel Components   A number of critical implications for individual microlevel components arose both directly from consideration of assumptions and indirectly from consideration of desired marketplace strategy change. The focal firm's own assumption "Alliances will be necessary to quickly benefit from emerging technologies" indicated the need to develop a capability to identify relevant alliance partners, negotiate alliance arrangements, and carry through on the alliances—a capability that the firm was sadly deficient in. This capability was rendered all the more necessary by another of the firm's fundamental assumptions, "Emergence of new substitute products are on the verge of changing the competitive context."

As with competitor consequences, potential marketplace strategy changes lead to assessment of whether and how the focal firm might be able to execute them. For the focal surgical instruments firm, development of new products required it to acquire and assimilate many types of new knowledge, to develop some new capabilities and to refine others, and to reorient its organization culture toward innovation and change (and away from the stability of doing the same things in the same old way). Every microlevel component would need to undergo significant change.

Errors in Assumption Assessment

An overarching error is that assessment is not pushed far enough. Analysts do not challenge the validity of assumptions beyond a cursory appraisal. As illustrated earlier in the discussion of the assessment of validity, critical learning central to outwitting competitors is thus most likely missed.

A manifestation of this error is that sometimes analysts pay insufficient heed to assessing which assumptions are truly important to a competitor's strategy or its potential future decisions. Hence, analysts may pay far too much attention to unimportant assumptions and fail to see the implications of the (more) important assumptions.

Another manifestation of not pushing assumption assessment is that once a competitor's assumptions are identified, the learning that accrues from identifying the strategy that would logically flow from those assumptions is entirely missed. This error occurs because there is little appreciation among decision makers of the need to project a competitor's likely strategy *given* its fundamental assumptions and then to compare and contrast the competitor's projected and actual strategies.

As emphasized throughout this chapter, the capacity to outwit is greatly aided when signals of change in competitors' assumptions are derived. Yet a common error is to ignore such signals or to downplay their importance. Analysts are preoccupied with specifying what the competitor's assumptions are, rather than assessing how the assumptions are changing.

Summary

Understanding competitors' assumptions provides a unique input into what it takes to outwit (and thus outmaneuver and outperform) current and future rivals. By the same token, understanding one's own assumptions generates unique self-learning. However, assumption learning poses severe tests to analysts' thinking capacities: evidence must be carefully formulated and critically assessed.

CHAPTER

11

Assets

WINNING ULTIMATELY IS MANIFEST IN AN ORGANIZATION'S MARKETPLACE ACTIONS and results. However, it is increasingly the consequence of outwitting, outmaneuvering, and outperforming both factor and end-product rivals in the acquisition, development, and deployment of chips.[1] A distinctive form of outwitting is knowing what chips are required to win and how to obtain them. Distinctive forms of outmaneuvering include developing new types of chips, augmenting existing chips, and partnering with key factor suppliers to develop and continually enhance critical chips. A distinctive form of outperforming is improving the quality of specific chips faster and better than rivals, and more broadly, achieving greater efficiency and effectiveness in their use.

Chips can be broadly segmented into an organization's assets, and capabilities and competencies. Assets constitute what the organization possesses. Capabilities and competencies,[2] on the other hand, constitute what the organization does or is able to do. Assets directly affect what competitors are able to do. They contribute to and constrain any organization's capabilities and competencies.[3] They influence potential responses to emerging and future opportunities. Knowledge of a competitor's assets also is integral to understanding choices competitors make with regard to each microlevel component such as the activity/value chain, alliances, and assumptions.

The intent of this chapter is to provide an integrated, though general, framework for the identification and assessment of competitors' assets. Since a broad definition of assets is adopted, the emphasis is on developing an analysis framework that can be used to identify and assess any *individual* class or type of asset. Other chapters address in detail many facets of specific assets (and thus can be viewed in part as asset analysis).[4] Because analysis frameworks are readily available and widely used for financial and human assets, this chapter pays more attention to other classes of assets. Some assets such as knowledge, relationships, and perceptions, as argued in Chapter 1, are rapidly becoming the dominant chips needed by organizations.

Understanding Assets

Definition

At the most general level, assets are what an organization possesses, as opposed to what it does. The asset *wherewithal* at an organization's (current and future) disposal as it strives to shape the strategy game and its marketplace rules extends well beyond the early economists' notions of land, labor, and capital. Indeed, "wherewithal" is intentionally vague. Its purpose is to suggest a broad, inclusive conception of assets. Wherewithal is also intended to affirm that organizations typically have a multiplicity of asset classes and types at their disposal.

A Typology of Assets

Despite early efforts to grapple with the variety, characteristics, and importance of assets,[5] the management literature is remarkably bereft of analytical frameworks that identify and categorize assets[6] and link them to strategy. There is no generally accepted typology of assets to facilitate depiction, analysis, and projection of a competitor's wherewithal.

The asset typology indicated in Figure 11.1 has proved useful in identifying and assessing competitors' assets. It provides a highly aggregative categorization of assets. Each asset category and some of its principal classes are briefly described. It conveys the breadth of assets competitors possess and the importance of each class.

Financial Financial wherewithal has received the most attention in asset assessment. As the most liquid and leveragable asset, it is used for many purposes. Equity, debt, liquidity, and cash, are among the classes typically considered in capturing a competitor's financial means. Potential financial wherewithal must also be considered. Frequently, organizations quickly augment their financial asset base through access to further equity, debt, and lines of credit, as well as through disposal or divestment of physical and other assets, or through alliances and mergers.

Human Human assets are commonly conceived as "demographics": the total number of personnel; the number by organization level, functional area, location, experience, and education and training. Yet organizations increasingly recognize that it is what personnel do (skills) and know (knowledge)

FIGURE 11.1
Assets: Categories and Principal Classes

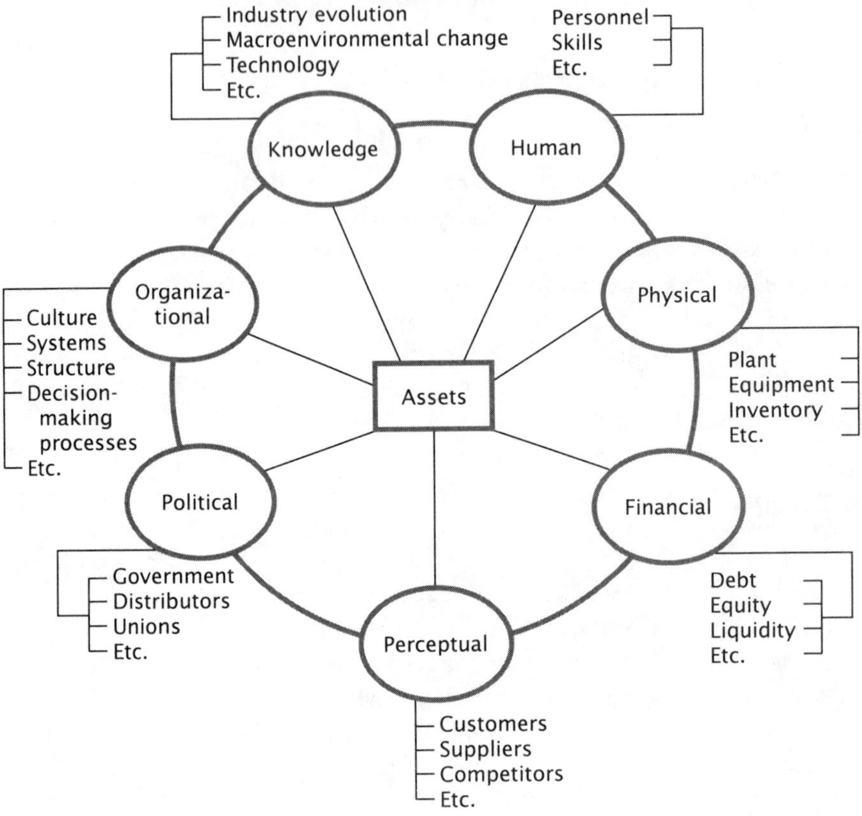

that matters. Skills are generally conceived as know-how: what individuals are skilled at, or able to do. Although no generally accepted categorization of skills exists, one useful approach is to relate skills and knowledge to specific types of jobs (such as brand managers or product design engineers) and to activities or processes (such as building and extending brands or developing new products). These in turn get combined to enable a capability or competency to exist and develop.

Knowledge Knowledge can be broadly defined as what people know (what they carry around in their heads) and what they can know (the knowledge they can develop).[7] As described in Chapter 2, processing (or analysis) transforms data into information that enables knowledge. At least three distinct though related classes of knowledge can be identified: people may possess knowledge about things or objects (e.g., scientific and technical knowledge, product knowledge), about systems and processes (e.g., manufacturing procedures, planning processes), and about entities (e.g., customers, suppliers, distributors, competitors, government, etc.). Increasingly, organizations view knowledge, rather than physical assets, as the source of both competitor-based and customer-based advantage.

Physical All organizations possess a base of distinct classes of physical assets including property (e.g., plant, buildings, land), equipment (e.g., manufacturing equipment, trucks, computers), and inventory (raw materials, work-in-progress, finished goods). Extensive variety exists in the types of assets subsumed within each class.

Perceptual Perceptual assets are sometimes not fully recognized or valued until organizations encounter negative perceptions about themselves or positive perceptions about their competitors. Classification of perceptions is typically based on who holds them. Principal classes include customers (e.g., brand loyalty, on-time delivery), suppliers (e.g., reputation as a customer), competitors (e.g., insistence on ethical behaviors), distributors (e.g., reputation for rapid delivery), the public (e.g., image as a good citizen), governmental agencies, and other external entities.

Perceptions sometimes constitute a formidable component of an organization's asset base. Some organizations invest heavily to establish, foster, and leverage perceptual assets such as brand loyalty, or an image with suppliers as a committed customer, or a reputation with customers for a willingness to listen to and work with them.

Political Organizations increasingly recognize that relationships with other entities contribute significantly to competitive success. Political relationships are classified based on with whom they are held. Organizations develop relationships with other competitive arena or industry entities such as suppliers, distributors, customers, competitors, industry and trade associations, consultants and technology experts, and broader macroenvironmental entities such as local community groups, public interest groups, governmental agencies, the courts, and unions. As discussed in Chapters 8 and 9, formal (in the case of alliances and networks) and informal, or special, relationships are often the source of significant competitor- and customer-based advantage.

Organizational Organizations must convert financial, human, knowledge, physical, perceptual, and political assets into outputs valued by customers. Many facets of an organization influence how well or how badly the transformation process is executed. Key organizational asset classes include culture, (e.g., values, beliefs, norms, and behaviors), systems (e.g., planning, control, and rewards), and decision-making processes. As illustrated in Chapters 14 and 15, a competitor's organization plays a pivotal role in shaping and sustaining winning strategies.

The asset typology represented in Figure 11.1 is neither exhaustive nor definitive. Although all organizations possess some stock of each asset category, analysts typically find it necessary to develop asset categories and classes that are more specific to individual businesses and competitors or that they deem more relevant to particular analysis purposes. For example, it is sometimes appropriate to identify and assess assets specific to functional areas or organizational subunits such as marketing, sales, R&D, technology,[8] logistics, information management, and human resources. As illustrated later in this chapter, assets also can be categorized using the activity/value chain.

The relevant types within each asset class typically vary greatly from one business to another—and sometimes even between look-alike competitors. It is only when broad asset categories—financial, human, knowledge, physical, perceptual, political, and organizational—are decomposed and related directly to winning in the marketplace, and to the development of capabilities and competencies, that a real understanding of a competitor's asset configuration is acquired.

Access and Control

Organizations do not need to own and control assets to have access to them or to leverage them for strategy purposes.[9] As discussed in Chapters 8 and 9 alliances, relationships, and networks can provide a critical advantage by allowing organizations to exploit assets that are at least partially owned and controlled by others. A competitor may use its long-standing relationship with a major distributor to keep rivals out of that channel or to make it more difficult for them to enter it. Many organizations outsource multiple activities such as logistics, data management, distribution, sales and, in some cases, elements of manufacturing. Outsourcing enables them to gain access to and benefit from assets that are superior to what they could develop internally. It also allows them to develop and leverage other assets by concentrating their efforts.

Stocks and Flows

Any organization's asset base is in a constant state of flux for many reasons. Assets are used up in transforming inputs (or factors) into outputs (products). The transformation process consumes asset inputs such as raw materials, inventory, and capital. The natural process of change within and outside the organization affects asset stock and flow. The development of new products, evolution of manufacturing processes, or the entry or exit of personnel adds to or depletes specific assets such as knowledge, skills, or key relationships. External shifts such as technology developments or the emergence of substitute competitors sometimes render obsolete any rival's core knowledge, skills, and technologies. Managers also choose for strategic reasons to reduce the stock of some assets.

Thus, any asset possessed or used by a competitor can be described and assessed at any point in time in terms of its *stock* (its amount or volume) and *flow* (whether the stock is increasing or declining). Stocks and flows represent the basic characteristics of assets and thus serve to focus the asset identification and assessment process.

Asset Attributes

Assets are not all alike. They vary widely along some key attributes. These differences are critical to how assets are acquired, retained, augmented, transformed into capabilities and competencies, and leveraged for marketplace advantage.

Availability   Assets vary in the extent to which they are available to individual competitors. *Internal* availability applies to asset stocks owned and controlled by the competitor. Availability slack is defined as that part of the stock of a specific asset that is not now used or leveraged and/or that can be generated for future use. Both dimensions of slack—what is not used and what can be generated—are important. A competitor may exhibit "slack" in such assets as capital, knowledge, skills, inventory, plant and equipment, perceptions, and relationships. Slack indicates available wherewithal that competitors can immediately leverage for purposes of winning.

External availability addresses whether it is possible to obtain specific assets exclusive of the competitor. Capital is widely available (though at a price) but essential data, information, or skills are sometimes in short supply, if available at all.[10] Intangible assets such as some types of perceptions and relationships can exist externally. It may be possible to procure favorable perceptions by the acquisition of organizations with well known and respected brand names or individuals who have strong relationships with key channels and end-customers.

Specificity   Any competitor's assets are specific to place, time, or space. The greater the asset specificity, the less it can be leveraged for diverse purposes by the competitor. Some types of knowledge are specific to a particular product technology or manufacturing process and thus afford little contribution to the competitor's efforts to diversify its product line. Skills are sometimes specific to a particular process or task. For example, a competitor's sales force is often skilled in selling a product line that requires only order taking and customer service but may be largely unskilled in selling another product line that requires detailing the product, and ascertaining and understanding customer requirements and specifications. Perceptions frequently are specific to particular products: one product has high brand loyalty, and another minimal, if any, loyalty.

Sustainability Competitors also reflect varying levels of ability to sustain existing stocks of assets. Declining performance depletes cash availability; product or factor competitors attract away personnel possessing key knowledge and skills; competitors' actions lessen customers' favorable perceptions of the firm and its products; the competitor sometimes cannot offer the inducements necessary to sustain relationships with unions, customers, or suppliers.

Replicability Assets that prove difficult to replicate, or that take time to replicate, are more likely sources of extensive advantage for competitors.[11] However, assets also vary greatly in their replicability. Capital is easy to replicate and often quickly, assuming its availability and that the competitor can afford to obtain it. Knowledge and skills may be extremely difficult to replicate, even when an organization commits extensive financial and human resources to doing so. Some intangible assets such as image and reputation for product reliability, or for fast service and rapid responsiveness to customer inquiries and complaints, often take years to replicate.

Substitutability Assets that are available, specific, sustainable, and difficult to replicate, however, are potentially substitutable: competitors are able to find a substitute for the asset. Some firms have spent years enhancing specific types of knowledge only to find that one or more rivals developed a form of knowledge that performs the same or a broadly similar function.

Indicators of Asset Change

Indicators of asset change are both direct and indirect. Moreover, indicators vary considerably from one asset type to another, and often across asset types within the same asset class.

Asset Change as Signals

Each asset type possesses signaling capacity. Changes in the stock and flow of each asset category are potentially alerting or confirming signals of profound and extensive change in the competitor's marketplace strategy. They frequently also indicate microlevel component changes as well as shifts in the emerging and potential product marketplace. Asset change as alerting signals of factor market change is often overlooked, in part because of the emphasis on the product marketplace in most organizations.

Identifying Competitors' Assets

To delineate fully the assets of a reasonably large independent business or stand-alone business unit, much less a corporation competing in multiple distinct businesses (such as General Electric, Emerson Electric, Siemens, or NEC), is a daunting and complex task. However, as is often the case in competitor analysis, complete specification of a competitor's assets, or indeed, of any specific asset category, is rarely required. Rather what is necessary is sufficient understanding of the competitor's asset configuration for the analytical purposes at hand. The analyst's challenge therefore is to determine how far to take asset identification and description. The principal guidance that can be offered reduces quickly to a general prescription in the form of four questions[12] that must be continually asked:

1. What does the organization know about specific assets of the competitor?
2. What might be learned about these assets?
3. What is the (potential) knowledge increment?
4. How can the knowledge increment be used in decision making?

Consideration of these four questions helps determine what needs to be learned and why. Building on these questions, a *guided* approach to asset identification, entails five steps (see Figure 11.2). The proposed sequence of steps enables the analyst to continually question how much further to take the analysis. A small, private, software competitor that was beginning to outperform its rivals is used to illustrate the approach.[13]

Determining What Needs to Be Learned and Why

Guided learning emphasizes determining the purpose of asset analysis. Sometimes the purpose is to develop an overview of one or more competitors' asset classes to identify which are most critical to their current and future marketplace strategies. Such analysis often reframes an organization's understanding of the importance of specific assets and provides critical guidance to its investments in asset acquisition and development. Many

FIGURE 11.2
Identifying a Competitor's Assets

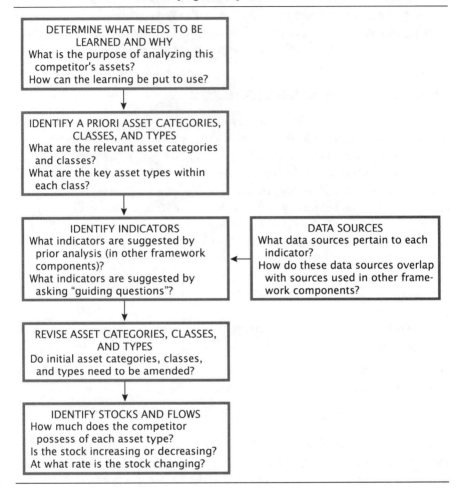

firms have discovered that their rivals have used networks[14] to reinvent or augment their stock of many different assets including raw materials, knowledge, and relationships with channels and customers.

A fundamentally different purpose, requiring much more systematic and detailed analysis, is to understand competitors' stock and flow of one or more asset classes, and perhaps even types within a particular class. Such analysis and the resulting learning can sharply influence what specific asset types an organization decides to develop and leverage. For example, one organization learned that its principal look-alike competitor had extensive knowledge of its corporate customers' changing technologies, thus allowing it to develop successful new products faster than many of its rivals. It also discovered that one of its functional substitute competitors was leveraging its relationships with and knowledge of the same customers to develop its next generation of products.

The focal software firm decided to investigate which assets were critical to the competitor's recent (and anticipated) success in launching some new products and how it acquired, augmented, and deployed these assets. It hoped that this learning would help guide its own asset development and deployment.

Identify Initial Asset Categories, Classes, and Types

Efficiency and effectiveness in a guided search are greatly aided by considering relevant asset categories and classes (see Figure 11.1) as a point of departure prior to data gathering. Consideration of an a priori set of categories and classes helps to avoid some of the errors noted later in this section, especially the common tendency to narrowly define the range of relevant assets.

Drawing on knowledge of their own organization, as well as of competitors and the competitive domain, analysts must consider which categories, and the classes within them, are most appropriate to the competitors being considered. Analysts sometimes find that they need to reconfigure the categories and classes noted in Figure 11.1 in several ways. Some categories are segmented and refined. For example, an airline might divide physical assets into two categories, capital equipment (airplanes) and other physical assets.

Identifying types within classes compels analysts to consider in specific terms the assets possessed by each competitor. Competitors possess many types of knowledge about corporate customers: their current and emerging needs and wants, purchasing personnel and their proclivities, buying behaviors and patterns, differences across activity/value chains, and product uses and applications.

The asset classes identified in the case of the software competitor are noted in Table 11.1. Many of the classes are peculiar to software organizations such as knowledge of software design and knowledge of specific software codes. Each class could be refined into asset types as analysts consider it necessary and beneficial to do so.

Identify Asset Indicators

In a guided analysis, indicators emanate from two complementary sources: other framework components and guiding questions (see Figure 11.3). Using

TABLE 11.1 A Software Competitor: Asset Stocks, Flows, and Data Sources

Asset Category	Asset Class	Sample Indicators	Data Sources
Capital	Equity Debt Cash Lines of credit	Capital committed by owners Funds provided by investors Credit provided by banks Calculations of cash availability	Statements by the competitor's managers Interviews conducted by consulting firm with industry experts and other participants Sales data provided by channels Calculations made by focal firm
Human	Total number of personnel Personnel by activity, function, or organization subunit Skills by groups or organization subunit	Employees Number in product development Number of design engineers Number of salespeople Ability of salespeople to sell	Statements by the competitor to the trade press Content of job advertisement Conversations by focal firm personnel at trade shows and other industry events Estimates of firm specializing in monitoring privately held businesses
Knowledge	Areas of knowledge: software design specific codes manufacturing corporate customers consumers marketing	Product functionality Product design Product features Purchase of process technology Statements of corporate customers	Product teardown Use of product in different customer contexts Interviews with machinery suppliers Interviews with a range of corporate customers and consumers
Physical	Plant and equipment Corporate headquarters Regional offices Inventory Work-in-progress Customer databases	Location of plant Types of machinery Types of equipment	Competitor press releases Visits to field offices and headquarters Statements by competitor to channel members Competitor's marketing activities and sales calls

Asset Stock	Asset Flow
Owner's equity approximately $10 million	Equity and debt base stable but could be easily augmented
Debt about $15 million	Cash flow is becoming increasingly positive as margins widen and volume increases
Cash on hand $2 million	
Line of credit about $3 million	Line of credit has also been increased (and probably could be extended even more)
450 employees	Modest increase in overall number of employees
40 devoted full time to new product development	Doubling of number devoted to new product development over the prior 2 years
10 involved in redesigning customers' channel relations	
35 salespersons dedicated to new product introduction	Marginal increase in salespersons committed to new product introduction
Extensive familiarity with key software codes	Using training and seminars to enhance knowledge of software codes
Detailed knowledge of latest manufacturing processes	Using outside sources to extend knowledge and skills
Intimate knowledge of key corporate customers' uses of specific products	Relationships with customers of all types devoted to extending customer knowledge
Well versed in how to do product testing with different groups of customers	Continually refining product testing and development of processes and skills
Exemplifies marketing know-how	
Extensive new production plant	Massive upgrade in quality of production plant and related machinery
Latest types of manufacturing machinery	
High level of inventory	Inventory continuing to rise
Extensive databases on current and potential corporate and consumer users	Continually upgrading extent and quality of data on customers of all types

(Continued)

TABLE 11.1 *(Continued)*

Asset Category	Asset Class	Sample Indicators	Data Sources
Political	Relationship with: customers channels trade associations universities research houses	Customer involvement in product testing and development Cooperative activity with channels Roles in trade association Hiring from specific universities	Statements by customers Interviews with channels Conversations with trade association leaders and other members Statements by the competitor's managers
Perceptual	Perceptions held by: customers channels competitors leading design engineers trade publications	Willingness of channels and corporate customers to work with the competitor Industry-wide survey measures Statements by leading software designers Actions of competitors	Statements by the competitor Interviews with channel members Industry secondary research (surveys) conducted by the focal firm and others Trade press reports of competitor's actions
Organizational	Infrastructure: information systems decision-making procedures/styles Culture: creativity commitment to quality work norms	Data gathering from customers Speed of decision making in response to competitor's actions Innovative products Innovative modes of competing in the marketplace Work habits	Reports by customers and channel members Comments by the competitor's personnel at a trade show Analysis of the competitor's products and actions in the marketplace Former employees

the two interrelated approaches helps ensure that analysts leverage analysis already conducted and that the asset categories and classes noted in Figure 11.1 are not ignored or downplayed.

First, many direct asset indicators emanate from the other framework components. For example, organization infrastructure and culture indicators (see

Asset Stock	*Asset Flow*
Very tight working relationships with many major corporate customers	Expending considerable efforts to extend and enhance connections to all types of customers and channels
Long-term cooperative relationships with key channel members	
Plays a leading role in the dominant trade association	Individuals seeking office in trade association and to be involved in many of its activities
Competitor viewed by corporate customers as the most innovative in its product sector	Customers, channels, and third parties seeing the competitor's products and services more favorably over time
Product features and functionality rated by consumers as highest among its peers	
Has strong reputation for product creativity among software design engineers	Competitors beginning to see how committed the competitor is to winning in its product segments
Viewed as tough and aggressive	Increasing frequency of favorable comments about the competitor in the trade publications
According to trade publications, an exemplar software developer and marketer	
Information system that gathers and disseminates data quickly	Seem to make marketing decisions more quickly and with greater commitment
Decision making that involves many individuals and integrates their input quickly	Respond to competitor's initiatives more quickly than previously
Culture that emphasizes being creative and continually enhancing quality in both products and interactions with all types of customers	Senior managers—emphasizing greater need for customer values and intimacy—now being reflected in managers and others spending more time with customers, suppliers, experts, etc.
Managers committed to working with outsiders—customers, experts—until problems are solved	

Chapters 14 and 15) are direct indicators of key categories of the competitor's organizational assets. As illustrated in Chapter 13, such is also the case with many technology indicators. Some marketplace posture dimensions such as image and reputation, and selling and relationships, provide direct indicators of perceptual assets and political assets, respectively.

FIGURE 11.3
**Identifying a Competitor's Assets: Guiding Questions from Framework
Components**

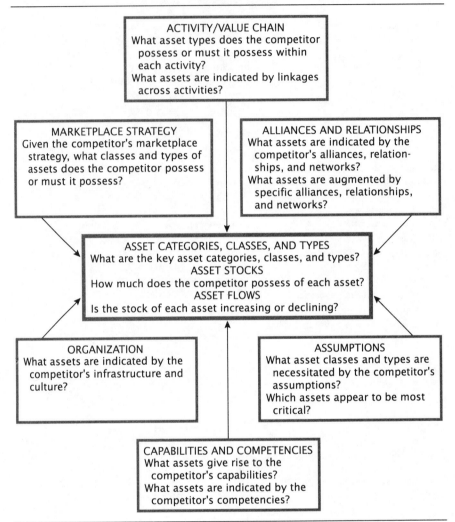

Many activities and tasks along the activity/value chain also furnish direct asset indicators.

However, most framework components generate indirect asset indicators. The analyst is obliged to draw inferences from them about the competitor's current and potential assets. Alliance and network indicators (see Chapters 8 and 9) often provide strong indirect indicators of asset acquisition and disposition.

A second but related means to generate asset indicators stems from asking "guiding component questions"[15] (see Figure 11.3). Once analysts develop a preliminary configuration of asset categories and classes, they ask questions about the assets the competitor has or must have. These questions typically lead to the generation of indicators already identified and some that have not. One side benefit of asking such questions is often added understanding of individual framework components. For example, how alliances and networks serve as generators or destroyers of assets helps to illuminate not just the role and importance of alliances and networks as a means of accessing assets that the competitor may not own or control, but also illustrates how alliances and networks are used to outwit, outmaneuver, and outperform rivals.

Consider, for example, marketplace strategy. An analysis of scope, posture, and goals sometimes generates extensive indicators of asset classes and types. Product evolution can indicate types of knowledge that the competitor possesses or needs to possess. The customer segments covered can indicate key distribution channel relationships. The rate of change in scope (e.g., speed of product introductions) sometimes indicates technology assets.

Each posture dimension also indicates asset classes and types. For example, functionality dimensions such as product performance characteristics frequently indicate specific types of technical knowledge and skills the competitor possesses or must possess. Image and reputation are likely to indicate perceptions held by customers and others.

Marketplace goals often indicate asset presence and requirements. A commitment to specific market share goals indicates required plant or production capacities, and sometimes indicates manufacturing technology characteristics and even relationships with vendors when projected sales are greater than the competitor's known production capacity.

The activity/value chain also provides a useful way to configure a competitor's assets. Each activity, along with the tasks within it,[16] serves as a guide for indicating asset classes and types. In the customer-focused activity/value chain, within the activity, understanding customers' needs, tasks such as meeting with customers, studying customers' operations, and specifying broad product or solution requirements, indicate asset types such as customer relationships, knowledge of customers' facilities, operating processes and their ways of doing business, and customer databases.

Many indicators gathered in the software example are noted in Table 11.1. Both direct and indirect indicators are evident. The importance of indirect indicators is particularly striking for every knowledge class. Knowledge of software design and codes was inferred from such indirect indicators as product functionality (what the software was able to do for users) and product features (specific capabilities built into the software).

Some Comments on Indicators and Data Sources

Before discussing the determination of asset stocks and flows, some comments on asset indicators and associated data collection issues are warranted. Much of the difficulty and complexity in conducting comprehensive competitor asset analysis arises because, as noted, the methodology for collecting and analyzing the requisite data to determine stocks and flows varies across asset classes and types. The indicators (or variables) along which stocks and flows are captured, tracked, and evaluated, as shown in Table 11.1, are specific to a class (and sometimes to types within a class). Ignoring these details causes many of the errors noted at the end of this section.

In view of these differences, analysts must develop a methodology appropriate to each asset class, and frequently for types within a class. It is necessary to identify for each asset class or type, the relevant indicators (by leveraging prior analysis and asking guiding questions as discussed), the types of data required, the pertinent internal and external data sources, the extent of the data required, and how best to collect the data. These tasks are closely related.[17] For example, the two knowledge classes, knowledge of corporate customers and knowledge of software design (see Table 11.1), involve distinct indicators, with different types of data, stemming from quite different data sources.

Revise Asset Categories, Classes, and Types

A priori asset categories, classes, and types guide initial efforts to identify relevant indicators and associated data sources. However, as analysts begin to capture and process data, the need to redefine categories, classes, and types typically arises. Indicators derived from framework component questions often suggest specific asset types. In the case of the software competitor, as indicators of knowledge were detected, key classes of knowledge were identified including knowledge of software design, of specific software codes, of manufacturing, of corporate customers, and of consumers and marketing. To choose one knowledge class—knowledge of corporate customers—as indicators were detected, distinct types of corporate customer knowledge were identified: knowledge of customer needs, of product use, of difficulties in product use, and of potential applications.

Identify Stocks and Flows

As relevant indicators are identified, the major task is to determine asset stocks and flows. Two central questions guide the analysis: What stock does the competitor possess of each asset type? Is the stock increasing or decreasing? Stocks and flows are effectively ascertained only at the level of types of assets.

Distinct modes of calculation, involving different types of judgments, characterize the methodologies pertaining to individual asset classes and types. For example, in determining *financial* stocks and flows, analysts often are required to execute multiple calculations.[18] In determining cash flow in the software example, analysts had to estimate revenues, margins, and costs. Each required a number of calculations. Revenues necessitated determination of sales units and prices. Product cost estimates required the analysts to identify each significant cost factor—raw materials, components, labor, energy sources, overhead, logistics, and marketing. Some judgments about margins were based on comments by the competitor's executives, knowledge of the focal firm's own margins and industry standards, and the relationship between estimates of the competitor's revenues and costs.

Judgments about a competitor's stock of knowledge often lack well-established methodologies (in particular, commonly accepted indicators) like those available for financial and many physical asset classes. The analysts in the software case, made several judgments pertaining to knowledge types (such as types of customer knowledge and manufacturing process knowledge) and then challenged each inference by asking what data supported or refuted each inference. The judgment that the competitor had an extensive stock of knowledge about many aspects of how to do product testing with different groups of customers is a case in point. It was buttressed by data along a number of indicators: measures from customer surveys, questions posed directly to channels and end-customers, statements by the competitor's managers, comments by industry observers in the trade press, and a detailed delineation of what the competitor did in product testing by the analysts themselves.

Open-Ended Search

Because they do not start with a preordained notion of the domain of assets, open-ended searches are more likely to cause analysts to adopt a broad understanding of the notion of assets and to ask how and why each asset type is potentially leveragable by competitors. In an open-ended search, analysts move from data about the competitor to a classification of asset categories, classes, and types. In principle, the search is unfocused in that the analyst is not committed a priori to any asset configuration, is not influenced by any prior analysis of the competitor and can scan all data types and sources. The analyst thus scans for indicators of the presence (and absence) of asset classes and their constituent types.

Common Errors in Asset Identification

Analysts commit a number of errors in identifying rivals assets. The discussion emphasizes errors specific to the concept[19] of assets and to the tasks inherent in collecting data and detecting indicators.

Not surprisingly, analysts sometimes conceive assets extremely narrowly. This occurs in two ways. Some asset categories—in particular, financial assets—are overly emphasized to the relative neglect of others.[20] Intangible assets (e.g., perceptual, political, and organizational) often receive only cursory appraisal. Although financial assets are important, the financial balance sheet captures only a subset of a competitor's assets and frequently does not capture the assets central to the attainment of customer—and competitor— advantage. Moreover, within asset categories, some classes receive disproportionate attention. Within perceptual assets, brand equity often receives detailed consideration while other classes, including perceptions held by other entities (e.g., other competitors, distributors, or suppliers) are accorded scarcely any attention.

Relatedly, the domain of assets is most often restricted to those owned or controlled by the competitor. Alliances, relationships, and networks, are not considered as sources of assets. Consequently, the competitor's current and potential asset base may be severely underestimated.

A common and major error occurs when analysts seek specification of a competitor's assets at a level of detail way beyond its potential contribution to analysis and decision making. This leads to considerable inefficiency. It is not uncommon to find organizations seeking a greater degree of detail in specifying a competitor's stock and flow of particular asset types than it possesses for its own assets.[21]

Another basic error is insufficient attention to the distinction between asset stocks and asset flows. Analysts reach broad judgments about competitors' assets without carefully distinguishing between how much of an asset a competitor possesses (and can obtain) and whether the stock is increasing or decreasing. In some instances, the direction of change in an asset stock (as a signal) is more important than its absolute level.

Assessing Assets

Assets are assessed in several ways (see Figure 11.4). First, it is essential to determine the attributes of each asset class or key type. A preliminary assessment of which assets are most critical to the competitor's marketplace strategy and activity/value chain helps focus analysts' attention not only on identifying key assets but on learning how these assets are leveraged for customer- and competitor-based advantage.[22] Comparing and contrasting a competitor's assets to those of the focal firm and other rivals identifies asset

FIGURE 11.4
Assessing Assets

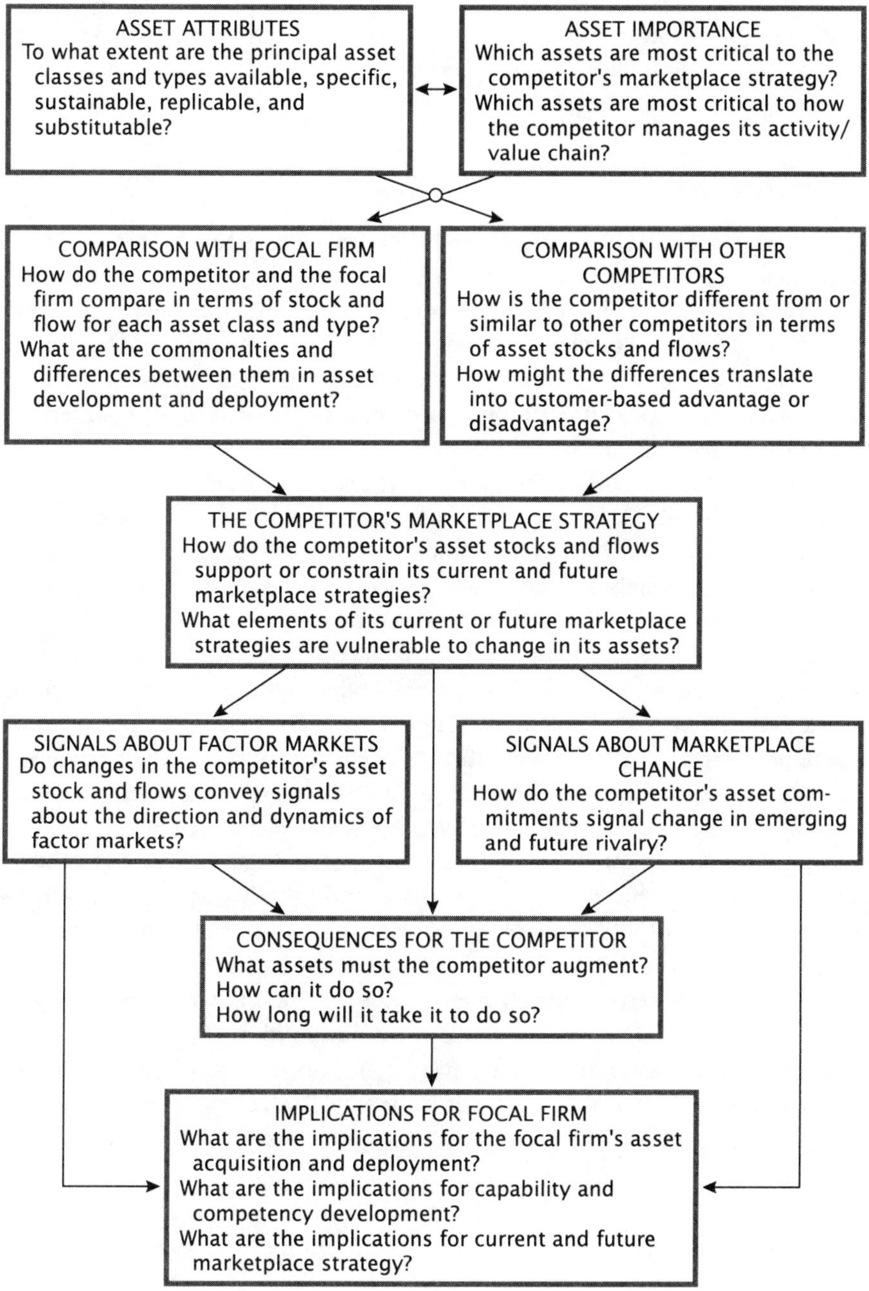

ASSET ATTRIBUTES
To what extent are the principal asset classes and types available, specific, sustainable, replicable, and substitutable?

ASSET IMPORTANCE
Which assets are most critical to the competitor's marketplace strategy? Which assets are most critical to how the competitor manages its activity/ value chain?

COMPARISON WITH FOCAL FIRM
How do the competitor and the focal firm compare in terms of stock and flow for each asset class and type? What are the commonalties and differences between them in asset development and deployment?

COMPARISON WITH OTHER COMPETITORS
How is the competitor different from or similar to other competitors in terms of asset stocks and flows? How might the differences translate into customer-based advantage or disadvantage?

THE COMPETITOR'S MARKETPLACE STRATEGY
How do the competitor's asset stocks and flows support or constrain its current and future marketplace strategies? What elements of its current or future marketplace strategies are vulnerable to change in its assets?

SIGNALS ABOUT FACTOR MARKETS
Do changes in the competitor's asset stock and flows convey signals about the direction and dynamics of factor markets?

SIGNALS ABOUT MARKETPLACE CHANGE
How do the competitor's asset commitments signal change in emerging and future rivalry?

CONSEQUENCES FOR THE COMPETITOR
What assets must the competitor augment? How can it do so? How long will it take it to do so?

IMPLICATIONS FOR FOCAL FIRM
What are the implications for the focal firm's asset acquisition and deployment? What are the implications for capability and competency development? What are the implications for current and future marketplace strategy?

superiority or inferiority in terms of stocks and flows. The analyst is then able to relate assets in detail to the competitor's current and future marketplace strategy. Asset assessment is also potentially a source of signals of change in particular factor markets and in the future product marketplace. Finally, assessment leads to the determination of competitor consequences and focal firm implications.

Asset Attributes

Each asset class and its principal types are assessed as to availability, specificity, sustainability, replicability, and substitutability. These assessments draw on analysts' knowledge of the competitor and its customer and factor competitive arenas. Even preliminary assessments of these attributes for the principal asset types[23] draw attention to significant asset issues for the competitor (and are thus critical inputs to comparisons with other competitors and with the focal firm).

In the software example, the competitor had significant slack available in its financial and physical assets. The analysts judged that it also had untapped slack in its perceptual assets. That is, it could better leverage positive perceptions of both channels and end-customers. The critical asset specificity occurred with regard to knowledge of software design and codes. While its perceptual assets would likely carry over to other (related) software products, its knowledge of software design and codes would not easily transfer to the design and development of unrelated[24] software products. Sustainability might prove to be an issue with three asset categories: capital, knowledge, and organization. Were the software competitor to suffer a decline in sales and/or an increase in marketplace rivalry, it would have severe difficulty in maintaining the level of free cash flow of the preceding two years. The departure of a small number of key individuals would greatly jeopardize its knowledge enhancement potential. As the organization grew in size, its innovative, high-contact culture would most likely prove difficult to sustain.

The analysts declared that all the competitor's assets were largely replicable. It would be difficult, though clearly possible, to replicate its knowledge of product development and testing, its positive perceptions, and its creative culture. Finally, if a substitute form of developing software code were to evolve, much of the competitor's specific knowledge might not be leveragable.

Asset Importance

Even in the early stages of asset assessment, it is useful to develop a preliminary judgment of which asset classes and types are most critical to the competitor's marketplace strategy and to how it manages specific product activity/value chains.[25] In the software case, two assets stood out as the source of current and potential value to customers: a small set of individuals who possessed critical software development knowledge and the competitor's culture, which undergirded its creativity and innovativeness.

Comparison with Focal Firm

When compared with the focal firm, asset stocks, flows, and deployment indicate relative asset abundance and use. *Stock* comparisons raise two related questions: How much of each asset type does each organization possess? And, which one has more or less of the asset? Such assessments are most meaningful at the level of asset types. An assertion of a greater endowment of perceptual or political assets is relatively meaningless until we know which types of perceptual or political assets are being addressed.

As noted, the distinct nature of asset types (even within a particular asset class) and the extensive differences among relevant indicators give rise to many types of judgments. In the case of the yogurt firm discussed in Chapters 5 and 6, assessment of relative endowment of perceptual assets required judgments about the image of the competitor and focal firm held by both distribution channels and many segments of consumers.

Comparisons were relatively straightforward in the software example. The competitor had considerably less financial and human wherewithal available to it, but it had more abundant knowledge of software design and code development (relative to this specific product); stronger relationships with channels, customers, and product-specific research establishments; higher quality perceptions; and a more creative organizational culture.

These judgments collectively suggested that the competitor, although it was less well endowed in terms of financial and physical assets, had outwitted and outmaneuvered the focal firm by developing and leveraging other types of assets to create distinct customer value.

Comparisons of asset *flow* also raised two related questions: Whose stocks are increasing or decreasing? and, What is the rate of change in their flow? Assessments of asset flows are often more critical than comparisons of *current* asset stocks. They are a strong signal of a competitor's *future* asset supply. Positive flows indicate enhanced asset availability and negative flows declining availability. Thus, in many instances, it is not so much greater (or lesser) asset stock endowment that is of importance but the direction and speed of change of asset flows. Again, a wide disparity exists in the ease with which the necessary judgments are made. One factor contributing to the difficulty in making judgments resides in the number of distinct indicators that may be necessary. It is relatively easy to determine if a hotel chain competitor is opening new properties at a much greater rate than the focal firm. However, to determine whether the yogurt competitor (see Chapters 5 and 6) is enhancing its image and reputation faster than the focal firm requires attention to many indicators including responses of customers and noncustomers (both consumers and channels) to survey and interview questions, unsolicited comments of customers about the products, and the rate of change in product purchases.

In the software example, the competitor was augmenting all assets other than financial and physical faster than the focal firm. It was investing time and money to enhance all knowledge types and to get closer to customers. Thus, it was reinforcing and extending perceptions held by customers, competitors, and others, and fostering its innovative culture. On the other hand, the focal firm was investing more in capital and hiring people. This raised two issues for the analyst team: How would the increments in financial and human assets be used to develop comparable or superior perceptual, political, and organizational assets compared with the competitor? How would the focal firm transform the increments in financial and human assets into skills and capabilities that could be leveraged to outmaneuver and outperform the competitor?

Comparisons with Other Competitors

As noted, asset comparisons are frequently flawed because of the choice of inappropriate competitors as the frame of reference. Horizontal versus vertical look-alike competitors typically generate radically different asset assessments. In some instances, analysts may judge that both the stock and flow of knowledge and skills are far superior to look-alike competitors with similar product lines but not to competitors with higher-end or lower-end product lines. For example, Compaq might favorably assess its customer knowledge and manufacturing skills compared with many of its direct competitors such as Dell and Gateway but might rate its software knowledge inferior compared with competitors that have broader product lines such as Digital, IBM, or Hitachi.

Distinct assessments also occur between look-alike and functional substitute competitors. When compared against current or emergent functional substitute competitors, many organizations have found that their prized and precious assets are not likely to generate the significant customer- and competitor-based advantage they had presumed or expected. To cite merely one example, a surgical instruments firm's stock of technology, political, and perceptual assets may suddenly seem exceptionally specific (to a particular form of the traditional handheld surgical product) in the face of the emergence of a laser technology based form of the product.

When stocks and flows are considered simultaneously, analysts sometimes judge that replicability is not a concern with current competitors but might emerge as a fundamental problem when considering new entrants. A potential entrant may be positioning itself to leapfrog the stock of customer knowledge of current competitors through its educational programs, hiring policies, and training practices.

The case of the software competitor emphasizes many of these points. Compared with its historic look-alike rivals, the competitor fared well in terms of availability and sustainability of knowledge, perceptual, political, and organizational assets. Yet when compared with some potential competitors such as large software organizations that could decide to enter its product-customer segments, it would not have their capital or human asset availability. These firms might replicate the competitor's strong and extensive political and perceptual assets such as relationships with key corporate customers and reputation for product quality.

Link to Current and Future Marketplace Strategy

Asset assessment ultimately must be related to the competitor's current and future marketplace strategy. Assets as a support base, and as a source of constraints and vulnerabilities, provide critical points of linkage to marketplace strategy.

Support Base   As noted previously, not all asset types are equally critical to a strategy. Thus, the intent here is to refine and extend which assets support or underlie each element of the competitor's marketplace strategy—scope, posture, and goals. For example, at the chemical firm discussed in Chapter 12, political assets in the form of long-standing, intimate, and cooperative relationships with many customers were central to all activities in its product development. The same was also true for the software competitor.

Constraints   Asset insufficiency and inappropriateness sometimes severely constrain marketplace strategy. Lack of capital, obsolete knowledge, static skills, deteriorating perceptions (e.g., declining brand loyalty), unraveling relationships, and disintegrating organizational systems and procedures can individually, or in any combination, constrain a competitor's ability to successfully compete in the marketplace. The computer competitor analyzed in Chapter 7 suffered a severe constraint in its supply of specific components, thus limiting the supply of finished products it could take to the marketplace. No dominant current asset constraints were evident for the software competitor. However, changes in strategic direction (e.g., the development of some types of product) were potentially severely constrained by its current stock of specific knowledge.

Vulnerability   Asset sufficiency and appropriateness do not eliminate vulnerability. Often forgotten is that any competitor's marketplace strategy is vulnerable not only to external events but also to changes in the organization's asset base. Some organizations' strategies are especially vulnerable to critical knowledge and skills exiting the organization. Some small organizations engaged in many types of professional services have quickly gone out of business once some key personnel departed either for competitors or to start their own enterprises. Departure of key personnel was a dominant vulnerability for the software competitor. Its reputation for product quality was also very vulnerable to assessments of reviewers in the trade press.

Signals about Factor Markets

Most types of labor, capital, physical equipment, components and supplies are purchased in factor markets. Thus, current and potential changes in competitors' stocks and flows of these asset types may signal imminent and future change in specific factor markets.

Such signals are derived in several ways.[26] How one or more competitors choose to add to their stock of labor, raw materials, components, or capital may critically affect the market for these assets. If a competitor decides to develop its own internal supply of components, rather than procuring them in the open market, it may greatly alter the supply-demand balance in the market for these components. A competitor's decision to use less of an asset may signal a demand downturn for the asset type in the factor market, especially if the competitor is a large consumer of the asset and/or it indicates that other users of it may also do likewise.

Signals of Marketplace Change

Since connections between asset change and marketplace change are directly and indirectly noted in many other chapters, the intent of the discussion here is to reinforce the importance of recognizing[27] that changes in competitors' asset stocks and flows can signal change in multiple facets of the emerging and potential marketplace. Such signals may pertain to products or solutions that will be offered to customers, the competitors that will be in the marketplace, and competitive dynamics. To cite merely one increasingly important asset indicator of potential marketplace change, assessment of the types of knowledge that one or more competitors are trying to develop may provide strong, and sometimes, long-lagged signals of the products they will put in the marketplace and the types of customers they will pursue.

Competitor Consequences

Assessment of consequences identifies asset issues and decisions confronting competitors that directly emanate from the analysis outlined above. Consideration of asset attributes—availability, specificity, sustainability, replicability, and substitutability—almost certainly generates concerns that a competitor should have about its supply of specific asset types, the leveragability of one or more assets, the capacity to acquire, extend, and augment its assets, and the extent to which some of its assets are potentially replicable by rivals. Flowing from the preceding discussion, the software competitor should be concerned that substantial elements of its knowledge are most likely specific to a narrow product range and that all its assets might be replicable in a relatively short period should a large software firm decide to enter its product segments.

Comparison with the focal firm and other rivals often indicates severe asset challenges confronting a specific competitor. Sometimes it becomes evident that a competitor has few options to alleviate a specific asset constraint such as limited availability of a particular raw material or component or a vulnerability such as dependence on a supplier with only one factory or product location.

As discussed, competitors may find that not only their current marketplace strategy but future alternatives are positively or negatively impacted by asset considerations. Marketplace opportunities are constrained, or even inhibited, by asset unavailability. The specificity of some assets, such as knowledge and skills, inhibits pursuit of some opportunities.

Focal Firm Implications

Analysis of competitors' assets compels comprehensive and critical assessment of the focal firm's own assets, including its future asset needs. Comparison of asset stocks and flows to rivals generates a new perspective on the availability, specificity, sustainability, replicability, and substitutability of its asset types. It therefore gives rise to asset implications that might otherwise go undetected.

A central focus in asset implications is the identification of asset *issues and decisions*. Each step in asset assessment potentially generates such issues and decisions. Consideration of each attribute typically identifies asset issues. For example, assessment of sustainability and replicability may indicate concerns pertaining to the intent to augment and extend specific asset types such as particular skills, forms of knowledge, or relationships with classes of customers. It may also demonstrate that competitors are able to develop and sustain these asset types; thus, by themselves, they are not likely to lead to any significant customer- or competitor-based advantage.

Comparisons with selected competitors may also indicate, as occurred in the software case, that some rivals are generating considerably more customer value out of smaller endowments of particular asset types. This raises critical issues pertaining to the transformation of assets into capabilities and competencies, and in turn, into products or solutions of value to customers. Asset assessment generates critical issues pertaining to the choice, development, and deployment of capabilities and competencies.[28]

Assessment of implications for the focal firm's current and future marketplace strategy also gives rise to specific issues and concerns. This occurs in a number of ways. Asset availability and sustainability can impact execution of the current marketplace strategy: an inability to lure and sustain personnel with the right kinds of knowledge and skills can lead to a void between planned and realized results. By comparison with some of its competitors, the focal software firm was already experiencing difficulty in recruiting and retaining key personnel.

Development of strategy alternatives, often intended to preempt or catch up to rivals, raises not only asset availability issues but concerns about replication and substitutability. The focal software firm was vitally concerned that any set of skilled personnel it put together to develop new products should be difficult to replicate or supersede.

In some instances, the dominant implication is the need to develop an "asset strategy": a set of programs to acquire and sustain key assets, extend their leveragability and make their imitability even more difficult.

Summary

Assessment of competitors' assets is difficult to separate from any component in the framework of analysis advocated in this book. However, it does compel analysts to comprehensively evaluate what an organization values about itself and whether what it values about itself is transformable into something of value to customers. It is thus a major element in self-learning.

Capabilities and Competencies

WINNING NECESSITATES CONTINUALLY CHANGING THE STRATEGY CONTEXT AND ITS marketplace rules. While assets provide the raw wherewithal to facilitate such change, capabilities and competencies spawn and sustain it. Creating a new strategy game[1] almost always requires the development of new, if not, unique[2] competencies or capabilities. Reconstructing an existing game typically demands, at a minimum, finding new ways to extend and leverage existing competencies and capabilities, and often the development and exploitation of new competencies and capabilities. Shifting the marketplace rules always requires the development and/or enhancement of existing capabilities. Customization has required many organizations to develop and integrate a mix of marketing, manufacturing, distribution, service, and sales capabilities.

Fundamental to outwitting therefore is recognizing which capabilities and competencies (C and C) are essential to winning in tomorrow's marketplace as well as how to develop, sustain, and leverage them. Outmaneuvering entails the actions and commitments necessary to develop and leverage the requisite C and C. Outperforming can be assessed in terms of developing unique C and C, refining common C and C better than rivals, or getting to specific levels of C and C faster and more efficiently than rivals.

This chapter begins by defining and distinguishing between competency and capability, delineating their importance, and identifying their key attributes. Because of the differences between C and C, the steps involved in identifying each are delineated separately. Assessment of C and C is treated simultaneously.

Because of the specific difficulties[3] encountered in many organizations in identifying competitors' C and C, this chapter particularly emphasizes the steps involved in capturing and processing data that were briefly outlined in Chapter 2.

Understanding Capabilities and Competencies

The Concepts of Capabilities and Competencies

Despite the burgeoning literature on C and C,[4] surprisingly little attention has been devoted to defining, categorizing, and distinguishing between these fundamental concepts.[5] C and C are both about the *ability* of the organization to *do* something. Conceptually, as defined and discussed in the previous chapter, an organization's abilities to do specific things are fundamentally distinct from its assets.[6]

For purposes of analyzing competitors, one useful way to distinguish between C and C is to consider the extent of the organization to which they apply. A *capability* is something a competitor does well at the subunit or local level. Thus, capabilities address how well an organization performs or executes specific activities, in either the customer-focused activity chain or the activity/value chain, as discussed in Chapter 7. Some capabilities such as the superb execution of integrated logistics (handling all materials, components, supplies, work-in-progress, and distribution out to the final customer) or rapid new product development involve considerable interlinking of activities (or, more specifically, tasks across activities) in the conventional or customer-focused activity/value.[7] Some organizations have a large number of capabilities. Individual capabilities sometimes change quickly and dramatically.

Competencies, on the other hand, constitute a corporatewide phenomenon: they are what an organization does well across multiple business units or product sectors. Marriott Hotels, for example, manages real estate exceptionally well (i.e., acquiring and developing sites, and building hotels to plan and budget) across the range of its hotels. Competencies, as illustrated later in this chapter, are the product of multiple capabilities from several different activities or processes. Organizations are likely to possess only a small number of competencies. Table 12.1 provides a listing of competencies that organizations in many different types of industries strive to develop and enhance. These competencies could not emanate from just one activity or process, or functional area. Because competencies are embedded across several product or business units, they are much less likely than capabilities to undergo sudden or dramatic change.

Although they are fundamentally distinct, the concepts of C and C can be refined in related ways. Competence and capability involve action: the focus

TABLE 12.1 Commonly Desired Competencies

The ability to:

1) Move product quickly from R&D to the marketplace

2) Anticipate and respond to market opportunities faster than competitors

3) Provide a unique solution to each customer

4) Hire, train, and retain the best personnel

5) Develop, nurture, and extend relationships with alliance partners

and emphasis is on what the competitor does (or does not do). A C or C is something an organization does well. A *distinctive* C or C is something that an organization does better than one or more competitors. A C or C is *unique* when an organization does something better than all its competitors. What an organization does badly is an incapability or incompetence (in-C or C). Noncapabilities and noncompetencies (non-C or C) are those things that an organization does not do at all.

C and C are often confused with both their inputs and consequences. As action—what the competitor does—they need to be clearly distinguished from assets—what the competitor possesses. Assets provide the raw material (such as knowledge, skills, capital, and relationships) out of which C and C evolve or are crafted. Access to components or supplies is not a C or C (though in some instances it is a pivotal asset) but the ability to locate and acquire components or supplies in a way that is distinctive or unique is a potential C or C that many organizations would love to possess. A substantial, and even increasing market share, or strong financial position are not themselves capabilities or competencies. However, they can contribute toward, and in part result from, a set of capabilities (or competencies) some of which may be distinctive or even unique.

Capabilities (and, to a lesser extent, competencies) potentially emanate exclusively from the asset base owned by a competitor. However, organizations of almost all types are increasingly using alliances, relationships and networks to attain, enhance, and extend C and C.[8]

The Importance of Capabilities and Competencies

Few facets of an organization are more crucial to winning than C and C. They are central to marketplace strategy: they undergird product development; they facilitate pursuit of customers; they imbue each mode of competition; they make possible the attainment of goals. Without C and C development and deployment, desired marketplace strategy—whether creating a new strategy game or simply shifting the marketplace rules—is likely to prove both illusive and illusory.[9]

Because of their importance to marketplace strategy, C and C serve (or should serve) as a focus of how the organization is managed. Every significant change to the activity/value chain must be assessed for its implications for C and C.[10] Alliances and networks are typically intended to establish new C and C or to augment and extend C and C. Changes in the organization's infrastructure and culture can facilitate or impede desired C and C change.

Core and Diverting Competencies and Capabilities

Because of their implications for winning, a distinction is required between *core and diverting* C and C. Core competencies are those that undergird a competitor's products across multiple competitive domains: they are central to customer- and competitor advantage, and to how a competitor manages its business. Honda's competence in engine design and development, which has contributed so much to its success in the motorcycle, automobile, boat, and lawn mower markets, is a frequently referenced illustration.[11]

Although competitors typically have only a small number of actual (corporatewide) competencies, it is still necessary to distinguish between those that are core and those that are not. Competencies that do not contribute to, or cannot be made to contribute to, customer- or competitor advantage *divert* the organization's attention, assets, and commitment from winning in the marketplace. Many organizations have developed significant technological C or C, only to find that they could not be leveraged into winning products.

Core capabilities also undergird a competitor's products and how it manages its business. Because it is possible for a competitor to possess a considerably larger number of capabilities than competencies, it is important to distinguish between core and secondary capabilities. Secondary capabilities are not necessarily unimportant; they just do not contribute as much to marketplace success or to how the competitor manages itself.

Tangible and Invisible Capabilities and Competencies

What organizations do is more or less observable or tangible. Thus, C and C are usefully segmented into whether they are *tangible or invisible.* Most attention has been focused on C and C that are relatively tangible or visible. The emphasis has been on those things one can observe the competitor doing such as delivering superior service, manufacturing higher quality products and integrating streams of technology.[12] Yet, less observable or invisible C or C such as the ability to consistently identify market opportunities, or to engage in continual organizational renewal, or to think strategically, are often critical core C or C: they may provide a central means of outwitting and outperforming the competition. Without understanding these invisible C or C, organizations are destined to play catch-up with their competitors.

The Importance of Understanding What Competitors Do Poorly or Not at All

Few if any organizations do everything well, much less better than most, or all, competitors. Although they frequently receive much less attention than competencies, in-C or C (what competitors do poorly) and non-C or C (what competitors do not do at all) deserve scrutiny since, as we shall see later in this chapter, they often reveal fundamental vulnerabilities, constraints, or weaknesses in competitors. What competitors do poorly or not at all may thus serve as the source of powerful signals of what competitors potentially cannot do in the future.

However, an in-C or C (or a non-C or C) does not necessarily indicate a weakness in a competitor. If the in-C or C is not critical to the competitor's strategy or if the competitor is able to compensate for the in-C or C, it may not reflect a weakness or vulnerability that is exploitable by others. Some firms possess little if any capability in the design, development, and manufacture of key components; they buy from vendors. If they develop alignments with vendors such that they are able to stay at the forefront of component development, then their own technology and manufacturing incapability may not constrain their marketplace strategy.

The Leveragability of Competencies and Capabilities

The distinction between *core* and *diverting* C and C reminds us that C and C are not ends in themselves: their value to organizations resides in the extent to which they are leveraged to create value for customers. Thus, the managerial challenge is to find ways to leverage C and C into offerings that attract, win, and retain customers. To do so requires that the organization continuously upgrade and extend each specific *competency or capability domain* (e.g., the ability to manufacture superior products, at low cost) and continuously explore for new ways to extend a C or C's *product domain* (the breadth and quality of solutions offered to customers).

Attributes of Competencies and Capabilities

All competencies and capabilities are not alike; they vary greatly with regard to some key attributes. Five attributes are critical in determining which C and C undergird a competitor's current and future strategies: (1) dynamism, (2) breadth, (3) robustness, (4) imitability, (5) augmentability.

Dynamism Competencies, and capabilities to a lesser extent, are not likely to remain stationary over time either in absolute or relative terms. They are thus either atrophying or enhancing: organizations are either losing or augmenting their ability to do whatever the C or C involves.[13] Dynamism exemplifies the relative nature of C or C: they are always augmenting or decaying compared with competitors. For example, an organization's competence such as its ability to identify new market opportunities is never likely to remain static vis-à-vis its rivals because of competitors' ongoing efforts to do the same.

Breadth of (C or C) Domain All C or C have specific bounds on the abilities entailed in them. For example, some firms are unable to fulfill orders in less than two days. A research competency includes specific technology areas and not others. A service capability encompasses certain types of service but excludes others. Specification of the C or C domain is essential to understanding its leveragability.

Robustness C and C also vary in their applicability to current and future product or business domains. A C or C is not necessarily applicable to all of a firm's *current* business or product-customer segments. Even if a C or C is applicable to all of a competitor's current product-customer segments, it may or may not be applicable to other product-customer segments (either within or outside its existing competitive domains) or products new to the marketplace. A competitor cannot always leverage a competence for new product development in specific new product domains or apply a capability for customer service to new products. For example, Bic, the ballpoint pen company was able to use its manufacturing, marketing and distribution competencies to successfully introduce and extend a line of Bic disposable cigarette lighters, but it was unable to leverage them into a line of Bic perfumes.

Imitability C and C vary in the degree to which they are imitable. Any organization would prefer that its core C or C be impossible or, at least, very difficult to imitate or replicate. Competitive advantages stemming from these C or C would then be secure. While it is sometimes difficult to replicate any type of C or C, invisible C and C, such as the ability to identify new market opportunities, are often extremely difficult to imitate because they are so interwoven into the infrastructure and culture of the organization.

Augmentability C and C that cannot be augmented or enhanced are not likely to be enduring sources of competitive advantage. Ideally, any C or C should be enhancable so that it adds to sustainable advantage and renders imitation more difficult.[14]

Indicators of Capability and Competency Change

Both direct and indirect indicators are specific to individual C and C. Direct indicators permit monitoring of change in a C or C over time. Indirect indicators, however, often alert analysts to emerging or potential change in one or more C and C. As shown in this chapter, the direct indicators pertaining to one C or C often serve as the indirect indicators of change in one or more other C or C.

Capability and Competency Change as Signals

Change in C and C enable the derivation of critical signals. Efforts to develop *new competencies,* to augment *existing competencies,* or to ameliorate *in-C or C or non-C or C* can signal future direction in marketplace strategy as well as change in microlevel components. For example, a competitor's alliance with a foreign firm to augment a competency in the design and manufacturing of products with certain functional features conveys a strong signal of its intent to introduce such products. As this example indicates, indicators of change in C or C sometimes are the source of long-lagged, early, and high-impact signals of future marketplace moves by competitors.

Identifying Competencies

Capturing and assessing a competitor's competency[15] (and capability) profile requires analysts to ask radically different questions compared with any other microlevel component. It also demands that analysts go beyond first impressions of competitors' competencies: they need to carefully search for evidence of *actual* competencies and incompetencies. The key steps in a guided analysis are shown in Figure 12.1. A large multibusiness competitor, principally composed of industrial and commercial product sectors, is used for the purposes of illustration.

Because identifying competencies requires multiple difficult judgments on the part of analysts in identifying, assimilating and integrating data, this section addresses many issues involved in capturing and processing (Cells 2 and 3 in Figure 2.1).

Assimilate Prior Analysis

The fundamental question in identifying competencies is: What does the competitor do well (or badly) *as an organization,* that is, *across* (most or all of) its business sectors, units, or product groups? Answering this question requires that analysts leverage prior analysis of the corporate or multibusiness

FIGURE 12.1
Identifying Competencies and Capabilities

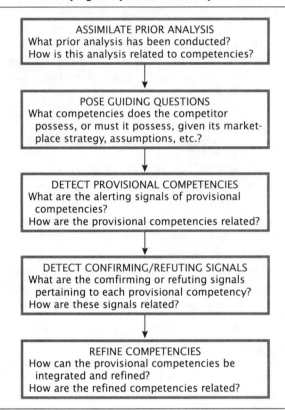

ASSIMILATE PRIOR ANALYSIS
What prior analysis has been conducted?
How is this analysis related to competencies?

POSE GUIDING QUESTIONS
What competencies does the competitor
possess, or must it possess, given its marketplace strategy, assumptions, etc.?

DETECT PROVISIONAL COMPETENCIES
What are the alerting signals of provisional
competencies?
How are the provisional competencies related?

DETECT CONFIRMING/REFUTING SIGNALS
What are the comfirming or refuting signals
pertaining to each provisional competency?
How are these signals related?

REFINE COMPETENCIES
How can the provisional competencies be
integrated and refined?
How are the refined competencies related?

entity such as its marketplace strategy, alliances and networks, assumptions, technology, and organization infrastructure and culture.

Pose Guiding Questions

Many of the requisite questions across framework components are noted in Figure 12.2. Each component causes analysts to ask distinctive questions. The vantage point inherent in each component gives rise to particular indicators that might not emanate from other components.

These questions must be asked from two related perspectives: What competencies does the competitor possess *now?* And, what competencies *must* it possess, given its current and projected marketplace strategy, alliances, networks, and assumptions. The emphasis on the competencies it must possess is critical for two reasons. First, both tangible and invisible competencies often are not obviously evident; thus, analysts need to ask what

FIGURE 12.2
Identifying Core (In)Competencies: Guiding Questions from Framework Components

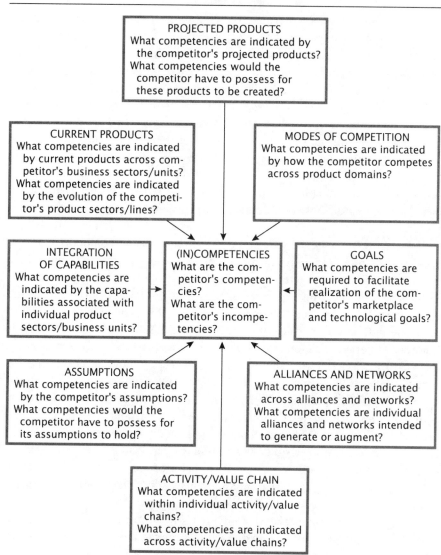

competencies must underlie or facilitate products with certain functionality and features across multiple business sectors, or core assumptions, or espoused technology goals. Second, asking what competencies the competitor must possess emphasizes (again) the importance of *indirect* indicators and the need to explicate the logic that suggests the presence (or potential presence) of (in)competencies.

The questions noted in Figure 12.2 generate the *inputs* necessary for competency identification: they suggest categories of *required data* from which alerting signals are derived. Some of these data categories are not obvious. For example, a multibusiness enterprise's assumptions often suggest competencies that it presumes it possesses or is able to develop. One corporation's assumptions about the success of its planned entry into a particular telecommunications market indicated a competency in related technologies that it would have to presume to possess or to be able to develop to win in that market.

The guiding questions also suggest likely primary and secondary *data sources.* Consideration of the questions noted in Figure 12.2 strongly suggests the need to involve multiple individuals and groups both inside and outside the focal organization. Access to multiple external observers of the competitor broadens the range of alerting indicators. Interviews with consultants, academics, and others knowledgeable about the competitor's competitive arenas often generate a host of potential[16] or provisional[17] competencies. Industry and technology experts often can provide a short list of provisional competencies. Interviews with other participants in the competitive arenas such as distribution channel members, end-customers, suppliers, and substitute competitors may also indicate provisional competencies.

Because there is often supporting and refuting evidence pertaining to the existence and importance of individual competencies, the judgments of more than one individual or group of individuals are essential to avoid the biases inherent in dependence on any single data source (and premature closure in the identification and assessment process). Thus, the guiding questions also suggest some *data collection* processes. Beyond the typical means of collecting data such as in-person and phone interviews, it is advisable to bring together groups of individuals within the focal firm, and if possible, some outsiders, to generate alerting signals of provisional competencies. Consideration of one or more provisional competencies may lead to the identification of other provisional competencies. Discussion of some tangible competencies (e.g., new product development or manufacturing) sometimes raises questions about possible intangible competencies (e.g., capacity of a competitor to learn about markets). Individuals pursuing some set of guiding questions are likely to jump from one competency to another as they develop a better understanding of the competitor.

Detect Alerting Signals of Provisional Competencies

The questions pertaining to each component generate indicators of *provisional* competencies. Analysts need to note each provisional competency because it helps focus the search for confirming and refuting signals. Related provisional competencies, or indeed the same competency, are often generated from more than one component.

TABLE 12.2 Current, Past, and Projected Products as Indicators of Provisional Competencies: A Multibusiness Enterprise

Indicators	Alerting Signals of Provisional Competencies
Has introduced a stream of successful new products in almost every product sector	Ability to anticipate customer needs and the direction of the marketplace
	Ability to lead the marketplace, that is, shape customer's needs
	Ability to do state-of-the-art research and development
New products almost always are viewed as significantly superior in terms of functionality vs. existing products	Ability to do product-specific research and development
	Ability to do advanced manufacturing
The majority of the new products seem to gain a major toehold in the marketplace	Ability to execute integrated marketing programs
	Ability to develop effective relationships and alliances

In the multibusiness firm example, marketplace strategy and networks yielded a number of related alerting signals. Consideration of current, past, and projected products across business sectors gave rise to a number of alerting signals of possible competencies (see Table 12.2). Each alerting signal was derived from a specific indicator.

The alerting signals generated by the firm's networks are noted in Table 12.3. Each network is the source of one or more indicators of specific

TABLE 12.3 Networks as Indicators of Provisional Competencies: A Multibusiness Enterprise

Indicators	Alerting Signals of Provisional Competencies
Multiple small networks of entities intended to aid the enterprise in doing research and development	Ability to do innovative and distinctive research
	Ability to do certain types of development work (outside the reach of other organizations)
Multiple small networks of alliances resulting in enhanced manufacturing	Ability to do specific types of manufacturing
A number of networks within business sectors involving multiple relationships and alliances with channels and end-customers	Ability to quickly move a lot of products into the marketplace
	Ability to build, sustain, and leverage complex channel and end-customer relationships
The number of small and large networks	Ability to develop and sustain networks

competencies. Multiple small interconnected networks serve as the basis of strong inferences about provisional competencies.

Consideration of the questions noted in Figure 12.2 may also lead to identification of possible incompetencies. Several such possible incompetencies and their associated indicators are noted in Table 12.4. Alerting signals of possible incompetencies often stem, not from a single corporate decision, action, or statement, but from an inference drawn by recognizing a pattern across a variety or series of indicators. A sequence of failed attempts (the indicator) on the part of the corporate competitor to compete head-to-head with rivals once they introduced largely similar products signaled a

TABLE 12.4 Competencies: A Multibusiness Enterprise

Competencies	Sample Indicators
Conduct innovative and distinctive research	A stream of new products in each product sector
	Awards for research from professional societies
Do advanced manufacturing	Product functionality and features
	Purchases of manufacturing process technologies
	Presentations by the firm at trade and industry shows
Identify and serve new customer needs	Success of most new products
	Statements of marketing personnel about how they learn about and from customers
Develop and enhance complex channel end-customer relationships	Reports by customers of the firm's commitment to working with them in solving technical/operational problems
Develop and enhance alliances and networks	A long list of successful alliances and network-like linkages with a variety of external entities
	Most alliances continue to contribute to product development and competing in the marketplace
Incompetencies (Inability to)	
Compete successfully once competitors respond with new product introductions	Has not fared well in many product segments once rivals introduce a largely look-alike or superior product
Manage total costs to meet profit expectations	Persistent statements from the firm that costs exceed projections
	Variability in profit performance

major incompetence: the inability to respond successfully to the new product introductions of competitors.

Detect Confirming/Refuting Signals

As provisional competencies are identified, analysts immediately turn their attention to confirming or refuting their existence. It is at this stage that general knowledge about the competitor generated from prior analysis becomes essential because provisional competencies are often highly interrelated and indicators pertaining to any individual competency may stem from any microlevel component of the competitor. In their search for confirming and refuting signals, analysts *order, select,* and *interpret* data pertaining to provisional competencies.

For the multibusiness firm, the provisional competency noted in Table 12.2—the ability to lead the marketplace (to shape customers' needs), provoked a search for other indicators that would help confirm or refute the firm's ability across business sectors to shape customers' needs. The indicators the analysts looked at included the extent to which the firm's new products leapfrogged those of rivals; the extent to which customers waited for the firm's announced products; the extent to which customers collaborated with the firm in product development; the extent to which customers viewed the firm as the innovator and product leader in the marketplace. The data strongly indicated the corporate competitor's ability to shape customers' needs across product sectors.

Ordering and *selecting* data often become critical in the search for refuting evidence. Analysts must proactively seek data that would question the alleged competencies. Sometimes, it is necessary to identify a priori what data would disconfirm a provisional competence[18] and then seek that data from specific sources. Thus analysts might seek data from research and technology experts about the multibusiness enterprise's ability to do specific types of research and development.

Refine Competencies

Because of the likelihood of a high degree of overlap among provisional competencies, analysts need to reduce and integrate provisional competencies into a small(er) number of distinct competencies. As further indicators emerge and are considered, individual provisional competencies are often restated or two or more competencies are integrated. As each provisional competency is considered, analysts develop a more complete understanding of the competitor's competencies: how various provisional competencies are related to each other; which competencies are truly distinct; and, the competency domain, and product or business domain, pertaining to individual possible competencies. For example, as networks were detailed and examined, the analysts reached the judgment that the core competence of the multibusiness enterprise was its ability to develop and continually enhance alliances and networks.

Two challenges are unavoidable in *interpretation*. One is the need to specify the product or business domain specific to each individual competency. As noted, competencies relate to all or most business or product sectors. In the multibusiness enterprise competitor, the ability to do advanced manufacturing was relevant to all business sectors with one or two exceptions. Thus, to allege that this competency pertained to all the firm's business sectors could lead to potentially grave errors in inferences about the focal firm's actions.

A second, and related, challenge is to specify the competency domain. In one firm, a refined competitor competency was initially stated as "the ability of the competitor to do research and development." Yet strong evidence was generated that the competitor did not have a consistently stellar record in development. In at least one business sector, the competitor generated a significant stream of applied research that did not result in new or innovative products. Thus, the analysis team restated the organizationwide competency as "the ability to do research in specific product/technology/ knowledge areas."

Several competencies and incompetencies were attributed to the multibusiness enterprise competitor (see Table 12.4). Each resulted from the integration and refinement of a number of provisional (in)competencies.

Some Errors in the Identification of Competencies

Although many errors are common to the identification of competencies and capabilities, a number particularly germane to competencies are noted here.

First, in many instances, the concept of competency is not delineated and communicated. As a consequence, capabilities and competencies are confused, data is poorly organized, and analysis is prone to degenerate into divergent camps that are unable to communicate with each other.[19]

Analysts often fail to take sufficient care when identifying the relevant product or business domain. For some corporations with highly distinct businesses such as GE, ITT, and Allied Signal, some competencies are typically associated only with a particular set of business or product sectors and not the entire corporation. It is still appropriate to consider the entire corporation as the relevant domain for other competencies.

A common tendency persists to emphasize tangible competencies such as those that are technology-based at the expense of invisible competencies. Thus, key competencies are missed.

Sometimes, there is such haste to identify core competencies that provisional competencies are not carefully noted, detailed, or documented. Consequently, analysts miss much of the valuable learning entailed in integrating and refining competencies and often do not understand the results as well as they think they do.

Relatedly, analysts often do not seek out, assimilate, and articulate evidence counter to provisional and refined competencies. The presumption often is that the evidence is overwhelming. Yet, as some of the examples above attest, consideration of refuting evidence often enables rejection of alleged competencies, or more commonly, the redefinition of the domain of competencies.

Identifying Capabilities

Since the identification of capabilities essentially follows the same steps as discussed for competencies (see Figure 12.1), the following discussion emphasizes peculiarities relevant to capabilities. A small plastics manufacturer that had begun to gain significant market share is used for illustration.

Assimilate Prior Analysis

Marketplace strategy and activity/value chain analyses are particularly critical to the identification of capabilities. In a guided analysis, these two analyses are conducted prior to capability identification.[20]

Pose Guiding Questions

Each framework component contributes many questions to initiate the search (see Figure 12.3). In posing these questions, the analyst engages primarily in the process of inferencing: capturing indicators and deriving from them signals of likely capabilities.[21]

Capture Alerting and Confirming/Refuting Signals

The initial task is to detect and perceive *alerting* signals of provisional (non)capabilities. As with competencies, provisional capabilities are emphasized here because alerting signals sometimes are not substantiated in later analysis.

The plastics competitor's marketplace strategy generated alerting signals of several capabilities (see Table 12.5). The ability to identify emerging market niches and customer needs was initially inferred from a sequence of successful new products. The frequency with which the competitor was first to market new product types (some of which were extensions of existing products)

FIGURE 12.3
Identifying a Competitor's Capabilities: Questions from Framework Components

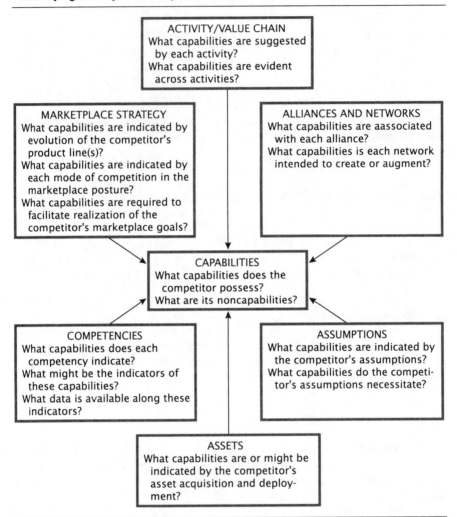

led to the hypothesis that the competitor must possess the capability to sense emerging marketplace needs. This invisible capability was distinguished from the ability to successfully manufacture new products with superior functionality—a much more tangible or observable capability—the alerting signal of which was a variety of product comparisons to those of rivals. Another capability, the ability to provide consistently superior service, was suggested by the competitor's emphasis on service and the details of its customer service programs.

TABLE 12.5 Capabilities of a Small Plastics Manufacturer

Indicators	Capabilities
Alerting indicators A stream of new products *Confirming indicators* Product modifications Close relationship with innovative customers	Ability to identify emerging market niches/customer needs
Alerting indicators Product comparisons with other competitors *Confirming indicators* Evaluations of different customer groups	Ability to manufacture products with superior functionality
Alerting indicators Product development process *Confirming indicators* Working relationships with vendors	Ability to acquire raw materials and components and to use them as a source of product development
Alerting indicators Comparison of customer service details to rivals *Confirming indicators* Evaluations of different customer groups	Ability to provide innovative and consistently superior customer service
Alerting indicators A description of the firm's training program *Confirming indicators* Customer's comments Statements of the firm's executives	Ability to imbue new technical knowledge into the organization through training and education

The inferencing process also provides guidance as to "signals about what." This occurs when the analyst asks such questions as:

- What *must* the competitor do well to make its marketplace strategy possible?

- What is the competitor doing poorly that accounts for its lack of success in the marketplace?

These questions compel the analyst to assess a priori what (non)capabilities might be possessed by the competitor *before* searching for (confirming or refuting) signals. For the plastics competitor, these questions led directly to hypothesizing the presence of two capabilities. Because of its ability to continuously lead the marketplace in new product introductions, it was inferred that the competitor must have developed the ability to imbue new product and technical knowledge into the organization through training, education, and development, as well as the ability to acquire necessary raw materials and components for use in product development.

Consideration of marketplace strategy may also lead to identification of noncapabilities. The principal guiding questions include:

- What does the competitor not do well with regard to its marketplace strategy?
- What does the competitor not do at all with regard to its marketplace strategy?

For the plastics competitor, a manifest noncapability was its inability to customize its offerings to individual customers. The competitor, like all its rivals, had not yet endeavored to do so.

The activity/value chain almost always is critical to guided searches for capabilities. The search is for alerting signals not just of capabilities within individual activities but of capabilities that cut across multiple activities. The plastics competitor's activity/value chain quickly generated alerting signals of two capabilities: the ability to manufacture products with multiple forms of functionality and the ability to develop new products within a relatively short period.

In many respects, the activity/value chain complements a marketplace strategy guided search. The marketplace strategy of the plastics competitor indicated the presence of the ability to provide consistently superior service. The activity/value chain was then examined for supporting or refuting indicators. Just-in-time delivery, attention to quality in all activities, and a streamlined distribution system indicated a commitment to delivering consistent high-quality service to all customers.

Alliances, relationships and networks may also indicate existing or emerging capabilities. The plastics competitor's long-standing relationships with some suppliers was central to its ability to acquire raw materials and components for use in product development. This capability was predicated on a high level of intimacy and sharing of information and purposes between the competitor and its suppliers.

Capturing Confirming/Refuting Signals

Once capabilities are provisionally identified through *alerting* signals, the search turns to generating *confirming* and/or *refuting* signals. Again, the analyst seeks multiple indicators of the existence and extent of specific capabilities.

For the plastics competitor, confirming and refuting indicators were sought for each of the capabilities discussed above (see Table 12.5). The competitor's close working relationships with innovative or leading customers in multiple product segments served as a key confirming indicator of its ability to identify emerging market niches and customer needs. By working closely with such customers, the competitor was in fact able to shape the needs and wants of many other customers in the broader marketplace.

Indicators generated from various microlevel components become important sources of confirming and refuting signals. In this respect, the activity/value chain analysis again complements a marketplace strategy guided search. The manufacturing capability inferred from the plastics competitor's marketplace strategy—the ability to manufacture products with superior functionality—was strongly supported through the indicators derived from its activity/value chain including access to critical raw materials, state of manufacturing process technologies, and experience and training of key manufacturing personnel.

The search for indicators refuting the existence of provisional capabilities often enlightens confirming judgments. By asking which indicators associated with the plastics competitor's activity/value chain *did not support* the provisional capability, the ability to manufacture products with superior functionality, the analysts challenged each indicator that had previously supported the existence of the capability. Moreover, they reviewed every critical task along the activity/value chain for indicators of current or potential difficulties in developing and sustaining the manufacture of products with increasing functionality.

Refine and Elaborate Individual Capabilities

As supporting and refuting evidence is collected and evaluated, the provisional capabilities noted in Table 12.5 are refined and elaborated. Analysts are principally concerned with ensuring that strong inferences (compelling data and convincing logic) support each capability. Each of the provisional capabilities of the plastics competitor "made the cut." They were refined in terms of wording but were included in the list of final capabilities.

Open-Ended Search

Open-ended search frequently draws analysts' attention to capabilities that previously they were either unaware of or had not considered important. This is especially likely to occur when they are influenced by what their own organization considers the key activities or processes, and the important capabilities that any competitor should possess within them.

In an open-ended search, the analyst scans, monitors, and analyzes data types and sources to detect alerting signals of the presence or absence of capabilities. Types of secondary data include published analyses or commentaries on the competitor conducted by financial institutions, security analysts, consulting firms, industry and trade associations or more generally, reports in the popular press and trade publications.

In most cases, however, scanning secondary sources will be of limited value since few publications deal explicitly with organizations' competencies and capabilities. It will therefore be necessary to scan primary sources. In particular, analysts need to identify individuals both inside and outside their organization who are in a position to make judgments about competitors' competencies and capabilities. The analyst can ask for judgments about the presence or absence of competencies or capabilities as well as the evidence for these inferences or conclusions.

Errors in Identifying Capabilities

Organizations sometimes allow their own (often presumed) capabilities to unduly contaminate the identification (and assessment) of competitors' capabilities. Analysts search for indicators of capabilities exhibited by their own organization; they ignore or neglect indicators that signal different capabilities; and they downplay capabilities that they don't fully understand.

Analysts often do not seek multiple confirming indicators of a capability. Thus, provisional capabilities are too quickly accorded the status of actual capabilities.

Relatedly, analysts may not carefully articulate the logic asserting what the competitor does in reference to a specific capability. Therefore, the capability is simply not understood. The capability domain as well as the relevant product domain are frequently misstated.

The contribution of incapabilities or noncapabilities to providing an understanding of capabilities is often not recognized. Much of the learning that emanates from the dialogue of simultaneously considering capabilities and incapabilities is missed.

Assessing Competencies and Capabilities

Assessing C and C involves a set of highly interrelated steps (see Figure 12.4). Assessing attributes unavoidably entails identification of change in C and C and contributes to determining which C and C are core and secondary. Identifying and projecting change in C and C, and comparisons with the focal firm and with other rivals, contribute directly to assessing consequences for the competitor's current and future marketplace strategy. Because of the

FIGURE 12.4
Assessing a Competitor's Capabilities or Competencies

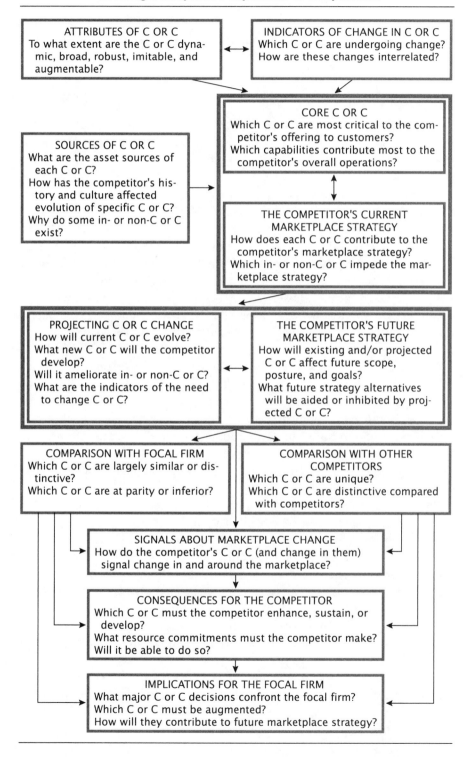

ATTRIBUTES OF C OR C
To what extent are the C or C dynamic, broad, robust, imitable, and augmentable?

INDICATORS OF CHANGE IN C OR C
Which C or C are undergoing change?
How are these changes interrelated?

CORE C OR C
Which C or C are most critical to the competitor's offering to customers?
Which capabilities contribute most to the competitor's overall operations?

SOURCES OF C OR C
What are the asset sources of each C or C?
How has the competitor's history and culture affected evolution of specific C or C?
Why do some in- or non-C or C exist?

THE COMPETITOR'S CURRENT MARKETPLACE STRATEGY
How does each C or C contribute to the competitor's marketplace strategy?
Which in- or non-C or C impede the marketplace strategy?

PROJECTING C OR C CHANGE
How will current C or C evolve?
What new C or C will the competitor develop?
Will it ameliorate in- or non-C or C?
What are the indicators of the need to change C or C?

THE COMPETITOR'S FUTURE MARKETPLACE STRATEGY
How will existing and/or projected C or C affect future scope, posture, and goals?
What future strategy alternatives will be aided or inhibited by projected C or C?

COMPARISON WITH FOCAL FIRM
Which C or C are largely similar or distinctive?
Which C or C are at parity or inferior?

COMPARISON WITH OTHER COMPETITORS
Which C or C are unique?
Which C or C are distinctive compared with competitors?

SIGNALS ABOUT MARKETPLACE CHANGE
How do the competitor's C or C (and change in them) signal change in and around the marketplace?

CONSEQUENCES FOR THE COMPETITOR
Which C or C must the competitor enhance, sustain, or develop?
What resource commitments must the competitor make?
Will it be able to do so?

IMPLICATIONS FOR THE FOCAL FIRM
What major C or C decisions confront the focal firm?
Which C or C must be augmented?
How will they contribute to future marketplace strategy?

difficulties in defining, articulating, and communicating the concept and content of C and C, particular emphasis is placed on the logic and data necessarily entailed in the judgments involved in assessment.

Attribute Change

Each attribute informs assessments of the importance of specific C and C, the relationships among them, and the competitor's commitment to and rationale for investing in them. Different judgments are involved in assessing each attribute.

Assessing *dynamism* requires the analyst to search for evidence at two levels: direct and indirect indicators of change in the C or C itself, and of the competitor's efforts and intentions to change it.[22] In judging the plastics competitor's after-sales service capability, the analyst might investigate which service elements are provided, whether the competitor is enlarging or lowering the number of service elements, or adding more personnel to deliver service or provide faster response times. Indicators of future change might include statements by the competitor's management about the importance of the ability to deliver and enhance after-sales service, announcements of new training programs, and the extension of existing programs.

Assessing C and C *domain* requires the analyst to delineate the bounds of each C or C. The multibusiness enterprise's ability to conduct innovative and distinctive research was limited to a specific set of technological domains; some technologies germane to its business were not encompassed in its research domain. The plastics competitor's ability to provide innovative and superior customer service consisted of a set of specific service elements (even though these elements were broader than offered by most competitors).

The assessment of *robustness* requires the analyst to assess whether it is possible to extend individual C or C to that portion of a competitor's product-customer portfolio to which they do not currently apply, to product-customer segments that the competitor is not currently in, to emerging and potential product-customer segments, and to potential products new to the marketplace. Robustness inherently questions whether the small plastics manufacturer can leverage its capabilities in manufacturing and in acquiring raw material and components as a major source of new products, and whether it can extend these capabilities to embrace and extend emerging new products in the industry.

The analyst must make judgments about whether individual competencies are *imitable*. Such judgments require an understanding of the nature of the competence, its sources, the resource commitments underlying it, and the length of time required to imitate it. Emulating the plastics competitor's ability to continually invigorate its product and technical knowledge through its human resource practices could prove enormously difficult. An itemization of what the focal plastics firm would have to do to imitate and outperform the competitor along one or more C or C often drives home to managers how difficult it is to replicate C or C that are embedded in the competitor's organizational practices, routines, and culture.[23]

Many of the other steps in assessment require that the analyst assess the extent to which a C or C can be *augmented* and whether the competitor has the capacity and inclination to do so. Again, this requires complex judgments. To determine the plastics competitor's manufacturing capability, the analyst needs to investigate the relevant manufacturing process technology developments external to the competitor and what the gap is between these advances and the competitor's current technology. The analyst must also identify what the competitor is doing to augment its manufacturing capability even though it may not do what is technologically feasible.

Even if a C or C can be further augmented, it does not imply that the competitor is able, or will do so. Constraints that can prevent C or C augmentation include asset limitations, lack of awareness of the importance of the C or C, or the unwillingness of management to risk organization discomfort due to the necessary changes.

Change in Capabilities and Competencies

As attributes are assessed, current changes in C and C are listed and documented (see Tables 12.6 and 12.7). Such change serves as an indicator of the direction and extent of emerging and potential C and C change, provides insight into what the competitor considers as its core or critical C or C, and, in turn, raises issues pertaining to attribute change.

Determining Core (In)Competencies or (In)Capabilities

Any listing of C or C must be reduced to those that are core. Unless analysts identify core C and C, they frequently waste considerable time and effort in tracking and analyzing diverting, or peripheral C or C.

Determination of core C or C requires the analyst to make judgments about the importance of individual C or C to the competitor's marketplace strategy and organizational operations. The analyst must first carefully delineate *how* each C or C contributes to the competitor's marketplace strategy and operations *before* making such judgments. The plastics competitor's ability to identify emerging market niches/customer needs contributed to marketplace strategy in several ways: by identifying potential customer needs, the competitor was able to consider what types of products would

TABLE 12.6 Change in Capabilities: The Small Plastics Manufacturer

Capability	Change in Capability
Ability to identify emerging market niches/customers needs	Building relationships with multiple types of customers
	Doing research into new technology areas
Ability to manufacture products with superior functionality	Adding new types of manufacturing technologies
	Working with customers on new product formulations
Ability to acquire raw materials and components and to use them as a source of product development	Intensifying relationships with key suppliers
	Developing new means of product testing in conjunction with customers
Ability to provide innovative and consistently superior customer service	Adding new elements to particular types of service
Ability to imbue new technical knowledge into the organization through training and education	Adding new training programs
	Continually bringing in outside sources of technology knowledge

TABLE 12.7 Change in Competencies: The Multibusiness Enterprise

Competencies	Change in Competencies
Conduct innovative and distinctive research	Applying research competency to wider array of products
Do advanced manufacturing	Continually adding new manufacturing technologies
Identify and serve new customer needs	Adding alliance partners to augment competency
Develop and enhance complex channel and end-customer relationships	Continually extending nature of relationship with channels and end-customers
Develop and enhance alliances and networks	Individual networks being extended

Incompetencies	Change in Incompetencies
Compete successfully once competitors respond with new product introductions	Statements about the need "to remedy this vulnerability"
	Some new marketing personnel
Manage total costs to meet profit expectations	Statements about the need for better cost management

satisfy these specific needs; by doing research into specific technology areas, the competitor could develop potential product prototypes and match these against identified needs or ask what applications might be spawned by emerging technologies; the relationships the competitor developed with both customers and technology sources allowed it to test product concepts and product prototypes more efficiently and effectively than any of its current look-alike rivals.

Analysts must tease through these types of (logic) linkages before they make judgments about whether a specific C or C is core or secondary, or diverting. Articulating these linkages is essential because in many cases they are not apparent. For example, how a human asset based C or C (such as the ability to hire, train, and retain the best people) contributes to marketplace strategy, or to key aspects of organizational operations such as cost management or reduction of product development cycle times, often is not immediately obvious. Thus, it is likely that the importance of a particular C or C is badly over- or understated.

As part of the analysis, often two or more C or C initially identified collapse into one. One multibusiness firm found that two provisional competencies (the ability to identify new market opportunities and the ability to successfully introduce new products) could be integrated into one competence: the ability to identify and satisfy new market opportunities.

Sources of Competencies and Capabilities

C and C do not mushroom overnight. It frequently takes years to develop the types of C and C noted in Tables 12.4 and 12.5. Each of the assets/classes (see Chapter 11) can contribute directly or indirectly to C or C evolution. Sometimes, one C or C plays a large role in the emergence and evolution of another. Moreover, individual C and C rarely evolve from a single source. Understanding what gives rise to and sustains a C or C provides at least a partial explanation of its attributes as well as its likely future direction. The analyst therefore needs to investigate what combination of sources undergird a particular C or C, in what ways individual sources contribute to two or more C or C, how the sources might reinforce or conflict with each other, and how change in the sources might facilitate or jeopardize the development and evolution of individual or multiple C or C.

Each of the capabilities of the small plastics manufacturer (see Table 12.5) was associated with specific sources (see Table 12.8). As in the case of linking C or C to marketplace strategy, it is imperative that analysts carefully articulate how each source contributes to the development and evolution of a particular C or C. Only by doing so can each source be specifically related to the essence of the capability: the work that the organization actually

TABLE 12.8   Sources of Capabilities: The Small Plastics Manufacturer

Capability	Source of Capability
Ability to identify emerging market niches/customers needs	Relationships with customers Norms of behaving with customers
Ability to manufacture products with superior functionality	History of imbuing learning into work practices Alliances with technology providers
Ability to acquire raw materials and components and to use them as a source of product development	Skills of manufacturing and marketing personnel in product development Partnerships with many component suppliers
Ability to provide innovative and consistently superior customer service	Norms of customer service inculcated into all individuals in the organization
Ability to imbue new technical knowledge into the organization through training and education	Financial resources to fund the training Long-standing values around the importance of training and learning

does. The ability of the plastics competitor to provide innovative and consistently superior customer service (and to persistently augment the capability) was deemed to reside largely in behavioral norms[24] that were taken almost for granted within the competitor's organization. Norms such as "always go the extra mile to serve customers," and "never hesitate to take initiatives that will be appreciated by customers," emboldened individuals to act and behave as if their jobs depended on the quality of the service they delivered to all customers.

Sources that contribute to two or more capabilities are typically especially important. For the plastics competitor, behavioral norms emerged as a key source in many capabilities. The culture fostered by the competitor was a direct cause or source of many of its capabilities.

Projecting Competency and Capability Change

Three types of highly interrelated C or C change should be projected: change in existing C or C, development of new C and C, and amelioration of in-C or C. Indicators of the competitor's need for C or C change generate anticipated signals of such change, thereby drawing analysts' attention to potential change in C and C before it takes place.

The assessment of attributes, change in C and C and sources of C and C, provide considerable input into projecting the domain, direction, and magnitude of change in current C and C. Consider the plastics competitor's ability to manufacture products with superior functionality. Indicators of this capability such as product functionality and features, purchases and use of manufacturing technologies, presentations by competitor personnel of the firm's manufacturing investments and commitments, as well as development of existing alliances and the creation of new alliances, cumulatively allow strong inferences about change in the domain of the competency (e.g., the types of manufacturing the firm will be able to do), and the direction and magnitude of the change (e.g., the volume of products with particular features that might be produced over some specified time period).

The development of C or C *new to the competitor* are critical to assessing linkages between C and C and projected marketplace strategy (the next assessment step to be discussed). Frequently, new C or C evolve out of existing C and C and/or the amelioration of in-C or C or non-C or C. New C or C take a considerable period to develop. Thus, a multitude of indicators usually indicate which C or C the competitor is seeking to develop, which sources are contributing to them, and the potential rate of evolution. Considerable evidence was emerging of the multibusiness enterprise's commitment to develop a supplier management competency: the ability to identify critical suppliers, develop partnering relationships with them, and generate superior outputs (e.g., components, supplies, products) compared with rivals.

As noted, rectifying in-C or C can lead to new C or C or change in existing C and C. A competitor that turns its inability to attract, recruit, train, and retain the best people in its industry segment into the C or C to do so, not only eliminates an in-C or C but creates a new C or C for itself. The analyst therefore seeks indicators of the competitor's efforts to rectify in-C or C. A number of indicators provided evidence that the multibusiness enterprise was beginning to try to turn its inability to win in the face of intense rivalry into a competency to do so. It was beginning to address the dominance of technology and manufacturing in its culture (as opposed to a culture dedicated to learning about the marketplace); it had begun to compete differently against new entrants in some of its markets; senior executives had discussed the importance of these changes on many public occasions.

Identifying a competitor's *need* to alter its C and C profile, as well as its understanding of the need to do so, is central to projecting both the development of new C and C and/or change in existing in-C or C. Indicators of the need to alter C and C include the attributes of existing C and C, performance results, anticipated strategy changes, vulnerabilities and constraints, comparison with other competitors, and changes in the relevant competitive arenas. Atrophy, restricted domain, constrained robustness, comparatively easy imitability, and limited augmentability are indicators of C and C that are not likely to buttress sustainable advantage over competitors.

To cite one other indicator of the need for C and C development, performance results such as loss of market share or loss of key accounts may indicate the need for both core and secondary C and C change. One firm that lost a series of governmental bids decided to completely revamp its entire approach to ascertaining customer requirements and developing initial job specifications for customer reaction—a core marketing and sales competency in its type of business.

Linking Competencies and Capabilities to Potential Marketplace Strategy

In conjunction with the trajectories associated with current marketplace strategy,[25] current and projected change in its C and C profile constitutes a critical indicator of any competitor's *emerging and future* marketplace strategy. It is useful to relate C and C change to each of the elements of marketplace strategy: scope, posture, and goals.

Scope C and C change sometimes indicates likely future products or solutions long before they appear in the marketplace. In the case of the multibusiness enterprise, the domain of its innovative and distinctive research, allied with the advanced manufacturing technologies it was investing in and the alliances and networks it was orchestrating, strongly indicated not only the types of products it wanted to bring to the marketplace but many of their attributes.

For the plastics competitor, its capabilities pertaining to identifying emerging market niches/customer needs and to imbuing new technical knowledge into the organization, served as indicators of product direction. By monitoring which customers the competitor was working with, which issues it was addressing with these customers, and which product trials it was conducting, the focal firm was able to project which new products or variations around existing products it would likely introduce.

Posture Change in capabilities is always directly linked to posture change.[26] Each change in the plastics competitor's capabilities indicated specific posture changes. Changes in its manufacturing capability led directly to enhancement of product functionality, in part, through working with customers on new product formulations.

By the same token, in-C or C sometimes indicates posture directions that are not possible. The plastics competitor did not possess the requisite capabilities to move rapidly toward customization. The multibusiness enterprise did not possess the requisite marketing and sales competencies to quickly become an aggressive competitor in many of its product sectors.

Goals Implicit in projected scope and posture direction is change in marketplace goals. For the plastics competitor, all the changes in its capabilities suggested a commitment to further enhancing differentiation along all modes of competition. The multibusiness enterprise's commitment to augmenting its ability to do innovative and distinctive research and to identifying and serving new customer needs indicated a goal of extending current product lines, and possibly adding new product lines.

Comparison with the Focal Firm

A competitor's core C and C create competitor- and customer-based advantage to the extent they are distinctive or unique. A determination of distinctiveness and uniqueness stems from a comparison with other competitors and the focal firm. The value of carefully identifying and assessing competitors' C and C is that they offer a means for the focal organization to critically evaluate what it currently does well and poorly, and what it may need to do well to win in the future marketplace. Because organizations seem to frequently overstate both the extent of their own C and C and their marketplace value, few bases of comparison induce a greater sense of humility than when managers are forced to compare and contrast their own organization's alleged C and C with those of rivals.

Great care must be taken in comparing and contrasting C and C. A number of caveats are warranted. Any two competitors, by accident or design, may over time have developed both common and different C and C. Because a competitor evidences a particular C or C, it does not follow that the focal firm should also develop it. The competitor may have different current or planned marketplace strategies or the C or C is not robust or augmentable. Also, differing asset endowments of rivals may lead them to develop different C and C. These caveats are especially germane in the case of assessing competencies.

A prelude to any comparison is the identification and listing of the focal firm's own C and C. Competencies and incompetencies for the multibusiness enterprise and the focal firm are noted in Table 12.9. Comparison proceeds along a number of lines.

Similar Competencies The previously noted issues of competency domain and business domain assume particular importance in the comparison of (apparently) similar competencies. Competencies that at first glance seem to refer to a common competency domain may not do so. Both firms possessed a research-based competency; both firms used applied research and development[27] as a central source of many new products. Yet the competency domains were reasonably distinct. The competitor's research and

TABLE 12.9 Competencies: Comparison between the Focal Firm and the Multibusiness Enterprise

Competitor	Focal Firm
Competencies (Ability to)	
Conduct innovative and distinctive research	Develop innovative products pulling from own research and that of others
Do advanced manufacturing	Introduce products quickly into the marketplace
Identify and serve new customer needs	Do flexible manufacturing
Develop and enhance complex channel and end-customer relationships	Manage all costs (with a view to being low, if not lowest, cost competitor)
Develop and enhance alliances and networks	
Incompetencies (Inability to)	
Compete successfully once competitors respond with new product introductions	Do research that is distinct and unique
Manage total costs to meet profit expectations	Create and leverage new customer needs

development domain was much broader than the focal firm's: its research embraced a wider swath of technological areas and challenges. In terms of competency sources, the focal firm was more dependent on its alliances with other organizations.

Although both firms possessed clear and specific manufacturing competency, the relevant competency and business domains were quite distinct. The competitor continued to augment its ability to adopt and extend the latest manufacturing technologies, tools, and processes. These technologies related to almost every business unit. The focal firm, on the other hand, emphasized its ability to augment its manufacturing flexibility—its ability to adapt manufacturing to marketplace needs at short notice. However, its manufacturing competency manifested a narrower domain and was much less robust than the competitor's.

Dissimilar Competencies Competencies evidenced by one organization and not by the other shed considerable light on how and why each is winning (or losing). The competitor's competency in identifying and shaping new customer needs (reflecting its marketing assets), allied with its demonstrated competency in developing and enhancing customer relationships that were related to all phases of product development), helped explain why it was the preferred supplier of choice by most "early adopter" customers.

The focal firm by combining its competencies in flexible manufacturing and quick product introductions was able to compensate somewhat for its incompetency compared with the competitor in developing innovative, leading edge products.

Incompetencies The competitor's incompetencies somewhat mirrored some of the focal firm's competencies. More importantly, they revealed why the focal firm was able to compete so successfully against it over a number of years. The competitor had never developed a competency (across its business units) to compete aggressively for market share and position once a rival had succeeded in catching up to it with comparable or superior products. Rather than engage in head-to-head competition, the competitor employed its R&D and other competencies to, in effect, initiate another strategy game by introducing a product that was new to the marketplace. Hence, by using its own competency to rapidly introduce new products, the focal multibusiness firm was able to move into the competitor's product domain and to outmaneuver and outperform it within two or three years.

The focal firm's incompetencies were also revealing. Its inability to do innovative and unique R&D greatly constrained its strategic intent and vision. It could not aspire to being the leading product innovator in its chosen business sectors unless it radically overhauled its approach to R&D and/or its disinclination to enter into alliances and networks intended to result in breakthrough products.

Comparison with Others: Distinctive and Unique Competencies and Capabilities

Comparison with a range of look-alike, selected functional substitute, and even some extended competitors, can quickly confirm whether, and to what extent, a competitor's C and C are distinct or unique. Such assessment challenges the robustness of an organization's C and C: a functional substitute competitor's C or C can suddenly reveal that the organization's C or C is not leverable into the products required to win in the marketplace.

Not surprisingly, the multibusiness enterprise's substitute competitors varied from one business unit to another. Thus, the distinctiveness of its core competencies (as identified in Table 12.4) and their likelihood of continuing to be core competencies that would contribute to winning in the marketplace needed to be specifically assessed within each product sector. Again, not surprisingly, the results varied from one product unit to another. Its manufacturing competency would likely contribute to continued success in some product units, but in one or two cases, it could potentially do little to fend off the arrival and the penetration of substitute products.

The plastics competitor, when compared with its look-alike rivals, was able to identify emerging market niches/customer needs—a unique capability. The evidence appeared to suggest that none of its look-alike rivals was even remotely comparable in the ability to discern market opportunities. Its ability to manufacture products with superior functionality and to provide innovative and consistently superior service were probably distinctive compared with almost all its look-alike rivals, but only slightly so in the case of one or two rivals.

Signals of Marketplace Change

Assessment of C and C sometimes generates signals of emerging and future marketplace change. Such change includes potential products, the emergence of new competitors, scope, and dynamics of rivalry, as well as relations and interactions (e.g., alliances and networks) between various entities in and around the competitive domain.

As illustrated by the plastics manufacturer case, assessment of capability change across multiple competitors contributes to determining the future scope and profile of products or solutions offered to customers. Moreover, change in competitors' capabilities occasionally augurs configurations of products or solutions that are vastly different from those presently on the market.

Similarly, developments in competitors' C or C directly shape the dynamics of rivalry. As individual competitors ameliorate non-C or C, develop new and enhance existing C or C, the battle within and across each mode of competition as discussed in Chapter 5—product line width, functionality, features, service, availability, image and reputation, selling and relationships, and price—may change dramatically.

Consequences for the Competitor

Determination of competitor consequences should be viewed in part as the integration and extension of the prior steps. It usually raises issues and questions about the following fundamental C or C consequences:

- Which core C or C are in danger of atrophying, either despite the competitor's best efforts or through inattention?
- Which core C and C are in danger of losing their marketplace relevance?
- Which C or C should the competitor retain and augment?
- Which C or C is the competitor augmenting that might not create marketplace value?

- Which C or C must be better integrated and coordinated?
- Which new C or C need to be developed?
- Which in-C or C must or should be rectified and enhanced?

It was abundantly clear that one of the multibusiness enterprise's historic core competencies—identifying and shaping new customer needs—needed renewal and reinvigorating. The firm was increasingly relying on its R&D output to drive customer needs: it had a number of recent relatively unsuccessful product introductions, and customers were beginning to cite its newfound arrogance. And, as discussed, the competitor needed to develop a competitive marketing competency that would enable it to take on rivals in the battle to attract, win, and retain customers, once three or more rivals were battling for supremacy in any competitive domain.

Determination of these general C or C consequences raises in turn the next layer of considerations:[28]

- What are the consequences for the competitor's current marketplace strategy if it is able, or not able, to augment existing C or C, develop new C or C, or ameliorate in-C or C?
- What are the consequences for the competitor's future marketplace strategy if it can, or cannot, make the suggested C or C changes?

Assessment of these considerations may generate exciting or troubling consequences for the competitor. In the multibusiness enterprise case, the consequences were potentially troubling. It could quickly lose much of its marketplace dominance in some product sectors, and find itself confronting newly successful rivals in other product sectors. It thus needed to embark on an aggressive set of initiatives to upgrade and better leverage the competencies it required to compete successfully.

Determination of these consequences raises additional considerations:

- Does the competitor have the assets to augment specific C or C or to develop new C or C?
- Is the competitor sufficiently committed to doing so?
- Are the competitor's leaders fully aware of the extent of the necessary C or C change?

The multibusiness enterprise competitor did possess sufficient assets (and could gain access to considerable external assets through capital and debt acquisition, alliances, technology agreements, etc.) to change its competency profile. However, important questions were raised as to whether its leaders were fully cognizant of the degree of competency change required (at least as judged by the focal firm's analysts). Unless the multibusiness competitor committed itself to related action programs to extend and augment its competency profile, it risked being extensively outwitted, outmaneuvered, and outperformed by its rivals.

Implications for the Focal Firm

Implications for C and C, marketplace strategy, and other microlevel components are so closely interlinked that they are almost inseparable. Assessing these factors feeds directly into determining action programs to manage C and C.

Linking C and C and Marketplace Strategy Sometimes a dominant implication pertains to what the focal firm must do to better *leverage its current core C and C* for value in the marketplace. By analyzing competitors, hidden customer value is often discovered in existing C and C. In the multibusiness case, the focal firm could greatly extend its business domain in product sectors by extending the competency domain of its ability to flexibly manufacture. It could produce a greater variety of products, with greater speed and efficiency, and yet with superior functionality and features to many competitors. This insight became apparent only after extensive competency analysis. For the focal plastics firm, a parallel implication was derived. Once it recognized that its ability to identify emerging market niches and customer needs was truly a distinctive capability, the commitment to ferreting out new customer opportunities became a central focus of everything the organization did.

Sometimes, it is unmistakably apparent that unless the focal firm creates one or more C or C, it cannot renovate or reinvent its marketplace strategy. Such was the case for the focal plastics firm. New capabilities were needed before the firm could pursue a posture built around the customization of its solutions.

Ameliorating in-C or C may also lead directly to specific marketplace strategy implications. For the focal multibusiness firm, investing to rectify its incompetence in competing against rivals in established product-customer segments could cause a significant shift in the dynamics of these segments, send an unambiguous indication of its intentions to its rivals, and result in an increase in cash generated from these businesses. Developing this competence was necessary if the focal firm hoped to cease being outmaneuvered and outperformed in product segments it had largely created.

Linking C and C to Micro Components Change in C and C often has major implications for other micro components. The multibusiness firm, once it became evident that its core competencies required significant investment, realized that its core assumptions also needed critical review. In particular, an assumption that its current competencies (without significant augmentation) were sufficient to outmaneuver and outperform rivals for the immediate future was probably false. Moreover, competency development and augmentation would probably require it to enter into some new alliances and relationships and to extend and develop almost all its key asset types.

If the focal plastics firm decided to develop a customization capability, it would signify a radical shift in its assumptions about what it took to win in the marketplace. It would also require the firm to manage its activity/value chain very differently, and to develop new relationships with almost all its customers.

Management of C and C Implications also include what the focal firm must do to manage its C and C. Analysts can weave their way through C and C issues, alternatives, decisions, and action programs. Issues pertaining to C and C (such as the plastics firm's need to develop a customization capability) lead to the identification of alternative ways of responding to them. Alternatives in turn give rise to C and C decisions—the choice of action programs to augment existing C and C, develop new C and C, and ameliorate in-C or C.

Errors in the Assessment of Capabilities or Competencies

Because of the difficulties encountered by many organizations in conducting C and C analysis, this section identifies some key errors associated with the steps in assessing competitors C and C (see Figure 12.4).

First, inattention to the robustness of individual C or C results in analysts not anticipating the development and introduction of new products or major extensions of existing product lines. This error is especially critical if the competitor aims to create a new strategy game or reconstruct an existing game.

Sometimes insufficient attention is paid to assessing whether a competitor is willing and able to augment a particular C or C. Hence, projections of C or C development greatly over- or understate what the competitor may be able to do.

When analysts do not carefully identify and challenge the sources of a particular C or C, they are more likely to misunderstand its attributes, misconstrue why it is changing, and misspecify its potential development. As discussed in the case of the plastics competitor, analysts are thus also likely to fail to detect the influence of individual sources such as elements of the competitor's culture on the direction and development of two or more C or C simultaneously.

Analysts greatly exacerbate the difficulties inherent in projecting C and C when they do not attempt to identify indicators of the need for a competitor to alter its C or C. Without such anticipated indicators, analysts are ill-equipped to track and project emerging and potential C or C change.

Sometimes analysts fail to carefully trace the links between C or C change and specific emerging and future consequences for the competitor's marketplace strategy. Analysts who do not articulate such links are not likely to recognize which indicators pertain to potential change in the competitor's marketplace strategy.

In their haste to draw comparisons with rivals, analysts may not adequately specify the relevant domains of specific C or C. As a consequence, they are likely to derive inappropriate decision implications.

Finally, in assessing focal firm implications, analysts sometimes do not adequately detail the implications of C or C change for individual micro components such as the activity/value chain or assumptions. A failure to do so leads analysts to make recommendations for C or C change without fully understanding their implications.

Summary

Identifying and assessing competitors' C and C allows analysts to integrate and leverage analysis of every framework component—marketplace strategy and each microlevel component from activity/value chain through organization infrastructure and culture. It also provides a unique perspective on competitors: what they do well or badly.

CHAPTER

13

Technology

FEW PHENOMENA ARE AS UBIQUITOUS AS TECHNOLOGY IN THEIR EFFECTS ON THE capacity of organizations to outwit, outmaneuver, and outperform competitors. It affects everything an organization does and how it does it. It undergirds entrepreneurship and innovation, and thus marketplace strategy. It impacts every activity or process—every stage of the activity/value chain. It contributes to every form of capability and competency. It influences every interaction with external entities.

This chapter presents a comprehensive and integrated set of frameworks for the analysis of competitors' technology. It begins by outlining a broad conception of technology, highlighting its importance and pervasiveness. It illustrates how to use the product technology chain and the activity/value chain to identify and assess the state of an individual competitor's technology.

This chapter emphasizes the multiple *outputs* that can be generated through competitor technology analysis. It illustrates the inherent connection between technology and marketplace strategy and each micro component. Assets specific to technology and technology's role in capabilities and competencies receive particular attention.

The Competitive Implications of Technology

Definition of Technology

Technology is a complex phenomenon. Simple but embracive definitions of it have proved elusive. Some authors[1] and organizations take great care to specify what technology entails while others avoid the issue.[2] The most common thread among definitions and descriptions of technology is that it incorporates or refers to how an organization *does* things: for example, how

---

361

it develops new products; how it manages processes; how it moves data and information; how it develops connections to external entities.

In the spirit of technology as "doing" or "encapsulated doing," this chapter defines technology as the research, development, and application or use, involved in products, processes, and materials. Although, research, development, and application represent three distinctly different facets of technology, the object or focus of each is essentially similar: the generation and use of knowledge. In research, knowledge is typically new to the world or the firm. In development, it is often an extension of existing knowledge. Application predominantly entails the use of knowledge that already exists and which may even be widely disseminated.

Technology represents the encapsulation of knowledge for three purposes: developing or enhancing products or offerings for customers; developing and enhancing organizational activities and processes, both those largely or exclusively within the organization and those that connect the organization to external entities such as suppliers, distributors and end-customers; and developing or enhancing raw materials, components, or supplies.

Technology Strategy

All organizations have a technology strategy. Although it is often largely implicit, it is the sum of a set of investment programs in research, development, and application, in particular technology domains that are intended to achieve specific technology goals.[3] For example, a video production firm might have programs in domains such as video development, video production, distribution, and customer support services. Each program typically consists of a number of projects.

Specific *technology* goals are associated with individual programs. Sometimes the dominant goal is *undisputed leadership* in a particular (technology) domain such as the creation of the most sophisticated or technically advanced video reproduction. The goal of many programs is merely to *catch up* to or attain relative parity compared with specific competitors. Other programs aim to *remedy a technology deficiency* without attaining leadership or parity.

The Product Technology Chain

A "product technology chain" incorporating distinct stages offers an analysis framework to identify and monitor the research, development, and application of competitors' products. Each of the generic stages is briefly described and defined in Figure 13.1. Although the demarcation lines

FIGURE 13.1
The Product Technology Chain

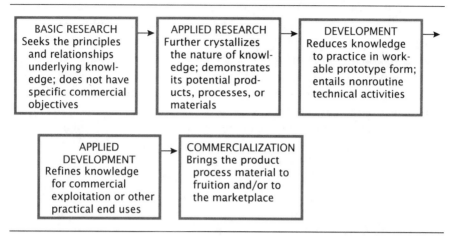

between these stages are often hazy and ill-defined, the execution of each stage within any organization involves a series of phases or steps as detailed later in the chapter.

Research and applied research embrace what is often referred to as "invention." Fundamental or basic research (as opposed to applied research) is conducted by a small number of firms in a relatively small subset of businesses such as pharmaceuticals, raw materials, semiconductors, electronics, and chemicals. Its focus is the discovery of knowledge not now known. Applied research, on the other hand, is much more bounded and focused. Many more firms in a wider variety of businesses or industries engage in applied research. It both enables and is enabled by basic research.

Compared with research, development is clear, targeted, and specific. The purpose of development is to transform knowledge (often that generated in pure and applied research) into practical use—to *apply* scientific, engineering, or other "research" knowledge. Frequently, the transformation involves the extension and expansion of such knowledge. Almost always it involves connecting knowledge in one field with that in other fields. Development seeks to take product (or process)[4] knowledge through a series of defined steps to test, refine, and prepare it for practical use, either in the form of products to sell in the marketplace or processes that improve internal operations. These steps vary greatly from one business to another, and sometimes even from one situation to another within the same firm; hence, the need to identify the phases within each stage and the connections across stages (as detailed later in this chapter).

Technology and the Activity/Value Chain

The activity/value chain described in detail in Chapter 7 greatly facilitates identification and analysis of a competitor's use of technology. The emphasis is on development and application; basic (scientific) research typically does not aim to enhance activities such as logistics, marketing, and service. Many other types of research, however, aim to generate and deploy knowledge relevant to specific activities or processes such as market research, business intelligence, and benchmarking technology use in other organizations.

Technology offers multiple opportunities to enhance the efficiency and effectiveness of each activity (see Figure 13.2). Competitors use technology to radically transform how they execute each activity or to incrementally improve the performance of each task within an activity. The strategic relevance of technology is greatly enhanced by its capacity to interrelate and integrate the activities. Information and materials handling technologies increasingly allow firms to do things they could not previously do. As a consequence, organizations continually develop, adopt, and apply technologies as one means to add superior value to their customer offerings—a critical form of outmaneuvering and outperforming rivals.

Technology Assets

The development and execution of technology programs and projects along either the product or activity/value chain requires critical assets. Technology assets (or technology wherewithal)[5] represent a specific application of

FIGURE 13.2
The Activity/Value Chain: Key Technologies

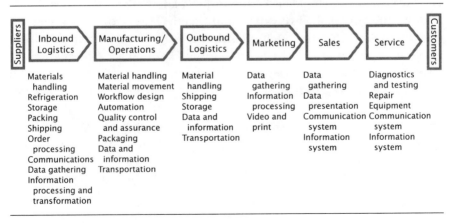

Suppliers	Inbound Logistics	Manufacturing/ Operations	Outbound Logistics	Marketing	Sales	Service	Customers
	Materials handling	Material handling	Material handling	Data gathering	Data gathering	Diagnostics and testing	
	Refrigeration	Material movement	Shipping	Information processing	Data presentation	Repair	
	Storage	Workflow design	Storage	Video and print	Communication system	Equipment	
	Packing	Automation	Data and information		Information system	Communication system	
	Shipping	Quality control and assurance	Transportation			Information system	
	Order processing	Packaging					
	Communications	Data and information					
	Data gathering	Transportation					
	Information processing and transformation						

the asset framework outlined in Chapter 11. Thus, assets specific to technology are delineated and assessed in terms of financial, human, knowledge, physical, perceptual, political, and organizational categories. Relating these categories to a competitor's technology strategy, or to specific programs and projects, facilitates assessment of the sources of the competitor's technology capabilities or competencies.

Identification and assessment of a competitor's technology assets is essential for several reasons. Technology assets sometimes are highly *specific:* they are limited in use or application to a particular type of product or organizational activity or process. Other technology assets have multiple uses. Information technology that connects a competitor to its channels and end-customers can be used to track product flows, depict sales patterns, research customer needs, and monitor broad market trends. Technology asset configurations sometimes indicate key competitor constraints and vulnerabilities. These sometimes take a long time to eradicate or require major strategic or operating responses. Finally, changes in the stocks and flows of technology assets often lead to strong signals of emerging or potential changes in marketplace strategy.

Technology Capabilities and Competencies

Since technology, as noted, is essentially about "doing," it is integrally related to any competitor's capabilities and competencies. However, a careful distinction must be drawn between technological capabilities and competencies, that is, what the competitor does well technologically, and technology's role in or contribution to other capabilities and competencies (e.g., learning about customers faster and better than rivals).

Some capabilities and competencies are innately technological: they are what the organization does well technologically. An organization might have varying degrees of capability in many of the technologies noted in Figures 13.1 and 13.2. Many organizations through the use of information technology have developed distinct capability in gathering, analyzing, and transmitting vast amounts of data and information in a timely and integrated manner. Many organizations develop, adopt, and integrate multiple logistics technologies so that they outperform rivals in moving materials, components, supplies, and finished products.

Some organizations also manifest technology competencies in research, development, and application that cross multiple product lines or business units. Classic examples include the ability to do pure research; the ability to adapt, extend, and leverage the research knowledge developed by other organizations; the ability to manufacture multiple distinct but related product lines, at low cost and high quality, and with great variation.

In most instances, however, the contribution of technology to other capabilities and competencies, rather than technological capabilities and competencies, per se, is of particular interest and relevance in understanding and projecting competitors' future marketplace strategy and other behaviors. For example, information and materials-handling technologies often combine to facilitate development and enhancement of order fulfillment and service capabilities. Many market research, data analysis, brand development, advertising, and communications technologies are likely to contribute to a marketing competency desired by all organizations: the ability to anticipate and shape customers' needs.

Indicators of Technology Change

The relevant *direct* indicators vary significantly across the stages in the product technology chain and in the activity/value chain. Indicators of progress or change in research are fundamentally distinct from indicators pertaining to development or to activities across the activity/value chain. Indeed, direct indicators are peculiar to phases within research and development and to the relevant technologies in the activity/value chain. As an aid to efficient and effective search, analysts therefore need to develop a priori lists of relevant indicators across the product technology chain and the activity/value chain.

Indirect indicators of technology change across both chains are also many and varied. A decline in marketplace results in one product area sometimes indicates a likely increase in asset commitment to research in another product area. Similarly, changes in product functionalities or features often indicate some (as yet) unknown changes in manufacturing technology.

As evidenced in this chapter, data sources pertaining to indicators vary significantly across the stages in each chain, especially the product technology chain. Personal sources are typically critical in research; secondary sources are sometimes more useful in development than in research.

Technology Change as Signals

Technology change often provides strong, high impact, signals at all three levels of competitor analysis—system, competitor, and micro components. It frequently serves as the source of strong signals at the *system* level: the emergence, entry, and decline of look-alike rivals and substitute rivals; and the migration of rivals from one product-customer segment to another. Relatedly, competitors' technology change furnishes alerting and strong signals of change in and around the marketplace.[6] A fundamental rationale for analysis of the product technology and activity/value chains, as presented in this chapter, is that technology change often gives rise to strong signals of change in competitors' marketplace strategy. Sometimes these signals have a long change lag, thus providing a substantial time period in which to develop a preemptive or other type of response. As explained later in this chapter, although technology change affects every microlevel component, it often provides particularly insightful signals of recent, emerging, and potential change in competitors' assumptions, capabilities and competencies, and alliances and networks.

Identifying a Competitor's Technology State

Guided and open-ended approaches are essential to capturing the state of competitors' technologies. Because of the scope and complexity of technology, this chapter presents guided frameworks that demonstrate what analysis can be conducted and how to do so. However, the same scope and complexity also makes an open-ended approach highly desirable because analysts often do not know a priori what the relevant indicators are, indicators frequently show up in unexpected sources, and a greater variety of data sources are required than for any other framework component.

Distinct guided types of analysis (see Figure 13.3) contribute to depicting the prevailing state of a competitor's technology. Each addresses particular facets of a competitor; each adds unique insight into the state of a competitor's technology.

FIGURE 13.3
Identifying the State of a Competitor's Technology

Focus of Analysis	What Is Learned
Product technology chain ⟶	How technology contributes to the organization's products.
Activity/value chain ⟶	The impact of technology on the organization's key activities.
Marketplace strategy ⟶	The technologies the competitor has (or must have) as indicated by change in its marketplace strategy.
Assets ⟶	The stock of technology-specific assets possessed by the competitor.
Capabilities and competencies ⟶	The competitor's technology capabilities and competencies.
Alliances and networks ⟶	How they contribute to the competitor's technology state.

Product Research, Development, and Application

Identifying a competitor's product technology chain(s) is closely inter-related with other framework components such as marketplace strategy, customer-focused activity chains, alliances, and networks. Partly as a consequence, it is often straightforward to develop *first-cut*[7] product technology chain(s) for many competitors using a guided analysis (see Figure 13.4). A major research initiative by a large pharmaceutical competitor is used for illustration (see Table 13.1).

Key Products　It is first necessary to identify the competitor's key current and emerging products or product categories, as well as the research

FIGURE 13.4
Identifying a Competitor's Product Technology

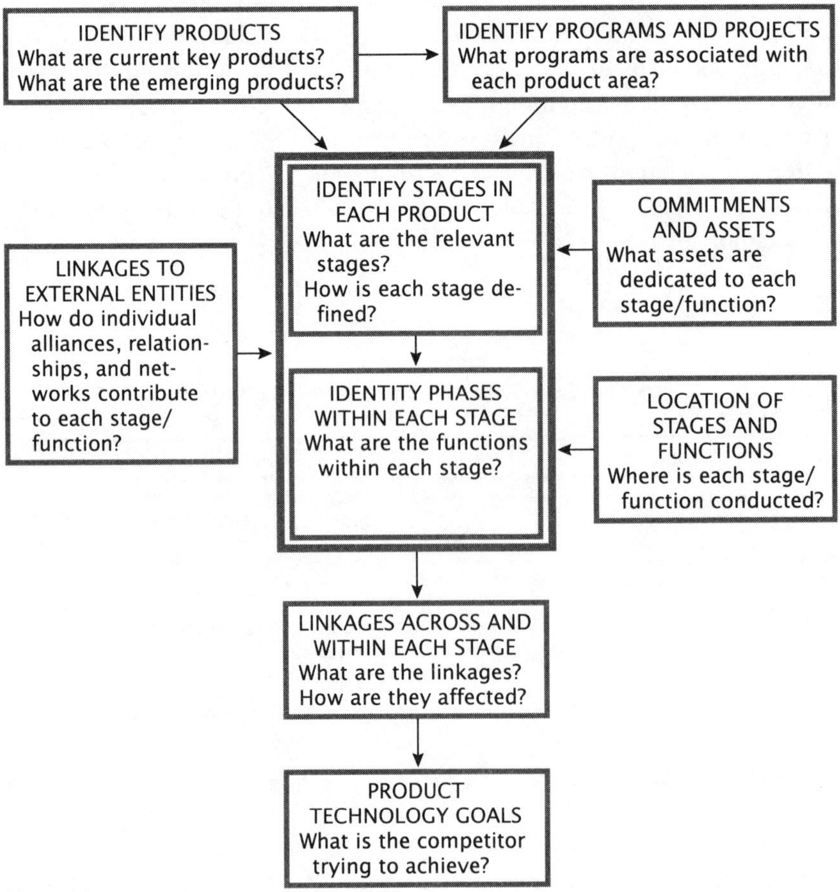

TABLE 13.1   Stages and Phases in a Product Technology Chain: A Pharmaceutical Competitor

Stages and Phases within Each Stage	Sample Data Sources
Basic research: Research in compounds Development of product concept	Competitor statements Relevant science/discipline experts Consultants and others specializing in research
Applied research: Synthesis Biological testing Pharmacological screening	Conference presentations Specialized journal articles Competitor announcements Patents
Clinical development: "Phase 1" testing "Phase 2" testing "Phase 3" testing	Governmental agency reports Experts' testimony Competitor reports and comments
Regulatory approval: Submission of materials Review hurdles	Regulatory agency statements Competitor announcements Science/trade press comments
Commercialization: Post-marketing safety monitoring Large-scale manufacturing Distribution Sales Service Education	Competitor announcements Comments by industry members: channels, hospitals, medical associations, etc. Reports by popular and trade press

domains that could lead to new products. This step is essential because distinctly different stages and phases are often evident within research and development across product groups. Even products within the same product group occasionally have distinct product technology chains. Also, potential products that might result from current research and development sometimes manifest a distinctly different product technology chain from those that have already reached the marketplace.

The pharmaceutical competitor's *potential* product was a drug that would treat a common medical condition. The research domain addressed the development of a new drug compound. Many of its rivals, including the focal firm, were also doing research in the same research domain.

Key Programs and Projects   Analysts next identify key programs and projects for each product (group) and/or research domain. These provide a focus for the subsequent steps in identifying stages and phases. The pharmaceutical competitor had initiated a research program several years previously that had now resulted in a clear and specific research direction. The competitor's senior research scientists had discussed their projects, that is, individual research tracks, in public seminars.

Relevant Stages Configuration of the specific stages for each product technology chain is often heavily influenced by the relevant industry. Typical stages in the pharmaceutical industry are noted in Table 13.1. However, judgments on the part of analysts are still required to delineate a broad definition and scope for each stage. Distinctions between development and applied development cause extensive debate in many industries.

Key Phases As with the activity/value chain, the more difficult challenge is to delineate the key phases or tasks within each stage. Again, phases within research, development, and commercialization are peculiar to individual industries. Common phases in the pharmaceutical industry (see Table 13.1) provided a point of departure to determine what the competitor had so far accomplished and what it had yet to achieve. It was heavily engaged in each of the phases associated with applied research.

Location of Tasks Stages within the chain and even phases within an individual stage are often conducted in different locations. An understanding of the geographic location of the specific stages and phases is important for at least three reasons. It often provides strong indicators of the focus and type of work conducted as well as the assets possessed by and potentially available to the competitor. It raises issues about the competitor's use of organizational technologies such as data and information management to coordinate the geographic locations. The pharmaceutical competitor was conducting its applied research in its two principal research sites.

Linkages to External Entities Increasingly, firms' product technology activities are connected to other organizations through alliances, relationships, and networks. The alliance and network analyses presented in Chapters 8 and 9 respectively, help identify external current and potential linkages along the product technology chain.

The pharmaceutical competitor had prominent external linkages with specific universities, biotechnology entities, individual research scientists, and independent testing facilities. Each might be useful at later phases in the evolution of the potential product.

Linkages within Stages Geographic disparity, management alliance/network relationships, differences in task content, and knowledge transfer considerations all suggest why developing and sustaining integrated linkages across phases within individual stages is sometimes problematic. Thus, how competitors build bridges across phases within each stage typically needs to be examined.

The pharmaceutical competitor was well known for its ability to move expeditiously through the applied research phases. The analysts identified the steps the competitor had to complete in each phase of applied research, the typical time involved in each step and when the research outcomes might move to clinical trials.

Commitments and Assets   It is also possible to describe the stock and flow of asset commitments pertaining to each stage. Sometimes, it is even necessary to do so for specific phases within individual stages. The pharmaceutical firm had indicated through statements of senior executives that this research program would not suffer from asset impediments.

Linkages across Stages   The stages in the product technology chain are not independent and isolated. If research, development, and engineering are not to some degree integrated, a common result is the generation of research that does not translate into products or solutions that customers value. The relevant indicators of linkages across the stages vary greatly from one industry or product category to another.

The pharmaceutical competitor had a well-earned reputation for its ability to move expeditiously through the stages and to successfully commercialize its research.

Goals   Analysis of the preceding steps furnishes sufficient data to develop at least some preliminary judgments about the competitor's product-related technology goals. In particular, it is critical to develop some judgments (and provide both the supporting logic and data) with respect to the following product goal dimensions:

- *Product Invention.*   Sometimes the indicators allow an unmistakable inference that the competitor is intent on creating a market through a new product or a series of related products. This was the intent of the pharmaceutical competitor.

- *Product Leadership.*   A distinct goal is to attain recognized leadership in a particular product category or group. This is achieved by using research and development to leapfrog rivals' products or through a series of advances, none of which alone is revolutionary, to cumulatively overtake the product offerings of rivals.

- *Product Invigoration.*   Not infrequently, one or more rivals endeavor to (re)invigorate a product or product group such that parity or maybe marginal superiority is attained with rivals.

- *Product Replacement.* Here the purpose is to replace an existing product with a new product that serves the same functional ends. Sometimes it leads to attracting new customers.

The Activity/Value Added Chain

A *guided* analysis (see Figure 13.5) seeks to identify the technologies associated with each activity and key tasks, as well as how technologies serve to

FIGURE 13.5
Identifying the Role of Technology in a Competitor's Activity/Value Chain

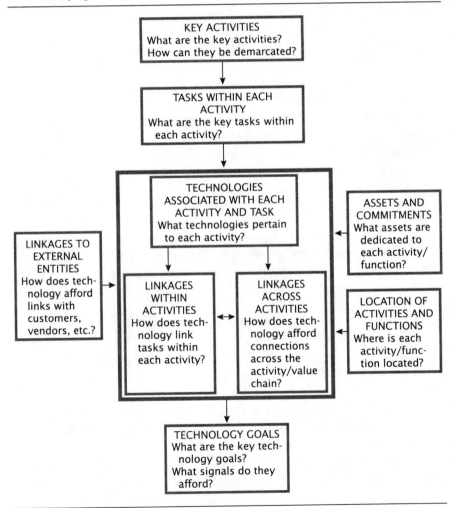

connect activities. A specialized food manufacturer's competitor is used for illustration.

Key Activities and Tasks Key activities and tasks are identified using the methodology detailed in Chapter 7.

Technology Associated with Activities and Tasks The essence of technology analysis at the level of the activity/value chain is to delineate the role and importance of technology for each activity, and if possible, for each task. A technology perspective may generate a somewhat different configuration of activities than might be the output of a conventional activity/value chain analysis. Attention to technology may suggest the need to include research as a separate activity. Doing so reinforces the importance of research in the minds of analysts and managers.

At a general level, analysts begin by identifying which technologies are relevant to each task. Of central import is to consider *how* technology affects or could influence each task. One point of departure is to consider each of the technologies noted in Figure 13.2. Based on analysts' own knowledge, it is often useful to develop a listing of the technologies pertaining to each task or set of tasks. Identifying which technologies affect each task within the focal organization is an essential input to developing a list of potentially relevant technologies.

For the consumer food product competitor (see Table 13.2), specific technologies are associated with each task. Individuals *within* the focal organization often possess sufficient knowledge about the technologies involved in each task and about a competitor (and especially so if it is a competitor they have been competing against for many years) to quickly develop a first-cut delineation[8] of not just the relevant technologies but some of the technology details noted in Table 13.2.

Technology often differentially affects tasks *within* an activity. For example, different technologies are germane to marketing tasks such as gathering market data, generating new product ideas, testing product prototypes with customers, creating and communicating image and reputation, developing and sustaining distribution alliances, and running market trials of the final product with selected end-customers. In the food product competitor analysis, video and print technologies pertain to advertising and promotion, while distinct information technologies pertain to consumer research and product trials.

Linkage within Activities Technology often links tasks within an activity. For example, information technology directly involves marketing by linking customers' product usage with distribution channel management

TABLE 13.2   Technologies across the Activity/Value Chain: A Consumer Food Competitor

Activities/Tasks	Relevant Technologies
Inbound logistics:	
Shipping of raw materials from vendors to plant	Refrigeration technology Packaging technology
Movement of raw materials within plant	Materials handling technology
Quality inspection	Sampling technology
Manufacturing:	
Processing	Manufacturing process technologies
Ensuring freshness	Airtight packaging technology
Outbound logistics:	
Warehousing	Storage technologies
Shipping	Storage technologies
Service to distribution channel members	Information technologies
Marketing:	
Market research	Information technologies
Brand development	Information technologies
Advertising	Video and print technologies (connected to print shops)
Sales and service:	
Customer hot line	Information technology
Sales force coverage	Information technology
On-site customer capabilities	Proprietary equipment technology
On-site service	Repair technologies

and decisions about which product varieties to develop and promote. Material handling technologies often connect every manufacturing task.

Information technologies provided the integrating mechanism for the consumer product competitor across the sales and service tasks. Information technology allowed selected customer hot-line calls to be directed quickly to specific salespeople and allowed on-site customer service personnel to be in direct contact with each other in the field and with the regional and national sales offices.

Linkage across Activities   Technology's most powerful and pervasive impact often is how it links or integrates tasks across activities. Many technologies noted in Figures 13.1 and 13.2 speed the flow of materials and information across activities, enhancing the quality of data and information within each of those activities. Indeed, in many instances, data and information cross activity boundaries in real time. The information technologies of the consumer product firm track the flow of raw materials, products in process, finished products, and service-related spare parts.

Linkage to External Entities Technology provides the means to integrate the competitor's own value-creating activities and those of its vendors, distribution channels, end-customers, logistics providers, governmental agencies, and other knowledge-generating entities such as consultants, universities, and market research organizations. Information technology increasingly allows direct connections between vendors, manufacturing, distribution channels, and end-customers.

Information technology allowed the consumer product competitor to have just-in-time delivery of key raw materials from certain suppliers. Materials handling, storage, and information technologies combined to facilitate codesign and oversight of the flow of finished products between the firm's warehouses and distributors' central storage locations—thus minimizing storage time and costs, as well as product deterioration.

Goals Analysis as outlined also provides insight into the competitor's technology goals in related ways. Two key technology goals were strongly indicated by the consumer product competitor's investments in technology: to dramatically improve its material-handling technologies in every facet of its operations and to use information technologies to speed the flow and enhance the quality of data and information within and across all activities. It was also using technology to facilitate and reinforce its marketplace strategy goals, especially the enhancement of its posture. For example, technology was being used to augment customer functionality by allowing the customer to use the product under increasingly wider circumstances. Technology, as noted, was being used to initiate new means of servicing customers and to augment existing modes of service.

Marketplace Strategy

Marketplace strategy often suggests multiple *indirect* indicators of a competitor's technology (see Table 13.3). Attention to these indicators alerts decision makers and analysts to the powerful connections between marketplace strategy and technology. It also helps shape some of the questions that guide product technology chain and activity/value chain analysis. This is especially so if analysts ask what technologies the competitor would have to possess for its marketplace strategy to materialize or what technologies it must augment or acquire to enhance its marketplace strategy.

TABLE 13.3 Marketplace Strategy as an Indicator of Technology

Marketplace Strategy Elements	Detecting Technologies: Key Questions
Products	What research activities underlie or must underlie each product?
	What development activities underlie or must underlie each product?
	What manufacturing technologies underlie each product?
Customers	What technologies allow access to particular groups of customers?
	What technologies allow the competitor to customize its products?
	What technologies aid the competitor's customer retention rates?
Posture	What technologies give rise to or facilitate:
	—Specific product features?
	—Different types of product functionality?
	—Different forms of service?
	—Different types of distribution?
	—Different facets of image and reputation?
	—Different facets of selling and relationships?
	—Various pricing levels?
Goals	What changes in goals indicate technology change?

Technologies can be connected to *products* in a number of ways. Many manufactured and service products are reverse engineered and decomposed to determine the role of technology in their development and delivery. Technology issues or questions are then raised with regard to each product or product group:

- What research is required to generate it?
- What development technologies are necessary?
- What process technology is required to manufacture it?
- Does the competitor have the necessary technologies?
- If not, how does it acquire the necessary technologies?
- Who is "world-class" in each technology (within or outside the business or industry)?
- Does the competitor have access to the necessary product and process technology through alliances or networks?

Changes in products over time are the source of retrospective and prospective signals[9] of technology change. A comparison of product features or product components from one time to another indicates technology changes that must have occurred within the competitor.[10]

Changes in *customer focus* also give rise to technology signals. Frequently, a competitor's sudden ability to reach new customers is a consequence of its development and/or use of technology. Many personal computer, software, and electronics manufacturers are now reaching both consumers and industrial customers through innovative adaptation of information and physical distribution technologies. As firms move toward greater degrees of customization, they require a more extensive use and integration of manufacturing, marketing, sales, and service technologies.

Changes in *posture* often generate pointed technology signals. Changes in product line width, features, and functionality typically have their source in some form of product and/or process technologies. Other elements of posture such as image and reputation, selling and relationships, and service, are also often intimately connected to competitors' use of the many technologies noted in Figures 13.1 and 13.2.[11]

A competitor's changes in marketplace goals, either announced or inferred by analysts, may provide important technology signals. Announcements of intention to provide superior service sometimes guide analysts to investigate what information and other technologies these competitors require to attain their stated customer service goals.

Technology Assets

As with any form of asset, the challenge is to delineate the stock and flow of the relevant technology asset categories. The emphasis here is on technology-specific assets (assets currently or potentially associated with the development and exploitation of technology programs and projects).

In a guided analysis, the initial task is to identify a priori specific asset categories, using the categories noted in Chapter 11 (financial, human, knowledge, physical, perceptual, political, organizational) as an initial point of departure. Asset categories and classes are then arrayed along the product technology chain or the activity/value chain. The relevant asset classes and types are always somewhat specific to individual technologies.

The categories and classes identified in the case of a video production firm, as well as associated indicators and data sources, are shown in Table 13.4. Two categories of knowledge were deemed important. Knowledge that the competitor possessed about entities such as customers, vendors, distributors, and standards bodies was essential to all stages of product development and product delivery. A distinct knowledge category was knowledge embedded in some of the competitor's key operating processes. It included classes of knowledge such as the actual production of videos, all the operations involved in postproduction, and project management (each

TABLE 13.4   The Competitor's Stock of Technology Assets: A Video Production Firm

Asset Category	Sample Asset Types	Sample Indicators
KNOWLEDGE ABOUT ENTITIES	Customers Distributors Vendors	Product development process Working relationships with these entities
KNOWLEDGE ABOUT PROCESSES	Preproduction Production Postproduction Project management Opportunity identification	How the firm works with potential and actual customers and vendors in all stages of product development and delivery
PHYSICAL	Production equipment Editing equipment Database	Types of equipment Changes in equipment

HUMAN	Number of people with:
	  specific types of knowledge
	  specific skills
		Total number of people
		Hiring practices
		Work practices

PERCEPTUAL	Perceptions held by:
	  customers
	  distributors
	  vendors
	  competitors
	  potential alliance partners
		Comments passed by these groups
		Reactions of customers and distributors to the competitor's product development

RELATIONAL	Relationships with:
	  equipment developers
	  equipment suppliers
	  venture capitalists
	  distributors
	  lead customers
		Number and type of formal and informal agreements with these parties
		Extent and type of involvement of these parties in each phase of product development

ORGANIZATIONAL	Beliefs about importance of technology Processes for developing and transmitting technology knowledge	Statements about technology Task forces Committees

video could be viewed as a "project" involving multiple tasks and coordination with many internal functions and external entities). Perceptual technology assets address the perceptions held by others about the current and future state of the competitor's technology. In this case, it became evident from comments of corporate users that the competitor was viewed by some customer segments as possessing significantly superior technical capability in many phases of video production. Relational (or political) technology assets refer to the competitor's technology-related relationships with other entities. The video competitor had a close working relationship with one equipment supplier; thus, it appeared to obtain the latest production equipment earlier than its rivals and some of the equipment was designed specifically to its specifications.

Technology Capabilities and Competencies

The product technology chain, activity/value chain, marketplace strategy, alliances and networks, assets, and organizational capabilities and competencies serve as the basis of a guided identification of a competitor's technology capabilities and competencies. One approach is to identify what the competitor does well in terms of *technology* within each stage along both chains, as illustrated in Figure 13.6 (as distinct from the contribution of technology to other types of capabilities and competencies). Another approach is to infer technology capabilities and competencies from the competitor's marketplace strategy—an extension of the analysis discussed earlier. It is also possible to first identify the competitor's key capabilities and competencies and then to work backward to the role technology plays in their generation and development.[12]

The food product competitor's technology capabilities were reasonably straightforward to identify given the analysis reflected in Table 13.2. Two

FIGURE 13.6
Identifying Technology Capabilities and Competencies

Product Technology Chain

| Research | Applied Research | Development | Applied Development | Application |

Technology Capabilities and Competencies

| Inbound Logistics | Operations | Outbound Logistics | Sales | Service |

Activity/Value Chain

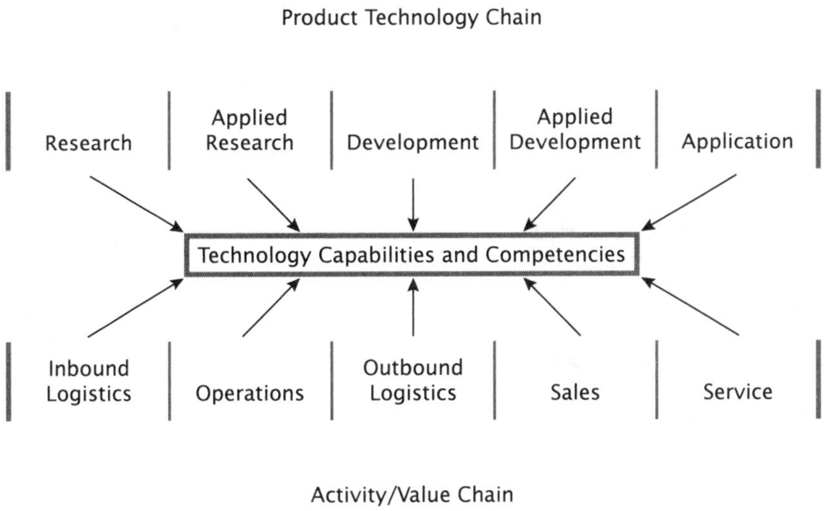

core capabilities were evident. It now had extensive information technology capability: it was able to track all phases of its total operations—raw materials acquisition, storage, manufacturing, distribution, sales, and customer service. It also had a superior logistics capability: it could acquire, refrigerate, store, and move produce in a timely fashion. One surprising secondary technology capability was the firm's ability to use video and print technologies to create innovative and eye-catching advertising.

Key organizational capabilities of the video production competitor along its activity/value chain, and the technology associated with them are shown in Table 13.5. Specific technology capabilities are evident in each activity. The more these technologies are distinct from each other (i.e., do not emanate from the same underlying technology assets or stocks of knowledge), the more difficult it is for rivals to emulate and supersede the competitor's organizational capabilities. The video firm's dominant and integrating technology capability allowed it to custom-tailor videos irrespective of whether

TABLE 13.5 From Organization to Technology Capabilities: The Video Production Competitor

Concept Development	Product Specification	Preparation for Production	Video Production	Service
ORGANIZATIONAL:				
Ability to quickly develop innovative alternative concepts for one or more current or potential clients	Ability to quickly and cheaply design multiple product specifications	Ability to quickly assemble people, supplies, and sites	Ability to work on many production projects at one time Ability to produce a video at a lower cost than any key rivals	Ability to customize service to the needs of each customer
⬆	⬆	⬆	⬆	⬆
TECHNOLOGICAL:				
Ability to use computer-aided graphics, print, information, and other technologies to show alternative concepts to current and potential clients in their own offices	Ability to use video, sound, and related technologies to develop distinctly different product designs	Ability to link with suppliers and components	Ability to quickly extend technology base Ability to use technologies in place of personnel and other overhead burdens	Ability to use technologies to interact with customers Ability to repair, re-edit videos, and upgrade video content

the customer was a commercial, corporate, not-for-profit, or governmental entity. This was a consequence of the many technology capabilities noted in Table 13.5.

Assessing a Competitor's Technology

Assessing any competitor's technology centers on two distinct though related foci: the current and projected *state* of the technology, and its current and potential contribution to marketplace strategy and microlevel components. Although they are often difficult to separate, it is generally necessary to develop a thorough understanding of the competitor's technology state, and in particular, its technology strategy, before assessing its (potential) contribution to marketplace strategy and microlevel components.

Technology Strategy

Assessment of a competitor's (implicit) technology strategy is especially important if the competitor is engaged in multiple businesses or in multiple product groups within a single business because different businesses or product groups typically manifest different technology thrusts. A number of technology thrusts are common (see Table 13.6).

Pursuing New Technology Competitors sometimes aim to generate new knowledge (pure research) or to create process technologies that represent new ways of doing thing. Essentially, the pursuit of fundamental research

TABLE 13.6 Identifying Overall Technology Thrust

Technology Thrust	Direction	Indicators
Pursue new technology domain	Seek a technology domain that no one else occupies	Newness of knowledge Research outputs
Extending technology domain	Extend current research and development	Program initiation/termination
	Extend scope of existing organizational technologies	Project continuation/modification/deletion
Reinforcing existing technology domain	Improve and refine existing technologies	Personnel allocation
Narrowing technology domain	Reduce the number of domains	Investment commitments Personnel changes/allocations
	Narrow scope of an existing domain	Alliance change Announcements

means that competitors either are already in or are moving into technology (knowledge) domains that few, if any, other organizations occupy.

Extending Technology A persistent trait of most technology programs and projects is that they are intended to extend a competitor's prevailing technology domain. Typical of this technology thrust is further advancement along a competitor's *product* research and development path or extension of the (technological) scope of its organization technologies.

Reinforcing Existing Technology Many organizations commit their technology investment programs to reinforce and enhance one or more existing technology domains. Software firms invest considerable resources to refine existing software. Manufacturing firms invest in technology projects to improve their existing production processes.

Narrowing the Technology Base In part because of the competitive difficulties of attaining and sustaining marketplace success in multiple product areas and the escalating costs associated with enhancing technology in multiple technology domains, firms frequently narrow their technology programs to a set of selected domains. Narrowing the technology base occurs in two ways. Competitors reduce the number of distinct domains or they narrow the scope of one or more domains.

Linking Technology and Marketplace Strategies

The preceding technology thrusts give rise to or support different marketplace strategies. Thus, it is critical to identify which marketplace strategy thrust is associated with each technology thrust for each product or product group (see Figure 13.7). The following marketplace thrusts merit attention.

Create Fundamental New Business Competitors often use a combination of product and organization technology programs to create a business that is new to the world—a new strategy game. Research and development generates one or more products that create a new customer need. The intended customers often extend beyond the competitor's existing customers. Such was the case with the pharmaceutical firm.

Generate New Business for the Competitor More commonly, technology generates a new business (new products) for the competitor that is not new to the world. The new products are intended to challenge or jump ahead of what others are already offering or plan to offer—to reconstruct an existing strategy game. However, the *basic* or underlying customer functionality is

FIGURE 13.7
Linking Technology and Marketplace Strategy Thrusts

Technology Thrust \ Strategy Thrust	Create Fundamental New Business	Generate New Business for the Competitor	Extend Existing Business Scope	Enhance Position Within Existing Business Scope	Business Synergy
Pursuing New Technologies					
Extending Existing Technologies					
Reinforcing Existing Technologies					
Narrowing the Technology Base					

not new to the marketplace. The new products created by the video production competitor fall into this category.

Extend Existing Business Scope Most often, technology extends the competitor's existing products or allows it to reposition its existing products to attract or reach new customers. Research and development may enable product line extensions. Organization technologies such as more adroit use of information technologies often facilitate the attraction and retention of new segments of customers. The consumer food firm's competitor used multiple technologies to extend its existing products and to reach new customers.

Enhance Position within Existing Business Scope Technology is often directly intended to enhance the value a competitor delivers to its existing customers—to change the marketplace rules. Research and development can lead to product design improvements. Technology enhancements in engineering and manufacturing frequently improve product functionality (e.g., enhanced reliability and performance).

Business Synergy Sometimes technology contributes to some combination of the preceding four marketplace directions by facilitating linkages among a competitor's existing businesses or between its existing and intended businesses. The video production firm, as discussed later in this chapter, was using technology to attract new customers and to develop new products for existing customers.

Product Technology: Research and Development

The critical dimensions, indicators, and data sources, associated with each stage in a *guided* assessment of a competitor's product technology chain vary considerably (see Table 13.7). The new research initiative of the pharmaceutical competitor is used for illustration.

Knowledge Newness Both research and applied research generate new knowledge. However, the spectrum of "newness" ranges from the genuinely new that is characteristic of pure research or science to some forms of development in which the knowledge output constitutes only an incremental advancement.

Many questions need to be posed (see Table 13.8). Developing even first-cut answers to these questions requires both the development of appropriate indicators and criteria, and the judgment of individuals with relevant technology expertise. For example, the content of the work of scientists as they generate genuinely new knowledge often can be judged only by other scientists with the relevant knowledge and background. However, this does not mean that substantial disputes and disagreements do not occur about whether specific research programs are likely to succeed in generating new knowledge, the value of such knowledge (both from a scientific and commercial vantage point), the degree of uncertainty involved, and whether a particular competitor has the technology assets to generate specific forms of new knowledge.

The pharmaceutical competitor's research program if successful would generate radical new knowledge leading to a breakthrough product.

Uncertainties Generating new knowledge, by definition, involves uncertainties. Once the degree of newness is established, knowledge uncertainty is assessed. The degree of uncertainty depends not just on the newness of the knowledge domain but also on the stage of the research and the results attained to date. Again, the judgments of individuals with relevant technological expertise are essential.

Critical uncertainties pertained to each phase of the pharmaceutical competitor's research program. For example, scientists in the focal firm pointed

TABLE 13.7 Evaluating Product Technology

Criteria	Dimensions	Indicators
Knowledge newness	Fundamental	Focus of research
	Radical	Research programs
	Incremental	Research projects
Knowledge uncertainty	High	Newness of knowledge
	Average	Type of knowledge
	Low	
Lead time	Long	Stages in product evolution
	Medium	
	Short	
Investment	Total amount	Dollars spent
	By program	Allocation to programs and
	Growth rate	projects
Personnel	Knowledge	Number of people
	Skills and capabilities	Types of people
	Training/background of individuals	Hiring and remuneration practices
External linkages	Alliances	Alliance partners
	Networks	Nature of alliance
		Network members
Potential products	Breakthrough	Projected product attributes
	Innovative	
	Extension	
Sustainability of advantage	Uniqueness of knowledge	Competitor's knowledge
	Product functionality	and product projections
Historic outcomes	Past record in technology development	Research outputs
		Patents
		Commercialized products

TABLE 13.8 Assessing Product Research: Key Questions

Fundamental Research

What are the specific research programs?

What are some of the key research projects?

Is the intended knowledge new to the world?

Could the research, as being pursued by the competitor, generate genuine knowledge breakthrough?

What are the differences between the intended knowledge and the competitor's current state of knowledge?

What are the key uncertainties pertaining to the research?

What is the timeline of the research?

to average to high uncertainties about the potential drug compound's results once tests were conducted outside of test tubes.

Lead Time Projections of the likely timeline associated with a product technology are developed by estimating the time associated with the phases within research, development and application. Familiarity with the nuances of research and development specific to individual products (or industries) is essential to determining such estimates. It would be at least three to five years before the pharmaceutical competitor's potential drug compound would enter preclinical trials and another four to six years before it would be subjected to regulatory review and approval.

Investment Although there is no correlation between the amount invested in research and development and its results, assessing a competitor's current and potential investment commitments furnishes indicators of its ability to stay the course. Often, organizations are unable to fund the intended or required technology programs. By assessing whether a competitor can sustain or increase its investment, analysts are better able to develop potential product development timelines. Critical issues to assess therefore are what financial (and other) assets are required to see a program or specific project through to completion and how the competitor might obtain them.

The pharmaceutical competitor was cash rich. The critical issue, however, was how the competitor evaluated the likely returns from investing in this research program compared with its other investment opportunities.

People Assessing a competitor's personnel often helps to reveal the direction and speed of its product technology. Sometimes, it is possible to develop a deep understanding of the relevance of the knowledge possessed by a competitor's key scientists, engineers, and others to the attainment of particular technology goals.

In the judgment of the focal firm's scientists and managers, the pharmaceutical competitor had access to sufficient personnel with the relevant knowledge and skills (including those available to it through its external alliances and relationships) to complete the research program.

External Linkages As emphasized earlier, linkages to external entities are critical to assessing product technology. They are often the source of essential knowledge. Sometimes they provide the impetus to generation and development of the desired knowledge. Such external linkages did not seem to be critical to the early stages of this particular research program of the pharmaceutical competitor.

Potential Products Success in terms of technology does not imply success in the marketplace—what technologists and others refer to as commercial success. Hence, the analyst must try to assess the attributes of the products that could flow from the research and development. A number of guiding questions are offered in Table 13.9.

It was generally agreed that the pharmaceutical competitor's research program, if successful, would generate a breakthrough product that would create a new product-customer segment.

Sustainability of Advantage When a product eventually reaches the marketplace, it may possess limited or extensive sustainable advantage. Product, market, and technological risks must be considered. Assessment of each of these risks entails unavoidable judgments. A much broader range of individuals including marketing and sales personnel, customers, and industry experts are asked for their judgments than is the case in the assessment of research. The relevant individuals vary by the assessment dimension or criterion.

Sustainability is assessed along a number of dimensions. The imitability of the underlying knowledge by current or potential competitors always merits appraisal. The uniqueness of the product and customer functionality is always scrutinized. Also, other competitors' technology may create superior products in the short or long run.

It was possible that the pharmaceutical competitor would have a lead time of three to five years over its rivals before they could introduce a similar or superior product.

TABLE 13.9 Assessing Product Development: Key Questions

What is the product scope?
—A series of related products?
—One or two significant stand-alone products?
What are the marketplace scope implications?
—Product(s) new to the marketplace?
—Product(s) new to the competitor?
—Extensions of the competitor's current product line(s)?
—Enhancements of existing products?
How are the products different from and superior to:
—Their nearest look-alike products?
—Their substitute products?
What is the timeline associated with their evolution?
How sustainable will be the product advantages?
—How easy or difficult will it be for competitors to replicate the products?
—How long will it take competitors to do so?

TABLE 13.10   Evaluating Technology along the Activity/Value Chain

Criteria	Key Dimensions	Indicators
Technology goals	Across the activity/value chain Program goals Project goals	Investments Commitments Statements
Technology newness	New to world Internally developed Adapted from others	Thrust of technology programs and projects
Technology risks	Knowledge development Knowledge use Knowledge obsolescence	Knowledge evolution Knowledge integration into the organization

Technology sources	Suppliers of knowledge,
	   materials, equipment, etc.
		Individual suppliers
		Relationships with the
		   organization

Investments	Total amount in dollars Commitment to programs Growth rate of investment	Dollars spent Allocations to programs and projects

Personnel	Knowledge
	Skills and capabilities
	Training/backgrounds of
	   individuals
		Number of individuals
		Types of individuals
		Hiring and
		   remuneration
		   practices

External linkages	Alliances Networks	Alliance partners Nature of alliances Network membership
Individual activities	Impact on tasks Cross-task linkages	Volumes/throughputs Product quality Cycle times Costs
Across activities	Linkage across activities	Cycle times Parallel processes Costs
Products	Product evolution Product enhancement	Product development
Posture	Product line width Features, functionality, etc.	Product lines/types Product attributes Product performances, etc.
Goals	Market penetration Customer satisfaction, etc.	Market results statements

TABLE 13.10 *(Continued)*

Criteria	Key Dimensions	Indicators
Sustainability of advantages	Technology elements: Newness, risks, etc.	Competitors' projected marketplace strategies
	Marketplace elements: Product superiority, service, etc.	Customer responses
Historic outcomes	Past record in developing and leveraging technology	Technology developments
		Impact on activities
		Impact on marketplace strategy

Historic Outcomes Finally, it is often insightful to develop a profile of the competitor's historic track record in successful research and development. It reveals the competitor's ability to bring different types of research to fruition. The pharmaceutical competitor had a long and illustrious track record in being first to market with new products and in penetrating the market with these products.

Organization Technology

A guided analysis of organization technology also separates evaluation of technology from its implications for the competitor's marketplace strategy and microlevel components. Key dimensions, related indicators, and data sources, also vary along each step in a guided assessment (see Table 13.10). The analysis is illustrated in the case of the consumer food competitor discussed earlier.

Technology Programs A useful point of departure is to review (and perhaps redefine) the programs noted in identifying the competitor's technologies. Sometimes connections among programs that were initially missed, such as the amount of funding committed to them, or their external sources, become evident. Also, for major programs it may be appropriate to further refine the distinctions between specific projects.

Technology Goals Goals provide a sense of the direction the competitor wants to pursue with its technology programs. At the level of the entire activity/value chain, a competitor might aim toward the broad technology goal directions noted at the beginning of this section: the development of new technology, extending existing technology, or reinforcing existing technology. Programs and projects have more specific goals associated with them such as achieving a specific technology state by a specific time (e.g., linking all key corporate customers through information technologies).

The consumer food competitor's aggregate goal was clear: to install new technologies and to upgrade existing technologies so it would have at least parity with its major competitors in every technology domain.

Technology Newness Technology programs and projects may be developed by the competitor itself, be extensions or adaptations of technologies developed by others, or simply involve the execution of well-disseminated technologies. Each of these three types of technology generates significant improvements in key activities and processes, and thus potentially competitor-based and customer advantage.

None of the technologies of the consumer food competitor were new to the world; they involved adaptations and extensions of others' technologies, and in some cases they involved the execution of widely available technologies.

Technology Risks Risks are always associated with developing organization technologies, or adapting, enhancing, and using technologies provided by others, or retaining existing technologies. Different types of risks are associated with different technologies. The following are common risks: the underlying knowledge pertaining to a specific technology becomes outdated; the firm is not able to develop the knowledge it has identified as necessary; even if the knowledge is developed, the firm is not able to fully use or exploit it in its activities (or tasks within activities).

Distinct technology risks were evident for the consumer food competitor. Unless it moved more quickly than was so far apparent to update some of its manufacturing plant technology, the risk of becoming a follower in manufacturing technology was high. Its commitment to further upgrading its packaging technology was highly dependent on its alliance with the developer of the technology. In its efforts to become a "first mover" in its business segment with this new technology, the competitor might have to bear many of the debugging difficulties often associated with the adoption of a new technology.

Technology Sources The risks associated with internal technology development make it particularly important to assess the competitor's technology assets and capabilities. Many organizational difficulties are also associated with assimilating and applying externally acquired technologies.

The consumer food competitor was not developing any major or significant technology itself. However, it was heavily committed to extending and adapting many technologies it acquired from external sources. It was also working with external sources to develop specific technologies. Of particular importance were its efforts to work closely with a computer services organization to design and install an integrated information system to link all data, materials, and product flows.

Investments As in the product technology chain, current and projected commitments of capital to specific programs and projects often give rise to a strong signal of the competitor's commitment to technology development and change.

The consumer food competitor was devoting extensive cash commitments to a number of the technology programs previously noted.

People The number, experience, knowledge, and background of the competitor's personnel involved in specific programs or projects are an indicator of the likely success of technology programs. However, there is often significant variation across programs and projects.

The consumer product firm did not have any prior experience in the new form of airtight packaging technology that it was acquiring from an outside vendor. The vendor reported some difficulties the competitor was experiencing in getting up to speed with the new technology and raised some doubts as to whether the competitor would be able to fully utilize the technology without extensive further assistance.

External Linkages Relationships with external entities are important irrespective of whether the competitor is developing new technology or extending and adapting installed technologies. Linkages with customers, vendors, and technology experts are critical not just to technology development and enhancement but to selecting those technologies that will generate the greatest organization effects and marketplace advantage.

External relationships were playing a major role in the consumer food competitor's efforts to upgrade almost all the technologies identified in Table 13.2. Vendors were active in the installation and upgrading of several technologies.

Effects on Activities The fundamental purpose of using technology is to enhance each activity or process. Without attention to these consequences, investments in technology programs and projects often take on a life of their own with the attainment of technology goals displacing attention to their broader organizational consequences.

Specific effects were already evident in the case of the consumer food competitor. Manufacturing could now handle a greater volume of throughput; product quality appeared to be more consistent; certain cost efficiencies were also likely; and less wastage was probably occurring. Information technology was leading to faster cycles in both acquiring supplies and delivering products to customers.

Effects on Marketplace Strategy Organization technology directly affects each element of marketplace strategy: products, posture, and goals. The adroit use of many technologies enabled the consumer food competitor to continually upgrade and reinforce its marketplace strategy. The enhancements in storage, packaging, materials handling, and manufacturing process technologies all contributed to the availability of a larger volume of product—thus, among other things, the competitor could seek new customer segments. Moreover, the effect of individual technologies could be traced to each dimension of posture. For example, the airtight packaging technologies enhanced functionality: the product would last longer and taste better. Information technologies facilitated a greater variety of services to customers and faster delivery of some services through directly connecting customers' channel locations with the firm's service locations. Advancement in some print technologies allowed the competitor to develop a new type of print advertising—thus probably enhancing the competitor's image.

Sustainability of Advantages The organizational capabilities and marketplace advantages, sourced in part, in a competitor's use of organization technologies are often not sustainable. Many of the elements discussed— technology newness, risks, sources, investments, people, external linkages— contribute to assessing whether a competitor is able to sustain its technology direction and thus its competitor- and customer-based advantages. Comparison with current and potential competitors is the other key ingredient in this analysis.

The overall assessment for the consumer food competitor was that it did not currently possess significant customer-based advantage over its two or three major look-alike competitors. This assessment was based on customer survey responses and judgments of the management team in comparing their respective offerings. Yet the assessment was also made that if the competitor maintained its momentum in investing in the array of technologies noted earlier, it could achieve parity within a year or two. It might then be in a position to gain customer-based advantage because of the experience gained in acquiring, extending, and adapting technologies.

State of Technology Assets

The importance of assessing the stock and flow of a competitor's technology assets is evident in the preceding discussion.[13] The stock of these assets undergirds or undermines the attainment of technology goals. The flow of technology assets constitutes indicators of technology direction. The assessment criteria detailed in Chapter 11 are applicable. The video production firm discussed earlier is used as an example.

Availability The video competitor possessed little slack in its physical and human assets—they were stretched to the limit. But it appeared to possess significant slack in its perceptual and political assets: it did not seem to be adequately leveraging its highly positive corporate and brand names or its solid relationships with the channels and vendors. However, it did appear to be leveraging in multiple ways its stocks of knowledge about entities and processes.

Specificity Many of the video competitor's knowledge stocks about processes had little if any specificity: they were applicable to all products and customers. Yet, a large portion of its knowledge stocks about other entities such as customer groups and vendors were highly specific. Because of the singular needs and requirements of specific corporate customers, offering the same video "solution" to every customer would have been extremely foolhardy.

Sustainability Although positive flows of some key assets were evident, indicating ready external availability, each of the video manufacturer's asset categories presents sustainability concerns. Knowledge about entities and processes must be continually upgraded and replaced. As customers and channels specialize with regard to solutions, it becomes increasingly important for the competitor to anticipate future customer needs. Physical assets such as equipment require extensive cash investment; a decline in margins and profits could jeopardize its current quality. Sustained channel and customer perceptions require that the firm continue to provide innovative solutions.

Replicability As noted in the discussion of both the product technology chain and the activity/value chain, the replicability of technology assets by competitors greatly influences the sustainability of competitor-based and customer-based advantage. The most difficult assets to replicate in the case of the video production competitor might be its process-based knowledge and the intimacy of its relationships with vendors and its venture capital support group.

Technology Capabilities and Competencies

Analysts assess technology capabilities and competencies using the criteria noted in the previous chapter: dynamism, domain breadth, robustness, imitability, and augmentability. Consider, for example, the video competitor's core technology capability: the ability to custom-tailor its videos for each customer across its distinct customer categories. It is *dynamic:* the competitor is investing to continually enhance it. Its (technology) domain is broad: a variety of technologies contribute to the ability to customize customer solutions. It is also *robust:* it is applicable to all current products and customers, and it is highly likely that it could be leveraged to attract, win, and retain new categories of customers. It is *imitable* but it would not be easy to do so. A competitor would not only have to develop many different types of technology capabilities but it would also have to fashion an organization infrastructure and culture to support and sustain the capability: the latter thus greatly contribute to the imitation difficulties. Finally, the capability is probably considerably *augmentable:* the competitor has already committed a number of investments and related personnel developments to augmenting it.

Comparison with Focal Firm

The product technology chain, activity/value chain, assets, capabilities and competencies, and projected technology change, furnish a basis for comparison between one or more competitors and the focal firm. An effective way to generate self-learning is to assess in which product domains and/or technological programs the focal firm leads or lags a specific competitor. Such assessments provide insight into both consequences for the competitor and implications for the focal firm.

In the pharmaceutical example, comparison with the focal firm quickly pointed up some research domains in which the competitor was committing extensive assets, one or two programs in which the competitor was much further advanced, and two programs in which the focal firm was somewhat further advanced. The potential product development results were dramatic for both firms: in common research domains, one firm could easily get a product to the market as much as five years ahead of the other; and each could potentially develop products for which the other would not possess a rival offering.

In the consumer food example, the focal firm discovered that the competitor was outmaneuvering and outperforming it in the use of technology in almost every activity. The competitor had transformed all facets of its sales and service through the use of information, equipment, and repair technologies resulting in extensive customer advantages such as quicker response times to customer inquiries and complaints, greater flexibility for retail outlets to serve end-customers, and much greater ease of use in equipment.

In the video production example, even a preliminary comparison compelled the focal firm to recognize grave deficiencies in both its assets and its capabilities. It did not possess anything comparable to the competitor's knowledge base pertaining to customers or production processes. Although it had historically been proud of its ability to develop and deliver customer-specific solutions, the focal firm was vastly inferior in terms of the competitor's overarching capability: the ability to customize solutions.

Comparison with Multiple Competitors

Comparison with selected look-alike and functional substitute competitors generates an overall assessment of the extent to which an organization currently or potentially leads or lags in specific technology domains. Some *guiding* questions are set out in Table 13.11.

Current Technology Leadership Indicators relevant to leadership are highly dependent on the technology program. In general terms, leadership is assessed in terms of indicators such as stock and flow of technology assets, superiority of technology capabilities and competencies, and the range and quality of technology outputs—products, processes, and materials. Technology leaders are also indicated by the efforts of others to play catch-up. Technology leaders set the pace and direction of change in the specific technology domain.

Future Technology Leadership Because current technology (and marketplace) leaders so often fall behind their rivals, future technology leadership must be separated from current leadership. An assessment of future technology leadership requires a direct comparison of the timelines, progress, and likely outcomes of the product and organization technology programs between a competitor and its rivals as well as with the focal firm. The criteria, dimensions, and indicators noted in Tables 13.6 and 13.7 are also used as a basis for comparison across rivals.

Current Parity A competitor may be neither a distinct leader nor a follower in many technology domains. It has modest leadership in one or a few technology (or product) areas and lags somewhat in others. It is important to assess whether such competitors are able to sustain or enhance their current parity. This raises issues pertaining to the stock and flow of their technology assets (such as those raised about the consumer food competitor) and the applicability of their technology capabilities or competencies (such as those raised about the video production competitor).

Persistent Follower Some competitors are a persistent follower in particular technologies or programs. It is instructive to assess what such a

TABLE 13.11   Comparisons to Competitors

Current technology research	In which products does the competitor now have technology leadership?
	In which technology domains is the competitor setting the pace and direction?
	In which technology assets does the competitor have leadership?
	What distinct technology competencies has the competitor developed?
	What is the base of its superiority?
Future technology leadership	Will the competitor's research and development generate product leadership at some other date?
	What would the competitor have to do to achieve this leadership?
	What are the signals that the competitor will be ahead of specific rivals?
Current parity	In what stages of the product technology chain does the competitor have approximate parity with the focal firm or other specific rivals?
	In what activities in the activity/value chain does the competitor have approximate parity with the focal firm of other specific rivals?
	Are there signals that the competitor can move from parity to possible leadership (against the focal firm or other specific rivals) in one or more technology domains?
Persistent follower	In which stages of the product technology chain does the competitor lag?
	In which activities of the activity/value chain does the competitor lag?
	What would the competitor have to do to gain parity in one or more technology domains?
	Are there signals that the competitor is trying to move out of its followship status?
Laggard	How far behind is the competitor in specific technology domains?
	What would the competitor have to do to relieve its laggard status in each major technology domain?
	What are its most viable options?

competitor would have to do (and why it would do so) to gain parity or superiority vis-à-vis specific rivals: it provides a benchmark against which the
competitor's assets, and capabilities and competencies, are evaluated.

Laggard   Laggards are hopelessly behind one or more rivals in most or all
technology domains. Their chances of attaining parity, much less leadership,
in important technologies are slim.

Signals of Marketplace Change

Competitors' technology change is often a source of signals of change in all the arenas noted in Chapter 1—customers, channels, factors, institutions, and geography. The signals may be both strong and weak; they may indicate continuous or discontinuous change; the change may be short or long-lagged; and, many signals may be high-impact for the focal firm. The breadth of the change potentially signaled is briefly illustrated.

Competitors' product technology change gives rise to both strong and weak signals about future product change. A competitor's potential products are often the source of a strong signal of discontinuity in product evolution causing other competitors to respond in their product development and facilitating the entry of new competitors. Relatedly, projections of the likely posture of rivals (and thus, competitive dynamics among rivals) might look considerably different from prevailing modes of competition. Thus, a scenario of the competitive (product) arena at some future point could suggest a fundamentally different industry structure and definition.

Technology change also often indicates new configurations of competitors—alliances, relationships, and networks. A competitor's technological breakthrough causes other rivals to enter into alliances or even to begin developing a network to play catch-up or to create the technological capacity to leapfrog the breakthrough. Hence, a major technology change is sometimes an early, though weak, signal of a reconfiguring of the players.

Competitors' technology change often indicates significant channel, customer, and vendor (factor) change. A single competitor's technology-based linkup with one or more channels initially may be a weak signal of the distribution channels of the "future." New or emergent competitors are often the source of such signals. They indicate changing customer needs, buying behaviors, and preferences. As illustrated in the pharmaceutical case, a competitors' technology change resulting in new products or solutions often creates new customer needs.

Projecting Technology Thrust and Competencies

Projections of competitors' future technology direction are embedded in each of the assessment steps previously discussed. However, it is always useful to project change in a competitor's overall technology direction (as opposed to analyzing the current state of technology) as well as in its technology assets, and capabilities and competencies.

The analysis discussed provides the necessary technology (and other) signals of likely change in the key technology domains. Projecting future technology change requires that analysts identify, interpret, and assess such signals. Analysis of the video production competitor and the food competitor generated many signals pertaining to investments in assets, commitments to enhance capabilities and competencies, and joint work with external entities such as vendors.

It is frequently possible to develop technology-specific scenarios around a competitor's likely future technology direction. Scenarios involve more complex projections based on judgments of what the analysts consider might happen or could be made to happen by the competitor. These scenarios identify indicators that analysts in turn monitor. A scenario asserting that the video production firm would continue to invest in technology, ultimately becoming the unquestioned technology leader in its business, might suggest that investments in new state-of-the-art technologies and linkages to leading vendors would need to be carefully monitored.

Competitor Consequences

Analysts summarize and integrate competitor consequences with regard to technology management, marketplace strategy, and other microlevel components. These consequences are integrally related. They also help identify focal firm implications.

Assessment of a competitor's technology always identifies key technology issues confronting the competitor, including technology constraints and vulnerabilities. These in turn indicate technology assets that need to be acquired or developed, technology capabilities and competencies that need to be enhanced and augmented, as well as assets, capabilities, and competencies that are not being adequately leveraged.

The extent and importance of marketplace strategy consequences were illustrated as part of each assessment step. Frequently, as illustrated with the consumer food and the video production competitors, how a competitor manages its product and organization technologies has direct consequences for product range, customer reach, each mode of competition, and marketplace goals. Moreover, technology often underlies a competitor's ability to generate and sustain some degree of customer-based advantage.

Finally, analysts must assess the consequences of the state of a competitor's technology for each microlevel component. The pharmaceutical competitor would have to determine how it could best leverage its existing alliances and networks to speed up its projected research and then take its new product to market. For the consumer food competitor, success in technology program execution most likely would require reconsideration of historic assumptions about marketplace success and what it takes to win.

Focal Firm Implications

Implications for the focal firm are also assessed with regard to technology management, marketplace strategy, and microlevel components. These implications in most instances lead to significant issues and questions about the firm's capacity to win in both technology and the marketplace.

As illustrated in comparing a competitor's technology with the focal firm and with multiple rivals, the focal firm assesses whether and how it is outmaneuvering and outperforming specific rivals in terms of technology along each stage and activity in the product and activity/value chains respectively. Assessment of its current and potential technology leadership position in terms of the stock and flow of key technology assets and robust technology capabilities, as well as the range and quality of the outputs of technology—products, processes, and materials—has identified critical technology issues for many firms. The consumer food firm discussed in this chapter, discovered that its principal competitor was outperforming it with the use of technology in every activity. It thus had to develop a new technology strategy to gain at least technology parity with the competitor in many activities.

Assessment of the focal firm's current and potential technology assets, and capabilities and competencies, compared with current and emerging competitors often has critical implications for its current and potential marketplace strategies. These assessments sometimes save a firm from pursuing doomed strategy alternatives and point it in the direction of strategy alternatives more likely to win. For example, the focal pharmaceutical firm chose to reduce its investment in a research domain in which the competitor was likely to make a product breakthrough. The video firm decided to concentrate on a product sector in which it could focus its technology assets and capabilities, rather than try to compete against all competitors in all product sectors. The consumer food firm recognized that every strategy alternative would be jeopardized unless it quickly developed a technology strategy to at least play catch-up with its dominant rival.

Implications for other microlevel components stem in large measure from the assessments pertaining to technology management and marketplace strategy. Technology constraints, deficiencies, and vulnerabilities often quickly suggest the need for specific types of alliances and relationships, and sometimes even point to particular partners.

A Note on Open-Ended Inquiry

An open-ended orientation is often essential to the execution of each guided analysis framework in this chapter. Analysts need to continually challenge their own understanding of technology: which technologies are important to the future of their business; which organizations might develop and promote them; how they are likely to evolve; and what their implications might be for the focal organization. Many of the key technology analysis challenges—for example, determining what technology entails, defining the scope of the analysis, identifying key stages and phases in a product technology chain, delineating technology assets, identifying linkages between technology and organization capabilities, and assessing competitor consequences and focal firm implications—require analysts to ask questions from multiple perspectives, to seek inputs from multiple data sources within and external to the focal firm, and to develop alternative logics that suggest different consequences and implications. Without an open-ended orientation, decision makers and technology analysts are more likely to view technology solely from the historic or dominant perspective of their own organization.

Errors in the Identification and Assessment of Competitors' Technology

Many of the learning errors noted in previous chapters also apply to technology analysis. This section highlights some errors that critically affect the outputs of such analysis.

A reluctance to grapple with the definition and meaning of technology often results in overly narrow specification of what needs to be learned about competitors' technology. By default, analysts address only those individual technologies, or facets of them, deemed important by their own organizations.

A partial outgrowth of the preceding error is that analysts sometimes zero in on one or two technology programs before they identify and preliminarily assess the competitor's range of programs. As a consequence, the scope and potential of competitors' technologies is often gravely understated.

Product technology is often analyzed in isolation; it is not connected to the competitor's current or future marketplace strategy. Hence, the benefits to the competitor are not fully understood, and signals of marketplace change are missed.

Also, technology is not directly linked to change in microlevel components. Relating technology to a specific activity/value chain and to capabilities or competencies, as illustrated throughout this chapter, illuminates the contribution of technology to what the competitor does and how it is accomplished.

Analysts often shy away from projections of competitors' product or organization technologies. Thus, relevant anticipated indicators are not identified, and potential competitor consequences and focal firm implications of likely technology directions are missed.

A final error worth noting is the unwillingness of decision makers and analysts to adopt multiple perspectives in technology analysis. Hence, the range of questions asked and the types of analysis conducted are greatly circumscribed.

Summary

Technology is intimately linked to the analysis of each framework component. Thus, analysts must avoid the temptation to conduct isolated technology analysis. The guided frameworks in this chapter facilitate tight connections to particular components—activity/ value chain, assets, and capabilities and competencies. However, an open-ended orientation reminds analysts to continually question prevailing wisdom about technology, to analyze technology from multiple perspectives, and to emphasize questions rather than quick answers.

CHAPTER 14

Organizational Infrastructure

SUSTAINED WINNING IS NEVER ACCIDENTAL OR RANDOM. IT OCCURS WHEN AN organization is better prepared to outwit, outmaneuver, and outperform its rivals: it is willing to change and adapt to current and anticipated marketplace conditions. But what constitutes an organization? For purposes of understanding competitors, an organization is usefully segmented into two related components: infrastructure and culture. How well a competitor manages its infrastructure and culture strongly influences the extent to which it wins (or does not do so). Infrastructure is addressed in this chapter and culture in the next.

This chapter begins by delineating the elements of a competitor's infrastructure and their key attributes. Drawing on two extensive cases, the body of the chapter details analysis issues in the derivation and use of signals. It especially emphasizes the temporal nature of signal analysis. The final section describes a number of common errors in signal analysis.

Understanding Organizational Infrastructure

Elements of Infrastructure

An organization's infrastructure consists of four elements. Although they are highly interrelated, each element represents a distinct facet of an organization.

Structure Structure consists of an organization's units and the interrelationships among them. In a multibusiness enterprise such as Emerson Electric, General Electric, Toshiba, or Mercedes-Benz, the units include the corporate headquarters, business sectors, and divisions or business units. Within any business unit or stand-alone business, structure typically revolves around a hierarchy of reporting relationships involving senior line management, functional units (such as manufacturing, marketing, finance, and sales), or other pockets of expertise (such as strategic planning, business development, or business intelligence generation).

Systems Any organization's structure, however innovative its design, is merely a shell. Systems are required to move information through the structure, oversee and control the flow of resources, and reward and motivate organizational members. Information, control, and reward systems provide the grease that makes the structure work.

People Structure and systems do not have purpose, energy, or focus without people who learn, make decisions, and take action.[1] The recruitment (or loss) of even a few key personnel can have an uplifting (or devastating) effect on an enterprise.

Decision-Making Processes Structures, systems, and people always influence (and are influenced by) how organizational members come together to make decisions. Decision-making processes may be largely formal, hierarchial, and bureaucratic as is sometimes evident in strategic planning systems or in the review and assessment procedures evident in many large corporate enterprises. In some organizations, authoritarian routines dominate: decisions are made by one person or by a small group of individuals, and all others fall in line to execute them.

Attributes of Infrastructure

Because organizations continually try to anticipate, cope with, and leverage change in and around the marketplace, infrastructure is never likely to remain stagnant for long. Despite such change, however, three attributes of infrastructure critically affect an organization's capacity to win: (1) integration, (2) alignment, and (3) external focus.

Integration The subelements or dimensions *within* each infrastructure element need to be integrated. Multiple conflicts and inconsistencies often characterize how organizations are structured, how systems are designed, which individuals are hired and promoted, and how decisions get made.

Many multibusiness enterprises have found that a rigid corporate structure inhibits related businesses from working with each other. The difficulties involved in working with other business sectors or business units render it almost impossible to pool resources and to develop a cooperative strategy. Rather than being mutually reinforcing, individual systems often are at loggerheads with each other. Incentive systems that promote commitment to long-run investments often run counter to control and financial systems that are geared to enhancing short-run performance goals.

Alignment The infrastructure elements also must be aligned with each other. Systems are sometimes incongruent with the way organizations would like to make decisions. To cite merely one example, information systems often do not provide data and information in a timely fashion. Some firms maintain relatively small business or operating units to promote risk-taking behavior and then inhibit such behavior through the imposition of reward and financial control systems that severely penalize senior personnel if they do not reach prescribed financial goals or if decisions do not lead to promised results.

External Focus The elements of infrastructure, individually and collectively, ultimately need to be focused on winning in the marketplace. All too often, the focus predominantly is on internal issues, decisions, and concerns. Systems and decision-making processes are sometimes preoccupied with attaining internal goals such as achieving manufacturing standards, adhering to budget timelines, or executing strategic planning routines.

Marketplace Strategy: The Importance of Infrastructure

When an infrastructure is integrated, aligned, and externally focused, it serves to direct, support, and reinforce an organization's efforts to win in the marketplace. Structure, systems, and decision processes must be designed to coordinate and guide resources toward the detection and pursuit of marketplace opportunities. This is especially manifest in the development of winning products. Some successful corporations such as Emerson Electric and Thermo Electron endeavor to keep business units relatively small so that the focus is on entrepreneurial activity. Getting people with knowledge, experience, and leadership skills that are appropriate to current and potential marketplace conditions is a never-ending pursuit for all organizations. If information, remuneration, and control systems are not integrated, they often hobble managers who might otherwise create innovative marketplace postures.

Linkage to Microlevel Components

Infrastructure change assumes importance in part because it is often the result or partial cause of change in other microlevel components. Change in an activity/value chain such as greater internal connectedness[2] often requires change in systems and decision-making processes. Change in alliances and networks often leads to a need for structure and personnel change. New alliances such as joint ventures sometimes create a new organization unit. Efforts to reallocate assets, enhance capabilities, or leverage technology usually give rise to change in structure, systems, and personnel.

Indicators of Infrastructure Change

Direct indicators are common in the case of structure, systems, people, and decision-making processes. Competitors often make highly visible announcements about structure and people, indicating structure changes and specific characteristics of the personnel being hired, promoted, or terminated. Sometimes specific attributes of systems and decision making processes are also discussed in public.

Infrastructure Change as Signals

Patterns of infrastructure change often generate strong and high-impact signals of change in marketplace strategy and in specific microlevel components. Changes over time in structure, systems, personnel, and decision-making processes may collectively signal intent to change marketplace goals such as the commitment to win in a particular product-customer segment or to change how the competitor competes in the marketplace. A pattern in a sequence of infrastructure changes over time generates the data and logic to allow the derivation of strong inferences, as is evident in the cases discussed later in this chapter.

However, individual infrastructure changes often give rise to alerting signals that in turn direct analysts' attention to seek confirming or refuting signals. Infrastructure changes such as the establishment of a new division, the hiring of new personnel, the creation of new incentive systems, or modification of decision-making processes, cause analysts to draw initial inferences about specific past, current, and future competitor change.

Often, as evidenced in prior chapters, infrastructure change serves as confirming or refuting signals of change in marketplace strategy or other microlevel components. Change in structure, systems, personnel, and decision-making processes follows actual or projected change in marketplace scope, posture, or goals, or change in microlevel components such as

activity/value chain, assumptions, assets, and capabilities. Once infrastructure change is detected, it allows inferences (signals) to be drawn that confirm or refute prior inferences.

Identifying and Assessing Infrastructure Change

Because this section emphasizes the role and importance of drawing inferences, and then competitor consequences and focal firm implications, it
combines identification and assessment. Two distinct cases are used for
illustration.

Case 1: A Competitor Announces a New President

Few infrastructure changes receive so much publicity as the appointment of
new senior executives. They are viewed as the harbingers of change not just
in other infrastructure elements—structure, systems and decision-making
processes—but in shifts in marketplace strategy and other microlevel components. Witness the scrutiny accorded in the past year or two to senior executive changes in such firms as Apple, Kodak, Honda, AT&T, Cable and
Wireless, Disney, and CBS.

Context The case discussed here involves two capital equipment suppliers. The focal firm, IndComp, was the marketplace leader in terms of market
share, product innovation, and customer relationships. The competitor,
CompDiv, a division of a large corporate enterprise, was its principal rival in
most geographic regions in North America for this particular product line.
CompDiv had suffered market share erosion for the previous five years. It
had made relatively little change in its historic product line during that time.
Not surprisingly, though it was still profitable, the division's financial performance had deteriorated considerably, especially in the prior two years.

Anticipated Indicators The focal firm, IndComp,[3] expected CompDiv, in
part compelled by the expectations of its corporate parent, to take remedial
action. As part of its ongoing monitoring of competitors, IndComp listed a
number of anticipated indicators pertaining to CompDiv's expected actions:

- A precipitous decline in marketplace and/or financial performance.
- Comments by executives from the corporate parent about the need to
  improve the division's performance.
- The (forced) retirement of one or more of the current senior management team.

- The announcement of an alliance intended to upgrade the product line.
- A licensing agreement to allow it to sell the products of another rival, perhaps a foreign enterprise.
- The appointment of new executives.

In monitoring for the emergence of each anticipated indicator, IndComp sought to ensure that both the *detection lag*[4] and the *inference lag* were as short as possible. It wished to capture these indicators as soon as they became available. Also, once one or more anticipated and subsequent indicators were detected, analysts would begin immediately to draw some tentative inferences about both competitor consequences and focal firm implications. These inferences would then lead to and guide further data collection and indicator detection.

Alerting Indicator IndComp was somewhat surprised by the alerting indicator that eventually transpired. Rather than an announcement of impending retirements or statements by the corporate parent that the division's performance had to be turned around, the corporate parent issued a one-page press release announcing the appointment of a new division president. A daily newspaper and the industry's trade publications reported key items from the release. The new president was a senior marketing executive with another large corporation known for its well-honed management systems. His expertise was in new product development and product innovation. In the trade press, he was described by an executive in another firm as "abrasive, arrogant, and impetuous." It was his first presidency.

Alerting Inference The alerting inference was quite straightforward: the division was now *publicly* committing itself to turning around its recent poor marketplace and financial performance.

However, the initial announcement, as reported in the daily newspaper and industry publications, contained a number of related indicators, each of which allowed analysts to draw signals about the potential scope and direction of the changes that might be wrought by the new president (see Table 14.1). It is the pattern across these signals that generates insight, not any single inference by itself.

Preliminary Consequences and Implications When considered in *context,* even somewhat vague and fuzzy indicators can lead to early and high-impact signals. The analysis team began to use these signals to identify preliminary competitor consequences and focal firm implications. For example, since the new president had been employed for a number of years by a corporation

TABLE 14.1   A Personnel Change: Announcement of the Hiring of a New President

Data/Indicators	Signals	Implications/Actions
MAY 15:		
Announcements in a national newspaper that the division had hired a new president. He would assume the position on October 1	Division is now committed to turning around its recent poor performance	Monitor actions taken by the division before the new president assumes his position
		Consider what actions he might take
His previous firm is known for its formal management systems	He would bring a more disciplined style of management to the division	Change is possible in responses by the division to the firm's own decisions
He has a reputation for marketing expertise and involvement in new product development	He would add marketing resources, build a coherent marketing approach, and emphasize product development and line extensions	Analysts need to detail likely new marketing initiatives and programs by the division as an input to the firm's own marketing decisions
He was described as abrasive, arrogant and impetuous; this is his first division presidency	He would make changes, create "waves" within the division and do so quickly	The firm would have to take the new president seriously—he would make changes
JUNE 6:		
The CEO of the division's parent announces that the new president is being hired to turn around the division's marketplace and financial performance	Corporation was willing to make the necessary commitments to win	Need to articulate what the division's likely strategies might be
	New president would have to take quick actions	Identify possible actions to preempt specific strategies
JULY:		
Two senior vice-presidents announce that they are resigning to seek other business opportunities	New president now has more opportunity to reorganize the top management team; thus, action is even more likely	If early action is highly likely, need to develop scenarios that play out both the division's possible actions and the firm's own actions
EARLY AUGUST:		
Statement by the new president in a trade publication that little product innovation was apparent in the recent history of the industry	He would reorient the division to the development of new products	If the division were to introduce new products, what should be the firm's actions in the short run and in the long run
	He might be willing to enter into alliances or make other major strategic moves	

renowned for its formal management and executive education systems, the analysis team hypothesized that he would seek greater infrastructure integration, alignment, and external focus. Some managers then in the division would likely find it difficult to adapt to a new management philosophy and approach. One implication for IndComp was that CompDiv might react very differently in the future to its marketplace initiatives such as extending a product line, offering price breaks to a particular region, or entering new distribution channels.

Another *early indicator* considered was the president's alleged marketing expertise, and particularly, his interest and involvement in new product development. The inference drawn by the analysis team was that he would commit more resources to all facets of marketing and quickly commit the organization to develop new products or, at a minimum, extend existing product lines. This signal had high-impact implications for IndComp: If CompDiv reinvigorated its product line over the next three years, it had no choice but to begin to immediately identify and assess what actions it should take. It was in the strategic interests of IndComp to take action before CompDiv had turned itself around; otherwise it would have conceded the strategic upper hand to CompDiv.

New Anticipated Indicators The analyst team in IndComp within a few days of deriving the preceding alerting signals asked itself what set of anticipated indicators might now be expected. The specific question they asked was: Which indicators should we now seek that would confirm CompDiv's intent to change its marketplace strategy and supporting microlevel components? IndComp wished to assess whether the appointment of the new president was merely a cosmetic change or an indicator of real strategic and operational change. Again, they identified a tentative list of indicators that might emerge *before* the new president took office:

- Statements by corporate officers, the new president, and others within IndComp.
- Statements by third parties such as key customers, channels, and industry consultants.
- Announcement of changes in personnel.
- Marketing actions by CompDiv such as changes in sales, promotion, and other programs.
- Changes in infrastructure—structure, systems, and decision-making processes.
- Changes in mode and content of interactions with channels and end-customers.

Confirming Signals Within a month, a significant confirming signal was derived. The CEO of CompDiv's parent corporation said at a meeting with security analysts that the new president was "being brought on board to turn around the division's poor performance." He further stated that very clear goals had been established for the new president. The analysis team drew the inference that the new president would have to take quick action; he did not have two or more years to analyze the situation and then conclude what he should do. An interesting consequence for CompDiv was now apparent: Would its historic "laid-back" culture facilitate commitment to quick actions? The implication derived for IndComp was that it would have to quickly articulate and develop what changes might be necessary to its current and planned marketplace strategy, given different actions that the new president might initiate.

A short time later, another confirming signal emerged from an indicator that had been anticipated. Within a few days of each other, the trade press reported that two senior executives, both of whom would have been direct reports to the new president, had announced their retirement from the CompDiv "for personal reasons" and "to pursue other business opportunities." The analysis team interpreted these resignations as an opportunity for the new president to move even more quickly than might otherwise be expected to (among other things) reorganize the top management team, including hiring new executives. It could also be an opportunity for him to "send strong messages" to the organization that many facets of its culture would have to be changed and that everyone in the organization would have to contribute to changing the culture and to accepting the necessary changes.

One implication of the stream of confirming signals for IndComp began to crystallize for the analysis team. It was necessary to develop a set of scenarios that would address the interactions of what CompDiv might do and how it might react to what IndComp might do. These scenarios would then serve as an input to assessing what actions IndComp should take and when.

Approximately a month before he was to assume his position, the president designate, as reported in one of the trade publications, said that he was shocked at how little product development had occurred in the industry within the past 10 years. The analysis team inferred that he would not only reorient the division to the development of new products, but that to introduce some new products within a 2-year period, given the personnel, technology resources and culture of the CompDiv, he would have to enter into several alliances.

Competitor Consequences A number of *consequences* for CompDiv were immediately considered: Who would be the potential alliance partners?

What types of alliances might be possible with each type of alliance part-ner? Could the division manage alliance relationships?[5]

Implications and Actions A number of related *implications* were derived for IndComp. Should it also not consider alliances as a means of rapidly ex-tending and enhancing its own product development efforts? If an obvious alliance partner emerged for CompDiv, or any other competitor, should it think about preempting its rivals by aligning with that partner? Within the scenarios that were being developed, what actions were suggested that might preempt the competitor's intent to enter into alliances?[6]

Consideration of these implications also caused discussion within Ind-Comp as to whether its marketplace goals were sufficiently *stretching*[7] the organization. A strong argument was made that its product development and introduction goals were surprisingly easy to accomplish. IndComp was con-tent with being a market share leader as opposed to being the organization recognized for its innovative technologies, the source of new leading ideas in the industry, and the place where the best talent in the industry should work. Thus, one implication that could not be avoided was the need to de-velop and adopt a more demanding set of marketplace and related goals.

The intent of assessment, as noted in Chapter 2, is to *influence decisions.* The projections of what the competitor might do within each scenario—in effect, *signals of potential marketplace change*—led the analysis team to conclude that a number of distinct action plans were open to the new presi-dent of CompDiv. The analysis team was particularly worried that some of these actions could be detrimental both to IndComp and to the industry in general. For example, the new president might be tempted to drop prices to gain a quick upturn in market share and to develop some leverage with cus-tomers. A price war would likely be the result of a significant price reduction by CompDiv, especially if one or two other competitors decided to reduce prices still further. The new division president also might be tempted to make announcements of new products or new product development activi-ties to slow down customers' purchases from rivals, including IndComp.

IndComp's assessment of the options open to the new president and his obvious need to do something quickly, led it to take some *actions before* he assumed his new position. First, a senior executive granted an interview to a trade publication in which he outlined IndComp's understanding of the current industry, its immediate future, and the firm's likely responses to marketplace moves that any new entrant might make or that might be made by the new management team in any existing competitors. The intent was to convey in a thinly disguised manner to CompDiv's new president that Ind-Comp would take strong retaliatory actions in response to any effort by "buy market share."

Second, senior executives visited key customer accounts. The intent was to strengthen IndComp's relationship with each customer and thus make it more difficult for CompDiv, or any other competitor, to take sales from these customers.

Third, a new product development program and an actual product line extension were announced shortly before the new division president took office. Although the new product program had been underway for some time, IndComp had initially decided not to announce its existence until specific products were ready for market introduction. The program was formally announced prior to a trade conference with the intent of conveying to CompDiv and other rivals, and especially to channels and end-customers, that IndComp was now seriously committed to being the product leader in this segment of the industry. In this way, IndComp hoped to preempt any moves by CompDiv that would give them a long-term customer advantage.

Finally, IndComp revitalized and extended its competitor scanning and monitoring program. The intent was to capture competitor change as it happened and before it took place (in part, through the use of anticipated indicators). In this way, IndComp hoped to institutionalize what it had learned through the experience previously recounted.

Case 2: A Competitor's Restructuring Program

Most organizations encounter competitors undergoing some form of restructuring. Corporations shed whole business sectors or a number of business units to "focus on their core businesses." Others realign their businesses into new (related) product sectors. Still others restructure around alliances with rivals or firms in related businesses.

Because changes in structure often do not lead to projected or anticipated results, inferences drawn from the restructuring efforts of competitors about likely marketplace strategy change, operational improvements, and financial performance sometimes prove false. If the focal firm acts on these false inferences, it is likely to make decisions and commitments that hamper rather than aid the focal firm's strategic and operating goals. Indeed, experience suggests that such incorrect inferences have led to severely deleterious results in some organizations. Thus, analysts must critically assess inferences before acting on them in the case of competitors' structural change.[8]

The Alerting Indicator A large U.S. corporation, USCorp, exemplifies the need for such careful analysis. It was surprised by an announcement from a large European competitor, EuroCorp, that it planned to restructure one of its business sectors. EuroCorp announced it would create a number of smaller business units that would focus on specific products, technologies, and customer needs. Such units, the announcement asserted, could then unleash their entrepreneurial zeal to create new products, reinvigorate existing product lines and develop new ways of providing value to customers. EuroCorp's headquarters staff would work with the subunits to try to identify and achieve potential synergies—ways in which they could cooperate to mutual advantage. The intent of the restructuring was to build the organization that would allow EuroCorp to leapfrog its rivals to attain and extend global marketplace leadership—in the language of Chapter 1, to reconstruct the existing strategy game and possibly to create a new one.

Context USCorp and EuroCorp were direct competitors in most of the products in the business sector affected by EuroCorp's proposed new structure. EuroCorp had significantly more market share in Europe and USCorp had four times EuroCorp's market share in the United States. Both firms had launched major investment programs to penetrate the Asian market.

Initial Inference The surprise announcement—the alerting indicator— quickly led to an initial inference: the European competitor was now committed to achieving global prominence, and possibly, global dominance, in this product sector. The logic was simple and apparently compelling. EuroCorp was already a technology leader in many of these product segments; most of these products were generating extensive amounts of cash; the firm had a reputation for entrepreneurial flair; a series of prior investments had indicated its commitment to winning on a global scale; its cosmopolitan senior management team had consistently said for several years that it must have a significant strategic presence in every geographic region of the world. EuroCorp appeared to have both the intent and the capacity to use its announced restructuring program to advance its strategic purposes.

Preliminary Consequences The analysis team quickly concluded that the proposed restructuring could have (and most likely would have) *significant consequences* for EuroCorp and *high-impact implications* for USCorp. If successful, the restructuring would generate considerable momentum for EuroCorp in each product area. It would allow the managers of each product sector to embark on strategic initiatives that previously might have been difficult, if not impossible, such as joint product development ventures with technology partners and others, joint marketing and sales activities with channels, and special deals with high-volume end-customers. However, announcing a restructuring program was not the same as executing it. EuroCorp would have to create the business subunits, establish the appropriate management teams, build liaison across the units, and develop and implement a series of strategies initiatives for each business unit.

Potential Implications Among other implications, USCorp would find it-self confronting another committed and financially well-endowed competi-tor—one with a new stated goal of winning in the U.S. market. Its announced intentions would be interpreted by all rivals as a signal of potential major change in the U.S. marketplace, thus compelling each rival to review its strategy options and plans.

The potential strategy and actions inferred from the announced restruc-turing constituted both *discontinuous* and *short-lag* change, each of which was a major source of concern to the analysis team. The structure change could lead to a new marketplace strategy: new products that would be dis-tinctively different from the firm's current products; radical new ways of competing to attract, win, and retain customers, and goals that would be sig-nificantly unlike the firm's historic marketplace goals. These discontinuous changes could be affected in the relative short-run, within 6 to 12 months. Largely because of the short change lag, the alerting signal, if correctly de-rived, would give USCorp little time to consider its own initiatives in re-sponse to the projected actions of EuroCorp (and the subsequent changes that might occur in the broader competitive context).

Partly in response to EuroCorp's anticipated strategy changes, USCorp im-mediately evaluated three nonmutually exclusive strategic initiatives:

1. Launch "a counteroffensive" move: commit new resources to winning in Europe.
2. Initiate a marketing program to protect and enhance the firm's posi-tion in the United States.
3. Embark on a major program to quickly gain a position in the dominant Asian countries, possibly including a number of alliances with Asian organizations.

Assessment before Committing to Action As USCorp began to assess its strategy options, it asked: What if the strong inference that EuroCorp would leverage its structure change into an aggressive strategy to quickly gain mar-ket share turned out not to be completely true? It considered whether its own actions such as launching a counteroffensive in Europe might lead to unde-sired results such as a price war. It then evaluated each of its strategy op-tions, in the presence and absence of EuroCorp's intended strategy change. A major outcome of this assessment was a decision to monitor EuroCorp's exe-cution to determine whether it was truly committed to the new strategy.

Monitoring Projected Competitor Change Part of the intrigue, complex-ity, and difficulty of competitor analysis is that occasionally what appears to be a compelling logic at one point in time leading to an *apparently strong* inference turns out to be the result of poor reasoning and limited or inappropriate data. One way to avoid such deleterious discoveries is to assiduously monitor projected competitor change. Strong inferences that transpire as partially or completely incorrect reinforce the importance of anticipated indicators as a means to monitor whether a projection is panning out. Analysts can use such indicators to project a timeline around anticipated events or actions.[9]

Analysts often overlook that these indicators also facilitate tracking what is not taking place. For example, if USCorp developed a set of anticipated indicators pertaining to EuroCorp's development of new products and then discovered that it was not capturing any relevant data, it could then raise critical questions as to whether EuroCorp was indeed committing resources to create and launch new products.

USCorp, however, did not formally identify a set of anticipated indicators to monitor and assess EuroCorp's execution of its structure change and the strategy and operations actions that might follow from it. Instead, over the first six months following the structure announcement, it monitored each structure event and associated strategy and actions as they occurred. These included announcements of the establishment of new subunits, personnel appointments, and planned marketplace strategy changes including the development of new products, rationalization of some product lines, creation of new "buying opportunities" for certain customers, and new marketing approaches.

In the following six-month period, USCorp through its monitoring program continued to capture and document each major statement and action by EuroCorp.

What became apparent throughout the second year was that EuroCorp was not executing an aggressive strategy to quickly acquire market share in all major regional markets—as initially anticipated. This inference was derived from a pattern across a number of indicators: products were not being introduced as initially announced; marketing programs were not being rolled out; few initiatives were evident to end-customers.

Rather, the inference drawn from these indicators was that EuroCorp was experiencing serious difficulty in creating the planned organizational structure, and in making the structure work. Some organization units had undergone two or more changes of chief executive. Senior corporate executives had stated publicly that they were unhappy with the rate of progress in putting the new structure in place. Rumors were rife that disagreements had arisen between the senior managers of different units. A management consulting firm indicated that based on its industry sources "technology turf battles" had emerged between units within EuroCorp. Financial analysts suggested that a clear sense of strategic leadership had not yet taken hold in this product sector of EuroCorp.

Implications: A Series of Specific Decisions As it monitored EuroCorp's actions, and the broader competitive arena, USCorp made key decisions. In the six-month period following EuroCorp's announcement, it decided not to change its marketplace strategy solely based on EuroCorp's potential strategy evolution (even though its initial impulse, as discussed, was to do so). During the same period, it committed to reviewing its strategy options and to considering the implications of a range of its own actions partly in response to EuroCorp's announcement. In the next six-month period, USCorp decided to carefully track EuroCorp's execution of its announced restructuring and its associated strategy moves. During the following year, it decided that EuroCorp would not successfully execute the structural change without a fundamental cultural and leadership shift. USCorp arrived at a series of key judgments over almost two years that resulted in a sequence of specific decisions.

Errors in the Identification and Assessment of Infrastructure Change

The preceding cases suggest common errors in how organizations identify and assess infrastructure change. This section emphasizes errors specific to each of the stages in signal analysis described in Chapter 4 (see Figure 4.1): capture, detection, perception, interpretation, and assessment of signals. Many of these errors also apply to the identification and assessment of culture,[10] which is the subject of Chapter 15.

First, analysts often emphasize description and documentation of (individual) infrastructure elements (capture) at the expense of drawing inferences (perception and interpretation). They develop lengthy profiles of structure, systems, people, and decision-making processes with little attention to noting indicators that might serve as the sources of signals (detection). An emphasis on infrastructure detail to the neglect of detecting indicators and drawing inferences constitutes a particularly egregious error for two reasons. As noted earlier in this chapter, competitors' infrastructures change continually and sometimes precipitously. Thus, as soon as an analyst has detailed a competitor's structure or systems, they are already undergoing change. Second, analysts are more likely to pay less heed to the patterns across infrastructure changes that typically underpin strong inferences.

Implicit in this error is that analysts forget or ignore that signals emanate from the extent and direction of infrastructure change, and not from descriptions of infrastructure alone. This oversight is most unfortunate because once analysts detect infrastructure change, it is often easy to determine its extent and direction. Organizations making structure announcements generally indicate what the prior structure was. Incentive system changes almost always are presented by organizations in relation to what constituted the prior incentive system. Organizations enumerate the deficiencies of prior processes to highlight the benefits of the proposed processes. Analysts do not need detailed and comprehensive descriptions of infrastructure change to detect and assess signals with high-impact implications, especially for major infrastructure change such as the establishment of a new corporate structure, the appointment of new senior executives, the introduction of new systems, or radical change in decision processes.

However, as the cases in this chapter also demonstrate, patterns in infrastructure change over time give rise to stronger inferences than any one change alone. Frequently, unless analysts seek patterns across indicators, they miss specific signals.

Also, the temporal nature of signal analysis requires analysts to continually assess inferences they have previously derived. A failure to do so simply inhibits learning. As illustrated in the USCorp-EuroCorp case, a pattern discerned across multiple indicators over a number of months sometimes causes analysts to modify a prior strong inference.

Analysts also are prone to overlook that infrastructure change is not an end in itself: interpretation should contribute to assessment. It is a means to anticipate or confirm *change* in the competitor's marketplace strategy and in other microlevel components. Hence, the focus must be on *interpretation and assessment:* the inferences about other types of change that can be drawn from change in infrastructure.

The preceding errors contribute in part to a lack of attention to *alerting signals.* Analysts must always be attentive to the signaling capacity of indicators (perception). Thus, even when infrastructure change appears insignificant by itself, or the indicators are vague and fuzzy, it is still often possible to generate inferences that alert analysts to (potential) significant current, past, or future competitor change. If the analysis team in IndComp had not recognized the signaling capacity of the appointment of the new president for CompDiv, even in the first few days when they knew relatively little about him, the analysis process simply would not have taken place as quickly as it did.

Relatedly, as noted earlier, analysts should move quickly to draw tentative or preliminary signals once indicators are detected. As illustrated in both cases in this chapter, such signals quickly alert analysts to potential implications and guide further data collection including the determination of anticipated indicators.

Inferences derived from infrastructure change must always be generated with reference to their *context*.[11] The *future*, rather than the past or present, often constitutes the relevant context. USCorp's inference that EuroCorp would move quickly to execute its new strategic direction was based on its understanding of EuroCorp's past and current actions and proclivities. However, as the relevant context changed—a deterioration in sales and profits in the product sector, the emergence of disagreements between the business units, some change in product technologies—USCorp's initial inference proved more and more incorrect.

As noted in Chapter 2, the essence of (competitor) learning is the *detection and correction of errors* in both the stock of knowledge and the processes of learning. Hence the importance of monitoring whether inferences, that is, what is inferred, are panning out. Thus, another critical error is the failure to track the projection(s) that are central to any inference.

The error just noted arises in part because the pertinent *(anticipated)* indicators are not identified. Both cases discussed in this chapter highlight the role and importance of identifying such indicators. Had USCorp identified the indicators necessary to monitor how well EuroCorp was executing the new structure, it most likely would have detected earlier than it did that problems and difficulties were slowing down execution of the projected strategy.

Summary

Infrastructure analysis should not be isolated from other competitor analysis components. It is a common source of alerting and confirming or refuting signals. This analysis emphasizes the importance of understanding the temporal nature of the signal perception, interpretation, and assessment as well as the context of signals.

CHAPTER

15

Culture

MARKETPLACE STRATEGY, ACTIVITY/VALUE CHAIN, ALLIANCES AND RELATIONSHIPS, assets, and capabilities and competencies indicate what a competitor *can* do. However, by themselves, they are insufficient to determine what a competitor *may* do. The competitor's culture (in conjunction with assumptions)[1] offers extensive insight into *why* a competitor is pursuing its current strategy, what strategy alternatives it may (or may not) consider, and what actions it may (or may not) entertain. Understanding competitors' organizational cultures greatly facilitates the chances of outwitting, outmaneuvering, and outperforming them.

This chapter begins by defining culture and outlining its importance. It next delineates the key elements of culture—values, beliefs, norms, and behaviors—and how these elements are interrelated. It then details the methodology to identify and assess a competitor's culture. The final section notes some errors specific to culture analysis.

Because of the pervasiveness and influence of culture in any organization, this chapter emphasizes interrelationships among the framework components. It also highlights the role and importance of open-ended inquiry.

Understanding Culture

Definition and Importance of Culture

Few concepts in the management literature are defined in as many ways as organizational culture[2] or are used in as many ways in everyday discourse within organizations. It is sometimes depicted in broad terms as "how we do things around here." Yet, most authors go beyond merely describing what things are done and how they are done: they also delve into shared rationales

419

and understandings that underpin and guide the organization's actions and individuals' behaviors. Their concern and focus is not just what an organization does but why. Organization culture thus can be broadly defined as the collectivity of norms and behaviors (the substance of individuals' behaviors within an organizational setting) and their underlying explicit or implicit rationales such as values, beliefs, and principles.[3]

Culture provides a cohesive bond among what otherwise might be disparate subunits, groups, and individuals. The bond in part consists of a shared understanding of what is important: Should individuals pay attention to serving customers or adhering to internal policies and standards? It also conveys shared meanings[4] around key concepts, principles, and ideas: Does customer satisfaction imply that individuals do heroic things to delight customers or merely do what is prescribed in the work manual? Culture is integrally entwined in every facet of what an organization does and how it does it.

The Elements of Culture

Since the focus in this book is understanding competitors, the emphasis is on capturing those critical elements of a competitor's culture that can be obtained without extensive (or indeed any) access to the inside of the competitor's organization. Thus, we address four key elements of organization culture: behaviors, norms, beliefs, and values.[5] These elements constitute a hierarchy ranging from a base of core values that represent what the organization considers important, to innumerable behaviors that are generally evident (see Figure 15.1). These four culture elements are highly interrelated but they differ greatly in their visibility and accessibility. Each is discussed briefly. The differences between a product-centered culture and a customer-oriented culture—a critical aspect of any competitor's culture—are used to illustrate the four elements (see Figure 15.2).

Behaviors Behaviors refer to the everyday activities of individuals in their organizational capacity: what they do and how they do it. Common patterns of behaviors are often aggregated and described as organizational practices: how products are designed; how data are collected from vendors, channels, and end-customers; how customers are treated; how organizational members dress; how they speak; how they interact with each other; how they relate to or deal with outsiders.

Behaviors reside at the culture's surface; they are its most visible element. It is possible to observe many behaviors of the members of a competitor that take place outside the confines of the competitor's organization. Any person who comes in contact with a competitor can serve as an informant: they report the specific behaviors they observe.

FIGURE 15.1
A Hierarchy of Culture Elements

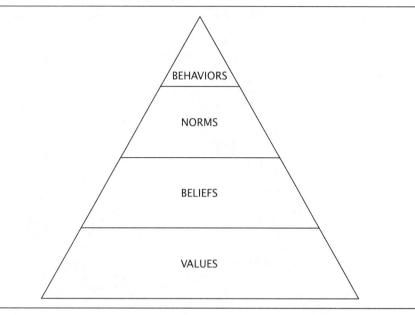

In product- and customer-oriented cultures, quite distinct behaviors are readily observable. Customer-centered cultures manifest organizational practices such as visits to customers by many different levels of managers; observation of customers using the firm's products; testing new product ideas with customers; bringing customers into the organization to provide a customer perspective as part of the deliberations around specific decisions.[6] On the other hand, in product-oriented cultures, individuals' behaviors and organizational practices are executed with little reference to customers. Individuals spend considerable time researching and investigating the latest technologies, solely with a view to designing and developing the most technologically advanced product (irrespective of its value to customers). In dealing with customers, individuals spend more time talking than listening.

Norms Norms underlie, support, and justify individual behaviors, and more broadly, organizational practices. They encompass the explanations and rationalizations used by organizational members for their behaviors. As such, norms are the behavioral "rules of the game" that govern daily interaction among organizational members *and* interactions with external entities.

Norms are reflected in general organizational practices or behavior patterns (e.g., always make the boss look good; never share information unless you have to; always subjugate your own interests to those of the team,

FIGURE 15.2
Comparison of Product- and Customer-Oriented Cultures

Culture Elements \ Culture Orientation	Product or Technology Orientation	Customer or Marketplace Orientation
Values	The pursuit of the perfect product is what is most important	Customer satisfaction and excitement is the rationale for being in business
	Customers purchase our products after we are finished with them	Customers must be involved in every phase of product design and development
	Efficiency in production and delivery is the appropriate decision-making criterion	Customer criteria must be an integral element in the making of every decision
Beliefs	The most technically sophisticated products will sell themselves	Only products that deliver superior value to customers will sell in the marketplace
	Customer involvement in product design and development will only lead to unproductive delays	Customer inputs can enhance every phase of product development and every activity of the organization
Norms	Products are continually tested for their conformance to predetermined functional standards	Customers are continually asked for their assessment of the firm's products and actual usage
	Customers don't understand the nature and complexity of our products	Customers often surprise product providers with their insight
Behaviors	Customers are only visited as a last resort	Customers are continually visited
	Extensive time is spent assessing the latest product technologies and product developments	Executives persistently ask questions about customers' reactions to products

group, or organization). Norms also are apparent in dealings with external entities such as customers and suppliers (e.g., act in an ethical manner in dealing with suppliers and customers; never disparage competitors in conversation with any external parties; always allow customers the opportunity to ask questions before closing the sale).

Norms don't just happen: they are learned, assimilated, and reinforced. Through the processes of acculturation, new organizational members observe and learn how others behave. Often the behaviors or practices embodied in norms are consciously imbued in new members, as when salespersons are taught how "to make a sale" and how to behave in the presence of customers. Behaviors inconsistent with norms are disapproved (e.g., inappropriate dress, "speaking out of turn," failure to follow procedures in reporting visits to customers).

Distinct norms characterize product- and customer-oriented organization cultures. In customer cultures, driving norms typically include: always pay attention to what the customer says; use every interaction with customers to test new product ideas or solicit their assessments of existing products; incorporate as quickly as possible customer responses and suggestions into product ideas and modifications. In product cultures, dominant norms include: always test the product for conformance to design standards; customers don't know enough about emerging technologies to be able to offer any insights in product evolution; if the technology is available, it should be built into the product.

Beliefs Most organization theorists suggest that behaviors and norms flow from underlying beliefs and values, although the latter also may be reinforced through behaviors and norms. Beliefs are the cause-effect understandings that a group of individuals share about their world. Stemming from their own education, training, organizational experience, and observations, individuals develop understandings of "how the world works," what succeeds and what doesn't.[7] Solutions to problems are incorporated into the experience set of individuals and thus get transformed into beliefs. Beliefs are less specific than the norms governing daily behavior; they offer more general guidelines about how organizational members should act to obtain desired results.

Organizations develop a vast repertoire of beliefs over time about matters internal or external to the organization. Critical externally focused beliefs are about strategy and the competitive environment: how to win in the marketplace, what environmental change is taking place, and the forces shaping the market segments the firm is in or wants to enter. Such beliefs are often about customers, suppliers, technology, government and, of course, competitors.

Internally focused beliefs are about attributes of the organization, and how to manage and lead the organization. Core beliefs often address what good management means, what the prerequisites are to good management, and what a successful organization looks like. Dominant beliefs in some organizations address organization structure (e.g., "a flat organization structure leads to more rapid and effective decision making"), costs ("we need to invest heavily in order to reduce our breakeven point"), manufacturing ("our antiquated machinery is inhibiting the production of products with superior functionality") and personnel ("the investment in executive education and development has led to the savviest management team in the industry").

Distinct belief structures dominate product- and customer-oriented cultures. Customer culture beliefs might include: only products that continuously add new customer benefits will sell in an increasingly competitive marketplace; constantly experimenting with total customer solutions will lead to enhanced customer satisfaction; products developed in partnership with customers are more likely to succeed in the marketplace. By contrast, product culture beliefs might include: the most technically sophisticated products will sell themselves; customer involvement in product development will only lead to intolerable delays; the firm's own knowledge is sufficient for foreseeable product development requirements.

Values Values constitute culture's deepest level. They are defined as what the organization (and its members) consider important, or profess to care about. As such, values are statements or assertions of what ought to be or of what is desirable. Values communicate to organizational members what the organization stands for, what it believes in. Values espouse or suggest desired end states or results the organization seeks.

Values also typically address internal and external concerns. Internal values often deal with treatment of employees (e.g., "all individuals must be treated with respect and integrity irrespective of their background"), commitment to excellence (e.g., "we shall strive to attain excellence in everything that we do") and innovation (e.g., "innovation is the lifeblood of our enterprise"). External values often emphasize desired orientation toward customers (e.g., "satisfying customers is the end purpose of all our efforts within this organization").

Values are the most inaccessible element of culture. They must be *inferred* by analysts. Although some organizations make freely available their dominant espoused values, analysts are still well advised to seek evidence in the organization's decisions, actions, and statements that they truly influence the organization.

Not surprisingly, distinct value sets characterize product- and customer-oriented cultures. Customer culture values typically include: the raison d'être of the organization is satisfied and excited customers; all decisions must be assessed from the vantage point of how they impact the provision of value to customers; the customer is always right. Product culture values are quite different, and typically include: design and development of the perfect product is what is important; efficiency in operations is the dominant decision criterion.

Linkages among the Culture Elements Values and beliefs underpin norms and behaviors (see Figure 15.1). They embody how an organization wants to conduct business and for what purposes.[8] Without a guiding set of beliefs and values, an organization is rudderless; it has no anchors by which organizational members can test their behaviors, assess prevailing norms, or determine the relevance or desirabilty of planned actions. An organization's core or fundamental beliefs and values are often surprisingly enduring, thus the importance of detecting and assessing competitors' guiding beliefs and values.

Linking Strategy and Culture

An organization's culture significantly affects scope, posture, and goals. Organizations such as 3M, Hewlett-Packard, and Rubbermaid hold values and beliefs that espouse innovation, risk taking, and entrepreneurship,[9] which translate into behaviors and practices such as product development, continual efforts to enhance differentiation and the persistent pursuit of "stretch"[10] goals. Their commitment is to continual product change and innovation in virtually every operational process; they are willing to engage in trial-and-error learning in the marketplace; they tolerate failure, even learn from it; creating change is their way of life. On the other hand, organizations dominated by bureaucratic values and traditional industry beliefs often find it extremely difficult to engage in sustained product innovation, to dramatically change operational processes or to reflect on their long-held assumptions.

Key Culture Attributes

As with all other framework components, cultures vary greatly along a number of attributes. The five most important attributes for diagnosing culture's affect on a competitor's strategy and operations are integration, embeddedness, alignment, durability, and adaptability.

Integration Tremendous variation exists in the extent to which values, beliefs, norms, and behaviors reinforce each other within organizations. As illustrated in the customer oriented culture (see Figure 15.2), strongly integrated cultures send consistent messages to all organization members and to external audiences such as customers, suppliers, and competitors.

Embeddedness Any organization with multiple businesses, departments, or functions, and/or geographic locations, contains myriad *local* cultures. Thus, an organization typically consists of many local cultures that are integrated to varying degrees across locations. For example, significant differences often exist between the values and beliefs of the R&D or technology functions, and the marketing and sales functions of firms. Visitors to the European, U.S., and Japanese operations of large global businesses are often struck by the diversity in their local cultures. Thus, analysts must pay close attention to the extent to which culture is embedded or uniformly shared throughout a competitor's organization.

Alignment Two distinct though related types of alignment need to be assessed when diagnosing a competitor's culture. Internal alignment refers to whether culture is aligned with the organization's infrastructure: its structure, systems, and decision-making processes. For example, values and beliefs may support entrepreneurship and innovation; however, reward and incentive systems may encourage individuals not to rock the boat, not to take risks, to sustain the status quo. External alignment refers to whether the culture is congruent with the direction of change in the competitive environment. For example, many firms are now desperately trying to amend their historic bureaucracy-laden cultures to meet the organizational requirements of increasing customization of their product offerings.

Durability Whether they are intentionally crafted or they unwittingly evolve, cultures are surprisingly enduring. Behaviors and norms, once they become an accepted way of life, are terribly difficult to change. Beliefs and values often require major external jolts and/or deterioration in performance before organizations willingly confront their relevance to changed marketplace circumstances.

Adaptability Independent of the extent to which a culture is integrated, embedded, aligned, and durable, is whether it encourages an organization to adapt to its changing environment. Do the values and beliefs support risk taking, entrepreneurialism, and leadership that stresses innovation and commitment to changing marketplace strategy? Are norms oriented to maintaining the status quo within the organization or to challenging beliefs, values, and assumptions?

Indicators of Culture Change

It is possible to establish the broad contours of a competitor's culture without access to the inner workings of the competitor. Multiple direct and indirect indicators of the four culture elements are readily available in most circumstances such that internal access to a competitor is not required (though it is obviously helpful) to develop a profile of its culture.

If values, beliefs, and norms truly guide an organization's decisions and actions, then how it acts and the choices, or decisions, it makes under specific circumstances ought to indicate underlying values, beliefs, and norms. Decisions and actions in the end-customer, channel, factor, and institutional arenas therefore are critical *indirect* indicators of values, beliefs, and norms. The analyst can thus draw inferences that connect the decisions and actions to the culture elements.

Statements constitute both direct and indirect indicators of the culture elements. Organizations frequently address their values and beliefs in many public formal statements and informal comments.[11] As explained later in this chapter, statements also often provide indirect indicators of values, beliefs, and norms.

Cultural Change as Signals

Culture change sometimes generates strong, high-impact, early signals of marketplace change. A shift from a product- or technology-driven culture to a marketplace or customer-oriented culture typically signals significant emerging or potential changes in the scope, posture, and goals of marketplace strategy.[12] Changes in the attributes of culture—integration, embeddedness, alignment, durability, and adaptability—often signal change in the coherence and direction of marketplace strategy as well as in each of the framework components. Because it takes so long to change a culture, alerting signals of culture change often provide long lead times for the focal organization to develop and execute appropriate strategic and organizational responses.

It should also be noted that items absent in the culture elements are sometimes also a source of signals. For example, many organizations have carefully noted the noncustomer orientation in the culture of their competitors. Of course, efforts by a competitor to fill in the missing culture items itself becomes a source of signals.

Identifying a Competitor's Culture

Culture exemplifies the need for each component in the competitor analysis framework to be carefully delineated prior to data collection and analysis. Although analysts obviously possess the option to define and specify the culture elements, a clear understanding of values, beliefs, norms, and behaviors guides initial search activity. The steps and associated key questions in a guided analysis are shown in Figure 15.3.

Accumulate Prior Analysis

A guided approach to culture identification derives prevailing values, beliefs, norms, and behaviors from prior analysis of the framework components. Each component—marketplace strategy, activity/value chain, alliances and

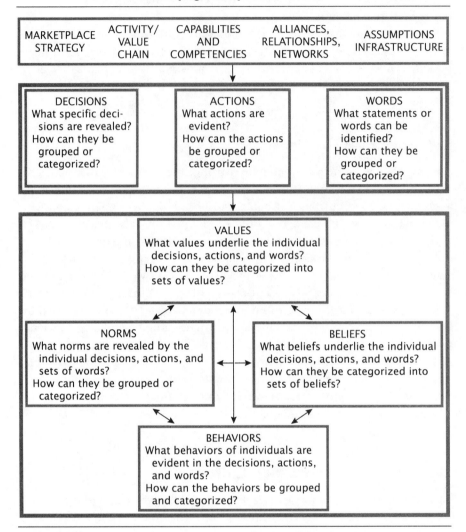

FIGURE 15.3
Identifying a Competitor's Culture

relationships, networks, assumptions, assets, capabilities and competencies, technology, and the organization's infrastructure—furnishes culture indicators (see Figure 15.3). Each can be reviewed to identify individual decisions and actions.

Prior analysis is also the source of culture-relevant statements. Much of the data from which each framework component is derived also furnish many statements from and about the competitor that may refer directly to the culture elements. In some instances, statements directly describe specific behaviors.

Sometimes specific analysis is conducted for culture identification purposes. It is possible to document and analyze the behaviors and statements of a competitor's personnel in public settings such as trade and industry shows, governmental hearings, and conferences. Some organizations have chosen to identify and analyze the values and beliefs inherent in the behaviors and statements of one or more executives in one or a select set of competitors.

Detecting Indicators

Three key indicators—decisions, actions, and statements—are especially useful in identifying a competitor's culture.

Decisions Decisions represent choices that the competitor made (or is making) given a range of alternatives. For example, competitors choose to develop a particular type of relationship with select large end-customers, to change its hiring policies or to respond to a crisis in one particular way rather than others. The presumption is that such choices reflect underlying values, beliefs, and norms.

A modest number of decisions, and in some cases, even a single decision, can be highly indicative of a competitor's values and beliefs or change in values and beliefs. Decisions of major organizational or strategic import often facilitate detection of strong, high-impact signals of underlying values and beliefs. This is even more likely to be the case when the decision has consequences that are visible both to those within and outside the organization. For example, Johnson & Johnson's decision to immediately pull Tylenol from all retail shelves on the first indication that its product had been tampered with, strongly indicated underlying values pertaining to the need to maintain the company's consumer franchise irrespective of the costs of doing so and beliefs pertaining to the relationship between customers' perceptions of the firm and its market position and financial returns.[13]

Decisions should be searched for at the level of the elements or subelements of the framework components. In the case of marketplace strategy, what decisions are evident in the context of the competitor's scope, posture, and goals? Individual alliances generate distinct decisions. Individual capabilities and competencies also typically give rise to different decisions. Changes in assumptions are likely to reveal still different decisions.

Key *marketplace strategy* decisions for the electronics firm included (see Table 15.1): To speed up the introduction of new products; to add greater variety to existing product lines; to give added emphasis to service, image and reputation, and relationships as means of attracting and retaining customers; to aim for greater market share and presence, even at some cost to short-run profitability. Key decisions along its *activity/value*

**TABLE 15.1   Detecting Raw Values, Beliefs, and Norms: Marketplace Strategy and
Activity/Value Chain as Sources of Indicators**

Marketplace Strategy and Activity/Value Chain Decisions	Raw Values, Beliefs, Norms	
To speed up the introduction of new products	Value:	The importance of new products (innovation)
	Belief:	New products will lead to competitive gains
To add greater variety to existing product lines	Value:	The importance of sustained differentiation
	Belief:	Greater product variety leads to marketplace success
To give added emphasis to service, image, and reputation, as a means to attract and retain customers	Belief:	Nonfunctional dimensions of posture lead to success
To aim for greater market share (even at the cost of short-run profitability)	Belief:	Market share leads to long-run profitability
To support a vendor in financial difficulty	Value:	Adheres to its promises and commitments
	Norm:	Acts in an ethical manner in dealing with external entities
To look for new alliances to augment its technology base in R&D and manufacturing	Belief:	Current technology is insufficient for long-run success
To do micromarketing; To customize service, delivery, and relationships	Value:	Customers must receive individual attention
	Belief:	Individualized attention to customers leads to greater success in the marketplace

chain included: To support a vendor in financial difficulty; to look for new
alliance partners to augment its technology base in research and manufacturing; to add considerable resources to its marketing and sales budget for
the purposes of what it called "micromarketing."

Patterns among decisions are even stronger indicators of the underlying
culture. Analysts might search for patterns in decisions pertaining to each
of the arenas discussed in Chapter 1—end-customers, channels, factors, and
institutions. At a more micro level, patterns are often evident within each
framework component such as assets or capabilities.

Actions   Actions refer to what the competitor actually did or is doing
under particular circumstances. Actions reflect and result from decisions.[14]
Most of a competitor's actions in the end-customer, channel, factor, and

institutional arenas are largely visible. Actions within the organization vary in visibility. As with decisions, patterns among actions provide stronger signals of the underlying culture.

Again, actions can be identified within the elements and subelements of the framework components. In some instances, a single action strongly signals specific culture elements. The visit by a competitor's senior vice-president to a relatively small customer (including the amount of time spent with the customer, the questions he asked, and the commitments he made) served as a strong alerting signal that this competitor was endeavoring to become much more customer oriented.

A number of key actions were identified along the activity/value chain of the electronics firm:

- Reduced modestly the overall number of suppliers.
- Pushed logistics providers to move toward electronic data interchange.
- Upgraded most of its key manufacturing process technologies.
- Hired a new marketing manager.
- Compelled all members of the sales force to undergo training in "relationship marketing" and compelled all its service personnel to undergo training in the latest technologies relevant to the delivery of rapid, high-quality service.

As with decisions, patterns among actions within and across framework components add strength to inferences about a competitor's culture. It is often revealing to consider the actions of key executives in competitor organizations. One organization monitors very carefully the actions of competitors' senior executives at trade shows.

Statements Statements serve as direct and indirect indicators of culture in two ways. Each prior analysis component is reviewed for words associated with key decisions and behaviors[15] that help indicate the underlying culture. Analysts also scan for words that alert them to decisions and actions. As with decisions and actions, it is imperative to search for patterns in statements.

Raw Values, Beliefs, Norms, and Behaviors

Raw values, beliefs, norms, and behaviors are those inferred or derived from individual decisions, actions, and statements (see Figure 15.3). They are raw in the sense that they are associated with *only one* decision, action, or statement.

Decisions, actions, and statements quickly generate listings of diverse values, beliefs, norms, and behaviors. However, significant differences characterize the process of derivation. Decisions and actions are largely indirect indicators of values and beliefs (see Figure 15.3). Values and beliefs undergirding decisions and actions are therefore often not immediately self-evident: in all cases, analysts must *infer* the values and beliefs. Thus, they must be especially attentive to the logic[16] that generates a specific value or belief. Many of the questions that analysts must ask are noted in Figure 15.3.

Norms are also indirectly indicated by decisions, actions, and behaviors and are sometimes directly indicated by statements. Norms often place particular onus on articulating the *logic* involved in their derivation from decisions and actions. In the electronics firm case, "dealing in an ethical manner with external entities," was inferred from a specific decision, "to commit resources to helping a supplier in financial difficulty." The electronics firm had multiple options in reacting to the supplier's difficulties, yet it chose to speed up its payments to the supplier and to commit to continuing to use its components. The general inference was that the firm would not exploit for its own gain the difficulties encountered by other organizations with which it had a business relationship.

Statements, as noted earlier, often provide direct indicators of values, beliefs, norms, and behaviors. For the electronics firm, the statement "we always look for internal replacements," provided a direct indicator of a prevailing norm, a strong preference for promoting from within. Sometimes statements indirectly indicate aspects of the culture elements. The statement "we take every opportunity to meet customers in their location" indirectly suggests values associated with the need to infuse internal decision making with an external orientation.

Refined Values, Beliefs, Norms, and Behaviors

The long listing of raw values, beliefs, norms, and behaviors that often ensues needs to be aggregated or refined to identify those that are most critical to understanding the competitor's culture. Refined values, beliefs, norms, and behaviors refer to those that are dominant in a particular domain such as customers, technology, or decision making. Since no a priori listing of domains is likely to be relevant to every competitor setting, analysts must review the raw items to identify pertinent domains. An emphasis on key words or sets of words such as customers, vendors, technology, and winning in the marketplace can help identify domains.

Analysts must then make judgments as to the integrative (that is, refined) values, beliefs, norms, and behaviors in each domain. Although there are no prescribed rules for doing so, analysts often find themselves having to reduce a listing of 5, 10, or more raw values down to a smaller set of 1 or 2, and in some cases, 3 or more, in each domain (such as customers, vendors, technology).[17] The refined values in the case of customers and technology in the case of the electronics firm are shown in Figure 15.4.

Core Values, Beliefs, Norms, and Behaviors

Core values, beliefs, norms, and behaviors are those that analysts consider fundamental to understanding the competitor's strategies in the market-place and its internal organization. The core values, beliefs, norms, and behaviors for the electronics firm are shown in Table 15.2.

In some instances, the core and refined items are largely similar. This is more likely when the competitor is a relatively small organization or analysts have had particular difficulty in finding culture-relevant data. In other in-stances, the refined items require further integration and aggregation. This tends to happen when analysts have generated a reasonably long list of refined items in each culture element.

Open-Ended Inquiry

Open-ended analysis is particularly important and useful in detecting a competitor's culture. It is not always easy to anticipate culture indicators. There are no simple algorithms as to what data to search for or what data sources

FIGURE 15.4
Refined Values, Beliefs, Norms, and Behaviors: The Domains of Customers and Technology

Culture Element	Customers	Technology
Values	We must always strive to add value for our customers	Technology must be pushed to its limits
Beliefs	Customer satisfaction is the key to business success	Technology leads to new products that lead to the ability to stay ahead of rivals
Norms	Always do what the customer asks	Pursue each technology advance as if the firm's future depended on it
Behaviors	Managers spend time with customers at their locations	Managers spend extensive time with external technology sources

434 COMPETITORS

TABLE 15.2 First-Cut Culture Profile for an Electronics Firm

Dimensions		Indicators
VALUES:		
Customer satisfaction is our fundamental purpose	Statement:	"Our primary reason in being is to create satisfied customers"
	Decision:	To replace faulty products
Treat all employees with dignity	Statements:	"We must respect all employees at all times"
Train managers and employees to do best possible job		"Everything possible must be done so that we have the most competent people in the business"
	Decisions:	To develop training and educational program
		To institute new employee review and assessment programs
Ensure open communications between all organizational levels	Statements:	"We are doing all that is possible to open interaction among and between all levels"
The organization must strive for excellence in all it does		"Excellence is our only organizational imperative"
	Action:	Personnel changes
The firm adheres to its commitments and promises	Statement:	"We go through walls to help carry through on our commitments"
	Decision:	To support vendor in difficulty
	Action:	Follow-up on promises to customers
BELIEFS:		
Customer satisfaction is the key to business success	Statement:	"Customer satisfaction leads to better margins"
	Decision:	To allocate resources in a particular way
Technology development is the key to long-run success	Statement:	"Technology generates new break-through products"
	Decision:	To commit funds to R&D
	Action:	Personnel appointments
Satisfied employees generate organizational commitment	Statement:	"Employees that are excited about their work commit to the organization"
	Decision:	To initiate rewards and recognition programs
	Action:	Publicly highlights outstanding achievements
NORMS:		
Always do what the customer wants	Statement:	"Customer cannot be left unsatisfied"
	Decision:	To accept product returns
	Action:	Listen attentively to customers' complaints

TABLE 15.2 *(Continued)*

Dimensions	Indicators	
There is strong preference for promoting within	Statement:	"We always look first for internal replacements"
	Decision:	To promote special individuals
Open-door communications policy is propagated	Statement:	"Anybody can reach any superior if they wish to"
BEHAVIORS:		
Individuals in public settings always wear formal business attire	Statement:	"Personnel are expected to dress properly"
	Action:	The way individuals dress
Managers spend time with customers at their locations	Statement:	"We take every opportunity to meet customers in their location"
	Decision:	To allocate time
	Action:	Time spent with customers

are likely to prove most useful. Indeed, some sources of data may surprise analysts. Thus, an open-ended search is likely to turn up useful but unanticipated indicators. An open-ended orientation also pushes analysts to continue searching for confirming and refuting indicators. As with other framework components, one danger with a guided culture analysis is that conclusions are reached too quickly. Also, an open-ended culture inquiry serves as a useful check and balance on analysis of the other framework components.

Data Sources Both primary and secondary sources need to be scanned and monitored. Electronic databases often furnish some *direct* indicators of values and beliefs. It is not uncommon for industry leaders and senior executives of large organizations to make statements in public arenas (e.g., presentations to industry and trade associations, financial analysts, customers, and suppliers) about both their organization's and their own values and beliefs. Companies of all sizes occasionally describe their *espoused* core values and related beliefs in varying levels of detail in company documents such as annual reports and financial filings. Many firms develop value statements that receive wide internal and external distribution. Executives often address in interviews with the popular and trade press what they consider important and essential to the firm's continued marketplace success.

Direct indicators of norms and behaviors can be found in secondary sources. Statements by a competitor's personnel often refer to how things are done within their organization. Behaviors of individuals are sometimes described in trade and other publications.

Open-ended culture inquiry makes especially valuable use of *primary* data sources for both direct and indirect culture indicators. Questions are posed to any person outside the focal firm who has had direct contact with the competitor such as vendors, channels, end-customers, consultants, alliance partners, technology experts, security analysts, and industry and trade press personnel. As prescribed in other chapters, it is usually beneficial to begin with personnel within the focal firm who have an understanding of some elements of the competitor's culture. Each person can be asked to describe incidents or items (such as decisions, actions, or statements) that they consider indicative of the competitor's culture. They can also be asked more direct questions such as what they consider to be the competitor's dominant values, beliefs, norms, and behaviors.

Alerting Signals The search of both primary and secondary data sources is for alerting indicators of each culture element. Analysts are on the lookout for indicators that draw attention to specific aspects of the competitor's culture. In this way, they are sensitive to both direct and indirect culture indicators.

Confirming/Refuting Signals Open-ended inquiry necessitates a search for confirming and/or refuting evidence for each initial alerting culture signal. This is especially important for *indirect* signals. Consider values, beliefs, and norms. Because they are not directly visible, analysts' attention must be particularly focused on detecting alerting *indirect* indicators. It is necessary to search for confirming or refuting indirect indicators even in those situations in which the analyst finds that a competitor has articulated (what it believes to be) its key values and beliefs. It is prudent for the analyst to corroborate, indeed challenge, the stated beliefs and values by inferring what they are or must be. As noted, there may be significant differences between espoused and actual beliefs and values. And because values and beliefs change over time, the analyst may detect alerting signals of belief and value change before they are generally recognized within the competitor.

Assessing Culture

Culture change can be the source of strong and weak signals about both short-term and long-term competitor change with significant consequences for the competitor and the high-impact implications for the focal firm. The steps and key questions in a guided analysis are shown in Figure 15.5. The electronics firm is used for illustration.

FIGURE 15.5
Assessing a Competitor's Culture

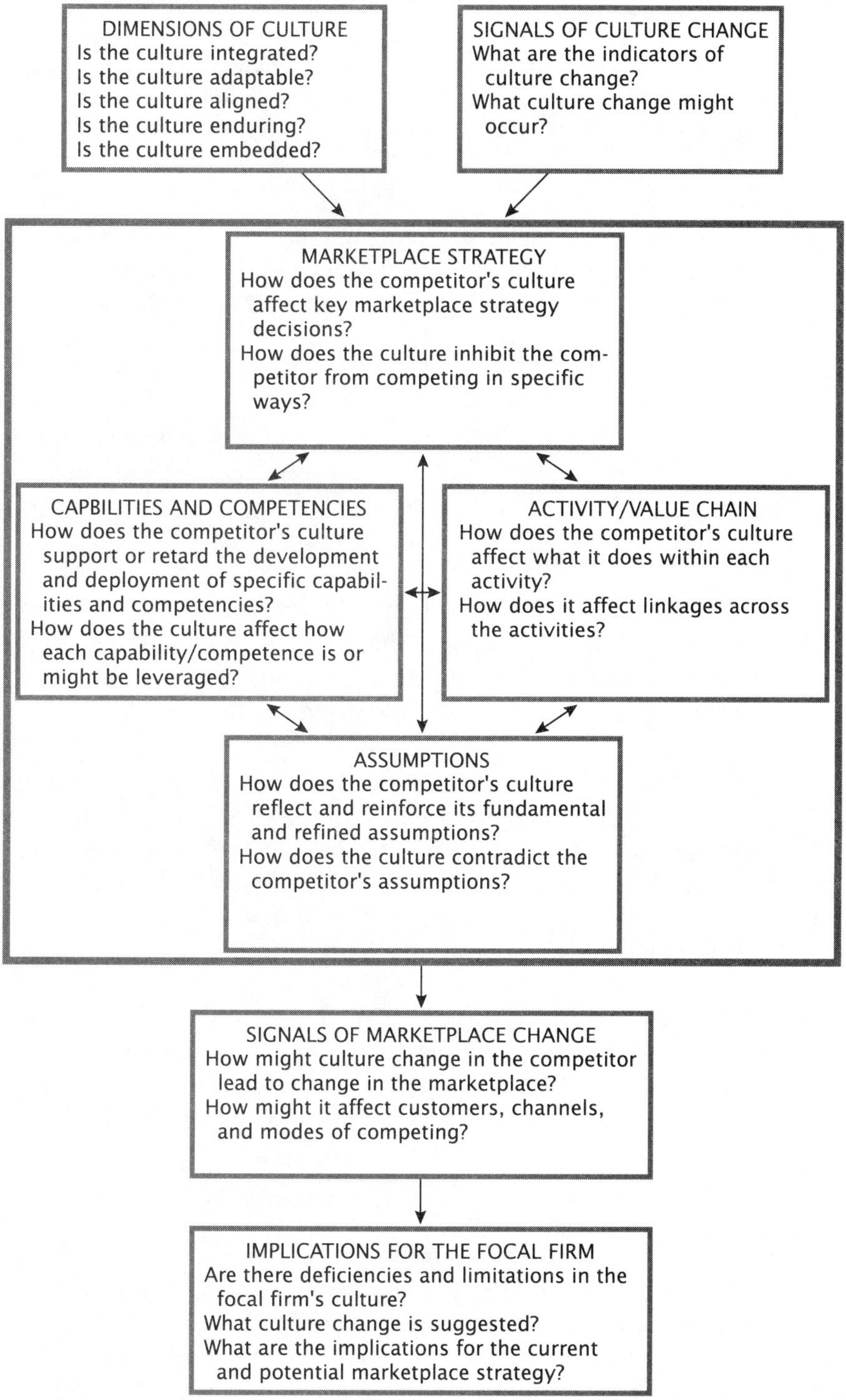

DIMENSIONS OF CULTURE
Is the culture integrated?
Is the culture adaptable?
Is the culture aligned?
Is the culture enduring?
Is the culture embedded?

SIGNALS OF CULTURE CHANGE
What are the indicators of
culture change?
What culture change might
occur?

MARKETPLACE STRATEGY
How does the competitor's culture
affect key marketplace strategy
decisions?
How does the culture inhibit the competitor from competing in specific
ways?

CAPBILITIES AND COMPETENCIES
How does the competitor's culture
support or retard the development
and deployment of specific capabilities and competencies?
How does the culture affect how
each capability/competence is or
might be leveraged?

ACTIVITY/VALUE CHAIN
How does the competitor's culture
affect what it does within each
activity?
How does it affect linkages across
the activities?

ASSUMPTIONS
How does the competitor's culture
reflect and reinforce its fundamental
and refined assumptions?
How does the culture contradict the
competitor's assumptions?

SIGNALS OF MARKETPLACE CHANGE
How might culture change in the competitor
lead to change in the marketplace?
How might it affect customers, channels,
and modes of competing?

IMPLICATIONS FOR THE FOCAL FIRM
Are there deficiencies and limitations in the
focal firm's culture?
What culture change is suggested?
What are the implications for the current
and potential marketplace strategy?

The Attributes of Culture

Each of the five major culture attributes discussed earlier provides different insights into a competitor's culture. Assessment of each generates fundamental questions not just about culture but about an organization's capacity to win.

Integration   The less the degree of integration across the four culture elements, the less likely that a competitor's culture will buttress or provoke significant strategic change. The analysis team concluded that the electronic firm's culture was somewhat bifurcated: integration was evident within values and beliefs, and within norms and behaviors, but not between them. Values and beliefs were tightly integrated around the importance of customer satisfaction and the need for persistent technology development and investment in human resources. Behaviors and norms exemplified a strong internal orientation evidenced by the strong preference for promotion from within, and strict adherence to a formal dress code.

Embeddedness   The bifurcated culture seemed to be strongly embedded in all organizational units. All levels of the organization appeared to be customer oriented; technology seemed to be regarded by all units of the organization as the source of future marketplace success.

Alignment   The culture was strongly internally aligned but weakly externally aligned. The norms and behaviors were driven by the reward, remuneration, and control systems. The customer orientation and commitment to technology might not be well aligned with changing customers needs and expectations: an old concept of customer satisfaction might actually be impeding the competitor's capacity to shape and lead customers.[18]

Durability   Based on the judgments of key informants (customers, channel members, and long-time employees in the focal organization), the dominant threads of the culture—a strong customer orientation, a commitment to technology—had endured for more than 15 years.

Adaptiveness   In many respects, the foregoing analysis is a prelude to answering the following question: what is the evidence that the culture will facilitate (or impede) the firm's adaptation to the emerging competitive environment? Grave questions existed about the ability of the electronic firm's culture to lead the organization through an expected tidal wave of marketplace change. Customers appeared to be increasingly willing to purchase products that did not incorporate every last item of advanced technology.

This tendency clashed with the competitor's avowed commitment to put in the marketplace only the "most sophisticated technically advanced products."

Signals of Culture Change

Even if a culture endures, its individual elements are likely to undergo modest change. At the extreme, analysts may detect significant change across the four culture elements. In either case, the direction and intensity of culture change must be assessed. Since major culture change takes so long to show its effects, analysts are often able to *project* potential culture change and assess its competitor consequences and focal firm implications long before the change fully occurs.

The culture of the electronics firm was becoming more customer focused. Change in that direction was occurring along several indicators. For example, multiple actions constituted indicators of increasing attention to customer satisfaction (a dominant value), the importance of customer satisfaction as a source of marketplace performance (a dominant belief), and behaviors oriented toward the provision of attention to customers. Some new indicators were also evident: a relatively recent change in behaviors—managers holding on-site meetings with customers—was a key *alerting* signal to the *elevated* importance of attention to customers within the competitor's organization.

It is also useful for analysts to *project* how culture change might unfold or evolve. Among other things, such projections cause analysts to ask whether there are any current indicators of such change. Analysts might ask to what extent the electronics firm would have to adapt its culture to win if customization[19] were a dominant feature of the competitive environment. The firm's customer- and technology-related values, beliefs, and norms might have to be significantly changed to support a movement toward the development and delivery of customized solutions. For example, the firm's deeply embedded customer orientation may not include values and beliefs necessary to develop and sustain an organization dedicated to customization.[20]

Linkage to Framework Components

Because culture is so pervasive in its effects on what an organization does, it is imperative to assess a culture's consequences for the competitor in all the framework's components. In many instances, this assessment helps explain *why* a competitor does (or does not) do certain things, as well as how it does them. Frequently, individual items in the culture elements help explain a competitor's predilection to make (or avoid) specific decisions or to engage in particular patterns of actions.

Many of the guiding questions in this analysis are noted in Figure 15.5. For example, one might expect to find the electronics firm's increased customer orientation to be reflected in linkages across the activity/value chain. Indeed, this was the case. The competitor had initiated team visits to customers. The teams then were expected to identify ways that individual activities might be redesigned to add value for customers as well as ways to build bridges across activities for the same purpose.

It is always instructive to consider a competitor's culture in conjunction with its assumptions.[21] Values, beliefs, and assumptions should be highly interrelated. To return to the product and customer cultures discussed at the beginning of this chapter, one would expect the customer-oriented values and beliefs (see Figure 15.2) to stem from and in turn reinforce specific assumptions (e.g., where they are in conflict, customers must be given higher priority than execution of internal policies; customers' expectations and demands will continue to require increased customization of solutions). The electronics firm's technology values and beliefs (see Table 15.2) were consistent with its apparent dominant technology assumption that technology developments would be the source of products that customers would value and purchase.

The importance of culture is further highlighted when analysts consider (and *project*) future developments pertaining to the framework components. Sometimes clashes among the culture elements make it difficult to assess the consequences for individual components. Consider likely alliances for the electronics firm. Its technology-related values and beliefs might suggest it would engage in some alliances to stay at the forefront of technology developments. Yet its norms and behaviors would suggest some difficulties in shaping and executing alliances: strong preferences for promoting from within (norm) and the desire to have individuals always wear formal business attire (behaviors) might make it difficult to consummate and foster an alliance with some potential partners. Thus, attention to a competitor's culture greatly aids in both anticipating likely competitor actions and assessing whether they will succeed.

The Competitor's Current and Future Marketplace Strategy

As noted, culture frequently buttresses and reinforces a competitor's current marketplace strategy—its scope, posture, and goals. However, it also often inhibits both the consideration and adoption of particular strategy alternatives.

The culture changes noted for the electronics firm (e.g., the increased orientation within each culture element toward customers) could potentially affect each posture dimension. Some evidence existed that it was already beginning to do so. For example, its service activity was becoming more "customer friendly": customers were reporting that more service options were available and service personnel were more amenable to their queries and suggestions.

It is insightful to go beyond the current strategy to assess what potential strategy alternatives would be congruent or incongruent with the competitor's current culture and its *projected* direction. Congruent alternatives thus should not contain any surprise for the focal firm.

Of particular relevance to outwitting competitors is consideration of how a competitor's prevailing culture might constrain or impede development and execution of specific strategy alternatives. Embedded and enduring values and beliefs around the importance of internally developed products and internally funded growth, for example, would suggest that certain strategy options such as acquisitions and mergers would receive, at best, secondary attention. More narrowly, a culture that supports a (low) price marketplace posture is not easily adaptable to a differentiation-oriented posture reflected in relatively higher prices. Analysts made the judgment that the electronics firm would incur severe difficulty in forming an alliance with aggressive technology-driven organizations that could serve as the source of new products, largely because of its rigid norms and behaviors.

Culture is also a critical input to assessing a competitor's likely responses to changes in the focal firm's marketplace strategy. Competitors driven by an embedded and enduring culture that supports a high image, high price posture often do not immediately, if at all, respond to one firm's price reductions. Relatedly, early signals of culture change alert an organization to likely changes in a competitor's response patterns.

Signals of Marketplace Change

Current and projected competitor culture change often is a source of signals of emerging and potential marketplace change. A moment's reflection on the extensive culture changes undergone or being embarked on by highly visible U.S. firms such as General Motors, Ford, IBM, Digital Equipment Corporation, Westinghouse, Kodak, and Xerox, and European firms such as Phillips and Unilever, attest to the capacity of culture change to signal emergent or potential marketplace change in terms of the products that could be brought to market, the speed with which new products reach the market, changes in firms' posture and, as a consequence, the dynamics of rivalry among competitors.

Comparisons of culture change across competitors may reveal greater stress being placed on lowering cost structures, thus suggesting greater intensity in price competition. In some product sectors, values and beliefs associated with the need to develop and offer higher value-added products or to provide greater variability in solutions, might suggest greater segmentation in the marketplace.

Comparison with the Focal Firm

Comparison against the culture of one or more competitors causes the focal firm to critically assess the content and direction of its own culture. One immediate outcome of such comparisons is to illuminate the focal firm's culture. A related benefit is that individuals are sensitized to the importance of culture as a facilitator of and impediment to desired marketplace and organizational changes. Comparisons with other firms often identify key culture implications for the focal firm.

In comparing the electronics firm competitor, the focal firm found it necessary to identify its own values, beliefs, norms, and behaviors as evidenced in its decisions, actions, and statements, and in how its members behaved in different circumstances.[22] The electronics firm afforded a foil against which the focal firm could assess its own culture.

Consequences for the Competitor

Many of the comments pertaining to the electronics firm highlight how assessment of culture alerts analysts to significant current and potential consequences for a competitor. The analysts identified the following three key consequences for the electronics firm:[23]

1. The need to more tightly integrate and align values and beliefs with norms and behaviors. Until it did so, the analysts believed that the competitor could not execute an aggressive and coordinated marketplace strategy.

2. The need to adapt its culture to fit a rapidly changing electronics marketplace. Unless it did so, the analysts argued that it would be "stuck" in its old way of doing business and therefore could not win in the emerging marketplace.

3. The need to change its culture so that it could more easily and effectively initiate and execute alliances with organizations that possessed different cultures from its own. In the absence of an ability to do so, the analysts judged that the electronics firm would simply not have access to the resources necessary to generate new products or reinvigorate its existing product lines.

Implications for the Focal Firm

Ultimately, the focal firm must identify the relevant implications for its own marketplace strategy and microlevel components with particular reference to its own culture.

Analysts can begin by addressing implications for the focal firm's own culture. Each of the prior assessment segments is used to identify and assess the quality of the firm's own culture: its strengths and leveragability, and its weaknesses and vulnerabilities relative to current and potential competitors. These judgments necessarily entail consideration of the current, emerging, and projected competitive environment.

Analysts in the focal firm identified key implications in the following four domains:

1. The focal firm's own *culture* was in many respects similar to its rival discussed throughout this chapter. Its culture, too, was in large measure a creature of a competitive era that was now past. Thus, its values, beliefs, norms, and behaviors needed to be critically assessed in conjunction with a rapidly changing competitive environment.

2. The analysts became particularly sensitive to how the focal firm's culture had for years constrained its *marketplace strategy*. The organization was not inclined to critically review its strategies, irrespective of the performance results. Also, there was little inclination to identify strategy alternatives that might take the organization in new scope, posture, and goal directions. Strategy changes were predominantly extensions or modifications to the historic marketplace direction and thrust. Culture change was thus a necessary prelude to developing and executing winning marketplace strategies.

3. Several microlevel implications were identified. For example, integration of activities across the activity/value chain was being impeded by an absence of supporting values, beliefs, and norms. Compared with the electronics rival, the focal firm had not developed a set of integrated and embedded values and beliefs that facilitated and exhorted functions such as engineering, manufacturing, and marketing to work closely together in product design, development, and delivery.

4. Finally, implications for the behaviors of senior executives were identified. First, they would have to demonstrate that they were culture sensitive: that they recognized the importance of tackling the many culture issues confronting the organization. Second, they themselves would have to lead the culture change; they ought not to hand it over to others such as the human resources team and then disengage from

its execution. Third, they would need to be seen by others in the organization as open to discussing what culture change was needed and how best to achieve the desired change.

Errors in Detecting and Assessing Competitors' Culture

Many of the errors associated with infrastructure analysis—emphasizing description at the expense of inferences, downplaying change as the source of signals, a lack of attention to alerting signals, not identifying anticipated indicators, and not recognizing that the future rather than the past often constitutes the relevant context—also pertain to identifying and assessing competitors' culture. This section addresses additional errors that are germane to culture analysis.

A pervasive error in many organizations is the belief that it is essentially impossible to detect and describe any competitor's culture without extensive access to the inner workings of the competitor's organization. A related error is the belief that extensive data are necessary to conduct useful culture analysis. As the analysis in this chapter demonstrates, both beliefs are simply not true.

Analysts sometimes do not fully appreciate that culture represents the heartbeat and lifeblood of an organization: it is not just a statement of values and beliefs, and a listing of norms and behaviors. Thus, the purpose is not to describe and understand a competitor's culture per se, but rather to understand how the culture affects decisions taken by the competitor.

Relatedly, because culture pervades what an organization stands for (its values and beliefs) and how it operates and behaves, any single culture element—values, beliefs, norms, or behaviors—should not receive disproportionate attention. However, in part reflecting the importance accorded values in their own organization, analysts sometimes pay considerably more attention to values than the other culture elements. The result is an unbalanced view of competitors' cultures. It likely leads to misinterpretations—false or misleading signals.

Often, analysts fail to use culture as a source of questions about other micro components. As illustrated in the analysis of the electronics competitor, culture often provides unique insight into how a rival manages its activity/value chain or why it does not make specific marketplace strategy moves.

Different insights emerge when the cultures of multiple competitors are assessed. Even first-cut culture descriptions allow analysts to investigate how differences in the attributes of competitors' cultures—integration, embeddedness, alignment, durability, and adaptability—facilitate or inhibit winning. These differences are then used for self-learning—how the focal organization might better manage its own culture.

Organizations are often extremely reluctant to raise thorny issues and difficult questions about their own culture. Thus, a cardinal error is not to use competitors' cultures to identify and assess the focal organization's prevailing culture. While the reluctance to engage in critical self-learning is understandable, the reference point afforded by descriptions of one or more competitors' cultures encourages the focal organization to detect and assess its own *actual* values, beliefs, norms, and behaviors—as opposed to those it presumes to possess.

Finally, a guided culture analysis often greatly benefits from an open-ended perspective. It encourages analysts to be open to unexpected indicators, and to draw inferences from them. The result is sometimes unanticipated insights into the competitor's culture. A desire to execute efficient analysis sometimes drives out open-ended tendencies.

 ## Summary

Identifying and assessing any competitor's culture does not require exhaustive data gathering and extensive processing. It is possible to develop tentative first-cuts of competitors' cultures with surprisingly little data. Analysts then decide how much further learning might result by extending the analysis.

16

Projecting the Competitor's Future Marketplace Strategies

WINNING REQUIRES KNOWLEDGE ABOUT THE FUTURE.[1] DECISION MAKERS NEED TO develop facts,[2] perceptions, beliefs, assumptions, and projections about particular states of the future and about how these states might evolve from the present. In particular, analysts must develop knowledge about future states of individual (or groups of) competitors such as their future marketplace strategies, and of competitive domains such as the dynamics of rivalry among competitors.[3]

This chapter demonstrates the relevance and use of scenarios to develop knowledge of competitors' futures. It begins by delineating what a scenario is, as well as the scope, purpose, and characteristics of scenarios. After some specific guidelines for scenario development and use are noted, the content of scenarios is then briefly illustrated. The body of the chapter details how to construct and assess competitor scenarios and concludes by noting some common errors in scenario development and use.

Projecting Competitor Futures: The Use of Scenarios

Scenarios are a widely used methodology[4] to help decision makers understand how the future may evolve, how they themselves "see" the future (and, as a consequence, the present), and the decision implications of different "futures."

What a Scenario Is

Scenarios are descriptive narratives of plausible alternative projections of how some future will evolve. For our purposes, the *future* may assume many varied foci. It may refer to the future end-state[5] of an industry or competitive domain such as the number of players in it, their relationships with suppliers and channels, and the nature of its competitive dynamics. It may also refer to a competitor's future marketplace strategy.

A single scenario lacks a referent point. *Alternative* projections facilitate comparing and contrasting what could unfold under distinct conditions and assumptions. For example, scenarios depicting how a competitor could gain and lose significant market share quickly point to different events and conditions that would have to happen for each end-state (the gain or loss of market share) to occur.

Scenarios as depictions of the future are narratives in the sense that they represent explicit *descriptions* of plausible alternative competitive domain (or industry) evolutions or of the strategy options that a competitor might pursue. These descriptions have been called the plot[6] and "logics" of a scenario. They involve delineating not only what may evolve and how it may do so (the plot), but also why it may occur (the logics).

The descriptions (as well as the end-states) that lie at the heart of a scenario are best conceived as *projections.* Projections should not be confused with predictions. A projection should be interpreted as one view of the future that is based on some specific rationales, whereas predictions tend to be forecasts of things or events that *will* take place or happen. One might predict when new entrants will be enticed into a particular competitive domain or when a competitor will lower price on a particular product line. However, a projection (as the plot and "logics" of a scenario) would include the set of events that might occur that would lead to the emergence of new entrants or to a competitor lowering price.

Scenarios are *plausible* in that there is, or should be, some degree of evidence to support the projections they contain. Scenarios therefore are not random, off-the-wall, or blind projections; rather the logics buttressing the plot leading to particular end-states or outcomes can be tested for their plausibility.

A Range of Scenarios

Scenarios have many distinct applications in competitor learning depending on the type of scenario and the level of analysis (see Figure 16.1). Two types of projections merit attention. *Simple projections* entail plots and logics that are based on the intersection of current events and trends, and are likely to continue unabated, with modest change, for some time period.[7] They are thus largely extrapolations of the present into the future.

Scenarios, on the other hand, are *complex* projections or *alternative futures.* They represent possible futures. They stem from analysts' judgments, embodied in the articulated plots and logics, about how the future may evolve or be made to happen by one or more competitors and/or other organizations (including the focal firm).

Simple projections and alternative futures can be developed at the three analysis levels noted in Chapter 3: system level, competitor level, and microlevel. System-level scenarios address the future states of a competitive domain or industry. Competitor-level scenarios address competitors' possible marketplace strategies. Microlevel scenarios address the future of individual microlevel components such as projections around an individual competitor's assumptions or the evolution of its alliances or networks.

FIGURE 16.1
Types of Scenarios

Level \ Type	Simple Projections	Complex Projections: Alternative Futures
System	If current key industry trends continued, what would the industry look like 2 or 3 years from now?	What might be fundamentally different "futures" for the industry over the next 2 to 5 years?
Competitor	How would the competitor's strategy evolve if current trends in the marketplace remained constant and the competitor did not change itself in any significant way?	How might marketplace and other forces converge to lead the competitor to adopt radically different strategies compared with its strategy today?
Micro	If the competitor continued on its historic path, what would its activity/value chain look like 2 or 3 years from now?	How might forces internal and external to the competitor combine to cause it to manage its activity/value chain in different ways (and how would they differ from its activity/value chain today)?

Guided and Open-Ended Scenarios

Constructing and using scenarios draws heavily from both the guided and open-ended perspectives. Scenarios represent perhaps the only methodology detailed in this book that naturally integrates many key aspects of both approaches: they require an analytical structure for their execution but a mentality that is as unconstricted as possible.

Scenarios are *guided* in that they are generated with a view to deriving implications for particular strategies, decisions, or issues. Also, specific questions guide each step in constructing and assessing one or more scenarios. Reference to particular strategic decisions or challenges confronting an organization serves to bound scenario construction and assessment. For example, a set of scenarios might be developed to better understand the technology choices currently being appraised by a firm considering a significant shift in its marketplace strategy.

However, scenarios are (or should be) inherently open-ended. They are open-ended to the extent that presumptions are not made about the decisions or issues to which they are relevant. Often, it is only when scenarios are fully articulated and their implications are derived, that their relevance to specific strategies or decisions becomes evident. Moreover, successful scenario development requires analysts to suspend their presumptions and viewpoints about the future. It requires that no question, perspective, or issue is ruled inadmissible in constructing and considering the ramifications of scenarios. The open-ended approach also suggests that analysts should seek not only unconventional viewpoints and welcome inputs from sources external to the organization, but that scenarios should be used to challenge the prevailing wisdom and strategic perspectives within their own organization.[8]

Purpose of Scenarios

Scenarios are not an end in themselves. Their ultimate purpose is twofold: to enhance the knowledge of decision makers and (partly as a consequence) to augment the quality of decision making.

Enhancing Knowledge A fundamental purpose of scenarios is to enhance each of the knowledge elements discussed in Chapter 2: facts, perceptions, beliefs, assumptions, and projections. As participants in the analytical and organizational processes[9] involved in developing and using scenarios, decision makers often (explicitly and tacitly) create new knowledge. Because they require detailed depictions of how various futures could unfold, scenarios lead decision makers to question and challenge many aspects of their own and their organization's prior knowledge.

The essence of scenarios is a methodology by which organizations formally develop and test complex *projections* about the world around them. These projections, as detailed descriptions of various futures, such as how a competitive domain might unfold or how a competitor might adopt an entirely new strategy, frequently supersede previously shared or implicit expectations (projections) about the future.

Developing alternative projections (and considering their decision ramifications) often causes decision makers to question the relevance of specific *facts* previously deemed important, to see a different relationship among a given set of facts, and to unearth new facts.

Scenarios, perhaps, most affect decision makers' *perceptions* of the world around them. Well-constructed scenarios often reshape decision makers' impressions or opinions about what a competitor might be able to do, why it might do so, and what the results might be. Thus, scenarios sometimes dramatically reconfigure decision makers' tacit knowledge (perceptions, beliefs, assumptions, and projections they may not be consciously aware of).

Scenarios also affect decision makers' *beliefs* in multiple ways. They often lead to new beliefs about future actions of competitors and their consequences (e.g., if a competitor introduces a specific product, it will not result in a significant increment in market share). Also, many long-held beliefs about what is driving change in an industry may be replaced or discarded.

Because scenarios are complex projections of what might happen in the future, their implications for *assumptions* are extensive. Scenarios inevitably confront decision makers with challenges to prevailing assumptions, often resulting in the modification of existing assumptions and/or the adoption of new assumptions pertaining to the emerging and future marketplace, competitors' likely strategy moves, and what the focal organization itself must do to win.

Augmenting Decision Making The ultimate purpose of scenarios is not to enhance knowledge for its own sake but rather to augment the making of decisions. This occurs in at least three ways. First, scenarios sometimes bring *new decisions* to the organization's attention. As a result of constructing and assessing a set of industry scenarios, one organization decided to invest in a synthetic form of its core product, something that had previously received almost no consideration.

Second, scenarios often *reconfigure existing decisions* by either altering the array of alternatives or affecting the organization's viewpoint on individual alternatives. Compelled by an unexpectedly negative set of implications derived from competitor scenarios, one organization decided to divest a particular product group. This alternative had previously been explored but rejected.

Third, scenarios cause managers to *speed up or slow down* the making of particular decisions. Two or three distinct scenarios that all lead to a consistent implication (e.g., invest in research and development) frequently result in the suggested actions being executed more quickly than might otherwise be the case.

Key Attributes of Scenarios

The following characteristics are key attributes of well-constructed scenarios.

Articulated Plot and Logics The essence of each scenario should be a clearly articulated plot with supporting logics: a story that allows any individual to follow a set of events and to trace through the set of rationales that undergird the projected events and their results. Without such articulated logics, decision makers and others will find it impossible to decipher and test a scenario's plausibility.

Internal Consistency The logics must be internally consistent: each link in the chain of a scenario's story or plot must be logically connected to prior and subsequent links. A competitor that is selling 99 percent of its manufacturing capacity in one year cannot be projected to double its sales in the following year in the absence of any increment to its manufacturing capacity unless it can obtain supplies from other sources.

Specified Time Frame Key events, actions, and results, must be identified within some specified time frame. Otherwise, the scenario is difficult, if not impossible, to follow, understand, and assess.

Decision/Action Oriented Whether guided or open-ended, implications of scenarios for the organization's current and future decisions must be derived and demonstrated. Otherwise, scenarios are likely to degenerate into an exercise for their own sake.[10]

The Content of Competitor Scenarios

The preceding discussion suggests several elements that must be contained in any *competitor* scenario.

End-State This is the outcome at some point in the future such as the state of a particular competitor's marketplace strategy.

Plot The plot consists of what the competitor must do to get to the endstate. Plots address the actions the competitor takes to get from where it is today to the conditions delineated in the end-state. Plots therefore in part identify competitor consequences.

Driving Forces Plots and end-states are not merely the invention of imaginative minds. They are constructed out of driving forces: the conditions, trends, events, and other circumstances that shape or drive the story described in a particular plot. Many of these forces are specific to the competitor such as the ambitions of its senior executive team, or its assets, capabilities, or culture. Other forces are external to the competitor, such as changing demographics, technology developments, industry structure shifts, and regulatory change.

Analysts often need to distinguish between individual driving forces and *aggregate driving forces or uncertainties.* The latter are typically an amalgam of individual driving forces. They are the factors that analysts choose to investigate or manipulate[11] as the drivers of scenario outcomes. They are uncertain in that their direction and rate of change are difficult to anticipate. These factors are critical in that how they change is likely to greatly affect key scenario outcomes. Analysts thus often spend considerable time discussing and analyzing individual driving forces before choosing a small set of aggregate forces around which to create distinct scenario end-states and plots.[12]

On the other hand, some driving forces (i.e., specific conditions, events, circumstances) may be expected not to change, or to change very little, over the duration of the scenario time period—which we refer to as *accepteds.* For example, decision makers might accept that a competitor's commitment to doing what it takes to win in a particular product sector will show little, if any, change over the relevant scenario time period. They might also accept that the growth rate of a specific product sector would not increase by any substantial amount over the scenario timeline.

Some driving forces are *yet-to-be-played-outs:* changes (such as events, commitments, decisions) that have already occurred but consequences of which have not yet unfolded or have not yet played out. For example, a competitor has begun to build a new plant but it has not yet been completed and thus its output has not yet reached the marketplace.

It is also useful to identify *impossibles:* conditions or events that analysis shows cannot occur or that are extremely unlikely to happen during the scenario period. Although great care must be taken in determining what is impossible, attention to what may be impossible (and why it is so) sharpens analysts' understanding of the scenario context. For example, analysis may show that it is impossible for a competitor, using its current technology programs, to launch a major new breakthrough product within the next two years.[13]

Logics Scenario logics constitute the evidence or rationales for the content of the end-state and the plot—the "why" underlying the "what" and "how" of a plot.[14] Logics explain why specific forces, industry players, macroenvironmental actors (such as community groups or governmental institutions) behave as they do.

Types of Competitor Scenarios

Competitor scenarios can be developed in multiple ways. Three distinct though related approaches are briefly outlined. Each type of scenario is intended to identify and assess potential competitor strategy shifts, their plausibility, competitor consequences, and focal firm implications.

Emergent scenarios begin with the competitor's current marketplace strategy and ask: What strategy directions might evolve from it? By searching for patterns in the competitor's actions and words, analysts depict alternative plots and logics that provide insight into how the competitor might develop and adapt its current marketplace strategy.[15] Often, these scenarios alert decision makers to potential strategy alternatives that might already be underway or that the competitor could easily undertake.

Unconstrained what-if scenarios are generated when analysts ask open-ended or unconstrained what-if questions that suggest possible end-states, such as a completely new strategy. These then require the development of a plot and logics that would allow the competitor to trace a path to that future end-state from its current strategy.

Constrained what-if scenarios arise when analysts ask what the competitor would do under distinctly different competitive or industry conditions or end-states. These end-states typically result from the intersection of two or three key *uncertainties*.[16] These constrained what-if questions generate scenarios requiring the development of very different plots and supporting logics, which enable decision makers to project and assess widely disparate sets of competitor actions and their results.

Unconstrained and constrained what-if scenarios are especially appropriate for dealing with discontinuous competitor strategy change, which is often unanticipated by rivals. As a consequence, these scenarios often challenge decision makers' understanding of their competitive environment, and thus present a new perspective on what it takes for their organization to win.

Constructing Competitor Scenarios

As discussed, competitor scenarios necessitate careful development of projected end-states, plots and logics, competitor consequences, and focal firm implications. Each is briefly addressed in the case of an *unconstrained* what-if scenario using the yogurt competitor discussed in Chapters 5 and 6 for illustration. The steps in guided scenario construction (see Figure 16.2) are highly iterative and interrelated.

Decision Focus and Context

The focal yogurt firm was struggling with a classic strategic decision: how could it leverage its successful marketplace strategy in new geographic regions? In moving from being a regional to a national yogurt competitor, it would have to confront national rivals who had an established position and reputation in all geographic areas.

Identify Potential End-States: Possible Strategy Alternatives

The essence of competitor scenario development is identifying (and testing) likely plausible strategies that one or more competitors might pursue. Analysts therefore begin by generating the range of potential strategy alternatives that might be available to the competitor. It is not the intent at this stage either to develop fully or to assess these alternatives; rather the purpose is to identify what strategy possibilities might be open to the competitor. In doing so, analysts must step outside the bounds of conventional wisdom, the dictates of accepted analytical orthodoxy,[17] and the organizational pressures to develop "forecasts of what will happen."[18] There is no presumption at this stage that the competitor might pursue one strategy in preference to others.

In asking unconstrained what-if competitor strategy questions, two principles should guide the initial selection of possible strategy alternatives. First, they should be distinctly different: they should not be variants of one basic type of strategy. Strategies as different as "grow only through internal development" versus "grow through acquisitions" provide a broader frame of reference than a range of possibilities of growth through internal development. Second, they must be informed by knowledge both of the competitor *and* the broader competitive context. It is never enough to depend only on knowledge of an individual competitor; what a competitor may or may not do is greatly affected by what might occur in the broader competitive environment.

In the yogurt case, three fundamentally different potential marketplace strategies were identified (see Table 16.1). These strategies present distinct combinations of projected scope, posture, and goals. Each clearly constitutes distinct end-states. They also involve distinct plots and supporting

FIGURE 16.2
Constructing an Unconstrained What-If Scenario

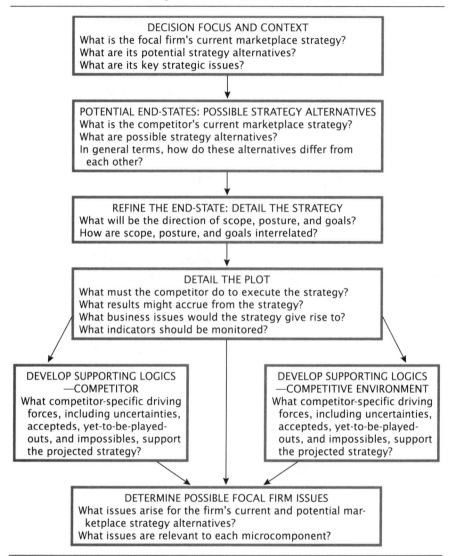

logics, and give rise to some distinct competitor consequences and focal firm implications.[19]

Merely identifying a range of apparently[20] plausible alternatives causes analysts to question and challenge the organization's (implicit and explicit) knowledge. For example, recognition that the yogurt competitor might enter the low-price market sector compelled some managers in the focal firm to

TABLE 16.1 Three Distinct Marketplace Strategies

Aggressive penetration of high-price market	Scope:	Add new product lines Add new varieties to existing lines Focus on all types of customers
	Posture:	Same general posture as now Emphasize coverage in all distribution channels Build cooperative relationships with channels
	Goals:	Dominate the high-price segment within 3 to 5 years Gain at least 3 market share points per year Add to profitability each year
Low-price market entry	Scope:	New product line New brand name Focus is on customer's now purchasing rivals' low-price products
	Posture:	Build new brand image through extensive advertising Use mass distribution aggressively Create deals with large channels Price at middle of low-price range
	Goals:	10% plus market share within 3 years Penetrate all key channels within 1 year Generate profits in second year
Maintaining present strategy projectory	Scope:	Continue with additions to existing product lines Continue to penetrate existing channels Add selected new channels
	Posture:	Add to perceived image as high-end product Continue to innovate with packaging Experiment further with service to channels Use salespersons to penetrate new, institutional, and other customers Maintain higher prices than most rivals
	Goals:	Pursue 2 market share points per year for at least 3 or 4 years Increase cash flow each year (in spite of continued investments) Internally, reduce costs (in part as a means to increase cash flow)

reconsider their long-held assumption that it was inconceivable that this competitor would enter, much less, launch an all-out attack on the low-price end of the market.

Identifying potential strategies is itself an iterative process. As analysts think about possible ways that a competitor might move into the future, a long listing of potential strategies often ensues. They then consider how these strategies might be grouped and how different the thrust of the groups are from each other. Eventually, they prune these down to a small set of distinctly different strategies, often choosing only three or four strategies that are then fully articulated.[21]

Detail Alternative Strategies (Refine the End-State)

Identifying a possible strategy end-state provides little of its details. Analysts need to project each marketplace strategy element: scope, posture, and goals. A projection for the strategy alternative, Win in the Low-Price Segment (see Figure 16.3), addresses product-customer direction (e.g., what products will be added to existing lines and the customers they are aimed at), posture (e.g., introduce a new brand name, provide higher service than is typically the case in the product segment, etc.), and goals (e.g., take market share from rivals in the low-price segment, thus making it more difficult for them to compete in the high(er) price segments).

Although there are no hard-and-fast rules as to how detailed a projected strategy should be, the more specified the alternative, the easier it is to determine what the competitor must do to execute it (the plot) and to identify and consider rationales that support or refute it (the logics). The details of a projected strategy illustrate to analysts and others how it might evolve; thus, it is in the details that understanding of the strategy resides.

Detail the Plot (Determine Competitor Consequences)

Delineating a strategy end-state does not identify what the competitor needs to do to *execute* it. A full understanding of what the strategy entails can be attained only by detailing what the competitor has to do to make strategy happen. Also, every projected strategy leads to outcomes or *results* (such as success or failure of new product introductions) that in turn give rise to *issues* for the competitor, further refinement of individual *uncertainties,* and key items to *monitor.* Identifying such consequences as an explicit part of any competitor scenario provides a critical linkage to the focal firm's decision making.[22] A number of scenarios typically give rise to both distinct and common competitor consequences.

Strategy Execution Greater clarity is obtained about a projected strategy's feasibility and viability[23] when analysts specify what the competitor *must do* to execute the strategy. This requires nothing short of delineating in a time-sequenced manner the actual steps involved in bringing the strategy to fruition: the decisions and action points that the competitor must execute to get products to the marketplace, and attract, win, and retain customers.

FIGURE 16.3
One Yogurt Competitor Scenario: Low-Price Market Entry

PROJECTED STRATEGY ALTERNATIVE
Add to existing product lines, a low-price line
Aimed at "generic" product customers
Different brand name
High service level, same national distribution, superior image,
   at price about same as low-end rivals
To provide competition for rival's low-end products
—Gain 10 percent of low-end sector within three years
—Achieve financial break-even within one year

SUPPORTING LOGICS—COMPETITOR
Needs to extend its product offering
   both to gain economies of scope
   and to preempt competitors
Can acquire product supply from
   vendors with whom it already has
   strong relationships
Has demonstrated capacity to build
   alliances as required
Fits with its apparent core assumptions that distinct market segments
   exist
Would leverage its extensive marketing and sales capabilities
Would be supported by an organization culture that values being "the
   best in the industry"

SUPPORTING LOGICS—COMPETITIVE
ENVIRONMENT
Projected growth rate of current seg-
   ments will not support the competi-
   tor's announced revenue targets
Higher growth in low-end segments
Channels demanding broad product
   coverage from suppliers
Successful competitors in low end
   might then move up the product
   ladder
Emergence of vendors specializing in
   providing products to branded
   competitors
Strategy will be especially successful
   if:
—Competitor can quickly establish
   a brand name
—With superior image
—At comparatively low price
—With strong channel support

CONSEQUENCES FOR THE COMPETITOR
Determine product content
Develop product
Acquire vendors
Establish own manufacturing
Create marketing programs
Build relationship with trade for new product line
Organize sales force
Could gain significant early market penetration
Significant issues around how best to differentiate the product,
   build brand name image, and leverage distribution channels
Need to monitor each execution step

IMPLICATIONS FOR THE FOCAL FIRM
Direct threat to current marketplace
   strategy
Similar products
—Going after the same customers
—Through the same channels
May eliminate potential sources of
   supply
May jeopardize potential alliance
   partners

Radically changes current marketplace assumptions
Existing capabilities may be insufficient to sustain sales growth
Introduce new options
May need to introduce new product
   line more quickly than planned

The following critical steps were identified in the low-price scenario:

- Determine product content.
- Develop products.
- Acquire vendors.
- Establish own manufacturing.
- Create manufacturing programs.
- Build relationships with the trade for product introductions and promotions.
- Organize sales force.

Strategy Results Without identifying a projected strategy's potential results, analysts have no way of knowing whether, and to what extent, the competitor will benefit from the projected strategy. The following questions are typically raised:

- If the strategy is successfully executed, what would be the marketplace results?
- In which market segments would the competitor be a leader?
- What would be the impact on the competitor's financial performance?
- If the strategy proved successful, would it lead to a reshaping of the stakes for the players?

Whether the yogurt competitor pursued a full-scale or low-key strategy, it would most likely gain (at least modest) penetration of the low-price market because of its assets and capabilities (to be discussed) and the difficulties that existing players might experience in fending off this new entrant. Stated differently, the analysts judged that the chances of the competitor failing completely or not attracting customers at all in the low-price segment were slim to none.

Business Issues Even a cursory review of a projected strategy, and what must be done to execute it, gives rise to issues that the competitor must confront, assess, and manage. Issues are broadly defined as challenges that the competitor must manage. Challenges involve choices among alternatives, requiring understanding of current and emergent change, and anticipating the shape and direction of future change. They take many forms such as critical decisions (in which the competitor may confront distinct, and sometimes, conflicting options), commitments of assets (in which the competitor is confronted with timing concerns or the irrevocability of some commitments such as building a manufacturing facility), distinct interpretations of how the future might evolve (such as projections of market growth or how competitors might respond to its own actions), bottlenecks (such as manufacturing constraints), or key events (such as an alliance with a supplier or cooperative agreement with a competitor) that need careful management.

Individual steps in strategy execution often have specific, and sometimes unique, issues associated with them. Also, as a strategy is implemented over time, issues that had not been anticipated are detected.

In the low-price strategy alternative, three overarching issues were detected:

1. How to best differentiate the new product line.

2. How to build the new brand name without jeopardizing the firm's existing lines.

3. How to build and sustain the support of multiple channels of distribution.

Each issue presented alternative courses of action. Success in managing each issue was central to strategy execution.

Uncertainties One side benefit of delineating what it takes to execute a strategy as well as its associated business issues is an identification of further uncertainties and/or refinement of previously noted uncertainties.[24] In the low-price scenario, each of the issues noted led to specific uncertainties. Channel management emerged as a specific uncertainty that was not previously appreciated: the competitor could choose to pursue all channels or only a select number.

What Should Be Monitored One major output of scenarios is that they alert analysts to those facets of a competitor (and the competitive environment) they should monitor. Each step in strategy execution may provide unique foci of monitoring.[25] Issues and uncertainties also suggest what should be monitored. Of particular importance to monitor in the competitor's low-price scenario were the early steps in product development and preparation for product launch. Indicators such as the acquisition of vendors, manufacturing program changes, and approaches to the channels would signal strong commitment to pursing this strategy.

Develop Supporting Logics

Insight into competitors, the marketplace, and the focal firm stems not from a competitor's projected strategy alternative, per se, but from the "logics"—

the rationales or arguments—that support it. Logics articulate how and why the projected strategy end-state and plot possess plausibility: the evidence that supports the projection; why it might make sense for the competitor; how and why it might be feasible; how it might fit with emerging and projected change in the marketplace.

Both competitor and competitive logics must always be considered. Competitor logics address competitor-specific rationales. Competitive logics address rationales pertaining to the environment surrounding the competitor (and the focal firm).

Competitor Logics For each projected strategy, analysts ask what competitor-specific (1) driving forces, (2) uncertainties, (3) accepteds, (4) yet-to-be-played-outs,[26] and (5) impossibles are leading or might lead the competitor in that marketplace direction.

1. *Driving forces.* What is it about a competitor that might lead it in a specific strategic direction? In the low-price scenario, two competitor-specific driving forces were judged to be dominant: the need to extend its product offering to gain both economies of scope and scale, and the need to preempt or impede competitors' current and potential marketplace moves. By adding a new product line to attract customers that were at best low-usage purchasers of its existing product lines, the competitor would attain economies of scope. Economies of scale would accrue in distribution, promotion, and sales activities, and to a lesser degree in manufacturing. Preempting and impeding current and potential competitors' marketplace moves (such as entry into the low-price segment) was a dominant driving force in that it served as the goal that was inspiring the competitor to undertake the strategy.

2. *Uncertainties.* Competitor-specific uncertainties constitute factors under the competitor's control that would most directly affect the projected marketplace strategy. Uncertainties, by definition, represent options or choices open to the competitor: they consist of factors the competitor can manipulate or manage.

Two uncertainties merited particular attention. How extensive would be the low-price product line that the competitor might develop and over what time period? To what extent would the competitor commit its resources to achieve rapid penetration of the low-price sector? The competitor might introduce a narrow product line, do so over a lengthy period, and commit only a modicum of resources to the strategy. Or, at the other extreme, it might develop a full product line, and do so as quickly as possible by committing extensive resources.

Both of these uncertainties would significantly affect each element in the projected marketplace strategy, and thus what the competitor would have to do to execute the strategy (and therefore its implications for the focal firm and other rivals).

3. *Accepteds.* Each framework component[27] is analyzed for accepteds, or "facilitators" of the projected strategy that could be accepted as unlikely to change.[28] Although there is no a priori reason to expect that one or more accepteds will emanate from each component, consideration of all components helps ensure that significant accepteds are not missed.

A number of accepteds were identified. First, the yogurt firm's apparent dominant assumption was that distinct business segments existed; this would allow the introduction of a product line under another brand name with minimal cannibalization of its existing product lines. Second, an organization culture that promotes being "the best in the industry" would motivate the competitor to do as well as it possibly could, should it decide to go after the low-price segment. Third, its strong marketing and sales capabilities were not likely to dissipate in the near future. Fourth, its already strong financial condition was likely to get stronger rather than weaker.[29]

4. *Yet-to-be-played-outs.* Consideration of yet-to-be-played-outs always compels analysts to develop linkages between the competitor's present and future. It helps to ground the development and assessment of scenarios in an understanding of how what the competitor is doing today, or has already done, is likely to shape what the competitor does at different points in the future.

It was too early to tell how a few key initiatives of the yogurt competitor would unfold. Yet each initiative could severely affect the outcome of the low-price scenario. One or two key alliances with providers of yogurt might not work out, thus potentially jeopardizing product supply. Most of the decisions and actions central to the low-price strategy had yet to be taken and executed.

5. *Impossibles.* Consideration of impossibles draws analysts' attention to further facets of a competitor that could critically shape a particular scenario. Some of these factors might not otherwise be explicitly articulated.

The analysts agreed on two key impossibles. First, the competitor could not introduce its potential new product line in less than 9 to 12 months: it would take that long to put in place required manufacturing, marketing, distribution, and sales programs. Second, it would be impossible for the competitor, irrespective of what marketing program it developed, to single-handedly raise the growth rate of the total yogurt market by more than one percent per year.[30]

Competitive Logics   A competitor's potential marketplace strategy may be facilitated or inhibited by current, emerging, and projected developments in and around the marketplace.

Often easily discernible trends and patterns in the competitive environment coalesce to provide a compelling rationale for a particular projected strategy. Sometimes, one trend or pattern alone is not convincing, but a number of such forces pushing in the same direction add significantly to the likelihood that a competitor will move (or ought to move) in a particular direction.

Marketplace forces might drive the yogurt competitor to enter the low-price market segment. Growth in this segment was considerably higher than in the higher priced segments; current competitors that succeeded in the low-price segment would be better positioned to win in the higher priced segments; and many distribution channels were demanding that suppliers offer them the broadest possible coverage.

A competitive context may present a few or a multiplicity of uncertainties. The uncertainties analysts choose to investigate typically generate distinct competitive environments in which a competitor's projected strategy would play out.

Two uncertainties were deemed to be of particular relevance to the yogurt scenarios. First, would competitors continue to invest heavily in marketing, promotion, and sales activities? Second, could substitute products emerge that would further retard growth of the yogurt sector? These two uncertainties generate four radically different competitive contexts (see Figure 16.4). Analysts can now begin to ask how the projected strategy would play out in each of these environments.

Accepteds often provide a base of givens relevant to competitive environments such as those noted in Figure 16.4.

Two accepteds were deemed to be intimately related to the driving forces and uncertainties previously noted. First, the overall growth of the yogurt market was not likely to increase; indeed, it was most likely to remain at or about the mostly stagnant level of the prior five years. Second, most competitors would continue to innovate in their efforts to manage the marketplace rules to attract, win, and retain customers. Thus, the intensity of rivalry was not expected to abate.

Competitive domains are always witnessing the unfolding of the ramifications of prior decisions, commitments, and events. As in the case of driving forces and uncertainties, it is the interaction of these yet-to-be-played-outs that generates insight.

Such was the case in the yogurt marketplace. A few competitors had introduced new products or extended existing product lines. The success or failure of these products could lead to quite different competitive dynamics in specific price/image categories or within specific geographic regions. A number of competitors had either extended their manufacturing capacity or had

FIGURE 16.4
Four Competitive Contexts

		Emergence of Substitute Products	
		Yes	**No**
Marketing/Sales Expenditures	**High**	DOG-EAT-DOG-WARFARE In this competitive environment, rivals compete for every individual channel, retail account, and end-customer as if their lives depended on it.	COMPETITIVE INTENSITY In this competitive environment, rivals compete against each other largely to defend existing customer base, and with the expectation that they can achieve modest gains at the expense of others.
	Low	CONTROLLED AGGRESSION In this competitive environment, rivals do not seek to upstage each other; they are willing to share the spoils among themselves.	LIVE AND LET LIVE In this competitive environment, rivals are generally comfortable with their market position and do not try to upset the balance among themselves.

announced their intention to do so. When these additional product supplies appeared, the market could also affect pricing and other competitive dynamics. Almost all competitors had changed the focus and content of their advertising. It was still unclear how these efforts would affect product image and consequent sales. Some large supermarket channels had raised concerns about the number of brands and the amount of shelf space they consumed, thus implying questions about the profitability of the product sector for them.

All alleged impossibles at the competitive level must be treated with great caution since change is so unpredictable and sometimes occurs with surprising speed. However, one short-run impossible was noted. No single competitor would "break from the pack." Given the approximately equal market share of the leading competitors, the presence of strongly entrenched local competitors in many geographic regions, and the prohibitive cost of "buying market share," it did not seem likely that any single competitor could attain a dominant market position within the succeeding two or three years.

Determine Possible Focal Firm Issues

Competitor scenarios are connected to the focal firm when implications for its current and future decisions are derived. Without this connection, scenarios remain as nice-to-know depictions of what competitors might do and why they might do so. The intent here is to identify current and future issues,[31] not to determine what to do about them; action implications are identified as one of the final elements in assessing scenarios.

Possible focal firm issues must be included in scenario construction for at least two reasons. First, as issues are identified, they sometimes cause decision makers to reflect on, challenge, and alter their own knowledge. Issues often suggest new questions about the competitor (and the competitive context) or a new emphasis on previously considered questions. Second, issues sometimes generate new decisions or lead to a reframing of existing decisions.

In keeping with the competitor analysis framework advanced throughout this book, possible issues can be considered about the focal firm's marketplace strategy and its microlevel components.

Marketplace Strategy Projections of competitors' strategies often quickly generate specific positive and/or negative issues for the focal firm's *current* marketplace strategy. Strategies intended to alter the strategy game[32] and/or its marketplace rules can put the focal firm's current strategy at severe risk, irrespective of its historic results. This is well exemplified in the low-price scenario. The competitor's projected product line would constitute a direct threat to the focal firm's existing products; both firms would be offering essentially similar products, going after the same customer segment, through the same distribution channels, and with reasonably similar prices. Were the competitor to carry through with the projected strategy, the competitive dynamics of the low-price segment would be radically altered.

Competitors' projected strategies also generate issues pertaining to the focal firm's *potential strategy alternatives.* They often identify substantial threats to the focal firm's planned products, some of which may be at an advanced stage of development. More positively, competitors' projected strategies sometimes direct the focal firm's attention to emerging product change, to potential market opportunities, to the possibility of following one or more competitors into a specific customer niche. In the low-price scenario, the focal firm's long-term goal of moving into higher priced products might be jeopardized if its cash flow from existing product lines were reduced.

Micro Components Consideration of each micro component can help identify potential implications that might not be self-evident from a quick perusal of a competitor's projected strategy including what it takes to execute it, and its associated issues and uncertainties. Moreover, linkages among issues often lead to consideration of decisions and actions that might not necessarily emanate from any single component or individual issue.

Some issues pertaining to each microlevel component of the low-price strategy are noted in Table 16.2. A few of these (activity/value chain, networks, and assets) are briefly discussed.

1. *Activity/value chain.* The competitor's need for external sources of product supply (to meet its sales goals) might eliminate potential supply sources for the focal firm. Thus, a severe constraint might be imposed on its ability to dramatically increase its product sales. A possible need to more rapidly introduce one or more products (to preempt some of the benefits that might accrue to one or more competitors introducing specific types of product) implies a much tighter integration of all the activities and tasks across the activity/value chain.

2. *Networks.* Although the competitor may not have intended to do so, its alliances and relationships with many entities such as vendors, suppliers, distribution channels, and logistics firms, in effect create a network. The resultant benefits such as extended and guaranteed supply of product compel the focal organization to reappraise its historic approach to dealing with both ends of its activity/value chain—its supplier base and its distribution channels.

3. *Assets.* The low-price projected strategy indicates that the competitor could successfully fund and execute a major new marketplace initiative while simultaneously aggressively pursuing stretch goals[33] in the high-price end of the market. Thus, an unavoidable issue for the focal firm is whether it could obtain the necessary assets to simultaneously compete in both high-price and low-price ends of the market.

Assessing Competitor Scenarios

Learning accrues when scenarios are assessed for their knowledge and decision ramifications. A guided approach begins by (re)sensitizing analysts to the specific elements of the projected strategy and to the scenario's attributes (see Figure 16.5). The scenario's plausibility is then tested: logics must be challenged. Finally, it is always necessary to determine competitor consequences and focal firm implications.

Understanding the Projected Strategy

Assessment usefully begins by (re)sensitizing analysts to both the general contours of a projected strategy and its unique features. Since it is all too

TABLE 16.2   Issues for the Focal Firm: Microlevel Components

Microlevel Components	Issues for the Focal Firm	Outwitting, Outmaneuvering, and Outperforming
Activity/value chain	The competitor's stated desire to better integrate all activities as a prelude to introducing its new product line implies a need for the focal firm to review and assess management of its own activity/value chain	The competitor may outmaneuver the focal firm by more effectively integrating all the activities across its value chain; one result being shorter time to market
Alliances and relationships	The competitor's success in acquiring new external sources of supply might eliminate potential supply sources for the focal firm	The competitor may see the need for an extended supply base and therefore change in the marketplace
Networks	The competitor's mix of formal and informal relationships with "industry" participants may be allowing it to do a better job than the focal firm in leveraging resources that it does not own	The focal firm may be outwitted due to an outdated perspective on appropriate relationships with other entities in and around its industry
Assumptions	The competitor's implied assumptions about its ability to win in the low-price segment compel the focal firm to review its own assumptions about what it takes to win in every price segment	The competitor may be outwitting its rivals; it may have figured out a way to win convincingly in the low-price segment
Assets	The competitor's capacity to "resource" a major entry into the low-price segment while simultaneously competing aggressively in all other segments raises the issue of whether and how the focal firm might also be able to do so	The competitor may be able to outmaneuver and outperform all rivals by being better able to initiate and sustain multiple innovative ways of competing in the marketplace
Capabilities and competencies	The competitor's ability to build and sustain distinct images around its different product lines should cause the focal firm to ask whether it could do so, if so, how	The focal firm may need to assess its entire marketing approach if it aspires to outperform this competitor
Technology	The competitor is using information and other technologies to speed up the flow of information from and to channels and end-customers, and others including vendors and suppliers	The competitor may be outmaneuvering the focal firm and others through its use of technology
Organization	The competitor's values and beliefs that are driving its intense will to win require the focal firm to appraise its own culture, especially if it has to confront another aggressive, well-funded competitor	The competitor may have outwitted many of its rivals by recognizing that winning in the marketplace is heavily influenced by the culture created within the organization

FIGURE 16.5
Assessing Competitor Scenarios

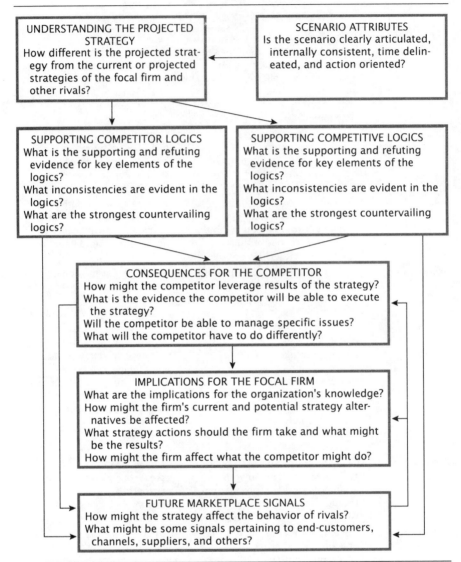

easy to get lost in the details of any single scenario,[34] analysts sometimes find themselves assessing specific elements of a scenario (such as the degree of integration of the projected posture) rather than the scenario as an integrated whole. A focus on the overall scenario—its marketplace strategy content, underlying plot and logics, competitor consequences, and focal firm implications—is more likely to direct analysts' attention to the central and critical assessment issues and questions.

A sense of the uniqueness of a potential strategy, gleaned through comparison with the current (and projected) strategies of the focal firm or other competitors, also sensitizes analysts to central and important assessment issues and questions. Even a preliminary comparison may highlight the need for thorough and careful assessment. Such preliminary comparisons sometimes indicate that a competitor could potentially develop a dominant strategy that would likely win irrespective of what some other rivals did.

Consideration of some of the key judgments about the competitor itself and the competitive environment (such as the choice of uncertainties) on which the scenario hinges also helps to inform analysts about key assessment issues and questions.

Scenario Attributes

Assessment of its attributes also sharpens analysts' understanding of a scenario in multiple ways. Assessment of the extent to which it is clearly articulated, internally consistent, time delineated, and action oriented, compels consideration of a scenario as an interrelated and integrated whole rather than as a set of isolated and stand-alone elements.

The low-price strategy was judged to be extensively articulated (i.e., competitor and competitive logics were elaborated), well delineated with regard to time (time-dependent sequences were specified), and with an emphasis on its action consequences for the competitor (what the competitor had to do to execute the strategy was outlined).

Scenarios often founder on the rock of internal consistency. Key internal consistency questions can be raised with regard to the strategy projection, the plot and logics, and the connection between the logics and the projection. Although assessing internal consistency and scenario plausibility are obviously intimately related,[35] the argument here is that if internal consistency is assessed, even at a general level *before* scenario plausibility, the focus in testing scenario plausibility can be sharpened. Some sample questions include:[36]

- Are the scope, posture, and goals mutually consistent and reinforcing?
- Are the projected modes of competing within posture consistent?
- What inconsistencies might arise among the goals?
- Are the driving forces and key uncertainties consistent?

- Will the driving forces and key uncertainties lead to the scope, posture, and goals in the projected strategy?

Particular attention was paid to the internal consistency of the projection in the low-price scenario. One concern was whether entry into the low-price segment would be inconsistent with the competitor's long-established commitment to winning in the high-price, high-image, market segment. The judgment of the analyst team was that it would be possible to win in both segments with distinct brand names.[37] The projected posture was also assessed for its internal consistency: each mode of competition was deemed appropriate to winning in the low-price market segment.

Assessing Plausibility

Logics must be critically appraised beyond its consistency.[38] It is necessary to review, challenge, and assess each major link in the causal chain of reasoning represented in the logics. Apparently persuasive and convincing arguments sometimes dissipate in the face of testing the evidence. Both supportive and countervailing evidence must be treated. As illustrated throughout this book, articulating the strongest countervailing arguments often results in modifications to the interpretation or outcomes of the initial "supporting logic." It might be argued that real understanding of the logics emerges only in this stage: in endeavoring to answer the types of questions noted earlier, analysts often refine the individual relationships in the causal chains linking driving forces and uncertainties to that which is projected.

As in constructing a scenario, competitor and competitive logics are separately assessed and then integrated (see Figure 16.6).

Competitor Logics Assessment of competitor logics requires a thorough appraisal of each line of argument or individual logics, such as individual driving forces or accepteds, as well as their collective logics. To control some of the inevitable biases,[39] as much as possible, analysts should assess the individual and collective logics, independent of or before the strongest countervailing logics is developed. Guiding questions include:

- What is the supporting evidence for each argument or line of logics?
- Are the alleged driving forces compelling?
- Could the driving forces lead to what is projected?
- If the presumed results did accrue, of what benefit would they be to the competitor?
- Does the competitor possess the asserted capability or competency?

FIGURE 16.6
Assessing a Yogurt Competitor's Scenario

PROJECTED STRATEGY ALTERNATIVE
Opposite, but complementary to, the competitor's
current marketplace strategy
But, in large measure similar to focal firm's
Key judgments:
  Assumption about growth of low-end segment
  Ability to develop a new brand name
  Absence of effective retaliatory responses on the
  part of existing competitors

SCENARIO ATTRIBUTES
Logical increment to
  existing strategy
Could be achieved over
  a 3-year timeline
Is expressly action
  oriented

SUPPORTING LOGICS—COMPETITOR
Supporting Logics:
  Competitor could potentially gain
  strong economies of scope by adding a distinct new product line
  Every activity in its activity/value
  chain can be leveraged in developing and introducing the new line
  Competitor has the financial wherewithal to build its own manufacturing capacity should the initial
  launch prove successful
Countervailing Logics:
  No other competitor has successfully launched a low-end brand
  Would preempt competitors only if
  successful; could be vulnerable to
  a strong attack by one or more
  competitors
  Product supply could be vulnerable
  to interruption of vendors'
  capacities
  Has no proven record in competing
  in the low-price market segment
  Organization culture strongly
  oriented to high-price, high-end
  image; thus, could have severe difficulty in reorienting toward the
  low end

SUPPORTING LOGICS—COMPETITIVE
ENVIRONMENT
Supporting Logics:
  Little evidence that overall growth
  rate of the industry will increase beyond recent experience
  However, growth in lower end could
  decline from recent rates due to
  saturation of market and marketing
  responses of high-price competitors
  The competitor's success in the low-
  price end would make it more difficult for current low-price rivals to
  move up the product ladder
Countervailing Logics:
  Increased intensity of rivalry in low-
  price end, in part due to the com-
  petititor's entry, will lower prices
  further, cause marketing and distribution costs to rise, thus making if
  difficult for the competitor to reach
  its market share and profit goals
  Some large retail channels may not
  be nearly as receptive as anticipated to a new low-end brand

CONSEQUENCES FOR THE COMPETITOR
If the competitor succeeds with the new product, it will have a unique
  position in the business
Major initiative is development of a new brand, something the com-
  petitor has never done in the yogurt business
All other major elements in the required action plan do not present
  anything that is new for the competitor
Strategy is compatible with current goals
Strategy will require the competitor to overcome supply constraints—
  would appear it can do so

(Continued)

FIGURE 16.6   *(Continued)*

IMPLICATIONS FOR THE FOCAL FIRM
Potential significant negative implications—the competitor's potential
  strategy represents a real threat to the focal firm's existing business
Alters current assumptions and marketplace projections so that significant strategy change is required
Suggests the need to develop alternative strategy responses
New product at a higher price point than current product line if introduced more quickly than currently planned may cushion negative
  implications

FUTURE MARKETPLACE SIGNALS
Competitor's entry could precipitate a new set of competitive dynam-
  ics in the low-price segment, including a possible price war
If other competitors imitate the strategy, then all existing competitors
  can expect less market share, less margins, less profits
Power of channels vis-à-vis manufacturers would further increase

---

In the low-price case, the *driving forces* were indeed compelling. The yogurt competitor could gain significant economies of scope and scale
through the introduction of the low-price product line. These economies
could potentially grant the competitor substantial competitor and customer
advantage.

Assessment of linkage between driving forces and accepteds also sheds
light on a scenario's plausibility. Economies of scope would obviously be
more difficult to gain if the total yogurt market remained essentially stagnant and if competitive intensity continued to increase in all sectors of the
market.

Competitive Logics   Competitive logics are assessed in the same manner
as competitor logics. Again, the analysts' charge is to test the supporting or
refuting evidence for individual logics as well as the collective logics. Frequently, analysts must make unavoidable judgments about emerging and projected competitive change. For purposes of illustration, we will emphasize
assessment as the level of the collective logics.

The projected low-price strategy is supported by a strong *competitive*
rationale. There was no evidence to support an upturn in market growth
in the high-price product sectors; success in the low-price sector would be
increasingly important to winning in the overall yogurt marketplace. Distribution channels were already increasingly favoring those competitors
with full product lines. Also, the resultant competitive dynamics of a
major new entrant in the low-price segment would make it considerably
more difficult for current low-price players and other potential entrants

to use their success in the low-price segment as either a stepping-stone to involvement in the higher price segments or to use the consequent cash throw-off in the high-end segments.

Little plausible countervailing evidence was apparent. However, if multiple other rivals also entered the low-price segment (most likely after the competitor under review did so), the competitor might well meet with little success in its efforts to penetrate this segment.

Consequences for the Competitor

Every projected strategy gives rise to specific competitor consequences—strategy results, strategy execution, business issues, and uncertainties. Assessing these consequences affords an opportunity to test whether the strategy will generate acceptable returns for the competitor and whether the competitor is able to execute the strategy. Each consequence is briefly discussed.

Results A distinction must be made between alternative scenario results (such as marketplace and financial returns for the competitor, and changes in the strategy game and marketplace rules), and whether the competitor would be content with particular results, including how it might leverage one set of results compared with others. Typical guiding questions include:

- What range of results might ensue?
- Do the results meet or exceed the competitor's goals?
- What actions of the competitor are most critical to attaining specific results?
- Which other players might affect the results, what might they do, and are they likely to do so?
- How might the competitor take advantage of the results?

In the low-price scenario, if the yogurt competitor successfully penetrated the low-price segment, it would attain a unique position in the business: it would be the only competitor with distinct leading brands in every major price segment. Such a result would contribute greatly to the competitor's espoused strategic intent of becoming the dominant supplier in the business.

Its consequent dominant position could then be leveraged with distribution channels, many of which (as previously noted) were reviewing their need to carry a large number of vendors. Also, some of the incremental cash thrown off could be directed toward further product development.

These results would influence and affect other competitors. One conse-quence might be added difficulty for other rivals both to enter and to sustain their position in some channels. The stakes in all segments of the market would be affected: many competitors might well attain lower returns than expected or customary in the low-price sector.

Strategy Execution   Assessment of results presumes that the competitor is able to execute the strategy necessary to attain them. Often this is not the case. Assessing a competitor's capacity to implement a projected strategy draws on analysts' knowledge of the competitor generated through the types of analysis addressed in Chapters 5 through 15. Guiding questions include:

- What new initiatives and actions does the strategy necessitate?
- Where are the bottlenecks likely to be?
- What assets does the strategy require? Does the competitor now pos-sess these assets or can it attain them?
- What capabilities and competencies are required? How do they fit with the competitor's current capability and competency profile?
- How will the competitor's organizational infrastructure and culture fa-cilitate or impede specific actions?
- Which of the competitor's current constraints, limitations, and vulner-abilities are most likely to affect execution of the strategy?

None of the strategy execution steps required the competitor to do any-thing that was new to it, with the exception of developing a new brand. Moreover, it did not appear that the competitor suffered any financial, phys-ical, or organizational asset deficiencies or limitations that would impede or retard execution of the projected strategy. However, the competitor would have to develop a new set of perceptual assets: a new brand name, customer loyalty to the new brand, and strong channel perceptions of both the brand and its ability to introduce and sustain the new brand.

Issues   Assessment of issues offers a more pointed focus to assessment. In particular, it directs attention to what the competitor may do in the future.[40] Guiding questions typically include:

- What has the competitor done to date to manage the issue and what have been the results?
- What options are available to the competitor in managing the issue?
- Why might the competitor pursue one option rather than others?

- How might the competitor be constrained in pursuing any of the options?

In the low-price scenario, each of the issues noted previously was central to winning in the low-price market segment. Each presented critical assessment challenges. For example, assessment of "how best to differentiate the new product line" required analysts to assess whether and how the competitor might specifically succeed in differentiating its new product from existing and potential rivals. Analysts were able to lay out how the competitor might do so, what assets and capabilities it would require, and what the results might be.

Uncertainties Including attention to competitor-specific uncertainties reminds analysts that scenario construction and assessment is always necessarily iterative and that learning is inherently continuous. For example, monitoring the emergence and evolution of substitute products generates extensive learning about product change, customers' responses to alternative products, and rivalry between the providers of the competing products.

Future Marketplace Signals

A competitor's projected strategy and its associated logics typically allow the derivation of multiple signals about the marketplace in which the strategy will play out. An understanding of the potential marketplace context is an unavoidable input into assessing scenario plausibility, competitor consequences, and focal firm implications. Typical *guiding* questions include:

- How might the strategy cause other competitors to act?
- What might be the ramifications for channels, end-customers, suppliers, and other entities?
- What might be the resultant dynamics among rivals?
- How might the focus of competition be different from what it is now?
- What might be the marketplace results for individual (and classes of) competitors?

Were the yogurt competitor to pursue and successfully execute the projected strategy, several marketplace ramifications would ensue. Current providers of yogurt would follow the competitor into the low-price segment; competition among rivals in the low-price segment would continually intensify resulting in downward pressure on prices, margins, and profits; as a consequence, over time some rivals would suffer a decline in profitability to the point they probably would be compelled to withdraw from the segment; many channels would experience an increase in power versus suppliers; and end-customers would see greater product variety and lower prices.

Implications for Focal Firm

The purpose of assessment to this point is to aid the specification and choice of decision and action implications for the focal firm—what the focal firm should do, how it should do so, and why. In keeping with the thrust of the analysis framework presented throughout this book, implications are segmented into the following three elements: knowledge, marketplace strategy, and micro components. Implications across these elements are highly interrelated.

Knowledge Projecting a competitor's potential marketplace strategy, developing and assessing its plot and underlying logics, and deriving competitor consequences and focal firm implications, often directly causes both single- and double-loop learning.[41] In either case, the organization's facts, perceptions, beliefs, assumptions, and projections are likely to be altered, and sometimes dramatically so. It is in this sense that the purpose of scenarios is often cited as changing management's understanding of the current world around them and the future world that soon may be upon them.

In the yogurt case, the focal firm's knowledge did undergo considerable change. It adopted new *projections* about the likely actions of both the competitor and other rivals, the future state of the yogurt marketplace, and its own potential actions. In short, its view of the future was altered.

Change was evident even in the case of *facts.* Some new facts were accepted. For example, the focal firm's leading position in its historic geographic area was not as secure as the firm had traditionally believed.

The focal firm's *perceptions* about both the competitor and the potential competitive context, it seems fair to say, were shattered. The perception of the competitor as a docile, slow-moving rival, shifted to that of a potentially aggressive, path-breaking rival that could irrevocably alter the playing field in all segments of the yogurt market.

Some fundamental *beliefs* also changed. First, the focal firm recognized that its own historic strategy, if it did not undergo significant change, would not continue to generate the returns to which the firm had become accustomed. Second, it accepted that new entrants would cause a lowering of profitability for all participants in the low-price end of the yogurt market. Third, it also decided that entering the high-price segment or moving beyond its historic geographic boundaries would not lead to the sales growth or profit increments previously anticipated.

Perhaps the most fundamental knowledge shift occurred in *assumptions*. The focal firm was now willing to assume that new entrants into the low-price segment would take place; that these entrants would be aggressive pursuers of market share; that the historic stability of the low price segment would be destroyed; and that it needed to move beyond its historic niche in the low-price segment.

These shifts in knowledge directly affect development and evaluation of marketplace strategy alternatives as well as options within each micro component (and, in turn, are affected by consideration of these alternatives and options).

Marketplace Strategy Significant strategy implications emerged. First and foremost, the focal yogurt firm's current marketplace strategy would come under severe threat if the competitor (or another similar competitor) were to enter the low-price segment. Thus, two dominant implications were manifest: the need to buttress and reinforce the focal firm's marketplace strategy in its historic geographic area, and the need to develop and execute strategy alternatives that would alleviate the firm's dependence on, and thus vulnerability to, the low-price segment.

Buttressing the firm's historic strategy led to specific sets of actions. To leverage its strong local image, the firm decided to develop a new advertising program to emphasize its local roots and perceived superiority to rivals. It also decided to target many institutional customers such as hospitals, cafeterias, and restaurant chains that previously had largely been ignored.

However, the competitor's low-price scenario clearly identified the focal firm's vulnerability to attack by existing and new rivals if it restricted its marketplace scope to its historic geographic area. Thus, for the first time, the firm identified and assessed strategy alternatives that entailed moving beyond its existing marketplace scope. The options included:

- Developing a high-price product line to compete directly against the entrenched high-end rivals.
- Entering adjacent geographic regions.
- Acquiring or merging with a competitor outside its current region.

Since the firm did not have the resources to acquire another competitor, and its senior managers did not want to entertain the option of a merger (in large part because it might jeopardize the firm's culture), the first two options received extensive analysis. The management team decided to enter adjacent regions slowly, carefully, and methodically.

Microlevel Components As illustrated in the focal firm microlevel issues noted earlier (see Table 16.2), scenarios around even a single competitor's potential strategies can lead to significant microlevel implications. The potential scope and scale of microlevel implications are reinforced when marketplace strategy implications such as those noted for the focal firm (e.g., moving into contiguous geographic areas) are taken into account. The early detection and superior execution of microlevel implications often contribute greatly to outwitting, outmaneuvering, and outperforming competitors.

The microlevel implications were indeed extensive for the focal firm (see Table 16.3). Key decisions and actions pertained to each microlevel component. Rather than discuss each microlevel component in detail, we will highlight key implications and interactions among them.

Preparing for the entrance of one or more competitors into its historic "home" market while also planning to enter contiguous regions, would

TABLE 16.3 Microlevel Implications: The Yogurt Firm

Microlevel Components	*General Implications*	*Some Consequent Decisions/Actions*
Activity/Value chain	Integrate all activities	Conduct detailed cost analysis
	Manage costs more carefully with each activity	Establish cross-functional teams
Alliances and relationships	Build stronger relationships with every external entity	Assign responsibility for major customers to key individuals
Networks	View itself as part of a larger network of entities seeking common goals	Conduct analysis of how to lead and contribute to the network
Assumptions	Challenge long-held assumptions about the market, what it takes to win, and itself	Make specific changes in its assumptions about specific price segments, rivals, and itself
Assets	Direct resources toward winning in new geographic markets	Develop programs to acquire and leverage additional resources
Capabilities and competencies	Build new customer capabilities	Assign teams to develop action plans
	Build new cost control capabilities	
Technology	Investigate technologies needed to develop better data and information	Work with third-parties to develop the requisite technologies
Organization	Review how culture inhibits necessary decisions and actions	Develop cross-functional teams to identify required culture change

require the focal firm to pay detailed attention (for the first time) to integrating the activities across its activity/value chain. For example, in the interest of achieving significantly greater cost efficiencies, logistics would have to be managed so that inventories of raw materials, work-in-progress, and finished products were kept to a minimum.

Successful execution of these changes required cross-functional teams for greater coordination across activities. Such infrastructural change would require an extensive change in the organization's culture: its values, beliefs, norms, and behaviors were still mired in a departmentalized and functional "stovepipe" mode of operating.

Developing a new mode of managing the business would in turn necessitate a new way of thinking about the business—a new mentality or sets of assumptions about how best to run and manage the business.[42]

Assessing Implications across Multiple Scenarios

Assessment, as outlined, must be conducted across two or more scenarios. Robust implications (common to two or more scenarios; see Figure 16.7)

FIGURE 16.7
Industry or Competitor Scenarios

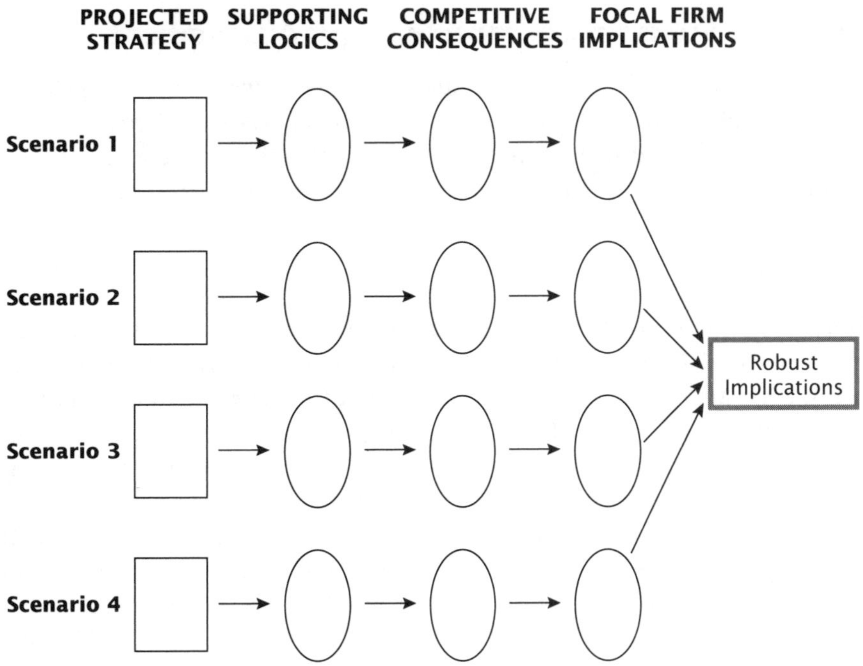

typically indicate decisions and actions that demand serious consideration. The scenarios developed around the marketplace strategies briefly sketched in Table 16.1 led to two common implications. First, the need to consider extending the firm's current product line emerged as imperative if the focal firm desired to escape becoming a captive of its current product-customer segment. Second, the need to pay specific attention to managing the firm's cost structure would become increasingly urgent as rivalry intensified in the marketplace.

Assessing Multiple Competitors' Scenarios

Assessing scenarios of two or more competitors generates projections of the future marketplace, the dynamics of likely rivalry, and consequences for specific groups of competitors. These projections in turn suggest implications for the focal firm; some of these implications may differ from those derived from any single competitor's scenarios. Scenarios developed around two or more competitors' marketplace strategies, intended to reconstruct a market segment or competitive arena, can indicate the broad contours of the marketplace any competitor might face at some future point: the products that would be offered; the value that would be provided to customers; and the focus of the rivalry among competitors.

Errors in Scenario Construction and Assessment

Critical scenario errors pertain to the disposition of analysts (and especially decision makers) toward scenarios, and to the analysis and organizational processes associated with scenario development and use. These errors have specific implications for the learning model outlined in Chapter 2.

Disposition

Some of the most fundamental scenario errors stem from decision makers' incorrect preconceptions of scenario learning. A pervasive problem is that many analysts view scenarios as assertions of what will happen (predictions) rather than as articulations of what could happen (projections). This error essentially precludes individuals from asking open-ended questions about what could or might happen in the future.

A related error is the unwillingness of individuals to (try to) suspend their beliefs, suppositions, and presumptions about the future. They do not enter into scenario construction with an open mind as to how the future might unfold. Thus, they do not allow scenarios to become a means to identify, challenge, and if need be, change their core beliefs and assumptions about how competitors might change the strategy game in the long run or alter marketplace rules in the short run. Stated differently, double-loop learning is not likely to occur.

A final error worth noting here is that many analysts are often unclear about the purposes and uses of scenarios. They become obsessed with the nuances and details of individual scenarios and differences across them. They forget that the purpose of scenarios is not just to develop understanding of alternative competitor futures but to augment the quality of decision making.

Analysis

A common analytical error occurs when analysts do not allow scenario development and assessment to be adequately open-ended: sufficient attention is not paid to choosing uncertainties (the variables around which end-states are crafted); end-states are not compared and contrasted; different relationships among driving forces are not examined; and individuals simply don't ask with enough vigor—could this future really evolve? For example, could a competitor make this type of marketplace strategy work?

A reflection of this error is a tendency to partially predetermine scenario content by choosing two or three scenarios to cover a spectrum of possibilities such as optimistic, pessimistic, and middle-of-the-road views of the future. Such forced categories inhibit the development of scenarios more likely to offer greater insight for decision making. Hence, knowledge is shortchanged.

Sometimes, analysts do not fully appreciate the iterative nature of scenario construction and use. As illustrated in the yogurt example, the steps in scenario development and use are tightly interrelated. Treating the steps as a simple sequential process gravely impedes refinement of scenarios and thus learning.

Organization Processes

The most critical organizational error is the separation of those who develop scenarios from those who must integrate scenario content into decision making. In this way, only a small part of the knowledge that accrues to the developers of scenarios is transferred to those who need it—the decision makers.

Another error, perhaps embedded in many of those already noted, is an inclination to rush through the scenario process. If not enough time is allowed for reflection, often entailing consideration of questions that might not otherwise be raised, scenario development degenerates into a mere

routine: the completion of a task because someone in authority asked that
it be done.

Summary

Projecting competitors' marketplace strategies, as well as the broader
competitive arenas, provides a fundamentally different focus for
learning than depicting what competitors are doing now. It generates
knowledge about the competitive arena, the competitors, and the
organization itself.[43] It requires that all those involved in scenario development and use must be willing to continually challenge their
own and each other's knowledge. However, it also requires that analysts, and especially decision makers, must be willing to become true
learners: not just developing knowledge but putting it into action,
and then learning from their actions.

PART
THREE

An Organizational Perspective on Competitor Learning

17

Integrating Competitor Analysis and Decision Making

COMPETITOR LEARNING, AS ARGUED IN CHAPTER 2, MUST BE TIGHTLY INTEGRATED with decision making. This chapter provides guidelines to effect such integration. It deals with the *organizational* side of competitor learning, as opposed to the predominantly analytical focus of the previous chapters. It addresses how decision makers, competitor analysis professionals (CAPs), and others can be organized, structured, and managed so that the doing and using of competitor analysis is fully integrated into every facet of decision making.

It is not the intent of this chapter to provide a blueprint or recipe for managing competitor learning. Rather it is to identify errors associated with the way many organizations approach competitor analysis and to suggest how to avoid these mistakes. By exposing why competitor analysis often does not deliver on its promises or expectations, both decision makers and CAPs will understand how they can enhance both its efficiency and effectiveness.

In keeping with the theme and thrust of this book, this chapter adopts a learning perspective: the identification of errors that impede more efficient and effective synthesis between competitor analysis and decision making. It identifies key errors associated with the organizational processes of learning: how individuals work together to develop and use competitor (and other types of) knowledge. Guided and open-ended approaches are then used to suggest ways to avoid and ameliorate each set of errors.

Central Organizational Errors

The essence of learning, as argued in Chapter 2, is the detection and correction of errors in our stock of knowledge and in our processes of learning (or knowing). Chapters 5 through 16 identified and addressed many common and potential analysis errors that affect the stock of (competitor) knowledge in any organization. At the risk of oversimplification, these can be reduced to five core analysis errors:

1. Competitor analysis is largely focused on a narrowly defined set of (typically larger look-alike) competitors: thus, extensive potential competitor learning is missed.

2. Analysis is preoccupied with competitors' current and past states; thus, critical learning associated with competitors' future direction and actions is never obtained.

3. Description is emphasized at the expense of assessment: thus, implications for the focal organization receive at best only cursory consideration.

4. Competitor analysis is not extended to include augmented and self-learning: thus, knowledge about current and potential customers, suppliers, technology, and marketplace dynamics, and the firm itself is never attained.

5. Different, and at times directly conflicting, logics or lines of reasoning are not created and assessed: thus, learning takes place within a narrow frame of reference.

While these core *analysis* errors occur and persist in many organizations for many reasons, the thesis in this chapter is that the following five *organizational* errors contribute greatly to their existence:

1. Managers adopt a structural rather then a cultural approach to dealing with competitor analysis: thus, most of the underlying organizational obstacles (as discussed in this chapter) to doing and using competitor analysis remain untouched.

2. Competitor analysis professionals (CAPs) take as their primary role "the doing of analysis," rather than educating others about competitor

learning: thus, they quickly run out of time, energy, and resources to meet the analysis demands that decision makers foist on them.

3. Decision makers, and especially senior managers, do not understand how their own behaviors, attitudes, and inclinations impede (or facilitate) competitor learning: thus, they do not know what analysis questions to ask; how to identify and challenge the logic, or reasoning, supporting inferences, conclusions or recommendations; or how to energize and motivate CAPs and others to enhance the quality of competitor learning.

4. There is limited shared understanding of key concepts and analysis tools and techniques among decision makers, CAPs, and others: thus, the content and range of analysis is constrained.

5. Capturing, processing, and crafting are viewed as the responsibility of CAPs and other analysts while assessment is considered the prerogative of decision makers—the problem of "vertical linkage": thus, the opportunity for real dialogue inspired by mutual learning is difficult to generate and foster.

Link to Decisions

The preceding analysis and organizational errors severely hamper the *effectiveness* of competitor learning. Most critically, they result in a fundamental disconnect between decisions and competitor analysis. Decision makers are not as well informed by competitor analysis as they should be. Decisions are not as influenced by the outputs of competitor analysis as they should be. A central aim of any systematic and sustained effort to build and sustain competitor learning therefore must be to eliminate this disconnect.

Competitor analysis, no matter how well its learning activities and tasks are executed, is likely to have minimal influence on decisions in the presence of the following widespread errors:

- Key current decisions are not carefully identified and publicized; thus, the relevance of competitor analysis (outputs) is difficult to discern and demonstrate.

- Possible future decisions are disregarded: thus, the potential relevance of competitor analysis is difficult to recognize.

- Generating relevant current and potential decisions[1] is not a recognized purpose of competitor analysis: thus, the thrust and content of analysis is unnecessarily constrained.

While these decision-related errors seem surprising at first glance, a simple exercise has convinced individuals in many organizations of their pervasiveness. Ask a small number of colleagues to identify the most important decisions currently confronting their department or unit, and the organization as a whole, as well as a short list of those that will be faced in the immediate future. The variations in the responses will quickly identify the difficulties faced in many organizations in connecting competitor learning and decisions.[2]

A guided approach to integrating competitor analysis and decisions begins with the identification of current and future decisions. The central learning questions noted in Chapter 2 suggest the following four guiding questions:

1. What current and future decisions are currently the focus of the organization's attention?
2. What current and future decisions should be the center of attention?
3. What is the decision gap?
4. What are the implications of these decisions for competitor analysis, including the execution of learning activities and desired outputs?

Individuals at multiple organization levels—the total enterprise, business units or product sectors, and functional groups or departmental units (such as marketing, manufacturing, R&D, and finance)—can ask these questions as one means to initiate a systematic effort to avoid the three decision errors noted earlier. Asking these questions leads to recursive analysis.[3] Identifying future decisions often sheds new light on existing decisions. A growing awareness of emerging R&D decisions such as which research programs should be funded and what alliances should be considered within individual research programs often sheds new light on current decisions such as whether to extend funding for one or more existing R&D programs.

While there are no simple algorithms to complete the task, the following questions serve as a guide to generating a listing of individual *current* decisions:

- What marketplace strategy decisions confront the organization?
- What are the current decisions pertaining to each microlevel component: activity/value chain, alliances and relationships, networks, assumptions, assets, capabilities and competencies, technology, and organization infrastructure and culture?

Individual decision makers and other analysts can list the decisions they are involved in shaping and making.

The analysis frameworks presented earlier to identify and analyze current and emerging individual and classes of competitors, provide critical input to determine the current and future decisions that *should* warrant managerial attention. While space does not allow a systematic treatment of this linkage, analysts must ask which decisions should receive serious managerial attention stemming from:

- The identification of current look-alike, functional substitute, and extended competitors.
- The identification of emerging and projected look-alike, functional substitute, and extended competitors.
- Competitors' current and projected marketplace strategies.
- Current and projected change in competitors' microlevel components.

Assessment of current and potential implications of each decision helps determine the relatively short set of *core* or critical decisions that should be the focus of the organization or a particular subunit. The framework of analysis presented in Chapter 1 offers one guide to such assessment. Analysts need to ask the following types of questions:

- How could each decision contribute to creating a new strategy game, reconstructing an existing game, or changing marketplace rules?
- How could each decision contribute to the firm's efforts to reshape stakes, to reconceive chips, or to redefine how score is kept?
- How could each decision contribute to outwitting, outmaneuvering, and outperforming current and future competitors?

Although the steps noted earlier constitute a mundane and tedious exercise, they are essential and unavoidable if more effective competitor learning is the organization's goal. The outcome, however, is a short list of core decisions that play a central role in determining intelligence needs.

The pure *open-ended* orientation, as described in Chapter 2, begins by identifying and analyzing current and potential competitors. It then derives current and future decisions that deserve organizational attention. The outside-in thrust alleviates the bias inherent in preoccupation with current and imminent events in the life of the organization.

It is, however, important to note that the guided and open-ended approaches are complementary. The open-ended approach, because it explicitly addresses competitor change (including what we have referred to as augmented learning) before considering implications for the focal organization, is especially likely to detect and highlight emerging or potential decisions. For example, projections of competitors' technology change sometimes indicate technology issues and decisions that the focal firm may not have contemplated. In the same way, the open-ended approach also draws attention to future decisions that should receive current attention as well as current decisions that should receive more serious attention.

An open-ended orientation is also helpful in dealing with the guiding questions noted earlier. Since answers to many of these questions are often not immediately self-evident, an open-ended approach encourages individuals to work in groups to identify core current and future decisions. It also suggests avoiding constraints on who is asked these guiding questions, both inside and outside the organization.

Link Decisions to Decision Makers

Competitor analysis connects to decisions through decision makers: it is individuals who create and leverage knowledge. It may be a participatory connection as when decision makers are involved in capturing, processing, and crafting as well as assessment. Or it may be a constrained connection as when decision makers receive competitor analysis outputs that have been generated by CAPs and others. Thus, it is never enough to determine core decisions; those who are involved in making the decisions must be identified.[4]

If the relevant decision makers are not identified, errors ensue:

- Some decision participants are likely to be ignored: thus, it is unlikely that they will be involved in competitor analysis, and it will be difficult to direct outputs to all appropriate decision makers.
- The intelligence needs of individual decision makers are more likely to be misspecified: thus, the effectiveness of competitor analysis is severely jeopardized.
- Differences in intelligence needs across groups of individuals are less likely to be detected and appreciated: thus, opportunities to customize outputs are missed.

When those involved in making and executing each major decision are not carefully identified, it is too easy for competitor analysis to drift and assume a life and a purpose that is isolated from the intelligence needs of individual decision makers.

A *guided* approach again addresses four central questions:

1. Who is involved in each decision?
2. Who should be involved in each decision?
3. What are the differences in the participants across decisions?
4. What are the implications for competitor analysis outputs and learning activities?

The initial task is to develop a first-cut listing of decision makers. In most business units, this exercise is typically straightforward. However, the initial listing is often so long that the development of groups of decision makers becomes necessary. One danger is that if the level of aggregation becomes too high (e.g., all marketing personnel), much of the benefit of the exercise may be lost.

It is then necessary to identify which individuals, or sets of individuals, are involved in each major decision (or groups of decisions). Again, there are no simple a priori rules to simplify this task. The outcome of this exercise is a matrix such as that shown in Figure 17.1. It provides an array of decision makers pertaining to individual decisions or groups of decisions.

It is also imperative to consider which individuals are not involved in these decisions, but who should be, based on their organizational role, position, or knowledge. Sometimes, organization routines and historic ways of doing things lead to the exclusion of individuals, or groups of individuals, who should be contributors to specific decisions. In many organizations, marketing and other functional area personnel often have little opportunity to participate in key research and development decisions.

Significant variation is often evident in the relevant decision-making groups. Those involved in a key pricing decision are often strikingly different from those involved in a decision to determine how much capital should be committed to upgrading the firm's manufacturing technology. These differences are critical to determining intelligence needs and to customizing analysis outputs.

An *open-ended* approach makes no presumptions about who is or should be involved in making specific decisions. It begins by asking, Who should be involved in each major decision and why? It thus endeavors to bring an unconstrained perspective to the second guided question—Who should be involved in each decision?

FIGURE 17.1
Linking Decision Makers and Decisions

Decisions

Decision Makers				

Decisions and Decision Makers: Discerning Intelligence Needs

Knowing which decisions are the focus of the organization's attention, and which managers and others are involved in shaping and making them, is necessary but not sufficient to identify competitor intelligence[5] needs. Each major current and potential decision must be carefully examined for the knowledge required to make the decision. Decision makers and others must be systematically questioned to identify how different types of knowledge could contribute to the making of specific decisions.

Assumption errors have greatly exacerbated the difficulties inherent in deriving intelligence needs. Three in particular seem to be prevalent:

1. Decision makers know what intelligence they need.[6]
2. Intelligence needs are reasonably stable.
3. Intelligence needs can always be quickly met.

Partly as a consequence of these assumption errors, determination of intelligence needs is often marked by the following errors:

- The intelligence that decision makers say they need is accepted: thus, the intelligence that decision makers actually need is likely to be misconstrued.
- Change in intelligence needs over time is not tracked: thus, competitor analysis outputs are likely to be mismatched with intelligence needs.
- Decision makers and CAPs make little effort to anticipate intelligence needs: thus, they often find themselves scurrying to quickly develop "answers" to critical questions or issues.
- Outputs are not viewed as a means to identify intelligence needs; thus, potential intelligence needs are missed.[7]

Determination of intelligence needs at the level of the organization or any of its subunits, as well as at the level of individual decision makers, is often done in a cursory manner. Key executives are asked a few questions; some documents are assessed for hints of inputs required by specific managers; and, little dialogue occurs between decision makers, CAPs, and others.

A *guided* approach leads to a highly structured and systematic approach to identifying intelligence needs specific to individual decisions and/or decision makers. The central learning questions again suggest the following four steps:

1. Determine what information ideally would be required for each major decision or set of decisions.

2. Identify the information now being used (or the data and information intended to be used).

3. Determine the intelligence gap.

4. Identify the competitor analysis outputs required to fill the intelligence gap (this step is considered in detail in the next section).

Consideration of ideal intelligence needs allows decision makers and CAPs to step outside the types of analysis typically conducted, the information historically used in making specific decisions, and individual decision makers' propensities to prefer particular types of data and information.

The following steps typically contribute to identifying ideal intelligence needs. First, analysts identify a priori what intelligence they believe would be required to make a specific decision or would be required by a specific decision maker to perform his or her job. Such first-cut intelligence specifications provide a benchmark against which to assess the breadth and quality of the intelligence currently employed.

Second, analysts can ask decision makers to identify what they consider the ideal intelligence for specific decisions. As they ponder this question, decision makers often articulate a need for data and information they previously had not considered or had downplayed or ignored.

Third, analysts can ask outsiders such as industry experts, customers, suppliers, technology specialists, and management consultants, what intelligence they consider critical for specific decisions. Each external source may suggest new kinds of data and information that analysts had not previously considered relevant to a specific decision or type of decision maker.

Finally, by observing decision makers at work, analysts sometimes discern intelligence needs they themselves did not anticipate or that decision makers did not articulate. Listening to questions decision makers ask in meetings, noting the issues they ask analysts and others to consider, and observing the data and information they seek, often suggests critical intelligence needs.

Consider, for example, one firm's decision whether to build a new manufacturing plant. Analysts determined that ideal *external* intelligence included:

- Competitors' current and planned plant capacities.
- The state of technology in each current and projected plant.
- The functionalities, features, and other attributes of products produced in each plant.

- Competitors' marketplace strategy.

- Competitors' manufacturing reactions to the firm's announcement of its intention to build a new plant.

- Technological changes that might affect the anticipated manufacturing advantage.

- Customers' assessments of products produced in the new plant compared with those of rivals.

To determine an intelligence gap, analysts need to identify what knowledge is currently used or desired. Doing so is not nearly as straightforward as is often presumed or asserted. Again, it must be approached in different ways simultaneously. Ask decision makers to identify how they use specific types of data and information in making each major decision. Observe decision makers at work: listen to the questions they ask, the responses they make to the comments and contributions of others, and the analyses they request. Also, review relevant documents such as meeting summaries, reports, and specific analyses.

In the new manufacturing plant case, most of the intelligence needs previously identified pertained to *internal* data and information: superiority of the proposed manufacturing technologies compared with the plant being replaced; projected cost efficiencies; anticipated product functionalities and features; and responses of existing customers to the plant's output. External intelligence needs had received relatively little attention.

An *open-ended* approach to the determination of intelligence needs assumes special importance because the future cannot be known with certainty. Decision makers therefore need to be alert to how the present may be unfolding into a future that is radically different from the past.[8] Managers and others tend to be blinded by the biases associated with their own organization's success, their professional background and training, and the normal preoccupations of current and impending decisions.

An open-ended perspective suggests the need for multiple different approaches to identifying current and potential intelligence needs. It emphasizes the importance of interactions among individuals from different organization levels, functions, and units to explore current and potential intelligence needs. In many instances, since decision makers are not presumed to know what the ideal intelligence is, and often find it difficult to articulate how they make decisions, and what data and information they find useful, such interactions generate unexpected intelligence needs.[9]

It encourages decision makers, CAPs, and others to approach analysis "by leaving their biases and preoccupations at the door." A genuinely open-ended mind-set in exploring the implications of alternative futures through scenarios grants individuals the permission and freedom to ask tough questions about possible industry, technology, or competitor futures. The result is often the generation of intelligence needs that lie outside those identified in the guided approach.

Projections of the strategies and actions of "invented" competitors also cause decision makers and CAPs to step outside the bounds of conventional competitors. The result is frequently the identification of new intelligence needs. One firm discovered the importance of potential alliances and their implications for the strategies of all its rivals by determining how an invented competitor could develop and leverage a modest network to radically reshape solutions that would be relevant to both existing and new customers.

Leveraging Outputs: The Link to Decisions and Intelligence Needs

Intelligence needs are identified so that both existing and new competitor analysis outputs are more effectively leveraged. Leveraging outputs demands considerable attention because individual outputs such as alternative projections of a competitor's marketplace strategy, or the implications of change in a competitor's assumptions, are often inputs to making multiple decisions. In one company, comparison of multiple competitors' capabilities to those of the focal firm, had specific implications for which products to produce, how best to revamp manufacturing, and whether to enter specific new product-customer segments. Moreover, outputs such as projections of competitors' marketplace strategies, networks, and capabilities are frequently useful to decision makers in multiple organization functions or departments such as research and development, manufacturing, engineering, marketing, sales, mergers and acquisitions, and line management.

Inattention to linking outputs to intelligence needs leads to serious errors:

- Decision makers are unaware of output possibilities: thus, they do not receive intelligence that others in the organization could easily generate.
- CAPs do not appreciate the outputs it is possible to craft:[10] thus, their ability to tailor or customize outputs to the intelligence needs of specific decisions and individual decision makers is severely constricted.
- Analysis routines and processes dictate the generation of outputs: thus, outputs become an end in themselves.[11]

In shaping, critiquing, and communicating outputs—the three core tasks in crafting outputs—meeting deadlines and adhering to historic organization practices are frequently the operative goals in too many organizations.

How different types of output can be leveraged by decision makers receives only passing attention. Also, decision makers themselves do not reflect on how they could use specific outputs in making different types of decisions.

The guided approach suggests that competitor analysis outputs must be customized or tailored to meet decision makers' specific intelligence needs. Customizing outputs is guided by the following four questions:

1. What outputs are required to satisfy each intelligence need?
2. What is the output gap—the difference between existing and desired outputs?
3. What new outputs must be developed?
4. How can each type of output be tailored to better meet the needs of each decision or each decision maker's needs?

Each item in the list of intelligence needs helps identify necessary outputs. In the manufacturing plant example, one required intelligence item was competitors' current and planned plant capacities. Current plant capacities required several indicators including plant size, throughput of products, type of equipment, and state of process technologies. Determination of competitors' planned plant capacities required, among other things, announcements of plant extensions and projections of the types of product to be manufactured, likely process technologies, and potential plant efficiencies.

The impact of shaping (and critiquing) outputs on how they are leveraged should now be evident. Different types of output provide specific value or intelligence to decision makers (see Table 17.1). For example, *updates* keep decision makers and others abreast of events and change relevant to competitors. *Alerts* forewarn managers and others of imminent competitor change. *Projections* of rivals' marketplace strategies serve as a foil against which the focal firm's planned strategy is compared and assessed.

Determining the specific competitor analysis outputs required to satisfy a particular intelligence need always gives rise to judgments about the appropriate type and form of output. A guided approach suggests the development of relevant norms to aid CAPs and others involved in crafting outputs. In one organization, the following norms pertain to all types of competitor analysis outputs:

- Keep each output short and simple.
- Identify key competitor change.
- Emphasize implications for specific decisions or decision makers.

Central to the guided approach is determining specific *new* outputs required to meet particular intelligence needs. These outputs then guide

TABLE 17.1 Types of Outputs and Potential Value to Decision Makers

Sample Types of Output	Value to Decision Makers (Examples)
Alerts: Delineation of a single event or change (e.g., a product announcement or hiring of a new executive or a price change)	Helps decision makers ask further questions or reframe prior questions Allows decision makers to consider its implications
Updates: Provides updated details on some facet of competitor change (e.g., latest actions in a new product introduction)	Allows decision makers to compare competitor's actions with those previously projected Helps decision makers anticipate next actions by the competitor
Description of one competitor's marketplace strategy	Helps decision makers understand what the competitor is currently doing in the marketplace Allows decision makers to ask specific questions about the competitor's marketplace strategy
Description and comparison of multiple competitors' current marketplace strategies	Helps decision makers understand what differences exist across competitors, why these differences exist, and what their implications might be for the focal firm's own current and potential strategic moves
Assessment of the focal firm's competitive posture against one or more competitors	Facilitates analysis of customer-based advantage against one or more rivals Provides guidance for changing the current marketplace strategy
Projections of two or more competitors' marketplace strategies	Gives decision makers a foil against which to assess the firm's potential strategies Provides possible alternatives for the firm to consider
Description of current state of one or more microlevel components of a specific competitor (e.g., its assumptions)	Allows decision makers to assess the validity of the competitor's assumptions, and, thus, to assess the firm's own assumptions Aids the efforts of decision makers to explicate and test their own assumptions
Projections of change within a specific microlevel component, (e.g., a competitor's activity/value chain)	Gives decision makers an opportunity to assess how a competitor might be outwitting and outmaneuvering the focal firm Gives decision makers a frame of reference to ask questions about the focal firm's own investments and commitments
Delineation of emerging and projected functional substitute competitors	Decision makers can compare and assess value delivered to customers across types of products or solutions as an input to enhancing current and future marketplace strategy
Augmented learning: description and projection of change pertaining to endcustomers, channels, suppliers, etc.	Decision makers can assess current assumptions about the competitive environment Decision makers can challenge merits of existing and potential strategy alternatives

analysis. A set of senior executives in one firm declared that they needed more timely information on change in and around the marketplace. This request caused CAPs and others to recognize that they were not capturing what they were learning about the competitive context beyond individual rivals as they engaged in competitor and customer analysis. They then crafted specific outputs pertaining to change in and around end-customers, channels, suppliers, substitute products, and changing competitive dynamics.[12] Consideration of new outputs ensures that analysts do not fall victim to the malaise of continually generating outputs of the same type and form.

Yet generating new outputs by itself is not enough. They must be customized to meet the intelligence needs of individual or groups of decision makers. Few other acts so clearly distinguish competitor learning from what passes for competitor analysis in so many organizations: knowledge becomes intelligence when it is useful to decision makers.[13] Analysis of a competitor's marketplace can be customized to generate specific outputs for marketing managers (detailed descriptions of the strategy and its implications), sales managers (selected elements of the strategy and their implications), line managers (a summary of the strategy and its implications).

The *open-ended* approach assumes importance in linking outputs to decisions and decision makers because analysts and decision makers are often surprised by the implications they derive from outputs. When individuals are encouraged to suspend their concerns with the nuances and details of specific outputs such as a competitor's marketplace strategy or a set of competitor scenarios, they often detect the relevance and value of outputs for specific decision makers or decisions that others may have missed. A set of analysts in one firm, when asked to consider how specific outputs might be useful to any decision maker, quickly identified how specific decisions made by the head of each functional area (including R&D, engineering, manufacturing, marketing, and sales) could benefit from an understanding of the current and projected marketplace strategies of competitors.

Thus, the open-ended approach starts with current and potential competitor outputs and then asks who could use them, how they could do so, and what difference they would make to specific decisions or decision makers. A firm might craft detailed descriptions of its augmented learning—current and potential change with regard to distribution channels, end-customers, suppliers, and competitive dynamics—and then ask how they might be useful to particular decision makers in making specific decisions. A marketing manager might thus ask how projected channel and end-customer change might affect new product development, marketing strategy, or pricing decisions. In this way, the marketing manager is likely to identify intelligence needed as input to these decisions.

Also, the open-ended perspective emphasizes development of alternative types of outputs. There are no a priori constraints on output design or form.

Analysts have poetic license to develop any form of output. Such freedom encourages analysts to *explore:* to approach analysis from many distinct perspectives; to step outside the conventional wisdom pertaining to output forms and types; to develop and test alternative logics. As a consequence, there is greater likelihood that decision makers' mind-sets will be confronted and challenged through the provision of unanticipated outputs. Analysts and decision makers may be surprised by the consequences and implications of their own interpretations (inferences) and assessments.

Link to Decision Making: Refining Intelligence Needs

The bridge between intelligence needs and outputs is further refined by taking into account how organizations make decisions. Key marketplace strategy and important operations decisions take considerable time. Profound differences are typically evident across decision stages: how the organization gathers data to understand the decision context, identifies possible alternatives, develops specific options, chooses a preferred course of action, and then executes it.[14] Individuals at different levels in the organization play diverse roles during these stages. The generation and use of intelligence is not a one-time event over the course of any single decision.[15]

In linking competitor learning to decision making, several errors are prevalent:

- Differences in the way decisions are made and executed, including the process, speed, and degree of deliberation, are neglected: thus, opportunities to influence the content of decisions are missed.

- Differences in the sets of individuals involved in a decision as it ebbs and flows through the organization are not taken into account: thus, opportunities to engage decision makers in competitor learning activities are missed.

- Differences in intelligence needs as individuals proceed through the decision stages are disregarded: thus, opportunities to customize competitor analysis outputs are missed.

A guided approach raises four questions:

1. What are the stages in each major decision?
2. What intelligence ideally is required at each stage?
3. What is (or might be) the intelligence gap?
4. How might current outputs be leveraged and what new outputs are required?

The guided approach advocates mapping decision paths: the timeline for the decision; the key analysis steps; the intelligence involved at each step; and the individuals involved in each step. The intent is to identify what intelligence is required at each stage of the decision and how it might be provided.

Table 17.2 provides an example of an R&D decision: whether to invest in a particular research initiative. Each stage, or phase, in making the decision gives rise to specific organizational issues or concerns. Competitor analysis outputs contribute significantly to the analysis of these issues and concerns. In the initial stage, understanding the decision context, a primary concern is developing a rich understanding of the current and future competitive

TABLE 17.2   Phases in an R&D Decision: The Contribution of Competitor Analysis Outputs

Phases In Making the Decision	Decision Issues and Concerns	Sample Contributions of Competitor Analysis Outputs (re Competitors)
Understanding the decision context	What opportunities are evident?	What R&D competitors are conducting
	What are competitors doing?	Projected results of their R&D programs
Delineating the decision	Where should the firm invest its R&D dollars?	Potential reactions of competitors to possible resource commitments
	Where else might this capital be allocated?	
Identifying decision alternatives	What are the broad R&D program alternatives?	General scope and direction of competitors' research programs
	How do they differ from each other?	
Developing decision alternatives	What are the details of each program?	Details of how individual competitors are conducting the research
	What is the timeline?	
	How much resources are required?	
Evaluating decision alternatives	What might be the outcomes of each program?	Projections of competitors' research commitments and their likely results
Choosing the preferred alternative	What might affect projected results?	All of the above
Implementing the chosen alternative	What factors might affect execution of the program?	Outputs of monitoring of competitors' research programs

context. Competitor analysis outputs such as descriptions of competitors' current and projected R&D programs and projects contribute greatly to detailing the competitive R&D context. Stemming in part from analysis of competitors' R&D programs, augmented learning addressing likely marketplace change such as the emergence of new products also contributes to understanding the competitive context.

As the decision proceeds through the phases indicated in Table 17.2, decision makers and CAPs can identify what intelligence is employed, what is needed, and thus what the intelligence gap is. For example, in developing decision alternatives, decision makers may require assessments of how competitors are conducting specific types of research broadly similar to that being proposed and evaluated. If these are not available, one element of the intelligence gap is identified.

An *open-ended* perspective ideally compels an open-minded evaluation of the four questions noted earlier. Organizations, like individuals, often view themselves through tainted and rose-colored glasses. Hence, it is useful to contact outsiders to initiate and ignite such self-evaluation. Sometimes, something as simple as comparisons with how other organizations (and not just current competitors) make decisions, what intelligence they employ, and how they do so, can bring a sweeping breath of fresh air to reflections on the routines that typically dominate how an organization goes about making key decisions.

Beyond Decisions: Creating Access Points for Competitor Analysis

If competitor analysis outputs are to be integral to decision making, they must be connected to the systems and processes that are intended to support and facilitate knowledge generation for decision makers, as well as the development and execution of key decisions. Systems and processes such as strategic planning, budgeting, and information management provide many opportunities for direct connections to the key learning activities and tasks (see Figure 2.1). Thus, it is necessary to identify those aspects of specific systems and processes (the access points) in which competitor analysis outputs can be used.

In linking competitor analysis outputs to access points, errors may occur:

- Many potential access points are never identified: thus, vital connections between competitor learning and individuals' learning are missed.

- Competitor analysis outputs remain isolated from central organization processes (e.g., strategic planning), and systems (e.g., information systems): thus, competitor learning's potential to influence the shaping and making of decisions is constrained.

- Outputs are not linked to the content of individuals' jobs, to tasks assigned committees, to task forces, and to other work groups: thus, they are not perceived as central to decisions, decision makers, or decision making.

Again, guided and open-ended approaches suggest two distinct but complementary ways to identify and connect to access points. The guided approach begins with a priori identification of all significant systems and processes and how they might afford access points. In the spirit of the central learning questions noted in Chapter 2, decision makers and others need to address these four questions:

1. What systems and processes exist and what are the potential access points within each?
2. To what extent are competitor analysis outputs already integrated into these access points? What is the evidence?
3. What is the opportunity to do so (beyond what is already occurring)?
4. Which decision makers would be informed by doing so and what decisions would be affected?

The intent in this section is to illustrate how competitor analysis outputs are useful in key systems and processes (see Table 17.3).

The *strategic planning* process offers a multitude of access points. Each analysis stage in the typical strategic planning sequence—environmental analysis, organization assessment, development of strategy options, choice of strategy, development of actions plans and budgets—can benefit from competitor analysis outputs. For example, environmental analysis, usually the first stage in most strategic planning processes, is greatly aided by identification of key competitor change, projections of competitors' strategies, and augmented learning—change relevant to suppliers, channels, end-customers, and technology.

The *capital allocation* process typically receives much less attention as a potential access point in most organizations than the strategic planning process. Yet the need for competitor knowledge as an input to capital allocation is often paramount. This is true for projects consuming large, moderate, and small amounts of capital. For example, capital expenditure projects such as investments in research and development, or plant and equipment, might be subjected to following questions:

TABLE 17.3   Linking Analysis Outputs and Access Points

System Process	Sample Access Points within System/Process	Potential Contribution of CA Outputs
Strategic planning	Environmental analysis Assumptions Potential opportunities Assessment of potential strategies Monitoring strategy execution	Identify key competitor (and other) trends and patterns Competitors' assumptions serve as one referent point in assumption development
Capital allocation	The opportunity or threats embedded in each project Projected returns Evaluation of projects What might not pan out in executing projects	Furnishes nonfinancial criteria to test the "business case" associated with each project Enables decision makers to identify and challenge project assumptions
Budgeting	Determination of budget priorities Allocation of budget to projects, units, etc. Timing of budget expenditures	Provides decision makers with an external context for budget decisions Generates questions about budgets that otherwise would not be asked
Information system	Dissemination of CA outputs to decision makers	Provides a specific external focus to the content of what moves through the information system
Control and evaluation system	Indicators along which performance is monitored and measured	Externally focused indicators External assessment criteria
Issues management	Identification of issues Assessment of potential implications Ranking of importance of issues	Help to identify current, emerging, and potential issues
Remuneration and incentive systems	Performance criteria against which performance is assessed	Specific external criteria
Reengineering	Choice of processes to reengineer Analysis leading to reengineering execution	Help identify processes to reengineer Provide competitor criteria to assess potential results
Task forces	Purpose of task forces Content and sequence of work	Inputs to deliberations of the task force

- How might the current strategies of specific competitors affect the project's projected revenue stream?

- What potential strategies of these competitors might cause one or more of the project's underlying assumptions to be changed?

- How might specific assumptions underlying a specific product differ from those of one or more competitors?

- How might successful execution of the project affect competitors' marketplace strategy choices and implementation of their current strategies?

- What augmented learning is relevant to the project's future?

The *budgeting* process is rarely connected to competitor knowledge. Yet, it is often a significant access point. Yearly, quarterly, and monthly budgets can be tested for their contribution to outwitting and outmaneuvering competitors by asking these questions:

- How do specific expenditures help to create or sustain action programs that help to outmaneuver specific rivals?

- What discretion exists to change budget allocations as a consequence of commitments and moves by competitors?

- How can the budget be reallocated to take advantage of marketplace opportunities that present themselves?

The *information* system is an obvious key access point. Increasingly, data and information collection processes are used to identify and capture competitor data. Many organizations use the formal information system to disseminate both customized and general outputs. Yet, in most instances, information systems have as yet only touched the surface of how they might contribute to competitor learning. Decision makers need to consider the following issues:

- How can information technology be used to gather critical competitor data and transmit it to the appropriate analysts or decision makers?

- How can the formal information system be used to shape and transmit customized outputs to meet specific decision makers' intelligence needs?

The formal financial and operating *control and evaluation* system in most organizations pays little if any attention to monitoring the current and potential strategies and actions of competitors. The focus typically is on execution of internal decisions, operating processes, and financial results.

Many organizations now possess a well-established *issues analysis system.* The purpose of the system is to identify the critical issues confronting each product sector or business, how each issue might evolve, and how they might affect the future success of the business. Competitor analysis outputs should serve as a critical input to identifying current, emerging, and potential issues.

Even *remuneration and incentive* systems are not immune from the benefits of competitor analysis outputs. For example, such outputs aid in identifying relevant competitors to serve as benchmarks against which organizational and managerial performance can be evaluated.

Less standard systems or processes are also worthy of attention. For illustration purposes, we will use reengineering and quality management. The *reengineering process,* as practiced in many organizations, tends to overly emphasize internal metrics and measures. Outputs such as competitors' marketplace strategies, and capabilities and competencies, provide external referent points against which to assess reengineered processes.

As practiced in many organizations, the *quality management process* could also benefit from assessment against the practices and performance of current and potential competitors.

Finally, *committees* and *task forces,* two quasi-formal processes in almost all organizations, often present rich opportunities for the use of competitor analysis outputs. Key questions that any committee or task force might ask, irrespective of its charge or terms of reference, include:

- How might actions of competitors affect the issues or decisions central to the deliberations of the committee or task force?

- What should the committee or task force know about competitors' current and future marketplace strategies, alliances, assumptions, and capabilities?

The open-ended approach encourages those crafting outputs as well as decision makers (if they are not involved in output development) to consider how specific types of outputs might be used in any system or process anywhere in the organization. There are no constraints in thinking about potential uses or access points. Decision makers, for example, might consider how an understanding of competitors' assumptions could be applied in each system or process.

A significant outcome of the open-ended approach is often the creation of new access points. For example, line managers may want to have new insights into competitors' marketplace strategies, assumptions, and capabilities presented to their monthly or quarterly strategy review meetings. Specific decision makers often decide that they would like to receive regular updates of changes in competitors' marketplace strategies or activity/value chains.

A Dedicated Structure for Competitor Analysis?

Increasingly, organizations create a dedicated organization structure to facilitate, motivate, and lead competitor analysis. Specific individuals—whom we have referred to as competitor analysis professionals or CAPs—are assigned the charge of "doing" competitor analysis. Many organizations have established a formal competitor analysis unit.

At least three errors or pitfalls are commonly associated with efforts to effect a structural approach to competitor analysis:

- Dedicated competitor analysis units are given organizationwide responsibility for doing competitor analysis: thus, others outside the unit assume they can wash their hands of involvement.

- Dedicated units see "doing analysis" as their predominant and, in many instances, only role: thus, the value of educating others to do analysis, and to be involved in analysis, assumes secondary importance.

- Senior managers and other decision makers overburden the dedicated unit with data requests: thus, the time available for CAPs to create value-adding analysis is severely constrained.

As a direct result of these errors, structured groups of CAPs, despite their best efforts, often generate surprisingly little value for decision makers. Their commitment, zeal, and capabilities are misused and misguided. They are asked to do analysis that other groups or units such as marketing, sales, research and development, and finance, should do for themselves. Moreover, they have limited time to meet all the analysis requests; and their time is consumed answering managers irrelevant "1–800" questions.[16]

The guided approach addresses four questions:

1. What is the current structure?
2. What are the merits and limitations of alternative structures?
3. What is the structure gap?
4. What are the implications of changing the structure?

It is always useful to identify the prevailing structure. It alerts decision makers and others to "who does what" with regard to the analysis of competitors. Frequently, the structure is largely informal: individuals are assigned competitor analysis as part of other responsibilities.

Even a cursory effort to identify and evaluate the merits and limitations of alternative structures often suggests ways to improve the current structure. Alternative dedicated structures are designed around answers to the following issues: How many CAPs should be involved? What reporting relationships should they have among themselves? What department or unit should they report to or be located in? How should they be monitored and remunerated? What should be the leadership role of managers and other decision makers? An underlying criterion is how each structure could potentially contribute to the making of specific decisions.

What is clear from the success and failure of many different types of dedicated competitor analysis structures across many firms in the past few years is that there is no single best or optimal structure. For example, some multi-business enterprises have successfully leveraged work done by a dedicated competitor analysis unit located at corporate headquarters. Other such enterprises have singularly failed to do so.

The *open-ended* approach tends to shy away from rigid or formalized structures. It emphasizes informal and changing relationships: individuals engaged in doing competitor analysis should not be constrained by preset or rigid reporting relationships. Informal structures encourage both CAPs and decision makers to be opportunistic in linking intelligence needs with the availability of CAPs and other analysis resources. It encourages individuals and groups to try different roles as they see fit, to exploit opportunities to engage in competitor learning as they arise, and to develop procedures (which are discussed in the next section) on a trial-and-error basis.

Organization Procedures: Bringing Individuals Together to Do Competitor Analysis Work

Individuals must work together to complete the many types of competitor analysis tasks noted throughout this book, such as projecting marketplace strategy, analyzing an activity/value chain, or assessing an invented competitor's capabilities. Many of the tasks noted in this chapter such as determining the key decisions confronting the organization, its intelligence needs, and how outputs can be leveraged, also require that individuals work together. Thus, procedures must be established that bring decision makers and others together to get the required competitor analysis work done and integrated into decision making. In developing and sustaining procedures, several errors arise:

- Individuals assigned to competitor analysis tasks such as collecting data from external data sources, interpreting data, and critiquing outputs, are drawn from a narrow set of organization units, functions, or departments: thus, the data and analysis inputs to learning are often unnecessarily constrained.

- The roles and responsibilities associated with competitor analysis tasks are perceived as "add-ons" to individuals' jobs: thus, the commitment and motivation of individuals to participate in competitor analysis activities is low and in some cases zero.

- Prescribed roles address only capturing, processing, and crafting but not assessment; thus, the link to decisions and decision making is missed.

CAPs simply do not have the time, resources, or capabilities to generate, disseminate, and leverage the outputs required to meet all the organization's intelligence needs. Even in the presence of a dedicated structure, the work entailed in the doing and using of competitor analysis must extend to individuals beyond it. In the absence of a dedicated structure, organization procedures are the only means available to get the work done.

A guided approach strives to design procedures that aid both the efficiency and effectiveness of competitor analysis. Four questions guide the analysis:

1. What procedures are currently used to accomplish which competitor analysis tasks?
2. What might be ideal procedures?
3. What is the procedure gap?
4. What procedures need to be put in place and how will they contribute to efficient and effective competitor analysis?

Current procedures can be identified with respect to the key tasks within each core learning activity—capturing, processing, crafting, and assessment or to the organizational challenges identified in this chapter. Table 17.4 lists procedures that various organizations have developed to bring together individuals from different organization levels, units, and backgrounds to accomplish competitor analysis work.

Each procedure is then evaluated for its efficiency and effectiveness. For example, do the data collection procedures result in quickly getting to the best data sources both inside and outside the organization? Do the relevant analysis procedures lead to higher quality outputs?

In designing many procedures such as cross-functional teams or ad hoc groups, a guided approach pays considerable attention to specifying the roles that individuals can play, or should play, given their positions, backgrounds, interests, experience, and aspirations. Table 17.5 lists a sampling of roles related to the key tasks within each learning activity.

TABLE 17.4 Organizational Procedures Designed to Execute Competitor Learning Activities and Tasks

A group of mid-level managers, CAPs, and others meet over time to identify the organization's key current and future decisions

A group of managers and representatives from various staff functions meet regularly to identify intelligence needs pertaining to specific decisions or groups of decision makers (such as the senior marketing managers)

Cross-functional teams are created for a specified period to conduct an integrated analysis of one or more competitors

An ad hoc team of managers and CAPs develops a set of scenarios around competitors' likely future strategies

Special occasions are created so that individuals who have visited competitors' operations, evaluated competitors' offerings at trade shows, or completed some analysis can present their data and findings to each other or management gatherings

Ad hoc groups are asked to update a competitor profile

Special half-day of one-day events are designed so that managers, staff, and CAPs can meet to discuss each others' intelligence issues

Market research and competitor analysis groups meet occasionally to share their competitor and customer knowledge

Competitor analysis staff make periodic presentations to line management and individual departments as part of the strategic planning process

Senior managers meet periodically to identify what competitor analysis issues confront the firm, what questions should be raised, what analysis should be conducted

CAPs hold an "open forum" to which all managers and staff are invited. The purpose is to present analysis findings and implications

Heads of all functional areas meet monthly to discuss customer and competitor issues. Agenda is typically open

Competitor analysts provide one-on-one updates on competitors' strategies to individual managers

An open-ended perspective must always complement a guided approach to designing and managing organization procedures. Individuals and groups must be encouraged to be opportunistic in creating and adapting procedures to meet circumstances: to try different roles as they see fit, to exploit opportunities to engage in competitor learning as they arise and to develop procedures on a trial-and-error basis.

A Competitor Learning Culture

Everything discussed so far—decisions, decision makers, decision making, intelligence needs, structure, procedures—is influenced and shaped by the organization's culture. How (and why) individuals or groups generate and use knowledge cannot be separated from the organization's values, beliefs, norms, and behaviors.[17] The enthusiasm and commitment individuals bring to key competitor learning tasks such as capturing data, detecting indicators, perceiving and interpreting signals, and assessing consequences and implications, is a function of the values and beliefs associated with knowledge and learning, and the norms and behaviors pertaining to how things get done. In the absence of a supportive learning culture, competitor analysis is difficult to initiate, foster, and sustain.

Three common errors render it especially difficult to develop a competitor learning culture:

1. Senior managers see their (exclusive) role as providing and overseeing the requisite organization structure and procedures: thus, establishing a learning culture is neglected.

2. Initiatives to create a competitor learning culture are undertaken at the enterprisewide level: thus, too much is expected to change too quickly, promises emerge that cannot be delivered, and the initiatives peter out.

3. CAPs do not understand their own role in shaping a learning culture: thus, many opportunities to affect a learning culture are not realized.

Competitor learning is therefore largely left to the vagaries of the current culture. All too often, the prevailing values and beliefs do not buttress the trials and difficulties of competitor learning. And the prevailing norms and behaviors simply do not allow the requisite competitor learning activities and tasks to be accomplished.

A guided approach is driven by attention to four central questions:

1. How does the organization's culture affect key competitor learning activities and tasks?

2. What might be some elements of an ideal competitor learning culture?

3. What is the culture gap and what actions are required to improve the competitor learning culture?

4. How would the enhanced culture affect the execution of competitor learning activities and tasks?

The framework of culture analysis delineated in Chapter 15 is equally applicable to the focal organization. The *guided* approach begins by diagnosing how the organization's culture—values, beliefs, norms, and behaviors—supports or inhibits each learning activity and its constituent tasks.

One way to initiate a culture diagnosis is to observe and list the actions and statements of individuals or groups as they execute the doing and using of competitor analysis. It is equally important to note inactions[18]—what individuals and groups do not do. Decisions pertaining to competitor analysis are always indicative of underlying values, beliefs, and norms. One firm's decision to include competitor analysis as a key component in new product development, and another firm's R&D management's decision to drop projections of competitors' R&D programs as an input to the resource commitment, suggested specific (competitor learning) alerting values. These values were then confirmed by further indicators.[19]

Asking the types of questions noted in Table 17.5 leads to multiple indicators of the prevailing (competitor learning) culture. Even simple and straightforward questions sometimes lead to important insights into specific elements of the culture. By asking who is involved in particular competitor

TABLE 17.5   Determining the Focal Firm's Competitor Learning Culture: Sample Questions

Behaviors and Practices	Values, Beliefs, and Norms
Which decision makers involve themselves in the analysis of competitors?	What values and beliefs are reflected in these behaviors and practices about:
How do they do so?	The importance of understanding competitors?
What statements have decision makers made about the need for competitor analysis?	The importance of asking questions?
What types of questions do decision makers ask about competitors?	How decision makers and professional analysts should interact?
Which decision makers continually do so?	The types of dialogue that should occur as part of "analysis"?
Who gathers what types of data (and who doesn't)?	What norms are reflected in these behaviors and practices about:
Who asks for competitor analysis outputs?	How decision makers and professional analysts (should) interact?
Who uses competitor analysis outputs?	How data and information are (should be) transmitted?
Who is involved in competitor analysis projects or assignments?	Which individuals are (should be) involved in different competitor analysis tasks?
To what extent, and how, are competitor analysis outputs integrated into specific systems and processes?	How competitor analysis outputs are (should be) crafted?
What types of organization procedures are used?	How outputs are communicated to decision makers?
Who is involved in each procedure?	
Do decision makers challenge the logics inherent in analysis outputs?	

analysis projects, such as identifying and assessing competitors' market-place strategies or assumptions, analysts often are able to quickly draw strong *initial* inferences about the role of decision makers (such as specific levels of managers) in the "doing and using" of competitor analysis.

The culture gap is determined by comparing the results of the diagnosis with the outlines of an ideal competitor learning culture. Crafting an ideal culture is itself the source of considerable learning. Consideration of an ideal culture leads decision makers, CAPs, and others to consider what values, beliefs, and norms need to be reinforced or initiated, and what behaviors or roles they should adopt to affect desired culture change.

The culture gap thus guides determination of what culture change is required and how it might be affected. An action plan to leverage aspects of the existing culture, and to move toward a more supportive culture, always requires the identification of (at least) three types of desired behaviors or practices:

1. Actions by individual decision makers, CAPs, and others.
2. Refinement and development of procedures.
3. Integration of outputs into systems and processes.

Unless individuals modify their behavior, a supportive culture does not emerge. Consider the following commitments to behavior change adopted by one senior executive:

- To ask questions about competitors and customers in every meeting.
- To insist on competitor analysis outputs as part of the planning process for each product.
- To visit key customer accounts and ask questions about the value delivered by rivals.
- To make himself available to the CAPs and others engaged in analysis of individual competitors.

As the senior manager engages in each new behavior, it sends a message to multiple internal constituencies, including his peers and subordinates, that he is serious about supporting and leveraging competitor analysis.

An *open-ended* perspective must pervade any guided approach to diagnosing and shaping a competitor learning culture. Analysts need to have a completely free rein in identifying indicators of the current culture. They need to be able to observe individual decision makers and others in multiple situations and in multiple interactions among individuals. By the same token, they need to possess complete freedom to draw inferences about the content of the culture. Analysts must endeavor not to allow themselves to be constrained by the current culture.

Relatedly, an open-ended perspective allows decision makers and analysts to conduct small experiments and to initiate local efforts to see what works in shaping and changing the culture. Analysts could adopt different approaches to collecting data or employ different procedures to execute detailed activity/value chain analyses or to develop sets of competitor scenarios. As decision makers and analysts learn what does and does not work, they then can adapt and modify the analysis processes and organizational procedures.

Involving Decision Makers in Competitor Analysis

A central theme in the discussion throughout this book, and especially in this chapter, is that competitor learning, as the development and use of knowledge, cannot occur unless decision makers—executives, managers, and others who can use competitor analysis outputs—are intimately involved. It is appropriate therefore to conclude by identifying central errors in the way decision makers (and especially senior managers) in most organizations approach analysis of competitors:

- Some managers do not see themselves as providers of data inputs: thus, capturing and processing are severely limited.
- Decision makers do not engage in collaborative processing with CAPs or others: thus, they do not understand either the data or logic side of processing.
- Decision makers quickly judge the decision relevance and value of outputs (even when they have not been involved in their generation): thus, they often misconstrue the context underlying outputs.

Decision makers (often unwittingly) create and sustain a void between those who generate outputs and those who use them in decision making. A guided approach suggests that decision makers must review all the prescriptions and suggestions noted throughout this chapter. In particular, they must identify and assess various roles they could play (see Table 17.6), and how they should do so.

An open-ended approach encourages decision makers to experiment with different roles or behaviors, to monitor the results, and to learn and adapt as they observe the results. An open-ended perspective provides a continued stimulus to ask new questions, to challenge old answers, to seek new ways of learning and, above all, to engage with others in shared reflection about what works and does not.

TABLE 17.6 Learning Activities and Tasks: Roles and Responsibilities for Individuals

Learning Activities and Tasks	Individuals' Roles and Responsibilities (Samples)
CAPTURING	
Determining data needs	Specifying ideal data types
	Identifying desired indicators
Identifying data sources	Enumerating primary and secondary data sources, the types of data they possess, and the characteristics of the data
Collecting data	Identifying opportunities to collect specific types of data
	Collecting the data
PROCESSING	
Selecting data	Determining the relevant data and indicators
	Elaborating the context of data and information
Ordering data	Identifying analysis tools and techniques
	Doing different types of analysis
Interpreting data	Drawing, alerting, and confirming inferences from data
	Developing logics to support inferences
	Testing alternative logics
	Determining competitor consequences and focal firm implications
CRAFTING	
Shaping outputs	Developing different types of outputs
	Formatting outputs in different ways
	Customizing outputs
Critiquing outputs	Challenging the logic underlying outputs
	Developing countervailing data and logic
Communicating outputs	Presenting outputs to decision makers in different organizational settings
	Tailoring outputs to preferences of individual decision makers
DECISION MAKING	
Current decisions	Assessing the implications of competitor outputs for current (and past) decisions
	Reframing existing decisions
New decisions	Detecting new decisions
	Assessing implications of competitor outputs for potential

Summary

The intent of this chapter has been to surface critical errors in the way many organizations organize to do competitor analysis. While there is no one correct way, if these common pitfalls are avoided, competitor analysis is likely to be better integrated not only into the making of decisions but also into the broader fabric of the organization—its systems and processes, procedures, and culture.

APPENDIX

Data Sources

EACH ORGANIZATION MUST DEVELOP A DATABASE OF DATA SOURCES. THE TABLE ILLUSTRATES one way of organizing such a database. It requires a set of individuals to work together over time to identify each significant source of data relevant to competitors (and indeed the broader competitive environment) both within and outside the organization, the types of data they typically generate or possess, and how to obtain the data most efficiently and effectively (while adhering to legal guidelines and ethical guidelines). The entries are examples, a starting point that each organization can consider.

Sources	Primary (Individuals)	Secondary (Written)
Internal	Individuals within the organization who by virtue of their positions and roles pay attention to competitors (and the broader competitive context):	Written materials pertaining to competitors (in part or in whole) that are created or received by any individual, group, or unit within the organization
	Board members	Analysis of the relevant competitive context generated by personnel in any of the organizational domains or areas noted under the primary column
	Chief executive	
	Senior line managers	
	R&D	
	Marketing	Written materials received regularly by these personnel from external sources including governmental reports, security analysts' reports, industry and trade association outputs, newspapers
	Sales	
	Manufacturing	
	Financial	
	Accounting	
	Legal affairs	Written materials received periodically by these personnel such as clippings from specific publications, reports from specific experts or external organizations
	Public relations	
	Human resources	
	Logistics	
	Procurement	

Sources	Primary (Individuals)	Secondary (Written)
Internal *(continued)*	Information systems Strategic planning Mergers and acquisitions Business development Specialist analysis groups	Reports developed by these personnel following trips to visit domestic or foreign customers, channels, suppliers, trade shows, and sometimes even competitors
External	Current, past, and potential customers Customer focus groups Distribution channels (retailers, brokers, wholesalers) Suppliers/providers of raw materials, components, supplies Logistics providers Industry, trade, and professional associations Industry and trade publications News media Trade unions Advertising agencies Third-party service organizations Consulting firms Security analysts Financial services Local, state, and federal agencies Industry experts such as professors, former employees of industry members Specialist experts such as patent lawyers, technology researchers	All written outputs placed in the external environment by competitors such as annual reports; 10K and other financial statements; product catalogues; many types of governmental, judicial, and legislative filings; internet sites Presentations and comments by competitors in many public venues such as trade and industry shows, regulatory and legislative hearings Data pertaining to competitors in many types of publicly available databases Daily, regional, and local newspapers; trade and industry publications Reports generated by specialist industry analysis organizations, security analysts, financial services organizations, consulting firms, and firms specializing in providing data on individual firms Governmental agencies that develop data pertaining to specific competitive or market domains Business school cases

NOTES

CHAPTER 1

1. Many others have also used the notion of a game as a metaphor for rivalry among competitors.

2. *Webster's College Dictionary* defines intellect as: "The faculty of the mind by which one knows or understands, as distinguished from that by which one feels or wills; capacity for thinking or acquiring knowledge." *Webster's College Dictionary,* New York: Random House, 1991.

3. Errors in knowledge and knowledge processes are addressed in Chapter 2.

4. The concepts of data, information, and intelligence are more fully explored in Chapter 3.

5. The role and importance of networks in understanding competitors is the focus of Chapter 9.

6. Strategy without an entrepreneurial flavor or content is both a sterile and contradictory concept. A strategy that does not create and cause change is not likely to be distinctive in the marketplace.

7. The marketplace goals of firms are addressed in Chapter 6. Technological goals are addressed in Chapter 13.

8. A good example of this line of exhortation can be found in Gary Hamel and C.K. Prahalad, *Competing for the Future,* Boston, MA: Harvard Business School Press, 1994.

9. This view of strategy is entirely consistent with the stakeholder theory of strategy. See R.E. Freeman, *Strategic Management: A Stakeholder Approach,* Marshfield, MA: Pitman, 1984.

10. Throughout this book, we will use the phrase "competitive domain" instead of "industry" because the boundaries of so-called historic industries are breaking down and because of our emphasis on customers as the focus in determining which products (and thus which entities) compete against each other.

11. For this reason, "political" assets are included in Chapter 11 as one asset category in an organization's wherewithal that must be developed and leveraged in the battle against competitors. Relationships are also addressed in Chapter 8.

12. Winning in the institutional arena is increasingly addressed under the rubric of political strategy. See John M. Mahon, Barbara Bigelow, and Liam Fahey, "Political Strategy: Managing the Social and Political Environment," in Liam Fahey and Robert Randall (Eds.), *The Portable MBA in Strategy,* New York: John Wiley & Sons, 1994.

13. How stakes are conceived has significant implications for organizational goals and performance measurement—what is referred to later in this chapter as scorekeeping.

14. Such aspirations reflect the ambitions of many organizations discussed earlier.

15. This argument has recently been made by many others. See, for example, James Brian Quinn, *The Intelligent Enterprise,* New York: The Free Press, 1992.

16. Peter Drucker has made this point many times. See, for example, Peter Drucker, *Post-Capitalist Society,* New York: HarperBusiness, 1994.

17. Strategy authors have tended to ignore or downplay the importance of external relationships. A notable recent exception is John Kay, *Foundations of Corporate Success,* Oxford: Oxford University Press, 1993.

18. Perceptual chips are considered in more detail in Chapter 11.

19. Competitive reputation includes the perceptions that competitors might have about a particular rival's proclivity to engage in legal action to defend its patents, customer relationships, or market position. A strong reputation often deters competitors from taking certain actions.

20. See, for example, C.K. Prahalad and Gary Hamel, "The Core Competence of the Corporation," *Harvard Business Review,* May–June 1990, pp. 79–91; and James Brian Quinn, *The Intelligent Enterprise,* New York: The Free Press, 1992.

21. Others have also made the same point. See, for example, Milind M. Lele, *Creating Strategic Leverage,* New York: John Wiley & Sons, 1992.

22. How networks are exploited for this purpose is detailed in Chapter 9.

23. This is another manifestation of the aforementioned tendency of firms to develop and foster networks.

24. The activity/value chain is the focus of Chapter 7.

25. These modes of differentiation or competition are discussed in detail in Chapter 5.

26. Indeed, all too often firsthand knowledge of a firm's products and the firm itself becomes the very reason why customers do not want to become repeat purchasers.

27. The importance of the distinctions between products and solutions is discussed and illustrated in Chapter 5. These distinctions underlie the proposed concept of marketplace strategy and the methodology suggested for identifying and assessing competitors' marketplace strategy.

28. This tendency reflects the increased entrepreneurialism discussed earlier in this chapter.

29. Macroenvironmental refers to the political, regulatory, economic, social, and technological forces *outside* the industry or competitive domain. See Liam Fahey and V.K. Narayanan, *Macroenvironmental Analysis for Strategic Management,* St. Paul, MN: West, 1986.

30. The processes involved in perceiving and assessing signals are discussed in Chapter 4.

31. This mode of analysis or logic is the essence of scenario thinking, which is the subject of Chapter 16. See Liam Fahey and Robert Randall, *Learning from the Future: Competitive Foresight Scenarios,* New York: John Wiley & Sons, 1997; and Peter Schwartz, *The Art of the Long View,* New York: Doubleday/Currency, 1991.

32. These assertions lie at the heart of a learning organization. Learning is the focus of Chapter 2.

33. The premise underlying this assertion is that opportunity development and exploitation is the raison d'être of strategic management.

34. The need for and willingness of organizations to identify, assess and, if necessary, change their mind-set or mental models of the world around them is a core theme in the literature on organizational learning. See, for example, Peter Senge, *The Fifth Discipline: The Art and Practice of the Learning Organization,* New York: Doubleday/Currency, 1990. Learning (and unlearning) is the focus of Chapter 2.

35. These forms of rivalry are the focus of Chapters 11 and 12.

36. Many of the nuances of outmaneuvering rivals along the modes of competition in the channel and customer arenas are detailed and discussed in Chapter 5.

37. Others have referred to this as creating a new competitive space. See, for example, Gary Hamel and C.K. Prahalad, *Competing for the Future,* Boston, MA: Harvard Business School Press, 1994.

38. It may be useful to think of outwitting, outmaneuvering, and outperforming as the corners of a triangle to reinforce how intimately interconnected they are.

39. This observation reinforces the importance of outwitting competitors as a critical task in strategy.

CHAPTER 2

1. Any strategy is, by definition, based on some premises or assumptions about how the competitive domain and the broader social, political, and economic environment will evolve.

2. This point has been made by many others. For a particularly compelling argument, see Peter F. Drucker, *Innovation and Entrepreneurship, Practice and Principles,* New York: Harper & Row, 1985.

3. How to develop these alternative futures and develop strategy-relevant implications from them is the focus of Chapter 16.

4. Competitors should be interpreted here to include both look-alike and functional rivals.

5. Learning about the external environment and the focal firm are termed respectively augmented learning and self-learning later in this chapter.

6. The notion of mental models emphasizes that these views of the environment reside in the minds of organization members. The difficulties in changing these views of the external environment have been well chronicled by many others. See, for example, Peter Senge, *The Fifth Discipline,* New York: Doubleday/Currency, 1990.

7. This sentiment is perhaps most acutely captured in the notions of the "winner's curse" and that "nothing fails like success." See, for example, Richard Pascale, *Managing on the Edge,* New York: Simon & Schuster, 1991.

8. It must be noted here that not all learning theorists and authors subscribe to the notion that learning must be tightly integrated with action. Some authors largely view learning as the acquisition and development of knowledge.

9. Learning as (in part) reflection on one's own actions (and those of others) is central to the concept of learning advocated in this chapter and throughout this book.

10. This point has been emphasized by some organization learning theorists. See, for example, George Huber, "Organizational Learning: The Contributing

Processes and the Literatures," *Organization Science,* vol. 2, no. 1, February 1991, pp. 88–115.

11. The tasks or stages in each learning activity are only briefly sketched in this segment of the chapter. They are elaborated later in this chapter and extensively discussed in many other chapters.

12. The characteristics of data and information are considered in detail in Chapter 3. Many different types of data and information are noted in the remaining chapters in this book.

13. One major purpose of the analysis tools and techniques presented in Chapters 5–16 is to help clarify data requirements.

14. "Primary sources" as used throughout this book refers to human sources; "secondary sources" refers to written words.

15. I have chosen to use the verb *processing* instead of *analyzing* to emphasize that it is individuals who do the processing, that is, who interpret and make sense out of data. Also, analysis will be reserved to incorporate all four learning (knowledge) activities: capturing, processing, crafting (output development), and assessment (integration into decision making).

16. The role and importance of logic and the relationship between data and logic is examined in Chapter 3.

17. The concepts of indicators and signals, and the rationales for distinguishing between them, are detailed in Chapter 4.

18. As shown throughout later chapters, decision makers are often involved in all stages of learning. See especially Chapter 17.

19. These options are addressed in some detail in Chapter 17.

20. Assessment is more fully explicated in Chapters 3 and 4, and is illustrated in detail in each of the remaining chapters.

21. Monitoring, as an organized process of tracking competitors, is detailed in Chapter 3.

22. For an incisive and detailed treatment of the difficulties and complexities of shifting learning from the individual to the organization level, see Daniel H. Kim, "The Link between Individual and Organizational Learning," *Sloan Management Review,* Fall 1993, pp. 37–50.

23. This is the essence of many theorists' view of how knowledge is generated in organizational settings. See, for example, Ikujiro Nonaka and Hiro Takeuchi, *The Knowledge-Creating Company: How Japanese Companies Foster Creativity and Innovation for Competitive Advantage,* New York: Oxford University Press, 1995.

24. Many theorists have elaborated the connection between thinking and acting. See, for example, C. Argyris and D. Schon, *Organizational Learning: A Theory of Action Perspective,* Reading, MA: Addison-Wesley, 1978.

25. This point is strongly emphasized and developed in Peter Senge, *The Fifth Discipline,* New York: Doubleday/Currency, 1990.

26. The role and importance of concepts in managerial, analytical, and organizational frameworks is not widely appreciated. The influence of concepts is addressed at the beginning of Chapter 3.

27. Knowledge is tacit when we are not aware of it. The importance of tacit or implicit knowledge in shaping how individuals think and make decisions is now well established in the literature. See, for example, Ikujiro Nonaka and Hiro Takeuchi, *The Knowledge-Creating Company,* New York: Oxford University Press, 1995.

28. This is in keeping with the traditional epistemological definition of knowledge as justified true belief. The emphasis throughout this book is on justification as opposed to truth in an abstract, static, dictionary sense. Thus, we emphasize the data and logic or reasoning that supports a belief, an assumption, or a projection.

29. This is not as big a problem as may appear at first glance. I shall argue in Chapters 3 and 4 that a greater inhibitor to efficient and effective competitor analysis is the pursuit of unnecessary precision in data and information, and in many outputs of analysis. Stated differently, most data used in analysis do not meet the test of facts. Moreover, data that may not meet the test of facts can still be inordinately useful in competitor analysis. Indeed, if only facts could be used, analysis in all organizational domains would come to a grinding halt.

30. Although perceptions are descriptive, they frequently refer to the future state of a competitor because they may not be completely verifiable.

31. The distinctions between microlevel and macrolevel components of a competitor are delineated in Chapter 3.

32. Again, it is important to emphasize that the focus here is on the focal firm's beliefs about a competitor and not the competitor's beliefs. The latter will be treated as part of the competitor's culture. See Chapter 15.

33. The concept of assumptions is explored in detail in Chapter 10.

34. It is difficult to overstate the importance of tacit assumptions. As argued in Chapter 10, the existence of a competitor's tacit assumptions contributes to analysts in the focal firm often having a superior understanding of the competitor's assumptions than the competitor itself.

35. Judgments are based on data and logic: decision makers articulate the rationales for making the choice(s) that constitute a particular judgment.

36. Projecting, one of the core analysis processes in competitor analysis, is addressed in detail in Chapter 3.

37. Facts reflect judgments in a number of ways. Individuals always make judgments as to which facts to pay attention to, which facts are (more) important, or which facts should be included in an output such as a description of a competitor's marketplace strategy.

38. The concept of inferences and its role in shaping competitor knowledge are elaborated in Chapter 4.

39. This point is discussed at length in Paul C. Nystrom and William H. Starbuck, "To Avoid Organizational Crises, Unlearn," *Organizational Dynamics,* Spring 1984, pp. 53–65.

40. See, for example, Karl E. Weick, *Sense making in organizations.* Thousand Oaks, CA: Sage, 1995.

41. Errors are defined by Argyris as any feature of knowledge or knowing that inhibits learning. See Chris Argyris, "Usable Knowledge for Double-Loop Problems," in Ralph Kilmann and Associates, *Producing Useful Knowledge for Organizations,* pp. 377–394. New York: Prager, 1983.

42. Errors of knowing, or errors in the processes of learning, are discussed in the final section of this chapter and in more detail in Chapter 17.

43. Such reflection can also lead to new knowledge.

44. The notions of single-loop and double-loop learning were developed and explicated by Chris Argyris and Donald Schon. See their book, *Organizational Learning,* Reading, MA: Addison-Wesley, 1978.

45. Many different illustrations are provided throughout the remaining chapters in this book that collectively support this contention.

46. The number of individuals and groups or units dedicated to competitor analysis has risen substantially in the past five years. One indicator is the growth in membership of the Society of Competitor Intelligence Professionals.

47. Changes in organization attributes as an impetus to learning are addressed in Chapters 3 and 4.

48. Different types of current, emergent, and potential competitors are discussed in Chapters 5 and 6.

49. Signals of marketplace change are an explicit part of the analysis framework presented in Chapters 5-16.

50. These terms were defined and distinguished earlier in this chapter.

51. The concept of intelligence is developed in Chapter 3 and intelligence needs receives extensive treatment in Chapter 17.

52. It is for this reason that the role and importance of concepts is addressed at the beginning of Chapter 3 and the concept underlying each framework component—what we mean by, say, marketplace strategy, assets, or culture—is addressed at the beginning of Chapters 5-16.

53. This point has been forcefully made, by among others, Russell Ackoff, "Management Misinformation Systems, *Management Science,* December 1967, pp. B147-B156.

54. The importance of and distinctions between efficient and effective learning are described in Chapter 3.

55. Scanning and monitoring are discussed in detail in Chapter 3.

56. The nature and importance of logic in any learning mode or process is addressed in Chapters 3 and 4, and many examples are provided in later chapters.

CHAPTER 3

1. These examples relate to each of the principal learning activities in Figure 2.1.

2. In this vein, competitor learning, as a concept, assumes critical importance.

3. The notion of logic is developed later in this chapter.

4. See Chapters 5 and 6 for a detailed discussion of the types of data required to conduct an analysis of a competitor's marketplace strategy.

5. Many types of outputs are identified in Chapters 5-16. The organizational processes involved in the development and customization of outputs are addressed in Chapter 17.

6. The common usage of these terms, which often have quite different meanings even within the same organization, illustrates the importance of defining concepts.

7. A representative sample of such books includes: Leonard M. Fuld, *Competitor Intelligence: How to Get It; How to Use It,* New York: John Wiley & Sons, 1985; Benjamin Gilad and Tamar Gilad, *The Business Intelligence System: A New Tool for Competitive Advantage,* New York: American Management Association, 1988; Ruth Stanat, *The Intelligent Corporation: Creating a Shared Network for Information and Profit,* New York: American Management Association, 1990; John E. Prescott and Patrick T. Gibbons (Eds.), *Global Perspectives on Competitive Intelligence,* Alexandria, VA: Society of Competitive Intelligence Professionals, 1993; John J.

McGonagle, Jr. and Carolyn M. Vella, *A New Archtype for Competitive Intelligence,* Westport, CT: Quorom Books, 1996.

8. Listings of topics to be covered in most frameworks tend not to be integrated; the linkages and relationships among and between topics is typically poorly treated.

9. Identifying and assessing these strategies is the focus of Chapters 5 and 6. Projecting competitors' marketplace strategies is addressed in Chapter 16.

10. The role and importance of culture in understanding competitors is detailed in Chapter 15.

11. Organization learning theorists consistently emphasize that organizational learning cannot occur unless individuals first learn. See, for example, Peter Senge, *The Fifth Discipline,* New York: Doubleday/Currency, 1990.

12. It is in this sense that organization theorists talk about decision makers thinking their way into acting and acting their way into thinking. See, for example, Karl Weick, *The Social Psychology of Organizing* (2nd ed.), Reading, MA: Addison-Wesley, 1969.

13. The role of CAPs is addressed in detail in Chapter 17.

14. These and many related points regarding errors in the processes of knowing (learning) were discussed in the concluding section of Chapter 2. They are discussed in more detail in Chapter 17.

15. The importance of context is explicitly treated in the discussion of signals in Chapter 4 and in many other places in succeeding chapters.

16. The pursuit of accuracy or precision in data that does not add value from a decision-making perspective is another common error in the process of knowing.

17. The following fallacies about data draw heavily (with permission) from Liam Fahey, "Mis- Intelligence," *Across the Board,* April 1989, pp. 26–31.

18. This case is a good example of the aforementioned error of misconstruing an opinion for a projection of what will actually take place.

19. Issues raised in this example about the roles of data that alert analysts to potentially important signals and confirming and refuting data are addressed in Chapter 4.

20. Established competitors refer to organizations the focal firm has been competing against for at least two or three years.

21. In almost every instance brought to my attention in which organizations engaged in illegal and/or unethical conduct, the desired data could have been obtained through ethical and legal means.

22. This is clearly unethical behavior because it requires that one or more individuals within the firm misrepresent who they are.

23. It is essential that decision makers and other analysts be fully cognizant of the legal and ethical guidelines advocated by their own organization.

24. This implies that knowledge exists only in individuals' heads.

25. The presumption here is that the individual has some justification or solid base of reasoning (what we refer to as logic) as a basis to accept the content of the information.

26. The fallacy of misplaced concreteness was coined by the philosopher, Alfred North Whitehead.

27. It is in this sense that one can argue that intelligence (knowledge that informs decision makers and influences decision making) cannot be gathered; it can only be created.

28. Stated differently, the value of information is its decision relevance: individuals can put the information to use (information thus becomes intelligence or knowledge in use).

29. This is a good example of descriptive learning, as discussed in Chapter 2.

30. The steps involved in getting from the acquisition of a single piece of data to intelligence are identified and discussed in detail in Chapter 4.

31. These types of intelligence are neither exhaustive nor mutually exclusive.

32. How competitor analysis outputs are integrated into decision making and organizational processes such as strategic planning, capital allocation, budgeting, and others, is considered in detail in Chapter 17.

33. This section draws heavily from Liam Fahey and V.K. Narayanan, *Macroenvironmental Analysis for Strategy Formulation,* St. Paul, MN: West Publishing, 1986.

34. The internal focus of scanning is noted here because the impulse in most organizations is to scan external sources rather than internal sources. As noted earlier, however, in the case of many long-standing competitors, much of the required data already exist *inside* the focal organization.

35. Distinctions among types of indicators and their roles in alerting analysts to past, current, and potential competitor change are fully developed in Chapter 4.

36. This surprise element in scanning reinforces the importance of open-ended scanning.

37. Perhaps more important than search guidelines is an understanding of the role and importance of the act of perception necessary to detect indicators and signals, which is discussed Chapter 4.

38. How these types of competitors arise is addressed in Chapter 5.

39. Again, the role and importance of primary sources, that is individuals, in scanning should be emphasized. Structured or open-ended interviews with informed sources can generate data that simply cannot be obtained through secondary sources.

40. Discerning and delineating here constitute interpretation, a central item in processing, as discussed in Chapter 2.

41. Indicators are discussed in detail in Chapter 4.

42. Monitoring these trends is discussed in detail in Chapter 5 as part of tracking competitors' marketplace strategies.

43. Monitoring sequences of events and streams of actions is specifically addressed in Chapter 7 as part of the analysis of competitors' activity/value chains.

44. All of these, and many related, judgments are the focus of much attention in succeeding chapters.

45. Knowledge, as described in Chapter 2, includes facts, perceptions, beliefs, assumptions, and projections. Projections are inherently about the future. However, as illustrated in Chapter 2, facts, perceptions, beliefs, and assumptions also can be about the future.

46. This particular scenario is detailed in Chapter 16.

47. This illustrates the tight linkage between projecting and assessment in guided analysis.

48. These and many related forces (or factors) will be considered and illustrated as part of delineating and discussing projections in later chapters pertaining to marketplace strategy, alliances, networks, assumptions, assets, and capabilities and competencies.

49. This example of augmented learning is examined in detail in Chapter 5.

50. In the remaining chapters, *consequences* will be used (instead of *implications*) in the case of competitors. Implications will be used exclusively in the case of the focal firm.

51. These types of competitor consequences are addressed in every chapter in the book and are especially detailed in the competitor scenarios discussed in Chapter 16.

52. Implications are also addressed in detail in the remaining chapters.

CHAPTER 4

1. The concepts of data and information were detailed in Chapter 3.

2. The distinction between *consequences* for a competitor and *implications* for the focal firm are maintained throughout this chapter, and indeed, the remainder of the book.

3. This assertion follows from the definition of a signal presented in the previous paragraph.

4. Michael E. Porter, *Competitive Strategy: Techniques for Analyzing Industries and Competitors,* New York: The Free Press, 1980, p. 75.

5. Oliver Heil and Tom Robertson, "Toward a Theory of Competitive Market Signalling: A Research Agenda," *Strategic Management Journal,* vol. 12, 1991, p. 403.

6. These connections are elaborated later in this chapter.

7. These are the indicators principally noted in the definitions of signals offered by Porter, and Heil and Robertson, quoted in the prior paragraph.

8. This point is strongly supported in the organization learning, social psychology, and other literatures. See, for example, James G. March and J.P. Olsen, *Ambiguity and Choice in Organizations* (2nd ed.), Berger: Universitetsforlaget, 1979.

9. The relationship between signals and change is detailed later in this chapter.

10. The content of projections and assessments was discussed in Chapter 3.

11. These elements of knowledge and processes of knowing were developed in Chapter 2.

12. This is a good example of selecting and ordering data, two core tasks in processing.

13. Interpretation was identified in Chapter 2 as one of the core tasks in processing.

14. Assessment here is a more specific example of assessment as discussed in Chapter 3.

15. Assessing implications for the industry or broader competitive domain is augmented learning, as discussed in Chapter 2.

16. Some of these errors are noted in the final section of this chapter.

17. This is a more specific illustration of the recursive nature of competitor learning discussed in Chapter 2.

18. Signaling capacity is the phrase used in the management literature to suggest the potential of one thing to give rise to a signal about something else.

19. Inaction as an indicator reinforces the need to separate the detection of indicators from perception of signals, as depicted in Figure 4.1, and discussed earlier in this chapter.

20. Sometimes newsletters are intentionally made available to external parties such as distribution channels, end-customers, security analysts, and others. Often,

newsletters and other news documents are written with the presumption that they will in one way or another make their way into the public milieu.

21. Asset categories, classes, and types are delineated in Chapter 11.

22. Asset attributes of course pertain to the notion of chips developed in Chapter 1.

23. These elements of culture are described and discussed in Chapter 15. Behaviors as an element of culture refer to the behaviors of individual organization members as they interact with external entities such as customers, channels, suppliers, and others.

24. Again, these attributes are detailed in Chapter 11.

25. The power of assumption change as a signal of strategy change is discussed in detail in Chapter 10.

26. Change indicated in assessment is a key output of the types of competitor learning identified in Chapter 3: descriptive, comparative, extended, and self-learning.

27. Prospective signals tend to be the sole focus of the treatment of signals in the management and economics literatures.

28. Scenarios as a means of generating anticipated signals are addressed in Chapter 16.

29. Searching for anticipated indicators is a good example of scanning in the prospective mode noted in Chapter 3.

30. The provision of misinformation in almost all circumstances violates common codes of ethical and moral behavior. It is doubly unfortunate because the untruth of statements, or "misinformation," is often easy to determine. Thus their purpose is quickly undermined. Moreover, when a competitor's attempt to engage in misinformation becomes public, it undermines the integrity of that competitor not only in the eyes of many external stakeholders beyond its rivals (including end-customers and channels) but also in the eyes of many of its employees.

31. The distinction between a competitor's motivation to "send a signal" and its purpose in terms of the behavior or response it seeks to evoke has received surprisingly little attention in the literature addressing signals.

32. These and other modes of differentiation or competitive posture are addressed in detail in Chapter 5.

33. This is the phrase that is so often used in common parlance. As noted earlier, in the conceptual framework developed in this chapter, signals cannot be sent; they can only be inferred.

34. *Message* and *information* are the words used in the strategy and economics literatures with regard to the substance conveyed in intended signals.

35. For further discussion of this point, see Michael E. Porter, *Competitive Strategy: Techniques for Analyzing Industries and Competitors,* New York: The Free Press, 1980. Bear in mind, however, that Porter treats indicators as signals.

36. This is in part because the analyst has the opportunity to judge the tone and tenor of the remarks, the emotion of the speaker, and the overall context of the statements.

37. The role and importance of plausible alternative logics in the case of both direct and indirect signals is treated in Chapter 10 with regard to assumptions.

38. Competitor consequences are examined throughout this book.

39. As noted, false inferences are judgments and projections that prove to be incorrect. False inferences can be about the past, present, or future.

CHAPTER 5

1. The concept of marketplace rules was outlined and discussed in some detail in Chapter 1.

2. The assessment of scope is addressed at the conclusion of Chapter 6 after the three elements of marketplace strategy—scope, posture, and goals—have been detailed.

3. These three questions refer respectively to the where, how, and why of marketplace strategy noted at the beginning of this paragraph.

4. A product line is a set of products that share similar functional attributes such as mainframe or personal computers. Product types represent product groupings within a line.

5. As shall be discussed shortly, these moves constitute direct indicators of change in scope.

6. The importance of distinguishing between end-customer and channel arenas was discussed in Chapter 1.

7. To emphasize the interconnectedness of the concepts of scope and posture, each is segregated into the same two items, position and direction.

8. The specificity of indicators to individual dimensions (within modes of competition) is extensively illustrated in the next section of this chapter.

9. Again, these are the components indicated in Figure 3.2: activity/value chain, alliances and relationships, networks, assumptions, assets, capabilities and competencies, technology, organizational infrastructure, and culture.

10. The emphasis here is on customer functionality. Product features often address different facets of product functionality.

11. Price/value relationship refers to the value customers perceive themselves receiving along all the modes of competition for some particular outlay. Price/performance refers to the benefits received in terms of functionality for some given price.

12. Analysis of this presumption again emphasizes the importance of context, as discussed in Chapter 3, in any endeavor to understand the behaviors and actions of competitors.

13. These are the generic strategies popularized by Michael E. Porter. See his book, *Competitive Strategy: Techniques for Analyzing Industries and Competitors*, New York: The Free Press, 1980.

14. For a detailed discussion of customization, see Joseph B. Pine, *Mass Customization: The New Frontier in Business Competition*, Boston, MA: Harvard Business School Press, 1993.

15. These strategies are described in detail in the case of Japanese firms in the U.S. marketplace in Philip Kotler, Liam Fahey, and Somkid Jatusripitak, *The New Competition: What Theory Z Didn't Tell You About—Marketing*, Englewood Cliffs, NJ: Prentice-Hall, 1985.

16. This also implies moving to the next stage or generation of customer needs.

17. Organizations' willingness to incur the risks necessarily involved in bypass moves is also related to the notion of stakes discussed in Chapter 1. Organizations recognize the rewards of winning and the difficulties caused by losing a round in the competitive game—the costs of getting back into the game are escalating.

18. Change in each microlevel component as an indicator of marketplace strategy change is discussed in each of the next nine chapters.

19. Competitors' assumptions are addressed in detail in Chapter 10.

20. These signals are discussed at length in Chapter 13.

21. The analysis frameworks offered in this book are intended to address the visibility of competitors' future behaviors *before* they are entered into or implemented.

22. The importance of the entrepreneurial content of strategy has been noted in many places already. See, for example, the discussion in Chapter 1.

23. This is not to imply that all entrepreneurial content contributes to winning; only that without some degree of entrepreneurial content, a strategy cannot deliver sustained superior returns compared with that of rivals.

24. For a discussion of stretch, see Gary Hamel and C.K. Prahalad, "Strategy as Stretch and Leverage," *Harvard Business Review,* March–April 1993.

25. It is important to emphasize again that product is intended to refer to all types of product: tangible and intangible; manufactured and service offerings; a single product (e.g., a computer or type of software) or a total solution (e.g., an integrated system including many different types of hardware and software).

26. This is why we begin the identification of a competitor's scope *before* we discuss data sources.

27. Both customers' needs and preferences are emphasized for two reasons. Customers may not be fully aware of their needs and wants and may have difficulty articulating what they are or will be. Preferences on the other hand can be more easily ascertained; they are also reflected in customers' actual choices.

28. Although they may be embedded, they are often not obvious.

29. These are the steps briefly delineated in Chapter 2 under "Capturing" in the competitor learning model (Cell 2 in Figure 2.1).

30. Identifying knowledge gaps is one of the key learning questions noted in Chapter 2. It is the focus of significant attention in Chapters 9 and 14.

31. An illustration of useful data sources is provided in the case of posture later in this chapter.

32. Mapping a competitor's moves and direction is an example of the steps involved in processing that were delineated in Chapter 2: selecting data, ordering data, and interpretation.

33. Projecting competitors' strategies is the focus of Chapter 16.

34. Shaping, critiquing, and communicating outputs are the three steps in Crafting noted in Figure 2.1.

35. This is again another example of outputs being crafted: shaped, critiqued, and communicated.

36. The yogurt competitor's goals are treated in detail in Chapter 6.

37. A learning benchmark refers here to the distinction between the first two key learning questions noted in Chapter 2: What do we know? What do we need to know?

38. "Institutionalizing" data sources and search processes means that the organization catalogs names, addresses, and phone numbers of *primary* data sources, the types of data they have provided and/or could potentially provide, as well as the preferred means of collecting data from the individual sources. It also means cataloging all the *secondary* sources of data and how the data can be most expeditiously obtained.

39. Again, this is merely a sample of the data sources available. Each organization must develop its own listing of relevant primary and secondary sources.

40. This is another example of the importance of logic as discussed in Chapters 3 and 4.

41. This is one of the posture types defined earlier in this chapter.

42. How posture is used for purposes of comparative and self-learning will be detailed in Chapter 6.

43. How to avoid this error is addressed in detail in many later chapters. See, for example, the detailed treatment of the temporal aspects of Capturing and Processing in Chapter 14.

44. One executive has observed to me that the real problem in much of the competitor and customer analysis he sees is not differentiating between the forest and trees. In his view, far too many individuals are preoccupied with distinctions between the tree and its bark.

CHAPTER 6

1. The strategy literature dating at least from A.D. Chandler, *Strategy and Structure: Chapters in the History of Industrial Enterprise,* Cambridge, MA: MIT Press, 1962, has long held that goals are a crucial and central element in any conception of strategy.

2. The management literature has a long tradition of arguing that an organization without some sense of its goals is a meaningless entity. For one of the earliest exponents of this view, see Herbert A. Simon, "On the Concept of Organizational Goal," *Administrative Science Quarterly,* vol. 9, no. 1 (June 1964), pp. 1-22.

3. Strategic intent and vision, which are discussed later in this chapter, embody the notions of goals as a rallying force and unifying force within an organization.

4. As noted, behaviors are a shorthand for a series of actions that are related to each other or are engaged in for a common purpose or end.

5. Using the competitor's aspirations as a strategy assessment criterion is considered under assessment later in this chapter.

6. See C.K. Prahalad, Liam Fahey, and Robert M. Randall, "A Strategy for Growth: The Role of Core Competencies in the Corporation," in Liam Fahey and Robert M. Randall, Eds., *The Portable MBA in Strategy,* New York: John Wiley & Sons, 1993.

7. These aims by themselves do not constitute a strategy within the framework presented in this and the previous chapter: strategy is the combination of behaviors and goals.

8. Gary Hamel and C.K. Prahalad, "Strategic Intent," *Harvard Business Review,* vol. 67, no. 3, 1989, pp. 63-76.

9. See, for example, James C. Collins and Jerry A. Porras, *Built to Last: Successful Habits of Visionary Companies,* New York: HarperBusiness, 1994.

10. Tom Peters and Robert Waterman, *In Search of Excellence,* New York: Harper & Row, 1982.

11. By first identifying a competitor's strategic thrusts and investment programs and then inferring the goals associated with them, an analyst is likely to be in a position to infer what the competitor's intent/vision is, or would have to be, given the thrusts and programs.

12. The quagmire that is the terminology associated with goals is well reflected in the different definitions and uses of objectives and goals. Some authors and companies use objectives and goals as proposed in these paragraphs. Others reverse them.

13. Parameters here are equivalent to indicators: they are what analysts or others monitor and measure to determine goal attainment.

14. See Chapter 5 for a discussion of these types of marketplace coverage.

15. Technological goals are discussed in detail in Chapter 13.

16. The relevant organization levels will have been identified as part of the determination of scope and posture.

17. The remaining errors discussed in this section can be viewed as a checklist for analysts to review and test the process by which they derive inferences.

18. The importance of this error and the process of challenging and refuting inferences is more fully discussed in Chapter 13.

19. The discussion here refers principally to the end-customer and channel arenas.

20. Parameters and criteria for scorekeeping in different arenas and domains are addressed throughout this book. See the initial discussion in Chapter 1. See also, for example, the discussion of scorekeeping pertaining to capabilities and competencies in Chapter 12 and to technology in Chapter 13.

21. It is for this reason that comparative and extended learning and self-learning were emphasized in Chapter 2 (and throughout this book).

22. Along with marketplace strategy, these items constitute the elements in the competitor analysis framework depicted in Figure 3.2 and discussed throughout this book.

23. The importance of cycling through the key learning questions as a means of avoiding this error is addressed in detail in Chapters 9 and 14.

24. This error largely corresponds to the error noted in Chapter 8 pertaining to analysts' missing the forest for the trees—the underlying structure of scope and posture.

25. These categories are not mutually exclusive.

26. Scenarios, as discussed in Chapter 16, offer a formal methodology to create and test the marketplace strategies of invented rivals.

27. Mythology was defined in Chapter 2 as an incongruence between what individuals take to be knowledge—what they know—and the reality inside or outside their organization.

CHAPTER 7

1. This chapter focuses on the core or primary activities in the value chain. Many of the secondary or support activities such as personnel, technology, and infrastructure are addressed in later chapters.

2. The value chain has been popularized by the work of Michael E. Porter. See his book, *Competitive Advantage,* New York: The Free Press, 1985, especially Chapters 2 and 3.

3. In this book, the designation A/VC refers to both the conventional value chain and the customer-focused activity chain.

4. This is an example of how what others (e.g., Porter, 1985) have termed secondary or support activities play an important role in connecting the firm to external parties rather than just connecting activities within the firm.

5. What is meant here is that it becomes difficult to separate what the competitor does from what the personnel and the customer do. Their contributions can be so tightly intertwined that it does not make a lot of sense to try to detail in highly specific terms who does what.

6. Differences in an organization's A/VC compared with those of rivals is a necessary but not sufficient condition for the generation of customer value by that organization. Customers must also appreciate the value that is generated.

7. These connections are discussed in Chapters 12 and 13 respectively.

8. First-cut is the term used throughout this book when analysts develop initial analysis outputs. They are often generated from data readily available to analysts, that is, a specific data search is not conducted before they are created. These first-cut outputs are then used to help determine what the next analysis steps should be.

9. Impetus is used here in the sense in which it was discussed in Chapter 2 as a central element in the competitor learning model.

10. These are examples of triggered competitor analysis, as discussed in Chapter 2: learning is triggered by what the competitor is doing and why it is succeeding.

11. This is an example of activated learning, as discussed in Chapter 2.

12. This is an example of initiated learning: the organization initiates competitor analysis in the absence of specific competitor change.

13. As discussed later in this chapter, these circumstances can be viewed as criteria to help determine which competitors' A/VCs should be identified and assessed.

14. This assertion is consistent with the four learning questions noted in Chapter 2 at the beginning of the section on guided learning.

15. This is an example of marketplace strategy serving as an indicator of activity/value chain elements.

16. This is especially appropriate advice in the case of customer-focused activity chains.

17. The small number of customers is sufficient because the competitor's customer-focused A/VC does not change in fundamental ways from one customer to another.

18. In the language of Chapter 2, these are examples respectively of self-learning and augmented learning.

19. Chapter 8 illustrates the use of these learning questions.

20. This occurs because decision makers and other analysts are not willing to expose their own organization to the challenges posed by comparison with competitors.

21. As discussed in Chapter 2, processing involves the transformation of data into information.

22. This is an example of recursiveness in assessment: a determination of the extent of uniqueness requires comparison across competitors' A/VCs which is a later step in assessment (see Figure 7.9).

23. These perceptions are the essence of superior image and reputation, one of the central components of a competitor's marketplace posture. As discussed in Chapter 11, these perceptions may also constitute a key resource or asset for a competitor: something that can be leveraged for marketplace success.

24. These linkages are identified in detail in Chapters 8 and 9.

25. An illustration of how to do so is provided in Chapter 11.

26. This linkage is elaborated in Chapter 12.

27. These linkages are treated in Chapter 10.

28. This point is central to the concept of competitor learning advanced in this book. It is discussed and emphasized in many chapters.

29. The role and importance of this metaphor was discussed in Chapters 2 and 3.

30. This is another example of the recursive nature of competitor analysis being emphasized in this chapter.

31. This point reinforces the importance of attention to indirect inferences and the reasoning that connects these indicators to specific inferences.

32. This is another reason for attaching importance to identifying change that is occurring or likely to take place in competitors' AV/Cs, as was discussed at the beginning of assessment.

33. These observations illustrate how technology could be used to improve both extraconnectedness and intraconnectedness. This point is discussed further in Chapter 13.

34. This is how real self-learning and augmented learning occur.

CHAPTER 8

1. This is a classic example of announcements, as a form of data and indicators, as discussed in Chapter 3.

2. These materials include the formal statements associated with the announcements of impending alliances.

3. Identifying a competitor's potential alliances is addressed in the final section of this chapter.

4. This point is discussed in more detail in the next chapter with reference to a competitor's networks.

5. The importance and contribution of preliminary assessments in competitor learning is developed in the next chapter in the case of networks.

6. This is the essence of the recursive nature of competitor analysis emphasized in this chapter.

7. The final section of this chapter addresses patterns across alliances.

8. Analysts may need to subject the alliance partner to the kinds of analysis detailed in this book and summarized in Figure 3.2.

9. The evolution of an alliance (or special relationship) constitutes a critical element of the competitor context which, as noted earlier in this chapter, must always be understood as a prelude to the derivation of signals.

10. These individuals may be describing either the special side of their own organization's relationship with the focal firm or that of another entity.

11. This is not always the case. The special side of a relationship may arise long after two or more organizations have been interacting with each other. For example, a supplier and a manufacturer may develop shared interests and commitments well into their formal working relationship.

12. The pharmaceutical firm appointed a group of managers with responsibility to understand every phase of the FDA procedures and processes, to build a working relationship with the agency's personnel, and to rapidly respond to all requests for data, etc.

13. Parameters can be viewed as indicators along which the evolution of the alliance is recorded.

14. Linkages across alliances are addressed in detail in Chapter 9 when we discuss networks.

15. Again, these concepts were introduced and developed in Chapter 1.

16. Analysis of constraints and vulnerabilities along a competitor's activity/value chain was discussed in detail in Chapter 7.

17. The mode of analysis here is largely similar to that discussed previously in the case of competitor consequences as part of the assessment of alliances.

CHAPTER 9

1. Networks have only begun to receive serious attention in the past five years or so. Most strategy textbooks still pay only modest attention to their role and importance. For thorough treatments of the topic, see Benjamin Gomes-Casseres, *The Alliances Revolution,* Boston, MA: Harvard University Press, 1998; and Nitin Nohria and Robert Eccles (Eds.), *Networks and Organizations: Structure, Form and Action,* Boston, MA: Harvard Business School Press, 1992.

2. For a good example of rivalry among a set of networks, see Benjamin Gomes-Casseres, "Group Versus Group: How Alliance Networks Compete," *Harvard Business Review,* July–August 1994, pp. 62–74.

3. The first four of these network types were identified and briefly discussed in Jordon D. Lewis, *Partnerships for Profit,* New York: The Free Press, 1990.

4. Technology networks are addressed in Chapter 13.

5. These primary suppliers can be viewed as second-level nodes in a network structure.

6. Some of these judgments are the focus of the errors in network analysis that are noted in the final section of this chapter.

7. The importance of reconfiguring a network is discussed later in the chapter.

8. In the terminology of Chapter 4, these can be viewed as the alerting indicators of the existence of some type of network.

9. As noted throughout this book, these types of judgment typify capturing and processing.

10. This is a good example of how assessment provides feedback to and thus influences the three earlier learning activities: capturing, processing, and crafting.

11. The philosophy and orientation of scenarios, and their use in competitor learning, is the focus of Chapter 16.

12. This point is further developed in the discussion of scenarios in Chapter 16.

13. These two items essentially refer to competitor consequences.

14. This task is a central focus in scenarios. See Chapter 16.

15. This type of analysis was treated in some detail in Chapter 8.

16. The analysis discussed previously under the heading, "Comparisons across Competitors," is relevant here.

17. Infrastructure is addressed in Chapter 14.

18. These tasks thus become anticipated indicators.

19. The analysis just discussed will help identify and inform many of the questions raised here.

20. These questions relate directly to the strategy framework of analysis outlined in Chapter 1.

21. This error is discussed in some detail in the section on errors in Chapter 14.

22. This error is fundamental in part because it is applicable to the analysis of marketplace strategy and each microlevel component.

CHAPTER 10

1. This definition follows that offered by Ian I. Mitroff and Richard Mason, *Challenging Strategic Planning Assumptions,* New York: John Wiley & Sons, 1981.

2. However, the explicit purpose of the methodology detailed in this chapter is to capture the *actual* assumptions of any competitor.

3. The role and importance of tacit assumptions in driving and explaining the behaviors of both individuals and organizations is extensively treated in the literatures on organization culture, organization decision making, and organizational knowledge. See, for example, Ikujiro Nonaka and Hirotaka Takeuchi, *The Knowledge-Creating Company,* New York: Oxford University Press, 1995.

4. The validity of most assumptions is time constrained.

5. These are the steps involved in the analysis of signals detailed in Chapter 4.

6. The process of doing so is addressed in detail later in this chapter.

7. Often outstanding performance along such parameters as market share and financial returns masks the need for fundamental strategy change (due to the change in the competitive environment such as the planned strategies of competitors).

8. This is consistent with the definition of assumptions provided earlier in the chapter: What the competitor takes for granted or as a given, or must take for granted.

9. Even though analysts may have already identified key recent signals, taking the time here to identify key changes often results in a more systematic identification of signals.

10. Actual core assumptions include both explicit and implicit assumptions. As argued earlier in this chapter, implicit or tacit assumptions may be more important as guides to competitors' future behaviors.

11. This error is a direct consequence of the fact, noted earlier, that so many organizations do not fully identify, develop, and assess their own assumptions.

12. Adhering to an assumption again emphasizes the importance of paying attention to tacit assumptions.

13. This test may not be applicable to all assumptions since some may not be stated in a form that easily allows its opposite to be considered.

14. Among other benefits, this serves as another check or balance in the identification and analysis of assumptions.

15. Again, this reflects the importance of tacit assumptions, as discussed earlier.

16. These elements in scenario development are treated fully in Chapter 16.

17. This example is used because of the differences in assumptions between the focal firm and the competitor. It seems safe to suggest that the diametrical differences reported in this example are not likely to be common. It is drawn heavily (and with permission) from Liam Fahey, "Understanding Your Competitor's Assumptions," in John E. Prescott, Ed., *Advances in Competitive Intelligence,* Vienna, VA: Society of Competitive Intelligence Professionals, 1989.

18. It is probably preferable to separate, as much as possible, identification of the focal firm's assumptions from those of competitors to avoid many types of bias (errors). One way of doing so, which was done by the industrial products firm, is to use a team that was not involved in the prior identification and evaluation of competitors' assumptions. In many instances, because of time pressures and the shortage of personnel, it is not possible to do so. The discussion here reflects the pervasive organizational error noted earlier.

19. These examples again reinforce the need to clearly define terms and concepts (as discussed in Chapter 3) and to communicate their meaning.

20. Domain assumptions refer to the refined assumptions discussed earlier.

21. Again, validity of assumptions refers to the truth of assumptions, not whether they are held by the competitor.

22. The rationale for this argument has already been made in Chapter 1: success often causes complacency and thus the organization only becomes self-critical *after* performance has suffered a serious deterioration.

CHAPTER 11

1. Chips is the general term used in Chapter 1 to refer to the assets, capabilities, and competencies required for successful strategy development and execution.

2. Capabilities and competencies, including the distinctions between them, are detailed and discussed in Chapter 12.

3. The relationship between assets and capabilities or competencies is often obscured in the management literature by a failure to distinguish between them. Assets can be viewed as nouns; we can think of them in terms of quantity. Capabilities and competencies, on the other hand, are best viewed as verbs; we think of them in terms of action—what the competitor does.

4. For example, relationships are addressed in Chapters 8 and 9, technology is the focus of Chapter 13, and organization is considered in Chapters 14 and 15.

5. See, for example, Peter Drucker, *The Practice of Management,* New York: Harper & Brothers, 1964; and H. Igor Ansoff, *Corporate Strategy,* New York: McGraw-Hill, 1965.

6. Even many proponents of the now popular "resource-based" view of strategy fail to carefully delineate and categorize the key resources that might be leveragable by organizations. They frequently refer to resources as combinations of assets and skills without specifying what constitutes either assets or capabilities in any thorough way, and as a consequence the differences between them.

7. The recent surge in interest in knowledge as an asset, and as the basis of capability and competence, has not yet led to generally accepted definitions or categorizations of what knowledge is or consists of.

8. Technology assets are discussed in some detail in Chapter 13.

9. This point has been made forcefully by others including James Brian Quinn, *The Intelligent Enterprise,* New York: The Free Press, 1991.

10. The notion that assets are available outside the competitor implies the existence of a market in which these types of assets can be bought and sold. For many assets such as perceptions, relationships, knowledge, and most organization attributes, this is not the case.

11. This is the focus of much discussion in the resource-based theory of the firm. See, for example, Margaret A. Peteraf, "The Cornerstones of Competitive Advantage," *Strategic Management Journal,* March 1993.

12. These questions are addressed in detail in Chapters 2 and 3.

13. The particular firm was chosen for illustration purposes for these reasons: First, software providers are service organizations. Thus, this competitor's principal assets are not absorbed in manufacturing. Second, as a private organization, it allows us to demonstrate how asset analysis can be conducted for nonpublicly quoted organizations. Third, it is sometimes easier to see the interconnections among assets in smaller firms.

14. The use of networks of alliances and relationships to create and augment assets is addressed in Chapter 8.

15. These questions are referred to as guided component questions to avoid confusion with the guided or central learning questions noted at the beginning of this section.

16. The relationship between activities and tasks is discussed in detail in Chapter 7.

17. The connections between these tasks have been addressed in many other chapters, and thus will not be considered in further detail here.

18. This is a good example of the importance of information—data that are transformed by analysts into information—as a source of indicators.

19. An understanding of the concept of assets helps to avoid many of the errors noted in this section.

20. I have seen analyses of competitors' assets that consider only financial assets.

21. See Chapter 3 for examples of this tendency and its implications.

22. It was noted at the beginning of this chapter that often it is not immediately obvious which assets undergird a competitor's marketplace strategy or activity/value chain.

23. In many instances, it is appropriate to begin assessment by determining the key or most important assets.

24. Unrelated refers here to software products that would require distinctly different (software) designs and codes.

25. Activity/value chain is in the plural here because as emphasized in Chapter 7, an individual organization with distinct products may have unique value chains associated with each product.

26. As noted, signals are inferences drawn by analysts.

27. These connections are emphasized here because in many organizations little attention is paid to asset change as a source of signals of future marketplace change.

28. This set of issues receives considerable attention in Chapter 12.

CHAPTER 12

1. The three levels of changing the strategy game—creating a new strategy game, reconstructing a strategy game, and shifting the marketplace rules—are discussed in Chapter 1.

2. Unique competencies or capabilities are those that no other organization possesses. Few organizations possess genuinely unique competencies or capabilities.

3. These difficulties (and many of their associated errors) are noted later in this chapter.

4. A veritable plethora of articles has emerged on these topics in the past five years. Among the most widely cited are: C.K. Prahalad and Gary Hamel, "The Core Competence of the Organization," *Harvard Business Review,* May/June 1990, pp. 79-91; George Stalk, Philip Evans, and Lawrence E. Shulman, "Competing on Capabilities: The New Rules of Corporate Strategy," *Harvard Business Review,* March/April 1992, pp. 57-69; and Dorothy Leonard-Barton, "Core Capabilities and Core Rigidities: A Paradox in Managing New Product Development," *Strategic Management Journal, 13,* 1992, pp. 111-125.

5. A few authors have been especially careful to define what they mean by a capability or a competence. See George S. Day, "The Capabilities of Market-Driven Organizations," *Journal of Marketing,* October 1994, pp. 37-52.

6. Capability or competence in the sense they address and involve doing or action are viewed as verbs, whereas assets, viewed raw wherewithal of an organization, are viewed as nouns.

7. The customer-focused activity chain is discussed in detail in Chapter 7.

8. The role and importance of alliances, relationships, and networks in creating and sustaining C and C are addressed in Chapters 8 and 9.

9. These assertions are the focus of much of the discussion in the remainder of this chapter.

10. How management of the activity/value chain and the customer-focused activity chain can affect C and C is explicated in detail in Chapter 7.

11. This illustration is briefly discussed in C.K. Prahalad, Liam Fahey, and Robert Randall, "A Strategy for Growth: The Role of Core Competencies in the Corporation," in *The Portable MBA in Strategy,* edited by Liam Fahey and Robert Randall, New York: John Wiley & Sons, 1994.

12. In their seminal article, "The Corporation's Core Competencies," (*Harvard Business Review,* 1990), C.K. Prahalad and Gary Hamel emphasize technology-based competencies, a manifestly observable competence, almost to the complete exclusion of intangible competencies.

13. Although dynamism may be argued to be implicit in the concept of competence or capability, it is separated out here because of its importance to the understanding of both concepts (i.e., capability and competence) and to reinforce that if competencies and capabilities are not nourished they will simply decay.

14. As with dynamism, the augmentability of a C or C is largely taken for granted or not considered in much of the C and C literature, yet how to augment or enhance a C or C is perhaps the fundamental C and C challenge confronting any organization. Therefore, this chapter focuses on the sources of C or C, their indicators, and change in the evolution of C and C.

15. Competencies are discussed before capabilities because they are a corporate phenomenon. Also, capabilities are closely related to activity/value chain analysis, addressed in Chapter 7.

16. Potential competencies here refers to competencies for which the analyst should be seeking alerting indicators.

17. Provisional competencies are those for which individuals provide actual alerting indicators pertaining to one or more specific competitors.

18. This is another example of anticipated indicators discussed in Chapter 4.

19. This common error reinforces the emphasis throughout this book on the need to delineate and communicate the meaning associated with key concepts such as capabilities and competencies.

20. Indeed, the intertwined nature of these three components will become evident as we proceed through this analysis.

21. This is the process of deriving signals described in Chapter 4.

22. It is here that analysts can and should identify and list the changes occurring in each C or C.

23. For further discussion of the importance of culture in the context of developing and sustaining C and C, see Chapter 15.

24. Norms, as an element of an organization's culture, are addressed in detail in Chapter 15.

25. Scope and posture trajectories are addressed in Chapter 5.

26. This is so because capabilities are a business- or product-unit phenomenon.

27. The concepts of applied research and development are more fully detailed in Chapter 13.

28. The discussion of competitor consequences in Chapters 5–15 could also be separated in a sequence of derived questions as is done in this chapter.

CHAPTER 13

1. See, for example, Philip A. Roussel, Kamal N. Saad, and Tamara J. Erickson, *Third Generation R&D,* Boston, MA: Harvard Business School Press, 1991.

2. Confusion about technology escalates when authors fail to offer some definition or, at least, boundaries as to what technology entails (and does not entail). Regrettably, many strategy textbooks have fallen into this trap.

3. This definition of technology strategy is consistent with the definition of marketplace strategy provided in Chapter 5. It views technology as consisting of investments and commitments (programs)—the behaviors—that are executed to attain specific goals.

4. Both products and processes are emphasized here because research and development frequently aims to enhance the organization's own processes (e.g., manufacturing processes).

5. As defined in Chapter 11, assets are the wherewithal at the competitor's disposal to compete against rivals.

6. Technology change as a source of augmented learning is addressed later in this chapter.

7. Again, by first-cut is meant a distillation of what analysts know about a competitor, sometimes aided by data quickly collected from external sources. The first-cut product technology chain is then further detailed and developed as analysts subject it to the usual analysis questions.

8. Such individuals often do not have an opportunity to develop this type of analysis, or if they do, they do not possess an analysis framework to guide and motivate the analysis.

9. See Chapter 4 for a discussion of these categories of signals, and their importance.

10. This is an example of product change serving as an alerting signal of technology change.

11. The connections between posture and technology are illustrated in a number of places throughout this chapter.

12. This would therefore be an extension of the analysis depicted in Chapters 11 and 12.

13. Specific reasons why the identification and assessment of assets is an essential part of technology assessment were also noted earlier in the chapter.

CHAPTER 14

1. People have already been defined as assets in Chapter 11. We emphasize change in people here as a source of signals.

2. This attribute of an activity/value chain is discussed in Chapter 7.

3. Both cases in this chapter are disguised due to the sensitivity of the analysis.

4. Detection lag and inference lag are defined and discussed in Chapter 4.

5. Much of the analysis outlined in Chapter 8 is relevant to these questions.

6. The analysis pertaining to these types of questions is detailed in Chapter 8.

7. The concept of stretch goals, and its importance, is discussed in Chapter 5.

8. This counsel is relevant to any significant inference.

9. The projected evolution of a competitor's alliance described and discussed in Chapter 8 is one example of how indicators can be used to lay out a projected timeline.

10. These errors also apply to any facet of the analysis of competitors.

11. This point has been emphasized in many places throughout this book.

CHAPTER 15

1. Although many authors view an organization's assumptions about the world around it as the core of its culture, for the purposes of analyzing competitors, we have separated the assumptions a competitor makes about its environment and itself (as delineated in Chapter 10) from other key elements of its culture—values, beliefs, norms, and behaviors.

2. Even chapters in books edited for the purposes of understanding organization culture often suggest very different definitions of what culture is (and how it should be managed). See, for example, Ralph Kilmann, Saxton, and Serpa, *Gaining Control of the Corporate Culture,* San Francisco: Jossey-Bass, 1986.

3. This is a more encompassing conception of culture than is found in the work of many authors who have specialized in studying culture. Behaviors and practices, the more explicit elements of culture, as delineated in this chapter, are included because they provide strong indicators of the underlying values and beliefs—the more difficult elements to capture in the case of competitors.

4. The importance of culture as a creator and conveyor of meanings has been emphasized by many culture theorists and researchers. See, for example, Merle Reis Louis, "An Investigator's Guide to Workplace Culture," in Peter J. Frost, Larry F. Moore, Meryl Reis Louis, Craig C. Lundberg, and Joanne Martin (Eds.), *Organizational Culture,* Beverly Hills: Sage Publications, 1985.

5. One articulation of culture that explicitly adopts these four elements can be found in John P. Kotter and James L. Heskett, *Corporate Culture and Performance,* New York: The Free Press, 1992.

6. Each of these practices can be viewed as indicators of the customer orientation of a competitor's culture.

7. These understandings reflect the type of processing described in Chapter 2 (see Figure 2.1). Individuals select and order data about the world around them and make sense out of it.

8. Sometimes this is referred to as the organization's philosophy of doing business.

9. For a discussion of the role of culture in shaping the strategies of these and many other companies, see James C. Collins and Jerry I. Porras, *Built to Last: Successful Habits of Visionary Companies,* New York: HarperBusiness, 1994.

10. See Chapter 6 for a discussion of the function and importance of stretch goals.

11. Chapters 3 and 4 address formal and informal statements in detail.

12. This assertion is fully developed in the remaining parts of this chapter.

13. Johnson & Johnson had several choices once the suspicion of tampering arose. Among other things, it could have chosen to do nothing until it was absolutely certain that its products had been tampered with.

14. Actions can be viewed as indicators of the underlying decision(s).

15. The linkage between actions and words in the context of indicators is discussed in Chapter 4.

16. The role and importance of logic in the inferencing process are addressed in Chapter 3.

17. The methodology here is largely similar to that already described for deriving refined assumptions in Chapter 10.

18. The electronics competitor may be constrained by a view that customer satisfaction is about enhancing the satisfaction of existing customers, thus not paying much attention to the needs and satisfaction of potential customers, or customers who have already walked away from its products.

19. See Chapter 5 for a detailed discussion of customization.

20. Although the competitor is customer oriented, it may possess little of the values and beliefs associated with organizations that truly customize their offerings to the needs and situation of individual customers.

21. Some authors view deeply embedded and widely shared assumptions as the essence of an organization's culture. See, for example, Edgar H. Schein, *Organizational Culture and Leadership,* 2nd ed., San Francisco: Jossey-Bass, 1992.

22. The methodology to do so is similar to that of identifying a competitor's culture with the added benefit that analysts obviously have access to considerable internal data. However, as argued in many places in this book, they must seriously address the biases inherent in addressing their own organization.

23. Since this is the final component in the analysis of individual competitors, the analysis here will emphasize specific consequences for the competitor and specific implications for the focal firm.

CHAPTER 16

1. Although at first glance, it may seem impossible to talk about "knowledge of the future," we are not talking about facts in a narrow sense (those things that are unambiguously true, as discussed in Chapter 2) but rather about decision makers' perceptions, beliefs, assumptions, and projections about possible states of the future.

2. Facts about the future, to be consistent with the definition of facts provided earlier in Chapter 2, refer to items that may be taken as true about the future with little question about their veracity. For example, we can take it as fact for the foreseeable future that a presidential election will be held in the United States every four years.

3. See Chapter 2 for a discussion of the argument linking learning and the need for future knowledge in the context of strategy making.

4. For a detailed discussion of the applicability of scenarios to organizational contexts and managerial decision making, see Liam Fahey and Robert Randall, *Learning from the Future: Competitive Foresight Scenarios,* New York: John Wiley & Sons, 1997.

5. End-state is the widely used term to denote the final outcome of the evolution of a competitive domain or the object of what is being projected.

6. See, for example, Peter Schwartz, *The Art of the Long View: Planning for the Future in an Uncertain World,* New York: Doubleday/Currency, 1991, pp. 141–169.

7. Simple projections are not scenarios (as defined in this chapter) since they do not involve the construction and modes of thinking typical of scenarios such as the choice of key uncertainties. We have introduced simple projections here for the purposes of a baseline against which complex projections can be assessed.

8. This orientation is essential to generating the double-loop learning discussed in Chapter 2.

9. The organizational processes involved in developing and using scenarios have received sparse attention in many treatments of scenarios. For a detailed discussion, see Liam Fahey and Robert Randall, *Learning from the Future: Competitive Foresight Scenarios,* New York: John Wiley & Sons, 1997.

10. This point is consistent with the argument in Chapter 2 that learning must be viewed as consisting of both knowledge generation and knowledge use.

11. By manipulate here, we mean that analysts play with various uncertainties to develop alternative plots that best characterize different futures the organization might confront.

12. The importance of the distinctions across these competitive contexts is evident in the discussion of the yogurt example later in this chapter.

13. Such a conclusion might be reached from the types of analysis covered in Chapter 13.

14. See, for example, Peter Schwartz, *The Art of the Long View,* New York: Doubleday/Currency, 1991; and, Norman E. Duncan and Pierre Wack, "Scenarios Designed to Improve Decision Making," *Planning Review,* July–August 1994, vol. 22, no. 4, pp. 18–25.

15. Emergent scenarios are not simple projections since they allow multiple distinct end-states and associated plots.

16. As noted, key uncertainties are aggregate driving forces that are critical to a specific future: how they change is likely to greatly affect key scenario outcomes. They are uncertain in that their direction and rate of change is difficult to anticipate.

17. Analysts must go beyond current knowledge, some of which is likely to be largely tacit, as discussed in Chapters 2 and 10.

18. It should be emphasized again that requests for "forecasts of what will happen" fly in the face of the purpose of scenarios, as discussed earlier, which is to provide alternative views of what the future might be.

19. Some distinct competitor consequences and focal firm implications are emphasized here because, as noted, radically different scenarios may lead to some similar, and even some identical consequences and implications.

20. We emphasize "apparently" plausible strategies here because they have not as yet been fully constructed and assessed.

21. In most instances, three or four strategies are sufficient to capture the breadth of opportunities confronting a competitor. Also, it is difficult for managers and others to maintain in their minds distinctions across more than three or four scenarios.

22. When consequences for the competitor are not clearly explicated as part of a scenario plot, deriving implications for the focal firm occurs without a full understanding of what the scenario implies for the competitor—not a desirable situation.

23. Feasibility refers here to whether the competitor can execute the strategy; viability refers to its likelihood of winning in the marketplace.

24. This is a good example of the iterative nature of the steps involved in constructing a scenario.

25. The role, intent, and importance of monitoring are detailed in Chapter 3.

26. Accepteds, yet-to-be-played-outs, and impossibles are identified before individual scenarios are developed.

27. Again, component here refers to the components in the competitor analysis framework outlined in Chapter 3 and detailed in Chapters 5–15.

28. Accepteds that might argue against the projected strategy are sought and considered as part of assessment.

29. The latter two accepteds illustrate how accepteds are often the result of analysis. Since the competitor was increasing both its operating margins and net profits, the likelihood of its financial condition deteriorating was very slim.

30. The overall market growth rate had been less than 2 percent per year for the prior three or four years.

31. The notion of what constitutes an issue was addressed earlier under the heading Business Issues (as part of the section Detail the Plot).

32. The strategy game is extensively delineated in Chapter 1.

33. The concept of stretch goals is discussed in Chapter 6.

34. This is especially likely when individuals have spent a considerable amount of time constructing a scenario.

35. If a scenario is internally inconsistent, its plausibility may be severely limited, if not completely impossible. On the other hand, an entirely consistent scenario may still be implausible; for example, it simply may not be possible or feasible.

36. These questions are also the focus of scrutiny in testing the plausibility of a scenario, in particular, the plausibility of the logics of a scenario.

37. Obviously, many other firms have successfully done so.

38. Even internally consistent scenarios may not be plausible.

39. Such biases include a tendency to seek data that support analysts' preconceptions or suppositions; a tendency to downplay data that are inconsistent with analysts' judgments; a tendency to accept supporting evidence from credible or authoritative sources.

40. This is because issues generate choices that the competitor is confronting or must confront; thus, they unavoidably generate a focus on what the competitor may do in the future.

41. Both types of learning are discussed in detail in Chapter 2.

42. Assumptions here are part of the change in the focal firm's knowledge base.

43. These constitute the augmented, comparative, and self-learning described in Chapter 2.

CHAPTER 17

1. Generating such decisions is one purpose of scenarios, as discussed in Chapter 16.

2. I have seen many small groups quickly conclude that if they can't agree on what key decisions confront their unit or organization, it will be extremely difficult to connect competitor analysis to decision making.

3. The recursive nature of analysis was noted and discussed in Chapter 2.

4. Note that we don't say, make decisions. Usually, many more individuals contribute to making a decision than those who have organizational authority or responsibility to "make the decision."

5. Intelligence as used in this chapter is consistent with its definition in Chapter 3: knowledge that is useful to decision makers.

6. This error received some attention in Chapter 2.

7. This is the essence of the open-ended perspective: generate the outputs and then assess which decision makers can use them in the making of current or potential decisions.

8. This orientation is fundamental to the construction and use of scenarios, as described in Chapter 16.

9. This point is further elaborated in the discussion of procedures later in the chapter.

10. This error illustrates the importance accorded to crafting outputs throughout this book.

11. This tendency is more likely to occur when analysts do not view analysis of competitors as a means to a broader end: to develop a more refined understanding of the competitive context and the organization itself. The importance of doing so was discussed in Chapter 2.

12. This is an illustration of augmented learning.

13. This distinction was developed in Chapter 2.

14. This is a simple description of the classic decision-making stages. Decision makers often cycle back and forth through these stages as they endeavor to understand the decision and its implications.

15. This assertion underlies the earlier error noted in this chapter: change in intelligence needs over time is not tracked.

16. Superficial "1-800 questions" are asked by decision makers or others who typically want a specific question answered by CAPs. All too often, these questions, even if answered quickly and correctly, contribute little to decision making. Hence, they are irrelevant and are dubbed 1-800 questions.

17. These key elements of culture were discussed in detail in Chapter 15.

18. Inactions were noted in Chapters 3 and 4 as significant indicators or sources of signals.

19. This is an example of the signals methodology outlined in Chapter 4 and illustrated in many other places throughout the book.

INDEX